# Bangkok

## Joe Cummings

D0109301

LONELY PLANET PUBLICATIONS
Melbourne • Oakland • London • Paris

**Bangkok**
**5th edition** – August 2001
**First published** – September 1992

**Published by**
**Lonely Planet Publications Pty Ltd**  ABN 36 005 607 983
90 Maribyrnong St, Footscray, Victoria 3011, Australia

**Lonely Planet Offices**
**Australia** Locked Bag 1, Footscray, Victoria 3011
**USA** 150 Linden St, Oakland, CA 94607
**UK** 10a Spring Place, London NW5 3BH
**France** 1 rue du Dahomey, 75011 Paris

**Photographs**
Many of the images in this guide are available for licensing from
Lonely Planet Images.
email: lpi@lonelyplanet.com.au

**Front cover photograph**
Food vendor preparing a meal at an evening market, Bangkok
(Jerry Alexander)

**Bangkok map section title page**
Mahboonkrong (MBK) shopping centre, Bangkok (Andrew Lubran)

ISBN 1 86450 285 1

Printed by The Bookmaker International Ltd
Printed in China

# Contents – Text

**THE AUTHOR** — 4

**THIS BOOK** — 5

**FOREWORD** — 6

**INTRODUCTION** — 9

**FACTS ABOUT BANGKOK** — 10

History ...............................10
Geography ......................13
Climate ...........................13
Ecology & Environment ....14
Government & Politics ......14
Economy ...........................15
Population & People ........17
Education .........................17
Arts .................................17
Society & Conduct ............25
Religion ...........................34

**FACTS FOR THE VISITOR** — 38

When to go ......................38
Orientation ......................38
Maps ..............................38
Tourist Offices ..................39
Visas & Documents ..........40
Embassies & Consulates ....43
Customs ..........................45
Money .............................46
Post & Communications ..51
Internet Resources ...........56
Books ..............................57
Newspapers &
Magazines .......................60
Radio ..............................60
TV ...................................60
Video Systems ..................62
Photography & Video ......62
Time ...............................63
Electricity .........................63
Weights & Measures ........63
Laundry ...........................63
Toilets & Showers ...........64
Health .............................65
Women Travellers ............74
Gay & Lesbian Travellers ..75
Disabled Travellers ...........76
Senior Travellers ...............77
Bangkok for Children ........77
Libraries ...........................77
Universities .....................78
Cultural Centres ...............78
Dangers & Annoyances ....79
Legal Matters ................81
Business Hours .................81
Public Holidays &
Special Events .................82
Doing Business ..............84
Work ...............................85

**GETTING THERE & AWAY** — 87

Air ..................................87
Road ...............................92
Train ...............................96
Boat ...............................100

**GETTING AROUND** — 101

The Airport ....................101
To/From the Airport ......102
Bus ................................104
Skytrain .........................105
Subway ..........................106
Car & Motorcycle ..........107
Taxi ...............................107
Motorcycle Taxi .............108
Túk-Túk ..........................108
Boat ...............................109
Walking ..........................109

**THINGS TO SEE & DO** — 110

Museums & Galleries ......110
Temples & Shrines ..........115
Churches ........................123
Old City Sights .............123
Parks .............................124
Other Attractions ...........125
River & Canal Trips ........126
Activities .......................131
Courses .........................132

**WALKING TOURS OF BANGKOK** — 135

Temples & River
Walking Tour .................136
Chinatown-Phahurat
Walking Tour .................139
Old Banglamphu
Walking Tour .................142

## PLACES TO STAY 145

Budget ...........................145
Mid-Range ...................153
Top End ......................157
Long-Term Rentals ..........163

## PLACES TO EAT 164

Districts .........................164
Tastes Of Bangkok ...........171
Dinner Cruises ...............184
Hotel Restaurants .........184
High Tea ........................185

## ENTERTAINMENT 186

Nightlife ........................186
Theatre & Dance ............192
Muay Thai (Thai Boxing) ...194
Cinemas ......................199
Video ..............................199
Spectator Sports ............200

## SHOPPING 201

What to Buy .................201
Where to Shop .............207
Guarantees ...................210

## EXCURSIONS 211

West of Bangkok ............211
North of Bangkok ..........211
North-East of Bangkok ..213
South of Bangkok ..........213
Ayuthaya ........................214
Bang Pa-In ....................221
Nakhon Pathom ............221
Around Nakhon Pathom ..224
Samut Sakhon ...............225
Samut Songkhram ..........227
Kanchanaburi ................229
Ko Samet ........................239

## LANGUAGE 248

Food ...............................256
Drink ..............................262
Health ............................255

## GLOSSARY 264

## THANKS 266

## INDEX 276

Text .................................276
Boxed Text ...................280

## MAP LEGEND back page

## METRIC CONVERSION inside back cover

# Contents – Maps

## THINGS TO SEE & DO

National Museum ..........111   Chao Phraya River Express ..128

## WALKING TOURS OF BANGKOK

Temples & River                Chinatown-Phahurat            Old Banglamphu
Walking Tour .................137   Walking Tour .................140   Walking Tour .................143

## SHOPPING

Chatuchak Weekend
Market ..........................207

## EXCURSIONS

Excursions ......................212   Damnoen Saduak               Ko Samet ........................240
Central Ayuthaya ............216   Floating Market ..............224
Nakhon Pathom ..........222   Kanchanaburi ...............230

## BANGKOK MAP SECTION

Greater Bangkok ........Map 1   Thanon Khao San               Chinatown–Bang Rak–
Central Bangkok ........Map 2   (Khao San Rd) ............Map 4   Thonburi ....................Map 6
Banglamphu &                   Pratunam & Victory            Lumphini Park–Th Ploenchit–
Ko Ratanakosin ..........Map 3   Monument ................Map 5   Samyan ......................Map 7

# The Author

## Joe Cummings

Born in the sub-tropical port of New Orleans, Joe began travelling in South-East Asia shortly after finishing university. Before writing became a full-time job, he played guitar in a succession of bands, volunteered for the Peace Corps, worked as a movie extra, and taught English in Thailand, Malaysia, Taiwan and the USA. Along the way he earned an MA degree in Thai language and art history.

He has written over 30 original guidebooks, phrasebooks and atlases for countries in Asia and North America. He is best known for authoring Lonely Planet's guides to *Thailand*, *Thailand's Islands & Beaches*, *Laos* and *Myanmar*, parts of *South-East Asia on a shoe-string*, and *Thai* and *Lao* phrasebooks, plus *World Food Thailand*. As a freelance journalist he has written for dozens of periodicals, including *Ambassador*, *Bangkok Post*, *International Herald Tribune*, *Geographical*, *The Nation*, *Outside*, *San Francisco Examiner*, *South China Morning Post* and *Wall Street Journal*.

## FROM THE AUTHOR

Thanks to the following people in and out of Thailand who assisted along the way: Avia Travel, André Barguirdjian and Mau Travel Service, Richard Barrow, Nancy and Nima Chandler, Kaneungnit Chotikakul, Nattawud Daoruang, Brent Madison, Theerada Suphaphong and ML Sompongvadee Vikitsreth.

The Tourism Authority of Thailand and its employees throughout Thailand, as usual, were of considerable assistance. My partner, Lynne Cummings, helped out immensely with proofreading, fact-checking, data entry, day-to-day organising, and 100 other things that made putting this book together an easier and more efficient task.

# This Book

## From the Publisher

The 5th edition of *Bangkok* was edited at Lonely Planet's Melbourne office by Rachael Antony. Sally Morgan did the design, mapping and layout at lightning speed, under the guiding eye of Chris Love. Kristin Odijk provided proofing wizardry and all kinds of helpful advice. Simon Bracken designed the cover and provided italics; Matt King organised illustrations; Simon Borg, Kelli Hamblet, Martin Harris and Mic Looby drew them; and Katie Butterworth designed the chapter ends. Proud father Kusnandar whipped-up the climate chart, and the Big Q handled the Language chapter; Leonie Mugavin provided updated air travel information and library resources; Shahara Ahmed went over the Health section with a fine flea comb; Cathy Viero gathered together the readers letters; Lyndal Hall gave us access to *World Food Thailand;* and Alex Landragin gave us the thumbs up on *Scoop.* Additional material was penned by Bruce Evans, Rachael Antony and Carly Hammond.

Special thanks go to Guru Bruce Evans for providing Thai expertise far beyond the call of duty; Jane Thompson, Kristin Odijk; Glenn Beanland at LPI; Mark Germanchis for Quark expertise; Carly Hammond for taking on the odious task of Bangkok's nightlife and wielding a camera for us; Dave Sulzer at Columbia; and finally, Adam Claridge-Chang at Rockefeller for his exploration of the bizarre, comical and surprising.

**THANKS**
Many thanks to the travellers who used the last edition and wrote to us with helpful hints, advice and interesting anecdotes. Your names appear in the back of this book.

# Foreword

## ABOUT LONELY PLANET GUIDEBOOKS

The story begins with a classic travel adventure: Tony and Maureen Wheeler's 1972 journey across Europe and Asia to Australia. Useful information about the overland trail did not exist at that time, so Tony and Maureen published the first Lonely Planet guidebook to meet a growing need.

From a kitchen table, then from a tiny office in Melbourne (Australia), Lonely Planet has become the largest independent travel publisher in the world, an international company with offices in Melbourne, Oakland (USA), London (UK) and Paris (France).

Today Lonely Planet guidebooks cover the globe. There is an ever-growing list of books and there's information in a variety of forms and media. Some things haven't changed. The main aim is still to help make it possible for adventurous travellers to get out there – to explore and better understand the world.

At Lonely Planet we believe travellers can make a positive contribution to the countries they visit – if they respect their host communities and spend their money wisely. Since 1986 a percentage of the income from each book has been donated to aid projects and human rights campaigns.

**Updates** Lonely Planet thoroughly updates each guidebook as often as possible. This usually means there are around two years between editions, although for more unusual or more stable destinations the gap can be longer. Check the imprint page (following the colour map at the beginning of the book) for publication dates.

Between editions up-to-date information is available in two free newsletters – the paper *Planet Talk* and email *Comet* (to subscribe, contact any Lonely Planet office) – and on our Web site at www.lonelyplanet.com. The *Upgrades* section of the Web site covers a number of important and volatile destinations and is regularly updated by Lonely Planet authors. *Scoop* covers news and current affairs relevant to travellers. And, lastly, the *Thorn Tree* bulletin board and *Postcards* section of the site carry unverified, but fascinating, reports from travellers.

**Correspondence** The process of creating new editions begins with the letters, postcards and emails received from travellers. This correspondence often includes suggestions, criticisms and comments about the current editions. Interesting excerpts are immediately passed on via newsletters and the Web site, and everything goes to our authors to be verified when they're researching on the road. We're keen to get more feedback from organisations or individuals who represent communities visited by travellers.

Lonely Planet gathers information for everyone who's curious about the planet – and especially for those who explore it first-hand. Through guidebooks, phrasebooks, activity guides, maps, literature, newsletters, image library, TV series and Web site we act as an information exchange for a worldwide community of travellers.

**Research** Authors aim to gather sufficient practical information to enable travellers to make informed choices and to make the mechanics of a journey run smoothly. They also research historical and cultural background to help enrich the travel experience and allow travellers to understand and respond appropriately to cultural and environmental issues.

Authors don't stay in every hotel because that would mean spending a couple of months in each medium-sized city and, no, they don't eat at every restaurant because that would mean stretching belts beyond capacity. They do visit hotels and restaurants to check standards and prices, but feedback based on readers' direct experiences can be very helpful.

Many of our authors work undercover, others aren't so secretive. None of them accept freebies in exchange for positive write-ups. And none of our guidebooks contain any advertising.

**Production** Authors submit their raw manuscripts and maps to offices in Australia, USA, UK or France. Editors and cartographers – all experienced travellers themselves – then begin the process of assembling the pieces. When the book finally hits the shops, some things are already out of date, we start getting feedback from readers and the process begins again ...

## WARNING & REQUEST

Things change – prices go up, schedules change, good places go bad and bad places go bankrupt – nothing stays the same. So, if you find things better or worse, recently opened or long since closed, please tell us and help make the next edition even more accurate and useful. We genuinely value all the feedback we receive. A well travelled team reads and acknowledges every letter, postcard and email and ensures that every morsel of information finds its way to the appropriate authors, editors and cartographers for verification.

Everyone who writes to us will find their name in the next edition of the appropriate guidebook. They will also receive the latest issue of *Planet Talk*, our quarterly printed newsletter, or *Comet*, our monthly email newsletter. Subscriptions to both newsletters are free. The very best contributions will be rewarded with a free guidebook.

Excerpts from your correspondence may appear in new editions of Lonely Planet guidebooks, the Lonely Planet Web site, *Planet Talk* or *Comet*, so please let us know if you *don't* want your letter published or your name acknowledged.

Send all correspondence to the Lonely Planet office closest to you:

**Australia:** Locked Bag 1, Footscray, Victoria 3011
**USA:** 150 Linden St, Oakland, CA 94607
**UK:** 10A Spring Place, London NW5 3BH
**France:** 1 rue du Dahomey, 75011 Paris

Or email us at: talk2us@lonelyplanet.com.au

**For news, views and updates see our Web site: www.lonelyplanet.com**

## HOW TO USE A LONELY PLANET GUIDEBOOK

The best way to use a Lonely Planet guidebook is any way you choose. At Lonely Planet we believe the most memorable travel experiences are often those that are unexpected, and the finest discoveries are those you make yourself. Guidebooks are not intended to be used as if they provide a detailed set of infallible instructions!

**Contents** All Lonely Planet guidebooks follow roughly the same format. The Facts about the Destination chapters or sections give background information ranging from history to weather. Facts for the Visitor gives practical information on issues like visas and health. Getting There & Away gives a brief starting point for researching travel to and from the destination. Getting Around gives an overview of the transport options when you arrive.

The peculiar demands of each destination determine how subsequent chapters are broken up, but some things remain constant. We always start with background, then proceed to sights, places to stay, places to eat, entertainment, getting there and away, and getting around information – in that order.

**Heading Hierarchy** Lonely Planet headings are used in a strict hierarchical structure that can be visualised as a set of Russian dolls. Each heading (and its following text) is encompassed by any preceding heading that is higher on the hierarchical ladder.

**Entry Points** We do not assume guidebooks will be read from beginning to end, but that people will dip into them. The traditional entry points are the list of contents and the index. In addition, however, some books have a complete list of maps and an index map illustrating map coverage.

There may also be a colour map that shows highlights. These highlights are dealt with in greater detail in the Facts for the Visitor chapter, along with planning questions and suggested itineraries. Each chapter covering a geographical region usually begins with a locator map and another list of highlights. Once you find something of interest in a list of highlights, turn to the index.

**Maps** Maps play a crucial role in Lonely Planet guidebooks and include a huge amount of information. A legend is printed on the back page. We seek to have complete consistency between maps and text, and to have every important place in the text captured on a map. Map key numbers usually start in the top left corner.

Although inclusion in a guidebook usually implies a recommendation we cannot list every good place. Exclusion does not necessarily imply criticism. In fact there are a number of reasons why we might exclude a place – sometimes it is simply inappropriate to encourage an influx of travellers.

# Introduction

Bangkok – the name explodes with images of the quintessential steamy, tropical Asian metropolis. With squeaky clean Singapore reigning as the Switzerland of Asia and Hong Kongs' reincarnation under the socialist bureaucracy of China, no city in South-East Asia can beat Bangkok for hardcore hedonism, chaos, capitalistic enterprise and perpetual surprise.

The economic boom of the early 1990's prompted an explosion of shopping malls, entertainment centres, apartment blocks and 'tuppies' – Thai yuppies – to fill them. Today abandoned skyscrapers still covered in scaffolding attest to the recent economic crash and serve as grim monuments to the desperate businessmen who threw themselves from high-rise roof-tops. For a while the Thai tabloids ran stories of high-profile empire builders who went from driving Mercedes to selling noodles on street corners overnight; a parable for the economy at large.

However, as the region stabilises, Bangkok is abuzz once more with cool bars, boutique stores, restaurants and nightclubs opening up every week; alongside an overwhelming proliferation of micro-economy ventures of curry stalls, fruit stands and soft-drink vendors dotting every corner.

Most intriguing is that beneath the veneer of this incredibly urbanised city lies an uncompromised *khwaam pen thai* – 'Thai-ness' – from the everyday 'wai' (palms together) greetings, to a gusty *chaiyo* (cheers) over a bottle of Mekong. It's this quality that melds

Bangkok's contrasts and contradictions; glass-and-steel buildings shaped like cartoon robots stand next to glittering temple spires; wreaths of jasmine flowers dangle from the rear-view mirrors of buses and taxis; shaven-headed, orange-robed monks walk barefoot along the street beneath a bank of giant Sony screens blasting MTV Asia.

At times Bangkok seems like it's hurtling toward disaster. The city is sinking as wells suck the water table dry beneath the spongy Chao Phraya flood plains upon which the city was laid out in the 18th century. During the dry season, a thick traffic-induced haze fills busy intersections – this is in a city where several hundred new vehicles are registered every day. About seven million people – around 10% of Thailand's population – live in the capital and every bus from the provinces brings in yet more fortune-seekers.

Maddening? Definitely. But the amazing thing is how well the city works. Public transport may be excruciatingly slow at times, but it is plentiful; try flagging a taxi in any other Asian capital at 3 am. You can buy a bowl of mouth-watering *kŭaytĭaw* from a street vendor while standing outside a US$200-a-night hotel; or have your muscles gently kneaded for 1½ hours at Wat Pho, the oldest temple in the city, for less than the price of a cinema ticket in most Western cities. Catch a ride aboard a canal taxi on the Thonburi side and you can disappear down shaded waterways where modern Bangkok is soon left behind.

# Facts about Bangkok

## HISTORY

Before it became the capital of Thailand in 1782, the settlement known as Bang Makok, meaning 'Place of Olive Plums', was only a very small part of what is today called Bangkok by foreigners. Bang Makok was, in fact, only an outlying district of Thonburi Si Mahasamut (now Thonburi) on the east bank of Mae Nam Chao Phraya (Chao Phraya River).

Thonburi was founded on the west bank by a group of wealthy Thais during the reign of King Chakkaphat (1548–68). It became an important trading city during the 17th and 18th centuries, when Siam's capital was in Ayuthaya to the north (see the Excursions chapter). Constantine Phaulkon, a Greek-born minister to Ayuthaya's King Narai, convinced the monarch to build a fortress on the banks of the Chao Phraya at the mouth of Khlong (Canal) Bangkok Yai.

Following the Burmese defeat of Ayuthaya in 1765, the Thai general Phraya Taksin made himself king in 1769 and established a new capital at Thonburi. Taksin, whose behaviour became increasingly violent and bizarre, eventually came to regard himself as the next Buddha, but his ministers, who did not approve of his religious

fantasies, deposed and then executed him in the custom reserved for royalty – by beating him to death in a velvet sack so that no royal blood touched the ground, in 1782.

Chao Phraya Chakri replaced Taksin and, as King Rama I, became the first king of the Chakri dynasty (the current monarch, King Bhumibol, is the ninth). In 1782 Rama I moved the capital to the Bangkok district on the river's eastern bank, believing the area to be more easily defended against naval attack.

The site chosen for the new royal palace and government buildings was occupied by a Chinese settlement; the Chinese were relocated to the Sampeng district, Bangkok's Chinatown today. Using thousands of Khmer prisoners of war, Chakri built 10km of city walls and expanded Bangkok's canal system to create a royal 'island' – Ko Ratanakosin. Sections of the 4.5m-thick walls are still standing in the area of Wat Saket and the Golden Mount, and water still flows, albeit sluggishly, around the canals of the original royal district.

Artisans from Ayuthaya contributed several new temples to the city. Upon completion of the new capital in 1785, at a three-day consecration ceremony, the city was given a new name:

Krungthep mahanakhon amon ratanakosin mahintara ayuthaya mahadilok popnopparat ratchathani burirom udomratchaniwet mahasathan amonpiman avatansathit sakkathattiya witsanukamprasit

Roughly translated, this tongue-twister means: 'Great city of angels, the repository of divine gems, the great land unconquerable, the grand and prominent realm, the royal and delightful capital city full of nine noble gems, the highest royal dwelling and grand palace, the divine shelter and living place of reincarnated spirits.' Fortunately, it is shortened to Krung Thep, meaning 'City of Angels' in everyday usage. The name Bangkok persisted among foreign traders, and today the

Metropolitan's Bangkok's official government seal depicts the capital's Grand Palace, emphasising the city's role as a royal as well as administrative centre.

capital of Thailand is still known by its old name to most outside the kingdom. (However, the original name lives on in modern memory thanks to Thai rock duo, Asanee & Wasan who had a big hit based on it, called 'Krung Thep Mahanakhon', an epic funk rave consisting of Bangkok's name chanted over a hypnotic rhythm! It appears on their 1989 album, *Fak Thong*.)

Temple construction remained the highlight of most early development in Bangkok through the reign of Rama III (1824–51). Around this time Thailand began to feel threatened by the British and French who were making colonial inroads to Cambodia, Laos and Burma. This prompted the construction of a great iron chain, around 1825, which was suspended across the Chao Phraya river from the fortress to guard against the entry of unauthorised ships.

Until King Mongkut's rule (Rama IV, 1851–68), Bangkok residents made their way around the city via the vast river and canal system established under the first three kings of the Chakri dynasty. These waterways were supplemented by a network of meagre footpaths.

After motorised transport arrived in the early 20th century, roadways were steadily added and the city expanded in all directions. After a bloodless revolution in 1932 transformed Thailand from an absolute monarchy, Bangkok became the nerve centre of a vast civil service, which, coupled with its growing success as a world port, transformed the city into a mecca for Thais seeking economic opportunity and contemporary culture.

During their invasion of South-East Asia in 1941, the Japanese outflanked Allied troops in Malaya and Burma. The Thai government, under the dictatorship of former military man Phibul Songkhram, complied with this action by allowing the Japanese access to the Gulf of Thailand. As Japanese troops briefly occupied parts of Bangkok on their way to the Thai-Burmese border to fight the British in Burma, the Thai economy stagnated. Phibul resigned in 1944 under pressure from the Thai underground resistance and, after V-J Day in 1945, Bangkok resumed its pace towards modernisation.

## The Original Siamese Twins

While walking along Bangkok's Mae Nam Chao Phraya one afternoon in 1824, English trader Robert Hunter spotted what he thought was a creature with eight limbs and two heads swimming in the river. When the oddity lifted itself onto a canoe, Hunter was surprised to see it was in fact two 13-year-old boys who were fused together at the chest. The Briton was so intrigued that he sponsored a medical examination of the boys (which showed they couldn't be surgically separated) and later introduced them to Bangkok's Western social circuits.

The boys, named Chang and Eng, left Siam five years later to tour Europe and the USA as physiological celebrities. They eventually settled in North Carolina, where they married two sisters and sired 22 children. In 1874 Chang passed away in his sleep; Eng followed him two hours later.

Thais have no known genetic disposition toward joined births (Chang and Eng were actually of Chinese descent), but ever since Hunter's 'discovery', the nonmedical world has used the term 'Siamese twins' to describe the phenomenon.

Over the next 15 years, bridges were built over Mae Nam Chao Phraya, canals were filled in to provide space for new roads and multistorey buildings began crowding out traditional teak structures.

From 1964 to 1973 – the peak years of the 1962–75 Indochina War – Thai army officers Thanom Kittikachorn and Praphat Charusathien ruled the nation and allowed the USA to establish several army bases within its borders in support of the US campaign in Vietnam, Laos and Cambodia. During this time Bangkok (along with nearby Pattaya) gained notoriety as a 'rest and recreation' (R&R) spot for foreign troops stationed in South-East Asia.

In October 1973 the military brutally suppressed a large pro-democracy student demonstration at Thammasat University in Bangkok, but King Bhumibol and General Krit Sivara, who sympathised with the students, refused to support further bloodshed,

**A view of 19th-century Bangkok.**

forcing Thanom and Praphat to leave Thailand. Oxford-educated Kukrit Pramoj took charge of a 14-party coalition government and steered a leftist agenda past a conservative parliament. Among Kukrit's lasting achievements were a national minimum wage, the repeal of anti-communist laws and the ejection of US military forces from Thailand.

The military regained control in 1976 after right-wing, paramilitary civilian groups assaulted a group of 2000 students holding a sit-in at Thammasat. Many students fled Bangkok and joined the People's Liberation Army of Thailand (PLAT), armed communist insurgency based in the hills who had been active in Thailand since the 1930s.

Thailand continued to seesaw back and forth between civilian and military rule for the next 15 years. Although a general amnesty in 1982 brought an end to the PLAT as students, workers and farmers returned to the cities, the new era of political tolerance exposed the military once again to civilian fire.

In May 1992 several huge demonstrations demanding the resignation of the latest dictator, General Suchinda Kraprayoon, rocked Bangkok and larger provincial capitals. Charismatic Bangkok governor Chamlong Srimuang, winner of the 1992 Magsaysay Award (a humanitarian service award issued by a foundation in the Philippines) for his role in galvanising the public to reject Suchinda, led the protests. After street confrontations between the protesters and the military near the Democracy Monument resulted in nearly 50 deaths and hundreds of injuries, King Bhumibol summoned both Suchinda and Chamlong to his royal presence for a rare public scolding. Suchinda resigned, having been premier for less than six weeks, and Chamlong's career was all but finished.

Since 1992 democratically elected civilian coalitions have administered the government. In 1997, following several months of warning signs which almost everyone in Thailand and in the international community chose to ignore (see Economy later in this chapter), the Thai currency fell into a deflationary tailspin and the national economy slowed to a virtual halt. Bangkok, which rode at the forefront of the 1980s double-digit economic boom, has been worse affected than any other city in the country in terms of job loss and income erosion. By early 2000, following a financial restructuring coached by the International Monetary Fund (IMF), the economy began to show signs of recovery.

Despite the financial slump, Bangkok remains the most exciting and dynamic city in South-East Asia with, for example, the region's largest foreign media correspondent base. Since the opening up of Vietnam, Cambodia, Laos and Myanmar to foreign investment, the city has served as the financial hub for mainland South-East Asia, a continuing role that should do much to see the city through the current economic crisis.

Although today it's a city groaning under the weight of an overburdened infrastructure, Bangkok continues to lure rural and working-class Thais, Asian and Western investors, and curious visitors from around the world with its phantasmagoria of the carnal, spiritual and entrepreneurial.

## GEOGRAPHY

Occupying a space roughly midway along Thailand's 1860km north-south axis, Bangkok lies approximately 14° north of the equator, putting it on a latitudinal level with Madras, Manila, Guatemala and Khartoum (Sudan). The rivers and tributaries of northern and central Thailand drain into the Gulf of Thailand via Mae Nam Chao Phraya delta surrounding Bangkok, creating a huge, flat and extremely fertile area known as 'the rice bowl of Asia'. More rice is grown here than in any other area of comparable size in all of Asia – Thailand has been the world's top exporter of rice for at least the last 30 years.

Metropolitan Bangkok – which covers 1569 sq km and extends into the neighbouring provinces of Nonthaburi, Samut Prakan and Samut Sakhon – sits smack in the middle of this delta area, just a few kilometres inland from the gulf. A network of natural and artificial canals criss-crosses the city, although they are fewer in number in urban Bangkok than in surrounding provinces. All feed into Thailand's hydraulic lifeline, the broad Mae Nam Chao Phraya, which snakes through the city centre and serves as an important transport link for cargo and passenger traffic both within the city and upcountry.

## CLIMATE
### Rainfall

Bangkok and Central Thailand are well within tropical latitudes and experience alternating periods of a dry and wet monsoon climate. The south-west monsoon arrives between May and July and lasts into October. This is followed by a dry period from November to May, a period that begins with lower relative temperatures until mid-February (because of the influences of the north-east monsoon, which bypasses this part of Thailand, but results in cool breezes), followed by much higher relative temperatures from March to May.

According to the official Thai agricultural calendar, the rains begin in July; however, the arrival of the monsoon can vary. Occasional rains in the dry season are known as 'mango showers'. In Bangkok it usually rains most during August and September, though it can flood in October since the ground has reached full saturation by then. If you are in Bangkok in early October, you may find yourself in hip-deep water in certain parts of the city. An umbrella can be invaluable – a raincoat will just make you hot.

### Temperatures

During the cool/dry season (November to February), night-time temperatures may dip as low as 12°C, with normal daytime temperatures averaging around 28°C. During the rainy months (June to October), the temperature averages 32°C in the daytime, and 26°C to 28°C at night. Add four or five degrees to the latter temperatures for the hot season (March to May) average.

As the city climate is very humid for most of the year, perceived temperatures

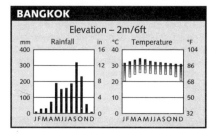

**BANGKOK**

Elevation – 2m/6ft

are often higher than thermometer readings; 34°C may feel more like 39°C. During the hot season the humidity is compounded by air pollution – the high level of particulate keeps the moisture in the air from evaporating. The lowest humidity occurs between November and May, especially when the occasional upland breeze arrives from the Khorat Plateau to the north-east and pushes back the humid delta air.

## ECOLOGY & ENVIRONMENT

Mae Nam Chao Phraya delta's natural environment has been forever altered by the founding and ongoing development of Bangkok. All of the city's canals as well as Mae Nam Chao Phraya itself would be considered polluted by most definitions, although plenty of Bangkok residents make daily use of these waterways for bathing, laundry, recreation and even drinking water (after treating it of course). The worst water quality is found in the almost black canals found on the Bangkok side of the river. The city has made efforts to clean up the canals

over the last couple of decades, with some limited success. Anyone who has been visiting Thailand for 20 years or more will have noticed some incremental improvements, particularly in the river. The current budget crisis in Thailand will probably slow, if not halt, any momentum gained in this direction.

Air quality varies from precinct to precinct but is generally worse at major traffic crossings. Along with carbon monoxide, lead and other poisons produced primarily by vehicle emissions, Bangkok's air has a fairly high concentration of particulate matter, including dust and debris brought in on the wheels of cars and trucks or created by ongoing construction projects. Relative to other cities in Asia, however, Bangkok doesn't even make the United Nations Environment Programme (UNEP) or World Health Organization (WHO) list of the region's five worst cities for air pollution – honours captured by Delhi, Xian, Beijing, Calcutta and Shenyang. Ambient noise ratios in Bangkok are comparable to those measured in Seoul, Chongqing and Ho Chi Minh City.

In addition to several parks filled with trees and other vegetation, Bangkok relies on immense green areas to the west of the city as a means of detoxifying the air. One of the greatest threats to the environment is not only continued development in the city centre, but developments in outlying areas and neighbouring provinces. Realising the importance of maintaining green 'lungs' for the city, the Thai government recently enacted strict controls on development in these areas. They've had less success controlling development in the inner city, and almost no success controlling vehicle circulation, one of the most obvious problem areas. The 1999 introduction of the BTS Skytrain, an elevated light rail system that runs above some of the city's more sluggish avenues, came as a welcome relief to those who live or work in adjacent areas. (See the Skytrain section in the Getting Around chapter for further information.)

## GOVERNMENT & POLITICS

The Bangkok Metropolitan Authority administers the capital, and the city boasts the only elected governorship in the nation

---

### Green Travel

Simple acts can make a big difference. While you're in Bangkok you can help make a positive contribution to the environment. Here's some hints to consider while on holiday (and even when you're at home!):

• Don't buy souvenirs or eat meals produced from endangered species and wildlife such as turtles and coral.
• Take reusable calico shopping bags and refuse plastic bags whenever possible – they end up clogging waterways.
• Reuse your straws or drink from your own cup – straws get stuck in dolphin's blowholes.
• As an alternative to fast-food packaging, take a reusable drink bottle and a light-weight aluminium or stainless-steel food container (readily available in camping stores) – they'll also be handy on long journeys.
• Use rechargeable batteries for your Walkman etc, which will cut down on the rubbish you leave behind.

(provincial governors are appointed). The mid-2000 elections saw tough-talking, 10-time former MP Samak Sundaravej take over as Bangkok governor.

In September 1997 the Thai parliament established a new constitution that guaranteed – at least on paper – more human and civil rights than had previously been codified in Thailand. As the first national charter to be prepared under civilian auspices, the 'people's constitution' fosters great hope in a nation battered by the ongoing economic crisis.

Prime Minister Chavalit Yongchaiyudh, was forced to resign in November 1997, after failing to deal effectively with Thailand's economic woes. An election brought former PM Chuan Leekpai back into office. Chuan's team of economists tried to right the economy from the top-down and thus neglected the rural and urban poor.

Chuan lost the election (the first ever compulsary elections held in Thailand as per the 1997 constitution) in 2001 to millionaire Thaksin Shinawatra who capitalised on widespread discontent and promised (among other things) 'a million baht' to every village if elected – which later turned into a 'loan'. Amid accusations of widespread vote-buying and violent protests in 16 provinces, Thailand's Election Commission launched an investigation into election conduct while the Counter-Corruption Commission checked into allegations of graft and 'wealth concealment' in Thaksin's past. As we went to press, Thaksin still had the helm, but how long he'll last before another election is called is anyone's guess.

## ECONOMY

Although only about 10% of the national population resides in Bangkok, roughly 60% of the country's wealth is concentrated here. Banking, finance, wholesale and retail trade, transportation, tourism and energy dominate the immediate municipality, while the surrounding metropolitan area adds manufacturing, shipping, food processing and intensive farming to the list of top revenue producers. Per capita income in metropolitan Bangkok runs well above the average in the rest of the country (US$7000

using the purchasing power parity measure), although it's second to that found in Phuket, an island province in the South.

The minimum daily wage in Bangkok and surrounding provinces, 162B (US$4.05), hasn't changed since 1996, although Thai legislators are currently lobbying to raise the figure to 180B. At the time of writing, the inflation rate was a low 2% per annum. As in most other countries, prices continue to rise.

The bursting of South-East Asia's economic bubble in 1997 for the most part stemmed from investor panic, with the rush to buy dollars to pay off debts creating a self-fulfilling collapse. Between 30 June and 31 October, the baht depreciated roughly 40% against the US dollar, and dollar-backed external debt rose to 52.4% of the country's GDP. Such currency problems echoed the European currency crisis of 1992–93 when sudden, unforeseen drops in the pound, lira and other currencies sounded the death knell of a long period of steady growth and economic stability.

Following the 1997 recession, the Thai economy shrank 10% in 1998, then grew 4% to 5% in 1999 and 2000. Exports in 1999 increased 13% over the previous year's while manufacturing rose 15%. This growth enabled Thailand to take an 'early exit' from The International Monetary Fund (IMF) US$17.2 billion rescue package of short-term loans in 2000.

At the time of writing, the economy was healthier than at any time since 1996, according to independent analysts. Despite the IMF bail-out and Thailand's subsequent move out of its recessions, the Thais are living in an era of self-imposed austerity and relatively high unemployment (7.5%). Some observers have concluded that this forced cooling off is the best thing that could have happened to the overheated economy, giving the nation time to focus on infrastructure priorities and offering the Thai citizenry an opportunity to re-assess cultural change.

The economic crisis has precipitated a national discussion about Thailand's role in globalisation. Many Thais with a shallow understanding of the situation believe that

## All Trunked Up But Nowhere to Go

The elephant is one of Thailand's most enduring (and loved) symbols – until 1917 a white elephant appeared on the Thai national flag, while today elephants are a major drawcard for tourists. Historically, Thais have worked side by side with elephants on farms and in the jungle, where they are still an important mode of transport. Around the year 1900 domesticated elephants in Thailand numbered around 100,000, now it's estimated a mere 3000 or 4000 remain and their survival (as well as that of wild elephants) is in peril.

Urbanisation, disruption of traditional lifestyles and concerns for deforestation, which recently led to banning teak logging, has resulted in elephants and their handlers *(mahouts)* being increasingly unemployed. Unsurprisingly, there are few employment vacancies listed in the *Bangkok Post* for grey, big-eared, banana-eating mammals!

The plight of these unemployed creatures has become an issue of national concern. Many domesticated elephants are increasingly neglected, mistreated or abandoned by owners who often cannot afford to care for them. These days working elephants wind up in the illegal logging industry along the Myanmar border (where they may be drugged with amphetamines to make them work faster), or turning tricks for the tourist trade by demonstrating now defunct logging skills, providing elephant rides, re-enacting historic battles or playing soccer matches.

Some mahouts are migrating to cities, like Bangkok, with their elephants in search of work, sometimes with disastrous results. City streets and crowds are not suited to the elephant's size or temperament – in 1998 an elephant died in Bangkok after getting one of its legs caught in a sewer culvert. Several incidents of pachyderm delinquency, one which involved a famished elephant running amok in a crowded street, led Bangkok officials to contemplate a blanket ban on elephants in the city.

A couple of high-profile novelty campaigns have helped raise awareness of the elephant's plight, including the world's first elephant orchestra launched by US expat Richard Lair, founder of the Thai Elephant Conservation Centre (TECC), in Lampang, Northern Thailand, and neuroscientist/avant-garde musician, Dave Soldier. Eleven elephants play sturdy, giant versions of traditional Thai instruments, such as slit drums, gongs, bow bass and xylophone-like *renats*. Their first CD recorded in the jungle might be described as 'abstract classical', with a new pop CD of Thai and American tunes planned for late 2001. Most of the profits will go towards funding the TECC and setting up a milk bank for orphaned elephants. You can purchase the CD or find out more at the Web site: www.mulatta.org.

Another well-publicised effort was implemented by Russian immigrant New York art pranksters, Komar and Melamid, who introduced 'Elephant Art' to Thailand, also at the TECC, in 1998.

While not all elephants can be taught to paint, some have taken to their new hobby with great enthusiasm – developing individual painting styles and colour preferences. Melamid was reported as saying, 'We try and stay out of artistic decisions'. Proceeds from the sales of the abstract paintings go towards elephant conservation – tourists are starting to buy up and a Christie's charity auction raised $US25,000 in 2000 – with one painting by six- year-old elephant, Ganesh, selling for US$2100.

To learn more about elephants in Thailand and how you might be able to help with donations or volunteer work, check out the Friends of the Asian Elephant Web site: www.elephant.tnet.co.th.

the IMF somehow forced this situation upon them. Many want to cut all ties with the IMF and World Bank. Some are calling for stronger tariffs on foreign goods. Others acknowledge that the reason Thailand fell into this recession in the first place was because so many middle- and upper-class Thais – not to mention banks – refused to practice any self discipline with regard to credit. As a recent *Bangkok Post* editorial pointed out, 'Developing nations may blame every ill on globalisation, but resistance only seems to widen the gulf between themselves and those who embrace it wholeheartedly'.

## POPULATION & PEOPLE

Official estimates place Metropolitan Bangkok's population at 7 million, though some sources claim this figure may be as much as a million short. The city's population density averages an astonishing 3600 persons per square kilometre.

The majority of the city's inhabitants are ethnic Thais (those born of Thai parentage who speak Thai as their first language). Up to 25% of the city's population may be of Chinese or mixed Thai and Chinese descent. The Chinese influence is strong throughout Central Thailand's Chao Phraya Delta and Bangkok is no exception. Even the Bangkok dialect shows Chinese influence in the common substitution of 'l' for 'r' in spoken Thai – even among non-Chinese. Many Bangkok Chinese-Thais speak both Thai and a Chinese dialect, such as Cantonese, Hokkien or Chiu Chau.

Bangkok's second largest Asian minority is of Indian descent. Most Indian-Thais can trace their heritage to northern India, and many are Sikhs who immigrated during the 1947 Partition of India. Many other South Asians in Bangkok – especially Nepalis, Bangladeshis and Pakistanis – are illegal immigrants who have overstayed their visitor visas in the hope of finding employment and permanent residence.

Caucasian residents number around 15,000, but since many of them live in Bangkok on Non-Immigrant Visas, which they renew every three or six months in Malaysia or Laos, it's difficult to pin their number down with any accuracy.

## EDUCATION

The literacy rate in Thailand is 93.8%, one of the highest rates in mainland South-East Asia. In 1993 the government raised compulsory schooling from six to nine years, and in 1997 it decreed that all citizens were entitled to free public schooling for 12 years. A high social value is placed on education as a way to achieve material success, the system itself favours rote learning at most levels.

Thailand's public school system is organised around six years at the *pràthŏm* (primary) level beginning at age six, followed by six years of *máthávom* (secondary) with the option of *udom* (tertiary) school. In reality less than nine years of formal education is the national norm. These statistics don't take into account the education provided by Buddhist wats in remote rural areas, where monastic schooling may be the only formal education available.

Private and international schools for the foreign and local elite are found in Bangkok and Chiang Mai, and to a lesser extent in other larger cities. The country has 12 public and five private universities, plus numerous trade schools and technical colleges. Two Bangkok universities, Thammasat and Chulalongkorn, are considered to be among the top 50 universities in Asia.

## ARTS
### Architecture

**Traditional** The table of Thai Art Styles is used by Thai art historians to categorise historical styles of Thai art, principally sculpture and architecture (since very little painting prior to the 19th century has survived).

In Bangkok you'll have the opportunity to view art from these eras in the excellent National Museum as well as at other smaller museums. Post-17th-century Thai art and architecture can also be seen in several of the city's older temples. To a lesser extent, Thai art can be seen in top-end antique shops.

**Modern** Modern Thai architects are among the most daring in South-East Asia, as even a short visit to Bangkok will confirm. Thais began mixing traditional Thai with European forms in the late 19th and early 20th centuries, as exemplified by Bangkok's Vimanmek Mansion, the Author's Wing of the Oriental Hotel, the Chakri Mahaprasat next to Wat Phra Kaew, the Thai-Chinese Chamber of Commerce on Thanon (Th) Sathon Tai, and any number of older residences and shophouses in Bangkok or provincial capitals throughout Thailand. This style is usually referred to as 'old Bangkok' or 'Ratanakosin'. The Old Siam Plaza shopping centre, adjacent to Bangkok's Chalermkrung Royal Theatre, is an attempt to revive the old Bangkok school.

## Thai Art Styles

| style | duration | centred in | characteristics |
|---|---|---|---|
| Mon Art (formerly Dvaravati) | 6th to 13th C | Central Thailand, also North and North-East | adaptation of Indian styles, principally Gupta |
| Khmer Art | 7th to 13th C | Central and North-East Thailand | post-classic Khmer styles accompanying spread of Khmer empires |
| Peninsular Art (formerly Srivijaya period) | | Chaiya and Nakhon Si Thammarat | Indian influence 3rd to 5th C, Mon and local influence 5th to 13th C, Khmer influence 11th to 14th C |
| Lan Na (formerly Chiang Saen) | 13th to 14th C | Chiang Mai, Chiang Rai, Phayao, Lamphun, Lampang | Shan/Burmese and Lao traditions mixed with local styles |
| Sukhothai | 13th to 15th C | Sukhothai, Si Satchanalai, Kamphaeng Phet, Phitsanulok | unique to Thailand |
| Lopburi | 10th to 13th C | Central Thailand | mix of Khmer, Pala and local styles |
| Suphanburi-Sangkhlaburi (formerly U Thong) | 13th to 15th C | Central Thailand | mix of Mon, Khmer, local styles; prototype for Ayuthaya style |
| Ayuthaya A | 1350–1488 | Central Thailand | Khmer influences gradually replaced by revived Sukhothai influences |
| Ayuthaya B | 1488–1630 | Central Thailand | ornamentation distinctive of Ayuthaya style begins, eg crowns and jewels on Buddhas |
| Ayuthaya C | 1630–1767 | Central Thailand | baroque stage and decline |
| Ratanakosin | 19th C to present | Bangkok | return to simpler designs, beginning of European influences |

In the 1920s and 1930s a simple Thai Deco style emerged, blending European Art Deco with modernist restraint. Surviving examples include the restored Chalermkrung Royal Theatre, the Royal Hotel, Ratchadamnoen Boxing Stadium, Hualamphong station, the main post office and several buildings along Th Ratchadamnoen Klang. Bangkok possesses the richest trove of Art Deco in South-East Asia, even surpassing the former colonial capitals of Jakarta, Kuala Lumpur, Singapore, Hanoi and Yangon (Rangoon).

Buildings of mixed heritage in the North and North-East of Thailand, exhibit French and English influences, while those in the South typically show Portuguese influence. Shophouses throughout the country, whether 100 years or 100 days old, share the basic Chinese shophouse *(hâwng thǎew)* design in which the ground floor is used for trading and the upper floors contain offices or residences.

Following WWII, Thai architecture underwent yet another transformation, abandoning traditional aesthetics for a functionalist approach that favoured quick, cheap and easy design and construction. This style of modern architecture popularised by the likes of Le Corbusier, was embraced across the globe. It was rarely welcomed for its aesthetic appeal (in fact it as often compared – unfavourably! – with things like egg cartons and transistor radios) but it facilitated the rapid growth and modernisation of cities such as Bangkok. However, the distinctive style of Thai's architecture all but disappeared during this time.

The building boom of the mid-'80s prompted Thai architects to begin experimenting again. Results included high-tech designs like Sumet Jumsai's famous robot-shaped Bank of Asia on Th Sathon Tai. Few people found the space-age look endearing, but at least it was different. Another trend was to affix gaudy Roman and Greek-style columns to rectangular Art Deco boxes in a post-modern parody of Western classical architecture. One of the outcomes of the latter fashion has been the widespread use of curvilinear balcony balustrades on almost every new shophouse, apartment or condominium throughout Thailand – often with visually disturbing results!

More recently, a handful of rebellious post-modern architects have begun reincorporating traditional Thai motifs – mixed with updated Western classics – in new buildings. Rangsan Torsuwan, a graduate of Massachusetts Institute of Technology, introduced the neoclassic (or neo-Thai) style, the best example of which is the Grand Hyatt Erawan. Another architect combining traditional Thai architecture with modern function is Pinyo Suwankiri, who has designed a number of government buildings in Bangkok as well as the Cittaphawan Buddhist School in Chonburi.

A good book for anyone with an interest in Thai architectural and interior design is William Warren's *Thai Style* (Asia Books), a coffee-table tome with excellent photography by Luca Invernizzi Tettoni.

## Painting

**Traditional** Except for a few prehistoric cave or rock-wall murals found in Ratburi, Ubon and Udon provinces, not much painting exists in Thailand predating the 18th century. Presumably there were a great number of temple murals in Ayuthaya that were destroyed by the Burmese invasion of 1767. The earliest surviving temples are found at Ayuthaya's Wat Ratburana (1424), Bangkok's Wat Chong Nonsi (1657–1707) and Phetburi's Wat Yai Suwannaram (late 17th century).

Nineteenth-century religious painting has fared better; Ratanakosin-style temples are in fact more highly esteemed for their painting than their sculpture or architecture. Typical temple murals feature rich colours and lively detail. Some of the finest are found in Bangkok, at Wat Phra Kaew's Wihaan Phutthaisawan (Buddhaisawan Chapel), the Grand Palace, and Wat Suwannaram in Thonburi.

**Modern** The beginnings of Thailand's modern art movement are usually attributed to Italian artist Corrado Feroci, who was invited to Thailand by King Rama VI in 1924. Feroci founded the country's first fine arts institute in 1933, which eventually developed into Silpakorn University, Thailand's premier training ground for artists and art historians. In gratitude for his contributions, the government gave Feroci the Thai name Silpa Bhirasri.

Modern painting and sculpture are exhibited at a number of Bangkok venues. One of the most important modern movements in Thai art was an updating of Buddhist themes, begun in the 1970s by painters Pichai Nirand, Thawan Duchanee and Prateung Emjaroen. The movement has grown stronger since their early efforts combined modern Western schemata with Thai motifs.

In the 1990s art with strong social comment became more popular, and such works moved out of the galleries to temporary 'installations' at streetside or in shopping centres. Performance art, focussed on the artists themselves, also briefly blossomed. Performance activist/artist Manit Sriwanichpoom earned the greatest notoriety for his 'pink man' appearances, in which he dressed entirely in pink while delivering anti-globalisation messages. In one such performance he stood behind a pink shopping cart below a sign reading 'Pepsi hilltribe culture conservation village'.

Today, Bangkok's luxury hotels act as important venues and sources of support for modern art. The largest collection of modern Thai painting anywhere in the world is found in the lobbies and public areas of the Grand Hyatt Erawan, with displays changing regularly. (See Art Galleries in the Things to See & Do chapter.)

## Music
Throughout Thailand you'll find a wide variety of musical genres and styles, from the serene court music that accompanies classical dance-drama to the chest-thumping house music played at Bangkok's latest discos. Even in Thai monasteries – where music is proscribed by the *vinaya* (monastic discipline) – the chanting of the monks has musical qualities.

**Traditional Classical** From a Western perspective, traditional Thai musical forms are some of the most bizarre on the planet, but acquiring a taste for them is well worth the effort. Classical, Central Thai music is spicy, like Thai food, and features an incredible array of textures and subtleties, hair-raising tempos and pastoral melodies. One reason classical Thai music may sound strange to the Western ear is that it does not use the tempered scale we have been accustomed to hearing since Bach's time. The standard scale does feature an eight-note octave, but it is arranged in seven full intervals, with no 'semi-tones'. Thai scales were first transcribed by Thai-German composer Phra Chen Duriyanga (Peter Feit), who also composed Thailand's national anthem in 1932.

Thai classical orchestra is called the *pìi-phâat* and can include as few as five players or more than 20. The pìi-phâat ensemble was originally developed to accompany classical dance-drama and shadow theatre, but can be heard in straightforward performance these days in temple fairs as well as concerts. Among the more common instruments is the *pìi*, a woodwind instrument that has a reed mouthpiece and is heard at Thai boxing matches. The pìi is a relative of a similar Indian instrument, while the *phin*, a banjo-like stringed instrument whose name comes from the Indian *vina*, is considered native to Thailand. A bowed instrument similar to ones played in China and Japan is aptly called the *saw*. The *ránâat èk* is the bamboo-keyed percussion instrument resembling the Western xylophone, while the *khlùi* is a wooden flute.

One of the more amazing Thai instruments is the *kháwng wong yài*, tuned gongs arranged in a semicircle. There are also several different kinds of drums, some played with the hands, some with sticks. The most important Thai percussion instrument is the *tà-phon* (or *thon*), a double-headed hand drum, which sets the tempo for the ensemble. Prior to a performance, the players make offerings of incense and flowers to the tà-phon, which is considered to be the 'conductor' of the music's spiritual content.

In the North and North-East there are several popular types of reed instruments with multiple bamboo pipes, which basically function like a mouth-organ. Chief among

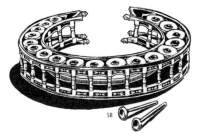

The kháwng wong yài consists of tuned gongs
arranged in a circular shape.

these is the *khaen,* which originated in Laos.
The khaen provides the backbone of *măw
lam,* a traditional style of music popular with
villages in Isan (North-Eastern Thailand).

**Resources** If you're interested in learning
how to play traditional Thai instruments,
contact the Bangkok YMCA (Map 7, ☎ 287
1900) to inquire about its weekly classes.
Recommended books on the subject are *The
Traditional Music of Thailand* by David
Morton and *Thai Music* by Phra Chen
Duriyanga (Peter Feit).

**Rock** Popular Thai music has borrowed
much from Western music, particularly its
instruments, but still retains a distinct
flavour of its own. Bangkok bar bands cover
everything from Jimi Hendrix to Madonna;
however, over the last 15 years the local
music scene has exploded with new stars
popping up on the charts every week.

One of Thailand's most famous and certainly most enduring rock groups is
Carabao, who have been recording and performing for more than 20 years. As well as
being Thailand's most popular group,
Carabao also scored hits in Malaysia, Singapore, Indonesia and the Philippines. The
band developed a reputation for being political thanks to nationalistic songs like
'Made in Thailand' (the chorus is in English), 'Thap Lang' which lobbied for the return of a stolen temple lintel on display at
the Art Institute of Chicago (lyrics included
the line: 'Keep Michael Jackson but give us

back the lintel'! The cover featured the
Statue of Liberty holding the lintel under
her arm), and the band's prominence during
the democracy demonstrations of 1992.

Carabao has crafted an exciting fusion of
Thai classical and *lûuk thûng* forms with
heavy metal. Carabao's influence was so
strong, that for a long time almost every
other Thai pop group sounded like a
Carabao clone. Members of the original
band later produced solo albums using the
now-classic Carabao sound.

Another major influence on Thai pop was
a 1970s group called Caravan, which created a modern Thai folk style known as
*phleng phêua chii-wít* (songs for life). Like
Western protest songs, music of this genre
has political and environmental subjects
rather than the usual moonstruck love
themes – during the authoritarian dictator-
ships of the 1970s many of Caravan's songs
were banned by the government. Following
the massacre of student demonstrators in
1976, some members of Caravan fled to the
hills to take up guerilla-type activities with
communist groups. Though the band dis-
solved in the early 1980s, they re-form for
the occasional live concert. The group's
most gifted songwriter, Surachai, continues
to record and release solo efforts.

Economic growth during the 1980s kick-
started the now thriving local pop scene –
with sales and promotion monopolised by
Thai's music industry heavyweight,
Grammy. Stars included the silky-throated
mega-star 'Bird' Thongchai MacIntryre,
who is also known for his on-screen film ex-
ploits playing several roles simultaneously;
and soft-rock duo brothers Asanee & Wasan
who remained popular into the 1990s.

The music scene soon became dominated
by production house packaged pop/TV star
artists with cute names, like 'Mos' and
'Nook'. Whether solo or group efforts, most
acts followed commercial formulae imported from the West or from Japan, with
Thai lyrics and melodies dominated by typical boy-group/teen-queen presentations.

Most popular of all were artists who
were *lûuk khrêung,* literally 'half child'
(ie, of mixed Thai and European heritage),

FACTS ABOUT BANGKOK

## Lûuk Thûng – Truckin' Music

Crawling along in Bangkok's peak-hour traffic from the backseat of a taxi, you may find yourself humming along to a tune weirdly reminiscent of schmaltzy Golden Hollywood soundtracks, rollicking Latino peasant ballads and Thai pop all rolled into one. Don't be alarmed – you've merely been seduced by the strange, but catchy strains of *lûuk thûng*, a kind of Thai country music that is the music of choice for many of Bangkok's migrant taxi drivers lonesome for their rural homes in the North-Eastern regions.

Whether it's slow and sentimental, or upbeat and corny, the popularity of lûuk thûng dims and shines with the times. But while Bangkok sophisticates snub it as country-bumpkin music, the launching of a 24-hour lûuk thûng national radio station (Lûuk thûng FM) in 1997 suggests that country is here to stay.

Lûuk thûng, which translates as 'Child of the Fields', emerged in the 1950s, a melding of Thai folk tunes with regional and Western influences, ranging from saccharine Hollywood soundtracks and Latin brass to – who could resist it? – yodelling. However, whether Western ears can discern these influences or not is debatable.

Part of the genre's popularity is due to the spectacular nature of lûuk thûng shows that tour temple fairs around the country, combining song, dance, comedy and large casts attired in a weird array of costumes – from royalty to rambutans. Country Thais enjoy the genre for its easy sing-a-long tunes and because they relate to its hard luck tales about poor hard-working farmers, lonely truck drivers and city waitresses far from home.

The genre's popularity skyrocketed in the 1960s with the stardom of Suraphon Sombatjalern, a kind of Thai country Dean Martin.

But the most popular lûuk thûng star of all was Pumpuang Duangjan, whose life mirrored the dreams and tragedies of the songs that she sung. The illiterate daughter of a farming family, Pumpuang left her rural town of Suphanbri to seek her fortune in the big city. She joined a band as a dancer at the age of 14 and soon after eloped with the saxophone player (who later ran off with her sister) before becoming the band's lead singer. She eventually became one of Thailand's most famous, if tragic, musical heroines. The extraordinary range of her voice ensured her nationwide success across all social levels; she once sang a song about *sôm tam* (Thailand's popular spicy papaya salad) penned for her by Princess Sirindhorn for a royal performance. At the same time her personal life was marked by heartbreak, and she suffered a string of much publicised failed love affairs. One of the most colourful rumours circulated was that she paid her married lover's wife so that she might keep him as her own, only to have him spend all her money, run her into debt and abandon her for his original wife. Pumpuang peaked in the 1980s when she pioneered the pop-style electronic lûuk thûng. She died in 1992, at the age of 31 from an immune system-related illness.

These days, big lûuk thûng stars include ex-soap opera star Got Chakraband, and Monsit Khamsoi, whose trademark silky, almost sleazy vocal style proved enormously popular with his hit, *Sang Nang*, which was played ad nauseam in 1999.

Would-be aficionados can track down modern and classical lûuk thûng in most Bangkok music stores.

**Rachael Antony with Bruce Evans**

including the still immensely popular performers Marsha Wattanapanich, Myria Nat Benedetti and especially Anita 'Tata' Young.

The 1990s saw a reaction to the packaging concept as an alternative pop scene grew in Bangkok. Hip-hop/ska group Joey Boy not only explored new musical frontiers but released lyrics that the Department of Culture banned. One such song included the common Thai euphemism for male masturbation, *chák wâo* (pull a kite), while another narrated a story of child abuse.

In 1992 Modern Dog, a Brit-pop inspired band of four Chulalongkorn University graduates, won the Coke Music Awards. They're generally credited with bringing independent Thai music into the mainstream, and their success prompted an explosion of similar bands and indie recording labels. Their self-titled album charted for years and at the time of writing they were recording a new album – like Joey Boy, they're on the Bakery Music label.

As the new millennium began, with more than 50 indie labels battling Grammy for airspace, crowd-pleasers Loso (from 'low society') updated Carabao's affinity for Thai folk melodies and rhythms with straight guitar rock. Grammy has responded with a rash of Thai headbangers designed to fill stadiums and outsell the indies. As in the West, some of the indies have been compelled to enter mergers to survive. Bakery Music was recently acquired by BMG Entertainment, a division of Bertelsmann AG, the world's largest media conglomerate.

If you'd like to know what the youngsters of Thailand are getting into, head to a music shop and ask to check out the bestsellers. As the world of Thai pop changes on a weekly basis, the best we can say is that at the time of writing the charts were dominated by female singers – perhaps teeny-bopper girls have the most to spend on music? Girls in the charts included Rudklao, Nong Pimluck, Nicole and Kat. Other bands winning the hearts and minds of Thai teenagers were P.O.P, Modern Dog, heart-throb singer and model Peter, LoSo, Silly Fools and girl-band Budokan.

**Jazz** Yet another inspiring movement in modern Thai music is the fusion of international jazz with Thai classical and folk motifs. The leading exponent of this newer genre is the composer and instrumentalist Tewan Sapsanyakorn (also known as Tong Tewan), whose performances mix Western and Thai instruments. The melodies of his compositions are often Thai-based, but the improvisations and rhythms are drawn from such heady sources as Sonny Rollins and Jean-Luc Ponty. Tewan himself plays

soprano and alto sax, violin and khlùi with equal virtuosity. When Tewan isn't touring internationally you may catch him and his band at various Bangkok clubs (see Live Music in the Entertainment chapter).

Other notable groups fusing international jazz and indigenous Thai music include Kangsadarn and Boy Thai; the latter adds Brazilian samba and reggae to the mix. Thai instrumentation in world music settings are specialities of Todd Lavelle and Nupap Savantrachas, each of whom scored hits in Thailand during the late 1990s. Fong Nam, a Thai orchestra led by American composer Bruce Gaston, performs an inspiring blend of Western and Thai classical motifs.

## Theatre & Dance

Traditional Thai theatre consists of six dramatic forms: *khŏn,* formal masked dance-drama depicting scenes from the *Ramakian* (the Thai version of the Indian classic, the *Ramayana*) and originally performed only for the royal court; *lákhon,* a general term covering several types of dance-dramas (usually for non-royal occasions) as well as Western theatre; *lí-keh* (pronounced likay), a partly improvised, often bawdy folk play with dancing and music; *mánohraa,* the southern Thai equivalent of lí-keh, but based on a 2000-year-old Indian story; *năng* (shadow plays), limited to southern Thailand; and *hùn lŭang* or *lákhon lék* (puppet theatre).

*Ramakian: The Thai Ramayana,* published by Naga Books, is a thorough exposition of the Thai version of Indian poet Valmiki's timeless epic.

**Khŏn** In all khŏn performances, four types of characters are represented – male humans, female humans, monkeys and demons. Monkey and demon figures are always masked with the elaborate head coverings often seen in tourist promo material. Behind the masks and make-up, all actors are male. Traditional khŏn is very expensive to produce – Ravana's retinue alone (Ravana is the story's principal villain) consists of over 100 demons, each with a distinctive mask. Perhaps because it was once limited to royal venues and hence never gained a popular following, the khŏn tradition nearly died out in Thailand. Until recently Bangkok's National Theatre was one of the few places where khŏn was still performed for the public. Now the renovated Chalermkrung Royal Theatre hosts weekly khŏn performances enhanced by laser graphics and high-tech audio.

Scenes performed in traditional khŏn (and lákhon performances) come from the *Ramayana*. The central story revolves around Prince Rama's search for his beloved Princess Sita, who has been abducted by the evil 10-headed demon Ravana and taken to the island of Lanka. Rama is assisted in his search, and in the final battle against Ravana, by a host of mythical half-animal, half-human characters, including the monkey-god Hanuman.

**Lákhon** The more formal *lákhon nai* (inner lákhon) was originally performed for lower nobility by all-female ensembles; today it's a dying art, even more so than royal khŏn. In addition to scenes from the *Ramakian,* lákhon nai performances may include traditional Thai folk tales; whatever the story, text is always sung.

*Lákhon nâwk* (outer lákhon) deals exclusively with folk tales and features a mix of sung and spoken text, sometimes with improvisation. Both male and female performers are permitted. Like khŏn and lákhon nai, performances are becoming increasingly rare. More common these days is the less-refined *lákhon chaatrii,* a fast-paced, costumed dance-drama usually performed at upcountry temple festivals or shrines (commissioned by a shrine devotee whose wish has been granted by the shrine deity).

A variation on chaatrii that has evolved specifically for shrine worship is *lákhon kâe bon.* This involves an ensemble of around 20 members, including musicians, who can be hired by worshippers to perform a dance of thanks to the spirits in return for answered prayers. You can see performances at Bangkok's Lak Meuang from 9 am and until 3 pm; each performance lasts 10 minutes or so. There is usually a long list of worshippers waiting to hire the troupe.

*Lákhon phûut* (spoken lákhon) is the equivalent of Western theatre based on the Greek model – all dialogue is spoken rather than sung. This is the most modern of Thailand's theatre traditions, but also the least popular. Live theatre's existence in Bangkok is limited to one serious venue, Patravadi Theatre (see the Entertainment chapter for details). If you're really desperate for English theatre you could consider checking out the amateur ex-pat offerings at the Playhouse Theater (☎ 02-319 7641), 84/2 Th Phetburi Tat Mai.

## Cinema

In 1922 film director Henry McRay came to Thailand to film the silent *Nang Sao Suwan,* which used Thai actors for all roles and was released in Thailand in 1923. The storyline followed the tribulations of a beautiful young Thai girl with too many suitors. However, no viewable print of this film appears to have survived. Silent films proved to be more popular than talkies right into the 1960s, and as late as 1969 Thai studios were producing up to 130 different silent films a year, all on colour 16mm stock. The usual practice for screening such films was to have live or recorded narrators on hand to accompany the projection.

In the 1970s and 1980s Thai film-production was limited almost entirely to cheap action or romance stories of low quality. The exceptions were a handful of films made for the international festival circuit, films that Thai audiences hardly ever saw or liked, such as Wichit Khunawut's *Khon Phu Khao* (Mountain People) and MC Chatri Yugala's *Khon Liang Chang* (Elephant Keeper) and the occasional period epic of quality, such as *Khunseuk* (Warrior; 1952 and 1976) and *Luk Isan* (Child of the North-East; 1983).

Notable films during the early 1990s include Prince Chatri's *Nong Mia* (The Song of Chao-Phraya). Named after the river running through Bangkok, *Nong Mia* is about a boatman who trawls through Bangkok's bars and brothels in search of his wife who has abandoned their hard-working river life for the pursuit of glamour and excitement in the big smoke.

Also popular was the entertaining *Galok Bang Tai Cha, Galok Bang Na Tai Gon* (The Dumb Die Fast, the Smart Die Slow). Directed by former underground political film maker, Manop Udomdej, it's a Thai take on the hard-boiled thriller genre, featuring a well-meaning service station owner, his scheming wife and a hitchhiker on the run.

Ironically the post-1997-recession years have seen a substantial leap in the quality of popular Thai cinema. *Fun Bar Karaoke,* a 1997 satire of Bangkok life in which the main characters are an ageing Thai playboy and his daughter, received critical acclaim for its realistic depiction of modern urban living mixed with sage humour. *Nang Nak*, based on a famous Thai ghost story in which a young pregnant woman (named Nak) and her baby die during childbirth, and later come back to haunt her husband, not only featured excellent acting and special effects, but brought out lots of interesting bits on Thai animism. The 1998 film became the largest-grossing film in Thai history, and is now available on video with English subtitles.

*Bangkok Dangerous*, a gritty Thai gangster film directed by Hong Kong brothers Oxide and Danny Pang, focussed on a deaf Thai hit man coming to the realisation that what he does for a living is wrong. Popular at international film festivals around the world in late 2000, the movie earned the International Film Critics Society's Fipresci Prize, which honours impressive international film debuts. Another 2000 debut, Wisit Sasanatieng's *Fah Talai Jone,* took viewers on a wild romp into Thailand's B-film past, mixing the anachronistic 'Thai Western' genre with vibrantly coloured landscapes and melodramatic romance.

The success of serious Thai screen efforts like *Nang Nak, Fun Bar Karaoke, Bangkok Dangerous* and *Fah Talai Jone* has led critics to herald the arrival of a 'Thai new wave' cinema.

The hilarious 2000 film *Satri Lek* (Iron Women), based on the true story of a Lampang volleyball team made up almost entirely of transvestites and transsexuals who won a national (men's) volleyball championship, became Thai cinema's second-largest grossing film thus far. When *Satri Lek* was released in Bangkok, a print with English subtitles was screened at one local cinema, probably a first for any major Thai theatre release. Like *Nang Nak,* the film is available with English subtitles on video.

The next Thai movie likely to garner some international attention is *Queen Suriyothai.* In the making for nearly two years, this film narrates a well-known episode in Thai history in which a queen in the Ayuthaya court sacrifices her life in a battle against Burma to save her husband's life.

Also look out for *Moon Hunter*; based on the life of academic Seksan Prasertkul, a leader of the mass student uprising of the 14 October 1973 it deals with his life and the events that ultimately toppled Thailand's military dictatorship. The script was co-written by Prasertkul and former reporter for *The Nation,* Bandhid Rittikol, who covered the 1973 protests. The film, which was in production at the time of writing, will be the first to deal with these historical events, which makers say was made with the 'wholehearted assistance' of the military.

## SOCIETY & CONDUCT
### Traditional Culture
The term 'culture' in Western society is often used to describe the fine arts, like theatre and painting, or obvious manifestations of culture such as cuisine or national dress. Thai culture, as discussed here, refers to the complex set of behavioural modes, and belief and value structures that guide all aspects of Thai life – from food and humour, to marriage, religious beliefs and daily interaction, including the way Thai culture interacts with Western influences.

In this broad sense, Thai culture has developed over time and through the course of Thai immigration through South-East Asia. Thai culture shares many similarities with related ethnic groups such as the Lao of neighbouring Laos, the Shan of north-eastern Myanmar, and isolated pockets of tribal Thais ranging from Dien Bien Phu, Vietnam, all the way to Assam, India.

Over time, the numerous ethnic groupings within Thailand have been largely

## Cut & Paste

Thai women have an expression they may invoke when seriously angry with their husbands or boyfriends, particularly in cases of sexual infidelity: 'If you don't behave, I'm going to cut it off and feed it to the ducks.' Unfortunately for Thai men, it's more than just an expression, as Thailand appears to have an unusually large number of cases in which jealous women have severed the penises of their lovers. Besides the proverbial duck feeding, other reported methods of disposal include tying the severed member to a helium balloon and allowing it to float into the firmament.

More than a few penises, however, are recovered more or less intact and reunited with their owners at Bangkok hospitals through a very complicated microsurgery procedure in which certain Thai hospitals excel. Thailand in fact performs more penis reattachments than any other nation.

Perhaps it's no coincidence then that Thailand is also a major world centre for transgender surgery, or what the Thai surgeons who specialise in the procedures prefer to call 'sex reassignment surgery'. So popular is the operation that some Bangkok clinics perform up to 10 sex re-assignment procedures per day. Many of the clients come from outside Thailand, primarily the Philippines, Japan, Scandinavia and the USA. These clients are primarily drawn by the skill of Thailand's plastic surgeons, although lower prices and legal laxity relative to other countries are also major factors.

The vast majority of the surgical transformations proceed from male to female, although a very few Thai surgeons do perform the much more difficult and costly female to male procedures. The typical male to female procedure complete with silicone breasts and an anatomically correct vagina (resplendent with a clitoris fashioned from the most sensitive part of the head of the penis) takes around 90 minutes and costs US$7000. By contrast the female to male procedure usually involves five separate surgical sessions at a cost of up to US$100,000.

assimilated into a culture recognisable as mainstream Thai. Though, regional particularities do exist, and the hill tribes of the Northern regions maintain their own distinct cultures.

Thai culture today clearly reflects recent Western influences, aspects that might be deemed 'Westernisation' by both Thais and foreigners, eg, the wearing of trousers instead of *phâakhamáa* (short sarong for men), the presence of automobiles, cinemas and 7-Eleven stores. While some regard this as an erosion of Thai culture, it's really just another instance of Thai culture incorporating external cultural influences as it has always done.

Such adaptations do not necessarily represent cultural loss. Ekawit Na Talang, a scholar of Thai culture and head of the government's National Culture Commission, defines culture as 'the system of thought and behaviour of a particular society – something which is dynamic and never static'. Cultures can not exist within a vacuum – all cultures evolve as the outside influences they come into contact with are naturalised. As Talang has said, 'Anything obsolete, people will reject and anything that has a relevant role in life, people will adopt and make it part of their culture'.

While not all merging has happy results, it can produce exciting cultural fusions, whereby one could argue that aspects of Western culture are actually 'Thai-ised', like Thai soap operas, pop music and modern Thai fashions. And of course, the latest Thai craze is as likely to be an import from Hong Kong or Japan as it is to hail from the USA.

The Thais themselves don't really have a word that corresponds to the English term 'culture'. The nearest equivalent, *wáthánátham*, emphasises fine arts and ceremonies over other aspects usually covered by the concept. So if you ask Thais to define their culture, they'll often talk about architecture, food, dance, festivals and the like. Religion – obviously a big influence on culture as defined in the Western sense – is considered more or less separate from wáthánátham.

Nevertheless there are certain aspects of Thai society that virtually everyone recognises as 'Thai' cultural markers.

## Sànùk

The Thai word *sànùk* means 'fun'. In Thailand anything worth doing, even work, should have an element of sànùk, otherwise it automatically becomes drudgery. This doesn't mean Thais don't want to work or strive, just that they tend to approach tasks with a sense of playfulness. Nothing condemns an activity more than the description *mâi sànùk,* 'not fun'. Sit down beside a rice field and watch workers planting, transplanting or harvesting rice while you're in Thailand. That it's back-breaking labour is obvious, but participants generally inject the activity with lots of sànùk – flirtation between the sexes, singing, trading insults and cracking jokes. The same goes in an office or a bank, or other white-collar work situations – at least when the office in question is predominantly Thai (businesses run by non-Thais don't necessarily exhibit sànùk). The famous Thai smile comes partially out of this desire to make sànùk.

## Face

Thais believe strongly in the concept of 'saving face', that is avoiding confrontation and endeavouring not to embarrass themselves or other people (except when it's sànùk to do so!). The ideal face-saver doesn't bring up negative topics in everyday conversation, and when they notice stress in another's life, they usually won't say anything unless that person complains or asks for help. Laughing at minor accidents – like when someone trips and falls down – may seem callous to outsiders but it's really just an attempt to save face on behalf of the person undergoing the mishap. This is another source of the Thai smile – it's the best possible face to put on in almost any situation.

## Status & Obligation

All relationships in traditional Thai society – and virtually all relationships in the modern Thai milieu as well – are governed by connections between *phûu yài* (literally, 'big person') and *phûu náwy* ('little person'). Phûu náwy are supposed to defer to phûu yài following simple lines of social rank defined by age, wealth, status, and personal and political power. Examples of 'automatic' phûu yài status include adults (vs children), bosses (vs employees), elder classmates (vs younger classmates), elder siblings (vs younger siblings), teachers (vs pupils), military (vs civilian), Thai (vs non-Thai) and so on.

While this tendency towards social ranking is to some degree shared by many societies around the world, the Thai twist lies in the set of mutual obligations linking phûu yài to phûu náwy. Sociologists have referred to this phenomenon as the 'patron-client relationship'. Phûu náwy are supposed to show a degree of obedience and respect (together these concepts are covered by the single Thai term *'kreng jai'*) towards phûu yài, but in return phûu yài are obligated to care for or 'sponsor' the phûu náwy they have frequent contact with. In such relationships phûu náwy can, for example, ask phûu yài for favours involving money or job access. Phûu yài re-affirm their rank by granting such requests when possible, to refuse would be to risk loss of face and status.

Age is a large determinant where other factors are absent or weak. In such cases the terms *phîi* (elder sibling) and *náwng* (younger sibling) apply more than phûu yài or phûu náwy, although the intertwined obligations remain the same. Even people unrelated by blood quickly establish who's phîi and who's náwng. This is why one of the first questions Thais ask new acquaintances is 'How old are you?'.

When dining, touring or entertaining, the phûu yài always picks up the tab; if a group is involved, the person with most social rank pays the check for everyone, even if it empties his or her wallet. For a phûu náwy to try and pay would risk loss of face. Money plays a large role in defining phûu yài status in most situations. A person who turned out to be successful in his or her post-school career would never think of allowing an ex-classmate of lesser success, even if they were once on an equal social footing, to pay the bill. Likewise a young, successful executive will pay an older person's way in spite of the age difference.

The implication is that whatever wealth you come into is to be shared – at least partially – with those who have been less fortunate. This doesn't apply to strangers – the average Thai isn't big on charity – but always comes into play with friends and relatives.

Foreigners often feel offended when they encounter such phenomena as two-tiered pricing for hotels or sightseeing attractions – one price for Thais, a higher price for foreigners. But this is simply another expression of the traditional patron-client relationship. On the one hand foreigners who can afford to travel to Thailand are seen to have more wealth than Thai citizens (on average this is self-evident), hence they're expected to help subsidise Thai enjoyment of these commodities; and at the same time, paradoxically, the Thais feel they are due certain special privileges as homelanders – what might be termed the 'home town discount'. Another example you might experience is in a post office line – Thais get served first as part of their nature-given national privilege.

## Comportment

Personal power (*baará-mii,* sometimes mistranslated as 'charisma') also has a bearing on one's social status, and can be gained by cleaving as close as possible to the ideal 'Thai' behaviour. *Khwaam pen thai* ('Thainess') is first and foremost defined, as might be expected, by the ability to speak Thai. It doesn't matter which dialect, although Southern Thai – with its Malay/Yawi influences – is slightly more suspect, mainly due to Southern Thailand's association with the 'foreign' religion of Islam.

Other hallmarks of the Thai ideal – heavily influenced by Thai Buddhism – include discrete behaviour towards the opposite sex, modest dress, a neat and clean appearance, and modes of expression and comportment that value the quiet, subtle and indirect rather than the loud, obvious and direct.

The degree to which Thais can conform to these ideals matches the degree of respect they receive from most of their asso-

ciates. Although high rank – based on age or civil, military or clerical roles – will exempt certain individuals from chastisement by their social 'inferiors', it doesn't exempt them from the way they are perceived by other Thais. This goes for foreigners as well, even though most first-time visitors can hardly be expected to speak idiomatic Thai. But if you do learn some Thai, and you make an effort to respect Thai social ideals, you'll come closer to enjoying some of the perks awarded for khwaam pen thai.

## Dos & Don'ts

Monarchy and religion are the two sacred cows in Thailand. Thais are tolerant of most kinds of behaviour as long as it doesn't insult either of these.

**King & Country** The monarchy is held in considerable respect in Thailand and visitors should be respectful too – avoid disparaging remarks about the king, queen or anyone in the royal family. One of Thailand's more outspoken intellectuals, Sulak Sivaraksa, was arrested in the early 1980s for lese-majesty because of a passing reference to the king's fondness for yachting (Sulak referred to His Majesty as 'the skipper') and again in 1991 when he referred to the royal family as 'ordinary people'. Although on the latter occasion he received a royal pardon, later in 1991 Sulak had to flee the country to avoid prosecution again for alleged remarks delivered at Thammasat University about the ruling military junta, with reference to the king (Sulak has since returned under a suspended sentence). The penalty for lese-majesty is seven years imprisonment.

While it's OK to criticise the Thai government and even Thai culture openly, it's considered a grave insult to Thai nationhood as well as to the monarchy not to stand when you hear the national or royal anthems. Radio and TV stations in Thailand broadcast the national anthem daily at 8 am and 6 pm. In towns and villages (even in some Bangkok neighbourhoods) this can be heard over public loudspeakers in the streets. The Thais stop whatever they're doing to stand during the anthem, (except in

## Rama V Cult

A new spirit cult venerating King Rama V (also known as King Chulalongkorn, or to the Thais as Chula Chom Klao), who reigned from 1868 to 1910, has swept Thailand since 1991. In Bangkok the most visible devotional activities are focused on a bronze statue of Rama V in Royal Plaza (Map 3) opposite Abhisek Dusit Throne Hall. The statue, intended only as a historical commemoration, has quite literally become a religious shrine. Every Tuesday evening thousands of Bangkokians come to offer candles, flowers (predominantly pink roses), incense and bottles of whisky to the newly ordained demigod. Worship of the statue begins around 9 pm and continues till early in the morning.

The cult is particularly strong in Bangkok and other large urban centres, since its members tend to be middle-class and nouveau riche Thais with careers in commerce or the professions. However, all over Thailand, Rama V portraits are selling briskly. Some devotees place the portraits at home altars, while others wear tiny, coloured porcelain likenesses of the king on gold chains around their necks in place of the usual *phrá phim* (Buddhist amulet). In some social circles Rama V amulets are now more common than any other phrá phim.

No single event occurred to ignite the Rama V movement. Its growth can, however, be traced to a series of events beginning with the 1991 military coup – which caused the intelligentsia to once again lose faith in the constitutional monarchy – and followed by the 1990-92 economic recession and 1997-98 baht crash. Along with worsening traffic and a host of other problems, these events brought about an unfocussed, general mistrust of modern politics, technology and affluence. Many Thais began looking for a new spiritual outlet with some historical relevancy. They seized on Rama V, a king who – without the help of a parliament or the military – brought Thai nationalism to the fore while fending off European colonialism. He is also considered a champion of the common person for his abolition of slavery and corvée (the requirement that every citizen be available for state labour when called).

Ironically, few Rama V cultists realise that Rama V conceded substantial Thai territory to French Indochina and British Malaya during his reign – a total loss of land greater than any Thai king had allowed since before the Sukhothai era. Rama V also deserves more of the blame for 'Westernisation' than any other single monarch. He was the first king to travel to Europe, which he did in 1897 and again in 1907. After seeing Europeans eating with forks, knives and spoons, he discouraged the Thai tradition of taking food with the hands; he also introduced chairs to the kingdom (before his reign, Thais sat on the floor or on floor cushions). Following one European visit he asked his No 1 concubine to grow her hair long after the European fashion; by custom Thai women had kept their hair cropped short since the Ayuthaya period.

---

Bangkok where nobody can hear anything above the street noise) and visitors are expected to do likewise. Visitors should keep an ear out for the anthem at Bangkok's Hualamphong station, and be aware that it will be played in cinemas throughout the country just before films are shown – again, the audience always stands until it's over.

**Religion** Correct behaviour in temples entails several considerations, the most important of which is to dress neatly and to take your shoes off when you enter any building that contains a Buddha image (as you would in a Thai home). Buddha images are sacred objects, so don't pose in front of them for pictures and definitely do not clamber upon them.

Shorts or sleeveless shirts are considered improper dress for both men and women when visiting temples. Some wats will offer trousers or long sarongs for rent so that tourists dressed in shorts may enter the compound.

Monks *(bhikkhu)* are not supposed to touch or be touched by women. If a woman wants to hand something to a monk, the object should be placed within reach of the monk, not handed directly to him – or alternatively placed on the monk's 'offering cloth'.

Keep your feet pointed away from any Buddha images. The usual way to do this is to sit in the 'mermaid' pose in which your legs are folded to the side, with the feet pointing backwards.

A few of the larger wats in Bangkok charge small entry fees. In others, offering a small donation before leaving the compound is appropriate but not mandatory. Usually there are donation boxes near the entry of the *bòt* (central sanctuary) or next to the central Buddha image at the rear. In rural wats, there may be no donation box available, in this case, it's OK to leave money on the floor next to the central image or even by the doorway, where temple attendants will collect it later.

**Social Gestures & Attitudes** Traditionally Thais greet each other not with a handshake but with a prayer-like palms-together gesture known as a *wâi*. If a Thai adult greets you with a wâi, you should wâi in response. Most urban Thais are familiar with the Western-style handshake and will offer the same to a foreigner, although a wâi is always appreciated.

Thais are often addressed by their first name with the honorific *khun* or other title preceding it. Other formal terms of address include *nai* (Mr) and *naang* (Miss or Mrs). Friends often use nicknames or kinship terms like *phîi* (elder sibling), *náwng* (younger sibling), *mâe* (mother) or *lung* (uncle), depending on the age difference.

A smile and the all purpose Thai greeting *sawàt-dii khráp* (if you're male) or *sawàt-dii khâ* (if you're female) goes a long way towards calming the initial trepidation that locals may feel upon seeing a foreigner, whether in the city or the countryside.

When handing things to other people you should use both hands or your right hand only, never the left hand (reserved for toilet ablutions). Books and other written material are given a special status over other secular objects. Hence you shouldn't slide books or documents across a table or counter-top, and never place them on the floor – use a chair if table space isn't available.

When encounters take a turn for the worse, try to refrain from getting angry – it won't help matters, since losing one's temper means loss of face for everyone present. Remember that this is Asia, where keeping your cool is paramount. Talking loudly is perceived as rude behaviour by cultured Thais, whatever the situation. See the previous entries on Face and Comportment regarding the rewards for khwaam pen thai – the pushy foreigner often gets served last.

**Feet & Head** The feet are the lowest part of the body (spiritually as well as physically) so don't point your feet at people or point at things with your feet. Don't prop your feet on chairs or tables while sitting. Never touch any part of someone's body with your foot.

In the same context, the head is regarded as the highest part of the body, so don't touch Thais on the head – or ruffle their hair – either. If you touch someone's head accidentally, offer an immediate apology or you'll be perceived as very rude.

Don't sit on pillows meant for sleeping – this represents a variant of the taboo against head-touching. I once watched a young woman on Ko Samet bring a bed pillow from her bungalow to sit on while watching TV; the Thai staff got very upset and she didn't understand why.

Never step over someone, even on a crowded 3rd-class train where people are sitting or lying on the floor. Instead squeeze around them or ask them to move.

**Dress & Nudity** Shorts (except knee-length walking shorts), sleeveless shirts, tank tops (singlets) and other beach-style attire are not considered appropriate dress in Thailand for anything other than sporting events. This kind of clothing is especially counterproductive if worn to government offices (eg, when applying for a visa extension). The attitude of 'This is how I dress at home and no one is going to stop me' gains nothing but contempt or disrespect from Thais.

Sandals or slip-on shoes are OK for almost any but the most formal occasions, likewise short-sleeved shirts and blouses with capped sleeves are quite acceptable.

Thais would never dream of going abroad and wearing dirty clothes, so they are often shocked to see Westerners travelling around Thailand in clothes that apparently haven't been washed for some time. If you keep up with your laundry, you'll receive much better treatment everywhere you go.

Regardless of what the Thais may or may not have been accustomed to centuries ago, they are quite offended by public nudity today. Bathing nude at beaches in Thailand is illegal. If you are at a truly deserted beach and are sure no Thais may come along, there's nothing stopping you; however, at most beaches travellers should wear suitable attire. Likewise, topless bathing for females is frowned upon in most places except on heavily touristed islands like Phuket, Samui, Samet and Pha-Ngan. According to Thailand's National Parks Act, any woman who goes topless on a national park beach (eg, Ko Chang, Ko Phi Phi, Ko Samet) is breaking the law. Many Thais say that nudity and topless sunbathing on the beaches is what bothers them most about foreign travellers. Nudity is seen as a sign of disrespect for the locals, rather than as a libertarian symbol or modern custom. Thais are extremely modest in this respect (Patpong-style go-go bars are widely regarded as cultural aberrations, hidden from public view and designed for foreign consumption) and it should not be the visitor's intention to 'reform' them.

**Shoes** Shoes are not worn inside people's homes, nor in some guesthouses and shops. If you see a pile of shoes at or near the entrance, you should respect the house custom and remove your shoes before entry. Several Thais have confided to me that they can't believe how oblivious some foreigners appear to be of this simple and obvious custom. For them the wearing of shoes indoors is disgusting and the behaviour of those who ignore the custom is nothing short of boorish.

**Visiting Homes** Thais can be very hospitable and it's not unusual to be invited home for a meal or a sociable drink. Even if your visit is very brief, you will be offered something to eat or drink, probably both – a glass of water, a cup of tea, a piece of fruit, a shot of rice liquor, or whatever they have on hand. You are expected to partake of whatever is offered; whether you've already eaten or not, whether you're thirsty or not, to refuse at least a taste is considered impolite.

As with temple buildings, you must remove your shoes before entering a Thai home.

### Treatment of Animals

Thailand is a signatory to the UN Convention on International Trade in Endangered Species (CITES). Public awareness has risen to the point that many international watchdog groups, such as the World Wildlife Fund and Wildlife Conservation Society, receive much local support. An illicit trade in endangered and threatened wildlife continues but appears to be much smaller than even 10 years ago. It's illegal for restaurants to serve dishes made with threatened or endangered species; I haven't seen any such restaurants in Bangkok for at least 10 years (there are still a few upcountry).

---

### Mutt Mayhem

Visitors to Bangkok can expect to encounter some of the sorriest-looking dogs on the planet. Unsurprisingly, these roaming mangy flea-depots are more likely to be considered an eyesore, a traffic hazard and a potential rabies incubator than man's best friend.

The number of dogs has become such a problem that the governor of Bangkok recently asked 300 temples in Bangkok to moonlight as dog kennels in a desperate bid to get stray dogs off the city's street.

City authorities have allocated four million baht to sterilise stray dogs, but no-one has figured out what to do with the creatures once their reproductive urges are stemmed. Animal welfare groups claim it will take a decade for sterilisation programs to have a visible effect, hence the governors' plea for temples to house the mutts until nature takes its course.

**From Lonely Planet Scoop travel news at www.lonelyplanet.com/scoop**

Depending on your general perspective on zoos and animal parks, Dusit Zoo and other wildlife viewing attractions in and around Bangkok seem reasonably humane in their treatment of animals. Harder to understand, at least for some of us, is the taking of monkeys, birds and other animals from the jungle to be kept as pets – usually tied by a rope or chain to a tree, or confined to small cages. Several NGOS in Thailand are working to educate the public as to the cruelty of such practices, and have initiated wildlife rescue and rehabilitation projects.

In any case, wildlife experts agree that the greatest danger faced by Thai fauna is neither hunting nor the illegal wildlife trade but rather habitat loss – as is true for most of the rest of the world.

## Prostitution

**History** Westerners often erroneously link the origins of Bangkok's infamous sex trade to tourism or to the 'R & R' tours of Western troops during the Indochina War. In fact the practise dates back centuries.

The Thais themselves generally blame 19th-century Chinese immigration for bringing prostitution to Thailand, but in reality Thailand was fertile ground because of its long-standing concubinary tradition, a legacy inherited from India.

The first known literary references to this tradition were recorded by Chinese visitors in the early 1400s. Dutch merchants visiting Pattani in 1604 commented that 'when foreigners come there from other lands to do their business...men come and ask them whether they do not desire a woman' and that in Ayuthaya most of their peers 'had concubines or mistresses, in order (so they said) to avoid the common whores'. Seventeenth-century Ayuthaya, in fact, had an official Thai government office in charge of operating a corps of 600 concubines.

Until 1934 Siam had no laws forbidding polygamy – or even a word for this Judaeo-Christian concept. Most men of wealth counted among their retinue at least one courtesan, or *sŏhphenii* (from the Sanskrit term for a woman trained in the Kamasutra and other amorous arts, often translated as 'prostitute'). In addition, the traditional Thai *mia yài mia náwy* (major wife, minor wife) system made it socially permissible for a man to keep several mistresses – all Thai kings up to Rama IV had *mia náwy* (or *sanŏm,* as the royal version was called), as did virtually any Thai male who could afford them until recent times. Even today talk of mia náwy hardly raises an eyebrow in Thailand as the tradition lives on among wealthy businessmen, *jâo phâw* (mafia 'godfathers') and politicians.

The first brothel district in Thailand was established by Chinese immigrants in Bangkok's Sampeng Lane area in the mid-19th century. At first, only Chinese women worked as prostitutes here; when Thai women became involved at the turn of the century, they usually took Chinese names. Prostitution eventually spread from Sampeng's 'green-lantern district' to Chinese neighbourhoods throughout Thailand and is now found in nearly every village, town and city in the kingdom. Ethnic Chinese still control most of the trade, although the sex workers themselves now come from almost every ethnic background. The demographic of the sex industry often mirrors global patterns of political and economic unrest; in the last few years Bangkok has even seen an influx of Russian and Central Asian women – most on Tourist Visas – participating in the sex trade through escort services. Women from nearby countries, particularly Myanmar and China have also found their way – both willingly and unwillingly – into the trade.

Prostitution wasn't declared illegal until the 1950s when Field Marshal Phibun bullied his way into the prime minister's seat. The numbers of women working as commercial sex workers (CSWs) increased immediately after prohibition, and the percentage of those aged between 15 and 19 increased from 15% to 25%. In the 1960s and 1970s the Vietnam War brought unprecedented numbers of foreign soldiers to Bangkok and Pattaya on R & R tours, creating a new class of sex workers who catered to foreigners rather than Thais.

**Sex Industry Today** Estimates of the number of Thai citizens directly involved in offering sex services vary wildly, but studies

Sunset by Mae Nam Chao Phraya with a silhouette of Wat Arun, the Temple of Dawn.

Seated buddhas at Wat Pho

Kinaree, half-bird half-woman, Wat Phra Kaew

Worshipping deva, Wat Pho roof carving

Lotus-motif ornamentation, Wat Mahathat

The majestic Grand Palace

Garuda's, mythical bird-like beings, guard Wat Phra Kaew (Temple of the Emerald Buddha).

by Chulalongkorn University estimate around 200,000 to 220,000. Although often portrayed as Asia's sex capital, Thailand actually ranks well behind Taiwan, the Philippines and India (not to mention several Western countries, such as the USA) in per-capita number of sex workers, according to international human development reports.

Sociologists estimate that as many as 75% of post-puberty single Thai males engage the services of a prostitute at an average of two times a month. In highly urban Bangkok, the rates are lower thanks to increasing acceptance of extramarital sex and corresponding decline in demand for paid sex services. Today the highest per-capita concentration of sex workers is found in the North. Brothels are less common in the southern provinces, except in Chinese-dominated Phuket, Hat Yai and Yala, and in Thai-Malaysian border towns, where the clientele is almost exclusively Malay.

**Sex Workers** Only an estimated 2.5% of all Thai sex workers work in bars and 1.3% in massage parlours. The remaining 96.2% work in 'cafes', barbershops and brothels only rarely patronised by non-Thai clients. In fact most of the country's sex industry is invisible to the visiting foreigner and it is thought that Thai-to-non-Thai transactions represent less than 5% of the total. Unlike Western prostitution, there are few 'pimps' (people who manage one or more prostitutes) in Thailand. Instead, a network of procurers/suppliers and brothel owners control the trade, taking a high proportion (or all) of the sex service fees. At its worst, the industry takes girls sold or indentured by their families, sometimes even kidnapped, and forces them to work in conditions of virtual slavery.

In the Patpong-style bar catering to foreigners, on the other hand, most bar girls or boys and go-go dancers are freelance agents; they earn their income from taking a percentage of drinks bought on their behalf and from sex liaisons arranged outside the premises – usually after closing (if they leave during working hours, a customer usually pays a 'bar fine' on their behalf). The average Patpong type bar girl or boy earns

---

### How You Can Help

Travellers visiting Thailand can make donations to, or do voluntary work, at Empower (www.empowerwomen.org), a non-profit grassroots organisation that offers support, education and health services to sex workers. It takes long-term volunteers (minimum three months) for activities, such as English-language classes (note, that it doesn't accept graduates pursuing research projects). It also has a shop that sells wares made by women at the centre.

Travellers to Thailand can report incidents of paedophilia to the tourist police or ECPAT International (☎ 215 3388, e) ecpatbkk@ksc15.th.com), 328 Th Phayathai, Bangkok 10400, Thailand.

---

6000B to 7000B per month directly from the bar they work in; fees for extracurricular services are negotiated between themselves and the customer and can run anywhere from 800B to 2000B per assignation – none of which goes to a controller.

Most CSWs come from village areas. Contributing factors to seeking work in the sex industry include lack of education or alternative employment opportunities, family debt or abuse, or a history of acceptance of sex work as a form of employment within the family or village.

Researchers estimate they have a maximum working life of 10 years, though the average is two years or less. Many women return to their villages – some with a nest egg for their families, others with nothing – where surprisingly they are often treated with a measure of respect. The ones that stay in the sex industry long-term appear to suffer the most; if they haven't saved up enough money to retire (few do), they're often unemployable due to mental and physical disabilities acquired during their short working lives. Various Thai volunteer groups are engaged in counselling Thailand's sex workers – helping them to leave the industry or educating them about the dangers of STDs, particularly AIDS. Thanks to such efforts, the latest surveys indicate that condom use among sex workers in Thailand averages 94%, and the rate in Bangkok is probably higher.

**Legal Aspects** The sex industry's annual turnover is nearly double the Thai government's annual budget – regulating such an economically powerful industry with its far reaching influence has proved difficult. Officially prostitution remains illegal, but the government has been either powerless or unwilling to enforce most laws forbidding the trade ever since it was first outlawed. Since 1993, when then-prime minister Chuan Leekpai initiated a crackdown on CSWs under the age of 18, Thailand has made quantifiable progress towards the reduction of under-age prostitution. In city establishments in particular, the presence of under-18 female and male sex workers has diminished.

Under current Thai law, a jail term of four to 20 years and/or a fine of 200,000B to 400,000B can be imposed on anyone caught having sex with prostitutes under 15 years of age (the age of consent in Thailand). If the child is under 13, the sentence can amount to life imprisonment. The Thai government is encouraging people to assist in the eradication of child prostitution by reporting child sexual abuses to the relevant authorities. Many Western countries have instituted extra-territorial legislation whereby citizens can be charged for child prostitution offences committed abroad.

Travellers visiting Thailand can help by making a report by contacting the tourist police or ECPAT International (☎ 215 3388, ⓔ ecpatbkk@ksc15.th.com), 328 Th Phayathai, Bangkok 10400. ECPAT, which stands for End Child Prostitution, Child Pornography, and Trafficking in Children for Sexual Purposes, lobbies on child prostitution issues and runs various education, preventative and rehabilitation campaigns in Thailand and around the world.

# RELIGION
## Buddhism

About 95% of the Thai citizenry are Theravada Buddhists. The Thais themselves frequently call their religion Lankavamsa

(Sinhalese lineage) Buddhism because Siam originally received this form of Buddhism from Sri Lanka during the Sukhothai period. Strictly speaking, Theravada refers to only the earliest forms of Buddhism practised during the Ashokan and immediate post-Ashokan periods in South Asia. The early Dvaravati and pre-Dvaravati forms of Buddhism – those that existed up until the 10th or 11th century – are not the same as that which developed in Thai territories after the 13th century.

Since the Sukhothai period, Thailand has maintained an unbroken canonical tradition and 'pure' ordination lineage, the only country among the Theravadin (using Theravada in its doctrinal sense) countries to have done so. Ironically, when the ordination lineage in Sri Lanka broke down during the 18th century under Dutch persecution, it was Siam that restored the Sangha (Buddhist brotherhood) there. To this day the major sect in Sri Lanka is called Siamopalivamsa (Siam-Upali lineage, Upali being the name of the Siamese monk who led the expedition to Ceylon), or simply Siam Nikaya (the Siamese sect).

Basically, the Theravada (literally, Teaching of the Elders) school of Buddhism is an earlier and, according to its followers, less corrupted form of Buddhism than the Mahayana schools found in East Asia or in the Himalayan lands. The Theravada school is also called the 'southern' school since it took the southern route from India, its place of origin, through South-East Asia (Myanmar, Thailand, Laos and Cambodia in this case); while the 'northern' school proceeded north into Nepal, Tibet, China, Korea, Mongolia, Vietnam and Japan. The Mahayana school was the 'great vehicle', because it built upon the earlier teachings, 'expanding' the doctrine in such a way as to respond more to the needs of lay people, or so it is claimed.

Theravada doctrine stresses the three principal aspects of existence: *dukkha* (suffering, unsatisfactoriness, disease); *anicca* (impermanence, transience of all things); and *anatta* (nonsubstantiality or nonessentiality of reality – no permanent 'soul'). The truth of anicca reveals that no experience, no state of mind and no physical object lasts. Trying to hold onto experience, states of mind and objects that are constantly changing creates dukkha, while anatta is the understanding that there is no part of the changing world we can point to and say, 'This is me' or 'This is God' or 'This is the soul'. These concepts, when 'discovered' by Siddhartha Gautama in the 6th century BC, were in direct contrast to the Hindu belief in an eternal, blissful self *(paramatman)*, hence Buddhism was originally a 'heresy' against India's Brahmanic religion.

Gautama, an Indian prince-turned-ascetic, subjected himself to many years of severe austerity before he realised that this was not the way to reach the end of suffering. He then turned his attention to investigating the arising and passing away of the mind and body in the present moment. Seeing that even the most blissful and refined states of mind were subject to decay, he abandoned all desire for what he now saw as unreliable and unsatisfying. He then became known as Buddha, 'the enlightened' or 'the awakened'.

Gautama Buddha spoke of four noble truths that had the power to liberate any human being who could realise them. These four noble truths are:

1. The truth of dukkha: 'All forms of existence are subject to dukkha (disease, unsatisfactoriness, stress, imperfection)'.
2. The truth of the cause of dukkha: 'Dukkha is caused by *tanha* (grasping)'.
3. The truth of the cessation of dukkha: 'Eliminate the cause of dukkha (ie, grasping) and dukkha will cease to arise'.
4. The truth of the path: 'The Eightfold Path is the way to eliminate grasping/extinguish dukkha'.

The Eightfold Path (Atthangika-Magga), which if followed will put an end to suffering, consists of:

1. Right understanding
2. Right mindedness (right thought)
3. Right speech
4. Right bodily conduct
5. Right livelihood
6. Right effort
7. Right attentiveness
8. Right concentration

These eight limbs belong to three different 'pillars' of practice: wisdom or *pañña* (1 and 2); morality or *sila* (3 to 5); and concentration or *samadhi* (6 to 8). The path is also called the Middle Way, since ideally it avoids both extreme austerity and extreme sensuality. Some Buddhists believe it is to be taken in successive stages, while others say the pillars and/or limbs are interdependent. Another key point is that the word 'right' can also be translated as 'complete' or 'full'.

The ultimate end of Theravada Buddhism is *nibbana* (Sanskrit: nirvana), which literally means the 'blowing out' or extinction of all grasping and thus of all suffering (dukkha). Effectively it is also an end to the cycle of rebirths (both moment-to-moment and life-to-life) that is existence. In reality, most Thai Buddhists aim for rebirth in a 'better' existence rather than the supramundane goal of nibbana, which is highly misunderstood by Asians as well as Westerners.

Many Thais express the feeling that they are somehow unworthy of nibbana. By feeding monks, giving donations to temples and performing regular worship at the local *wat* (temple), they hope to improve their lot, acquiring enough merit or *bun* (from the Pali-Sanskrit *puñña*) to prevent or at least lessen the number of rebirths. The making of merit *(tham bun)* is an important social and religious activity in Thailand. The concept of reincarnation is almost universally accepted in Thailand, even by non-Buddhists. The Buddhist theory of karma is well expressed in the Thai proverb: *tham dii, dâi dii; tham chûa, dâi chûa*, which means roughly, that good actions bring good results, bad actions bring bad results.

The Triratna (Triple Gems), highly respected by Thai Buddhists, include the Buddha, the Dhamma (the teachings) and the Sangha (the Buddhist brotherhood). All are quite visible in Thailand. The Buddha, in his myriad and omnipresent sculptural forms, is found on a high shelf in the lowliest roadside restaurants as well as in the lounges of expensive Bangkok hotels. The Dhamma is chanted morning and evening in every wat and taught to every Thai child in primary school. The Sangha is seen everywhere in the presence of orange-robed monks, especially in the early morning hours when they perform their alms-rounds, in what has almost become a travel-guide cliche in motion.

**Buddhist Monks** Socially, every Thai male is expected to become a monk for a short period in his life, optimally between the time he finishes school and the time he starts a career or marries. Men or boys under 20 years of age may enter the Sangha as novices – this is not unusual since a family earns great merit when one of its sons takes robe and bowl. Traditionally, the length of time spent in the wat is three months, during the Buddhist lent *(phansǎa)*, which begins in July and coincides with the rainy season. However, nowadays men may spend as little as a week or 15 days to accrue merit as monks. There are about 32,000 monasteries in Thailand and 460,000 monks; many of these monks ordain for life. Of these, a large percentage become scholars and teachers, while some specialise in healing and/or folk magic.

The Sangha is divided into two sects, the Mahanikai (Great Society) and the Thammayut (from the Pali *dhammayutika* or 'dharma-adhering'). The latter is a minority sect (the ratio being one Thammayut to 35 Mahanikai) begun by King Mongkut in the mid-19th century and patterned after an early Mon form of monastic discipline that he had practised as a monk. Members of both sects must adhere to 227 monastic vows or precepts as laid out in the Vinaya Pitaka – Buddhist scriptures dealing with monastic discipline. Generally, discipline for Thammayut monks is stricter. For example, they eat only once a day, before noon, and must eat only what is in their alms bowl, whereas Mahanikais eat twice before noon and may accept side dishes. Thammayut monks are expected to attain proficiency in meditation as well as Buddhist scholarship or scripture study; the Mahanikai monks typically 'specialise' in one or the other. Other factors may supersede sectarian divisions when it comes to disciplinary disparities. Monks who live in the city, for example, usually emphasise study of the Buddhist scriptures while those living in the forest tend to emphasise meditation.

**Buddhist Nuns** At one time the Theravada Buddhist world had a separate Buddhist monastic lineage for females, who were called *bhikkhuni* and observed more vows than monks did – 311 precepts as opposed to the 227 followed by monks. The bhikkhuni sangha (order) travelled from its birthplace in India to Sri Lanka around two centuries after Buddha's lifetime; it was taken there by the daughter of King Ashoka. However, this Sri Lankan tradition died out following the Hindu Chola invasion in the 13th century. Monks from Siam later travelled to Sri Lanka to restore the male sangha, but because there were no ordained bhikkhuni in Thailand at the time, Sri Lanka's bhikkhuni sangha was never restored.

In Thailand, the modern equivalent is the *mâe chii* (nun; literally 'mother priest') – women who live the monastic life as *atthasila* ('eight-precept' nuns). Their total number is estimated to be around 10,000. Thai nuns shave their heads, wear white robes and take vows in an ordination procedure similar to that undergone by monks. Generally speaking, ordination as a nun in Thailand isn't considered as 'prestigious' as monkhood. The average Thai Buddhist makes a great show of offering new robes and household items to the monks at their local wat but pays much less attention to the nuns. This is mainly due to the fact that nuns generally don't perform ceremonies on behalf of laypeople, so there is often less incentive for self-interested laypeople to make offerings to them.

This difference in prestige represents social Buddhism, however, and is not how those with a serious interest in Buddhist practice regard the mâe chii. Nuns engage in the same fundamental hermetic activities – meditation and Dhamma study – as monks do, activities that are the core of monastic life.

**Buddhism Resources** An increasing number of foreigners come to Thailand to be ordained as Buddhist monks and nuns, or to study with the meditation masters in

Bangkok and farther afield (see Courses in the Things to See & Do chapter).

There's a Buddhist bookshop across the street from the north entrance to Wat Bowonniwet that sells English-language books on Buddhism. Asia Books and DK Book House also stock Buddhist literature (see Bookshops in the Shopping Chapter).

If you wish to find out more about Buddhism you can contact the World Fellowship of Buddhists (Map 7, ☎ 661 1284/89, e wfbhq@asianet.co.th), 616 Soi 24, Th Sukhumvit. Senior *farang* (Western) monks hold Dhamma/meditation classes in English here on the first Sunday of each month from 2 to 6 pm; all are welcome.

# Facts for the Visitor

## WHEN TO GO

The best overall months for visiting Bangkok vis-à-vis climate are November to February – during these months it rains least and is not so hot. The most difficult months weather-wise are from April to May (the peak of the hot season) and September to October (the end of the rainy season). If you're in Bangkok during these months, be prepared to roast in April and do some wading in October.

Peak months for tourism are November, December, February, March and August, with secondary peak months in January and July. Consider travelling during the least crowded months of April, May, June, September and October if avoiding crowds of holiday-makers is your main objective and you want to take advantage of discounted rooms and other low-season rates.

## ORIENTATION

Greater Bangkok encompasses Thonburi, the former capital across the Mae Nam Chao Phraya (Chao Phraya River) to the west, along with Bangkok proper along the east side of the river. The latter is divided in two by the main north-south railway line. The portion between the river and the railway is 'old' Bangkok (often called Ko Ratanakosin) where most of the older temples and the original palace are located, as well as the Chinese and Indian districts. That part of the city east of the railway, which covers more than twice as much area as the old districts, is 'new' Bangkok. This latter part can be divided again into the business and tourist district wedged between Thanon (Th) Charoen Krung (New Rd) and Th Phra Ram IV, and the sprawling residential and tourist district stretching along Th Sukhumvit and Th Phet-buri Tat Mai.

This leaves the hard-to-classify areas below Th Sathon Tai (South Sathon Rd, which includes Khlong Toey, Bangkok's main port) and the area above Th Phra Ram IV between the train line and Th Withayu (Wireless Rd, which comprises an infinite variety of businesses, several cinemas, civil service offices, the shopping area of Siam Square, Chulalongkorn University and the National Stadium). The areas along the east bank of Mae Nam Chao Phraya underwent a surge of redevelopment during the 1980s and 1990s, seeing the construction of many new hotels, condos and other high rise structures.

On the opposite (west) side of Mae Nam Chao Phraya is Thonburi, which served as Thailand's capital for 15 years before Bangkok was founded. Few tourists ever step foot on the Thonburi side except to visit Wat Arun, the Temple of Dawn. Fang Thon (Thon Bank), as it's often called by Thais, seems an age away from the glittering high-rises on the river's east bank, although it is an up-and-coming area for condo development as well.

## MAPS

A map is essential for finding your way around Bangkok, and there are many competing for your attention. Lonely Planet's comprehensive *Bangkok* city map (150B), in a handy, laminated, fold-out sheet map form, includes a walking tour and is fully indexed.

A bus map is the best way to navigate Bangkok's economical bus system. The most popular is the durable *Tour 'n Guide Map to Bangkok Thailand* (40B), aka the 'blue map', which shows all bus routes and some walking tours. It's regularly updated, but inevitably some bus routes will be wrong, so take care. Other similar maps include the *Bangkok Bus Map* with lots of sightseeing tips and *Latest Tour's Map to Bangkok & Thailand* ('blue map' clone).

The Tourism Authority of Thailand (TAT) publishes and distributes the free *City Map of Bangkok,* a folded sheet map on coated stock with bus routes, major hotels, the latest expressways, sightseeing, hospitals, embassies and more – it's very useful though a bit hard to read due to the small print. Separate inset maps of popular areas are useful. You can pick it up at the airport TAT desk or at any Bangkok TAT office.

## Finding Addresses

Any city as large and unplanned as Bangkok can be tough to get around. Street names often seem unpronounceable to begin with, compounded by the inconsistency of Romanised Thai spellings. For example, the street often spelt as 'Rajdamri' is actually pronounced 'Ratchadamri' (with the appropriate tones, of course), or in abbreviated form as Rat'damri. The 'v' in Sukhumvit should be pronounced like a 'w'. One of the most popular location for foreign embassies is known both as Wireless Rd and Th Withayu (*wíthá yú* is Thai for 'radio').

Many street addresses show a string of numbers divided by slashes and hyphens, for example, 48/3-5 Soi 1, Th Sukhumvit. The reason is that undeveloped property in Bangkok was originally bought and sold in lots. The number before the slash refers to the original lot number. The numbers following the slash indicate buildings (or entrances to buildings) constructed within that lot. The pre-slash numbers appear in the order in which they were added to city plans, while the post-slash numbers are arbitrarily assigned by developers. As a result numbers along a given street don't always run consecutively.

The Thai word *thanŏn* means road, street or avenue. Hence Ratchadamnoen Rd (sometimes referred to as Ratchadamnoen Ave) is always called Thanon (Th) Ratchadamnoen in Thai.

A *soi* is a small street or lane that runs off a larger street. In our example, the address referred to as 48/3-5 Soi 1, Th Sukhumvit will be located off Th Sukhumvit on Soi 1. Alternative ways of writing the same address include 48/3-5 Th Sukhumvit Soi 1, or even just 48/3-5 Sukhumvit 1. Some Bangkok sois have become so large that they can be referred to both as thanŏn and soi, eg Soi Sarasin/Th Sarasin and Soi Asoke/Th Asoke.

Smaller than a soi is a *tràwk* (usually spelt 'trok') or alley. Well-known alleys in Bangkok include Chinatown's Trok Itsaranuphap and Banglamphu's Trok Rong Mai.

The long-running, oft-imitated and never equalled *Nancy Chandler's Map of Bangkok* (140B) contains information on out-of-the-way places and where to buy unusual things around the city. The six different water-coloured panels (Greater Bangkok, Chinatown, Th Sukhumvit, Chatuchak Weekend Market, Central Shopping Area and Markets of Central Bangkok) are all hand-drawn, hand-lettered and laid out by hand. A new edition is released every year. A detailed map covering a large portion of the city is *BangkokMap*, a 188 page hardcover street atlas put out by the Agency for Real Estate Affairs, a private company specialising in real estate surveys of the city. Each page features a colour-coded street grid showing various office and apartment buildings, hotels, restaurants and even many nightclubs. This atlas is available from most bookshops in Bangkok that carry English-language books.

## TOURIST OFFICES

Operated by the Bangkok Metropolitan Authority (BMA) and open 9 am to 7 pm daily,

the new Bangkok Tourist Bureau (☎ 02-225 7612), 17/1 Th Phra Athit, Banglamphu, is a very good spot for information. In addition to stocking a wealth of brochures, maps and event schedules, the bureau staff can answer questions and assist with the chartering of boats at the adjacent pier.

The Tourist Authority of Thailand (TAT) produces useful, informative and well-produced colourful brochures. Many of the staff speak English.

The TAT has a desk at Bangkok International Airport in the arrivals area of Terminal 1 (☎ 523 8972) and Terminal 2 (☎ 535 2669); both are open 8 am to midnight.

The TAT's information compound (☎ Map 3, 282 9773, fax 282 9775) on Th Ratchadamnoen Nok near the Ratchadamnoen Stadium is more convenient. It's open 8 am to 4.30 pm daily. The TAT also maintains a 24-hour Tourist Assistance Centre (TAC; ☎ 1155) in the compound for matters relating to theft and other mishaps, run by the paramilitary arm of the TAT, the Tourist Police. See the Tourist Police section in this chapter.

A smaller TAT office (☎ 272 4424) with fewer materials can be found at Chatuchak Market (Map 1); open 9 am to 4 pm Saturday and Sunday.

A tourist information booth at the Chana Songkhram police station on Th Chakraphong, a bit north of Th Khao San, distributes local bus maps for a donation (2B each).

## TAT Offices Abroad

**Australia**
(☎ 02-9247 7549, fax 9251 2465, ⓔ info@thailand.net.au) Level 2, 75 Pitt Street, Sydney, NSW 2000

**France**
(☎ 01-53 53 47 00, fax 45 63 78 88, ⓔ tatpar@wanadoo.fr) 90 Avenue des Champs Elysées, 75008 Paris

**Germany**
(☎ 069-138 1390, ⓔ tatfra@t-online.de) Bethmannstrasse 58, D-60311 Frankfurt/Main

**Hong Kong**
(☎ 2868 0732, fax 2868 4585, ⓔ tathkg@hk.super.net) Room 401, Fairmont House, 8 Cotton Tree Drive, Central

**Japan**
*Tokyo:* (☎ 03-3218 0337, fax 3218 0655, ⓔ tattky@crisscross.com), South Tower 2F, Room 259, Yurakucho Denki Bldg, 1-7-1 Yurakucho, Chiyoda-ku, Tokyo 100
*Osaka:* (☎ 06-6543 6654, fax 6543 6660, ⓔ tatosa@ca.mbn.or.jp) Technoble Yotsubashi Bldg 3F, 1-6-8 Kitahorie, Nishi-ku, Osaka 550-0014

**Laos** (☎ 21-217157, fax 217158) 79/9 Th Lan Xang, Vientiane, Lao PDR, or PO Box 12, Nong Khai 43000

**Malaysia**
(☎ 603-21623480, fax 603-21623486, ⓔ sawatdi@po.jaring.my) Suite 22.01, Level 22, Menara Lion, 165 Jalan Ampang, 50450 Kuala Lumpur

**Singapore**
(☎ 65-235 7694, fax 733 5653, ⓔ tatsin@mbox5.singnet.com.sg) c/o Royal Thai embassy, 370 Orchard Rd, 238870

**Taiwan**
(☎ 2502 1600, fax 2502 1603, ⓔ tattpe@ms3.hinet.net) 13th floor Boss Tower, 111 Sung Chiang Rd

**UK**
(☎ 020-7499 7679, ⓔ info@tat-uk.co.uk) 49 Albemarle St, London W1X 3 FE

**USA**
*New York:* (☎ 212-432 0433, toll-free ☎ 1-800 THAI LAND, fax 912 0920, ⓔ tatny@aol.com) Suite 3729, 1 World Trade Center, New York, NY 10048
*Los Angeles:* (☎ 323-461 9814, fax 461 9834, ⓔ tatla@ix.netcom.com) 1st floor, 611 North Larchmont Blvd, LA, CA 90004

## VISAS & DOCUMENTS
### Passports
Entry into Thailand requires a passport valid for at least six months from the time of entry. If you anticipate your passport may expire while you're in Thailand, you should obtain a new one before arrival or inquire from your government whether your embassy in Thailand can issue a new one after arrival (see Embassies & Consulates in Bangkok later in this chapter).

### Visas
Whichever type of visa you have, be sure to check your passport immediately after stamping. Overworked officials sometimes stamp 30 days on arrival even when you hold a longer visa; if you point out the error before you've left the immigration area at your port of entry, officials will make the necessary corrections. If you don't notice this until you've left the port of entry, go to Bangkok and plead your case at the central immigration office (☎ 287 3101).

Once a visa is issued, it must be used (ie, you must enter Thailand) within 90 days. The Royal Thai embassy in Washington, DC, maintains one of the best Internet sites for information about visas for Thailand: www.thaiembdc.org/consular/visa.

**Transit & Tourist Visas** The Thai government allows 57 different nationalities to enter the country without a visa for 30 days at no charge. Seventy-eight other nationalities – those from smaller European countries like Andorra or Liechtenstein or from West Africa, South Asia or Latin America – can obtain 15-day Transit Visas on arrival upon payment of a 300B fee.

A few nationalities, eg, Hungarians, must obtain a visa in advance of arrival or they'll be turned back. Check with a Thai embassy or consulate if you plan on arriving without a visa.

Without proof of an onward ticket and sufficient funds for one's projected stay any visitor can be denied entry, but in practice your ticket and funds are rarely checked if you're dressed neatly for the immigration check. See Exchange Control under Money in this chapter for the amount of funds required per visa type.

Next in length of validity is the Tourist Visa, which is good for 60 days and costs US$15. Two passport photos must accompany all applications.

**Non-Immigrant Visas** There are two types of Non-Immigrant Visas. The general Non-Immigrant Visa is valid for 90 days, costs US$20 and must be obtained from a Thai embassy or consulate in your home country. Study, retirement and extended family visits are among the purposes considered valid. Non-Immigrant Visas are available in single-entry versions only. This means if you want to stay longer than 90 days, you must obtain a new visa for each 90 day period you want to stay or apply for a Re-Entry Permit after you arrive in Thailand (see Re-Entry Permits further in this section).

If you know you'll be staying beyond 90 days, you can also obtain multiple visas in advance. For example, you can buy two back-to-back 90-day Non-Immigrant Visas for US$40 and this will allow you six months in the country, as long as you cross a border with immigration facilities by the end of your first three months. The second visa is validated as soon as you recross the Thai border, so there is no need to go to a Thai embassy or consulate abroad. You can buy up to four 90-day Non-Immigrant Visas in advance.

**Visa Exceptions** Citizens of Brazil, Korea and Peru may enter Thailand without a visa, in accordance with inter-governmental agreements, for a maximum stay of 90 days for purposes of tourism or temporary business only. No extension of stay will be granted, however.

**Re-Entry Permits** If you need to leave and re-enter the kingdom before your visa expires, eg a return trip to Laos, apply for a Re-Entry Permit at a Thai immigration office. The cost is 500B and you'll need to supply one passport photo. There is no limit to the number of Re-Entry Permits you can apply for and use during the validity of your visa.

**Visa Extensions & Renewals** Sixty-day Tourist Visas may be extended up to 30 days at the discretion of Thai immigration authorities. The Bangkok office (☎ 287 3101) is on Soi Suan Phlu, Th Sathon Tai, but you can apply at any immigration office in the country – every province that borders a neighbouring country has at least one. The usual fee for extension of a Tourist Visa is 500B. Bring along one photo and one copy each of the photo and visa pages of your passport. Usually only one 30-day extension is granted.

The 30-day no-visa stay can be extended for seven to 10 days (depending on the immigration office) for 500B. You can also leave the country and return immediately to obtain another 30-day stay. There is no limit on the number of times you can do this, nor is there a minimum interval you must spend outside the country.

Extension of the 15-day on-arrival Transit Visa is only allowed if you hold a passport from a country that has no Thai embassy.

If you overstay your visa, the usual penalty is a fine of 200B each extra day, with a 20,000B limit. Fines can be paid at the airport or in advance at the Investigation Unit (Map 7, ☎ 287 3101/10), Immigration Bureau, Room 416, 4th floor, Old Bldg, Soi Suan Plu, Th Sathon Tai. If you've overstayed only one day, you don't have to pay. Children under 14 travelling with a parent do not have to pay the penalty.

Other than paying the 500B extension fee, extending a Non-Immigrant Visa mostly depends on how the officials feel about you – neat appearance and polite behaviour help. Typically, one must collect a number of signatures and go through various interviews which result in a 'provisional' extension. You may then have to report to a local immigration office every 10 to 14 days for the next three months until the actual extension comes through. Becoming a monk doesn't guarantee an extension.

Retirees 55 years of age or older may extend the 90-day Non-Immigrant Visa one year at a time. To do this you will need to take to the Immigration Bureau: a copy of your passport, one photo, a 500B extension fee and proof of your financial status or pension. The requirement is that foreigners aged 60 or older must show proof of an income of not less than 200,000B per year (or 20,000B per month for extensions of less than a year); for those who are aged 55 to 59 the minimum is raised to 500,000/50,000B. According to immigration regulations: 'If the alien is ill, or has weak health and is sensitive to colder climates, or has resided in Thailand for a long period, and is 55 to 59 years of age, special considerations will be granted'.

Foreigners with Non-Immigrant Visas who have resided in Thailand continuously for three years – on one-year extensions – may apply for permanent residency at Section 1, Subdivision 1, Immigration Division 1, Room 301, 3rd floor, Immigration Bureau, Soi Suan Phlu, Th Sathon Tai (☎ 287 3117/01); foreigners who receive permanent residence must carry an 'alien identification card' at all times.

The government has a One-Stop Visa Centre (Map 1, ☎ 693 9333, fax 693 9340), 207 Th Ratchadaphisek, Krisda Plaza, where Non-Immigrant Visas for investors, businesspeople and foreign correspondents can be renewed in less than three hours.

Various law offices in Thailand, especially in Bangkok, can assist with visa extensions, renewals and applications – for a fee of course. Two that have been around for a while are Siam Visa (☎ 238 2989, fax 238 2987, ⒠ siamvisa@loxinfo.co.th), Kasemkit Bldg, 7th floor, Th Silom; and Express Visa Service (☎ 617 7258 ext 418, fax 272 3764, ⒠ thaivisa@usa.net), Sirida Place, 278 Th Vibhavadi Rangsit, Soi 3 Yak 10, Latyao, Chatuchak. This does not constitute an endorsement of either agency – be cautious and ask plenty of questions before plonking down your money.

### Onward Tickets
Thai immigration does not seem very concerned with whether or not you arrive with proof of onward travel. Legally speaking, all holders of Tourist Visas or the no-visa 30-day stay permit are *supposed* to carry proof of some kind. In all my years of frequent travel in and out of the kingdom, my onward travel documents haven't once been checked.

### Travel Insurance
A travel insurance policy to cover theft, loss and medical problems is a good idea. Some policies offer lower and higher medical-expense options; the higher ones are chiefly for countries such as the USA, which have extremely high medical costs. There is a wide variety of policies available, so check the small print.

Some policies specifically exclude 'dangerous activities', which can include scuba diving, motorcycling, even trekking. A locally acquired motorcycle licence is not valid under some policies.

You may prefer a policy that pays doctors or hospitals directly rather than you having to pay on the spot and claim later. If you have to claim later make sure you keep all documentation. Some policies ask you to call back (reverse charges) to a centre in your home country where an immediate assessment of your problem is made.

Check that the policy covers ambulances or an emergency flight home.

### Driving Licence & Permits
An International Driving Permit is necessary for any visitor who intends to drive a motorised vehicle while in Thailand. These are usually available from motoring organisations such as AAA (USA) or BAA (UK) in your home country.

### Hostel Cards
Hostelling International (HI), formerly known as the International Youth Hostel Federation, issues a membership card that will allow you to stay at Thailand's member hostels. Without this card or a temporary membership you won't be admitted. There is only one hostel in Bangkok, and it's not particularly recommended, so if your visit is limited to Bangkok a card may not be of much use.

Memberships are sold at any member hostel worldwide. For further information, check HI's Web site at www.iyhf.org.

## Student Cards

International Student Identity Cards (ISIC) can be used as identification to qualify for the student discount at some museums in Thailand (though these are rare). It's probably not worth getting just for a visit to Thailand, but if you already have one, or plan to use one elsewhere in Asia, then bring it along.

ISIC cards are issued via student-oriented travel agencies with ISIC agreements around the world. Check www.istc.org to fine the issuing agency closest to you.

## Tax Clearance

Anyone who receives income while in Thailand must obtain a tax clearance certificate from the Revenue Department before they'll be permitted to leave the country. The Bangkok office (☎ 281 5777, 282 9899) of the Revenue Department is on Th Chakkapong not far from the Democracy Monument. There are also Revenue Department offices in every provincial capital.

## Copies

All important documents (passport data page and visa page, credit cards, travel insurance policy, air/bus/train tickets, driving licence etc) should be photocopied before you leave home. Leave one copy with someone at home and keep another with you, separate from the originals.

You might like to store details of your vital travel documents in Lonely Planet's free online Travel Vault in case you lose the photocopies or can't be bothered with them. Your password-protected Travel Vault is accessible online anywhere in the world – create it at www.ekno.lonelyplanet.com.

## EMBASSIES & CONSULATES
## Thai Embassies & Consulates

To apply for a visa, contact the Royal Thai embassy (or consulate) in any of the following countries. In many cases, if you apply in person you may receive a Tourist or Non-Immigrant Visa on the day of application.

Mail applications generally take anywhere from two to six weeks.

**Australia**
*Canberra:* (☎ 02-6273 1149, 6273 2937) 111 Empire Circuit, Yarralumla, Canberra, ACT 2600
*Sydney:* (☎ 02-9241 2542) 8th floor, 131 Macquarie St, Sydney, NSW 2000
**Canada**
*Ottawa:* (☎ 613-722 4444) 180 Island Park Drive, Ottawa, Ontario K1Y OA2
*Vancouver:* (☎ 604-687 1143) 1040 Burrard St, Vancouver, BC V6Z 2R9
**China**
*Beijing:* (☎ 010-6532 1903) 40 Guanghua Lu, Beijing 100600
*Guangzhou:* (☎ 020-8188 6968, ext 3301-03) White Swan Hotel, Southern St, Shamian Island, Guangzhou
*Kunming:* (☎ 871-316 8916) King World Hotel, 145 Dong Feng Dong Lu, Kunming, Yunnan Province 650051
*Shanghai:* (☎ 021-6321 9442) 7 Zhongshan Rd, East 1, Shanghai 200002
**France**
*Paris:* (☎ 01-56 26 50 50) 8 Rue Greuze, 75116 Paris
**Germany**
*Berlin:* (☎ 30-794810) Lepsiusstrasse 64-66, 12162 Berlin
**Hong Kong**
(☎ 02-2521 6481/5) 8th floor, Fairmont House, 8 Cotton Tree Drive, Central
**India**
*New Delhi:* (☎ 021-6321 9442) 56-N Nyaya Marg, Chanakyapuri, New Delhi, 110021
*Calcutta:* (☎ 033-440 7836, 440 3230/1) 18-B, Mandeville Gardens, Ballygunge, Calcutta 700 019
*Mumbai:* (☎ 022-363 1404, 369 2543) Malabar View, 4th floor, 33 Marine Drive St, Chowpatty Sea Face, Mumbai 400 007
**Indonesia**
*Jakarta:* (☎ 021-390 4052/3/4) Jalan Imam Bonjol 74, Jakarta Pusat 10310
**Japan**
*Tokyo:* (☎ 03-3441 1386/7) 3-14-6 Kami-Osaki, Shinagawa-ku, Tokyo 141
*Osaka:* (☎ 06-243 5563, 243 5569) 4th floor, Konoike East Bldg, 3-6-9, Kitakyohoji-machi, Chuo-ku, Osaka 541-0057
**Laos**
*Vientiane:* (☎ 21-214581/3) Th Phonkheng, Vientiane Poste 128
**Malaysia**
*Kuala Lumpur:* (☎ 03-248 8222, 248 8350) 206 Jalan Ampang, Kuala Lumpur

*Kota Bharu:* (☎ 09-744 5266, 748 2545) 4426 Jalan Pengkalan Chepa, 15400 Kota Bharu, Kelantan
*Penang:* (☎ 04-226 8029, 226 9484) No 1, Jalan Tunku Abdul Rahman, 10350 Penang
**Myanmar** (Burma)
*Yangon:* (☎ 01-512017, 512018) 437 Pyay Rd, 8 Ward, Kamayut township, Yangon
**Nepal**
*Kathmandu:* (☎ 01-371410, 371411) Ward No 3, Bansbari, PO Box 3333, Kathmandu
**Netherlands**
*The Hague:* (☎ 070-345 9703) Laan Copes van Cattenburch 123, 2585 EZ The Hague
**New Zealand**
*Wellington:* (☎ 04-476 8618/9) 2 Cook St, Karori, PO Box 17226, Wellington 5
**Philippines**
*Manila:* (☎ 02-810 3833, 815 4219) 107B Rada St, Legaspi Village, Makati, Metro Manila
**Singapore**
(☎ 65-737 2644, 737 2158) 370 Orchard Rd, 238870
**UK & Northern Ireland**
*London:* (☎ 020-7589 0173, 7589 2944) 29-30 Queen's Gate, London SW7 5JB
**USA**
*Washington:* (☎ 202-944 3600) 1024 Wisconsin Ave NW, Washington, DC 20007
*Chicago:* (☎ 312-664 3129) 700 N Rush St, Chicago, Illinois 60611
*Los Angeles:* (☎ 213-962 9574/77) 2nd floor, 611 N Larchmont Blvd, Los Angeles, CA 90004
*New York:* (☎ 212-754 1770, 754 2536/8) 351 East 52nd St, New York, NY 10022
**Vietnam**
*Hanoi:* (☎ 04-823 5092/94) 63-65 Hoang Dieu St, Hanoi
*Ho Chi Minh City:* (☎ 08-822 2637-8) 77 Tran Quoc Thao St, District 3, Ho Chi Minh City

## Embassies & Consulates in Bangkok

Bangkok is a good place to collect visas for onward travel. The visa sections of most embassies and consulates are open from around 8.30 to 11.30 am Monday to Friday only (call first, as some are open only two or three days a week).

You'll need visas for onward travel to India, Mynamar, Nepal and Laos – contact the relevant embassies. If you're heading on to India you'll definitely need a visa, and if

you're going to Nepal it's highly advisable to have one even though they can be obtained on arrival.

For visits to Myanmar, visas are necessary and available direct from the Myanmar embassy. For Laos, visas can be acquired from the Lao embassy in Bangkok or the Lao consulate in Khon Kaen, on arrival at airports in Vientiane and Luang Prabang, or at the Thai-Lao Friendship Bridge crossing near Nong Khai. Visas are available on arrival in Malaysia, Cambodia and Vietnam.

Countries with diplomatic representation in Bangkok include:

**Australia** (Map 7, ☎ 287 2680) 37 Th Sathon Tai
**Austria** (Map 7, ☎ 287 3970–2) 14 Soi Nantha, Th Sathon Tai
**Bangladesh** (☎ 392 9437) 727 Soi 55, Th Sukhumvit
**Belgium** (Map 7, ☎ 236 0150) 44 Soi Phipat, Th Silom
**Cambodia** (Map 7, ☎ 254 6630) 185 Th Ratchadamri, Lumphini
**Canada** (Map 7, ☎ 636 0540) 15th floor, Abdulrahim Bldg, 990 Th Rama IV
**China** (Map 1, ☎ 245 7043) 57 Th Ratchadaphisek
**Denmark** (Map 7, ☎ 213 2021–5) 10 Soi 1, Th Sathon Tai
**France** (Map 7, ☎ 266 8250–6) 35 Soi 36, Th Charoen Krung; (☎ 287 2585–87) consular section (visas), 29 Th Sathon Tai
**Germany** (Map 7, ☎ 287 9000) 9 Th Sathon Tai
**India** (☎ 258 0300–6) 46 Soi Prasanmit (Soi 23), Th Sukhumvit
**Indonesia** (Map 5, ☎ 252 3135) 600-602 Th Phetburi
**Israel** (Map 7, ☎ 260 4854–9) 75 Ocean Tower 2, 25th floor, Soi 19, Th Sukhumvit
**Japan** (Map 5, ☎ 252 6151–9) 1674 Th Phetburi Tat Mai
**Korea** (South) (Map 1, ☎ 247 7537) 23 Th Thiam-Ruammit, Huay Khwang, Sam Saen Nok
**Laos** (Map 1, ☎ 539 6667, 539 7341) 520/1-3 Soi 39, Th Ramkhamhaeng
**Malaysia** (Map 7, ☎ 679 2190–9) 33-35 Th Sathon Tai
**Myanmar** (Burma) (Map 7, ☎ 233 2237, 234 4698) 132 Th Sathon Neua
**Nepal** (Map 1, ☎ 391 7240) 89 Soi Phuengsuk (Soi 71), Th Sukhumvit
**Netherlands** (Map 7, ☎ 254 7701, 252 6103–5) 106 Th Withayu
**New Zealand** (Map 7, ☎ 254 2530–3) 93 Th Withayu

**Norway** (Map 5, ☎ 261 0230–5) 18th floor, UBC II Bldg, 591 Soi 33 Th Sukhumvit
**Philippines** (Map 1, ☎ 259 0139) 760 Th Sukhumvit
**Portugal** (Map 6, ☎ 234 0372/2123) 26 Captain Bush Lane, New Rd, Bangrak.
**Singapore** (Map 7, ☎ 286 2111, 286 1434) 29 Th Sathon Tai
**South Africa** (☎ 253 8473) 6th floor, Park Place, 231 Th Sarasin
**Spain** (Map 7, ☎ 252 5132) 701 Diethelm Tower, 7th floor, 93/1 Th Withayu
**Sri Lanka** (Map 5, ☎ 261 1934–5) 13th floor, Ocean Tower II Bldg, 75/6 Soi 19, Th Sukhumvit
**Sweden** (Map 7, ☎ 254 4954–5) 20th floor, Pacific Place, 140 Th Sukhumvit
**Switzerland** (Map 7, ☎ 253 0156–60) 5 Th Withayu Neua
**UK & Northern Ireland** (Map 7, ☎ 253 0191–9) 1031 Th Withayu
**USA** (Map 7, ☎ 205 4000) 120-122 Th Withayu
**Vietnam** (Map 7, ☎ 251 5836–8) 83/1 Th Withayu

### Your Own Embassy

As a tourist, it's important to realise what your own embassy – the embassy of the country of which you are a citizen – can and can't do.

Generally speaking, it won't be much help in emergencies if the trouble you're in is remotely your own fault. Remember that you are bound by the laws of the country you are in. Your embassy will not be sympathetic if you end up in jail after committing a crime locally, even if such actions are legal in your own country.

In genuine emergencies you might get some assistance, but only if other channels have been exhausted. For example, if you need to get home urgently, a free ticket is exceedingly unlikely – the embassy would expect you to have insurance. If you have all your money and documents stolen, it might assist with getting a new passport, but a loan for onward travel is out of the question.

### CUSTOMS

Like most countries, Thailand prohibits the importation of illegal drugs, firearms and ammunition (unless registered in advance with the Police Department) and pornographic media. A reasonable amount of clothing for personal use, toiletries and professional instruments are allowed in duty-free, as is one still or one movie or video camera with five rolls of still film or three rolls of movie film or videotape. Up to 200 cigarettes can be brought into the country without paying duty, or for other smoking materials a total of up to 250g. One litre of wine or spirits is allowed in duty-free.

Electronic goods like personal stereos, calculators and computers can be a problem if the customs officials have reason to believe you're bringing them in for resale. As long as you don't carry more than one of each, you should be OK.

For information on currency import or export, see Exchange Control in the Money section of this chapter.

### Antiques & Art

When leaving Thailand, you must obtain an export licence for any antiques or objects of art you want to take with you. An antique as defined by the Department for Fine Arts (DFA) is any:

'archaic movable property whether produced by man or by nature, any part of ancient structure, human skeleton or animal carcass, which by its age or characteristic of production or historical evidence is useful in the field of art, history or archaeology.'

An object of art is a 'thing produced by craftsmanship and appreciated as being valuable in the field of art'. Obviously these are very sweeping definitions, so if in doubt, go to the Department of Fine Arts for inspection and licensing.

Export licence applications can be made by submitting two front-view photos of the object(s), with no more than five objects to a photo, and a photocopy of your passport, along with the object(s) in question, to one of three locations in Thailand: the Bangkok National Museum, the Chiang Mai National Museum (Northern Thailand) or the Songkhla National Museum (Southern Thailand). You need to allow three to five days for the application and inspection process to be completed.

Thailand has special regulations for taking a Buddha or other deity image (or any part thereof) out of the country. These require not only a licence from the Department of Fine Arts but a permit from the Ministry of Commerce as well. The one exception to this are the small Buddha images *(phrá phim* or *phrá khrêuang)* that are meant to be worn on a chain around the neck. These may be exported without a licence as long as the reported purpose is religious.

## Temporary Vehicle Importation

Passenger vehicles (car, van, truck or motorcycle) can be brought into Thailand for tourist purposes for up to six months. Documents needed are: a valid international driving permit; passport; vehicle registration papers (or in the case of a borrowed or hired vehicle, authorisation from the owner); and a cash or bank guarantee equal to the value of the vehicle plus 20%. For entry through Khlong Toey port or Bangkok International Airport, this means a letter of bank credit. For overland crossings via Malaysia, a 'self-guarantee' filled in at the border is sufficient.

## Home Country Customs

Be sure to check the import regulations in your home country before bringing or sending back a large quantity of high valued Thailand purchases. The USA, for example, allows US$400 worth of foreign-purchased goods to enter without duty (with no limit on handicrafts and unset gems), while in Australia the total value is limited to A$400.

## MONEY
## Currency

The basic unit of Thai currency is the *baht*. There are 100 *satang* in one baht; coins include 25-satang and 50-satang pieces and baht in 1B, 5B and 10B coins. Older coins have Thai numerals only, while newer coins have Thai and Arabic numerals. Twenty-five satang equals one *saleung* in colloquial Thai, so a price of six saleung in the market, say, for a banana this means 1.50B. The term is becoming increasingly rare as ongoing inflation makes purchases of less than 1B or 2B almost non-existent.

Paper currency comes in denominations of 10B (brown), 20B (green), 50B (blue), 100B (red), 500B (purple) and 1000B (beige). A 10,000B bill was on the way when the 1997 cash crunch came, but has been tabled for the moment. Ten-baht bills are being phased out in favour of the 10B coin and have become rather uncommon. Fortunately for newcomers to Thailand, numerals are printed in Arabic as well as Thai forms. Notes are also scaled according to the amount; the larger the denomination, the larger the note. Large denominations – 500B and especially 1000B bills – can be hard to change in small towns, but banks will always change them.

## Exchange Rates

Exchange rates at the time of writing include:

| country | unit | | baht |
|---|---|---|---|
| Australia | A$1 | = | 23.0 |
| Canada | C$1 | = | 29.0 |
| European Union | €1 | = | 40.4 |
| France | 1FF | = | 6.0 |
| Germany | 1DM | = | 20.6 |
| Hong Kong | HK$1 | = | 5.8 |
| Japan | ¥100 | = | 34.5 |
| New Zealand | NZ$1 | = | 18.4 |
| Singapore | S$1 | = | 25.0 |
| UK | UK£1 | = | 65.3 |
| USA | US$1 | = | 40.5 |

Prior to June 1997 the baht was pegged to a basket of currencies heavily weighted towards the US dollar, and for over 20 years it hardly varied beyond 20B to 26B to the dollar. A year after flotation, in June 1998, the baht had slipped approximately 30% against the dollar.

Exchange rates slipped again, slightly, in late 2000, and there's always a chance the Thai currency will go for another roller coaster ride. Hence it's a good idea to stay abreast of exchange rates during your stay in Thailand – changing currencies at the right time could extend your budget significantly. Exchange rates are printed in the *Bangkok Post* and *The Nation* every day, or you can walk into any Thai bank and ask to see a daily rate sheet.

## Exchanging Money

There is no black-market money exchange for baht, so there's no reason to bring in any Thai currency. Banks or legal moneychangers offer the best exchange rate within the country. When buying baht, US dollars are the most readily acceptable currency and travellers cheques get better rates than cash. As banks charge up to 23B commission and duty for each travellers cheque cashed, you'll save on commissions if you use larger cheque denominations (eg, a US$50 cheque will only cost 23B while five US$10 cheques will cost 115B). British pounds are second to the US dollar in general acceptability.

Note that you can't exchange Malaysian ringgit, Indonesian rupiah, Nepali rupees, Cambodian riel, Lao kip, Vietnamese dong or Myanmar (Burma) kyat into Thai currency at banks, though some Bangkok moneychangers along Th Charoen Krung and Th Silom carry these currencies. The latter can in fact be good places to buy these currencies if you're going to any of these countries. Rates are comparable with black-market rates in countries with discrepancies between the 'official' and free-market currency values.

Visa and MasterCard credit-card holders can get cash advances of up to US$500 (in baht only) per day through some branches of the Thai Farmers Bank, Bangkok Bank and Siam Commercial Bank (and also at the night-time exchange windows in well-touristed spots like Banglamphu).

American Express card holders can also get advances, but only in travellers cheques. The Amex agent is SEA Tours (☎ 216 5783, 216 5934), 8th floor, Suite 88-92, Payathai Plaza (Map 5), 128 Th Phayathai, Bangkok.

See the Business Hours section later in this chapter for information on bank opening hours.

**Exchange Control** Legally, any traveller arriving in Thailand must have at least the following amount of money in cash, travellers cheques, bank draft or letter of credit, according to visa category: Non-Immigrant Visa, US$500 per person or US$1000 per family; Tourist Visa, US$250 per person or US$500 per family; and Transit Visa or no visa, US$125 per person or US$250 per family. This may be checked if you arrive on a one-way ticket or if you look as if you're at 'the end of the road'.

Legally there are no limits to the amounts of Thai or foreign currency you may bring into the country. Upon leaving Thailand, you're permitted to take no more than 50,000B per person without special authorisation; export of foreign currencies is unrestricted. It's legal to open a US dollar account at any commercial bank in Thailand. As long as the funds originate from abroad, there are no restrictions on their maintenance or withdrawal.

**ATMs & Credit/Debit Cards** An alternative to carrying around large amounts of cash or travellers cheques is to open an account at a Thai bank and request an automatic teller machines (ATM) card. Major banks in Thailand now have ATMs in provincial capitals and in many smaller towns as well, open 24 hours. Once you have a card you'll be able to withdraw cash at machines throughout Thailand, whether those machines belong to your bank or another Thai bank. ATM cards issued by Thai Farmers Bank or Bangkok Bank can be used with the ATMs of 14 major banks – there are over 3000 machines throughout the country. A 10B transaction charge is usually deducted for using an ATM belonging to a bank with whom you don't have an account.

Debit cards (also known as cash cards or check cards) issued by a bank in your own country can also be used at several Thai banks to withdraw cash (in Thai baht only) directly from your cheque or savings account back home, thus avoiding all commissions and finance charges. You can use Master-Card debit cards to buy baht at foreign-exchange booths or desks at either the Bangkok Bank or Siam Commercial Bank. Visa debit cards can buy cash through the Thai Farmers Bank exchange services.

These cards can also be used at many Thai ATMs, though a surcharge of around US$1 is usually subtracted from your home account each time you complete a machine transaction. Some travellers now use debit or

ATM cards in lieu of travellers cheques because they're quicker and more convenient, although it's a good idea to bring along an emergency travellers cheque fund in case you lose your card. One disadvantage of debit card accounts, as opposed to credit-card accounts, is that you can't arrange a 'charge back' for unsatisfactory purchases after the transaction is completed – once the money's drawn from your account it's gone.

Credit cards as well as debit cards can be used for purchases at many shops, hotels and restaurants. The most commonly accepted cards are Visa and MasterCard, followed by American Express (AmEx) and Japan Card Bureau (JCB). Diner's Club and Carte Blanche are of much more limited use.

**Card Problems** Occasionally when you try to use a card at upcountry hotels or shops, the staff may try to tell you that only cards issued by Thai Farmers Bank or Siam Commercial Bank are acceptable. With a little patience, you should be able to make them understand that the Thai Farmers Bank will pay the merchant and that your bank will pay the Thai Farmers Bank – and that any Visa or MasterCard issued anywhere in the world is indeed acceptable.

Another problem concerns illegal surcharges on credit-card purchases. It's against Thai law to pass on to the customer the 3% merchant fee charged by banks, but almost all merchants in Thailand do it anyway. Some even ask 4% or 5%! The only exception seems to be hotels – though even a few hotels will. If you don't agree to the surcharge they'll simply refuse to accept your card. Begging and pleading or pointing out the law doesn't seem to help.

The best way to get around the illegal surcharge is to politely ask that the credit-card receipt be itemised with cost of product or service and the surcharge listed separately. Then when you pay your bill, photocopy all receipts showing the surcharge and request a 'charge back'. Not all banks in all countries will offer such refunds – the banks in the UK, for example, refuse to issue such refunds, while the banks in the USA usually will.

To report a lost or stolen credit/debit card, call the following telephone hotlines in Bangkok:

| | |
|---|---|
| **AmEx** | ☎ 273 0022 |
| **Diners Club** | ☎ 238 3660 |
| **MasterCard** | ☎ 260 8572 |
| **Visa** | ☎ 256 7326 |

See the Dangers & Annoyances section in this chapter for important warnings on credit-card theft and fraud.

**International Transfers** If you have a reliable place to receive mail in Thailand, one of the safest and cheapest ways to get money from overseas is to have an international cashier's cheque (or international money order) sent by courier. It usually takes no more than four days for courier mail to reach Thailand from anywhere in the world.

If you have a bank account in Thailand or your home bank has a branch in Bangkok, you can have money wired direct via a telegraphic transfer. This costs a bit more than having a cheque sent; telegraphic transfers take anywhere from two days to a week to arrive. International banks with branches in Bangkok include Bank of America, Bank of Tokyo, Banque Indosuez, Banque Nationale de Paris, Citibank, Deutsche Bank, HongkongBank, Chase Manhattan Bank, Merrill Lynch International Bank, Sakura Bank, Standard Chartered Bank, United Malayan Bank and many others.

Western Union (☎ 254 9121), justifiably claiming to be 'the fastest way to send money worldwide', has an office in Central department store at 1027 Th Ploenchit as well as in other branches of Central around the city.

## Security

Give some thought in advance as to how you're going to organise your finances – whether travellers cheques, cash, credit and debit cards, or some combination of these. Many travellers favour hidden pouches that can be worn beneath clothing. Hip-pocket wallets are easy marks for thieves. Pickpockets work markets and crowded buses throughout the country, so it pays to keep your money concealed. See Dangers & Annoyances later in this chapter for more on petty crime.

It's a good idea not to keep all your money in one place; keep an 'emergency' stash well concealed in a piece of luggage separate from other money. Long-term travellers might even consider renting a safety deposit box at a bank. Keep your onward tickets, a copy of your passport, a list of all credit-card numbers and some money in the box just in case all your belongings are stolen. See Copies in the Documents section earlier in this chapter.

## Costs

While food and accommodation outside the capital are usually cheaper, costs in Bangkok are also very reasonable, especially considering the value vis-à-vis other countries in South and South-East Asia. Since the baht devaluation, prices have dropped even lower, at least with regard to hard currencies. If measured against the US dollar, for example, the cost of the average hotel room dropped 20% to 25% between June 1997 and June 2000, the price of the average hotel buffet came down 30%, a bowl of rice noodles cost 15% less, and the fare between Bangkok and Phuket fell 25%. With current inflation of baht prices running just 2% per year, these savings will slowly evaporate over the life of this guidebook edition, of course.

In Bangkok there's no limit to the amount you *could* spend, but if you live frugally, avoid the tourist ghettos and ride the public bus system you can get by on only slightly more than you would spend upcountry. Acommodation is of primary importance, as it's generally a good deal more expensive than in the provinces. Outside Bangkok, budget-squeezers should be able to get by on 240B per day – this estimate includes basic guesthouse accommodation, food, non-alcoholic beverages and local transport, but not camera film, souvenirs, tours, long-distance transport or vehicle hire. Add another 60B to 85B per day for every large beer (30B to 55B for small bottles) you drink.

However, in Bangkok, the visitor typically spends more than 400B per day just for accommodation – this is generally the minimum for air-con (in a twin room). On the other hand, if you can do without air-con, rooms can be found for as little as 75B per person. It is usually the noise, heat and pollution in Bangkok that drives many budget travellers to seek more comfort than they might need upcountry.

Those seeking international-class accommodation and food will spend at least 1500B to 2000B a day for a room with all the modern amenities – IDD phone, 24-hour hot water and air-conditioning, carpeting, a fitness centre, swimming pool and all-night room service.

Food is somewhat more expensive in Bangkok than in the provinces. However, in Thonburi (Bangkok's 'Left Bank'), many dishes are often cheaper than they are upcountry, due to the availability of fresh ingredients. This is also true for the working-class districts on the Bangkok side, like Khlong Toey or Makkasan.

Bangkok is a typical 'primary city', meaning that most goods produced by the country as a whole end up in Bangkok. The glaring exception is Western food, which Bangkok has more of than anywhere else in the kingdom, but charges the most for. International fast-food chains can be real budget-busters. Eat only Thai and Chinese food if you're trying to spend as little as possible. After all, why go to Thailand to eat steak and potatoes?

Throughout Thailand you might discover that there are two rates of entry fees – one for Thais and another, more expensive one for non-Thais. Before you get upset about the discount entry rate for locals, remember that most Thai people would be unable to afford higher entry fees. By paying a little more, tourists help keep entry fees for Thais affordable, which keeps museums, galleries etc more accessible for locals.

## Tipping & Bargaining

Tipping is not normal practice in Thailand, although they're getting used to it in expensive hotels and restaurants. Elsewhere don't bother. The exception is loose change left from a large Thai restaurant bill; for example, if a meal costs 288B and you pay with a 500B note, some Thais and foreign residents will leave the 12B coin change on the change tray. It's not so much a tip as a way of saying 'I'm not so money-grubbing as to grab every last baht'. On the other hand, change from a 50B note for a 44B bill will usually not be left behind.

Good bargaining takes practice and is another way to cut costs. Items sold by street vendors in markets or in most shops are flexibly priced – that is, the price is negotiable (this includes most hotel souvenir shops).

The only places you'll see fixed prices in Bangkok is in department stores. If the same kind of merchandise is offered in a department store and a small shop or market, it would be a good idea to check the department store price for a point of reference. Sometimes the department store price will be lower than the market price, sometimes it won't – but it will almost always be a fairly realistic figure. For items that aren't available in department stores, like antiques, your best research will be accomplished by shopping around. Unless you already know the fair price on a certain item, you needn't take the first opportunity to purchase – not only because you might find a better price, but because better quality or selection may be just around the corner.

Sometimes accommodation rates can be bargained down. Bargain hard in heavily touristed areas as the one-week, all-air-con type of visitor often pays whatever's asked, creating an artificial price zone between the local and tourist market that the budgeter must deal with.

Keep your sense of perspective and use some discretion when going for the bone on a price. There's a fine line between bargaining and niggling – getting hot under the collar over 5B makes both seller and buyer lose face. Remember most prices – even tourist rates – are much lower than you would·pay for at home.

Thais respect a good haggler. Always let the vendor make the first offer then ask 'Is that your best price?' or 'Can you lower the price?'. This usually results is an immediate discount from the first price. Now it's your turn to make a counter-offer; always start low but don't bargain at all unless you're

serious about buying. Negotiations continue back and forth until a price is agreed upon – there's no set discount from the asking price as some vendors start ridiculously high, others closer to the 'real' price.

Most vendors will offer a set of excuses for why they can go no lower, but since you have no way to assess the validity of such excuses you can only go with your instincts as to what the merchandise is really worth. It helps if you've done your homework by shopping around, and the whole process becomes easier with practice. It helps immeasurably to keep the negotiations relaxed and friendly, and to speak slowly and clearly (but not in a condescending manner). Vendors will almost always give a better price to someone they like.

One sure way to keep prices down is to avoid shopping in the company of touts, tour guides or 'friendly strangers' as they will inevitably – no matter what they say – take a commission on anything you buy, thus driving prices up.

The cost of transport within Bangkok and between it and other cities is very reasonable. Again, bargaining (when hiring a vehicle) can save you a lot of baht. See the Getting Around chapter.

## Value-Added Tax

Thailand has a 7% value-added tax (VAT). The tax applies only to certain goods and services but, unfortunately, no-one seems to know what's subject to VAT and what's not, so the whole situation can be rather confusing. Legally the tax is supposed to be applied to a retailer's cost for the product. For example, if a merchant's wholesale price is 100B for an item that retails at 200B, the maximum adjusted retail including VAT should be 207B, not 214B. But this rarely stops Thai merchants from adding 'VAT' surcharges to their sales.

Visitors to Thailand who hold valid tourist visas and who depart Thailand by air may apply for a VAT refund on purchases made at designated shops and department stores. However, the labyrinth of rules and restrictions are so complicated that few visitors bother to apply. First, you must bear a valid tourist visa and not have been in Thailand for more than 180 days in a calendar year. Second, VAT refunds are available only to visitors departing the country by air, and are available only at the departure halls of Thailand's international airports, where you must fill out a VAT refund application and present it to customs officers along with purchased goods and receipts. For more information, contact the VAT Refund office at Bangkok International Airport (☎ 535-6576-79) or the VAT Refund for Tourist Office, Revenue Department, Phaholyothin Rd, Bangkok 10400, Thailand (☎ 272-9387-8, fax 617-3559). This Web site also carries information: www.thaistudents.com/guidebook/vat.

## Other Consumer Taxes

Tourist hotels will usually add a 10% hotel tax, and sometimes an 8% to 10% service charge as well, to your room bill.

## POST & COMMUNICATIONS

Thailand has a very efficient postal service and within the country postage is very cheap. Bangkok's main post office (Map 6) on Th Charoen Krung (New Rd) is open from 8 am to 8 pm weekdays, and from 8 am to 1 pm on weekends and holidays. A 24-hour international telecommunications service (including telephone, fax, telex and telegram) is located in a separate building to the right and slightly in front of the main post office building.

The 1927 Thai Art Deco building is a treat in itself. During the short-lived Japanese assault on Bangkok in 1941, a bomb came through the roof and landed on the floor of the main hall without exploding. Italian sculptor Corrado Feroci, considered the father of Thai modern art, crafted the garuda sculptures perched atop either side of the building's central tower.

The easiest way to get to there is via the Chao Phraya River Express, which stops at Tha (pier) Meuang Khae at the river end of Soi Charoen Krung 34, next to Wat Meuang Khae, just south of the post office.

## Postal Rates

Air mail letters weighing 10g or less cost 14B to anywhere in Asia and the Middle East (Zone 1 in Thai postal parlance), 17B to Europe, Africa, Australia and New Zealand (Zone 2), and 19B to the Americas (Zone 3). Each additional 10g costs 5B, 7B and 9B respectively. Aerograms cost 15B regardless of the destination, while postcards are 12B to 15B depending on size. Printed matter and small packets up to 20g cost 12B, 16B or 18B depending on the zone.

Letters sent by registered mail cost 25B in addition to regular air mail postage. International express mail (EMS) fees vary according to 15 zones of destination radiating out from Thailand, ranging from 310B for a document sent to Zone 1 to 2050B for a document sent to Zone 15. EMS packages range from 460B to 2400B. Within Thailand, this service costs only 25B in addition to regular postage.

The rates for parcels shipped by international post vary according to weight (rising in 1kg increments), country of destination and whether they're shipped by surface (takes up to two months) or air (one to two weeks). Sample air rates include: Singapore, 560B for the first kilo, then 100B for each additional kilo; UK 990B first kilo, 400B for each additional kilo; and USA 775B and 300B.

A service called Economy Air SAL (for Sea, Air, Land) uses a combination of surface and air mail modes with rates beginning at 20B per 50g, plus 7B for each additional 25g after that. As a comparison, a 2kg parcel sent to the USA by regular air mail would cost 1810B, while the same parcel sent via Economy Air SAL would cost only 888B. There are a few variations depending on what's in the package eg printed matter travels by air more cheaply than other goods.

Parcels sent domestically cost 15B for the first kilogram, plus 10B for each additional kilogram.

You can insure the contents of a package at the cost of 7B for every US$20 of the value of the goods within, plus an 'operation charge' of 25B.

## Sending Mail

**Courier Services** The following companies will pick up mail or parcels anywhere in Bangkok for overnight delivery to other towns in Thailand or to most places in the world, and deliver within three to four days. DHL has the best reputation for punctuality and efficiency. Be sure to allow plenty of time between your call and the expected pick-up time for traffic jams.

**DHL Worldwide** (☎ 207 0600) 22nd floor, Grand Amarin Tower, Th Phetburi, Tat Mai
**Federal Express** (☎ 367 3222) 8th floor, Green Tower, Th Phra Ram IV
**UPS** (☎ 712 3300) 16/1 Soi 44/1, Th Sukhumvit

**Packaging** There's an efficient and inexpensive packaging service at the main post office, or you can simply buy the materials at the counter and do it yourself. The packaging counter is open 8 am to 4.30 pm weekdays and 9 am to noon Saturday. When the parcel counter is closed (weekday evenings and Sunday mornings), an informal packing service (using recycled materials) is open behind the service windows at the centre rear of the building.

Branch post offices throughout the city also offer parcel services.

### Receiving Mail

**Poste Restante** The poste restante counter at the main post office on Th Charoen Krung is open from 8 am to 8 pm weekdays, and 8 am to 1 pm on weekends. Each letter you collect costs 1B, parcels 2B. The poste restante service is very efficient and reliable, although during the high season you may have to wait in line.

As with many Asian countries, confusion at poste restante is most likely to arise over given names and surnames. Ask whoever will be writing to you to print your surname clearly and to underline it. If you're certain a letter should be waiting for you and it cannot be found, it's always wise to check it hasn't been filed under your given name. Branch post offices throughout Bangkok also offer poste restante service.

***American Express*** The AmEx office (☎ 216 5757, 273 0022), 8th floor, Suite 88-92, Payathai Plaza (Map 5), 128 Th Phayathai, will also take mail on behalf of AmEx

card holders. Opening hours are from 8.30 am to noon and 1 to 4.30 pm on weekdays, and 8.30 to 11.30 am on Saturday. AmEx won't accept courier packets that require your signature. The mail window staff have a reputation for being less than helpful.

### Telephone

The telephone system in Thailand, operated by the government-subsidised but privately owned Telephone Organisation of Thailand (TOT) under the Communications Authority of Thailand (CAT), is efficient if costly, and from Bangkok you can usually direct-dial most major centres with little difficulty.

The telephone country code for Thailand is ☎ 66 and Bangkok's is ☎ 02. See the Area Codes table in this section for telephone area codes throughout Thailand.

**International Calls** To direct-dial an international number from a private phone, simply dial ☎ 001 before the number (for calls to Malaysia and Laos, see the following entry). For operator-assisted international calls, dial ☎ 100.

A service called Home Country Direct is available at Bangkok's main post office (Map 6), Bangkok International Airport, Queen Sirikit National Convention Center (Map 7, World Trade Center), Sogo department store (Map 7), and at the Banglamphu (Map 4) and Hualamphong post offices. Home Country Direct phones offer easy one-button connection to international operators in 40-odd countries around the world.

You can also direct-dial Home Country Direct access numbers from any private phone (most hotel phones wont work) in Thailand.

For Home Country Direct, dial ☎ 001-999 followed by:

| | |
|---|---|
| **Australia (OTC)** | 61-1000 |
| **Australia (Optus)** | 61-2000 |
| **Canada** | 15-1000 |
| **Canada (AT&T)** | 15-2000 |
| **Denmark** | 45-1000 |
| **Finland** | 358-1000 |
| **France** | 33-1000 |
| **Germany** | 49-1000 |
| **Israel** | 972-1000 |

## Area Codes

The country code for Thailand is ☎ 66. Area codes include:

| | |
|---|---|
| Bangkok, Thonburi, Nonthaburi, Pathum Thani, Samut Prakan | ☎ 02 |
| Phetchaburi, Cha-am, Prachuap Khiri Khan, Pranburi, Ratchaburi | ☎ 032 |
| Kanchanaburi, Nakhon Pathom, Samut Sakhon, Samut Songkhram | ☎ 034 |
| Ang Thong, Ayuthaya, Suphanburi | ☎ 035 |
| Lopburi, Saraburi, Singburi | ☎ 036 |
| Nakhon Nayok, Prachinburi, Aranya Prathet | ☎ 037 |
| Chachoengsao, Chonburi, Pattaya, Rayong, Si Racha | ☎ 038 |
| Chanthaburi, Trat | ☎ 039 |
| Loei, Chiang Khan, Mukdahan, Nakhon Phanom | ☎ 042 |
| Nong Khai, Sakon Nakhon, Udon Thani | ☎ 042 |
| Kalasin, Khon Kaen, Mahasarakham, Roi Et | ☎ 043 |
| Buriram, Chaiyaphum, Nakhon Ratchasima (Khorat) | ☎ 044 |
| Si Saket, Surin, Ubon Ratchathani, Yasothon | ☎ 045 |
| Chiang Mai, Chiang Rai, Lamphun, Mae Hong Song | ☎ 053 |
| Lampang, Nan, Phayao, Phrae | ☎ 054 |
| Kamphaeng Phet, Phitsanulok, Sukhothai, Tak, Mae Sot, Uttaradit | ☎ 055 |
| Nakhon Sawan, Phetchabun, Phichit, Uthai Thani | ☎ 056 |
| Narathiwat, Sungai Kolok, Pattani, Yala | ☎ 073 |
| Hat Yai, Phattalung, Satun, Songkhla | ☎ 074 |
| Krabi, Nakhon Si Thammarat, Trang | ☎ 075 |
| Phang-Nga, Phuket | ☎ 076 |
| Chumphon, Ranong, Surat Thani, Chaiya, Ko Samui | ☎ 077 |

| | | |
|---|---|---|
| **Italy** | 39-1000 | |
| **Japan** | 81-0051 | |
| **Korea** | 82-1000 | |
| **Netherlands** | 31-1035 | |
| **New Zealand** | 64-1066 | |
| **Norway** | 47-1000 | |
| **Singapore** | 65-0000 | |
| **Sweden** | 46-1000 | (telephone 1) |
| **Sweden** | 41-2000 | (telephone 2) |
| **Switzerland** | 41-1000 | |
| **UK (BT)** | 44-1066 | |
| **UK (MCL)** | 44-2000 | |
| **USA (AT&T)** | 11-1111 | |
| **USA (MCI)** | 12001 | |
| **USA (Sprint)** | 13877 | |
| **USA - Hawaii** | 14424 | |

Hotels generally add surcharges (sometimes as much as 30% over and above the CAT rate) for international long-distance calls, so it's always cheaper to call abroad from a CAT telephone office. A useful CAT office is near the main post office (Map 6).

You can also make long-distance calls and faxes at the TOT office (Map 7) on Th Ploenchit – but this office accepts cash only, no reverse-charge or credit-card calls.

To make an international long-distance call *(thorásàp ráwàang pràthêt)* first fill out a bilingual form with your name and details pertaining to the call's destination. Except for reverse-charge calls, you must estimate the time you'll be on the phone and pay a deposit equal to the time and distance rate. There is always a minimum three-minute charge, refunded if your call doesn't go through.

Usually, only cash or international phone credit cards are acceptable at CAT offices. If the call doesn't go through you must pay a 30B service charge anyway – unless you're calling reverse-charges *(kèp plaithaang)*. For reverse-charge calls it's the opposite, you must pay the 30B charge only if the call goes through. Depending on where you're calling, reimbursing someone later for a reverse-charge call to your home country may be less expensive than paying CAT/TOT charges – it pays to compare rates at source and destination.

There are also private long-distance telephone offices but these are usually only for calls within Thailand. Private offices with international service always charge more than the government offices, although private office surcharges are usually lower than hotel rates. They typically collect a 10B surcharge for long-distance domestic calls and 50B for international calls, and accept cash only.

Whichever type of phone service you use, the least expensive time of day to make calls is from midnight to 5 am (30% discount from standard rates), followed by 9 pm to midnight or 5 to 7 am (20% discount). You pay full price from 7 am to 9 pm (this rate is reduced 20% on Sunday). Some sample rates for a three-minute call during the daytime: Africa 55B, Asia 40B, Australia 34B, Europe 46B (UK 42B).

If you're calling from someone's private phone, you must dial the international access code ☎ 001 before dialling the country code, area code and phone number you wish to reach.

**Malaysia & Laos** CAT does not offer long-distance service to Malaysia or Laos. To call these countries you must go through the TOT. For Laos, you can direct-dial ☎ 007 and country code 856, followed by the area code and number you want to reach. Malaysia can be dialled direct by prefixing the Malaysian number (including area code) with the code ☎ 09. If you're dialling from any area code in Thailand that begins with ☎ 07, the rate is 10B to 15B per minute. All other area codes are 20B to 30B per minute, depending on time of day.

**Telephone Office Hours** Bangkok's CAT international phone office, at the Th Charoen Krung main post office (Map 6), is open 24 hours.

**Pay Phones** There are three kinds of public pay phones in Thailand: 'red', 'blue' and 'green'. The red phones are for local city calls, the blue are for both local and long-distance calls (within Thailand), and the green ones are for use with phonecards. Local calls from pay phones cost 1B for 164 seconds (add more coins for more time). Local calls from private phones cost 3B, with no time limit. Some hotels and guesthouses have private pay phones that cost 5B per call.

Card phones are available at the information counter or gift shops of Bangkok International Airport, as well as at major shopping centres. Phonecards come in 25B, 50B, 100B, 200B and 240B denominations, all roughly the same size as a credit card, and can be purchased at any TOT office.

Another way to pay for domestic calls is to use the Pin Phone 108 system, which allows you to dial '108' from any phone – including cellular phones and public pay phones, then enter a PIN code to call any number in Thailand. To use this system, however, you must have your own phone number in Thailand.

**Cellular Phones** The TOT authorises the use of private cell phones using two systems, NMT 900MHz (Cellular 900) and GSM, and the older NMT 470MHz. The former system is becoming more common.

It costs 1000B to register a phone and 500B per month for 'number rental' with the 900MHz and GSM, or 300B for 470MHz. Rates are 3B per minute within the same area code, 8B per minute to adjacent area codes and 12B per minute to other area codes. Cell phone users must pay for incoming as well as outgoing calls. Keep this in mind whenever you consider calling a number that begins with the code ☎ 01. This means you're calling a cell phone number and will be charged accordingly. Note also that the zero in '01' needs to be dialled.

In Bangkok, you'll see sidewalk tables where it's possible to make pirate cell phone calls to anywhere in Thailand for 3B to 5B per minute. The vendors are able to do this by repeatedly taking advantage of special promotions on new cell phone accounts.

### eKno Communication Service
Lonely Planet's eKno global communication service provides low-cost international

calls – for local calls you're usually better off with a local phonecard. eKno also offers free messaging services, email, travel information and an online travel vault, where you can securely store all your important documents. You can join online at www.ekno .lonelyplanet.com, where you will find the local-access numbers for the 24-hour customer-service centre. Once you have joined, always check the eKno Web site for the latest access numbers for each country and updates on new features.

### Fax
The main post office CAT office offers fax, telegraph and telex services in addition to regular phone services. There's no need to bring your own paper as the post offices supply their own forms. A few TOT offices also offer fax services. International faxes typically cost 100B to 130B for the first page, 70B to 100B per page for following pages, depending on the size of the paper and destination.

Larger hotels with business centres offer the same telecommunication services, but always at higher rates.

### Email & Internet Access
The Internet is rapidly gaining popularity in Thailand, especially as more and more local, Thai-language pages go online and folks get their Internet software installed for Thai language.

The scene is changing rapidly and nowadays Thailand's better ISPs offer upcountry dial-up points in over a dozen towns and cities around the country, which means you won't necessarily have to pay long-distance charges to Bangkok if you are travelling with a laptop.

The major limitation in email and Internet access continues to be the CAT, which connects all ISPs via the Thailand Internet Exchange (THIX) at relatively low speeds by international standards. The CAT also collects a hefty access charge from local ISPs, which keeps rates high relative to the local economy.

Nevertheless, at the time of writing Thailand was more advanced in the cyberspace world than any other country in South-East Asia.

Nowadays most ISPs worldwide offer the option of Web-based email, so if you already have an Internet account at home, you can check your email anywhere in Thailand simply by logging onto your ISP's Web site using an Internet browser (such as Microsoft Internet Explorer or Netscape). If you have any doubts about whether your home ISP offers Web-based email, check before you leave home. You may want to register with one of the many free Web-based email services, such as MS Hotmail, Yahoo!, Juno or Lonely Planet's own eKno. You can log onto these services at any cybercafe in Thailand.

**Plugging in Your Own Machine** RJ11 phone jacks are the standard in new hotels, but in older hotels and guesthouses the phones may still be hard-wired (bring along an acoustic coupler just in case). Some hotels and guesthouses that feature room phones without RJ11 jacks may have a fax line in the office, and virtually all fax machines in Thailand are connected via RJ11 jacks. Some places will allow guests to use the house fax line for laptop modems, provided online time is kept short.

Longer-term visitors may want to consider opening a monthly Internet account. Local ISPs – of which there were 18 at last count – typically charge around 400B to 500B per month for 20 hours of Net access, 700B to 800B for 40 hours. Low-grade, text-only services are available for as low as 200B a month. With any of these accounts additional per-hour charges are incurred if you exceed your online time.

Temporary Internet accounts are also available from several Thai ISPs. One of the better ones is WebNet, offered by Loxinfo (www.loxinfo.co.th). You can buy a block of 25 hours (500B), or 45 hours (750B), good for up to one year. Purchasers are provided with a user ID, password, web-browser software, local phone access numbers and log-on procedures, all via email. You'll be able to navigate the Internet, check email at your online home address and access any online services you subscribe to.

**Email Centres & Cyber Cafes** Internet users can check their email or skim the Net at dozens of Internet cafes, bars and centres throughout the city. For the visitor who only needs to log on once in a while, these are a less expensive alternative to getting your own account – and it certainly beats lugging around a laptop. The going rate is 1B or 2B per on- and off-line minute, although we've seen a few places where slower connections are available at a half baht per minute. If past experience is any measure, rates will continue to drop.

Th Khao San has the highest concentration of access points in the city (over 30 at last count), so if it's choice you want, head there. Other good areas for Internet centres include Th Silom, Th Ploenchit and Siam Square. Additionally many Bangkok guesthouses and hotels nowadays offer Internet access on the premises.

There's not much point in recommending one place over another as they're all struggling to keep up with their competitors, and hence the equipment and functionality changes from month to month. Some places are little more than one terminal set up in the corner of a *ráan cham* (sundries shop), while the better spots offer scanner and printer services for additional charges.

A couple of places we've had good experiences with include Cyber Café (Map 7, ☎ 656 8473, ⓔ cybercafe@cyercafe-th.com), 2nd floor, Ploenchit Center, Th Ploenchit, and Bangkok Internet Café (Map 4, ☎ 629 3015), next to Prakorp's House & Restaurant (Map 4), Th Khao San.

## INTERNET RESOURCES

A growing number of World Wide Web (WWW) sites offer information on Bangkok. Remember that all URL's (Uniform Resource Locators) mentioned here are subject to change without notice – and of course the quality of content is volatile. You can use your own Web browser to conduct searches; there's a lot of information out there. A quick search on Yahoo at the time of writing yielded a list of nearly 1000 Web sites devoted to Thailand, plus 242,000 Web pages that mentioned the word 'Bangkok'.

Consider starting your Bangkok info search with the Lonely Planet Web site (www.lonelyplanet.com). You'll find colourful summaries on travelling to most places on earth, postcards from other travellers and the Thorn Tree bulletin board, where you can ask questions before you go or dispense advice when you get back. You can also find travel news and updates to this edition, while the subWWWay section links you to the most useful travel resources elsewhere on the Web.

Many Web sites focussing on Bangkok travel earn revenue from hotel bookings and advertising paid for by travel suppliers, hence you should take any recommendations they make with a huge grain of salt. Useful websites include:

**Asia Travel** This is among the best of the many commercial sites with travel booking capabilities.
www.asiatravel.com/thaiinfo

**Bangkok Metro** The online version of the printed publication, this site is good for entertainment and event listings in Bangkok.
www.bkkmetro.com

**Bangkok Post** Posts its entire newspaper – save for ads and wire stories – daily, and archives many stories for several years.
www.bangkokpost.com

**Bangkok Thailand Today** Contains a wealth of neighbourhood maps, travel information, local news, and lists of hotels and restaurants in the city.
www.bangkok.thailandtoday.com

**Bangkok.com** In spite if its million-dollar domain name, this site so far carries little of interest – although it has potential.
www.bangkok.com

**Kidon Media-Link** This site has the best set of Thai newspaper links – 10 at last count, including two in Thai and eight in English.
www.kidon.com/media-link/thailand

**Mahidol University** From the university in Bangkok, this is a useful site that's searchable by keyword.
www.mahidol.ac.th

**National Electronics and Computer Technology Center** This site contains links on everything from a list of all Thai embassies and consulates abroad and details of visa requirements to weather updates.
www.nectec.or.th

**ThaiIndex Pages** Includes general information, government-office listings, travel listings, a hotel directory and other web links.
www.thaiindex.com

**ThaiStudents.com** Maintained by the students at Sriwittayapaknam School in Samut Prakan, this is a complex of highly informative sites, including the largest English-language Web site in Thailand with over 2000 pages on tap at last count. Included are continually updated pages on Thai student life and more unbiased information on Thailand travel than any site we've seen – and there's no advertising. www.thaistudents.com

**The Nation** This is another good source of local news with a comprehensive searchable archive. www.nationmultimedia.com

**Tourism Authority of Thailand (TAT)** The TAT maintains a well-designed Web site containing a province-by-province guide, numerous and up-to-date press releases, tourism statistics, TAT contact information and trip planning hints. www.tat.or.th

You could also try the usenet newsgroup, soc.culture.thai. This is a chat outlet for anyone who thinks they have something to say about Thailand – we can't vouch for the quality, but it's not a bad place to start.

## BOOKS
Most books are published in different editions by different publishers in different countries. Your local bookshop or library at home is best placed to help you track down the following recommendations.

### Lonely Planet
*Thailand,* by the same author as this guide, has gone through nine editions since its first publication in 1982, and remains one of the most comprehensive guidebooks to Thailand available. *Thailand's Islands & Beaches* goes into more detail on the kingdom's coastal and marine destinations. Lonely Planet also publishes a *Thailand travel atlas, Thai phrasebook* and *Thai Hill Tribes phrasebook,* plus *World Food: Thailand.* A *Chiang Mai & Northern Thailand* guide is forthcoming.

### Description & Travel
The earliest Western literature of note on Thailand, Guy Tachard's *A Relation of the Voyage to Siam,* recounts a 1680s French expedition through parts of the country with little literary flair. Shortly after, Simon de la Loubére's 1693 *New Historical Relation of the Kingdom of Siam* chronicled the French mission to the Ayuthaya court in great detail.

Frank Vincent's *The Land of the White Elephant,* first published in 1873, is a very readable account of an American merchant's travels in Siam. Carl Bock's illustrated *Temples and Elephants* covered similar territory in 1884. Tachard, Loubére, Vincent and Bock have all been republished by Bangkok publisher White Lotus and are available in bookshops in Bangkok. Other reprints to look for if you're interested in historical travel writing include Ernest Young's *The Kingdom of the Yellow Robe* (1898) and the anonymous *An Englishman's Siamese Journals* (1890–93).

The infamous Anna Leonowens published *The English Governess at the Siamese Court* in 1870. Its largely unauthentic descriptions of Siamese life have since been transformed into four Hollywood movies (including one animated version) and a Broadway musical.

Joseph Conrad evoked Thailand in several of his pre-WWII novels and short stories, most notably in his 1920s *The Secret Sharer* and *Falk: A Reminiscence.* More detail from the 1920s can be found in *Teak Wallah,* by Reginald Campbell, a Briton who worked as a teak inspector in Northern Thailand.

### History & Politics
One of the more readable general histories written in the latter half of the 20th century is David Wyatt's *Thailand: A Short History* (Trasvin Publications, Chiang Mai, 1982).

Thailand's *Boom and Bust,* by Phongpaichit, Pasuk & Chris Baker (1998), was published just after the currency crash. It traces the boom – and the bust – as well as providing interesting insights into Thailand's contemporary culture.

At first glance *Siam Mapped: A History of the Geo-Body of a Nation* by Thongchai Winichakul appears to be a simple history of the mapping of Thailand. But a thorough reading will uncover a profound and very well-researched study of Thai notions of identity and sovereignty within the context of South-East Asian history and European involvement in the region.

Concentrating on post-revolutionary Thailand, *The Balancing Act: A History of*

*Modern Thailand* (Asia Books, 1991), by Joseph Wright Jr, starts with the 1932 revolution and ends with the February 1991 coup. Wright's most demonstrable thesis is that, despite the revolution, democracy has never gained a firm foothold in Thai society.

The best source of information on Thailand's political scene during the turbulent 1960s and 1970s is *Political Conflict in Thailand: Reform, Reaction, Revolution* by David Morrell & Chaianan Samudavanija.

Although it's tough to find, *The Devil's Discus* (Cassell & Co Ltd, London, 1964) by Rayne Kruger focuses on the circumstances surrounding the mysterious death of Rama VIII. It's banned in Thailand because of its police-blotter-style analysis of a taboo topic.

## Culture & Society

*Naga: Cultural Origins in Siam & the Western Pacific* by Sumet Jumsai (Chalermnit Press/DD Books, 1997) is an inspired piece of speculative theory on the oceanic origins of Thai people and culture. The book outlines how the myths, symbols and architecture common to Thailand and other mainland South-East Asian civilisations, in particular the *naga* or sea dragon motif, stem from an earlier phase in Asian-Western Pacific history when most of the peoples of the region inhabited islands and lived largely seafaring lives. The proposed confrontation between 'water-based' Thai culture and 'land-based' Khmer (and later Western) culture is fascinating.

*Culture Shock! Thailand & How to Survive It* by Robert & Nanthapa Cooper is an interesting outline on getting along with the Thai way of life, and is heavily oriented towards Bangkok. *Letters from Thailand* by Botan (translated by Susan Fulop Kepner) and Carol Hollinger's *Mai Pen Rai Means Never Mind* can also be recommended for their insights into traditional Thai culture.

*Working with the Thais* by Henry Holmes & Suchada Tangtongtavy covers just about everything you might need to know before entering into a serious work situation in Thailand. Some of the sociological explanations are quite complex, though well substantiated. *Bangkok Post* reporter Denis Segaller's *Thai Ways* and *More Thai Ways* presents further expat insights into Thai culture.

Relatively new *Wondering into Thai Culture*, by Mont Redmond, is yet another collection of newspaper essays, this time culled from *The Nation*.

For a look at Bangkok's infamous Th Patpong (Patpong Rd) from a Western female's perspective, read Cleo Odzer's *Patpong Sisters* (1994). Odzer, an American who carried out unauthorised anthropological research on Patpong in the late 1980s, comes to the unique conclusion that prostitution is empowering work for women who grow up in Thailand with few other employment possibilities. Although such a conclusion flies in the face of statistics (which show that the percentage of women who make up the labour force in Thailand is greater than in either China or the USA), and generalises from atypical Patpong-style prostitution, the book nonetheless offers many insights.

*'Hello My Big Big Honey!' Love Letters to Bangkok Bar Girls and Their Revealing Interviews* (also published in French) by Richard Ehrlich & Dave Walker is a collection of letters between Thai bar workers and their *faràng* (foreigner of European descent) clients, and the verbatim, question-and-answer interviews with the women. It discloses more about the complex nature of these encounters than 10 academic treatises of similar size. The prologue by Thammasat University professor Dr Yos Santasombat adds further insight with convention-questioning ideas.

## Fiction

Thai wunderkind SP Somtow has written and published more titles in English than any other Thai writer. Born in Bangkok, educated at Eton and Cambridge, and now a commuter between two 'cities of angels' – Los Angeles and Bangkok – Somtow's prodigious output includes a string of well-reviewed science fiction/fantasy/horror stories, including *Moon Dance, Darker Angels* and *The Vampire's Beautiful Daughter*. He has also dabbled in avant-garde music (including a royal command ballet), cinema and theatre. The Somtow novel most evocative of Thailand and its culture is his 1995 *Jasmine Nights*, which also happens to be one of his most accessible reads. Following a 12-year-old Thai boy's friendship with an African-American boy near Bangkok in the 1960s, this semi-autobiographical work blends Thai, Greek and African myth, American Civil War lore and a dollop of magic realism into a seamless whole. Film rights for *Jasmine Nights* have been picked up by London's Spinfilm.

For a look at rural life in Thailand, Pira Sudham is unparalleled. Sudham was born into a poor family in North-Eastern Thailand and has written *Siamese Drama, Monsoon Country* and *People of Esarn*. These books are not translations – Sudham writes in English in order to reach a worldwide audience. These fiction titles are fairly easy to find in Bangkok but can be difficult to find overseas.

*In the Mirror* is an excellent, sometimes heartrending collection of modern Thai short stories influenced by political movements of the 1960s and 1970s. The book examines the effect of modernisation on traditional Thai lifestyles, values and village communities, such as hill-tribe peoples and *chao leh* (Sea Gypsies).

*The Lioness in Bloom* is an eye-opening collection of 11 short stories written by or about Thai women and translated by Susan Fulop Kepner. It explores a wide spectrum of Thai women's experience – from old to young, rural to city, and touches on issues often considered taboo, such as women's sexuality, spouse abuse and gender oppression.

Ex-prime minister Kukrit Pramoj's *Four Reigns* (*Si Phaendin*; 1935, translated 1981), the most widely read novel ever published in Thailand, examines the lives of Bangkok courtiers and the social changes that occurred during four monarchal reigns, from the late 19th century to the bombing raids of the 1940s. His late work, *Red Bamboo*, vividly portrays and predicts the conflict between the Thai communist movement and the establishment during the 1960s and 1970s.

Axel Aylwen's novel *The Falcon of Siam* and its sequel *The Falcon Takes Wing* are not up to Kukrit's literary standards but nonetheless capture the feel and historical detail of 17th-century Siam.

Jack Reynolds' 1950s *A Woman of Bangkok* (republished in 1985), a well-written and poignant story of a young Englishman's journey into the world of Thai brothels, remains the best novel yet published with this theme.

Expat writer Christopher G Moore covers the Thai underworld in his 1990s novels *A Killing Smile, Spirit House, A Bewitching Smile* and a raft of others, with an anchor firmly hooked into Bangkok's go-go bar scene. His description of Bangkok's meta-sleazy Thermae Coffee House (called 'Zeno' in *A Killing Smile*) is the closest literature comes to evoking the perpetual male adolescence such places cater to.

Expat Jake Raymond Needham's recently published *Tea Money* (1999) and *The Big Mango* (2000) are humorous, zippy thrillers set in modern Bangkok, which both received good reviews in Bangkok's local press.

## Food & Shopping

Lonely Planet's compact *World Food: Thailand*, by Joe Cummings, the same author of this guide, enables food-conscious visitors to Thailand as well as residents to appreciate the full range of Thai cuisine by providing explanations of the cooking methods, extensive menu glossaries, and lots of cultural and historical background.

Among the explosion of Thai cookbooks to appear in recent years, one of the best remains *Thai Cooking* (formerly *The Original Thai Cookbook*) by Jennifer Brennan. Though expensive and unwieldy, the huge, coffee-table book, *Thailand the Beautiful Cookbook* by Panurat Poladitmontri contains excellent photography and authentic recipes.

Kasma Lohaunchit's stylish *It Rains Fishes: Legends, Traditions and the Joys of Thai Cooking* brings together Thai culinary lore, cooking techniques and recipes geared toward the American kitchen. Kasma's *Dancing Shrimp* focuses on Thai seafood, with special attention paid to authenticity.

*Tropical Herbs & Spices of Thailand, Tropical Fruits of Thailand* and *Tropical Vegetables of Thailand* (Periplus Nature Guide series) make good additions to anyone's library of books on Thai cuisine.

*Shopping in Exotic Thailand* by Ronald & Caryl Rae Krannich is packed with general shopping tips as well as lists of speciality shops and markets throughout Thailand.

John Hoskins' slightly dated *Buyer's Guide to Thai Gems & Jewellery* is a must for anyone contemplating a foray into Thailand's gem market. *Arts and Crafts of Thailand* by William Warren, with photographs by Luca Invernizzi Tettoni, is a useful primer for the world of Thai handicrafts.

## NEWSPAPERS & MAGAZINES

Although Thailand's 1997 constitution guarantees freedom of the press, the National Police Department reserves power to suspend publishing licences for reasons of 'national security'. Consequently, editors exercise self-censorship in realms such as the monarchy's personal lives and business interests. However, Thailand is widely considered to have the most liberal and reliable print media in South-East Asia.

Two well-respected English-language newspapers are published daily in Thailand and distributed in most provincial capitals throughout the country – the *Bangkok Post* in the morning and *The Nation* in the afternoon. The *Bangkok Post* is Thailand's oldest English-language newspaper, established in 1946. Both papers publish online (see Internet Resources earlier in this chapter).

The Singapore edition of the *International Herald Tribune* is widely available in Bangkok.

The most popular Thai-language newspapers are *Thai Rath* and *Daily News,* but they're mostly full of blood-and-guts stories. The best Thai journalism is found in the somewhat less popular *Matichon* and *Siam Rath* dailies. Many Thais read the English-language dailies as they consider them better news sources.

English-language magazine publishing has faltered with the economic slowdown in Thailand and several magazines failed after 1997. Thailand's biggest selling English-language magazine, *Bangkok Metro,* continues to inject urban sophistication into the publishing scene with extensive Bangkok listings of art, culture, cuisine, film and music, along with less extensive Pattaya, Phuket and Chiang Mai pages. The monthly *Le Gavroche* offers news and features on Thailand for the Francophone community.

Popular international magazines are available in specialist bookshops (see Bookshops in the Shopping chapter).

## RADIO

Thailand has more than 400 radio stations, with 41 FM and 35 AM stations in Bangkok alone. Radio station 107 FM, affiliated with Radio Thailand and Channel 9 on Thai public television, broadcasts CNN Asian news coverage almost every hour (5 pm to 2 am daily) and features good music programs with British, Thai and American DJs.

Bilingual DJs at Star FM 102.5 present R&B, pop, rock and alternative music 24 hours a day.

DJs is Radio Bangkok (Gold FMX), 95.5 FM. It has English-speaking DJs and plays new and old international pop hits 24 hours a day.

Station 87.5 FM broadcasts classic Thai pop, including old *lûuk thûng* styles played on accordion.

Chulalongkorn University broadcasts classical, light classical, popular 'golden oldies' and jazz in the evening at 101.5 FM.

The Voice of America (VOA), BBC World Service, Radio Canada, Radio New Zealand, Singapore Broadcasting Company, Radio New Zealand and Radio Japan, and all have English and Thai-language broadcasts over short-wave radio. BBC and VOA are the most easily received by the average short-wave radio. Radio France Internationale and Deutsche Welle carry short-wave programs in French and German respectively. Deutsche Welle also broadcasts English programming three times daily.

For frequencies and program schedules, check *The Nation* and *Bangkok Post* newspapers.

## TV

Thailand has five VHF TV networks based in Bangkok. Apart from Channel 11 they offer the usual mix of Thai-language soap operas, game shows and dramas. Some

## Get Soapy

If you ever happen to stay with a Thai family, take a look at what they're watching on TV around 8 pm and discover the world of Thai soap operas, a realm of Mercedes Benz cars, designer clothes and a lifestyle so unreal you can only wish you were there.

Thai soapies always air on two or three consecutive days of the week, ensuring that you get nicely sucked into the plot. And given that each of the four commercial stations airs soaps every night of the week (making three different plays a week for each channel – a total of 12 programs to choose from), and that each story will only run for about three months, the output of these production companies is prodigious. Little wonder that some episodes are a little rushed  – you might even spot today's newspaper in one!

Thai soaps fall into a few main categories – romance, comedy, horror, action and historical patriotic epics – not unlike their Western counterparts, but there are a couple of essentially Thai themes. One is the recurring 'past-life' romances, such as appears in *Reuan Raem (Temporary Dwelling)*, in which a hero and heroine will be torn apart in one life only to be drawn inevitably towards each other in the next rebirth, often in obstructive circumstances (eg, being in different countries, from different social classes, of different ages, even of different realms – one human and the other a ghost). This is a theme that looms large in Thai consciousness – what we call 'love at first sight' is often explained in Thailand as a connection from a previous life.

Another favourite theme is the poor orphan girl who finds out she is somehow the long-lost heiress of a huge fortune, a la *Oliver Twist*, which is the theme of *Dao Phra Suk (Venus)*. And then there's the unabashedly kinky ones, such as *Phalang Rak (The Power of Love)*, which tells the story of the ambitious businessman who is killed one day by bandits but through sheer willpower continues to live his 'life', running his business and looking after his family (turning into a skeleton at night and materialising as a normal person during the day) in spite of being dead!

Certain roles are almost mandatory, especially in romances and romantic comedies. The servants, for example, often perform the function of piecing together bits of the story through their chatter in the kitchen; explaining, for example, the history of the heroine before she came to the house, or some shady detail about the villain's past. But the one character that can't be dispensed with is the *naang ìtchăa*, the 'jealous woman'. She is usually beautiful in a hard and sexy way, but nasty and vindictive, and she never gets the man. The heroine is, of course, angelic. The naang ìtchăa will usually subject her to two or three thoroughly humiliating incidents, for a while seeming to turn the hero against her, only to be foiled in the last episode or two and doomed to watch the hero and heroine once more live happily ever after.

Another genre is *chiiwít (Real Life)* a grittier genre of soap. And here you might even strike a gem: *Banlang Mek (Throne of Clouds, 1993)*, brilliantly played by veteran actors Soraphong Chatree, Patravadi Mejhudhon (founder of the Patravadi Theatre) and Sombat Methanee, was an enthralling tale of an ambitious social climber's roller-coaster scramble to the top of a powerful dynasty, only to see it all – wealth, family and happiness – reduced to nothing.

Don't be expecting fast action a la American or Chinese films – Thai plays are notoriously slow: lingering shots on the actors' faces and flashbacks of the past (made of footage from previous episodes repeated in black and white) are all too common, especially when the producers decide they have to extend the play's run for another week because the next story isn't ready. But if you're finding it too boring, spare a thought for the actors as they hold their expressions of fear, joy, love or hatred for 10 seconds or more while the camera pans in and the theme song kicks in – Hollywood never had it so easy.

**Bruce Evans**

English programming is available – check the TV programs in the *Bangkok Post* and *The Nation* for details.

The privately owned Channel 3 offers Thai comedy, dramas, news and movies, mostly in Thai-language only.

Channel 5 is a military network (the only one to operate during coups). It presents a mix of ABC, CNN International and English-subtitled Thai news programs between 5 and 7 am; English-language news is shown at noon.

Channel 7 is also military owned. One of its best features is the broadcasting of rustic *lûuk thûng* music videos between 12.15 and 2.10 pm. See the boxed text 'Lûuk Thûng – Truckin' Music' in the Facts about Bangkok chapter.

Channel 9, the national public TV station, broadcasts from 5.30 am until 2 am. An English-language soundtrack is simulcast with the evening news program at 7 pm Monday to Friday on radio station FM 107.

Channel 11, run by the Ministry of Education, features educational programs, including TV correspondence classes from Ramkhamhaeng and Sukhothai Thammathirat open universities. An English-language news simulcast comes over FM 88 at 8 pm.

Upcountry cities will generally receive only two networks – Channel 9 and a local private network with restricted hours.

### Satellite & Cable TV

As elsewhere in Asia, satellite and cable TV services are swiftly multiplying in Thailand, and competition for the largely untapped market is keen. The most successful cable company in Thailand is UBC, available via CaTV, MMDS and DTH systems. UBC carries a typical range of cable TV programming, such as CNN and MTV Asia and sports shows – some English-language movie channels are subject to Thai censorship. See the UBC Web site (www.ubctv .com) for details.

If you have a satellite dish, you might be able to pick up Thai and regional programming from Thailand, Vietnam, Mynamar and Malaysia.

## VIDEO SYSTEMS

The predominant video format in Thailand is PAL, a system compatible with that used in most of Europe (France's SECAM format is a notable exception) and Australia. You'll need to take your own VCR to play videotapes from the USA or Japan, which use the NTSC format, or acquire a 'multisystem' VCR, which plays NTSC and PAL (but not SECAM, except in black & white). Some video shops (especially those that carry pirated or unlicensed tapes) sell NTSC as well as PAL and SECAM tapes.

Video CD (VCD) has begun replacing VHS in Thailand as well as in most of the rest of Asia. VCDs can be played on a VCD player or on any computer with a CD-ROM drive. For the latter you'll need to install VCD software, which can be downloaded free from the Internet. Many video shops and street vendors in larger cities sell VCDs of both Thai and international movies.

Digital video discs (DVD) are still relatively rare in Thailand, though they are available at high-end audio shops and some video stores. Many Thai department stores and audio shops sell multiplayers that can play audio CDs, VCDs and DVDs.

## PHOTOGRAPHY & VIDEO
### Film & Equipment

Print film is fairly inexpensive and widely available throughout Thailand. Japanese print film costs around 100B per 36 exposures; US print film costs a bit more. Fujichrome Velvia and Provia slide films cost around 265B per roll, Kodak Ektachrome Elite is 230B and Ektachrome 200 about 270B. Slide film, especially Kodachrome, can be hard to find outside Bangkok and Chiang Mai.

VHS video cassettes of all sizes are readily available in Bangkok.

### Processing

Film processing is generally quite good in the larger cities in Thailand and also quite inexpensive. Dependable E6 processing is available at several labs in Bangkok. Kodachrome must be sent out of the country for processing, so it can take up to two weeks to get it back.

Camera pros will find a number of labs in Bangkok that offer same-day pick up and delivery at no extra cost within the city. IQ Lab offers the widest range of services, including all types of processing (except Kodachrome), slide duping, scanning, digital prints, OutPut slides, photo CDs and custom printing. For more details on places to buy and process film, see Camera Supplies, Film & Processing in the Shopping chapter.

## Technical Tips

Pack some silica gel with your camera to prevent mould growing on the inside of your lenses. A polarising filter is useful to cut down on tropical glare at certain times of day, particularly around water or highly polished glazed-tile work. Tripods are a must for shooting interiors in natural light.

## Photographing People

You can snap photos of Thais in Bangkok with much the same attitude as you would photograph people in major urban areas elsewhere in the world. Monks don't usually mind if you take their pictures, but it's polite to ask or gesture for permission first.

## Airport Security

The X-ray baggage inspection machines at Thailand's airports are all deemed film safe. Nevertheless if you're travelling with high-speed film (ISO 400 or above), you may want to have your film hand-inspected rather than X-rayed. Security inspectors are usually happy to comply. Packing your film in see-through plastic bags generally speeds up the hand inspection process. Some photographers pack their film in lead-lined bags to ward off potentially harmful rays.

## TIME
## Time Zone

Thailand's time zone is seven hours ahead of GMT/UTC (London). Thus, noon in Bangkok is 9 pm the previous day in Los Angeles (except during Daylight Savings Time, when it's 10 pm), midnight in New York (except during Daylight Savings Time, when it's 1 am), 5 am in London, 6 am in Paris, 1 pm in Perth, and 3 pm in Sydney and Melbourne.

## Thai Calendar

The official year in Thailand is reckoned from 543 BC, the beginning of the Buddhist Era, so that 2001 AD is 2544 BE, 2002 AD is 2545 BE etc.

## ELECTRICITY

Electric current is 220V, 50 cycles. Electrical wall outlets are usually of the round, two-pole type. Some outlets accept flat, two-bladed terminals, and some will accept either flat or round terminals. Any electrical supply shop will carry adapters for any international plug shape as well as voltage converters.

## WEIGHTS & MEASURES

In Thailand, dimensions and weight are usually expressed using the metric system. The exception is land measure, which is often quoted using the traditional system of *waa*, *ngaan* and *râi*. Old-timers in the provinces will occasionally use the traditional Thai system of weights and measures in speech, as will boatbuilders, carpenters and other craftspeople when talking about their work. Here are some useful conversions:

| | | |
|---|---|---|
| 1 sq waa | = | 4 sq metres |
| 1 ngaan (100 sq waa) | = | 400 sq metres |
| 1 râi (4 ngaan) | = | 1600 sq metres |
| 1 bàat | = | 15g |
| 1 taleung or tamleung (4 bàat) | = | 60g |
| 1 châng (20 taleung) | = | 1.2kg |
| 1 hàap (50 châng) | = | 60kg |
| 1 níu | = | about 2cm (or one inch) |
| 1 khêup (12 níu) | = | 25cm |
| 1 sàwk (2 khêup) | = | 50cm |
| 1 waa (4 sàwk) | = | 2m |
| 1 sên (20 waa) | = | 40m |
| 1 yôht (400 sên) | = | 16km |

## LAUNDRY

Virtually every hotel and guesthouse in Bangkok offers a laundry service. Rates are generally geared to room rates; the cheaper the accommodation, the cheaper the washing and ironing. Cheapest of all are public laundries where you pay by the kilogram. Laundry detergent is readily available in general mercantile shops and supermarkets.

For dry-cleaning, take clothes to a real dry-cleaner. Laundries that advertise dry-cleaning often don't really dry-clean (they just boil everything!) or do it badly. Luxury hotels usually have dependable dry-cleaning services.

Two reliable dry-cleaners in Bangkok are Erawan Dry Cleaners at the basement of Landmark Plaza, Soi 11, Th Sukhumvit, and Spotless Dry Cleaning & Laundry, 166 Soi 23, Th Sukhumvit. Both companies dry-clean large items like sleeping bags as well as clothing.

## TOILETS & SHOWERS

In Thailand, as in many other South-East Asian countries, the 'squat toilet' is the norm, except in hotels and guesthouses geared towards tourists and international business travellers. Instead of trying to approximate a chair or stool like a modern sit-down toilet, a traditional Asian toilet sits more or less flush with the surface of the floor, with two footpads on either side of the porcelain abyss. For persons who have never used a squat toilet it takes a bit of getting used to. If you find yourself feeling awkward the first couple of times you use one, console yourself with the knowledge that, according to those who study such matters, people who use squat toilets are much less likely to develop haemorrhoids than people who use sit-down toilets.

Next to the typical squat toilet is a bucket or reservoir filled with water with a plastic bowl usually floating on the water or placed on the floor nearby. This water supply has a two-fold function. The first is for toilet-goers to scoop water from the reservoir with the plastic bowl and use it to clean their nether regions while still squatting over the toilet. And the second is that since there is usually no mechanical flushing device attached to a squat toilet, a few extra scoops must be poured into the toilet basin to flush waste into the septic system. In larger towns, mechanical flushing systems are becoming increasingly common, even with squat toilets. More rustic toilets in rural areas may simply consist of a few planks over a hole in the ground.

Even in places where sit-down toilets are installed, the plumbing may not be designed to take toilet paper, so the standard washing bucket will be standing nearby or there will be a waste basket to place used toilet paper.

Public toilets are common in cinemas, department stores, bus and train stations, larger hotel lobbies and airports. On the road between towns and villages it is perfectly acceptable to go behind a tree or bush or even to use the roadside when nature calls.

### Bathing

Some hotels and most guesthouses in the country do not have hot water, though most tourist-oriented places in Bangkok do. Very few boiler-style water heaters are available outside larger international-style hotels. In the smaller places hot water is provided by small, in-line electric heaters.

Many private homes and some old guesthouses in Bangkok have washrooms where a large jar or cement trough is filled with water for bathing. A plastic or metal bowl is used to sluice water from the jar or trough over the body. Even in homes where showers are installed, heated water is uncommon. Most Thais bathe at least twice a day.

If ever you find yourself having to bathe in a public place you should wear a *phâakhamáa* or *phâasîn* (the cotton wraparounds); nude bathing is not the norm and most Thais will find it offensive.

### Hair & Beauty Treatments

Whether you're anxious to impress Thailand's immigration officials, trying to lure a romantic interest or simply feel like sprucing up, you might want to head off for a hair or beauty treatment – it's also a good excuse for some pampering in air-conditioned comfort.

Shopping centres are easy places to find good salons, particularly Emporium and Siam Center, which contain as many as one or two salons per floor. The area around the Sala Daeng Skytrain station is also studded with beauty salons, especially along Th Silom, Th Convent and Th Sala Daeng. Less expensive salons can be found among the sois of Siam Square.

In Bangkok there's a squillion salons to suit all budgets. The cost of a cut and blowdry starts at 100B at a simple row-of-chairs place

TOM COCKREM

Traditional Thai dancers perform at Erawan Spirit House.

KRAIG LIEB

Easy rider – Bangkok hippie

JOE CUMMINGS

Sacred Brahman cow with attendant at the ancient Brahman ritual, Royal Ploughing Ceremony.

DENNIS JOHNSON

There is a combination of old learning and new learning in Bangkok.

RICHARD I'ANSON

Roof detail of Wat Benchamabophit

JOHN HAY

Mosaic work at Wat Arun (Temple of Dawn)

STAEVEN VALLAK

Water lilies in a decorative pot at Grand Palace

JOHN ELK III

Keeping up with the latest news.

and increases up to 1000B for an ultra trendy 'do'. However, most 'upscale' places cost a bargain 400B to 500B. For extras, such as perms or tinting/highlighting, figure on 100B to 200B each. Most good salons also offer facials for 200B, and head/neck/shoulder massages for 100B. Often the latter is included at no charge. Some places also offer facilities for full-body massages and other quasi-spa treatments (eg, aromatherapy), often for 400B or less.

The term for beauty salon is *ráan sŏem sŭay* (literally, beauty enhancement shop). Virtually all beauty salons in Bangkok are unisex; however, prices for men's cuts are sometimes cheaper than women's. The cheapest place for a man to get his hair cut is a simple *ráan tàt phŏm*, which looks similar to barbershops in the West. A haircut at a barber's costs 60B to 100B. These are getting harder to find in central Bangkok, but are plentiful in the Phrakhanong district (near the triple-digit sois of Th Sukhumvit) and in Thonburi near Wong Wian Yai. For men who fancy looking like a high-level Thai government official, Sompot Barber, across the street from the Interior Ministry on Thanon Bamrung Meuang, east of Thanon Atsadang, is a spot where many politicians, including former Prime Minister Chuan Leekpai, have their hair cut.

## HEALTH

Travel health depends on your predeparture preparations, your daily health care while travelling and how you handle any medical problem that does develop. While the potential dangers can seem quite frightening, in reality few travellers experience anything more than an upset stomach.

### Predeparture planning

**Immunisations** Plan ahead for getting your vaccinations: some of them require more than one injection, while certain vaccinations should not be given together. Note that some vaccinations should not be given during pregnancy or to people with allergies – discuss with your doctor.

Although there is no risk of yellow fever in Thailand, you will need proof of vacci-

---

### Medical Kit Check List

Following is a list of items you should consider including in your medical kit – consult your pharmacist for brands available in your country. All are readily available in Bangkok.

☐ **Aspirin** or **paracetamol** (acetaminophen in the US) – for pain or fever.

☐ **Antihistamine** – for allergies, eg hay fever; to ease the itch from insect bites or stings; and to prevent motion sickness.

☐ **Loperamide** or **diphenoxylate** – 'blockers' for diarrhoea.

☐ **Prochlorperazine** or **metaclopramide** for nausea and vomiting.

☐ **Antifungal** cream or powder – for fungal skin infections and thrush.

☐ **Antiseptic** (such as povidone-iodine) – for cuts and grazes.

☐ **Bandages, Band-Aids** (plasters) and other wound dressings.

☐ **Scissors, tweezers** and a **thermometer** (note that mercury thermometers are prohibited by some airlines).

☐ **Cold and flu tablets, throat lozenges** and **nasal decongestant.**

---

FACTS FOR THE VISITOR

nation if you're coming from a yellow fever infected area (sub-Saharan Africa and parts of South America).

It is recommended you seek medical advice at least six weeks before travel. Be aware that there is often a greater risk of disease with children and during pregnancy.

It's a good idea to carry proof of your vaccinations. If you want to be immunised while in Thailand, immunisations are available from a number of sources, including both public hospitals and private clinics in Bangkok. Vaccinations you should consider having only if you plan to travel outside Bangkok include the following (for more information about the diseases see the individual entries later in this section):

**Diphtheria & Tetanus** Vaccinations for these two diseases are usually combined and are recommended for everyone. After an initial course of three injections (usually given in childhood), boosters are necessary every 10 years.

**Polio** Everyone should keep up to date with this vaccination, which is normally given in childhood. A booster every 10 years maintains immunity.

**Hepatitis A** Hepatitis A vaccine (eg, Avaxim, Havrix 1440 or VAQTA) provides long-term immunity (possibly more than 10 years) after an initial injection and a booster at six to 12 months. Alternatively, an injection of gamma globulin can provide short-term protection against hepatitis A – two to six months, depending on the dose given. It is not a vaccine, but is ready-made antibody collected from blood donations. It is reasonably effective and, unlike the vaccine, it is protective immediately, but because it is a blood product, there are current concerns about its long-term safety.

**Hepatitis A** This vaccine is also available in a combined form, Twinrix, with hepatitis B vaccine. Three injections over a six-month period are required, the first two providing substantial protection against hepatitis A.

**Typhoid** Vaccination against typhoid may be required if you are travelling for more than a couple of weeks in most parts of Asia, Africa, Central and South America, and Central and Eastern Europe. It is now available either as an injection or as capsules to be taken orally.

**Cholera** The current injectable vaccine against cholera is poorly protective and has many side effects, so it is not generally recommended for travellers. However, in some situations it may be necessary to have a certificate as travellers are very occasionally asked by immigration officials to present one, even though all countries and the WHO have dropped cholera immunisation as a health requirement for entry.

**Hepatitis B** Travellers who should consider vaccination against hepatitis B include those on a long trip, as well as those visiting countries where there are high levels of hepatitis B infection, where blood transfusions may not be adequately screened or where sexual contact or needle sharing is a possibility. Vaccination involves three injections, with a booster at 12 months. More rapid courses are available if necessary.

**Rabies** Vaccination should be considered by those who will spend a month or longer in Thailand, especially if they are cycling, handling animals, caving or travelling to remote areas, and for children (who may not report a bite). Pretravel rabies vaccination involves having three injections over 21 to 28 days. If someone who has been vaccinated, is bitten or scratched by an animal, they will require two booster injections of vaccine; those not vaccinated require more. Rabies vaccinations are available at practically every public clinic or hospital in Thailand.

**Japanese B Encephalitis** Consider vaccination against this disease if spending a month or longer in rural Northern Thailand, making repeated trips to a risk area or visiting during an epidemic. It involves three injections over 30 days.

**Tuberculosis** The risk of TB to travellers is usually very low, unless you will be living with or closely associated with local people in high risk areas. Vaccination against TB (BCG) is recommended for children and young adults living in these areas for three months or more.

**Malaria Medication** Urban Thailand, including Bangkok, is malaria-free so unless you plan to travel to Thailand's frontier regions you don't need to worry about malaria prevention.

Antimalarial drugs do not prevent you from being infected but kill the malaria parasites during a stage in their development and significantly reduce the risk of becoming very ill or dying. Expert advice on medication should be sought, as there are many factors to consider, including the area to be visited, the risk of exposure to malaria-carrying mosquitoes, the side effects of medication, your medical history, and whether you are a child or an adult or pregnant. Travellers to isolated area in high-risk countries may like to carry a treatment dose of medication for use if symptoms occur.

**Health Insurance** Make sure that you have adequate health insurance. See Travel Insurance under Visas & Documents in this chapter for details.

**Travel Health Guides** If you are planning to be away or travelling in remote areas for a long period of time, consider taking a more detailed health guide. Lonely Planet's *Healthy Travel Asia & India* is a handy pocket size and packed with useful information including pretrip planning, emergency first aid, immunisation and disease information, and what to do if you get sick on the road. Lonely Planet's *Travel with Children* also includes advice on travel health for younger children.

*Guide to Healthy Living in Thailand,* published jointly by the Thai Red Cross Society and US embassy, is available from the

'Snake Farm' (Queen Saovabha Memorial Institute) for 100B. This booklet is rich in practical health advice on safe eating, child care, tropical heat, immunisations and local hospitals. It contains wise titbits with a literary flair, including 'Bangkok is a stopping point for many travellers and restless souls. Acute psychiatric emergencies, including alcohol and drug abuse, are, unfortunately, not rare' and 'Bangkok's traffic poses a far greater danger than snakes and tropical diseases combined'.

There are also a number of excellent travel health sites on the Internet. From the Lonely Planet home page there are links at www .lonelyplanet.com/weblinks/wlheal.htm to the World Health Organization and the US Centers for Disease Control & Prevention.

**Other Preparations** Make sure you're healthy before you start travelling. If you are going on a long trip ensure that your teeth are OK. If you wear glasses take a spare pair and your prescription.

If you require a particular medication, take an adequate supply, as it may not be available locally. Take part of the packaging showing the generic name rather than the brand, which will make getting replacements easier. To avoid any problems it's a good idea to have a legible prescription or letter from your doctor to show that you legally use the medication.

### Basic Rules
**Food** Beware of ice cream that is sold in the street or anywhere it might have been melted and refrozen; if there's any doubt (eg, a power cut in the last day or two), steer well clear. Shellfish such as mussels, oysters and clams should be avoided as well as undercooked meat, particularly in the form of mince.

If a place looks clean and well run and the vendor also looks clean and healthy, the food is probably safe. In general, places that are packed with travellers or locals will be fine, while empty restaurants are questionable. The food in busy restaurants is cooked and eaten quite quickly with little standing around and is probably not reheated.

**Water** In Thailand all water served in restaurants or to guests in an office or home will be purified. Tap water in Bangkok is not fit to drink, so refrain from drinking it or brushing your teeth with it. Use bottled water instead. Fruit juices are made with purified water and are safe to drink. Milk in Thailand is always pasteurised.

Ice is generally produced from purified water under hygienic conditions and is therefore theoretically safe. During transit to the local restaurant, however, conditions are not so hygienic (you may see blocks of ice being dragged along the street), but ice is very difficult to resist in the hot season. The rule of thumb is that if it's chipped ice, it probably came from an ice block (which may not have been handled well), but if it's ice cubes or 'tubes', it was delivered from the ice factory in sealed plastic. In rural areas, villagers mostly drink collected rainwater – use common sense.

Try to purchase glass water bottles, whenever possible, as they are recyclable (unlike the plastic disposable ones).

### Medical Problems & Treatment
Self-diagnosis and treatment can be risky, so you should always seek medical help. Although drug dosages are indicated in this section, they are for emergency use only. Correct diagnosis is vital. An embassy, consulate or five-star hotel can usually recommend a local doctor or clinic.

In Thailand, medicine is generally available over the counter and the price will be much cheaper than in the West. However, be careful when buying drugs, particularly where the expiry date may have passed or correct storage conditions may not have been followed. Bogus drugs are not uncommon and it's possible that drugs that are no longer recommended, or have even been banned, in the West are still being dispensed in Thailand.

Antibiotics should ideally be administered only under medical supervision. Take only the recommended dose at the prescribed intervals and use the whole course, even if the illness seems to be cured earlier. Stop immediately if there are any serious reactions and don't use the antibiotic at all if you are unsure that you have the correct one. Some people are allergic to commonly prescribed antibiotics such as penicillin; carry this information (eg, on a bracelet) when travelling.

## Hospitals & Clinics

Bangkok is Thailand's leading health care centre, with three university research hospitals, 12 public and private hospitals, and hundreds of medical clinics. The Australian, USA and UK embassies usually keep up-to-date lists of doctors who can speak English. For doctors who speak other languages, contact the relevant embassy.

Several store-front clinics in the Th Ploenchit area specialise in lab tests for sexually transmitted diseases. According to *Bangkok Metro* magazine, Bangkok General Hospital has the most sophisticated HIV blood testing program. Bangkok's better hospitals include:

**Bangkok Adventist (Mission) Hospital** (Map 3, ☎ 281 1422, 282 1100) 430 Th Phitsanulok
**Bangkok Christian Hospital** (Map 7, ☎ 233 6981–9, 235 1000) 124 Th Silom
**Bangkok General Hospital** (☎ 318 0066, 310 3000) 2 Soi 47, Th Phetburi Tat Mai
**Bangkok Nursing Home** (Map 7, ☎ 233 2610–9) 9 Th Convent
**Bumrungrad Hospital** (Map 5, ☎ 667 1000) 33 Soi 3, Th Sukhumvit
**Chao Phraya Hospital** (☎ 434 0265, 884 7000) 113/44 Th Pinklao Nakhon-Chaisi, Bangkok Noi
**Mahesak Hospital** (Map 6, ☎ 234 2760) 46/7-9 Th Mahesak
**Phayathai Hospital 1** (Map 5, ☎ 245 2620) 364/1 Th Si Ayuthaya
**Samitivej Hospital** (☎ 381 6728, 381, 6831) 133 Soi 49, Th Sukhumvit
**St Louis Hospital** (Map 7, ☎ 212 0033–48) 215 Th Sathon Tai

Should you need urgent dental care, suggested contacts in Bangkok include:

**Dental Polyclinic** (☎ 314 4397) 2111/2113 Th Phetburi Tat Mai 02-662 2402) 593/6 Th Sukhumvit
**Siam Dental Clinic** (☎ 252 6660) 412/11-2 Soi 6, Siam Square

For urgent eye care, the best choices are also in Bangkok.

**Pirompesuy Eye Hospital** (☎ 252 4141) 117/1 Thanon Phayathai.
**Rutnin Eye Hospital** (☎ 258 0442) 80/1 Soi Asoke

There are plenty of Chinese doctors and herbal dispensaries in Bangkok's Sampeng district, in the vicinity of Th Ratchawong, Th Charoen Krung, Th Yaowarat and Th Songwat. The Pow Tai Dispensary, 572-574 Th Charoen Krung, has been preparing traditional Chinese medicines since 1941.

**Alcoholics Anonymous** Members of Alcoholics Anonymous who want to contact the Bangkok group or anyone needing help with a drinking problem can call AA at ☎ 253 6305 from 6 am to 6 pm or ☎ 256 6578 from 6 pm to 6 am for information. There are daily meetings held at the Holy Redeemer Catholic Church, 123/19 Soi Ruamrudee (Ruam Rudi), Bangkok.

**Air Ambulance** Medical Wings (☎ 535 4736, fax 535 4355, e ew@bkk.a-net .net.th), Domestic Terminal, Bangkok International Airport, offers aeromedical transportation to/from any of 30 domestic airports in Thailand on a 24-hour basis.

## Environmental Hazards

**Heat Exhaustion** Dehydration and salt deficiency can cause heat exhaustion. Take time to acclimatise to high temperatures, drink sufficient liquids and do not do anything too physically demanding.

Salt deficiency is characterised by fatigue, lethargy, headaches, giddiness and muscle cramps; salt tablets may help, but adding extra salt to your food is better.

Anhidrotic heat exhaustion is a rare form of heat exhaustion that is caused by an inability to sweat. It tends to affect people who have been in a hot climate for some time, rather than newcomers. It can progress to heatstroke. Treatment involves removal to a cooler climate.

**Heatstroke** This serious, occasionally fatal, condition can occur if the body's heat-regulating mechanism breaks down and the

## Bangkok's Big Smoke

If the sight of sad addicts huddled in the fug of Bangkok's International Airport smoking rooms doesn't deter you, Thailand's new shock-tactic anti-smoking campaign might drive you towards ditching the habit.

From 2001 pictures of clogged arteries and diseased lungs will be pictured on cigarette packets in Thailand, which the Thai anti-smoking lobby hopes will both deter would-be smokers and convince addicts to give up. In this case, the lobby decided that pictures spoke louder than words, especially as illiterate smokers are unable to read printed warnings.

The campaign is an attempt to curtail the disturbing number of young male Thais taking up smoking; over 90% of Thailand's 10.2 million Thailand's smokers are males, many of whom are unaware of the implications of smoking on their health.

This campaign is in addition to recent government-banning tobacco advertising in newspapers, radio and TV, and smoking in public places.

Recent surveys suggesting that young people were influenced by the chic factor of smoking in the entertainment industry has also led to banning smoking and cigarettes in film and TV – the strongest anti-tobacco censorship in the world. All images of people smoking, even in documentaries, have been digitally edited out – including people smoking in anti-smoking advertisements!

**Adapted from Lonely Planet Scoop travel news at www.lonelyplanet.com/scoop**

body temperature rises to dangerous levels. Long, continuous periods of exposure to high temperatures and insufficient fluids can leave you vulnerable to heatstroke.

The symptoms are feeling unwell, not sweating very much (or at all) and a high body temperature (39°C to 41°C or 102°F to 106°F). Where sweating has ceased, the skin becomes flushed and red. Severe, throbbing headaches and lack of coordination will also occur, and the sufferer may be confused or aggressive. Eventually the victim will become delirious or convulse. Hospitalisation is essential, but in the interim get victims out of the sun, remove their clothing, cover them with a wet sheet or towel and then fan continually. Give fluids if they are conscious.

**Prickly Heat** Prickly heat is an itchy rash caused by excessive perspiration trapped under the skin. It usually strikes people who have just arrived in a hot climate. Keeping cool, bathing often, drying the skin and using a mild talcum or prickly heat powder or resorting to air-conditioning may help.

**Sunburn** In the tropics you can get sunburnt surprisingly quickly, even through cloud cover. Use a sunscreen, a hat, and a barrier cream for your nose and lips. Calamine lotion or aloe vera are good for mild sunburn. Protect your eyes with good quality sunglasses, particularly if you will be near water or sand.

### Infectious Diseases

**Dengue Fever** This viral disease is transmitted by mosquitoes and occurs mainly in tropical and subtropical areas of the world. Generally, there is only a small risk to travellers except during epidemics, which are usually seasonal (during and just after the rainy season).

The *Aedes aegypti* mosquito, which transmits the dengue virus, is most active during the day, unlike the malaria mosquito, and is found mainly in urban areas in and around human dwellings.

Signs and symptoms of dengue fever include a sudden onset of high fever, headache, joint and muscle pains (hence its old name, 'breakbone fever'), and nausea and vomiting. A rash of small red spots appears three to four days after the onset of fever. Dengue is commonly mistaken for other infectious diseases, including influenza.

You should seek medical attention if you think you may be infected. Infection can be diagnosed by a blood test. There is no specific treatment for dengue. You should avoid aspirin, as it increases the risk of haemorrhaging.

Recovery may be prolonged, with tiredness lasting for several weeks. Severe complications are rare in travellers but include dengue haemorrhagic fever (DHF), which can be fatal without prompt medical treatment. DHF is thought to be a result of a second infection due to a different strain (there are four major strains) and it usually affects residents of the country rather than travellers.

In 2000 Thailand's Mahidol University announced the development of a vaccine for all serotypes of dengue. The new vaccine began human trials late that year, and if successful the vaccine should be available in 2003 or 2004. As with malaria, the best precaution is to avoid mosquito bites.

**Diarrhoea** Simple things like a change of water, food or climate can all cause a mild bout of diarrhoea, but a few rushed toilet trips with no other symptoms is not indicative of a major problem.

Dehydration is the main danger with any diarrhoea, particularly in children or the elderly as dehydration can occur quite quickly. Under all circumstances *fluid replacement* (at least equal to the volume being lost) is the most important thing to remember. Weak black tea with a little sugar, soda water, or soft drinks allowed to go flat and diluted 50% with clean water are all good.

With severe diarrhoea a rehydrating solution is preferable as it will replace the minerals and salts that have been lost. Commercially available oral rehydration salts (ORS) are very useful; add these salts to boiled or bottled water. In an emergency you can make up a solution of six teaspoons of sugar and a half teaspoon of salt to 1L of boiled or bottled water.

You need to drink at least the same volume of fluid that you are losing in bowel movements and vomiting. Urine is the best guide to the adequacy of replacement – if you have small amounts of concentrated urine, you need to drink more. Keep drinking small amounts often. Stick to a bland diet as you recover.

Gut-paralysing drugs such as loperamide diphenoxylate can be used to bring relief from the symptoms, although they do not actually cure the problem. Only use these drugs if you do not have access to toilets, eg, if you *must* travel. For children under 12

years these drugs are not recommended. Do not use these drugs if the person has a high fever or is severely dehydrated.

In certain situations antibiotics may be required: diarrhoea with blood or mucus (dysentery), any diarrhoea with fever, profuse watery diarrhoea, persistent diarrhoea not improving after 48 hours and severe diarrhoea. These suggest a more serious cause of diarrhoea and in these situations gut-paralysing drugs should be avoided.

In these situations, a stool test may be necessary to diagnose what bug is causing your diarrhoea, so you should seek medical help urgently. Where this is not possible the recommended drugs for bacterial diarrhoea (the most likely cause of severe diarrhoea in travellers) are norfloxacin 400mg twice daily for three days or ciprofloxacin 500mg twice daily for five days. These are not recommended for children or pregnant women. The drug of choice for children would be co-trimoxazole with the dosage dependent on the child's weight. A five-day course should be given. Ampicillin or amoxycillin may be given in pregnancy, but medical care is necessary.

Two other causes of persistent diarrhoea in travellers are giardiasis and amoebic dysentery. Giardiasis is caused by a common parasite, Giardia lamblia. The symptoms include stomach cramps, nausea, a bloated stomach, watery, foul-smelling diarrhoea and frequent gas (farts). Giardiasis can appear several weeks after you have been exposed to the parasite. The symptoms may disappear for a few days and then return. Unfortunately this can continue for several weeks.

Amoebic dysentery caused by the protozoan Entamoeba histolytica, is characterised by a gradual onset of low-grade diarrhoea, often with blood and mucus. Cramping abdominal pain and vomiting are less likely than in other types of diarrhoea, and fever may not be present. Amoebic dysentery will persist until treated and can recur and cause other health problems.

You should seek medical advice if you think you have giardiasis or amoebic dysentery, but where this is not possible, tinidazole or metronidazole are the recommended drugs. Treatment is a 2g single dose of tinidazole or 250mg of metronidazole three times daily for five to 10 days.

**Fungal Infections** Fungal infections occur more commonly in hot weather and are usually found on the scalp, between the toes (athlete's foot) or fingers, in the groin and on the body (ringworm). You get ringworm (which is a fungal infection, not a worm) from infected animals or other people. Moisture encourages these infections.

To prevent fungal infections wear loose, comfortable clothes, avoid artificial fibres, wash frequently and dry yourself carefully. If you do get an infection, wash the infected area at least daily with a disinfectant or medicated soap and water, and rinse and dry well. Apply an antifungal cream or powder like tolnaftate. Try to expose the infected area to air or sunlight as much as possible and wash all towels and underwear in hot water, change them often and let them dry in the sun.

**Hepatitis** Hepatitis is a general term for inflammation of the liver. It is a common disease worldwide. There are several different viruses that cause hepatitis, and they differ in the way that they are transmitted. The symptoms are similar in all forms of the illness, and include fever, chills, headache, fatigue, feelings of weakness and aches and pains, followed by loss of appetite, nausea, vomiting, abdominal pain, dark urine, light-coloured faeces, jaundiced (yellow) skin and yellowing of the whites of the eyes. People who have had hepatitis should avoid alcohol for some time after the illness, as the liver needs time to recover.

Hepatitis A is transmitted by contaminated food and drinking water. You should seek medical advice, but there is not much you can do apart from resting, drinking lots of fluids, eating lightly and avoiding fatty foods. Hepatitis E is transmitted in the same way as hepatitis A; it can be particularly serious in pregnant women.

There are almost 300 million chronic carriers of Hepatitis B in the world. It is spread through contact with infected blood, blood products or body fluids, for example through sexual contact, unsterilised needles and blood transfusions, or contact with blood via small breaks in the skin. Other risk situations include having a shave, tattoo or body piercing with contaminated equipment. The symptoms of hepatitis B may be more severe than type A and the disease can lead to long term problems such as chronic liver damage, liver cancer or a long term carrier state. Hepatitis C and D are spread in the same way as hepatitis B and can also lead to long term complications.

There are vaccines against hepatitis A and B, but there are currently no vaccines against the other types of hepatitis. Following the basic rules about food and water (hepatitis A and E) and avoiding risk situations (hepatitis B, C and D) are important preventative measures.

**HIV & AIDS** Infection with the human immunodeficiency virus (HIV) may lead to acquired immune deficiency syndrome (AIDS), which is a fatal disease. Any exposure to blood, blood products or body fluids may put the individual at risk.

Between 1991 and 1994 Thailand's overall infection rate dropped 77%, an achievement that earned Population Development Agency director Mechai Viravaidya the prestigious Magsaysay Award in 1994. According to the United Nations Human Development Programme, Thailand – like the USA, Australia and the UK – has belonged to the 'decrease or no growth' category since 1994. The World Health Organisation reports that the infection rate and projected future vulnerability for AIDS in Thailand is now lower than for any other country in South-East Asia. As elsewhere around the globe, however, absolute numbers will only increase with time until/unless a cure is discovered.

In Thailand transmission is predominantly through heterosexual sexual activity (over 80%). The second most common source of HIV infection is intravenous injection by drug users who share needles (about 6%). Apart from abstinence, the most effective preventative is always to practise safe sex using condoms and never share syringes, even those that have been bleached.

The Thai phrase for 'condom' is *thŭng anaamai*. Latex condoms are more effective than animal-membrane condoms in preventing disease transmission; to specify latex condoms ask for *thŭng yaang anaamai* – actually the latter are the only kinds we've ever seen in Thailand. Since the 1970s, when health educator Mechai Viravaidya initiated a vigorous national program aimed at educating the public about contraception, the most common Thai nickname for 'condom' has been 'Mechai'. Good-quality latex condoms are distributed free by offices of the Ministry of Public Health throughout the country – they come in numbered sizes, like shoes! Many Western men find that even the largest size issued by the MPH is too small; one of the better commercial brands available in Thailand is Durex.

HIV/AIDS can also be spread through infected blood transfusions although this risk is virtually nil in Thailand due to vigorous blood-screening procedures. It can also be spread by dirty needles – tattooing, vaccinations, acupuncture and body piercing can potentially be as dangerous as intravenous drug use if the equipment is not clean.

If you do need an injection, ask to see the syringe unwrapped in front of you, or take a needle and syringe pack with you.

**Japanese B Encephalitis** Mosquitoes transmit this viral infection of the brain. Most cases occur in rural areas as the virus exists in pigs and wading birds. Symptoms include fever, headache and alteration in consciousness. Hospitalisation is needed for correct diagnosis and treatment. There is a high mortality rate among those who have symptoms; of those who survive, many are intellectually disabled.

**Sexually Transmitted Infections** Gonorrhoea, herpes and syphilis are among these infections; sores, blisters or rashes around the genitals and discharges or pain when urinating are common symptoms. In some STIs, such as wart virus or chlamydia, symptoms may be less marked or not observed at all, especially in women. Syphilis symptoms eventually disappear completely but the disease continues and can cause severe problems in later years. In Thailand gonorrhoea, nonspecific urethritis (NSU) and syphilis are the most common of these diseases. The treatment of gonorrhoea and syphilis is with antibiotics. The different sexually transmitted diseases each require specific antibiotics.

**Typhoid** Typhoid fever is a dangerous gut infection caused by contaminated water and food. Medical help must be sought.

In its early stages sufferers may feel they have a bad cold or flu on the way, as early symptoms are a headache, body aches and a fever that rises a little each day until it is around 40°C (104°F) or more. The victim's pulse is often slow relative to the degree of fever present – unlike a normal fever where the pulse increases. There may be vomiting, abdominal pain, diarrhoea or constipation.

In the second week the high fever and slow pulse continue and a few pink spots may appear on the body; trembling, delirium, weakness, weight loss and dehydration may occur. Complications such as pneumonia, perforated bowel or meningitis may occur.

## Cuts, Bites & Stings

**Bedbugs & Lice** Bedbugs live in various places, but particularly in dirty mattresses and bedding, evidenced by spots of blood on bedclothes or on the wall. Bedbugs leave itchy bites in neat rows. Calamine lotion or a sting-relief spray may help.

All lice cause itching and discomfort. They make themselves at home in your hair (head lice), your clothing (body lice) or in your pubic hair (crabs). You catch lice through direct contact with infected people or by sharing combs, clothing and the like. Powder or shampoo treatment will kill the lice and infected clothing should then be washed in very hot, soapy water and left in the sun to dry.

**Bites & Stings** Bee and wasp stings are usually painful rather than dangerous. Calamine lotion or a sting-relief spray are good and ice packs will reduce the pain and swelling. However, in people who are allergic to them severe breathing difficulties may occur and require urgent medical care.

There are some spiders with dangerous bites but antivenins are usually available in local hospitals. Scorpion stings are notoriously painful. Scorpions often shelter in shoes or clothing.

There are various fish and other sea creatures that can sting or bite dangerously or that are dangerous to eat – be sure to seek local advice.

**Cuts & Scratches** Skin punctures can easily become infected in hot climates and may be difficult to heal. Wash well and treat any cut with an antiseptic such as povidone-iodine. Where possible avoid bandages and Band-Aids, which can keep wounds wet. Coral cuts are notoriously slow to heal and if they are not adequately cleaned, small pieces of coral can become embedded in the wound. Avoid touching and walking on fragile corals in the first place, but if you are near coral reefs, then wear shoes and clean any cut thoroughly.

## Women's Health
**Gynaecological Problems** Antibiotic use, synthetic underwear, sweating and contraceptive pills can lead to fungal vaginal infections, especially when travelling in hot climates. Fungal infections are characterised by a rash, itch and discharge and can be treated with a vinegar or lemon-juice douche, or with yoghurt. Nystatin, miconazole or clotrimazole pessaries or vaginal cream are the usual treatment. Maintaining good personal hygiene and wearing loose-fitting clothes and cotton underwear may help prevent these infections.

Sexually transmitted diseases are a major cause of vaginal problems. Symptoms include a smelly discharge, painful intercourse and sometimes a burning sensation when urinating. Medical attention should be sought and male sexual partners must also be treated. For more details see the section on Sexually Transmitted Infections earlier. Besides abstinence, the best thing is to practise safer sex using condoms.

**Pregnancy** It is not advisable to travel to some places while pregnant as some vaccinations normally used to prevent serious diseases are not advisable during pregnancy (eg, yellow fever). In addition, some diseases are much more serious for the mother (and may increase the risk of a stillborn child) in pregnancy (eg, malaria).

Most miscarriages occur during the first three months of pregnancy. Miscarriage is not uncommon and can occasionally lead to severe bleeding. The last three months should also be spent within reasonable distance of good medical care. A baby born as early as 24 weeks stands a chance of survival, but only in a good modern hospital. Pregnant women should avoid all unnecessary medication, although vaccinations and malarial prophylactics should still be taken where needed. Additional care should be taken to prevent illness and particular attention should be paid to diet and nutrition. Alcohol and nicotine, for example, should be avoided.

## Less Common Diseases
**Rabies** This fatal viral infection is known in Thailand. Many animals can be infected (such as dogs, cats, bats and monkeys) and it is their saliva that is infectious. Any bite, scratch or even lick from an animal should be cleaned promptly and thoroughly. Scrub with soap and running water, and then apply alcohol or iodine solution. It is important that you seek medical help immediately to receive a course of injections.

**Tetanus** This disease is caused by a germ that lives in soil and in the faeces of horses and other animals. It enters the body via breaks in the skin. The first symptom may be discomfort in swallowing, or stiffening of the jaw and neck; this is followed by painful convulsions of the jaw and whole body. The disease can be fatal. It can be prevented by vaccination.

**Tuberculosis (TB)** There is a world-wide resurgence of TB, and in Thailand it's the seventh leading cause of death. TB is a bacterial infection usually transmitted from person to person by coughing but which may be transmitted through consumption of unpasteurised milk. Milk that has been boiled is safe to drink, and the souring of milk to make yoghurt or cheese also kills the bacilli. Travellers are usually not at great risk as close household contact with the infected person is usually required before the disease is passed on. You may need to have a TB test before you travel as this can help diagnose the disease later if you become ill.

## WOMEN TRAVELLERS
### Attitudes towards Women

Chinese trader Ma Huan noted in 1433 that among the Thais 'All affairs are managed by their wives, all trading transactions large or small'. In rural areas female family members typically inherit land and throughout the country they tend to control family finances.

The most recent United Nations Development Programme (UNDP) Report noted that on the gender-related development index (GDI) Thailand ranks 40th among 130 countries, thus falling into the 'progressive' category. This ranking is 12 points higher than the overall UN human development index for Thailand, meaning gender-related development in Thailand is further along than the average of all other human development criteria for that country. The organisation also reports that the nation's GDI increase was greater than that of any country in the world between 1975 and 1995. According to the UNDP, Thailand 'has succeeded in building the basic human capabilities of both women and men, without substantial gender imparity'.

Thailand's workforce is 45% female, ranking it 27th on a worldwide scale, just ahead of China and the USA. So much for the good news. The bad news is that although women generally fare well in education, the labour force and in rural land inheritance, their cultural standing is a bit further from parity. An oft-repeated Thai saying reminds us that men form the front legs of the elephant and women the hind legs (at least they're pulling equal weight).

Thai Buddhism commonly holds that women must be reborn as men before they can attain nirvana, though many Thai dharma teachers point out that this presumption isn't supported by the *suttas* (discourses of the Buddha) or by the commentaries. But it is a common belief, supported by the availability of a fully ordained Buddhist monastic status for men and a less prestigious eight precept ordination for women. See the Religion section in the Facts about Bangkok chapter.

On a purely legal level, men enjoy more privilege. Men may divorce their wives for committing adultery, but the reverse does not apply. Men who take a foreign spouse continue to have the right to purchase and own land, while Thai women who marry foreign men lose this right.

Article 30 of the 1997-ratified Thai constitution states: 'Men and women hold equal rights', while few so-called developed countries in the Western world have charters containing equal rights clauses. Reformation of discriminatory laws can be expected as 'organic' legislation is put in place.

### Safety

Around 40% of all visitors to Thailand are women, a higher ratio than the worldwide average as measured by the World Tourism Organisation. This is on a par with Singapore and Hong Kong, and ahead of all other Asian countries (where the proportion of female visitors runs lower than 35%). This ratio is growing from year to year and the overall increase for women visitors has climbed faster than that for men for every year since 1993.

Everyday incidents of sexual harassment are much less common in Thailand than in India, Indonesia or Malaysia, and this may lull women familiar with those countries into thinking that Thailand is safer than it is. Over the past decade, several women have been attacked while travelling alone in remote areas, and in August 2000 a British woman was murdered at a guesthouse in Chiang Mai. Such incidents, however, are extremely rare. If you're a woman travelling alone, try to pair up with other travellers when travelling at night or in remote areas. Make sure hotel and guesthouse rooms are secure at night – if they're not, demand another room or move to another hotel or guesthouse.

When in the company of single Thai males, keep an eye on food and drink. In

1999 and 2000 we received a couple of reports from women who alleged they had been drugged and raped by Thai trekking guides in Chiang Mai.

## What to Bring

**Tampons etc** Most Thai women don't use tampons, so they can be difficult to find in Thailand. In general only the o.b. brand is available, usually in middle-class pharmacies or minimarts that carry toiletries, although in Bangkok more upscale pharmacies may also stock Tampax. Boots stores in Bangkok and Chiang Mai carry their own brand which are similar to Tampax tampons. So, if you're coming for a relatively short interval, it's best to bring your own supply. Pads, however, are widely available from minimarts and supermarkets throughout Thailand.

Many women have found that the Keeper Menstrual Cap, a reusable natural rubber device inserted to catch menstrual flow, is a convenient and environmentally friendly alternative to tampons or pads. For more information, contact Health Keeper (☎ 519-896 8032, 800-663 0427, fax 519-896 8031, e orderinfo@keeper.com), or check www .keeper.com.

## GAY & LESBIAN TRAVELLERS

Thai culture is very tolerant of homosexuality, both male and female. The nation has no laws that discriminate against homosexuals (a recent proposal to ban homosexuals from the public teaching profession was quickly shot down), and there is a fairly prominent gay and lesbian scene around the country. Hence there is no 'gay movement' in Thailand as such since there's no anti-gay establishment to move against. Whether speaking of dress or mannerism, lesbians and gays are generally accepted without comment.

Public displays of affection – whether heterosexual or homosexual – are frowned upon. As the guide *Thai Scene* (Gay Men's Press, Box 247, London N6 4AT, UK) has written:

For many gay travellers, Thailand is a nirvana with a long established gay bar scene, which, whilst often very Thai in culture, is particularly welcoming to tourists. There is little, if any, social appro-

bation (sic) towards gay people, providing Thai cultural mores are respected. What people do in bed, whether straight or gay, is not expected to be a topic of general conversation nor bragged about.

According to *Pink Ink:*

Thai lesbians prefer to call themselves tom (for tomboy) or dee (for lady), as the term 'lesbian', in Thailand, suggests pornographic videos produced for straight men. Tom and dee, by contrast, are reasonably accepted and integrated categories for Thai women, roughly corresponding to the Western terms 'butch' and 'femme'.

## Organisations & Publications

Utopia (☎ 259 1619, fax 258 3250, e info@utopia-asia.com), 116/1 Soi 23, Th Sukhumvit, Bangkok, is a gay and lesbian multipurpose centre consisting of a guesthouse, bar, cafe, gallery and gift shop. It maintains a well-organised Web site (www .utopia-asia.com) called the Southeast Asia Gay and Lesbian Resources or 'Utopia Homo Page'.

Information Thailand also has a good Web site on gay and lesbian venues in Bangkok (www.ithailand.com/living/entertainment/ bangkok/gay).

Monthly *Bangkok Metro* (www.bkkmetro .com) magazine stays abreast of gay and lesbian happenings in the capital, as does the 'Pink Page' of the monthly tourist rag *Guide to Bangkok* (also available at www.geocities .com/WestHollywood/5752/). *Pink Ink* (www .khsnet.com/pinkink), a Web-only publication by and for Bangkok's English-speaking gay and lesbian community, is another useful resource. Gay Media (www.gay-media .com) contains lots of information on Thailand travel with special attention to gay venues of all kinds.

Anjaree Group (☎/fax 477 1776), PO Box 322, Ratchadamnoen, Bangkok 10200, is Thailand's premier (and only) lesbian society. Anjaree sponsors various group activities and produces a Thai-only newsletter. Bilingual Thai-English Web sites of possible interest to visiting lesbians include www.lesla.com and lctpage.hypermart.net/ index.shtml.

Gay men may be interested in the services of the Long Yang Club (☎/fax 679 7727), PO Box 1077, Silom Post Office, Bangkok 10504 – a 'multicultural social group for male-oriented men who want to meet outside the gay scene', with branches in London, Amsterdam, Toronto, Canberra, Ottawa and Vancouver, or see its Web site (www.longyangclub.com).

*Lady Boys, Tom Boys, Rent Boys,* by Peter A Jackson, discusses health and gender identity issues in Thailand's gay and lesbian scene.

## DISABLED TRAVELLERS

Bangkok presents one large, ongoing obstacle course for the mobility-impaired. With its high curbs, uneven pavements and non-stop traffic, movement around the city can be particularly difficult – many streets must be crossed via pedestrian bridges flanked with steep stairways, while buses and boats don't stop long enough for even the mildly disabled. Rarely are there any ramps or other access points for wheelchairs.

The Hyatt International, Novotel Siam Square, Royal Orchid Sheraton, Holiday Inn Crowne Plaza and Westin Banyan Tree are the only hotels in the city that make consistent design efforts to provide handicapped access to their properties. Because of their high employee-to-guest ratios, home-grown luxury hotel chains such as those managed by Dusit, Amari, and Royal Garden Resorts are usually very good about accommodating the mobility-impaired by providing staff help where building design fails. For the rest, you're pretty much left to your own resources.

For wheelchair travellers, any trip to Thailand will require a good deal of advance planning; fortunately a growing network of information sources can put you in touch with those who have wheeled through Thailand before. A reader recently wrote with the following tips:

The difficulties you mention in your book are all there. However, travel in the streets is still possible, and enjoyable, providing you have a strong, ambulatory companion. Some obstacles may require two carriers; Thais are by nature helpful and could generally be counted on for assistance.

Don't feel you have to rely on organised tours to see the sights – these often leave in the early morning at times inconvenient to disabled people. It is far more convenient (and often cheaper) to take a taxi or hired car. It's also far more enjoyable as there is no feeling of holding others up.

Many taxis have an LPG tank in the boot (trunk), which makes it impossible to get a wheelchair in and close it. You might do better to hire a private car and driver (this usually costs no more – and sometimes less – than a taxi). A tuk-tuk is far easier to get in and out of and can carry two people and a wheelchair better than a taxi.

Be ready to try anything – in spite of my worries, riding an elephant proved quite easy.

## Organisations & Publications

Four international organisations that act as clearing-houses for information on world travel for the mobility-impaired are:

**Access Foundation** (☎ 516-887 5798), PO Box 356, Malverne, NY 11565, USA
**Accessible Journeys** (☎ 610-521 0339), 35 West Sellers Ave, Ridley Park, Pennsylvania, USA. Specialises in organising group travel for the mobility-impaired. Occasionally the agency offers Thailand trips. Check out its Web site: www.disabilitytravel.com.
**Mobility International USA** (☎ 541-343 1284, Ⓔ info@miusa.org), PO Box 10767, Eugene, OR 97440, USA
**Society for the Advancement of Travelers with Handicaps** (SATH; ☎ 212-447 7284, Ⓔ sathtravel@aol.com), Suite 610, 347 Fifth Ave, New York, NY 11242, USA. SATH has a very useful Web site (www.sat.org), full of information for travelling with handicaps of all kinds. It also publishes the magazine *Open Worlds,* following similar themes.

In Thailand you can also contact:

**Association of the Physically Handicapped of Thailand** (☎ 951 0569, fax 580 1098 ext 7) 73/7-8 Soi 8 (Soi Thepprasan), Th Tivanon, Talaat Kawan, Nonthaburi 11000
**Disabled Peoples International (Thailand)** (☎ 583 3021, fax 583 6518) 78/2 Th Tivanon, Pak Kret, Nonthaburi 11120

The book *Exotic Destinations for Wheelchair Travelers* by Ed Hansen & Bruce Gordon

(Full Data, San Francisco) contains a useful chapter on seven locations in Thailand. Others books of value include *Holidays and Travel Abroad – A Guide for Disabled People* (RADAR, London) and *Able to Travel* (Rough Guides, London, New York).

## SENIOR TRAVELLERS

Senior discounts aren't generally available in Thailand, but the Thais more than make up for this in the respect they typically show for the elderly. In traditional Thai culture, status comes with age – there isn't as heavy an emphasis on youth as in the Western world. Deference for age manifests itself in the way Thais go out of their way to help older people in and out of taxis or with luggage, and – usually, but not always – in serving them first in shops and post offices.

Nonetheless, some cultural spheres are reserved for youth. Cross-generation entertainment in particular is less common than in Western countries. For example, there is strict stratification among discos and nightclubs according to age group. One place will cater to teenagers, another to people in their early 20s, one for late 20s and 30s, yet another for those in their 40s and 50s, and once you've reached 60 you're considered too old to go clubbing! Exceptions to this rule include the more traditional entertainment venues, such as rural temple fairs and other wát-centred events, where young and old dance and eat together. For men, massage parlours are another place where old and young clientele mix.

## BANGKOK FOR CHILDREN

Like many places in South-East Asia, travelling with children in Thailand can be a lot of fun as long as you come well prepared with the right attitudes, physical requirements and the usual parental patience. Lonely Planet's *Travel with Children* by Maureen Wheeler and others contains useful advice on how to cope with kids on the road and what to bring along to make things go more smoothly, with special attention paid to travel in developing countries.

Thais love children and in many instances will shower attention on your offspring, who will find ready playmates among their Thai counterparts and a temporary nanny service at practically every stop.

For the most part, parents needn't worry too much about health concerns, though it pays to lay down a few ground rules – such as regular hand-washing – to head off potential medical problems. All the usual health precautions apply (see the Health section earlier in this chapter). Children should especially be warned not to play with animals as rabies is relatively common in Thailand.

### Fun for Kids

Bangkok has plenty of attractions for children. Among the most recommended are the centrally located Dusit Zoo, Queen Saovabha Memorial Institute (Snake Farm) and Lumphini Park. On the outskirts of Bangkok are Samphran Elephant Ground & Zoo and Safari World. See the Things to See & Do and Excursion chapters.

On the 8th floor of the World Trade Center (WTC, Map 7) is Bangkok's premier antidote to the tropics, the World Ice Skating Center. The WTC also contains a small children's play centre in the shopping centre (see the Shopping chapter). Most shopping centres offer these free diversions on their uppermost floors. These same play areas often have banks of video game machines off to one side.

## LIBRARIES

Besides offering an abundance of reading material, Bangkok's libraries make a peaceful escape from the heat, noise and traffic.

The National Library (Map 2, ☎ 281 5212) on Th Samsen is an impressive institution with a huge collection of Thai material dating back several centuries as well as smaller numbers of foreign-language books. Membership is free. The Siam Society, off Th Sukhumvit, and the National Museum also have collections of English-language materials on the history, art and culture of Thailand.

Both the American University Alumni (AUA, Map 7) on Th Ratchadamri, and the British Council (Map 7) have lending libraries. The British Council allows only members (residents over 16 years only) to borrow books, while the AUA has a free public lending service. Both libraries cater primarily to Thai members, hence the emphasis tends to be on English-language teaching rather than the latest fiction. Their main strengths are their up-to-date periodicals sections – the British Council's selection is strictly British of course while AUA's is all-American.

Although you won't be permitted to borrow books unless you're a 'Chula' student, the library in Chulalongkorn University (south of Siam Square, Map 7) is a good place to hang out – it's quiet and has air-conditioning.

In a class all of its own, the Neilson Hays Library (Map 6, ☎ 233 1731), 195 Th Surawong, next to the British Club, is a historical monument as well as a good, all-purpose lending library. Built in 1921 by Dr Heyward Hays as a memorial to his wife Jennie Neilson Hays, this classic colonial Asian edifice is operated by the more than 100-year-old Bangkok Library Association and is the oldest English-language library in Thailand. The collection encompasses over 20,000 volumes, including a good selection of children's books and titles on Thailand. The periodical section offers a few Thai magazines, and the library even has jigsaw puzzles that can be borrowed.

Although the building isn't air-conditioned (except for one reading room), the ancient ceiling fans do a good job of keeping the sitting areas cool. The library's Rotunda Gallery hosts monthly art exhibitions and occasional art sales. Opening hours are 9.30 am to 4 pm daily, but closes early at 2 pm on Sunday. Free parking for members is available at the library's small car park near the corner of Th Surawong and Th Naret.

## UNIVERSITIES

Bangkok has over 25 colleges and universities. The top ones are Chulalongkorn University (general, business), Mahidol University (medical studies), Thammasat University (political science and law), Silpakorn University (fine arts), Asian Institute of Technology (business and engineering), Kasetsart University (agriculture), Chula-

chomklao Military Academy (military affairs) and King Mongkut's Institute of Technology (science and engineering). Two universities, Sukhothai Thammathirat and Ramkhamhaeng, are 'open' universities offering general curricula consumed by huge numbers of students, many of whom 'attend' class via telecast or closed circuit TV.

Of the major universities, Chulalongkorn (☎ 215 0871, fax 215 4804, e info@chula.ac.th) has the most picturesque campus, a collection of mixed Thai and Western-style buildings spread over a large, semi-leafy expanse in the middle of the city between Th Henri Dunant and Th Phayathai.

A number of foreign students have graduated from Thailand's best universities, where naturally, fluency in Thai is required. Chula has a few non-degree Thai language and culture programs open to non-Thai-speaking foreign students (see Language & Culture in the Things to See & Do chapter).

## CULTURAL CENTRES

Various Thai and foreign associations organise and support cultural events of a wide-ranging nature. They can be good places to meet Thais with an international outlook as well as expat Bangkok residents. Some of the more active organisations include:

**Alliance Française** (Map 7, ☎ 213 2122, 286 3841) 29 Th Sathon Tai. French-language courses; translation services; monthly bulletin; French films; small library and bookshop; French and Thai cafeteria; and music, arts and lecture programs.

**American University Alumni** (AUA; Map 7, ☎ 252 4021) 179 Th Ratchadamri. English- and Thai-language courses; monthly newsletter; American films; TOEFL preparation; Thai cafeteria; library; and music, art and lecture programs.

**British Council** (Map 7, ☎ 652 5480, fax 253 5311, e bc.bangkok@britcoun.or.th) 254 Soi Chulalongkorn 64, Siam Square, Th Phra Ram I. English-language classes; monthly calendar of events; British films; music, art and drama programs; and inexpensive Internet services.

**Foreign Correspondents Club of Thailand** (FCCT; Map 7, ☎ 652 0580, fax 652 0582, e fcct@asiaaccess.net.th) Penthouse, Maneeya Center Bldg, 518/5 Th Ploenchit. Home to wayward journalists and anyone else interested in keeping up with current Thai news, the FCCT appears to be undergoing a renaissance. The club sponsors well-selected films every Monday evening and presents various programs with a news slant several other nights a week; bar and restaurant on the premises.

**Goethe-Institut** (Thai-German Cultural Centre; Map 7, ☎ 287 0942, e goethe@idn.co.th) 18/1 Soi Atakanprasit, on Soi Goethe between Th Sathon Tai and Soi Ngam Duphli. German-language classes; monthly calendar of events; German restaurant; German films; musical performances; and art exhibits.

**Thailand Cultural Centre** (TCC; Map 1, ☎ 245 7742) Th Ratchadaphisek, Huay Khwang. Important centre hosting a variety of local and international cultural events, including musical and theatrical performances, art exhibits, cultural workshops and seminars.

The TCC also sponsors the Cultural Information Service Centre, an information clearing-house that issues a bimonthly calendar of notable cultural events throughout the country. Many of the events listed are held in Bangkok at foreign culture associations, universities, art galleries, film societies, theatres and music centres. This is the best single source for cultural happenings in Thailand and it even keeps track of obscure provincial festivals. The calendar is available at the TCC as well as at the TAT office on Th Bamrung Meuang.

## DANGERS & ANNOYANCES
### General Precautions

Although Bangkok is in no way a dangerous city to visit, it's wise to be a little cautious, particularly if you're travelling alone. Solo women travellers should take special care on arrival at Bangkok International Airport, particularly at night. Don't take one of Bangkok's very unofficial taxis (black-and-white licence tags) by yourself – better a licensed taxi (yellow-and-black tags), or even a public bus. Both men and women should ensure their hotel rooms are securely locked and bolted at night. Inspect cheap rooms with thin walls for strategic peepholes.

When possible, keep valuables in a hotel safe. Make sure you obtain an itemised receipt for property left with hotels or guesthouses – note the exact quantity of travellers cheques and all other valuables.

### Credit Cards

When making credit-card purchases, don't let vendors take your credit card out of your sight to run it through the machine. Unscrupulous merchants have been known to rub off three or four or more receipts with one credit-card purchase. After the customer leaves the shop, they use the one legitimate receipt as a model to forge your signature on the blanks, then fill in astronomical 'purchases'. Sometimes they wait several weeks – even months – between submitting each charge receipt to the bank, so that you can't remember whether you'd been billed at the same vendor more than once.

### Druggings

When travelling by train, bus or taxi beware of friendly strangers offering cigarettes, drinks, biscuits (cookies) or sweets (candy) – criminal elements have been known to mix heavy sedatives or 'knockout' drugs with the proffered food.

Male travellers have also encountered drugged food or drink from friendly Thai women in bars and from prostitutes in their own hotel rooms. Female visitors have encountered the same with young Thai men, albeit less frequently. Thais are also occasional victims, especially at the Moh Chit bus terminal and Chatuchak Park, where young girls are drugged and sold to brothels. Conclusion – don't accept gifts from strangers.

### Touts

Touting – grabbing newcomers in the street or in train stations, bus terminals or airports to sell them a service – is a long tradition in Asia, and while Thailand doesn't have as many as, say, India, it has its share. In the popular tourist spots it seems like everyone – young boys waving flyers, túk-túk drivers, samlor drivers, schoolgirls – is touting something, usually hotels or guesthouses. For the most part they're completely harmless and sometimes they can be very informative. But take anything a tout says with two large grains of salt. Since touts work on commission and get paid just for delivering you to a guesthouse, hotel, or shop, they'll say anything to get you to the door.

Often the best (most honest and reliable) places refuse to pay tout commissions – so the average tout will try to steer you away from such places. Hence don't believe them if they tell you the hotel or guesthouse you're looking for is 'closed', 'full', 'dirty' or 'bad'. Sometimes (rarely) they're right but most times it's just a ruse to get you to a place that pays more commission. Always have a careful look yourself before checking into a place recommended by a tout. Túk-túk and samlor drivers often offer free or low-cost rides to the place they're touting; if you have another place you're interested in, you might agree to go with a driver only if he or she promises to deliver you to your first choice after you've had a look at the place being touted. If drivers refuse, chances are it's because they know your first choice is a better one.

This type of commission work isn't limited to low-budget guesthouses. Taxi drivers and even airline employees at airports reap commissions from the big hotels as well. At either end of the budget spectrum, the customer ends up paying the commission indirectly through raised room rates. Bangkok International Airport employees are notorious for talking newly arrived tourists into staying at badly located, overpriced hotels.

**Bus Touts** Watch out for touts wearing (presumably fake) TAT badges at Hualamphong station. They have been known to coerce travellers into buying tickets for private bus rides, saying the train is 'full' or 'takes too long'. Often the promised bus service turns out to be substandard and may take longer than the equivalent train ride due to the frequent changing of vehicles. You may be offered a 24 seat VIP 'sleeper' bus to Penang, for example, and end up stuffed into a minivan all the way. Such touts are 'bounty hunters' who receive a set fee for every tourist they deliver to the bus companies. Avoid the travel agencies (many of which bear 'TAT' or even 'Lonely Planet' signs) just outside the train station for the same reason. However, one reader wrote:

After reading your book's general chapters I was expecting a much worse situation. Compared to

travelling in countries like Morocco, Tunisia, Turkey etc I think travelling in Thailand is very easy and hassle-free. When people in Thailand tout something usually saying 'No' once – or rarely twice – persuades them that you are not interested. In some countries you have to invest much more energy to get rid of people trying to sell etc.

## Drugs

Opium, heroin, amphetamines, hallucinogens and marijuana are widely used in Thailand, but it is illegal to buy, sell or possess these drugs in any quantity. (The possession of opium for consumption – but not sale – among hill tribes is legal.) A lesser known narcotic, *kràthâwm* (a leaf of the *Mitragyna speciosa* tree), is used by workers and students as a stimulant – similar to Yemen's *qat*. A hundred kràthâwm leaves sell for around 200B, and are sold for 5B to 15B each. The leaf is illegal and said to be addictive.

Although in certain areas of the country drugs seem to be used with some impunity, enforcement is arbitrary – the only way not to risk getting caught is to avoid the scene entirely. Every year perhaps dozens of visiting foreigners are arrested in Thailand for drug use or trafficking and end up doing hard time. A smaller but significant number die of heroin overdoses. Th Khao San has become a target of infrequent drug enforcement sweeps.

The legal penalties for drug offences are stiff. If you're caught using marijuana, mushrooms or LSD, you face a fine (the going rate for escaping a small pot bust – or 'fine' if you wish – is 50,000B) and/or up to one year in prison, while for heroin or amphetamines, the penalty for use can be anywhere from six months to 10 years imprisonment, plus a fine of 5000B to 10,000B. The going rate for bribing one's way out of a small pot bust is 50,000B. Drug smuggling (defined as attempting to cross a border with drugs in your possession) carries considerably higher penalties, including execution. Recent arrest records show that residents of Myanmar, Laos, Malaysia, Cambodia and the UK top the list of those arrested in Thailand for drug trafficking, followed by Australia, Germany, the USA and Italy.

## LEGAL MATTERS

In general Thai police don't hassle foreigners, especially tourists. If anything they generally go out of their way not to arrest a foreigner breaking minor traffic laws, taking the approach that a friendly warning will suffice.

One major exception is drug laws (see the preceding Drugs entry). Most Thai police view drug takers as a social scourge and consequently see it as their duty to enforce the letter of the law – for others it's an opportunity to make untaxed income via bribes. Which direction they'll go often depends on dope quantities – small-time offenders are sometimes offered the chance to pay their way out of an arrest, while traffickers usually go to jail.

Be extra vigilant about where you dispose of cigarette butts and other refuse when in Bangkok. A strong anti-littering law was passed in Bangkok in 1997, and police won't hesitate to cite foreigners and collect fines of 2000B.

If you are arrested for any offence, the police will allow you the opportunity to make a phone call to your embassy or consulate in Thailand if you have one, or to a friend or relative if not. There's a whole set of legal codes governing the length of time and manner in which you can be detained by the police before being charged or put on trial, but a lot of discretion is left up to the police. With foreigners the police are more likely to bend these codes in your favour than the reverse. However, as with police worldwide, if you don't show respect to the men in brown you will only make matters worse.

Thai law does not presume an indicted detainee to be either 'guilty' or 'innocent' but rather a 'suspect' whose guilt or innocence will be decided in court. Trials are usually speedy.

### Tourist Police Hotline

The best way to deal with most serious hassles regarding rip offs or thefts is to contact the Tourist Police, who are used to dealing with foreigners, rather than the regular Thai police. The Tourist Police maintain a hotline 24 hours a day – dial ☎ 1155 from any phone in Thailand to lodge complaints or to

request assistance with regards to personal safety. You can also call this number between 8.30 am and 4.30 pm daily to request travel information.

The Tourist Police can also be very helpful in cases of arrest. Although they typically have no jurisdiction over the kinds of cases handled by regular cops, they may be able to help with translation or with contacting your embassy.

### Visiting Someone in Prison

If you would like to visit someone who is serving a prison sentence in Bangkok you should contact the prisoner's Bangkok embassy, tell the consular staff the prisoner's name and ask them to write a letter requesting you be permitted to see that prisoner. The embassy can provide directions to the prison and tell you the visiting hours. Usually visiting is only allowed a couple of days a week. Don't try going directly to the prison without a letter from the prisoner's embassy, as you may be refused entry.

Over the last couple of years – especially since the release of the film *Brokedown Palace,* about two backpackers who receive a long Bangkok pris.on sentence after getting caught smuggling heroin out of Thailand – visiting imprisoned foreigners in Bangkok has become something of a fad. With the resulting increase in inquiries, both embassy and prison staff are tightening up on the release of prisoner information. The Thai corrections system does not accept the Western notion that anonymous prisoners should receive visitors, although exceptions are sometimes made for missionaries.

For the latest information on visitation policies, contact your embassy in Bangkok.

### BUSINESS HOURS

Most government offices are open from 8.30 am to 4.30 pm on weekdays (closed noon to 1 pm for lunch). Regular bank hours in Bangkok are Monday to Friday from 10 am to 4 pm, but several banks have special foreign-exchange offices that are open longer hours (generally from 8.30 am until 8 pm) and every day of the week. Note that all government offices and banks are closed on public holidays (see below Public Holidays & Special Events for details).

Businesses usually operate between 8.30 am and 5 pm on weekdays and sometimes Saturday morning as well. Larger shops usually open from 10 am to 6.30 or 7 pm, but smaller shops may open earlier and close later.

## PUBLIC HOLIDAYS & SPECIAL EVENTS

The number and frequency of festivals and fairs in Thailand is incredible – there always seems to be something going on, especially during the cool season from November to February.

Dates for festivals may vary from year to year, either because of the lunar calendar, which isn't quite in sync with the solar calendar, or because local authorities decide to change festival days. The TAT publishes an up-to-date *Major Events & Festivals* calendar each year.

On dates noted as public holidays, all government offices and banks will be closed.

### January
**New Year's Day** A public holiday in deference to the Western calendar.

### February
**Magha Puja (Maakhá Buuchaa)** Held on the full moon of the third lunar month to commemorate the Buddha preaching to 1250 enlightened monks who came to hear him 'without prior summons'. A public holiday throughout the country, it culminates with a candle-lit walk around the main chapel at every wát.

### Late February to early March
**Chinese New Year** Called *trùt jiin* in Thai, Thai-Chinese all over Thailand celebrate their lunar new year (the date shifts from year to year) with a week of house-cleaning, lion dances and fireworks. The most impressive festivities take place Chinatown, Bangkok.

### March
**Bangkok International Jewellery Fair** Held in several large Bangkok hotels, this is Thailand's most important annual gem and jewellery trade show. It runs concurrently with the Department of Export Promotion's Gems & Jewellery Fair.

**Ngan Thetsakan Sak Thai (Thai Tattoo Festival)** Two-day festival at Wat Bang Phra, near Nakhon Chaisi, about 20km west of Bangkok (See the boxed text 'More Than Skin Deep' in this section).

### April
**Songkhran Festival** The New Year's celebration of the lunar year in Thailand. Buddha images are 'bathed', monks and elders receive the respect of younger Thais by the sprinkling of water over their hands, and a lot of water is generously tossed about for fun. Songkhran generally gives everyone a chance to release their frustrations and literally cool off during the peak of the hot season. Hide out in your room or expect to be soaked – the latter is a lot more fun.

**Chakri Day** A public holiday, held on 6 April, commemorating the founder of the Chakri Dynasty, Rama I.

### May
**Visakha Puja (Wísǎakhà Buuchaa)** A public holiday that falls on the 15th day of the waxing moon in the sixth lunar month. This is considered the date of the Buddha's birth, enlightenment and *parinibbana* (passing away). Activities are centred around the wát, with candle-lit processions, chanting and sermonising.

**Coronation Day** A public holiday. The king and queen preside at a ceremony on 5 May at Wat Phra Kaew in Bangkok, commemorating their 1946 coronation.

**Royal Ploughing Ceremony** To kick off the official rice-planting season, the king participates in this ancient Brahman ritual at Sanam Luang (the large field across from Wat Phra Kaew) in Bangkok. Thousands of Thais gather to watch, and traffic in this part of the city comes to a standstill. (See the boxed text 'Royal Ploughing Ceremony' in this section).

### July
**Asalha Puja (Àsǎanhà Buuchaa)** Commemorates the first sermon preached by the Buddha.

**Khao Phansaa** A public holiday and the beginning of Buddhist *phansǎa* (lent), this is the traditional time of year for young men to enter the monkhood for the rainy season and for all monks to station themselves in a monastery for the three months. It's a good time to observe a Buddhist ordination.

### August
**Queen's Birthday** A public holiday. In Bangkok, Th Ratchadamnoen Klang and the Grand Palace are festooned with coloured lights.

## More Than Skin Deep

Every year on an astrologically determined date in March, Wat Bang Phra, not far from Bangkok, hosts the two-day Ngan Thetsakan Sak Thai (Thai Tattoo Festival). Festival-goers come from all over Thailand and beyond to participate in the ritual tattooing – or to observe. Day one begins with a group trance session in which lay participants, temporarily 'possessed' by animal spirits under the monks' control, imitate the calls and movements of tigers, monkeys, bears and other creatures. Thus mentally prepared for the painful experience of hand-tattooing, the visitors line up to have their skins carefully stencilled by the monks. At Wat Bang Phra every new devotee of the tattoo cult must begin with an 'entry-level' *yan* (sacred design) across the upper back and shoulders. Most yan can be tattooed in 15 minutes or less. Wat Bang Phra is near Nakhon Chaisi, about 20km west of Bangkok.

**A long heavy silver stylus is used to transfer ink beneath the skin.**

Although their intricate, monochromatic designs are often beautiful, traditional Thai tattoos, *sák,* are intended not simply to decorate the body but to confer spiritual power on the wearer. There are two kinds of powers, one that protects the body from physical harm – popular among soldiers, truck drivers, policemen, Thai kickboxers and others working in dangerous professions – and one that acts like a love potion, drawing lovers and admirers to the wearer.

To the untrained eye the differences are subtle. Many *sák* consist of magical runes descended from an old Cambodian script known as *khǎwm* arranged to form maze-like designs. Some Thai tattoos also incorporate powerful animal forms, such as tigers or lions, while others depict mythical figures such as mermaids, angels or half-human, half-animal characters.

The most common place to be tattooed is the upper back, followed by the chest, arms, lower back and thighs. The designs are hammered into the skin using 60cm metal styluses, sharpened at one end and dipped into a thick, black ink concocted of powdered charcoal, oil, herbs and various secret ingredients known only to those who have mastered the tattooing art.

The tattooing tradition is passed on from generation to generation by highly respected Thai tattoo artists, many of whom are Buddhist monks or lay masters who have spent many years in the monkhood. Traditionally all artists are male, as are most of the tattoo recipients. Women who have themselves tattooed in the traditional style almost always choose an 'invisible' tattoo made with sesame oil rather than black ink. Often applied to the forehead, tongue or shoulder, such tattoos leave red welts at first but after a few days no physical trace remains.

Visible or not, the tattoo can only perform its shamanistic function if proper ritual is adhered to. Those who desire to be tattooed must make offerings to the tattoo master and pay a token fee, usually no more than 100B or so. During the procedure the artist or tattoo receiver may wear a gilded headdress of the kind worn by Thai classical dancers. Even after the tattoo has been applied, it carries no power until the master has chanted *káthǎa* (Pali verses), blown air from his cheeks on to the top of the tattoo wearer's head or struck the tattoo with the flat side of a sacred dagger. Thereafter, the wearer must keep the tattoo's potency alive by the daily repetition of prescribed *káthǎa* and, ideally, by keeping Buddhism's five moral precepts against killing, lying, stealing, sexual misconduct and intoxication.

## The Royal Ploughing Ceremony

One of the most colourful and important royal ceremonies performed each year takes place in May just before the annual rains typically arrive. Although the ceremony was very popular during the Ayuthaya era, it was abandoned when Thailand became a constitutional monarchy in the 1930s. King Bhumibol revived the Royal Ploughing Ceremony in 1960 to boost morale among Thai farmers.

The King, or members of his immediate family, presides over the event, for which a set of special pavilions is constructed on Sanam Luang, the parade grounds opposite Wat Phra Kaew. For the duration of the two-hour ceremony, Thailand's Permanent Secretary for Agriculture and Cooperatives serves as the Phraya Raek Na (Lord of the Ploughing). Dressed in the Merlin-like conical hat and glittering robes of his Ayuthaya predecessors, he follows a flower-garlanded pair of white oxen as they pull a red-and-gold plough in six ceremonial ovals around a consecrated area. Accompanied by a retinue of traditionally dressed male and female attendants, the Phraya sows rice seed – from the King's experimental rice fields at Chitrlada Palace – in the ploughed furrows in the nation's symbolic first planting of the year.

After the ploughing, the oxen are presented with seven buckets containing rice, corn, grass, beans, sesame seeds, alcohol and water. Their choice of feed is believed to predict not only agricultural production for the coming year but also the state of domestic transportation and foreign relations.

At this point the ceremonial ground is opened to Thai farmers who scramble to collect a few grains of the rice from the furrows. The farmers believe that the blessed grains can bring an abundant harvest if planted or lure wealth if kept in one's pocket.

### September
**Thailand International Swan-Boat Races**
These take place on Mae Nam Chao Phraya in Bangkok near the Rama IX Bridge.

### October
**Chulalongkorn Day** A public holiday in commemoration of King Chulalongkorn (Rama V).

### Mid-October to mid-November
**Thawt Kathin (Thâwt Kàthǐn)** A one-month period at the end of Buddhist phansǎa (lent) during which new monastic robes and requisites are offered to the Sangha. In Nan Province longboat races are held on the Mae Nam Nan.

### November
**Loi Krathong (Lawy Kràthong)** On the proper full-moon night, small lotus-shaped baskets or boats made of banana leaves containing flowers, incense, candles and a coin are floated on Thai rivers, lakes and canals. This is an intrinsically Thai festival that probably originated in Sukhothai and is best celebrated in the North. There are rather low-key celebrations along the banks of Mae Nam Chao Phraya, in Bangkok.

### December
**King's Birthday** This is a public holiday held on 5 December and celebrated with some fervour in Bangkok. As with the queen's birthday, it features lots of lights along Th Ratchadamnoen Klang. Some people erect temporary shrines to the king outside their homes or businesses.
**Constitution Day** A public holiday.

## DOING BUSINESS

Thailand's steady economic growth over the past 15 years has attracted much trade and investment, so the Thais, or at least Bangkok Thais, are quite used to doing business with foreigners.

See Society & Conduct in Facts about Bangkok for a discussion of social taboos and important information on social relationships, status and Thai concepts of saving face.

### Government Contacts

For a complete rundown of investment regulations, contact the Office of the Board of Investment (BOI; ☎ 537 8111, e head@boi .go.th), Th Vibhavadi Rangsit, Bangkok, Thailand 10900. Investment law in Thailand is quite complicated, but the government does offer certain tax deferments and other concessions for foreign businesses, depending on the business arena.

The BOI has offices in Australia, the USA, Germany, France and Japan – these can be contacted through the Thai embassy in each of these countries. There are four regional offices within Thailand for the Central, Southern, Northern and North-Eastern regions.

Those interested in import/export should contact the Thai Chamber of Commerce (☎ 662 1860, fax 225 3372, ⓔ tcc@tcc.or .th), 150 Th Ratchabophit, and the Board of Trade of Thailand (Map 3, ☎ 221 9350, fax 225 3995) at the same address.

## Other Resources

The Bangkok daily *Business Day,* focuses on business news, including Thai politics as it relates to trade and investment. Three helpful books are: *Working with Thais, Thais Mean Business* and *Starting and Operating a Business in Thailand,* all available at bookshops in Bangkok (see Bookshops in the Shopping chapter).

On the Internet, you can find the latest news on investments, trade, labour policy and other topics relevant to the Thai business world by doing a search for 'Thailand' on the Mondaq Business Briefing Web site (www.mondaq.com).

## Business Services

Most of the major hotels have business centres where fax, telecommunications, translation and secretarial services can be arranged for standard fees. Several private companies around the city also offer similar services.

**Business Centres** These offices provide a mixed bag of services, including secretarial, translation and fax services.

**Bangkok Business & Secretarial Office** (☎ 233 4768, 233 3572) 5/6 Soi Sala Daeng, Th Silom
**Executive Business Center** (☎ 236 6120) Sathorn Thani Tower, 2 Th Sathon Neua
**Girl Friday Business and Secretarial Services** (☎ 635 0182) 191/5 Soi Seuksa Withaya, Th Silom

**Translation Services** These companies can provide Thai-English and English-Thai translations, often very quickly.

**Impro Co Ltd** (☎ 618 67667, fax 618 6869, ⓔ improbob@box1.a-net.net.th) 220 Soi 18, Th Pradipat
**Interlanguage Translation Center** (☎ 252 4307, fax 252 9177) 554 Th Ploenchit
**International Translations Office** (☎ 233 7714, fax 235 6619, ⓔ intrans@asiaaccess .net.th) 22 Th Silom
**Siam Translation Center** (☎ 250 1656, fax 254 5582) 57/4 Th Withayu (Wireless Rd)
**World Translation Center** (☎ 251 7545) 1107 Th Phetburi Tat Mai

**Computer Equipment Rental** The following companies rent a wide variety of computer equipment – usually not the latest hardware, but adequate for most business needs.

**Computerist Company** (☎ 247 1282, 247 1283) Tada Bldg, 55 Th Ratchaprarop
**Computer System Connection** (☎ 466 2393) 212 Th Intharaphitak
**Cybernetics Company** (☎ 235 2916) 62/17-8 Th Thaniya
**Shinawatra Computer Co** (☎ 241 3161) 526 Th Phra Ram V

**Temporary Office Rental** MRCentre (☎ 631 1555), 23rd floor, Liberty Square, Th Silom, offers temporary office space (complete with answering and cleaning services, plus optional secretarial services) in the heart of the Silom financial district. Many real estate agencies in Bangkok can also arrange office rentals, whether short or long-term – see the Rental Agencies section of the *Greater Bangkok Telephone Directory* yellow pages. At the time of writing, it's a buyer's market in Bangkok so office space can be very inexpensive if you bargain and don't take the first place you see.

## WORK

Thailand's steady economic growth has provided a variety of work opportunities for foreigners, although in general it's not as easy to find a job as in the more developed countries. The one exception is English teaching; as in the rest of East and South-East Asia, there is a high demand for English speakers to provide instruction to Thai citizens. This is not due to a shortage of qualified Thai teachers with a good grasp of English grammar, but rather a desire to have native speaker models in the classroom.

## Teaching English

Those with academic credentials such as teaching certificates or degrees in English as a second language get first crack at the better-paying jobs, such as those at universities and international schools. But there are perhaps hundreds of private language teaching establishments that hire noncredentialed teachers by the hour throughout the country. Private tutoring is also a possibility. International oil companies pay the highest salaries for English instructors, but are also quite choosy.

If you're interested in looking for teaching work, start with the English-language *Greater Bangkok Metropolitan Telephone Directory* yellow pages, which contains many upcountry as well as Bangkok listings.

Organisations such as Teachers of English to Speakers of Other Languages (TESOL), Suite 300, 1600 Cameron St, Alexandria, Virginia 22314, USA, and the International Association of Teachers of English as a Foreign Language (IATEFL), 3 Kingsdown Chamber, Kingsdown Park, Whitstable, Kent CT52DJ, UK, publish newsletters with lists of jobs in foreign countries, including Thailand.

## Other Jobs & Volunteer Positions

Voluntary and paying positions with organisations that provide charitable services in education, development or public health are available for those with the right education and/or experience. Some contacts are:

**Overseas Service Bureau** (OSB; ☎ 03-9279 1788) in Melbourne, Australia
**US Peace Corps** (☎ 800-424-8580) in Washington, DC, USA
**Volunteer Service Abroad** (☎ 04-472 5759) in Wellington, New Zealand
**Voluntary Service Overseas** (VSO; ☎ 020-8780 7200) in London, UK
**Voluntary Service Overseas** (VSO; ☎ 613-234 1364) in Ottawa, Canada

The United Nations supports a number of ongoing projects in the country. In Bangkok try contacting:

**Food & Agriculture Organisation** (☎ 281 7844)
**Unesco** (☎ 391 0577)
**Unicef** (☎ 280 5931)
**United Nations Development Programme** (☎ 282 9619)
**UN World Food Program** (☎ 280 0427)
**World Health Organisation** (☎ 282 9700)

Mon, Karen and Burmese refugee camps along the Thailand-Myanmar border can use volunteer help. Since none of these camps are officially sanctioned by the Thai government, few of the big nongovernment organisations or multilateral organisations are involved. This means the level of overall support is low but the need for volunteers is definitely there. If this interests you, travel to the relevant areas (primarily Sangkhlaburi and Mae Sot) and ask around for the 'unofficial' camp locations.

Busking is illegal in Thailand, where it is legally lumped together with begging.

## Work Permits

All work in Thailand requires a Thai work permit. Thai law defines work as 'exerting one's physical energy or employing one's knowledge, whether or not for wages or other benefits', hence theoretically even volunteer work requires a permit. A 1979 royal decree closes 39 occupations to foreigners, including civil engineering, architecture, legal services and clerical or secretarial services. Several jobs on this list were reopened to foreigners in 1998, however.

Work permits should be obtained through an employer, who may file for the permit before the foreigner enters Thailand. The permit itself is not issued until the employee enters Thailand on a valid Non-Immigrant Visa.

The Work Permit Application and supporting documents should be submitted to the Labour Department of the Ministry of the Interior, Aliens Occupation Division (Map 3, ☎ 221 5140, 223 4912), Th Fuang Nakhon, Bangkok 10200.

# Getting There & Away

## AIR
### Departure Tax
All passengers departing Thailand on international flights are charged an international departure tax of 500B. This tax is not included in the price of the ticket and should be paid in baht at the ticket counter. Make sure you have enough baht left over at the end of your trip – or re-visit one of the currency exchange booths. For domestic flights within Thailand there is a tax of 30B, which is included in the price of the ticket.

## Other Parts of Thailand
Three domestic carriers, Thai Airways International (commonly known as THAI), Bangkok Airways and PB Air, make use of domestic airports in 28 cities around the country. Other fledgling airlines, including Angel Air and Orient Express Air, have attempted to supplement domestic services but each has so far failed to keep going. PB Air only offers domestic flights between Bangkok and Krabi at the moment, along with international service to Medan (Indonesia) and Singapore. Orient Express is licensed to offer charter services, while Angel Airways is completely sidelined at the moment.

**THAI Airways International** Most domestic air services are operated by THAI, and its offices can be found throughout Thailand. Its head office (Map 5, ☎ 513 0121, reservations 280 0060) is at 89 Thanon (Th) Vibhavadi Rangsit.

**Air Passes** THAI occasionally offers four-coupon passes – available only outside Thailand for foreign currency purchases – in which you can book any four domestic flights for one fare of around US$199 (50% less for children under 12) as long as you don't repeat the same leg. Unless you plan carefully, this isn't much of a saving since it's hard to avoid repeating the same leg in and out of Bangkok. Also, as the baht is so low these days it's often cheaper to make

domestic flying arrangements in Thailand rather than from abroad.

For more information on this special, known as the 'Amazing Thailand fare', inquire at any THAI office outside Thailand.

**Bangkok Airways** Bangkok Airways, owned by Sahakol Air, flies four main routes: Bangkok-Sukhothai-Chiang Mai, Bangkok-Ko Samui-Phuket, Bangkok-Ranong-Phuket and U Taphao (Pattaya)-Ko Samui.

The airline's head office (Map 7, ☎ 229 3434, reservations 229 3456) is at 60 Queen Sirikit National Convention Centre, Thanon (Th) Ratchadaphisek Tat Mai, Khlong Toey.

Note that through fares for both THAI and Bangkok Airways are generally less than the combination fares – Chiang Rai to Bangkok, for example, is less than the addition of Chiang Rai to Chiang Mai and Chiang Mai to Bangkok fares. This does not always apply to international fares, however. It's much cheaper to fly from Bangkok to Penang via Phuket or Hat Yai than direct, for example.

**PB Air** The head office (Map 7, ☎ 261 0220) is on the 17th floor of the UBC II Building at 591 Soi 33, Th Sukhumvit. The airline is owned by Boon Rawd Brewery of Singha beer fame, and uses tiny Fokker F28s on its Bangkok-Krabi route.

**Angel Air** On the sidelines is Angel Air, a Bangkok-based regional carrier that served several destinations in Thailand and neighbouring countries for a couple of years, then suddenly ceased operations in early 2000 due to financial conditions. The airlines' owners say service will be resurrected in the near future.

**Domestic Airport** Bangkok's Don Muang Airport stands a few hundred metres south of Bangkok International Airport (Map 1). Facilities include a post and telephone office on the ground floor, a snack bar in the departure lounge and a restaurant on the 2nd floor. THAI operates a free shuttle bus between the international and domestic terminals every 15 minutes between 6 am and 11.20 pm.

## Other Countries

The expense of getting to Bangkok per air kilometre varies quite a bit depending on your point of departure. However, you can take heart in the fact that Bangkok is one of the cheapest cities in the world to fly out of, due to the Thai government's loose restrictions on air fares and close competition between airlines and travel agencies. The result is that with a little shopping around, you can come up with some real bargains. If you can find a cheap one-way ticket to Bangkok, take it, because you are virtually guaranteed to find one of equal or lesser cost for the return trip once you get there.

From most places around the world your best bet will be budget, excursion or promotional fares – when inquiring from airlines ask for the various fares in that order. Each carries its own set of restrictions and it's up to you to decide which works best in your case. Fares fluctuate, but in general

they are cheaper from September to April (northern hemisphere) and from March to November (southern hemisphere).

Fares listed here should serve as a guideline – don't count on them staying this way for long (they may go down!).

**Australia** STA Travel and Flight Centre are major dealers in cheap air fares. Check the travel agents' ads in the *Yellow Pages* and ring around. From Australia, there are many travel options to Bangkok, with a number of airlines offering both direct flights and flights with stopovers via another Asian capital. Fares can vary considerably depending on the season (Christmas and school holidays are high season) and the length (35 days or one year) of the ticket. Shop around as many airlines do offer some especially good deals. From Melbourne and Sydney, direct low-season fares to Bangkok start from around A$839 with Olympic Airways, or A$987 with THAI. In the high season, return fares start from A$1170 with Olympic Airways or A$1374 with Qantas Airways.

**New Zealand** As in Australia, STA Travel and Flight Centre are popular travel agents. Flights from Auckland to Bangkok go via Australia or another Asian capital as there are no direct flights. From Auckland, THAI return low-season fares start from NZ$1299 while a return in the high season will cost around NZ$1549.

**The UK & Continental Europe** Discount air travel is big business in London, and London to Bangkok is arguably the most competitive air route in the world. Typical discounted air fares run UK£331 to UK£421 for a return trip. You may have to call around to get these fares, or better yet check the ads that appear in the travel pages of the weekend broadsheet newspapers, in *Time Out,* the *Evening Standard* or in the free magazine *TNT.*

For students or travellers under 26, popular travel agencies in the UK include STA Travel (☎ 020-7361 6262; www.statravel .co.uk), 86 Old Brompton Rd, London SW7, and Usit Campus (☎ 0870-240 1010;

www.usitcampus.co.uk), 52 Grosvenor Gardens, London SW1. Both also operate branches throughout the UK and although they cater especially to young people and students, they also gladly sell tickets to all travellers.

Other recommended travel agencies for all age groups include:

**Bridge the World** (☎ 020-7734 7447, www.b-t-w.co.uk), 4 Regent Place, London W1
**Flightbookers** (☎ 020-7757 2000, www.ebookers.com), 177-178 Tottenham Court Rd, London W1
**North-South Travel** (☎ 012-45 608 291; www.nstravel.demon.co.uk), Moulsham Mill, Parkway, Chelmsford, Essex CM2 7PX. North-South Travel donates part of its profit to projects in the developing world.
**Quest Travel** (☎ 020-8547 3123, www.questtravel.co.uk), 10 Richmond Rd, Kingston-upon-Thames, Surrey KT2 5HL
**Trailfinders** (☎ 020-7938 3939, www.trailfinders .co.uk), 194 Kensington High St, London W8
**Travel Bag** (☎ 020-7287 5158; www.travelbag.co.uk), 52 Regent St, Piccadilly, London, WIB 5DX

At least two dozen airlines will transport you between London and Bangkok, though only three of them – British Airways, Qantas Airways and THAI – fly non-stop. If you insist on a non-stop flight, you will probably have to pay between UK£500 and UK£800 return for the privilege (or around UK£100 less if you are a student or under 26). A one-way ticket is usually only slightly cheaper than a return ticket.

One of the cheapest deals going is on Tarom (Romania), which has Brussels-Bangkok-Brussels fares valid for one year. Uzbekistan Airways does a London to Bangkok flight via Tashkent. Other cheapies are Lauda Air from London (via Vienna) and Czech Airlines from Prague (via London, Frankfurt and Zurich).

Discount return air fares from other cities in Europe include Amsterdam f999 (on Malev-Hungarian Airlines); Munich DM 799; Berlin DM896; Paris 2950FF (on Pakistan Airlines); Stockholm 2720kr; and Zurich 840Sfr (on Kuwait Airways or Olympic Airways).

**The USA** The *New York Times, LA Times, Chicago Tribune* and *San Francisco Examiner* all produce weekly travel sections where you'll find any number of travel agents' ads. Council Travel and STA Travel have offices in major cities nationwide. The magazine *Travel Unlimited* (PO Box 1058, Allston, MA 02134) publishes details of the cheapest air fares and courier possibilities for worldwide destinations from the USA.

It is cheapest to fly to Bangkok via West Coast cities rather than from the East Coast. You can get some great deals through the many 'bucket shops' (who discount tickets by taking a cut in commissions) and consolidators (agencies that buy airline seats in bulk) operating in Los Angeles and San Francisco. From these agencies a return air fare to Bangkok from any of 10 West Coast cities starts at around US$750, with occasional specials (especially in May and September) at just US$525. If you're flying from the East Coast, add US$150 to US$200 to these fares.

One of the most reliable discounters is Avia Travel (☎ 800-950 AVIA, 510-558 2150, fax 558 2158, ⓔsales@aviatravel .com) at Suite E, 1029 Solano Ave, Albany CA 94706. Avia specialises in custom-designed around-the-world fares, eg, San Francisco/Los Angeles-Bangkok-Rome/ Paris/London-San Francisco/Los Angeles for US$1135, as well as 'Circle Pacific' fares travelling Los Angeles-Tokyo-Taipei-Singapore-Bangkok-Hong Kong-Los Angeles for US$1100. Check Avia's Web site, www.avia.com, for the latest fares. The agency sets aside a portion of its profits for Volunteers in Asia, a nonprofit organisation that sends grassroots volunteers to work in South-East Asia.

Another agency that works hard to get the cheapest deals is Ticket Planet (☎ 800-799 8888, 415-288 9999, fax 415-288 9839, ⓔ trips@ticketplanet.com), 3rd floor, 59 Grant Ave, San Francisco, CA 94108. One of its 'Circle Pacific' fares, for example, offers a San Francisco-Hong Kong-Bangkok-Kuala Lumpur-Denpasar-San Francisco ticket for US$1000 plus tax during the low season. You can add Honolulu, Singapore, Jakarta or Yogyakarta to this route for US$50 each stop. It

## Air Travel Glossary

**Alliances** Many of the world's leading airlines are now intimately involved with each other, sharing everything from reservations systems and check-in to aircraft and frequent-flyer schemes. Opponents say that alliances restrict competition. Whatever the arguments, there is no doubt that big alliances are the way of the future.

**Courier Fares** Businesses often need to send urgent documents or freight securely and quickly. Courier companies hire people to accompany the package through customs and, in return, offer a discount ticket which is sometimes a bargain. However, you may have to surrender all your baggage allowance and take only carry-on luggage.

**Fares** Airlines traditionally offer 1st class (coded F), business class (coded J) and economy class (coded Y) tickets. These days there are so many promotional and discounted fares available that few passengers pay full fare.

**Lost Tickets** If you lose your airline ticket, an airline will usually treat it like a travellers cheque and, after inquiries, issue you with another one. Legally, however, an airline is entitled to treat it like cash and if you lose it then it's gone forever. Take very good care of your tickets.

**Onward Tickets** An entry requirement for many countries is that you have a ticket out of the country. If you're unsure of your next move, the easiest solution is to buy the cheapest onward ticket to a neighbouring country or a ticket from a reliable airline which can later be refunded if you do not use it.

**Open-Jaw Tickets** These are return tickets where you fly out to one place but return from another. If available, this can save you backtracking to your arrival point.

**Overbooking** Since every flight has some passengers who fail to show up, airlines often book more passengers than they have seats. Usually excess passengers make up for the no-shows, but occasionally somebody gets 'bumped' onto the next available flight. Guess who it is most likely to be? The passengers who check in late. If you do get 'bumped', you are normally offered some form of compensation.

**Reconfirmation** Some airlines require you to reconfirm your flight at least 72 hours prior to departure. Check your travel documents to see if this is the case

**Restrictions** Discounted tickets often have various restrictions on them – such as needing to be paid for in advance and incurring a penalty to be altered or cancelled. Others are restrictions on the minimum and maximum period you must be away.

**Round-the-World Tickets** RTW tickets give you a limited period (usually a year) in which to circumnavigate the globe. You can go anywhere the carrying airlines go, as long as you don't backtrack. The number of stopovers or total number of separate flights is decided before you set off and they usually cost a bit more than a basic return flight.

**Ticketless Travel** Airlines are gradually waking up to the realisation that paper tickets are unnecessary encumbrances. On simple one-way or return trips, reservations details can be held on computer and the passenger merely shows ID to claim their seat.

**Transferred Tickets** Airline tickets cannot be transferred from one person to another. Travellers sometimes try to sell the return half of their ticket, but officials can ask you to prove that you are the person named on the ticket. On an international flight, tickets are compared with passports.

also offers round-the-world air fares for New York-Hong Kong-Bangkok-Bombay/Delhi-Europe-London-New York from US$1299. Ticket Planet's Web site, www.ticketplanet .com, will have the most up-to-date fares.

While airlines themselves can rarely match the prices of the discounters, they are worth checking if only to get benchmark prices to use for comparison. Tickets bought directly from airlines may also have fewer restrictions and/or less strict cancellation policies than those bought from discounters (though this is not always true).

Cheapest from the USA are: THAI, China Airlines, Korean Air, EVA Air and CP Air. Each has a budget and/or 'super Apex' fare that costs around US$800 to US$1200 return from Los Angeles, San Francisco or Seattle (add US$150 to US$200 from the East Coast). THAI is the most overbooked of these airlines from December to March and June to August, hence flights during these months may experience schedule delays (if you can get a seat at all). Korean Air occasionally runs special fares of just US$550 to US$600 return between San Francisco or Los Angeles and Bangkok. Several of the airlines mentioned also fly out of New York, Dallas, Chicago and Atlanta – add another US$150 to US$250 to their lowest fares.

EVA Air offers the 'Evergreen Deluxe' class between the USA and Bangkok, via Taipei, which has business-class sized seats and personal movie screens for about the same cost as regular economy fares on most other airlines.

**Canada** Travel CUTS has offices in all major cities. The Toronto *Globe & Mail* and the *Vancouver Sun* carry travel agents' ads.

Canadian Airlines International flies from Vancouver to Bangkok with fares beginning at around C$950 to C$1100 return for advance-purchase excursion fares. Travellers living in eastern Canada will usually find the best deals out of New York or San Francisco, adding fares from Toronto or Montreal (see The USA entry).

**Asia** There are regular flights to Bangkok International Airport from every major city in Asia, and it's not so difficult dealing with intra-Asia flights as most airlines offer similar fares. Here is a sample of estimated one-way intra-Asia fares from Bangkok, current at the time of writing. Travellers should note that some Bangkok travel agencies have a shocking reputation for taking money and then delaying or not coming through with the tickets, or providing tickets with limited validity periods or severe use restrictions. There are a lot of perfectly honest agents, but beware of the rogues.

Return tickets are usually double the one-way fare, though occasionally airlines run special discounts for such tickets, and you may be able to get around 25% off. For fares in the reverse direction, convert to local currency.

| around Asia | fare (US$) |
| --- | --- |
| Calcutta | 190 |
| Colombo | 264 |
| Denpasar | 340 |
| Ho Chi Minh City | 121 |
| Hong Kong | 185 |
| Kathmandu | 254 |
| Kuala Lumpur | 142 |
| Kunming | 137 |
| Manila | 270 |
| Mumbai (Bombay) | 482 |
| Osaka | 290 |
| Penang | 110 |
| Phnom Penh | 101 |
| Seoul | 460 |
| Singapore | 177 |
| Taipei | 303 |
| Tokyo | 483 |
| Vientiane | 68 |
| Yangon | 93 |

**Regional Services** Several carriers have regional air services to Myanmar (Burma), Vietnam, Laos and Cambodia. Routes to/from Thailand by foreign carriers include Yunnan Airways from Kunming to Bangkok; Silk Air between Singapore and Phuket; Dragonair between Hong Kong and Phuket; Malaysia Airlines between Kuala Lumpur and Hat Yai; Royal Air Cambodge between Bangkok and Phnom Penh; Lao Aviation between Bangkok and Vientiane; Myanmar Airways International and Biman Bangladesh

Airlines between Yangon and Bangkok; Vietnam Airlines between Bangkok and Ho Chi Minh City; and Air Mandalay between Chiang Mai and Mandalay.

**Booking Problems** The booking of flights in and out of Bangkok during the high season (December to March) can be difficult. For air travel during these months you should book as far in advance as possible. Also, be sure to reconfirm return or ongoing tickets when you arrive in Thailand (THAI claims this isn't necessary with its tickets). Failure to reconfirm can mean losing your reservation.

## Airline Offices
Bangkok is a major centre for international flights throughout Asia, and Bangkok International Airport is a busy one. Domestic flights operated by THAI and Bangkok Airways also fan out from Bangkok all over the country. Addresses of airline offices in Bangkok are:

**Air France** (☎ 635 1186, res 635 1199) 20th floor, Vorawat Bldg, 849 Th Silom

**Air New Zealand** (☎ 254 8440) 14th floor, Sindhorn Bldg, 130-132 Th Withayu

**All Nippon Airways** (ANA; ☎ 238 5121) 2nd & 4th floor, CP Tower, 313 Th Silom

**American Airlines** (☎ 254 1270) 518/5 Th Ploenchit

**Bangkok Airways** (☎ 229 3434, res 229 3456) Queen Sirikit National Convention Center, Th Ratchadaphisek Tat Mai, Khlong Toey

**British Airways** (☎ 636 1700) 990 Th Phra Ram IV

**Canadian Airlines International** (☎ 251 4521, 254 8376) Maneeya Bldg, 518/5 Th Ploenchit

**Cathay Pacific Airways** (☎ 263 0606) 11th floor, Ploenchit Tower, 898 Th Ploenchit

**EVA Air** (☎ 367 3388, res 240 0890) 2nd floor, Green Tower, 3656–4-5 Th Phra Ram IV

**Garuda Indonesia** (☎ 285 64703) 27th floor, Lumphini Tower, 1168/77 Th Phra Ram IV

**Japan Airlines** (JAL; ☎ 692 5185–6, res 692 5151/60) JAL Bldg, 254/1 Ratchadaphisek

**KLM-Royal Dutch Airlines** (☎ 679 1100, ext 2) 19th floor, Thai Wah Tower II, 21/133-134 Th Sathon Tai

**Korean Air** (☎ 267 0985, res 635 0465–72) 9th floor, Kongboonma Bldg, 699 Th Silom

**Lao Aviation** (☎ 236 9822–3) Ground floor, Silom Plaza, 491/17 Th Silom

**Lufthansa Airlines** (☎ 264 2484, res 264 2400) 18th floor, Q House, Asoke Bldg, 66 Soi 21, Th Sukhumvit

**Malaysia Airlines** (☎ 263 0520–32, res 263 0565/71) 20th floor, Ploenchit Tower, 898 Th Ploenchit

**Myanmar Airways International** (☎ 630 0334–8) 23rd floor, Jewelry Trade Center Bldg, 919/298 Th Silom

**Qantas Airways** (☎ 636 1770, res 636 1747) 14th floor, Abdulrahim Place, 990 Th Phra Ram IV

**Royal Air Cambodge** (☎ 653 2261, res 653 2261–6) 17th floor, Pacific Place Bldg, 142 Th Sukhumvit

**Royal Brunei Airlines** (☎ 233 0056) 4th floor, Charn Issara Tower, 942/135 Th Phra Ram IV

**Singapore Airlines** (SIA; ☎ 236 5301, res 236 0440) 12th floor, Silom Center Bldg, 2 Th Silom

**Swissair** (☎ 636 2160–6) 21st floor, Abdulrahim Place, 990 Th Phra Ram IV

**Thai Airways International** (THAI; head office, ☎ 513 0121, res 280 0060) 89 Th Vibhavadi Rangsit; (☎ 234 3100–19) 485 Th Silom; (☎ 280 0110, res 280 0060) 6 Th Lan Luang; (☎ 215 2020–1) Asia Hotel, 296 Th Phayathai; (☎ 535 2081–2, 523 6121) Bangkok International Airport, Don Muang; (☎ 223 9746–48) 3rd floor, Room 310-311, Grand China Bldg, 215 Th Yaowarat

**United Airlines** (☎ 253 0559, res 253 0558) 14th floor, Sindhorn Bldg, 130-132 Th Withayu

**Vietnam Airlines** (☎ 656 9056–8) 7th floor, Ploenchit Center Bldg, Soi 2 Th Sukhumvit

## ROAD
## Other Parts of Thailand
**Government Bus** Several types of buses ply the roads of Thailand. The cheapest but slowest are the ordinary government-run buses, *rót thamádaa,* that stop in every little town and for every waving hand along the highway. For some destinations, smaller towns especially, these orange buses are your only choice, but at least they leave frequently. The government also runs faster, more comfortable, but less frequent air-conditioned buses called *rót ae, rót pràp aakàat* or *rót thua;* painted with blue markings. If these are available to your destination, they are your best choice since they don't cost much more than the ordinary stop-in-every-town buses. The government bus company is called Baw Khaw Saw, an abbreviation of

Borisat Khon. Every city and town in Thailand linked by bus transportation has a Baw Khaw Saw terminal, even if it's just a patch of dirt by the roadside.

The service on the government air-con buses is usually quite good and includes a beverage service and video. On longer routes (eg, Bangkok–Chiang Mai, Bangkok–Nong Khai), the air-con buses even distribute claim checks (receipt dockets) for your baggage. Longer routes may also offer two classes of air-con bus, regular and 1st class; the latter has toilets. 'VIP' buses have fewer seats (30 to 34 instead of 44; some routes have Super VIP buses, with only 24 seats) so that each seat reclines more. Sometimes these are called *rót nawn* (sleepers). Occasionally you'll get a government air-con bus with broken air-con or seats that aren't up to standard, but in general they're more reliable than the private tour buses.

**Private Bus** Private buses run between Bangkok and major tourist and business destinations: Chiang Mai, Surat, Ko Samui, Phuket, Hat Yai, Pattaya, Hua Hin and a number of others. These can be booked through most hotels or any travel agency, although it's best to book directly through a bus office to ensure you get what you pay for.

Fares vary from company to company, but usually not by more than a few baht. However, fare differences between the government and private bus companies can be substantial. Using Surat Thani as an example, government buses cost around 180B for the ordinary bus or 346B (1st class) for the air-con, while the private companies charge up to 535B. On the other hand, to Chiang Mai the private buses often cost less than the government buses, although those that charge less offer inferior service. Departures for some private companies are more frequent than for the equivalent government-bus route.

The private air-con buses are usually no more comfortable than the government air-con buses and feature similarly narrow seats and a hair-raising ride. The trick the tour companies use to make their buses seem more comfortable is to make you think you're not on a bus by turning up the air-con until your knees knock (take warm clothes), handing out pillows and blankets, and serving free soft drinks. On overnight journeys the buses usually stop en route and passengers are woken up to get off the bus for a free meal of fried rice or rice soup. A few companies even treat you to a meal before a long overnight trip.

Like their state-run equivalents, the private companies offer VIP (sleeper) buses on long hauls. In general, private bus companies that deal mostly with Thais are good, while tourist-oriented ones are the worst as they know very few customers will be returning.

In recent years the service on many private lines has declined, especially on the Bangkok-Chiang Mai, Bangkok-Ko Samui, Surat-Phuket and Surat-Krabi routes.

Sometimes the cheaper lines – especially those booked on Th Khao San (Khao San Rd) – switch vehicles at the last moment so that instead of the roomy air-con bus advertised, you're stuck with a cramped van with broken air-con. Another problem with private companies is that they generally spend more time cruising the city for passengers before getting under way, meaning that they rarely leave at the advertised departure time.

Out of Bangkok, the safest, most reliable private bus services are the ones that operate from the three official Baw Khaw Saw terminals rather than from hotels or guesthouses. Picking up passengers from any points except these official terminals is actually illegal, and services promised are often not delivered. Although it can be a hassle getting out to the Baw Khaw Saw terminals, you're generally rewarded with safer, more reliable and punctual service. See the Bus Terminals entry in this section for further details.

**Safety & Service** Statistically, private buses meet with more accidents than government air-con buses. Turnovers on tight corners and head-on collisions with trucks are most likely due to driver inexperience on a particular route. This in turn is probably a result of the companies opening and folding so frequently, and because of the high priority given to making good time.

GETTING THERE & AWAY

As private bus fares are typically higher than government bus fares, the private bus companies attract a better heeled clientele among the Thais, as well as among foreign tourists. One result of this is that a private bus loaded with money or the promise of money is a temptation for upcountry bandits. Hence, private buses occasionally get robbed by bands of thieves. These incidents are diminishing, however, due to increased security under provincial administration.

Large-scale robberies never occur on the ordinary government buses, very rarely on the government air-con buses and rarely on the trains. Accidents, however, are not unknown on the government buses, so the train still comes out as the safest means of transport in Thailand.

Keep an eye on your bags when riding buses – pilfering by stealth is still the most popular form of robbery in Thailand, though again the risks are not that great – just be aware. Most pilfering seems to take place on the private bus runs between Bangkok and Chiang Mai, especially on the buses booked on Th Khao San. Keep zippered bags locked and well secured.

When travelling on night buses take particular care of your belongings. Some of the long-distance buses leaving from Bangkok now issue claim checks for luggage stored under the bus, but valuables are still best kept on your person or within reach.

**Bus Terminals** There are three main public bus (Baw Khaw Saw) terminals. The Northern & North-Eastern bus terminal (☎ 936 3660 for Northern routes, ☎ 936 0667 for North-Eastern routes) is on Th Kamphaeng Phet, just north of Chatuchak Park. It's also commonly called the Moh Chit station *(sathǎanii mǎw chít),* or, since it moved to a newer air-con building on the other side of the highway a little farther north, it's sometimes referred to as 'New' Moh Chit *(mǎw chít mài).* Buses depart from here for North and North-Eastern destinations like Chiang Mai and Nakhon Ratchasima (Khorat), as well as places closer to Bangkok such as Ayuthaya and Lopburi. Buses to Aranya Prathet also go from here, not from the Eastern

bus terminal as you might expect. Air-con city bus Nos 4, 10 and 29, along with a dozen or more ordinary city buses, all pass the terminal. The Mo Chit Skytrain station is also within walking distance of the bus terminal.

The Eastern bus terminal (☎ 391 2504), the departure point for buses to Pattaya, Rayong, Chanthaburi and other points east, is a long way out along Th Sukhumvit, at Soi 40 (Soi Ekamai) opposite Soi 63. Most folks call it Ekamai station *(sathǎanii èkamai).* Air-con bus Nos 1, 8, 11, 13 and 38 all pass this station, and the Skytrain stops at its own Ekamai station in front of Soi 40.

The Southern bus terminal (☎ 435 1200, 434 7192), for buses south to Phuket, Surat Thani and closer centres to the west like Nakhon Pathom and Kanchanaburi, has one Thonburi location for both ordinary and air-con buses at the intersection of Hwy 338 (Th Nakhon Chaisi) and Th Phra Pinklao. A convenient way to reach the station is by ordinary city bus Nos 124 and 127.

Allow an hour to reach the Northern bus terminal from Banglamphu or anywhere along the river, and more than an hour to reach the Southern bus terminal. The Eastern bus terminal takes 30 to 45 minutes under most traffic conditions. During gridlock, eg, Friday afternoons before a holiday, it can take up to three hours to get across town to the terminals by public transport.

### Other Countries

**Malaysia** You can cross the west coast border between Malaysia and Thailand by taking a bus to one side of the border and changing to another bus on the other side, the most obvious direct route being between Hat Yai and Alor Setar. This is the route used by taxis and buses, but there's a 1km-long stretch of no-man's land between the Thai border control at Sadao (also known as Dan Nok) and the Malaysian one at Changlun; which is a hassle because you'll have to walk.

It's much easier to go to Padang Besar, where the train line crosses the border. Here you can get a bus right up to the border, walk across and take another bus or taxi on the other side. On either side you'll most likely be mobbed by taxi and *moto* (small motorcycle) drivers wanting to take you to Immigration. It's better to walk over the railway by footbridge into Thailand, and then ignore the touts until you get to 'official' Thai taxis who will take you all the way to Hat Yai, with a stop at the immigration office (2.5km from the border) for around 50B. A relatively new immigration-and-customs office and bus/train station complex has been constructed on the Thai side, making the whole transition smoother.

A daily bus runs between Alor Setar, Hat Yai and Kota Bharu and reverse.

There's also a border crossing at Keroh (Thai side – Betong), right in the middle between the east and west coasts. This may be used more now that the Penang to Kota Bharu road is open.

**Laos** A 1174m-Australian-financed bridge across the Mekong River near Nong Khai opened in April 1994. Called the Thai-Lao Friendship Bridge (Saphan Mittaphap Thai-Lao), it spans a section of the river between Ban Jommani on the Thai side to Tha (pier) Na Leng on the Lao side – very near the old vehicle ferry.

Construction began in early 1996 on a second Mekong bridge to span the river between Thailand's Chiang Khong and Laos' Huay Xai. Although it was supposed to be operational by early 1998, the project was abandoned in 1997 following the drastic fall in the baht. If it ever resumes development, the bridge will link Thailand with China by road via Laos' Bokeo and Luang Nam Thai provinces – part of an ambitious transport project partially financed by the Asian Development Bank (ADB) and known as the Chiang Rai–Kunming Road.

Another bridge under discussion would span the Mekong at Mukdahan (opposite Savannakhet) to create a land link between Thailand and Vietnam. The ADB's vaunted title for this development project is 'the Thailand-Lao PDR-Vietnam East-West Corridor'. A similar plan for Nakhon Phanom (opposite Laos' Tha Khaek) is currently undergoing a feasibility study.

A land crossing from Pakse (Champasak Province) in Laos to Chong Mek in Thailand's Ubon Ratchathani Province is open to foreign visitors. You no longer need a special visa to use this crossing, except for a normal Lao visa if crossing from Thailand to Laos. In the opposite direction, from Laos to Thailand, you can receive a visa on arrival, although you will probably have to go to Phibun Mangsahan, near Ubon, to get the visa. The immigration officers at Chong Mek will allow you to cross the border into Thailand and proceed to Phibun for this purpose.

**Myanmar** Several border crossings between Thailand and Myanmar are open to day-trippers or short excursions in the vicinity. As yet none of these link up with routes to Yangon or Mandalay or other cities of any size. Nor are you permitted to enter Thailand by land from Myanmar.

**Cambodia** As of early 1998, there has been a legal border crossing between Cambodia and Thailand at Aranya Prathet, opposite the Cambodian town of Poi Pet. If you're coming from Cambodia by rail or road, you don't need a Thai visa (or rather you will be granted a free 30-day tourist visa on arrival), but in the reverse direction you will need a Cambodian visa. The latter is available from the Cambodian embassy in Bangkok.

Cambodian officials usually request a US$1 'departure tax' when you arrive at the Cambodian-Thai border. The border is open from 8 am to 6 pm daily. You'll have to take a taxi or moto an additional 4km from the crossing to reach Aranya Prathet itself, from where there are regular buses (and trains) onward to Bangkok and other points in Eastern Thailand.

Other areas along the border won't be safe for land crossings until mines and booby traps left over from the conflict between the Khmer Rouge and the Vietnamese are removed or detonated.

**China** Thailand, Laos, China and Myanmar have agreed to the construction of a ring road through all four countries. The western half of the loop will proceed from Mae Sai, Thailand, to Jinghong, China, via Myanmar's Tachileik (opposite Mae Sai),

GETTING THERE & AWAY

Kengtung and Mengla (near Dalau on the China-Myanmar border), while the eastern half will extend from Chiang Khong, Thailand, to Jinghong via Huay Xai, Laos (opposite Chiang Khong), and Boten, Laos (on the Yunnanese border south of Jinghong).

The stretch between Tachileik and Daluo is still under construction (some sections towards the Chinese border are complete) but it's possible to arrange one- to three-day trips as far as Kengtung in Myanmar's Shan State. A road between Huay Xai and Boten already exists (built by the Chinese in the 1960s and 1970s) but needs upgrading. Once the roads are built and visa formalities are worked out, this loop will provide alternative travel connections between China and South-East Asia, in much the same way as the Karakoram Hwy has forged new links between China and South Asia. It's difficult to predict when all the logistical variables will be settled, but progress so far points to a cleared path by 2006.

The eastern half of this loop, from Boten to Huay Xai, Laos, and across to Chiang Khong, Thailand, can be done relatively easily now, though roadways between Boten and Huay Xai are a little rough.

## TRAIN
### Other Parts of Thailand

The government railway network run by the State Railway of Thailand (SRT) is quite efficient and inexpensive. After travelling several thousand kilometres by train and bus, I have to say that the train wins hands down as the best form of public transport in the kingdom. The SRT operates passenger trains in three classes – 1st, 2nd and 3rd – but each class varies considerably depending on whether you're on an ordinary, rapid or express train. Third class is often the cheapest way to cover a long distance. A journey by 2nd class is about the same as a private tour bus but much safer and more comfortable. Trains take a bit longer than chartered buses on the same journey, but are worth the extra travel time, on overnight trips especially.

**Rail Routes** Four main rail lines cover 4500km along the northern, southern, north-eastern and eastern routes. There are several side routes, notably between Nakhon Pathom and Nam Tok (stopping in Kanchanaburi) in the western Central region, and between Thung Song and Kantang (stopping in Trang) in the South. The southern line splits at Hat Yai, one route going to Sungai Kolok on the Malaysian east-coast border, via Yala, and the other route going to Padang Besar in the west, also on the Malaysian border.

**Bangkok Terminals** Most long-distance trains originate from Bangkok's Hualamphong station. Before a railway bridge was constructed across the Chao Phraya River in 1932, all southbound trains left from Thonburi's Bangkok Noi station. Today this station services commuter and short-line trains to Kanchanaburi/Nam Tok, Suphanburi, Ratchaburi and Nakhon Pathom (Ratchaburi and Nakhon Pathom can also be reached by train from Hualamphong). A slow night train to Chumphon and Lang Suan, both in Southern Thailand, leaves nightly from Thonburi (Bangkok Noi) station but it's rarely used by long-distance travellers.

**Bookings** Trains can be especially difficult to book around holiday time, eg, the middle of April approaching the Songkhran Festival, during Chinese New Year (around January/February) and during the high season months of December and February. At any time of year, it's advisable to book trains out of Bangkok as far in advance as possible – a minimum of a week for popular routes such as the northern line to Chiang Mai and southern line to Hat Yai, especially if you want a sleeper. For the north-eastern and eastern lines a few days will suffice. Mid-week departures are always easier to book than weekends; during some months of the year you can easily book a sleeper even one day before departure as long as it's on a Tuesday, Wednesday or Thursday.

Advance bookings may be made one to 60 days before your intended date of departure. If you want to book tickets in advance, go to Hualamphong station in Bangkok, walk through the front of the station house and go straight to the back right-hand corner

PHILIP GAME

JOHN ELK III

PAUL BEINSSEN

JOE CUMMINGS

Bangkok traffic can be a little too much to handle sometimes – why not take a boat or a train to get around instead?

Vimanmek Teak Mansion, one of the world's largest teak buildings, was home to King Rama V.

Nineteenth-century buddha's are one treasure found at the city's many antique stores.

where a sign says 'Advance Booking' (open from 8.30 am to 4 pm daily). The other ticket windows, lined up in front of the platforms, are for same-day purchases, mostly 3rd class. From 5 to 8.30 am and from 4 to 11 pm, advance bookings can also be made at windows No 2 through 11.

At the Advance Booking office, you simply take a queue number, wait until your number appears on one of the electronic marquees, report to the desk above which your number appears and make your ticket arrangements. Only cash in baht is accepted.

Note that buying a return ticket does not necessarily guarantee you a seat on the way back, it only means you do not have to buy a ticket for the return. If you want a guaranteed seat reservation it's best to make that reservation for the return immediately upon arrival at your destination.

Booking trains back to Bangkok is generally not as complex as booking trains out of Bangkok; however, at some stations this can be quite difficult (eg, buying a ticket from Surat Thani to Bangkok).

Tickets between any stations in Thailand can be purchased at Hualamphong station (☎ 223 3762, 225 6964, 224 7788, or 225 0300, ext 5200 03). You can also make advance bookings at Don Muang station (across from Bangkok International Airport) and at the Advance Booking offices at train stations in the larger cities. Advance reservations can be made by phone from anywhere in Thailand. Throughout Thailand, SRT ticket offices are generally open from 8.30 am to 6 pm on weekdays and 8.30 am to noon on weekends and public holidays. Train tickets can also be purchased at certain travel agencies in Bangkok. It's much simpler to book trains through these agencies than to book them at the station; however, they usually add a surcharge of 50B to 100B to the ticket price.

**Charges & Surcharges** There is a 60B surcharge for express trains *(rót dùan),* 40B for rapid trains *(rót rehw).* These trains are somewhat faster than the ordinary trains, as they make fewer stops. On the northern line during the day there is a 70B surcharge for 2nd-class seats in air-con cars. For the special

express trains *(rót dùan phísèt)* that run between Bangkok and Padang Besar or between Bangkok and Chiang Mai, there is an 80B surcharge (or 120B if a meal is included – on special diesel railcars only), or 80B between Bangkok and Chiang Mai.

The charge for 2nd-class sleeping berths is 100B for an upper berth and 150B for a lower berth (or 130B and 200B respectively on a special express). The difference between upper and lower is that there is a window next to the lower berth and a little more headroom. The upper berth is still comfortable enough. For 2nd-class sleepers with air-con add 250/320B per upper/lower ticket. No sleepers are available in 3rd class.

Air-con really isn't necessary on night trains, since a steady breeze circulates through the train and cools things down quickly. In fact air-con 2nd class can become uncomfortably cold at night and cannot be regulated by passengers, so choosing non-air-con might be your best bet.

All 1st-class cabins come with individually controlled air-con. A two-bed cabin costs 520B per person. Single cabins are no longer available, so if you're travelling alone you may be paired with another rail passenger, although the SRT takes great care not to mix genders.

You can figure on 500km costing around 200B in 2nd class (not counting the surcharges for rapid/express services), roughly twice that in 1st class and less than half in 3rd. Surprisingly, fares have changed only slightly over the last decade, in spite of an overall inflation rate in Thailand of 5% to 10% per annum, although supplemental charges have increased steadily. Currently the government continues to subsidise train travel to some extent, particularly 3rd class. However, there has been some talk of privatising the railway – the International Monetary Fund (IMF) has even urged this – which would of course ring the death knell for the passenger rail system as it has in most other formerly rail-faring countries of the world.

**Eating Facilities** Meal service is available in dining cars and at your seat in 2nd- and 1st-class cars. Menus change as frequently as the SRT changes catering services. For a while there were two menus, a 'special food' menu with 'special' prices (generally given to tourists) and a cheaper, more extensive menu. Nowadays all the meals seem a bit overpriced (75B to 200B on average) by Thai standards – if you're concerned with saving baht, bring your own.

Drinking water is provided, albeit in plastic bottles; sometimes it's free, sometimes it costs 5B to 10B per bottle.

Several readers have written to complain about being overcharged by meal servers on trains. If you do purchase food on board, be sure to check prices on the menu rather than trusting server quotes. Also check the bill carefully to make sure you haven't been overcharged.

**Station Services** Accurate, up-to-date information on train travel is available at the Rail Travel Aids counter at Hualamphong station. You can pick up timetables or ask questions about fares and scheduling – someone behind the counter usually speaks a little English. There are two types of timetable available: four condensed English timetables with fares, schedules and routes for rapid, express and special express trains on the four trunk lines; and four Thai timetables for each trunk line, with side lines as well. The Thai timetables give fares and schedules for all trains – ordinary, rapid and express, while the English timetables only display a couple of the ordinary routes.

All train stations in Thailand have baggage storage services (sometimes called the 'cloak room'). The rates and hours of operation vary from station to station. At Hualamphong station the hours are from 4 am to 10.30 pm daily, and left luggage costs 10B per day per piece for up to five days, after which it goes up to 15B per day. Hualamphong station also has a 10B shower service in the rest rooms.

Hualamphong Station is jammed with modern coffee shops and a coupon-style cafeteria. All stations in the provincial capitals have restaurants or cafeterias as well as various snack vendors. These stations also offer an advance-booking service for rail travel anywhere in Thailand. Although Hat Yai station is the only one with a hotel attached, there are usually hotels within walking distance of other major stations.

Hualamphong station has a couple of travel agencies where other kinds of transport can be booked, but beware of touts who try and drag you there saying the trains are fully booked when they aren't. Avoid the travel agencies outside the station, which have very poor reputations. Near the front of the station, at one end of the foyer, a Mail Boxes Etc (MBE) provides mailing, courier and packing services from 7.30 am to 7.30 pm Monday to Friday, 9 am to 4 pm Saturday and 9 am to 8 pm Sunday.

**Rail Passes** The SRT issues a couple of rail passes that may save on fares if you plan to ride Thai trains extensively within a relatively short interval. These passes are available in Thailand only, and can be purchased at Hualamphong station.

The cost for 20 days of unlimited 2nd- or 3rd-class rail travel (blue pass) is 1100B, not including supplementary charges, or 2000B including all supplementary charges; children four to 12 pay half the adult fare. Supplementary charges include all extra charges for rapid, express, special express and air-con. Passes must be validated at a local station before boarding the first train. The price of the pass includes seat reservations that, if required, can be made at any SRT ticket office. The pass is valid until midnight on the last day of the pass. However, if the journey is commenced before midnight on the last day of validity, the passenger can use the pass until that train reaches its destination.

Do the passes represent a true savings over buying individual train tickets? The answer is yes, but only if you can average more than 110km by rail per day for 20 days. If you travel at these levels (or less), then you'll be paying the same amount (or more) as you would if you bought ordinary train tickets directly. On less crowded routes where there are plenty of available 2nd-class seats, passes save time that might otherwise be spent at ticket windows, but for high-demand routes (eg, from Bangkok to Chiang Mai or Hat Yai) you'll still need to make reservations.

## Malaysia

Riding the rails from Singapore to Bangkok via Butterworth in Malaysia, is a great way to travel to Thailand – as long as you don't count on making a smooth change between the Kereta Api Tanah Melayu (KTM; Malaysia's state railway) and State Railway of Thailand (SRT) trains. The Thai train almost always leaves on time, but the Malaysian train rarely arrives on time. Unfortunately, the Thai train leaves Padang Besar even if the Malaysian railway express from Kuala Lumpur (or the 2nd-class connection from Butterworth) is late. To be on the safe side, purchase the Malaysian and Thai portions of your ticket with departures on consecutive days and plan a Butterworth/Penang stopover.

**Eastern & Oriental Express** In 1991 the SRT, the KTM and Singapore's Eastern & Oriental Express Co (E&O) purchased the rights from Paris' Venice Simplon to operate the new *Eastern & Oriental Express* between Singapore and Bangkok. The original *Orient Express* ran between Paris and Constantinople in the 1880s and was considered the grandest train trip in the world; an updated version along the same route was resurrected around 20 years ago to great success. The Singapore-Bangkok version is the first to start and end in the Orient and appears to be even more successful than its historical antecedent. It is also the first rail journey ever to make a direct link between Singapore and Bangkok without a change of trains.

The *Eastern & Oriental Express* travels at an average speed of 60km/h, completing the 2043km Singapore to Bangkok journey in about 40 hours, with a two-hour Butterworth stopover and tour of Georgetown, Penang. As in Europe, this new train offers cruise-ship luxury on rails. Passengers dine, sleep and entertain in 22 train carriages imported from New Zealand and refurbished using lots of brass, teak and old-world tapestry, fitted in 1930s style by the same French designer who remodelled the *Orient Express* in Europe.

The train features two restaurant cars, a saloon car and a bar car, with a combination bar car and open-air observation deck bringing up the rear. All accommodation is in deluxe private cabins with shower, toilet and individually controlled air-con; passengers are attended by round-the-clock cabin stewards (nearly two-thirds of the front-line staff are Thai) in the true pukka tradition.

Tariffs begin at (brace yourself) US$1390 per person for the full route in the bunk-style sleeper and US$2060 in a more spacious state room; half-car presidential suites are available for a mere US$2800. These fares include all *table d'hote* meals aboard the train and sightseeing tours along the way. Half routes from Bangkok or Singapore to Butterworth or vice versa are available for a bit more than half the fare, no hotel included. Honeymoon couples comprise a significant part of the clientele.

The *Eastern & Oriental Express* continues on from Bangkok to Chiang Mai for a separate price of US$900/1150/1650. The train can be booked through E&O in Singapore (☎ 392 3500), Queensland, Australia (☎ 07-3247 6555) or through many travel agents in both cities. *Eastern & Oriental Express* reservations and information can also be obtained by calling the following numbers: UK (☎ 020-7805 5100); and USA (☎ 800-524 2420). Or visit its Web site at www.orient-express.com.

## Laos

A joint-venture agreement between the Lao government and a new company called Lao Railways Transportation was signed in 1998 to establish a railway line along the middle of the Friendship Bridge. After a feasibility study is completed, the line, which will reportedly extend to Vientiane and Luang Prabang, is supposed to become operational in four years. Like most other transport projects in Laos, however, it will probably take much longer – if it ever happens at all.

Another rail link undergoing a feasibility study is a spur eastward from Udon Thani, across the Mekong to Tha Khaek, Lao PDR, and across Laos to connect with the Ho Chi Minh City–Hanoi railway in Vietnam.

## China

At a 1995 summit meeting in Bangkok, representatives of the Association of South-East Asian Nations (ASEAN) proposed the completion of a regional rail network linking Singapore with China via Malaysia, Thailand, Laos and Vietnam. In all but Laos and Cambodia, railbeds for such a circuit already exist. Current plans call for the extension of a rail line across the Mekong River from Thailand to Laos via the existing Thai-Lao Friendship Bridge. If completed this line may someday connect with a proposed north-south line from Vientiane to Savannakhet in Laos and then with a west-east line from Savannakhet to Dong Ha, Vietnam.

## BOAT
## Malaysia

There are several ways of travelling between Thailand's southern peninsula and Malaysia by sea. Simplest is to take a long-tail boat between Satun, right down in the south-west corner of Thailand, and Kuala Perlis. The cost is about M$5, or 50B, and boats cross over fairly regularly.

You can also take a ferry to the Malaysian island of Langkawi from Satun. There are immigration posts at both ports so you can make the crossing quite officially.

From Satun you can take a bus to Hat Yai and then arrange transport to other points in the south or farther north. It's possible to bypass Hat Yai altogether by heading directly for Phuket or Krabi via Trang.

You can also take a ferry to Ban Taba on the east coast of Thailand from near Kota Bharu.

On-again, off-again passenger ferry services also run between Pulau Langkawi and Phuket, Thailand. These services never seem to last longer than nine months or so – your best bet is to make inquiries through local travel agents to find out the latest on sea transport to/from Langkawi.

## Laos

It's legal for non-Thai foreigners to cross the Mekong River by ferry between Thailand and Laos at the following points: Nakhon Phanom (opposite Tha Khaek), Chiang Khong (opposite Huay Xai) and Mukdahan (opposite Savannakhet).

Thais are permitted to cross at all of the above checkpoints plus at least a half-dozen others from Thailand's Chiang Rai, Loei and Nong Khai provinces, including Chiang Saen, Pak Chom, Chiang Khan, Beung Kan, Ban Pak Huay, Ban Nong Pheu and Ban Khok Phai. For the most part these checkpoints are only good for day crossings (Thai and Lao citizens only). In the future one or more of these may become available for entry by foreign visitors as well.

## Myanmar

It is legal to enter Thailand via Ranong by boat from Kawthoung, the port at Myanmar's southernmost tip. Boats run regularly throughout the day from the main pier area in Kawthoung and cost 50B per person or you can charter a boat for 150B or 200B. These boats moor at Saphan Pla, a large dock area about 6km south of the town of Ranong.

In the reverse direction you won't need a Myanmar visa for a day trip, but if you plan to stay overnight or to continue farther north, you'll need to arrive with a valid Myanmar visa in your passport.

## China

It's possible to reach Yunnan Province from Thailand by boat along the Mekong River. Several surveys of the waterway have been completed and a specially constructed express boat made its inaugural run between Sop Ruak, Chiang Rai Province and Yunnan Province in early 1994. At the time of writing, permission is restricted to very infrequent private tour groups, but it's reasonable to assume that in the future, if demand is high enough, a scheduled public service may become available. The boat trip takes six hours, which is considerably quicker than any currently possible road route. However, it's only navigable all the way to China during the rainy season and immediately after.

# Getting Around

Getting around Bangkok may be difficult for the uninitiated, but once you're familiar with the transport system the whole city is accessible. The main obstacle is traffic, which moves at a snail's pace during the day. This means advance planning is a must when you're attending scheduled events or making appointments. If you can, avoid the traffic and travel by river, canal or Skytrain.

Bangkok was once called the 'Venice of the East', but much of the original canal system has been filled in for road construction. Many smaller canals are hopelessly polluted and would probably have been filled in by now if it weren't for their important drainage function. Fortunately, in recent years several canal-boat services have been revived on the medium-sized canals.

## THE AIRPORT

A district directly north of Bangkok known as Don Muang is home to Bangkok International Airport, the busiest airport in South-East Asia. A second, larger airport is intended to replace Don Muang at Nong Ngu Hao, 20km east of Bangkok, in 2004.

During the past decade, the airport facilities at Bangkok International Airport have undergone a major redevelopment and are among the most modern and convenient in Asia. Immigration procedures are efficient, though it can be slow during peak arrival times (11 pm to midnight). Baggage claim is usually quick, and baggage trolleys are free for use inside the terminal.

The airport has the usual range of newsstands, souvenir shops and duty-free shopping. The book and magazine selection is better in the domestic terminal. If you've got time, there's a good bookshop at the Amari Airport; you can walk there across the enclosed footbridge from Terminal 1.

If you're feeling peckish or in need of a drink, we recommend the *Taurus Brewhouse* (☎ 535 6861) a large German-style brew pub towards the south end of Terminal 2 on the 4th floor with an interesting range of beers brewed on the premises and an international menu, open 6 pm to midnight daily. Otherwise, try the reasonably priced *Rajthanee Food Mall*, a small 24-hour cafeteria area, 4th floor, Terminal 1. If you're hungry and broke, the cheapest place to eat is the *Louie's Tavern Food Centre* off the hard-to-find parking corridor between the international and domestic terminals. As at many other urban food courts in Thailand, you buy refundable coupons from a separate booth to pay for dishes (15B to 35B) ordered at individual booths. It's open 8 am to 9 pm daily.

### Terminal Shuttle

Thai Airways International (THAI) operates free air-con shuttle buses plying two routes between the international and domestic terminals. Both routes go between Terminal 1 and the domestic terminal, so if you're just going between these buildings, you can jump on any bus that comes along. In addition Route A-1 continues on to cargo agent 1 building and the VIP rooms building. This shuttle runs from 5.20 to 11 pm daily, departing every 20 minutes.

### Currency Exchange

The foreign currency booths (Thai Military Bank, Bangkok Bank, Krung Thai Bank) on the ground floor of the arrival hall and in the departure lounge of both terminals give a good rate of exchange, so there's no need to wait till you're in the city centre to change money if you need Thai currency. Each of these banks also operates ATMs in the arrival and departure halls.

### Post & Telephone

There is a 24-hour post/telephone office with a Home Country Direct phone service in the departure hall (3rd floor) of Terminal 1. Another 24-hour post office is in the departure lounge; a third one, in the arrival hall, is open 9 am to 5 pm Monday to Friday.

The Communications Authority of Thailand (CAT) operates a 24-hour Telecommunications Center on the 2nd floor of Terminal 2, where you can make international phone calls using credit card, reverse-charge and Home Country Direct facilities.

## Email & Internet Access

The Telecommunications Center also offers three computer terminals rigged for quick email and Net access. A 300B CATnet card will give you five hours of Internet access on these or any other CAT terminal in Thailand, valid for one year.

On the 4th floor of Terminal 2, Net Center has about seven computer terminals, and charges 75B for the first 15 minutes, 5B per minute thereafter – pretty expensive for Thailand. It accepts credit cards.

## Left Luggage & Day Rooms

Left-luggage facilities (70B per piece for under 24 hours, after which the charge is 35B for every 12 hours) are available in the departure hall in both terminals. Both are open 24 hours. In the transit lounge of Terminal 1, clean day rooms with washing and toilet facilities can be rented for US$86 a double per eight hours. Less-expensive rooms without bathrooms are available for US$31 per four-hour block.

## Hotel Reservations

The hotel reservation desks operated by the Thai Hotels Association (THA) at the back of the arrival hall in both terminals offer a selection of accommodation options in the city, but above guesthouse level (roughly 900B and above) only. THA staff can often arrange room rates well below normal walk-in rates.

There have been reports that the THA desks occasionally claim a hotel is full when it isn't, just to move you into a hotel that pays higher commissions. If you protest, the staff may ask you to speak to the 'reservations desk' on the phone – usually an accomplice who confirms the hotel is full. Dial the hotel yourself if you want to be certain.

There are usually one or two other desks in the arrival hall offering similar services, but THA seems to be the most reliable.

## Near the Airport

If you leave the airport building area and cross the expressway on the pedestrian bridge (just north of the passenger terminal), you'll find yourself in the Don Muang town area where there are all sorts of shops, a market, lots of small restaurants and food stalls, even a wat (temple, monastery), all within 100m or so of the airport.

The modern and luxurious Amari Airport Hotel (Map 1, ☎ 566 1020/1) has its own air-conditioned, enclosed footbridge from Terminal 1 and 'special ministay' daytime rates (from 8 am to 6 pm) for stays of up to a maximum of three hours. For additional accommodation information in the Don Muang area, see the Places to Stay chapter.

The Amari also has a selection of decent restaurants serving Italian, Japanese and Thai food.

## TO/FROM THE AIRPORT

Bangkok International Airport is located in the Don Muang district, approximately 25km north of Bangkok. You have a choice of transport modes from the airport to the city ranging in cost from 3.50B to 300B.

## Airport Bus

A 21-seat airport express bus service operates from Bangkok International Airport to four different Bangkok districts for 100B per person. Buses run every 15 minutes from 6 am to midnight. A map showing the designated stops is available at the airport; buses on each route make approximately six stops in each direction. A great boon to travellers on a budget, these buses mean you can avoid hassling with taxi drivers to get a reasonable fare as well as forgo the slow pace of the regular bus routes.

The Airport Bus counter is around 200m to the left (with your back to Terminal 1) of the left-most terminal exit. The routes are:

**A-1** To the Silom business district via Pratunam and Thanon (Th) Ratchadamri, stopping at big hotels like the Century, Indra, Grand Hyatt Erawan, Regent Bangkok and Dusit Thani.

**A-2** To Sanam Luang via Th Phayathai, Th Lan Luang, Th Ratchadamnoen Klang and Th Tanao; this is the route you want if you're going to the

Victory Monument, Democracy Monument, Siam Square or Banglamphu areas. In Banglamphu, it stops opposite the Food & Agriculture Organization headquarters on Th Phra Athit.

**A-3** To the Phrakhanong district via Th Sukhumvit, including Ekamai bus terminal (for buses east to Pattaya and Trat) and Soi 55 (Soi Thong Lor). Hotel stops include Ambassador and Delta Grand Pacific.

**A-4** To Hualamphong station via Th Phra Ram IV, Th Phayathai with stops at Mahboonkrong shopping centre and the Siam Inter-Continental Hotel.

## Public Bus

Cheapest of all are the public buses to Bangkok that stop on the highway in front of the airport. There are four air-con and two non-air-con bus routes that visitors find particularly useful for getting into the city. However, ordinary buses no longer accept passengers carrying luggage (you may get away with carrying a backpack on board, but it's officially against policy). It's worth paying the extra 12.50B for the air-con and almost guaranteed seating, especially in the hot season, since the trip to central Bangkok by bus usually takes an hour or more. Even better is the 100B express Airport Bus, described earlier.

Bus routes are as follows:

**Air-con bus No 29** Costs 16B and plies one of the most useful, all-purpose routes from the airport into the city, passing through the Siam Square and Hualamphong areas. After entering the city limits via Th Phahonyothin (which turns into Th Phayathai), the bus passes Th Phetburi (where you'll want to get off to change buses for Banglamphu), then Th Phra Ram I at the Siam Square/Mahboonkrong intersection (Map 5) – for buses out to Th Sukhumvit, or to walk to Soi Kasem San 1 for various lodgings – and finally turns right on Th Phra Ram IV to go to the Hualamphong district (where the main train station is located). You'll want to go the opposite way on Th Phra Ram IV for the Soi Ngam Duphli lodging area. No 29 runs only from 5.45 am to 8.30 pm, so if you're arriving on a late-night flight you'll miss it.

**Air-con bus No 13** (16B; operates 4.30 am to 9 pm) Also goes to Bangkok from the airport, travelling down Th Phahonyothin (like No 29), turning left at the Victory Monument to Th Ratchaprarop, then south to Th Ploenchit, where

it goes east along Th Sukhumvit all the way to Bang Na. This is definitely the one to catch if you're heading for the Th Sukhumvit area.

**Air-con bus No 4** (16B; operates 5.45 am to 8 pm) Begins with a route parallel to that of the No 29 bus – down Th Vibhavadi Rangsit to Th Ratchaprarop and Th Ratchadamri (Pratunam district), crossing Th Phetburi, Th Phra Ram I, Th Ploenchit and Th Phra Ram IV, then down Th Silom, left on Th Charoen Krung and across the river to Thonburi.

**Air-con bus No 10** (16B; operates 11 pm to 5 am) Travels from the airport all the way to the Southern bus terminal in Thonburi.

**Ordinary bus No 59** Costs only 3.50B (5B between 10 pm and 6 am) and operates 24 hours – it zigzags through the city to Banglamphu (the Democracy Monument area) from the airport, a trip that can take up to 1½ hours or more in heavy traffic. (Air-con No 59 costs 18B and operates from 6 am to 10 pm.)

**Ordinary bus No 29** (3.50B, or 5B from 11 pm to 5 am; operates 24 hours) Plies much the same route as air-con bus No 29.

## Train

You can also get into Bangkok from the airport by train. Just after leaving Terminal 1, turn right (north), cross the highway via the pedestrian bridge, turn left and walk about 100m towards Bangkok. Opposite the big Amari Airport Hotel is the small Don Muang station from where trains depart regularly to Bangkok. The 3rd-class fare from Don Muang is only 5B on the ordinary and commuter trains. Tickets for rapid or express trains cost 45B and 65B respectively.

Trains run frequently between 4.49 am and 8.18 pm, and it takes about 45 minutes to reach Hualamphong, the main station in central Bangkok. In the opposite direction trains run frequently between 7.45 am and 10 pm. To get to Banglamphu, you can walk from Hualamphong station to the bus stop almost opposite Wat Traimit (Map 6) and catch bus No 53.

## Taxi

Metered taxis waiting near the arrival area of the airport are supposed to be airport-regulated. Ignore the touts waiting in the arrival hall and buy a taxi ticket from the public taxi booth near the kerb outside the hall. Also be wary of touts from the old airport taxi mafia who may approach you with fares of around 200B. Their taxis have white-and-black plates and are not licensed to carry passengers, so you have less legal recourse in the event of an incident than if you take a licensed taxi (yellow-and-black plates). Robberies have reportedly occurred in these taxis.

Taxi fares vary according to destination and resultant meter reading; most destinations in central Bangkok cost around 200B to 300B. You also have to pay a 50B airport surcharge, and reimburse drivers for any toll charges paid if they take the tollway into the city (20B to 50B) depending on where you get off the tollway. Taking the tollway almost always saves time.

If you end up taking a flat-rate taxi, the driver should pay all toll charges. Two, three or even four passengers (if they don't have much luggage) can split the fare.

A few metered taxi drivers still try to renegotiate the fare once you're inside the cab and quote a flat rate of 300B to 400B. Passengers now receive a bilingual Taxi-Meter Information sheet, issued by the Department of Land Transport, which indicates the name of the driver, the cab licence number, the date and the time. A phone number for registering complaints against the driver is listed on this sheet, so if you have a problem you should call and report the driver. The passenger – *not* the driver – is supposed to keep this sheet. The driver may want to glance at the sheet to read your destination, but you should receive it back immediately.

Metered taxis, flagged down on the highway in front of the airport (turn left from the arrival hall), are cheaper since they don't have to pay the 50B airport surcharge. When the queue at the public taxi desk is particularly long, it's sometimes faster to go upstairs or walk out to the highway and flag one down.

### THAI Limousine

Three companies maintain counters at the airport offering airport limousine service, which is really just a glorified air-con taxi. THAI Limousine (☎ 535 2801), Airport Associate Limousine (☎ 535 5905, 535-5361) and Prapirab Limousine (☎ 535 1894) all

have a starting rate of 650B to destinations in central Bangkok, more than double the usual meter taxi fare. The main advantage is not having to wait in the public taxi queue.

### Helicopter

The Shangri-La Hotel (Map 6, ☎ 236 7777) can arrange a helicopter service (for hotel guests only) from Bangkok International Airport to the hotel rooftop for around 14,000B per trip; minimum of three persons. An additional three people can fly for 5000B per person. The flight takes around 15 minutes.

### Pattaya

THAI operates direct air-con buses to Pattaya from the airport daily at 9 am, noon and 7 pm; the fare is 200B one way. Private sedans cost 1500B to 2500B per trip.

## BUS

You can save a lot of money in Bangkok by sticking to the Bangkok Metropolitan Transit Authority (BMTA) public buses, which cost 5B for any journey under 10km on the ordinary white-and-blue buses, or 3.50B on the red buses or smaller green buses. Smaller 'baht buses' plying the sois are painted red and maroon, and cost 2B each.

Cream-and-blue air-con buses are available for 6B for the first 8km, and increase by 2B increments up to 16B, depending on the distance travelled. New orange Euro 2 air-con buses cost 12B for any distance, while white-and-pink air-con buses cost 10B. The air-con buses are not only cooler, but are usually less crowded (all bets are off during rush hours).

Most bus lines run from 5 am to 11 pm, except for the all-night cream-and-red ordinary buses which run from 11 pm to 5 am on some routes, and cost 5B. Buddhist monks and novices ride for free.

One air-con service that's never overcrowded is the red-and-white painted Microbus – it stops taking passengers once every seat is filled. The fare is a flat rate of 25B – you deposit the money in a box at the front of the bus (exact change only). A couple of useful Microbus lines include: the No

## Novelty Bussing

Anyone who has tried to navigate Bangkok's public transport system knows that the experience can be, well…challenging! The Bangkok Mass Transit Authority (BMTA) recently trialed some novel services in an attempt to improve the system – or at least attract some media attention. We can't predict whether these services will become a permanent fixture on Bangkok's street, or if they'll simply fizzle like an outdated publicity-stunt, but at least we can lend insight into the creative minds at work at BMTA.

In 2000, the BMTA responded to women's complaints about harassment, pickpocketing and snatch thieves on Thailand's Bangkok's bus system, by trialing a ladies-only bus run in May 2000.

The BMTA claimed the innovation was such a success that Lady Buses are now running hourly every day along 16 routes in the city – easily identifiable by their lady-like pink signs! The following Lady Bus routes may be handy for women travellers: Rangsit-Hua Lampong (No 29), Min Buri-Silom (air-con No 2) and Pak Nam-Sai Tai Mai bus terminal (air con No 11).

Public enthusiasm for the service spurred the BMTA to launch yet another line – the well-mannered bus, or the Culture Bus service. On the Culture Bus, chivalry is the order of the day, with men obliged to give up their seats to women, children and the elderly, and conductors obliged to be outstandingly polite and helpful. The polite system will consist of 80 vehicles running on eight different routes around Bangkok. The route most likely to be useful to travellers is Wat Si Nuan – Sanam Luang (No 80, non-air-con).

**Adapted from Lonely Planet Scoop travel news at www.lonelyplanet.com/scoop**

6, which starts on Th Si Phraya (near the River City complex) and proceeds to the Siam Square area, then out to Th Sukhumvit; and the No 1, which runs between the Victory Monument area and Banglamphu district.

All bus routes are numbered, and you'll usually find the numbers displayed somewhere on the front and rear windscreens, as well as on the kerb-facing side of the bus, and on some buses in little windows along the front roofline. If the number placard is printed on a yellow background, it means that it's an 'express' bus that uses elevated expressways for much of the route. These can be tricky to use if you don't already know where you want to get off, as there are far fewer stops.

BMTA recently introduced a ladies-only bus line and the chivalrous Culture Bus service. For information see the boxed text 'Novelty Bussing' in this chapter.

### Bus Maps

The best source of all for routes and fares is BMTA's Web site, www.bmta.motc.go.th.

To do any serious bus riding you'll need a Bangkok bus map – for details see the Maps section in the Facts for the Visitor chapter.

### Bus Safety

There's no need to be paranoid, but be careful with your belongings while riding Bangkok buses. Dexterous thieves specialise in slashing backpacks, shoulder bags or even trouser pockets with a sharp razor and slipping your valuables out unnoticed. You are more likely to be 'razored' on crowded ordinary buses, than other forms of transport, particularly in the Hualamphong station area. Hold your bag close to your chest, and preferably carry money in a front shirt pocket (as the Thais do) and maintain a physical and visual awareness of these areas, especially if the bus is packed shoulder to shoulder.

### SKYTRAIN

The much ballyhooed Skytrain elevated rail network finally opened in December 1999 and has proved to be a tremendous boon to those wanting to escape the often horrendous traffic jams on Bangkok's streets. Originally proposed in 1986 and begun in

1994, the result so far is two lines officially known as the Bangkok Transit System (BTS) Skytrain, known to the Thais simply as *rót fai fáh* (sky train).

One line starts from the Mo Chit Skytrain station in the north, next to the Northern & North-Eastern bus terminal and Chatuchak Park, and ends at the On Nut station, near Soi 81, Th Sukhumvit. Often referred to as 'the Sukhumvit line', it will reportedly soon be extended 9km farther south-east to Samut Prakan. There is talk of extending this line as far as the new airport under construction in Nong Ngu Hao.

The second line – colloquially known as the 'Silom line' – runs from the National Stadium east to Siam Square, where it soon after makes an abrupt turn to the south-west, continuing above Th Ratchadamri, down Th Silom to Th Narathiwat Ratchanakharin, then along Th Sathon till it terminates next to the foot of Saphan Taksin on the banks of Mae Nam Chao Phraya. This line will be extended a farther 2km over the river and into Thonburi, or so we're told. The extensions are to be completed within three years.

Although the Skytrain has yet to make a sizeable dent in Bangkok traffic, it's estimated that on the average day there are 40,000 fewer cars on the road than before the train's 1999 launch, and a large number of city residents have switched from BMTA's crowded air-con buses. Consequently BMTA has lowered the number of buses on the road at any one time, perhaps making a very small contribution to improving city air.

Certainly the Skytrain has made a very tangible difference in the lives of many people for whom the Skytrain routes are convenient. In pre-Skytrain Bangkok, if you wanted to take a taxi from Th Ploenchit to Chatuchak Weekend Market, for example, the trip might take an hour or more. By Skytrain the same journey is covered in approximately 16 minutes! Getting from Th Sukhumvit to Th Silom – a nightmare trip by car or taxi during rush hour – can now be accomplished in 15 minutes or less via Skytrain.

Another advantage to the Skytrain is that it offers a pleasant semi-bird's eye view of the city, allowing glimpses of greenery and historic architecture not visible from street level due to high walls.

## Riding the Skytrain

Trains run frequently from 6 am to midnight along both lines. If you've ever ridden a modern light rail system that used ticket cards with magnetic stripes, you'll have no trouble figuring out the simple Skytrain system. You can change between the two lines at the double-height Siam station (also known as 'Central Station'), in front of Siam Square and Siam Center. Free maps are available at all Skytrain station ticket booths. All trains are air-conditioned, often heavily so.

From your point of departure, fares vary from 10B to 40B depending on which of 23 current stations you plan to disembark from. Ticket machines in each station accept 5B and 10B coins only. You can buy tickets from staffed station ticket booths if you don't have correct change. You can also buy a stored-value ticket or Sky Card valid for 100B worth of train trips for 70B plus 30B deposit. The deposit is returned when you return the used card. Sky Cards are also sold in multiples of 200B and 300B. These cards can be purchased at all station ticket booths, and at branches of Siam Commercial Bank, Black Canyon Coffee shops and Watsons drug stores. Fares are posted inside every station.

For further information call BTS at ☎ 617 7300 or check its Web site (www.bts .co.th). Although their English is limited, ticket staff at each station can be very helpful with advice.

## SUBWAY

Since 1998, the Metropolitan Rapid Transit Authority (MRTA) has been building the city's first subway. The 18-station line is designed to link Hualamphong near the river with Bang Seu in the north via the Queen Sirikit National Convention Centre. Although the line intersects BTS Skytrain routes at two points – near the Asoke Skytrain station and the Mo Chit Skytrain station – engineers have reportedly provided for no pedestrian links between the two services. The estimated launch date for the *rót fai tâi din* (underground railway) is December 2002.

## CAR & MOTORCYCLE

Cars and motorcycles are easily rented in Bangkok, if you can afford them and have nerves of steel. Rates start at around 1500B per day or 9000B per week for a small car, much less for a motorcycle, excluding insurance. For long-term rentals you can usually arrange a discount of up to 35%. An International Driving Permit and passport are required for all rentals.

For long, cross-country trips, you might consider buying a new or used motorcycle and reselling it when you leave – this can end up being cheaper than renting, especially if you buy a good used bike.

Here are the names and addresses of some car-rental companies:

**Avis Rent-A-Car** (☎ 255 5300–4, fax 253 3734) 2/12 Th Withayu; (☎ 535 4031, 535 4052) Bangkok International Airport; (☎ 254 1234) Grand Hyatt Erawan Hotel; (☎ 253 0444) Le Meridien President

**Budget Car Rental** (☎ 202 0250) 19/23 Bldg A, Royal City Avenue, Th Phetburi Tat Mai

**Grand Car Rent** (☎ 248 2991) 233-5 Th Asoke-Din Daeng

**Highway Car Rent** (☎ 266 9393) 1018/5 Th Phra Ram IV

**Inter Car Rent** (☎ 252 9223) 45 Th Sukhumvit, near Soi 3

**Krung Thai Car Rent** (☎ 246 0089, 246 1525) 233-5 Th Asoke-Din Daeng

**Lumpinee Car Rent** (☎ 255 1966, 255 3482) 167/4 Th Withayu

**National Car Rental** (☎ 928 1525) Amari Airport Hotel; (☎ 722 8487) 727 Th Si Nakharin

**Petchburee Car Rent** (☎ 319 7255) 23171 Th Phetburi Tat Mai

**Sathorn Car Rent** (☎ 633 8888) 6/8-9 Th Sathon Neua

**SMT Rent-A-Car** (see National Car Rental)

There are more car-rental agencies along Th Withayu and Th Phetburi Tat Mai. Some also rent motorcycles, but you're better off renting or leasing a motorcycle at a place that specialises in motorcycles. Here are three:

**Chusak Yont Shop** (☎ 251 9225) 1400 Th Phetburi Tat Mai

**SSK Co** (☎ 514 1290) 35/33 Th Lat Phrao

**Visit Laochaiwat** (☎ 278 1348) 1 Soi Prommit, Th Suthisan

---

### Platform Shoes Banned

The wearing of platform shoes will soon be illegal for drivers in Thailand. Thai authorities have expressed concern that the platform heel-fad that is sweeping the country is causing an increase in road accidents. Some of the shoes currently on sale have heels as high as 20cm. As was the case in Japan, the popular towering shoes are considered to severely hamper braking ability. Under the proposed new driving laws, not only will high platform heels be banned, but other dangerous driving acts, such as applying makeup behind the wheel, will also be made illegal.

It is not yet decided the maximum height of heel that will be allowed. Thai police have expressed concerns that enforcing the law will be difficult, and might require policemen to have to stop cars and regard the legs of female drivers.

**From Lonely Planet Scoop travel news at www.lonelyplanet.com/scoop**

---

## TAXI

Bangkok's metered taxis *(tháeksii miitôe)* now outnumber the old nonmetered taxis. Metered taxis have signs on top reading 'Taxi Meter', those without have 'Taxi Thai' or just 'Taxi' signs. Metered taxis are cheaper, but can be a little harder to flag down during peak commuter hours. Demand often outstrips supply from 8 to 9 am and 6 to 7 pm, and between 1 and 2 am when the bars are closing. As metered-taxi drivers use rented vehicles and must return them at the end of their shifts, they sometimes won't take longer fares as quitting time nears.

Metered taxis charge 35B at flagfall for the first 2km, then 4.50B for the next 10km, 5B for 13km to 20km and 5.50B for any distance over 20km, but only when the taxi travels at 6km/h or more; at speeds under 6km/h, a surcharge of 1.25B per minute kicks in. Freeway tolls – 20B to 40B depending where you start – must be paid by the passenger.

A 24-hour 'phone-a-cab' service (Siam Taxi, ☎ 377 1771) is available for an extra 20B over the regular metered fare. This is only really necessary if you're in an area where there aren't a lot of taxis.

For certain routes it can be very difficult to find a taxi driver who's willing to use the meter. One such instance is going from the Southern bus terminal across the river to Bangkok proper – most drivers will ask for a flat 350B but settle for 250B. In the reverse direction you can usually get them to use the meter.

For those times when you're forced to use a nonmetered taxi, you'll have to negotiate the fare. It's no use telling nonmetered taxi drivers what a comparable metered trip would cost – they know you wouldn't be wasting your time with them if a metered taxi were available. Fares to most places within central Bangkok are 60B to 80B, and you should add 10B or 20B if you're travelling during rush hour or after midnight. For trips to the airport the nonmeter guys want 200B to 300B. Perhaps sometime in the future there won't be any nonmetered taxis left on the street – until that time you'll probably be forced to use them occasionally.

You can hire a taxi all day for 1000B to 1500B depending on how much driving is involved.

## MOTORCYCLE TAXI

As passengers become more desperate in their attempts to beat rush-hour gridlocks, motorcycle taxis have moved from the soi to the main avenues. Fares for a motorcycle taxi are about the same as túk-túks except during heavy traffic, when they may cost a bit more. (See the following Túk-Túk section.)

Riding on the back of a speeding motorcycle taxi is even more of a kamikaze experience than riding in a túk-túk. Keep your legs tucked in – the drivers are used to carrying passengers with shorter legs than those of the average *farang* (Westerner) and they pass perilously close to other vehicles while weaving in and out of traffic.

## TÚK-TÚK

In heavy traffic, túk-túks are usually faster than taxis since they're able to weave in and out between cars and trucks. On the down side, túk-túks are not air-conditioned, so you have to breathe all that lead-soaked air (at its thickest in the middle of Bangkok's wide avenues), and they're also more dangerous since they easily flip when braking into a fast curve. The typical túk-túk fare nowadays offers no savings over a metered taxi –

---

### Túk-Túk Wars

In 18th-century Bangkok, residents got around on foot, by canal, or in human-drawn rickshaws called rót chék or 'Chinese vehicles' by the Thais. During the early 20th century the rickshaw gave way to the three-wheeled pedicab or samlor, which was then fitted with an inexpensive Japanese two-stroke engine after WWII to become the onomatopoeic túk túk.

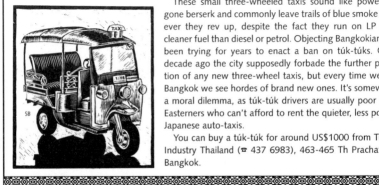

These small three-wheeled taxis sound like power saws gone berserk and commonly leave trails of blue smoke whenever they rev up, despite the fact they run on LP gas, a cleaner fuel than diesel or petrol. Objecting Bangkokians have been trying for years to enact a ban on túk-túks. Over a decade ago the city supposedly forbade the further production of any new three-wheel taxis, but every time we go to Bangkok we see hordes of brand new ones. It's somewhat of a moral dilemma, as túk-túk drivers are usually poor North-Easterners who can't afford to rent the quieter, less polluting Japanese auto-taxis.

You can buy a túk-túk for around US$1000 from Tuk-Tuk Industry Thailand (☎ 437 6983), 463-465 Th Prachathipok, Bangkok.

around 40B for a short hop (eg, Siam Square to Soi 2, Th Sukhumvit).

Túk-túk drivers tend to speak less English than taxi drivers, so many new arrivals have a hard time communicating their destinations. Although some travellers have complained about túk-túk drivers deliberately taking them to the wrong destination (to collect commissions from certain restaurants, gem shops or silk shops), others never seem to have a problem with túk-túks, and swear by them. Beware of túk-túk drivers who offer to take you on a sightseeing tour for 10B or 20B – it's a touting scheme designed to pressure you into purchasing overpriced goods. When in doubt, use a metered taxi rather than a túk-túk.

## BOAT

Although many of Bangkok's *khlong* (canals) have been paved over, there is still plenty of transport along and across the Chao Phraya River and up adjoining canals. River transport is one of the nicest ways of getting around Bangkok as well as often being much faster than other alternatives. For a start you get a different view of the city; secondly, it's much less of a hassle than tangling with the polluted, noisy, traffic-crowded streets.

Along the Chao Phraya River, the main transport consists of the Chao Phraya River Express (☎ 222 5330, 623 6342), which runs between Tha Wat Ratchasingkhon (Wat Ratchasingkhon pier) in south central Bangkok and Nonthaburi Province from 6 am to 6.40 pm daily. Fares range from 6B

to 10B, except for special express boats (denoted by a yellow flag or a red-and-orange striped flag), which run only from 6 to 9 am and 3 to 7 pm, cost 10B and stop at fewer piers along the way. See the Chao Phraya River Express map in the Things to See & Do chapter.

Other useful canal routes are: Khlong Saen Saep (Banglamphu to Bang Kapi), Khlong Phrakhanong (Th Sukhumvit to Sinakarin campus), Khlong Bang Luang/ Khlong Lat Phrao (Th Phetburi Tat Mai to Phahonyothin Bridge) and Khlong Phasi Charoen in Thonburi (Kaset Bang Khae port to Rama I Bridge). Although the canal boats can be crowded, the service is generally much faster than either a taxi or bus. Along Th Sukhumvit, however, the Skytrain is generally preferable.

See River & Canal Trips in the Things to See & Do chapter for more information.

## WALKING

At first glance Bangkok doesn't seem like a great town for walking – its main avenues are so choked with traffic that the noise and thick air tend to drive one indoors. However, quiet spots where walks are rewarding do exist, such as Lumphini Park or neighbourhoods off the main streets. Certain places are much more conveniently seen on foot, particularly the older sections of town along the Chao Phraya River where the roads are so narrow and twisting that bus lines don't go there. For interesting routes on foot see Walking Tours in the Things to See & Do chapter.

# Things to See & Do

If your visit to Bangkok is short, you won't begin to be able to see all the city has to offer. For visits of four or five days, must-dos include Wat Phra Kaew and the Grand Palace along with nearby Wat Pho, the National Museum, either the Lak Meuang or Erawan shrines, Jim Thompson's House, either Vimanmek Teak Mansion or Wang Suan Phakkat, and a river or canal trip.

For a three-day stopover, leave out the National Museum and the shrines. If you have longer – say a week or more – add Chatuchak Weekend Market, a morning at a floating market, a muay thai (Thai boxing) match and a *khŏn* performance. Looking for another temple or two? Wat Traimit's Golden Buddha never fails to impress, and Wat Arun also makes a pleasant cross-river excursion.

Evenings can be devoted to sampling Bangkok's incredible Thai restaurants – try at least one riverside place to soak up the languid ambience of old Bangkok. You should also seek out at least one Thai musical performance, whether traditional (at a dinner theatre) or modern (at one of the city's many nightclubs).

There's always plenty going on and visitors can supplement this chapter by taking a look in one of the English-language newspapers; the *Bangkok Post*, *The Nation* and *Bangkok Metro* for up-to-date listings of exhibitions, events and festivals.

Keep in mind also that the hectic pace of a short stop-over can soon be soothed by a traditional Thai massage.

Bangkok caters to diverse interests: there are temples, museums and other historic sites for those interested in traditional Thai culture; and for those seeking contemporary Krung Thep (Bangkok), there's an endless variety of good restaurants, clubs, international cultural and social events, movies in several languages and modern art galleries,

not to mention parks, markets and shopping. As the dean of expat authors in Thailand, William Warren, has said, 'The gift Bangkok offers me is the assurance I will never be bored'.

## MUSEUMS & GALLERIES
### National Museum (Map 3)
พิพิธภัณฑสถานแห่งชาติ

Just north-east of Tha Phra Chan, Thailand's National Museum is the largest museum in South-East Asia and an excellent place to learn about Thai art. All periods and styles are represented from Dvaravati to Ratanakosin, and English-language literature is available.

Room 23 contains a well-maintained collection of traditional musical instruments from Thailand, Laos, Cambodia and Indonesia. Other permanent exhibits include ceramics, clothing and textiles, woodcarving, royal regalia, Chinese art and weaponry.

The museum buildings were originally built in 1782 as the palace of Rama I's viceroy, Prince Wang Na. Rama V turned it into a museum in 1884.

In addition to the exhibition halls, the museum grounds contain the restored **Buddhaisawan (Phutthaisawan) Chapel**. Inside the chapel (built in 1795) are some well-preserved original murals and one of the country's most revered Buddha images, Phra Phuttha Sihing. Legend claims the image came from Ceylon, but art historians attribute it to the 13th-century Sukhothai period.

Free English tours of the museum are given by National Museum volunteers on Wednesday (Buddhism) and Thursday (Thai art, religion and culture), starting from the ticket pavilion at 9.30 am. These guided tours are excellent and many people have written to recommend them. The tours are also conducted in German (Thursday), French (Wednesday) and Japanese (Wednesday) all at 9.30am.

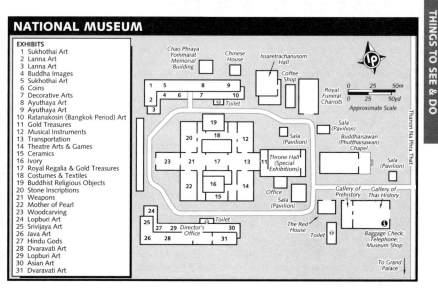

For more information on the tours, contact the volunteers on ☎ 215 8173. For general information call ☎ 224 1370. The museum is open 9 am to 4 pm Wednesday to Sunday; admission is 40B.

## Jim Thompson's House (Map 5)
บ้านจิมทอมป์สัน

Though it may sound corny when described, this is a great spot to visit for authentic Thai residential architecture and South-East Asian art. Located at the end of an undistinguished soi next to Khlong Saen Saep, the premises once belonged to the American silk entrepreneur Jim Thompson, who deserves most of the credit for the worldwide popularity of Thai silk.

Born in Delaware in 1906, Thompson was a New York architect who briefly served in the Office of Strategic Services (forerunner of the CIA) in Thailand during WWII. After the war he found New York too tame and moved to Bangkok. Thai silk caught his connoisseur's eye; he sent samples to fashion houses in Milan, London and Paris, gradually building a steady worldwide clientele for a craft that had been in danger of dying out.

A tireless promoter of traditional Thai arts and culture, Thompson collected parts of various derelict Thai homes in central Thailand and had them reassembled in the current location in 1959. Although for the most part assembled in typical Thai style, one striking departure from tradition is the way each wall has its exterior side facing the house's interior, thus exposing the wall's bracing system to residents and guests.

While out for an afternoon walk in the Cameron Highlands of west Malaysia in 1967, Thompson disappeared under mysterious circumstances and has never been heard from since. That same year his sister was murdered in the USA, fuelling various conspiracy theories to explain the disappearance. Was it communist spies? Business rivals? Or a man-eating tiger? The most recent theory – for which there is apparently some hard evidence – has it that the silk magnate was accidentally run over by a Malaysian truck driver who hid his remains.

*The Legendary American – The Remarkable Career & Strange Disappearance of Jim Thompson*, by William Warren, is an excellent book on Thompson, his career, residence and intriguing disappearance. In Thailand, it has been republished as *Jim Thompson: The Legendary American of Thailand* (Jim Thompson Thai Silk Co, Bangkok).

On display in the main house are his small but splendid Asian art collection and his personal belongings. The Jim Thompson Foundation has a table at the front where you can buy prints of old Siam maps and Siamese horoscopes in postcard and poster form, or you can shop for silks at an adjacent outlet of Jim Thompson Silk Co. A plush bar overlooking the canal offers cold drinks and occasional live jazz.

The house, on Soi Kasem San 2, Th Phra Ram I, is open 9 am to 4.30 pm daily. Admission is 100B (proceeds go to Bangkok's School for the Blind). Children and students under 25 years get in for 50B.

Call ☎ 216 7368 or 215 0122 for more information. The khlong at the end of the soi is one of Bangkok's most lively. Beware of well dressed touts in the soi who will tell you Thompson's house is closed – it's just a ruse to take you on a buying spree.

### Wang Suan Phakkat (Lettuce Farm Palace, Map 5)

วังสวนผักกาด

The Lettuce Farm Palace, once the residence of Princess Chumbon of Nakhon Sawan, is a collection of five traditional wooden Thai houses containing varied displays of art, antiques and furnishings. The landscaped grounds are a peaceful oasis complete with ducks and swans and a semi-enclosed garden reminiscent of Japanese gardens.

The diminutive **Lacquer Pavilion** at the back of the complex dates from the Ayuthaya period (the building originally sat in a monastery compound on Mae Nam Chao Phraya (Chao Phraya River), just south of Ayuthaya) and features gold-leaf *jataka* (stories of the Buddha) and *Ramayana* murals as well as scenes from daily Ayuthaya life. Larger residential structures at the front of the complex contain displays of Khmer Hindu and Buddhist art, Ban Chiang ceramics and a decent collection of historic Buddhas, including a beautiful late U Thong-style image. In the noise and confu-

sion of Bangkok, the gardens offer a tranquil retreat.

The grounds are open from 9 am to 4 pm daily and admission is 100B. It's on Th Si Ayuthaya, between Th Phayathai and Th Ratchaprarop; air-con bus No 3 passes by right out the front. Or it's a 500m walk from Phayathai station. Call ☎ 245 4934 for more information.

### Vimanmek Teak Mansion (Phrá Thîi Nâng Wímanmêhk, Map 2)

พระที่นั่งวิมานเมฆ

Originally constructed on Ko Si Chang in 1868 and moved to the present site in the Chitlada Palace grounds in 1910, this beautiful L-shaped, three-storey mansion contains 81 rooms, halls and anterooms, and is said to be the world's largest golden teak building. The huge staircases, octagonal rooms and lattice walls are nothing short of magnificent, in spite of which the mansion retains a surprisingly serene and intimate atmosphere.

Vimanmek was the first permanent building on the Chitlada Palace grounds. It served as Rama V's residence in the early 1900s, was closed in 1935 and reopened in 1982 for the Ratanakosin bicentennial. The interior of the mansion contains various personal effects of the king, and a treasure trove of early Ratanakosin art objects and antiques.

English-language tours leave every half-hour between 9.30 am and 3 pm. The tours cover around 30 rooms and last an hour. Smaller adjacent buildings display historic photography documenting the Chakri dynasty. Traditional Thai classical and folk dances are performed at 10.30 am and 2 pm in a pavilion off the canal side of the mansion.

Vimanmek is open from 9.30 am to 4 pm daily; admission is 50B for adults, 20B for children. It's free if you've already been to the Grand Palace and Wat Phra Kaew and kept the entry ticket for Vimanmek and Abhisek Dusit Throne Hall. As this is royal property, visitors wearing shorts or sleeveless shirts will be refused entry. Call ☎ 628 6300 for further details.

Vimanmek and Abhisek lie towards the northern end of the Chitlada Palace

A guardian of Wat Phra Kaew

Decorative detail of Wat Pho

The Golden Chedi at Bangkok's oldest temple, Wat Pho

Naga, mythical serpent beings, guard the Grand Palace

A traditional Chinese temple

Worshipping at a Bangkok temple.

One of the many Buddhist shrines in Bangkok.

A sleepy dog takes a break on Th Phra Ahtit...

...and a tired vegetable seller takes his break in a hammock slung across the back of his truck.

grounds, off Th U-Thong Nai (between Th Si Ayuthaya and Th Ratwithi), across from the western side of the Dusit Zoo. Air-con bus No 3 (Th Si Ayuthaya) or air-con bus No 10 (Th Ratwithi) will drop you nearby.

## Abhisek Dusit Throne Hall (Phrá Thîi Nâng Àphísèk Dusìt, Map 2)
พระที่นั่งอภิเศกดุสิต

This hall is a smaller wood and brick-and-stucco structure completed in 1904 for King Rama V. Typical of the finer architecture of the era, the Victorian-influenced gingerbread and Moorish porticoes blend to create a striking and distinctly Thai exterior. The hall now houses an excellent display of regional handiwork crafted by members of the Promotion of Supplementary Occupations & Related Techniques (SUPPORT) charity foundation sponsored by Queen Sirikit. Among the exhibits are *mát-mìi* cotton and silk, *málaeng tháp* collages (made from metallic, multicoloured beetle wings), damascene and niello ware, and *yaan lípao* basketry.

Abhisek is open from 10 am to 4 pm daily; admission is 50B (or free with a Grand Palace and Wat Phra Kaew ticket). There is a souvenir shop on the premises. As at Wat Phra Kaew and Vimanmek, visitors must be properly dressed. See the previous Vimanmek Teak Mansion entry for directions to Abhisek Dusit Throne Hall.

## Royal Elephant Museum (Map 2)
พิพิธภัณฑ์ช้างต้น

On the same grounds as the Vimanmek Teak Mansion and Abhisek Dusit Throne Hall, two large stables that once housed three 'white' elephants – animals whose auspicious albinism automatically made them crown property – are now a museum. One of the structures contains photos and artefacts outlining the importance of elephants in Thai history, and explains their various rankings according to physical characteristics. The second stable holds a sculptural representation of a living royal white elephant (now

kept at the Chitlada Palace, home to the current Thai king). Draped in royal vestments, the statue is more or less treated as a shrine by the visiting Thai public.

Admission to the Royal Elephant Museum is included in any admission to Vimanmek Teak Mansion and Abhisek Dusit Throne Hall.

## Royal Barges National Museum (Map 2)
เรือพระที่นั่ง

The royal barges are long, fantastically ornamented boats used in ceremonial processions on the river. The largest is 50m long and requires a rowing crew of 50 men, plus seven umbrella bearers, two helmsmen, two navigators, as well as a flagman, rhythm-keeper and chanter.

The barges are kept in sheds on the Thonburi side of the river, next to Khlong Bangkok Noi, near the Saphan Phra Pinklao. Suphannahong, the king's personal barge, is the most important of the boats; made from a single piece of timber, it's the largest dugout in the world. The name means 'golden swan', and a huge swan head has been carved into the bow. Lesser barges feature bows carved into other Hindu-Buddhist mythological shapes such as the *naga* (sea dragon) and the *garuda* (Vishnu's bird mount).

One of the best times to see the fleet in action on the river is during the royal *kathǐn* ceremony at the end of *phansǎa* (the Buddhist Rains Retreat, ending with an October or November new moon) when new robes are offered to the monastic contingent.

The barge shed (☎ 424 0004) is open from 8.30 am to 4.30 pm daily (except 31 December, 1 January and 12 to 14 April). Admission is 50B and you must pay an additional 100B if you want to take photos. To get there, take bus No 3 or 81 or take a ferry to Tha Rot Fai, then walk down the street parallel to the tracks until you come to a bridge over the khlong. Follow the bridge to a wooden walkway that leads to the museum. You can also get there by taking a khlong taxi (5B) up the canal and getting off near the bridge.

## Siam Society & Ban Kamthieng (Map 7)

สยามสมาคม/บ้านคำเที่ยง

At 131 Soi Asoke, Th Sukhumvit, the Siam Society is the publisher of the renowned *Journal of the Siam Society* and its members are valiant preservers of traditional Thai culture. The society headquarters is a good place to visit for those with a serious interest in Thailand. A reference library is open to visitors and Siam Society monographs are for sale. Almost anything you'd want to know about Thailand (outside the political sphere, since the society is sponsored by the royal family) can be researched here. An ethnological museum of sorts, exhibiting Thai folk art, is located on the Siam Society grounds in the Northern-style Kamthieng House. Ban Kamthieng is open 9 am to 5 pm Tuesday to Saturday. It was under renovation when we last visited, and as a result the usual 100B entry charge was being waived. For information call ☎ 661 6470.

## Other Museums

The **Museum of the Department of Forensic Medicine**, on the ground floor of the Forensic Medicine Building, Siriraj Hospital, Th Phrannok, near the Thonburi (Bangkok Noi) train station, is the most famous of 10 medical museums on the hospital premises. Among the grisly displays are the preserved bodies of famous Thai murderers. It's open Monday to Friday from 9 am to 4 pm; admission is free.

The **Hall of Railway Heritage** (Map 1), just north of Chatuchak Park, displays steam locomotives, model trains and other artefacts related to Thai railroad history. It's open Sunday only from 5 am to noon; admission is free. Call the Thai Railfan Club (☎ 243 2037) for further information.

The **Bangkok Doll Factory & Museum** (Map 5, ☎ 245 3008) at 85 Soi Ratchataphan (Soi Mo Leng), off Th Ratchaprarop in the Pratunam district, houses a colourful selection of traditional Thai dolls, both new and antique. Dolls are also available for purchase. It's open 8 am to 5 pm Monday to Saturday; admission is free.

Military aircraft aficionados shouldn't miss the **Royal Thai Air Force Museum** (Map 1), on Th Phahonyothin near Wing 6 of the Don Meuang Airport. Among the world-class collection of historic aircraft is the only existing Japanese Tachikawa trainer, along with a Spitfire and several Nieuports and Breguets. The museum is open 8.30 am to 4.30 pm weekdays and on the first weekend of each month; admission is free.

Bangkok also has a **Museum of Science** and a **planetarium**, both on Th Sukhumvit between sois 40 and 42 (Map 1). It's open daily 9am to 4pm, closed Monday and public holidays, entry is 40/20B adults/children under 12.

## Art Galleries

Housed in an early Ratanakosin-era building opposite the National Theatre, the **National Gallery** (Map 3, ☎ 282 8525, 281 2224) displays traditional and contemporary art, mostly by artists receiving government support. The general view is that it's not Thailand's best, but the gallery is worth a visit for die-hard art fans or if you're nearby. The gallery is open 9 am to 4 pm Wednesday to Sunday; entry is 30B.

**Silpakorn University** (Map 3, near Wat Phra Kaew) is Bangkok's premier fine arts university and has a gallery of student works. It's open 8 am to 7 pm weekdays, and 8 am to 4 pm weekends and holidays.

Bangkok's latest trend in public art consumption is the 'gallery pub', an effort to place art in a social context rather than leaving it to sterile galleries and museums. **About Studio/About Café** (Map 6, ☎ 623 1742), 418 Th Maitrichit, is the best of the several venues that attempt to combine gallery space with social space.

**Ruang Pung Art Community**, who pioneered this gallery style in Thailand around 12 years ago, is opposite section 13 in Chatuchak Weekend Market. It's open 11 am to 6 pm on weekends and features rotating exhibits. Also in Chatuchak Market is the very active **Sunday Gallery** (Sunday Plaza), which contrary to its name is open 10 am to 5 pm Monday, Wednesday and Friday, and 7 am to 7 pm on weekends.

The **Thailand Cultural Centre** (Map 1, ☎ 245 7742) on Th Ratchadaphisek (in the Huay Khwang district, between Soi Tiam Ruammit and Th Din Daeng) has a small gallery with rotating contemporary art exhibits, as does the **River City Complex** (Map 6) next to the Royal Orchid Sheraton.

Bangkok's **foreign cultural centres** hold regular exhibits of foreign and local artists – check the monthly bulletins issued by the American University Allumni (AUA), Alliance Française, the British Council and the Goethe Institut (see Cultural Centres in the Facts for the Visitor chapter).

The **Neilson Hays Library** (Map 6, ☎ 233 1731) at 195 Th Surawong occasionally hosts small exhibitions in its Rotunda Gallery.

Several of Bangkok's luxury hotels show top-quality contemporary art in their lobbies and other public areas. The **Grand Hyatt Erawan** (Map 7, on the corner of Th Ratchadamri and Th Ploenchit) and the **Landmark Hotel** (Map 7, Th Sukhumvit) have the best collections of contemporary art in Thailand. The Erawan alone has over 1900 works exhibited on a rotating basis.

For more information about Bangkok galleries, you can check out this Web site: www.rama9art.org.

## TEMPLES & SHRINES
## Wat Phra Kaew & Grand Palace (Map 3)

วัดพระแก้ว/พระบรมมหาราชวัง

Also called the Temple of the Emerald Buddha (Wat Phra Si Ratana Satsadaram), this wat adjoins the Grand Palace on common ground that was consecrated in 1782, the first year of Bangkok rule. The 945,000-sq-metre grounds encompass over 100 buildings that represent more than 200 years of royal history and architectural experimentation. Most of the architecture, royal or sacred, can be classified Ratanakosin or old Bangkok style, with minor variations. (See the boxed text 'The Emerald Buddha' in this section.)

The wat structures are extremely colourful, comprising gleaming, gilded *chedis* (stupas), polished orange and green roof tiles, mosaic-encrusted pillars and rich marble pediments. Extensive murals depicting scenes from the *Ramakian* (the Thai version of the Indian *Ramayana* epic) line the cloisters along the inside walls of the compound. Originally painted during Rama I's reign (1782-1809), the murals have undergone several restorations, including a major one finished in time for the 1982 Bangkok/Chakri dynasty bicentennial. Divided into 178 sections, the murals

## What's a Wat

A *wat* (from the Pali-Sanskrit *avasatha* or 'dwelling for pupils and ascetics') is a Buddhist compound where men or women can be ordained as monks or nuns. Virtually every village in Thailand has at least one wat, while in towns and cities they're quite numerous.

The typical wat compound in Thailand will contain: an *uposatha* (*bòt* in Thai), a consecrated chapel where monastic ordinations are held; a *vihara* (*wíhǎan*), where important Buddha images are housed; a *sala* (*sǎalaa*) or open-sided shelter for community meetings and Buddhist lectures; a number of *kùtì* (monastic quarters); a *hǎw trai* or *tripitaka* library where Buddhist scriptures are stored; a *hǎw klawng* (drum tower), sometimes with a *hǎw rákhang* (bell tower); various *chedia* (stupas); plus ancillary buildings – such as schools or clinics – that differ from wat to wat according to local community needs.

The typical wat is also a focus for much festival activity and is thus an important social centre for Thais. Especially lively are the *ngaan wát* (temple fairs); these take place regularly on certain auspicious dates (eg, the advent and end of the Rains Retreat; the anniversary of the Buddha's birth, enlightenment and death; and the anniversary of the first Dhamma lecture), and usually feature music, feasting and occasional fireworks. Another common type of celebration is the *ngaan sòp* (funeral ceremony), during which the deceased is cremated.

illustrate the epic in its entirety, beginning at the north gate and moving clockwise around the compound.

Except for an anteroom here and there, the **Grand Palace** (Phra Borom Maharatchawong), is today used by the king only for certain ceremonial occasions such as Coronation Day (his current residence is Chitlada Palace in the northern part of the city) and is closed to the public. The exteriors of the four buildings are worth a swift perusal, however, for their royal bombast.

**Borombhiman Hall** (east end), a French-inspired structure that served as a residence for Rama VI, is occasionally used to house visiting foreign dignitaries. In April 1981 General San Chitpatima used it as headquarters for an attempted coup. **Amarindra Hall**, to the west, was originally a hall of justice but is used today for coronation ceremonies.

Largest of the palace buildings is the triple-winged **Chakri Mahaprasat**, literally 'Great Holy Hall of Chakri' but usually translated as 'Grand Palace Hall'. Designed in 1882 by British architects, the exterior shows a peculiar blend of Italian Renaissance and traditional Thai architecture, a style often referred to as *faràng sài chá-daa* ('European wearing a Thai classical dancer's headdress'), because each wing is topped by a *mondòp*, a layered, heavily ornamented spire representing a Thai adaptation of the Hindu *mandapa* (shrine). The tallest of the mondòps, in the centre, contains the ashes of Chakri kings; the flanking mondòps enshrine the ashes of Chakri princes who failed to inherit the throne. Thai kings traditionally housed their huge harems in the mahaprasat's inner palace area, which was guarded by combat-trained female sentries.

Last from east to west is the Ratanakosin-style **Dusit Hall**, which initially served as a venue for royal audiences and later as a royal funerary hall.

## The Emerald Buddha (Phra Kaew)

The Emerald Buddha (actually carved from nephrite, a type of jade), for which Wat Phra Kaew is named, sits in a glassed-in, miniature prasat with an intricately carved, five-tiered roof, on a pedestal high above the heads of worshippers. At only 66cm high, the buddha is displayed in the huge bòt, built expressly to house the diminutive figure.

A definite aura of mystery surrounds the jade figure, enhanced by the fact that it cannot be examined closely, nor can it be photographed. Its lofty perch in part signifies the occult significance of the image, considered the 'talisman' of the Thai kingdom, the legitimator of Thai sovereignty.

Neither the origin nor the sculptor of the buddha is certain, but it first appeared on record in 15th-century Chiang Rai in North Thailand. Legend says it was sculpted in India and brought to Siam by way of Ceylon, but stylistically it seems to belong to the Chiang Saen or Lanna (Lan Na Thai) period of the 13th to 14th centuries.

Sometime in the 15th century, the buddha is said to have been covered with plaster and gold leaf and placed in Chiang Rai's own Wat Phra Kaew (literally, Temple of the Jewel Holy Image). While being transported to a new location after a storm had damaged the chedi containing the buddha, it supposedly lost its plaster covering in a fall. It next appeared in Lampang where it enjoyed a 32-year stay (again at a Wat Phra Kaew) until it was brought to Wat Chedi Luang in Chiang Mai.

Laotian invaders took the image from Chiang Mai in the mid-16th century and brought it to Luang Prabang in Laos. Later it was moved to Wiang Chan (Vientiane). When Thailand's King Taksin waged war against Laos 200 years later, the image was taken back to the then Thai capital of Thonburi by General Chakri, who later succeeded Taksin as Rama I, the founder of the Chakri dynasty.

Rama I had the Emerald Buddha moved to the new Thai capital in Bangkok and had two royal robes made for it, one to be worn in the hot season and one for the rainy season. Rama III added another seasonal robe – one to be worn in the cool season. The three robes are still solemnly changed at the beginning of each season by the king himself.

Admission to the Wat Phra Kaew and Grand Palace compound is 200B, and opening hours are from 8.30 to 11.30 am and 1 to 3.30 pm. For more information call ☎ 224 1833. The admission fee includes entry to the Royal Thai Decorations & Coins Pavilion (on the same grounds) and to both Vimanmek Teak Mansion and Abhisek Dusit Throne Hall, near the Dusit Zoo. (See the Vimanmek and Abhisek entries.)

Wats are sacred places to Thai Buddhists (see the boxed text 'What's a Wat' previously), this one particularly so because of its royal associations, visitors should dress and behave decently. If you wear shorts or sleeveless shirts you may be refused admission; sarongs and baggy pants are sometimes available on loan at the entry area. For walking in the courtyard areas you must wear shoes with closed heels and toes – thongs aren't permitted. As in any temple compound, shoes should be removed before entering the *bòt* (main chapel) or wíhǎan of Wat Phra Kaew.

The most economical way of reaching Wat Phra Kaew and the Grand Palace is by air-con bus No 8 or 12. You can also take the Chao Phraya River Express, disembarking at Tha Chang.

## Wat Pho (Wat Phra Chetuphon, Map 3)

วัดโพธิ์(วัดพระเชตุพน)

A long list of superlatives for this one: the oldest and largest wat in Bangkok, it features the longest reclining Buddha and the largest collection of Buddha images in Thailand, and was the earliest centre for public education. As a temple site, Wat Pho dates back to the 16th century, but its current history really begins in 1781 with the complete rebuilding of the original monastery.

Narrow Th Chetuphon divides the grounds in two, with each section surrounded by huge whitewashed walls. The most interesting part is the northern compound, which includes a very large bòt enclosed by a gallery of Buddha images and four wihǎan, four large chedis commemorating the first three Chakri kings (Rama III has two chedis), 91 smaller chedis, an old *tripitaka* (Buddhist scriptures)

library, a sermon hall, a large wihǎan that houses the reclining Buddha and a school building for classes in Abhidhamma (Buddhist philosophy), plus several less important structures. The temple is currently undergoing a 53-million baht renovation.

Wat Pho is the national headquarters for the teaching and preservation of traditional Thai medicine, including Thai massage. A **massage pavilion** convenes in the afternoon at the eastern end of the compound; a massage session costs 200B per hour (300B with herbs), 120B for a half-hour. You can also study massage here in seven to 10-day courses at the Wat Pho Thai Traditional Medical & Massage School on Th Sanam Chai, opposite the monastery's western wall. Other courses include Thai herbal therapy and traditional Thai medicine. A full course of all three takes one to three years to complete.

The tremendous **reclining Buddha**, 46m long and 15m high, illustrates the passing of the Buddha into nirvana. The figure is modelled out of plaster around a brick core and finished in gold leaf. Mother-of-pearl inlay adorns the eyes and feet of this colossal image, with the feet displaying 108 different auspicious *laksana* (characteristics of a Buddha). The images on display in the four wihǎan surrounding the main bòt in the eastern part of the compound are interesting. Particularly beautiful are the Phra Jinnarat and Phra Jinachi Buddhas, in the west and south chapels, both from Sukhothai. The galleries extending between the four chapels feature no less than 394 gilded Buddha images. Rama I's remains are interred in the base of the presiding Buddha image in the bòt.

The temple rubbings for sale at Wat Pho and elsewhere in Thailand come from the 152 *Ramakian* reliefs, carved in marble and obtained from the ruins of Ayuthaya, which line the base of the large bòt. The rubbings are no longer taken directly from the panels but are rubbed from cement casts of the panels made years ago.

You can hire English, French, German or Japanese-speaking guides for 150B for one visitor, 200B for two, 300B for three. Also on the premises are a few astrologers and palmists.

THINGS TO SEE & DO

The temple is open to the public from 8 am to 5 pm daily; admission is 20B. The ticket booth is closed from noon to 1 pm. Air-con bus Nos 8, 12 and 44 stop near Wat Pho. The nearest Chao Phraya River Express pier is Tha Tien. Call ☎ 221 9911 for more information.

## Wat Mahathat (Map 3)

วัดมหาธาตุ

Founded in the 1700s, Wat Mahathat is a national centre for the Mahanikai monastic sect and houses one of Bangkok's two Buddhist universities, Mahathat Rajavidyalaya. The university is the most important place of Buddhist learning in mainland South-East Asia today – the Lao, Vietnamese and Cambodian governments send selected monks to further their studies here.

Mahathat and the surrounding area have developed into an informal Thai cultural centre of sorts, though this may not be obvious at first glance. A daily **open-air market** features traditional Thai herbal medicine, and out on the street you'll find a string of shops selling herbal cures and offering Thai massage. On weekends, a large produce market held on the temple grounds brings people from all over Bangkok and beyond. Opposite the main entrance, on the other side of Th Maharat, is a large religious amulet market, known locally as *talàat phrá khrêuang* (holy amulet market).

The monastery offers **meditation** instruction in English on the second Saturday of every month from 2 to 6 pm in the Dhamma Vicaya Hall. Those interested in more intensive instruction should contact the monks in section 5 of the temple compound. See the Meditation entry in the Courses section later in this chapter.

The temple complex is officially open to visitors 9 am to 5 pm daily and on *wan phrá*, Buddhist holy days (the full and new moons every fortnight); admission is free.

Wat Mahathat is right across the street from Wat Phra Kaew, on the west side of Sanam Luang (Royal Field). Air-con bus Nos 8 and 12 pass by it, and the nearest Chao Phraya River Express pier is Tha Maharat.

## Wat Traimit (Map 6)

วัดไตรมิตร

The attraction at Wat Traimit (Temple of the Golden Buddha) is, of course, the impressive 3m-tall, 5.5-tonne, solid-gold Buddha image, which gleams like no other gold artefact I've ever seen.

Sculpted in the graceful Sukhothai style, the image was 'rediscovered' some 40 years ago beneath a stucco or plaster exterior when it fell from a crane while being moved to a new building within the temple compound. It has been theorised that the covering was added to protect it from 'marauding hordes', either during the late Sukhothai period or later in the Ayuthaya period when the city was under siege by the Burmese. The temple itself is said to date from the early 13th century.

The Golden Buddha can be seen every day from 9 am to 5 pm, and admission is 20B. Nowadays, lots of camera-toting tour groups haunt the place (there's even a moneychanger on the premises), so it pays to arrive in the early morning if you want a more traditional feel. Wat Traimit is near the intersection of Th Yaowarat and Th Charoen Krung, near Hualamphong station. Call ☎ 623 1226 for more information.

## Wat Arun (Map 6)

วัดอรุณฯ

The striking Temple of Dawn, named after the Indian god of dawn, Aruna, appears in all the tourist brochures and is located on the Thonburi side of Mae Nam Chao Phraya. The present wat was built on the site of 17th-century Wat Jang, which served as the palace and royal temple of King Taksin when Thonburi was the Thai capital; hence, it was the last home of the Emerald Buddha before Rama I brought it across the river to Bangkok. See the boxed text 'The Emerald Buddha (Phra Kaew)' in this section.

The 82m prang was constructed during the first half of the 19th century by Rama II and Rama III. The unique design elongates the typical Khmer prang into a distinctly Thai shape. Its brick core has a plaster covering embedded with a mosaic of broken, multi-hued Chinese porcelain, a common temple ornamentation in the early Ratanakosin period when Chinese ships calling at Bangkok used tonnes of old porcelain as ballast. Steep stairs reach a lookout point about halfway up the prang from where there are fine views of Thonburi and the river. During certain festivals, hundreds of lights illuminate the outline of the prang at night.

Also worth a look is the interior of the bòt. The main Buddha image is said to have been designed by Rama II himself. The murals date to the reign of Rama V; particularly impressive is one that depicts Prince Siddhartha encountering examples of birth, old age, sickness and death outside his palace walls, an experience that led him to abandon the worldly life. The ashes of Rama II are interred in the base of the bòt's presiding Buddha image.

The temple looks more impressive from the river than it does from up close, though the wat grounds make a peaceful retreat from the hustle and bustle of Bangkok. Between the prang and the ferry pier is a huge sacred banyan tree.

Wat Arun is open 8.30 am to 5.30 pm daily; admission is 10B. Call ☎ 466 3167 for more information. To reach Wat Arun from the Bangkok side, catch a cross-river ferry from Tha Tien at Th Thai Wang. Crossings are frequent and cost only 2B.

## Wat Benchamabophit (Map 3)
วัดเบญจมบพิตร (วัดเบญฯ)

This wat of white Carrara marble (hence its tourist name, 'Marble Temple') was built at the turn of the century under King Chulalongkorn (Rama V). The large cruciform bòt is a prime example of modern Thai wat architecture. The base of the central Buddha image, a copy of Phra Phuttha Chinnarat in Phitsanulok, contains the ashes of Rama V. The courtyard behind the bòt has 53 Buddha images (33 originals and 20 copies) representing famous figures and styles from all over Thailand and other Buddhist countries – an education in itself if you're interested in Buddhist iconography.

Wat Ben is on the corner of Th Si Ayuthaya and Th Phra Ram V, diagonally opposite the south-west corner of Chitlada Palace. It's open 8 am to 5.30 pm daily; admission is 20B. Bus Nos 3 (air-con), 5 and 72 stop nearby.

## Wat Saket & Golden Mount (Map 3)
วัดสระเกศ

Wat Saket is an undistinguished temple except for the Golden Mount (Phu Khao Thong), on the western side of the grounds with a good view out over Bangkok rooftops. This artificial hill was created when a large chedi under construction by Rama III collapsed because the soft soil would not support it. The resulting mud-and-brick hill was left to sprout weeds until Rama IV built a small chedi on its crest.

Frank Vincent, an American writer, describes his 1871 ascent in *The Land of the White Elephant*:

From the summit...may be obtained a fine view of the city of Bangkok and its surroundings; though this is hardly a correct statement, for you see very few of the dwelling-houses of the city; here and there a wat, the river with its shipping, the palace of the King, and a waving sea of cocoa-nut and betel-nut palms, is about all that distinctly appears. The general appearance of Bangkok is that of a large, primitive village, situated in and mostly concealed by a virgin forest of almost impenetrable density.

Rama V later added to the structure and housed a Buddha relic from India (given to him by the British government) in the chedi. The concrete walls were added during WWII to prevent the hill from eroding. Every November there is a big festival on the grounds of Wat Saket, which includes a candle-lit procession up the Golden Mount.

The wat is open 8 am to 5 pm. Admission is free except for the final approach to the summit of the Golden Mount, which costs 10B. The temple is within walking distance of the Democracy Monument; air-con bus Nos 11 and 12 pass nearby. For further information, call ☎ 223 4561.

## Wat Ratchanatda (Map 3)

วัดราชนัดดา

Across Th Mahachai from Wat Saket, this temple dates from the mid-19th century, built under Rama III in honour of his grand-daughter. Also spelt Wat Rajanadda, this wat was possibly influenced by Burmese models.

The wat has a well-known market selling Buddhist phrá khrêuang in all sizes, shapes and styles. The amulets not only feature images of the Buddha, but also famous Thai monks and Indian deities. Full Buddha images are also for sale. Wat Ratchanatda is an expensive place to purchase a charm, but a good place to look.

## Wat Bowonniwet (Map 3)

วัดบวรนิเวศ

Wat Bowonniwet (also less phonetically spelt Wat Bovornives and usually shortened to Wat Bowon), on Th Phra Sumen in Banglam-phu, is the national headquarters for the Thammayut monastic sect, the minority sect in Thai Buddhism. King Mongkut, founder of the Thammayuts, began a royal tradition by residing here as a monk – in fact he was the abbot of Wat Bowon for several years. King Bhumibol and Crown Prince Vajiralongkorn, as well as several other males in the royal family, have been temporarily ordained as monks here. The temple was founded in 1826, when it was known as Wat Mai.

Bangkok's second Buddhist university, Mahamakut University, is housed at Wat Bowon. India, Nepal and Sri Lanka all send selected monks to study here. Across the street from the main entrance to the wat are an English-language Buddhist bookshop and a Thai herbal clinic.

Because of its royal status, visitors should be particularly careful to dress properly for admittance to this wat – no shorts or sleeveless clothing.

## Lak Meuang (City Pillar, Map 3)

ศาลหลักเมือง

The City Pillar is across the street from the eastern wall of Wat Phra Kaew, at the south-ern end of Sanam Luang. This shrine en-closes a wooden pillar erected by Rama I in 1782 to represent the founding of the new Bangkok capital. Later, during the reign of Rama V, five other idols were added to the shrine. The spirit of the pillar, Phra Sayam Thewathirat ('Venerable Siam Deity of the State'), is considered the city's guardian deity and receives the daily supplications of count-less Thai worshippers, some of whom com-mission classical Thai dancers to perform *lákhon kâe bon* at the shrine. Some of the of-ferings include severed pig heads with sticks of incense sprouting from their foreheads.

## Sri Mariamman Temple (Map 6)

วัดพระศรีมหาอุมาเทวี

(วัดแขกสีลม)

Called Wat Phra Si Maha Umathewi in Thai, this small Hindu temple sits alongside busy Th Silom (near the Th Pan intersection) in Bangrak, a district with a high concentration of Indian residents. The principal temple structure, built in the 1860s by Tamil immi-grants, features a 6m facade of intertwined, full-colour Hindu deities, topped by a gold-plated copper dome. The temple's main shrine contains three main deities: Jao Mae Maha Umathewi (Uma Devi, also known as Shakti, Shiva's consort) at the centre; her son Phra Khanthakuman (Khanthakumara or Subramaniam) on the right; and her ele-phant-headed son Phra Phikkhanesawora (Ganesha) on the left. Along the left interior wall sit rows of Shivas, Vishnus and other Hindu deities, as well as a few Buddhas, so that just about any non-Muslim, non-Judaeo-Christian Asian can worship here – Thai and Chinese devotees come to pray along with Indians. Bright yellow marigold garlands are sold at the entrance for use as offerings to the deity images inside.

An interesting ritual takes place in the temple at noon on most days, when a priest brings out a tray carrying an oil lamp, coloured powders and holy water. He sprin-kles the water on the hands of worshippers who in turn pass their hands through the lamp flame for purification; they then dip their fingers in the coloured powder and daub prayer marks on their foreheads. On Friday at around 11.30 am, prasada (blessed vegetarian food) is offered to devotees.

Thais call this temple Wat Khaek – *khàek* is a colloquial expression for people of Indian descent. The literal translation is 'guest', an obvious euphemism for a group of people you don't particularly want as permanent residents; hence most Indian-Thais don't appreciate the term.

## Wat Thammamongkhon (Map 1)

วัดธรรมมงคล

East of Bangkok on Soi 101, Th Sukhumvit, this 95m-high chedi resulted from a monk's vision. While meditating in 1991, Phra Viriyang Sirintharo saw a giant jade boulder; at around the same time a 32-tonne block of solid jade was discovered in a Canadian riverbed. Viriyang raised over US$500,000 to purchase the block and commissioned a 14-tonne Buddha sculpture (carried out by Carrara sculptors) to go in a pavilion at Thammamongkhon. An image of this magnitude deserved a massive chedi. The chedi, which contains a hair of the Buddha presented to Thailand by Bangladesh's Sangharaja (head of a Theravada monastic order), features a lift so you can ride to the top. The chedi's grand opening ceremony was held in 1993.

A leftover 10-tonne chunk of jade was carved into a figure of Kuan Yin (the Chinese Buddhist goddess of compassion). Smaller leftovers – a total of nearly eight tonnes – were made into amulets and sold to worshippers for US$20 each, to raise money for 5000 daycare centres throughout Thailand.

## Other Temples & Shrines

Marked by its enormous, modern-style 32m-standing Buddha, **Wat Intharawihan** (Map 3) borders Th Wisut Kasat at the northern edge of Banglamphu. Check out the hollow air-con stupa with a lifelike image of Luang Phaw Toh. Entry is by donation.

**Wat Suthat** (Map 3), begun by Rama I and completed by Rama II and Rama III, boasts

a wihǎan with gilded bronze Buddha images (including Phra Si Sakayamuni, Thailand's largest surviving Sukhothai-period bronze) and colourful jataka murals depicting scenes from the Buddha's life. One of the oldest Ratanakosin-era religious structures in Bangkok, the main wihǎan bears wooden doors carved by several artisans, including King Rama II himself. Wat Suthat holds a special place in the national religion due to its association with Brahman priests who perform important ceremonies, eg, the Royal Ploughing Ceremony in May. These priests perform rites at two Hindu shrines near the wat – the Thewa Sathaan (Deva Sthan) across the street to the north-west and the smaller Saan Jao Phitsanu (Vishnu Shrine) to the east. The former contains images of Shiva and Ganesha while the latter is dedicated to Vishnu. The wat holds the rank of Rachavoramahavihan, the highest royal temple grade; the ashes of Rama VIII (Ananda Mahidol, the current king's deceased older brother) are contained in the base of the main Buddha image in Wat Suthat's wihǎan.

At nearby **Sao Ching-Cha** (Giant Swing, Map 3), a spectacular Brahman festival in honour of the Hindu God Shiva used to take place each year until it was stopped during the reign of Rama VII. Participants would swing in ever-heightening arcs in an effort to reach a bag of gold suspended from a 15m bamboo pole – many died trying. The Giant Swing is a block south of the Democracy Monument.

On the corner of Th Ratchaprarop and Th Ploenchit, next to the Grand Hyatt Erawan Hotel, is a large shrine **Saan Phra Phrom** (also known as the Erawan Shrine, Map 7), which was originally built to ward off bad luck during the construction of the first Erawan Hotel (torn down to make way for the Grand Hyatt Erawan some years ago). The four-headed deity at the centre of the shrine is Brahma (Phra Phrom in Thai), the Hindu god of creation. Apparently the developers of the original Erawan (named after Indra's three-headed elephant mount) first erected a typical Thai spirit house but decided to replace it with the impressive Brahman shrine after several serious mishaps delayed the

## Kickstart to Enlightenment

It will come as no surprise to football fans, but it appears the path to enlightenment may well start with a kick. Wander into a Bangkok temple and you can always expect to find a statue of the image of Buddha – at Bangkok's Wat Poriwat, you can also find a statue of British football star David Beckham.

A young Thai football fan Thongruang Haemhod worships the game so much that he has expressed his awe for his favourite player by sculpting a 30cm (one foot) high, gold leaf statue of the player. The gilded relief stands at the foot of the main Buddha image, which is surrounded by around 100 statues of minor deities.

Haemhod created the image of Beckham in order to sustain his memory for the next 1000 years – an action not without controversy. Some argue that it is sacrilegious to immortalise a transitory, Spice Boy sports star in a place usually reserved for religious deities. However, the temple's senior monk, Chan Theerapunyo, says that people should open their minds to contemporary art and the views of the next generation. 'Football has become a religion,' he said, 'so we have to open our minds and share the feelings of millions who admire Beckham'.

**Adapted from Lonely Planet Scoop travel news at www.lonelyplanet.com/scoop**

hotel construction. Worshippers who have a wish granted may return to the shrine to commission the musicians and dancers who are always on hand for an impromptu performance.

Since the success of the Erawan Shrine, several other flashy Brahman shrines have been erected around the city next to large hotels and office buildings. Next to the **World Trade Center** (Map 7) on Th Ploenchit is a large shrine containing a standing Brahma, a rather unusual posture for Thai Brahmans.

Another hotel shrine worth seeing is Saan Jao Mae Thap Thim, a **lingam (phallus) shrine**, behind the Hilton International (Map 5) in tiny Nai Loet Park off Th Withayu. Clusters of carved stone and wooden lingam surround a spirit house and shrine built by millionaire businessman Nai Loet to honour Jao Mae Thap Thim, a female deity thought to reside in the old banyan tree on the site. Someone who made an offering shortly thereafter had a baby, and the shrine has received a steady stream of worshippers – mostly young women seeking fertility – ever since. Nai Loet Park is fenced off so you must wind your way through the Hilton complex to visit the shrine; or come via the Khlong (canal) Saen Saep canal taxi; ask to get off at Saphan Withayu (Radio Bridge) – look for the TV3 building on the north side of the canal.

At the time of writing, the Hilton International announced it would only allow hotel guests to visit the shrine. Given its cultural significance to Bangkok Thais, this seems preposterous and untenable; however, if you take the back way as described above you can avoid the hotel grounds altogether.

**Wat Chong Nonsi** (Map 1), off Th Ratchadaphisek near the Bangkok side of the river, contains notable jataka murals painted between 1657 and 1707. It is the only surviving Ayuthaya-era temple in which both the murals and architecture are of the same period with no renovations. As a single, 'pure' architectural and painting unit, it's considered quite important for the study of late Ayuthaya art.

There are numerous less visited temples on the Thonburi side of the river. These include **Wat Kalayanamit** (Map 6) with its towering Buddha statue and the biggest bronze bell in Thailand; **Wat Pho Bang-O** with its carved gables and Rama III-era murals; **Wat Chaloem Phrakiat** (Map 1), tiled gables; and **Wat Thong Nophakhun** with its Chinese-influenced *uposatha* (bòt). **Wat Yannawa**, on the Bangkok bank of the river near Tha Sathon, was built during Rama II's reign and features a building resembling a Chinese junk. See the Chao Phraya River Express map in this chapter for the location of these wats; or for more detailed information, buy the Fine Arts Commission's Canals of Thonburi map, available from the Tourist Authority of Thailand (TAT).

Just off Th Chakraphet in the Phahurat district is a **Sikh temple (Sri Gurusingh Sabha, Map 6)** where visitors are welcome. Basically it's a large hall, somewhat reminiscent of a mosque interior, devoted to the worship of the Guru Granth Sahib, the 16th-century Sikh holy book, which is itself considered the last of the religion's 10 great gurus or teachers. Prasada is distributed among devotees every morning around 9 am, and if you arrive on a Sikh festival day you can partake in the *langar* (communal Sikh meal) served in the temple.

## CHURCHES

Several Catholic churches were founded in Bangkok in the 17th to 19th centuries. Worth seeing is the **Holy Rosary Church** (known in Thai as Wat Kalawan, from the Portuguese 'Calvario', Map 6) in Talat Noi near the River City Complex. Originally built in 1787 by the Portuguese, the Holy Rosary was rebuilt by Vietnamese and Cambodian Catholics around the turn of the century, hence the French inscriptions beneath the stations of the cross. This old church has a splendid set of Romanesque stained-glass windows, gilded ceilings and a very old Christ statue that is carried through the streets during Easter celebrations. The alley leading to the church is lined with Ratanakosin or 'old Bangkok' shophouse architecture.

The **Church of the Immaculate Conception** (Map 2), near Saphan Krungthon and north of Saphan Phra Pinklao, was also founded by the Portuguese and later taken over by Cambodians fleeing civil war. The present building is an 1837 reconstruction on the church's 1674 site. One of the original church buildings survives and is now used as a museum housing holy relics. Another Portuguese church, built in 1913, is the **Santa Cruz** (Wat Kuti Jiin, Map 6) on the Thonburi side near Memorial Bridge (Saphan Phra Phuttha Yot Fa, usually called Saphan Phut by Thais). The architecture shows Chinese influence, hence the Thai name 'Chinese monastic residence'.

**Christ Church**, at 11 Th Convent (Map 7) next to the Bangkok Nursing Home, was established as English Chapel in 1864. The current Gothic-style structure, opened in 1904, features thick walls and a tiled roof braced with teak beams; the carved teak ceiling fans date to 1919.

## OLD CITY SIGHTS

Bangkok's oldest residential and business district fans out along Mae Nam Chao Phraya between Saphan Phra Pinklao to the west and Hualamphong station to the east. It's an area originally inhabited by Chinese residents who were moved out of Ko Ratanakosin to make way for royal temples and palaces in the early 19th century, and today the local populace consists of a high percentage of Chinese and Indian ethnicities. It's a fascinating area to explore if you don't mind navigating the narrow and often congested streets. Although buses and taxis are abundantly available, it's an area best seen on foot.

## Chinatown (Sampeng, Map 6)
เยาวราช(สำเพ็ง)

Bangkok's Chinatown, off Th Yaowarat and Th Ratchawong, comprises a confusing and crowded array of jewellery, hardware, wholesale food, automotive and fabric shops, as well as dozens of other small businesses. It's a good place to shop as goods here are cheaper than almost anywhere else in Bangkok and the Chinese proprietors like to bargain, especially along Sampeng Lane (Soi Wanit 1). Chinese and Thai antiques in various grades of age and authenticity are available in Nakhon Kasem (the so-called Thieves' Market), but it's better for browsing than buying these days.

During the annual Vegetarian Festival, celebrated fervently by Thai Chinese for the first nine days of the ninth lunar month (September or October), Chinatown becomes a virtual orgy of vegetarian Thai and Chinese food. The festivities are centred around **Wat Mangkon Kamalawat (Neng Noi Yee)**, one of Chinatown's largest temples, on Th Charoen Krung. All along Th Charoen Krung in this vicinity, and on Th Yaowarat to the south, restaurants and noodle shops offer hundreds of different vegetarian dishes.

A Chinese population has been living in this area ever since the Chinese were moved here from Bang Kok (today's Ko Ratanakosin) by the royal government in 1782 to make room for the new capital. A census in the area taken exactly 100 years later found 245 opium dens, 154 pawnshops, 69 gambling establishments and 26 brothels. Pawnshops, along with myriad gold shops, remain a popular Chinatown business, while the other three vices have gone underground; brothels continue to exist under the guise of 'tea halls' *(rohng chaa)*, back-street heroin vendors have replaced the opium dens and illicit card games convene in the private upstairs rooms of certain restaurants. Four Chinese newspapers printed and distributed in the district have a total circulation of over 160,000.

At the south-eastern edge of Chinatown stands **Hualamphong station**, built by Dutch architects and engineers just before WWI. One of the city's earliest and most outstanding examples of the movement towards Thai Art Deco, the vaulted iron roof and neoclassical portico demonstrate engineering that was state-of-the-art in its time, while the patterned, two-toned skylights exemplify pure de Stijl Dutch modernism.

Fully realised examples of Thai Deco from the 1920s and 1930s can be found along Chinatown's main streets, particularly Th Yaowarat. Vertical towers over the main doorways are often surmounted with whimsical Deco-style sculptures – the Eiffel Tower, a lion, an elephant, a Moorish dome. Atop one commercial building on Th Songwat, near Tha Ratchawong, is a rusting model of a WWII vintage Japanese Zero warplane, undoubtedly placed there by the Japanese during their brief 1941 occupation of Bangkok; in style and proportion it fits the surrounding Thai-Deco elements.

## Phahurat (Map 6)

พาหุรัด

At the edge of Chinatown, around the intersection of Th Phahurat (Phahurat) and Th Chakraphet (Chakkaphet), is a small but thriving Indian district, generally called Phahurat. Here, dozens of Indian-owned shops sell all kinds of fabric and clothes. This is the best place in the city to bargain for these items, especially for silk. The selection is unbelievable, and Thai shoulder bags *(yâam)* sold here are the cheapest in Bangkok, perhaps in Thailand.

Behind the more obvious storefronts along these streets, in the 'bowels' of the blocks, is a seemingly endless Indian bazaar selling not only fabric but household items, food and other necessities. There are some good, reasonably priced Indian restaurants in this area too, and a Sikh temple (Sri Gurusingh Sabha) off Th Chakraphet (see Other Temples & Shrines earlier in this chapter).

## PARKS
## Lumphini Park (Map 7)

สวนลุมพินี

Named after the Buddha's birthplace in Nepal, this is Bangkok's largest and most popular park. It is bordered by Th Phra Ram IV to the south, Th Sarasin to the north, Th Withayu to the east and Th Ratchadamri to the west, with entrance gates on all sides. A large artificial lake in the centre is surrounded by broad, well-tended lawns, wooded areas and walking paths – it's the best outdoor escape from Bangkok without leaving town.

One of the best times to visit the park is in the early morning before 7 am when the air is fresh (well, relatively so for Bangkok) and legions of Chinese are practising t'ai chi. Meanwhile vendors set up tables to dispense fresh snake blood and bile, considered health tonics by many Thais and Chinese. A weight lifting area in one section becomes a miniature 'muscle beach' on weekends. Facilities include a snack bar, an asphalt jogging track, picnic area, restrooms and a couple of tables where women serve Chinese tea. Rowboats and paddle boats can be rented at the lake for 20B per half-hour.

During the kite flying season (mid-February to April), Lumphini becomes a favoured flight zone with kites *(wâo)* for sale in the park.

## Rama IX Royal Park (Map 1)

สวนหลวงร.๙

Opened in 1987 to commemorate King Bhumibol's 60th birthday, Bangkok's newest green area covers 81 hectares and includes a water park and botanical garden. Since its opening, the garden has developed into a significant horticultural research centre. A museum with an exhibition on the life of the king sits at the centre of the park. Take bus No 2, 23 or 25 to Soi Udomsuk (Soi 103), off Th Sukhumvit in Phrakhanong district, then a green minibus to the park – the trip takes about 15 minutes. Alternatively, you can take air-con bus No 145 from the Chatuchak Weekend Market, getting off at the first intersection after the two large shopping malls, Seacon Square and Seri Center. Turn left and catch either an orange minibus or songthaew for the remaining 10 minute ride; the whole trip takes about an hour. The park is open from 5 am to 6 pm daily; admission is 10B.

## Sanam Luang (Map 3)

สนามหลวง

Sanam Luang (Royal Field), just north of Wat Phra Kaew, is the traditional site for royal cremations and for the annual Ploughing Ceremony, in which the king officially initiates the rice-growing season (see 'The Royal Ploughing Ceremony' boxed text in the Facts for the Visitor chapter). The most recent ceremonial cremation took place here in March 1996, when the king presided over funeral rites for his mother. Before that the most recent Sanam Luang cremations were held in 1976 for Thai students killed in the demonstrations of that year.

A statue of Mae Thorani, the earth goddess (borrowed from Hindu mythology's Dharani), stands in a white pavilion at the northern end of the field. Erected in the late 19th century by King Chulalongkorn, the statue was originally attached to a well that provided drinking water to the public.

Before 1982, Bangkok's famous Weekend Market was regularly held at Sanam Luang (it's now at Chatuchak Park). Nowadays, the large field is most popularly used

as a picnic and recreational area. A large kite-flying competition is held here during the kite-flying season.

## OTHER ATTRACTIONS
## Dusit Zoo (Khao Din, Map 2 & 3)

สวนสัตว์ดุสิต(เขาดิน)

The collection of animals at Bangkok's 19-hectare zoo comprises over 300 mammals, 200 reptiles and 800 birds, including relatively rare indigenous species. Originally a private botanical garden for Rama V, it was converted to a zoo in 1938 and is now one of the premier zoological facilities in South-East Asia. The shady grounds feature trees labelled in English, Thai and Latin, plus a lake in the centre with paddle boats for rent. There's also a small children's playground.

If nothing else, the zoo is a nice place to get away from the noise of the city and observe how the Thais amuse themselves – mainly by eating. A couple of lakeside restaurants serve good, inexpensive Thai food.

It's open 9 am to 6 pm daily; entry is 20B for adults, 5B for children and 10B for those over 60. A small circus performs on weekends and holidays between 11 am and 2 pm. Sunday can be a bit crowded – if you want the zoo mostly to yourself, go on a weekday.

The zoo is in the Dusit district between Chitlada Palace and the National Assembly Hall; the main entrance is off Th Ratwithi. Buses that pass the entrance include the ordinary Nos 18 and 28 and the air-con No 10.

## Queen Saovabha Memorial Institute (Snake Farm, Map 7)

สถานเสาวภา

At this Thai Red Cross research institute (☎ 252 0161), formerly known as the Pasteur Institute, on Th Phra Ram IV (near Th Henri Dunant), venomous snakes – common cobra, king cobra, banded krait, Malayan pit viper, green pit viper and Russell's viper – are milked daily to make snake-bite antivenins, which are distributed throughout the country. When the institute was founded in 1923, it was only the second of its kind in the world (the first was in Brazil). The milking sessions – at 11 am and 2.30 pm weekdays, 11 am only on weekends and holidays – have become a major Bangkok tourist attraction. Unlike other 'snake farms' in Bangkok, this is a serious herpetological research facility; an informative half-hour slide show on snakes is presented before the milking sessions. Feeding time is 3 pm; admission is 70B.

The booklet *Guide to Healthy Living in Thailand,* published jointly by the Thai Red Cross and the US embassy, is available here for 100B. You can also get common vaccinations against cholera, typhoid, rabies, tetanus, polio, encephalitis, meningitis, smallpox and hepatitis A and B. If you're bitten by a strange animal, this is a good place to come for anti-rabies serum; bring the animal, dead or alive, if possible. The institute is open 8.30 to 11.30 am and 1 to 4.30 pm Monday to Friday.

There is also an anonymous STD clinic on the grounds of the institute.

## Monk's Bowl Village (Map 3)
บ้านบาตร

This is the only remaining village of three established in Bangkok by Rama I for the purpose of handcrafting *bàat* (monk's bowls). The black bàat, used by Thai monks to receive alms-food from faithful Buddhists every morning, are still made here in the traditional manner. Due to the expense of purchasing a handmade bowl, the 'village' has been reduced to a single alley in a district known as Ban Baht (*bâan bàat* or Monk's Bowl Village). About half a dozen families still hammer the bowls together from eight separate pieces of steel said to represent Buddhism's Eightfold Path. The joints are fused in a wood fire with bits of copper, and the bowl is polished and coated with several layers of black lacquer. A typical bàat-smith's output is one bowl per day.

To find the village, walk south on Th Boriphat, south of Th Bamrung Meuang, then left on Soi Baan Baht. The artisans who fashion the bowls are not always at work, so it's largely a matter of luck whether you'll see them in action. At any of the houses that

make them, you can purchase a fine quality alms bowl for around 400B to 500B. To see monks' robes and bowls on sale, wander down Th Bamrung Meuang in the vicinity of Sao Ching Cha.

## Phra Sumen Fort (Pâwm Phrá Súmehn) & Santichaiprakan Park (Map 3)
ป้อมพระสุเมรุ

In Banglamphu, next to the Chao Phraya River where Th Phra Athit meets Th Phra Sumen, stands one of Bangkok's original 18th-century forts. Built in 1783 to defend against potential naval invasions, and named for the mythical Mt Sumeru of Hindu-Buddhist cosmology, the octagonal, brick-and-stucco bunker was one of 14 city fortresses built along the city canal or Khlong Rop Krung (now Khlong Banglamphu).

Alongside the recently renovated fort, and fronting the river, a small grassy park and open-air Thai pavilion makes a good stop for river views, cool breezes or a picnic. The park is open 5 am to 10 pm daily.

A walkway zigzags along the river – in some cases suspended right over the river – from the fort all the way to Saphan Phra Pin Klao. Follow this walk and along the way you can catch glimpses of old Ratanakosin-style buildings not visible from the street, such as those housing parts of the Buddhist Society of Thailand and the Food & Agriculture Organization.

Eventually the walkway will continue beyond Saphan Phra Pin Klao all the way to Tha Mahathat.

## RIVER & CANAL TRIPS

In 1855 British envoy Sir John Bowring wrote: 'The highways of Bangkok are not streets or roads but the river and the canals. Boats are the universal means of conveyance and communication.' The wheeled motor vehicle has long since become Bangkok's conveyance of choice, but fortunately it hasn't yet become universal. A vast network of canals and river tributaries surrounding Bangkok still carry a motley fleet of watercraft, from paddled canoes to rice barges. In these areas many homes, trading houses and temples remain oriented towards water life and provide a fascinating glimpse into the past, when Thais still considered themselves *jâo náam* (water lords).

## Chao Phraya River Express

You can observe urban river life from the water for 1½ to three hours for only 10B to 15B by climbing aboard a Chao Phraya River Express boat at Tha Ratchasingkhon (see Chao Phraya River Express Map this chapter), just north of Saphan Krungthep. If you want to ride the entire length of the express route all the way to Nonthaburi, this is where you must begin (the trip takes about 40 minutes). Ordinary bus Nos 1, 17 and 75 and aircon bus No 4 pass Tha Ratchasingkhon. Or you could board at any other express boat pier in Bangkok for a shorter ride to Nonthaburi to the north. Express boats run about every 15 minutes from 6 am to 6 pm daily.

## Khlong Bangkok Noi & Khlong Om Canal Taxis

Another good boat trip is the Bangkok Noi canal taxi route which leaves from Tha Chang. The farther up Khlong Bangkok Noi you go, the better the scenery becomes, with teak houses on stilts, old wats and plenty of greenery. Stop off at Ayuthaya-era Wat Suwannaram to view 19th-century jataka murals painted by two of early Bangkok's foremost religious muralists. Art historians consider these the best surviving temple paintings in Bangkok.

A one-way fare anywhere is 10B to 30B depending on how far you go. The boats run 6.30 am to 11 pm, but are most frequent between 6 and 11 am. Nowadays a tourist boat makes the run for 60B per person; you may find that the regular canal taxis send you to this boat, since they receive a few baht commission from the tourist boat operators. The tourist boat makes fewer stops along the way, so visitors with less time may prefer them

Both boats terminate in Bang Yai, a district in Nonthaburi. From a pier at Wat Sao Thong Hin at Bang Yai you continue by boat taxi down picturesque Khlong Om and see durian plantations. Boats leave every 15 minutes

between 4 am and 8 pm, and the fare is 6B. If you want to make a loop, you can return from Tha Nonthaburi, via a Chao Phraya River Express, to any pier in central Bangkok (6B to 10B, depending on the distance).

You can also do this entire loop in reverse, starting at the Chao Phraya River Express pier at Tha Nonthaburi, continuing to Bang Yai, then down Khlong Bangkok Noi to Tha Chang.

Another way to return from Bang Yai is to board city bus No 1003 (8B), which terminates next to War Amarit on the east bank of Mae Nam Chao Phraya. A short cross-river ferry (2B) will take you to Tha Nonthaburi, where you can board a Chao Phraya River Express boat downriver.

## Other Canal Taxis

From Tha Tien near Wat Pho, get a canal taxi along **Khlong Mon** (leaving every half-hour from 6.30 am to 6 pm; 5B) for more typical canal scenery, including orchid farms. A longer excursion could be made by making a loop along khlongs Bangkok Noi, Chak Phra and Mon, an all-day trip. An outfit called Chao Phraya Chartered Company (☎ 622 7657, ext 111) runs a tour boat to Khlong Mon from River City shopping complex pier each afternoon from 2.30 to 4.30 pm for 420B per person, including refreshments.

Boats to **Khlong Bangkok Yai**, available from either Tha Tien or Tha Ratchini, pass Wat Intharam, where a chedi contains the ashes of Thonburi's King Taksin, assassinated in 1782 (see the History section in Facts about Bangkok). Fine gold and black lacquerwork adorning the main bòt doors depicts the mythical *naariiphŏn* tree, which bears fruit shaped like beautiful maidens.

From Tha Saphan Phut you can board a taxi boat that chugs along via Khlong Bangkok Yai and into **Khlong Bang Waek**, where you'll pass canal-side temples, stilted teak houses and orchid farms.

From Bangkok, it's possible to go as far as Suphanburi and Ratchaburi by boat, though this typically involves many boat connections.

For details on boat transport on the Bangkok side of the river, where four canal

# CHAO PHRAYA RIVER EXPRESS

**CHAO PHRAYA EXPRESS MAIN STOPS**

1 Tha Phibun Songkhram
2 Tha Phayap
3 Tha Thewet – for National Library, Tavee, Sawasdee & Paradise Guesthouses
4 Tha Saphan Phra Ram VIII – for Wat Intharawihan
5 Tha Samphraya (Tha Banglamphu)
6 Tha Saphan Phra Pin Klao
7 Tha Phra Athit – for Th Khao San Guesthouses
8 Tha Rot Fai – for Thonburi (Bangkok Noi) Train Station
9 Tha Phra Chan
10 Tha Wang Lang – for Supatra River House, Patravadi Theatre
11 Tha Maharat – for Silpakorn & Thammasat Universities
12 Tha Chang – for Grand Palace & Wat Phra Kaew
13 Tha Tien – for Wat Pho
14 Tha Ratchini
15 Tha Saphan Phut
16 Tha Ratchawong – for Chinatown
17 Tha Si Phraya – for River City Shopping Complex
18 Tha Meuang Khae – for Main Post Office
19 Tha Oriental
20 Tha Sathon – for Saphan Taskin Skytrain Station
21 Tha Ratchasingkhon

routes have been revived, see the Getting Around chapter. Although they provide quick transport, none of the four right-bank canal routes can be recommended for sightseeing.

## Boat Charters

If you want to see the Thonburi canals at your own pace, the best thing to do is charter a longtail boat – it needn't be expensive if you can get a small group together to share the costs. The usual price is 400B per hour and you can choose from among eight different canals in Thonburi alone. Beware of 'agents' who will try to put you on the boat and rake off an extra commission. Before travelling by boat, establish the price – you can't bargain when you're in the middle of the river!

The best piers for hiring a boat are Tha Chang, Tha Saphan Phut, Tha Khlong Banglamphu and Tha Si Phraya. Close to the latter, to the rear of the River City shopping complex, is the River City pier, where the Boat Tour Centre charges the same basic hourly price of 400B, and there are no hassles with touts or bargaining. Of these four piers, Tha Chang usually has the largest selection of boats.

Those interested in seeing Bangkok's deep-water port can hire longtail boats to Khlong Toey or as far downriver as Pak Nam, which means 'river mouth' in Thai. It's about two hours each way by boat, or a bit quicker if you return by bus or taxi.

## Dinner Cruises

A dozen or more companies in Bangkok run regular cruises along the Chao Phraya with rates ranging from 70B to 1200B per person, depending on distances and whether dinner is included with the fare. Most require advance phone reservations.

The less expensive, more casual boats allow you to order as little or as much as you want from moderately priced menus; a modest charge of 70B per person is added to the bill for the cruise. It's a fine way to dine outdoors when the weather is hot, away from city traffic and cooled by river breezes. Several of the dinner boats cruise under the illuminated Saphan Phra Ram IX, the longest single-span cable-suspension

bridge in the world. This engineering marvel supports the elevated expressway joining Bangkok's Th Tok district with Thonburi's Ratburana district. Dinner cruises offering an à-la-carte menu plus surcharge include:

**Khanap Nam Restaurant** (☎ 433 6611) Travels from Saphan Krungthon to Saphan Phra Ram IX; operates daily.

**Loy Nava** (☎ 437 4932, 437 7329) Travels from the Oriental Hotel pier to Tha Wasukri, offers a more swanky dinner cruise with a set price of 880B for the cruise and dinner; beer and liquor cost extra; operates 6 to 8 pm and 8 to 10 pm nightly.

**Marriott Royal Garden Riverside Hotel** (☎ 476 0021) Offers a three-hour dinner cruise aboard the *Manohra* for 1200B plus tax and service (about 1413B, drinks excluded); operates 7.30 pm nightly.

**Riverside Company** (☎ 434 0090) Travels from Saphan Krungthon to Saphan Phra Ram IX; operates Sunday to Thursday.

**Yok Yor Restaurant** (☎ 863 0565, 863 1708) Travels from Yok-Yor Restaurant (Tha Wisut Kasat) to Saphan Phra Ram IX; operates daily.

**Sunset Cruise** Before its regular 7.30 pm dinner cruise (2½ hours), the *Manohra* sails at 5 pm from the Marriott Royal Garden Riverside Hotel (☎ 476 0021) for an hourlong sunset cocktail cruise. Boarding costs 500B plus tax and service (about 589B), which includes one drink and a light snack. A free river taxi operates between the Tha River City (River City pier) and the Tha Royal Garden (Royal Garden pier) at 4 pm, just in time for the 5 pm cruise departure.

**Longer Cruises** All-day and overnight cruises on the river are also available. The Chao Phraya River Express Boat Co (☎ 222 5330, 225 3002–3) does a reasonably priced tour on Sunday only, starting from Tha Maharat at 8 am and returning at 5.30 pm, which includes visits to the Royal Folk Arts & Handicrafts Centre in Bang Sai, Bang Pa-In Palace near Ayuthaya and the bird sanctuary at Wat Phailom in Pathum Thani Province. The price is 280B per person excluding lunch, which you arrange yourself in Bang Pa-In.

Mit Chao Phraya Express Boat Co (☎ 225 6179) operates another moderately priced program through several Thonburi canals, with stops at several historic wats and the Royal Barges National Museum, and travels as far as Bang Pa-In. The tour departs from Tha Chang on Sunday at 8 am and returns at 5 pm. The program costs 280B, excluding admission fees to the aforementioned attractions.

The Oriental Hotel's luxurious all air-con *Oriental Queen* (☎ 236 0400–20) also does a cruise to Bang Pa-In that leaves at 8 am from Tha Oriental and returns by air-con bus at 5 pm. It costs 1800B, including lunch and guided tour.

Note that neither of the cruises that visit Bang Pa-In really allow enough time for you to see Ayuthaya properly, so if that's your primary intention, go on your own. On the other hand, I've had letters from history-weary readers who thought 15 to 30 minutes was plenty of time to see the ruins. Two other companies running similar Bang Pa-In/Ayuthaya tours for around 1500B per person are Horizon Cruise (☎ 266 8165) from the Shangri-La Hotel and River Sun Cruise (☎ 266 9316) from the River City Complex.

Royal Garden Resorts and the Menam Hotel maintain three restored 50- to 60-year-old teak rice barges that have been transformed into four- and 10-cabin cruisers. Decorated with antiques and Persian carpets, these craft represent the ultimate in Mae Nam Chao Phraya luxury, the nautical equivalent of the *Eastern & Oriental Express* train. These barges – two named *Mekhala,* one called *Manohra 2* – typically leave Bangkok in the afternoon and head upriver towards Ayuthaya (or downriver towards Bangkok on the return trip). In the evening they anchor at Wat Praket, where a candle-lit dinner is served. The next morning passengers offer food to the Wat Praket monks, and then the barge moves on to Bang Pa-In. After a tour of the Summer Palace, a longtail boat takes passengers on a tour of the ruins of Ayuthaya.

At present four Ayuthaya cruises are scheduled per week. The cost for the two-day cruise is variable depending on which barge is used, starting at 4800B to 5600B per person for the *Mekhala,* to US$308 to US$472 per person for the superdeluxe, four-cabin *Manohra 2* depending on time of year; prices include all meals and nonalcoholic beverages, accommodation, guide services, admission fees in Ayuthaya and hotel transfers. Shorter cruises are available by charter. Call ☎ 476 0021 at the Marriott Royal Garden Riverside Hotel *(Manohra 2)* or ☎ 256 7168 at the Menam Hotel *(Mekhala)* for details.

## Floating Markets

Among the most heavily published photo images of Thailand are those that depict wooden canoes laden with multicoloured fruits and vegetables, paddled by Thai women wearing indigo-hued clothes and wide-brimmed straw hats. Floating markets *(talàat náam)* are found throughout the huge canal system that surrounds Bangkok.

### Damnoen Saduak Floating Market
This is a large, if somewhat commercial, floating market on Khlong Damnoen Saduak in Ratchaburi Province, 104km south-west of Bangkok, between Nakhon Pathom and Samut Songkhram. You can get buses from the Southern bus terminal (Map 1) on Th Charan Sanitwong in Thonburi to Damnoen Saduak starting at 6 am. Get there as early in the morning as possible to escape the hordes. For more information, see Damnoen Saduak Floating Markets under Around Nakhon Pathom in the Excursions chapter.

### Wat Sai Floating Market
In recent years, visitors to the floating market near Wat Sai on Khlong Sanam Chai (off Khlong Dao Khanong) have outnumbered vendors to the point that opinions are now virtually unanimous – don't waste your time at this so-called market. Go to Damnoen Saduak instead, or find your own floating market.

If you're set on doing the Wat Sai trip, take one of the floating market tours that leave from Tha Oriental (at the end of Soi Oriental) or Tha Maharat – your only other alternative is to charter a whole boat at Tha Oriental, which can be quite expensive. Floating market tours cost from 50B, and give you only 20 minutes or so at the market (probably more than enough for this nonevent). Most tours charge 300B to 400B for 1½ hours.

## ACTIVITIES
### Athletic Facilities

The first and grandest of the city's sports facilities is the **Royal Bangkok Sports Club** (RBSC) between Th Henri Dunant and Th Ratchadamri (the green oval marked 'Turf' on the Bangkok bus maps). Facilities include a horse track, polo grounds, swimming pool, sauna, squash and tennis courts (both hard and grass), and an 18-hole golf course. There's a waiting list for membership, so the only way you're likely to mingle at this prestigious club is to be invited there by a lucky RBSC member.

Pricey membership at the **British Club** (☎ 234 0247), 189 Th Surawong, is open to citizens of Australia, Canada, New Zealand and the UK or to others by invitation. Among the sports facilities are a pool, golf driving range, and squash and tennis courts.

The least expensive swimming facility in Bangkok is the one operated by the **Department of Physical Education** (☎ 215 1535) at the National Stadium on Th Phra Ram I, next to Mahboonkrong shopping centre; membership costs just 300B per year plus 25B per hour.

The top-class **Clark Hatch Physical Fitness Centres**, with weight machines, pool, sauna and massage, can be found at the Hilton International Bangkok, Century Park, Amari Atrium and Amari Watergate hotels; nonhotel guests are welcome.

Other sports clubs open to the public include:

**Amorn & Sons** (☎ 392 8442) 8 Soi Amorn 3, Soi 49, Th Sukhumvit; tennis, squash, badminton

**The Bangkok Gym** (☎ 255 2440) 9th floor, Delta Grand Pacific Hotel, 259 Soi 19, Th Sukhumvit; weights, sauna, swimming, aerobics

**Bangna Tennis Court & Swimming Pool** (☎ 393 8276) 57.455 Soi Bangna; tennis, swimming

**Capitol Club** (☎ 661 1210) President Park Residential Complex, Th Sukhumvit; aerobics, rock-climbing wall, swimming, tennis, squash, weights, fitness machines

**Central Tennis Court** (☎ 213 1909) 13/1 Soi Atakanprasit, Th Sathon Tai; tennis

**Diana Women's Club** (☎ 278 1203) 33 Soi 2, Th Phahonyothin

**Kanpaibun Tennis Court** (☎ 391 8784, 392 1832) 10 Soi 40, Th Sukhumvit; tennis

**Saithip Swimming Pool** (☎ 331 2037) 140 Soi 56, Th Sukhumvit; tennis, badminton, swimming

**Sivalai Club Tennis Court & Swimming Pool** (☎ 411 2649) 168 Soi Anantaphum, Th Itsaraphap, Thonburi; tennis, swimming

**Soi Klang Racquet Club** (☎ 391 1194) 8 Soi 49, Th Sukhumvit; squash, tennis, racquetball, swimming, aerobics

### Traditional Massage

Traditional Thai massage, also called 'ancient' massage, is widely available in Bangkok. One of the best places to experience one is at **Wat Pho**, Bangkok's oldest temple. Massage here costs 200B per hour or 120B for half an hour. For those interested in studying massage, the temple offers two 30-hour courses – general Thai massage, and massage therapy – which you can attend three hours per day for 10 days, or two hours per day for 15 days. Tuition is 6000B. A nine-hour foot massage course costs 3000B.

The Wat Pho massage school has moved outside the temple compound to a new location in a nicely restored old Bangkok shophouse on Th Sanam Chai, opposite the temple's western wall. For those so inclined there are also longer one- to three-year programs that combine Thai herbal medicine with massage for a full curriculum in Thai traditional medicine. Call Wat Pho Thai Traditional Medical & Massage School on ☎ 221 2974 or [e] watpottm@netscape.net for further information.

Next to Wat Mahathat (towards Thammasat University at the south-east corner of Th Maharat and Th Phra Chan) is a strip of Thai herbal medicine shops offering good massage for a mere 100B an hour.

A more commercial area for Thai massage as well as Thai herbal saunas is Th Surawong near infamous Patpong. Here you'll find:

**Arima Onsen** (☎ 235 2142) 37/10-11 Soi Surawong Plaza; specialises in Japanese-style massage and reflexology

THINGS TO SEE & DO

**Eve House** (☎ 266 3846) 18/1 Th Surawong opposite Soi Thaniya; offers Thai herbal sauna as well as massage, but accepts women only

**Marble House** (☎ 235 3519) 37/18-19 Soi Surawong Plaza, Th Surawong

**Vejakorn** (☎ 237 5576) 37/25 Soi Surawong Plaza, Th Surawong

All of the places charge 150B per hour, 250B for 90 minutes or 300B for two hours.

Out on Th Sukhumvit you can find traditional Thai massage at:

**Buathip Thai Massage** (☎ 255 1045) 4/13 Soi 5, Th Sukhumvit

**Winwan** (☎ 251 7467) between sois 1 and 3, Th Sukhumvit

Fees for traditional massage should be no more than 300B per hour, some places have a 1½ hour minimum. Be aware not every place advertising traditional or ancient massage offers the real thing; sometimes the only thing 'ancient' about the pummelling is the age of the masseuse or masseur. Aficionados say that the best massages are given by blind masseurs (available at Marble House).

Most hotels also provide a legitimate massage service either through their health clubs or as part of room service. The highly praised **Oriental Hotel Spa** offers a 40-minute 'jet lag massage' designed to alleviate body-clock time differences.

## COURSES
### Language

Several language schools in Bangkok offer courses for foreigners in Thai language. Tuition fees average 250B per hour. Some places will let you trade English lessons for Thai lessons, or, if not, you can usually teach English on the side to offset tuition costs. If you can 'shop around', it's best to enrol in programs that offer plenty of opportunity for linguistic interaction rather than rote learning or the 'natural method', which focuses on teacher input rather than student practice.

Schools in Bangkok with the best reputations include:

**AUA Language Center** (☎ 252 8170) 179 Th Ratchadamri. American University Alumni

(AUA) runs one of the largest English-language teaching institutes in the world, so this is a good place to meet Thai students. Some foreigners who study Thai here complain that there's not enough interaction in class because of an emphasis on the 'natural method'. Others find the approach useful. Baw Hok courses are available.

**Nisa Thai Language School** (☎ 286 9323) YMCA Collins House, 27 Th Sathon Tai. Nisa has a fairly good reputation, though teachers may be less qualified than at Union or AUA language schools. In addition to all the usual levels, Nisa offers a course in preparing for the Baw Hok or Grade 6 examination, a must for anyone wishing to work in the public school system. A second location (☎ 671 3359) is at 32/14-6 Th Yen Akat.

**Siri Pattana Thai Language School** (☎ 213 1206) YWCA, 13 Th Sathon Tai, Bangkok. Offers Thai language lessons as well as preparation for the Baw Hok exam.

**Union Language School** (☎ 233 4482, 235 4030) Christ Church Thailand Bldg, 109 Th Surawong. Generally recognised as the best and most rigorous course. Employs a balance of structure-oriented and communication-oriented methodologies. Private tuition is also available.

## Language & Culture

Chulalongkorn University (Map 7, ☎ 218 3393, fax 218 3926, ⓔ surapeepan.c@chula.ac.th), the most prestigious university in Thailand, offers an intensive Thai studies course called 'Perspectives on Thailand'. The eight-week program includes Thai language, culture, history, politics, religion, art, geography, trade and economics. Classes meet six hours a day, five days a week and are offered once a year from the first Monday in July. Past students say the quality of instruction is excellent. The cost for this program, excluding airfare, meals and lodging, is US$950 per person. A fee for optional on-campus accommodation is US$200. For further information write to: Perspectives on Thailand, Continuing Education Center, 5th floor, Vidhyabhathan Bldg, 12 Soi Chulalongkorn, Chulalongkorn University, Bangkok 10330.

Since 1991 Chulalongkorn has also offered a two-year master's degree program in Thai Studies in English. Tuition and registration fees total 46,000B per semester. Contact Thai Studies Section, Faculty of Arts, Chulalongkorn University, Bangkok 10330, for further information. Non-degree students may enrol in courses offered in the Thai Studies program at a cost of 15,000B, plus a registration fee of 11,000B.

The Oriental Hotel (☎ 236 0400, ext 5) offers a lecture series across the river from the hotel as part of its Thai Cultural Programme. Lectures by some of Thailand's leading university professors run from Monday to Friday; cost is US$40 per person with a minimum of three persons in a class, including refreshments and trips (where applicable). Lectures include 'Thai Ways', 'Thai Beliefs', 'Thai Dances and Music', 'Contemporary Thailand' and 'Thai Art and Architecture'. Reservations are recommended. On request, the following additional lectures are available within 24 hours of paid reservation: Thai dance, martial arts and masked dance, Thai music lessons and meditation.

## Cooking

An increasing number of travellers are coming to Thailand just to learn how to cook. It's not uncommon to see foreign chefs seeking out recipe inspirations for the East-West fusion cuisine that seems to be taking the world by storm. Amaze your friends back home after attending a course in Thai cuisine at one of the following places:

**Modern Housewife Centre** (☎ 279 2834) 45/6-7 Th Sethsiri, Bangkok.

**Oriental Hotel Cooking School** (☎ 236 0400/39) Soi Oriental, Th Charoen Krung, Bangkok. Features a plush five-day course under the direction of well-known star chef Chali (Charlie) Amatyakul.

**Thai House** (☎ 280 0740, fax 280 0741) 3677/4 Mu, 8 Tambon Bang Meuang, Amphoe Bang Yai, Nonthaburi. Popular residential cooking course about 40 minutes north of Bangkok by boat. The program includes all meals, four nights' accommodation and transfer to/from Bangkok.

**UFM Food Centre** (☎ 259 0620–33) 593/29-39 Soi 33/1, Th Sukhumvit, Bangkok. The most serious and thorough cooking school in Thailand, with a multilayered curriculum; most classes are offered in Thai – minimum of four people necessary for an English-language class.

## Martial Arts

Many Westerners have had martial arts training in Thailand, but few last more than a week or two in a Thai camp – and fewer still have gone on to compete on Thailand's pro circuit.

**Muay Thai (Thai Boxing)** Training in muay thai takes place at dozens of boxing camps in Bangkok. Most would be relatively reluctant to take on foreign trainees, except in special cases where the applicant can prove a willingness to conform *totally* to the training system, diet, rustic accommodation and most of all learning the Thai language. Rates vary from US$50 to US$200 per week, including food and accommodation. Newcomers interested in training at a traditional muay thai camp can try the Fairtex Muay Thai (☎ 385 5148) outside Bangkok at 99/2 Mu 3, Soi Buthamanuson, Th Thaeparak, Bangpli, Samut Prakan, which accepts foreign students.

Jitti's Gym Thai Boxing & Homestay (Map 4, ☎ 282 3551), 13 Soi Krasab, Th Chakraphong, west Bamlamphu, specialises in training foreign students – women as well as men. A one-month stay here costs 10,000B and includes daily training sessions from 7 to 9 am and 3 to 7 pm, plus accommodation and evening meals. If you'd like to try a lesson without making a long-term commitment, you can train during any session for 200B.

Another place that specialises in international training is the Muay Thai Institute (☎ 992 0096, ⒠ khuna@muaythai.th.net), associated with the respected World Muay Thai Council. The Institute is located inside the Rangsit Muay Thai Stadium north of Bangkok International Airport. The Institute offers three main study programs: three basic muay thai courses of 10 days each plus a 90-day 'professional' course; three 15-day courses for muay thai instructors; and three 15-day courses for referees and judges. All text books are available in English, and there is accommodation on site. The fee is US$160 for 40 hours of instruction (half that for Thais). Most muay thai experts would express scepticism that muay thai could be learned in such relatively short intervals, but the school's credentials are 100% Thai.

In Thailand look for copies of *Muay Thai World,* a biannual periodical published by

Bangkok's World Muay Thai Council. Although it's basically a cheap martial-arts flick, Jean-Claude Van Damme's *Kick-boxer* gives a more comprehensive, if exaggerated, notion of muay thai than most films on the subject.

The Web site www.muaythai.com contains loads of information on muay thai in Thailand, including the addresses of training camps.

See the special section 'Traditional Thai Martial Arts' in the Entertainment chapter.

**Krabi-Krabong** A traditional Thai martial art, *kràbìi-kràbawng* (literally, sword-staff) is taught at several Thai colleges and universities, but the country's best training venue is the Buddhai (Phutthai) Sawan Fencing School of Thailand, 5/1 Th Phetkasem, Thonburi, where Ajahn Samai Mesamarna carries on traditions passed down from Wat Phutthaisawan. Several *farang* (foreigner of European descent) have trained here, including one American who became the first foreigner to attain *ajahn* (master) status.

See the special section 'Traditional Thai Martial Arts' in the Entertainment chapter.

## Meditation

Although at times Bangkok may seem like the most unlikely Buddhist city on earth, there are several places where interested foreigners can learn about Theravada Buddhist meditation. (See the Religion section in Facts about Bangkok for background information on Buddhism.) Thai language is usually the medium of instruction but several places also provide instruction in English. Some centres and monasteries teach both vipassana and samatha methods, others specialise in one or the other.

Instruction and accommodation are free of charge at temples, though donations are expected. Short-term students will find the two-month Tourist Visa is ample for most courses of study. Long-term students may want to consider getting a three- or six-month Non-Immigrant Visa. A few Westerners are ordained as monks or nuns in

order to take full advantage of the monastic environment. Monks and nuns are generally (but not always) allowed to stay in Thailand as long as they remain in robes.

For a detailed look at vipassana study in Thailand, including visa and ordination procedures, read *The Meditation Temples of Thailand: A Guide* (Silkworm Books, ☎ 053-271889, 104/5 Th Chiang Mai-Hot, Mu 7, Tambon Suthep, Chiang Mai 50100) or *A Guide to Buddhist Monasteries & Meditation Centres in Thailand* (available from the World Federation of Buddhists in Bangkok).

Useful reading material includes Jack Kornfield's *Living Dharma,* which contains short biographies and descriptions of the teaching methods of 12 well-known Theravada teachers, including six Thais. Serious meditators can study *The Path of Purification (Visuddhi Magga),* a classic commentary that reveals every detail of canonical Buddhist practice and includes a Pali-English glossary defining all the tricky terms like *kasina, jhana, nimitta, vipaka* and so on. These books are available at bookshops in Bangkok.

**Wat Mahathat (Map 3)** The International Buddhist Meditation Centre within this wat provides meditation instruction several times daily at section 5, a building near the monks' residences. Some of the Thai monks here speak English and there are often Western monks or long-term residents available to interpret. There is also a special Saturday session for foreigners at the Dhamma Vicaya Hall. Instruction is based on the Mahasi Sayadaw system of *sati-patthana* (mindfulness). Air-con bus No 8 or 12 both pass near the wat; the nearest Chao Phraya River Express pier is Tha Maharat.

**World Fellowship of Buddhists (Map 7)** The WFB (☎ 661 1284), in Benjasiri Park next to The Emporium, Soi 24, Th Sukhumvit, is a clearing house for information on Theravada Buddhism as well as dialogue between various schools of Buddhism. The centre hosts meditation classes from 2 to 5.30 pm on the first Sunday of every month.

Walking Tours of Bangkok

# Temples & River Walking Tour

This walk covers **Ko Ratanakosin** (Ratanakosin Island), which rests in a bend of the river in the middle of Bangkok and contains some of the city's most historic architecture – Wat Phra Kaew, the Grand Palace, Wat Pho and Wat Mahathat (see individual entries under Temples & Shrines in this chapter) – and prestigious universities. The river bank in this area is busy with piers and markets, worthwhile attractions in themselves. Despite its name, Ko Ratanakosin is not an island at all, though in the days when Bangkok was known as the 'Venice of the East', Khlong Banglamphu and Khlong Ong Ang – two lengthy adjoining canals to the east that run parallel to the river – were probably large enough that the area seemed like an island.

This circular walk (one to three hours depending on your pace) begins at **Lak Meuang (City Pillar)**, a shrine to Bangkok's city spirit. At the intersection of Thanon (Th) Ratchadamnoen Nai and Th Lak Meuang, opposite the southern end of **Sanam Luang (Royal Field)**, the shrine can be reached by taxi, by air-con bus No 1, 6, 7, 8, 12 or 39, by ordinary bus No 39, 44 or 47, or on foot if you're already in the Royal Hotel area. (If the Chao Phraya River Express is more convenient, you can start this walk from Tha Tien.)

Traditionally, every city in Thailand must have a foundation stone that embodies the city spirit *(phǐi meuang)* and from which intercity distances are measured. This shrine is Bangkok's most important site of animistic worship; believers throng the area day and night, bringing offerings of flowers, incense, whisky, fruit and even cooked food.

From the City Pillar, walk south across Th Lak Meuang and along Th Sanamchai with the Grand Palace/Wat Phra Kaew walls to your right until you come to Th Chetuphon on the right (the second street after the palace walls end, approximately 500m from the pillar). Turn right onto Th Chetuphon and enter **Wat Pho** through the second portico. Officially named Wat Phra Chetuphon, this is Bangkok's oldest temple and is famous for its huge reclining Buddha and its massage school. The school is the oldest in Thailand and is part of a traditional medical college that archives the country's principal texts on Thai medicine. After you've done the rounds of the various *wíhǎan* (sanctuaries) within the monastery grounds, exit through the same door and turn right onto Th Chetuphon, heading towards the river.

Th Chetuphon ends at Th Maharat after 100m or so. Turn right at Th Maharat and stroll north, passing the **market** area to your left. At the end of this block, Th Maharat crosses Th Thai Wang. On the southwestern corner is an older branch of the **Bangkok Bank**, where you turn left on Thai Wang to glimpse a row of rare, early **Ratanakosin-era shophouses**. If you continue along Th Thai Wang to the river you'll arrive at Tha Tien, one of the pier stops for the Chao Phraya River Express. From an adjacent pier you can catch one of the regular ferries

**Title page:** Chinese Statue at Wat Arun. (Photograph by Dennis Johnson)

# TEMPLES & RIVER WALKING TOUR

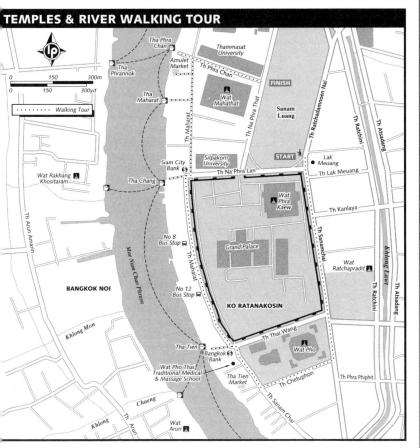

across the Chao Phraya to **Wat Arun**, which features one of Bangkok's most striking *prang*, a tall Hindu/Khmer-style pagoda (see Wat Arun under Temples & Shrines later in this chapter).

Stroll back along Th Thai Wang to Th Maharat and turn left to continue the walking tour. On the left along Th Maharat are two government buildings serving as headquarters for the departments of Internal Trade and Public Welfare. On the right are the whitewashed west walls of the Grand Palace. Two air-con city buses, Nos 8 and 12, stop along this stretch of Maharat – something to keep in mind when you've had enough walking. About 500m from the Th Thai Wang intersection, Th Maharat crosses Th Na Phra Lan; from here turn left to reach Tha Chang, another express boat stop, or right to reach the entrance to the Grand Palace and Wat Phra Kaew grounds.

The entrance to the **Grand Palace** and **Wat Phra Kaew** is on the right (south) side of Th Na Phra Lan less than 100m from Th Maharat. All visitors to the palace and temple grounds must be suitably attired – no shorts, tank tops or other dress considered unacceptable for temple visits – temple staff can provide wraparound sarongs for bare legs. Shops opposite the main entrance to the complex sell film, cold drinks, curries and noodles, and there's also a small post office. The Grand Palace has been supplanted by Chitlada Palace as the primary residence of the royal family, but it's still used for ceremonial occasions. Wat Phra Kaew is a gleaming example of Bangkok temple architecture at its most baroque.

After you've had enough of wandering around the palace and temple grounds, exit via the same doorway and turn left towards the river again. On the right you'll pass the entrance to **Silpakorn University and gallery**, Thailand's premier university for fine arts studies. Originally founded as the School of Fine Arts by Italian artist Corrado Feroci, the university campus includes part of an old Rama I palace. A small bookshop inside the gate to the left stocks English-language books on Thai art.

At Th Maharat, turn right (past the **Siam City Bank** on the corner) and almost immediately you'll see vendors selling cheap amulets representing various Hindu and Buddhist deities. Better quality religious amulets *(phrá khrêuang)* are found a bit farther north along Th Maharat in the large **amulet market** between the road and the river. Walk back into the market area to appreciate how extensive the amulet trade is. Opposite the amulet market on Th Maharat is **Wat Mahathat**, another of Bangkok's older temples and the headquarters for the country's largest monastic sect.

If you're hungry by now, this is a good place on the circuit to take time out for a snack or meal. Head back along Th Maharat from the amulet market just a few metres and turn right at Trok Thawiphon (the sign reads 'Thawephon'), which leads to Tha Maharat, yet another express boat stop. On either side of the pier is a riverside restaurant – *Maharat* to the left and *Lan Theh* to the right. Although the food at

KH

**Left:** The majestic Wat Phra Kaew.

both of these restaurants is quite adequate, most local residents head past the Lan Theh (no roman sign) and into a warren of smaller *restaurants* and food vendors along the river. The food here is very good and very inexpensive – to order, all you'll need is a pointing index finger.

Renewed and refuelled, start walking north again along Th Maharat past the amulet market and Wat Mahathat to Th Phra Chan, around 80m from Trok Thawiphon. Turn left for Tha Phra Chan if you want to catch an express boat north or south along the river, or turn right to reach **Sanam Luang**, the end of the tour. If you take the latter route, you'll pass **Thammasat University** on the left. Thammasat is known for its law and political science faculties; it was also the site of the bloody demonstrations of October 1976, when hundreds of Thai students were killed or wounded by military troops. Opposite the university entrance are several very good *noodle shops*.

# Chinatown-Phahurat Walking Tour

This route meanders through Bangkok's busy Chinese and Indian market districts – best explored on foot as vehicular traffic in the area is in almost constant gridlock. Depending on your pace and shopping intentions, this lengthy route could take from 1½ to three hours. You can also do this tour in reverse, beginning from the Phahurat fabric market.

Only head out on this walk if you can cope with extended crowd contact as well as the sometimes unpleasant sights and smells of a traditional fresh market. The reward for tolerating this attack on the senses is numerous glimpses into the 'real' day-to-day Bangkok, away from the modern-city facade of department stores and office buildings along Bangkok's main avenues – not to mention the opportunity for fabulous bargains. If you're planning a shopping spree, little English is spoken around here, so you might want to bring along a phrasebook, interpreter or brush up on your miming skills!

Start at **Wat Mangkon Kamalawat (Neng Noi Yee)**, Chinatown's largest and liveliest temple, on Th Charoen Krung between Th Mangkon and Trok Itsaranuphap. A taxi direct to the temple is recommended over taking a bus, simply because the district is so congested and street names don't always appear in roman script. If you're determined to go by bus, No 1, 4, 7, 25, 35, 40, 53 or 73 pass the temple going east (the temple entrance will be on the left), or you could take air-con bus No 1, 7 or 8 and get off near the Th Mangkon intersection on Th Yaowarat, a block south of Charoen Krung. Yet another alternative is to arrive by Chao Phraya River Express at Tha Ratchawong, then walk four blocks north-east along Th Ratchawong to Th Charoen Krung, turn right and walk one and a half blocks to the temple.

Whichever approach you choose, to help pinpoint the right area on Th Charoen Krung look for neighbouring shops selling fruit, cakes, incense and ritual burning paper for offerings at the temple. Inscriptions at the entrance to Wat Mangkon Kamalawat (Dragon Lotus Temple) appear in Chinese and Tibetan, while the labyrinthine interior features

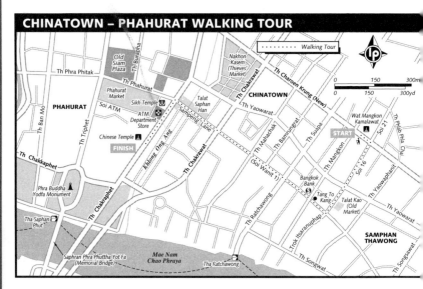

# CHINATOWN – PHAHURAT WALKING TOUR

a succession of **Mahayana Buddhist**, **Taoist** and **Confucian altars**. This temple is packed day and night with worshippers lighting incense, filling the ever-burning altar lamps with oil and praying to their ancestors.

Leaving the temple, walk left along Th Charoen Krung about 20m to the nearest pedestrian crossing (a policeman is usually directing traffic here), then cross the road and head down the alley on the other side. You're now heading south-west on **Trok Itsaranuphap**, one of Chinatown's main market lanes. This section is lined with vendors selling ready-to-eat or preserved foodstuffs, including cleaned chickens, duck and fish – though not for the squeamish, it's one of the cleanest looking fresh markets in Bangkok.

One hundred metres or so down Trok Itsaranuphap you'll cross **Th Yaowarat**, a main Chinatown thoroughfare. This section of Th Yaowarat is lined with large and small gold shops; for price and selection, this is probably the best place in Thailand to purchase a gold chain (sold by the *bàat*, a unit of weight equal to 15g). Cross to the other side (there's a pedestrian crossing 50m to your right on Th Yaowarat) and continue.

Down the lane almost immediately on your left is the Chinese-ornamented entrance to **Talat Kao (Old Market)**. The market section off Trok Itsaranuphap has been operating continuously for over 200 years. All manner and size of freshwater and saltwater fish and shellfish are displayed here, alive and filleted – or sometimes half-alive and half-filleted.

About 100m farther along Itsaranuphap, past rows of vendors selling mostly dried fish, you'll come to a major Chinatown market crossroads. Running perpendicular to Itsaranuphap in either direction is the famous **Sampeng Lane (Soi Wanit 1)**. Turn right into Sampeng Lane. This is usually the most crowded of Chinatown's market sois – a traffic jam of pedestrians, pushcarts and the occasional annoying motorbike twisting through the crowds. Shops along this section of Sampeng Lane sell dry goods, especially shoes, clothing, fabric, toys and kitchenware.

About 25m west, Sampeng Lane crosses Th Mangkon. On either side of the intersection are two of Bangkok's oldest commercial buildings, a **Bangkok Bank** and the venerable **Tang To Kang** gold shop, both over 100 years old. The exteriors of the buildings are classic early Ratanakosin (or 'old Bangkok'), showing lots of European influence; the interiors are heavy with hardwood panelling. Continue walking another 60m or so to the Th Ratchawong crossing (a traffic cop is usually stationed here to part the vehicular Red Sea for pedestrians), and cross and re-enter Sampeng Lane on the other side.

At this point, **fabric shops** – many of them operated by Indian (mostly Sikh) merchants – start to dominate as the western edge of Chinatown approaches the Indian district of Phahurat. If you're looking for good deals on Thai textiles you're in the right place, but hold off buying until you've had a chance to look through at least a dozen or more shops – they get better the farther you go. After about 65m is the small Th Mahachak crossing and then, after another 50m or so, the larger Th Chakrawat (Chakkawat) crossing, where yet another traffic cop assists. Along Th Chakrawat in this vicinity, as well as farther ahead along Sampeng Lane on the other side of Th Chakrawat, there are numerous gem and jewellery shops.

If you were to follow Th Chakrawat north from Sampeng Lane you could have a look around the Chinese-Thai antique shops of **Nakhon Kasem** (also known as the **Thieves' Market** because at one time stolen goods were commonly sold here) between Yaowarat and Charoen Krung. After you re-enter Sampeng Lane on the other side of Th Chakrawat, the jewellery shops are mixed with an eclectic array of housewares and clothing shops until you arrive, after another 50m, at the **Saphan Han** market area, named after a *saphaan* (bridge) over Khlong Ong Ang. Clustered along the khlong on either side of the bridge is a bevy of vendors selling noodles and snacks. On the other side of the bridge, Sampeng Lane ends at Th Chakraphet, the eastern edge of the Phahurat district.

**Th Chakraphet** This area is well known for its Indian restaurants and shops selling Indian sweets. One of the best eateries in the area is the *Royal India Restaurant*, which serves north Indian cuisine and is justly famous for its tasty selection of Indian breads. To get there, turn left onto Th Chakraphet and walk about 70m along the east (left) side of the road; look for the Royal India sign pointing down an alley on the left. On the opposite side of Th Chakraphet from the Royal India is a **Chinese temple**. North of this temple, in a back alley on the west side of the road, is a large **Sikh temple** (Sri Gurusingh Sabha) – turn left before the ATM department store to find the entrance. Visitors to the temple – reportedly the second largest Sikh temple outside of India – are welcome but they must remove their shoes. See Other Temples & Shrines in this chapter.

Several inexpensive Indian food stalls are found in an alley alongside the department store. Behind the store, stretching westward from Th Chakraphet to Th Triphet, is the **Phahurat Market**, devoted almost exclusively to textiles and clothing. Th Phahurat itself runs parallel to and just north of the market.

If you're ready to escape the market hustle and bustle, you can catch city buses on Th Chakraphet (heading north and then east to the Siam Square and Pratunam areas) or along Th Phahurat (heading west and then north along Th Ti Thong to the Banglamphu district). Or walk to the river and catch a Chao Phraya River Express boat from Tha Saphan Phut, which is just to the north-west of Saphan Phra Phuttha Yot Fa (Memorial Bridge). If you're doing this route in reverse, you can arrive by Chao Phraya River Express at Tha Saphan Phut.

# Old Banglamphu Walking Tour

One of the oldest districts in Bangkok, Banglamphu was originally settled by Thai farmers and produce merchants from Ayuthaya who followed the transfer of the royal court to Bangkok in the late 18th century. The name means 'Place of Lamphu', a reference to the *lamphuu* tree *(Duabanga grandiflora)* once prevalent in the area. By the time of King Rama IV (1851–68), Banglamphu had developed into a thriving commercial district by day, and an entertainment spot by night.

Although today Banglamphu is probably most famous for Th Khao San's backpacker scene, a number of historical sites can be found tucked away around the district. To see them on foot, start at the **Democracy Monument** at the traffic circle where Th Ratchadamnoen Klang and Th Din So (Saw) intersect.

From 'the Demo', walk north along the left-hand side of Th Din So. Many of the **shophouses** that line the road here date to the reigns of Rama V (1868-1910) and Rama VII (1925-9134). Since the entire block to the north-west of the Democracy Monument belongs to Wat Bowonniwet, the shop owners pay rent directly to the temple. Turn left from onto Din So, onto Th Phra Sumen, and immediately on your left you'll notice a short row of shops selling **Thai flags** and **Thai regalia**, including orange Buddhist flags, photos of the Thai royal family and window stickers reading *song phrá jaroen* ('long live the king').

Continue walking north-west along Th Phra Sumen. The long wall on your left encloses **Wat Bowonniwet**, one of the most highly venerated Buddhist monasteries in Bangkok and headquarters for the strict Thammayut monastic sect. (See the separate entry on Wat Bowonniwet in this chapter.) Opposite the monastery on the north side of the street, wedged between shophouses and Khlong Banglamphu, stands a former **city gate**, one of Bangkok's original 16. Originally built of timber, it was replaced by this larger brick-and-stucco version during the reign of Rama V and restored in 1981.

Farther along Th Phra Sumen, after crossing Th Bowonniwet, you'll pass a ruined brick **palace gate** on your left. Although the 18th-century

# OLD BANGLAMPHU WALKING TOUR

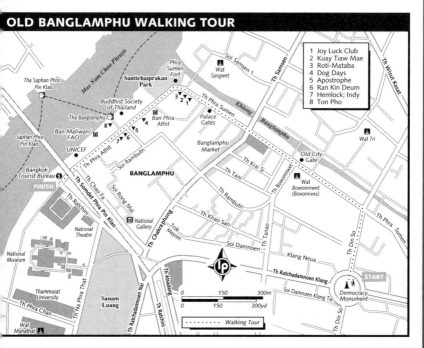

| | |
|---|---|
| 1 | Joy Luck Club |
| 2 | Kuay Tiaw Mae |
| 3 | Roti-Mataba |
| 4 | Dog Days |
| 5 | Apostrophe |
| 6 | Ran Kin Deum |
| 7 | Hemlock; Indy |
| 8 | Ton Pho |

palace, once the residence of Rama I's youngest brother, is long gone, local residents maintain a small spirit house in front of the gate out of respect for the Chakri dynasty.

As Th Phra Sumen approaches Mae Nam Chao Phraya, it bends southward and its name changes to Th Phra Athit. Looming over the riverine corner formed by the Chao Phraya and Khlong Banglamphu, 18th-century **Phra Sumen Fort** is the centrepiece of the recently developed **Santichaiprakan Park** (see the entry on Phra Sumen Fort in this chapter). The small grassy park makes a good stop for river views and cooling breezes. Standing in the park are Banglamphu's last two remaining lamphuu trees, only one of which is labelled. If you want to picnic by the riverside, several small eateries across the street can provide delicious takeaways, including Joy Luck Club, Kuay Tiaw Mae and Roti-Mataba (see the Places to Eat chapter). If you've tired of sightseeing by this point, but want to see more of the river, a **riverfront promenade** follows Mae Nam Chao Phraya south-west from the park.

If you continue walking south-west along Th Phra Athit, you'll pass a mixture of modern shophouses and old mansions on either side of the road, the latter built to house Thai nobility during the late 19th and early 20th centuries. **Ban Phra Athit**, at No 201/1, once belonged to Chao Phraya Vorapongpipat, finance minister during the reigns of

Ramas V, VI, and VII. One of the most splendidly restored Ratanakosin-era buildings in the neighbourhood, it now belongs to a private company, but is easily viewed from the street.

For a cold beer or hot espresso, drop into one of the several Th Phra Athit bistros popular among Thai writers, artists and university students: *Hemlock*, *Indy*, *Ran Kin Deum*, *Apostrophe* and *Dog Days*. If you feel like something more substantial, the riverside *Ton Pho* serves excellent Thai seafood.

To one side of Ton Pho is **Tha Banglamphu**, a pier for Chao Phraya River Express boats, and on the other side is the **Buddhist Society of Thailand**. The latter, housed in an attractive Ratanakosin-era building, provides a library and other services geared primarily to Thais (foreigners interested in Buddhism should visit the World Fellowship of Buddhists, near Soi 24, Th Sukhumvit).

Farther south-west on the river side of Th Phra Athit stands **Ban Maliwan**, a striking mansion designed and built in 1910-25 by Italian architect Ercole Manfredi. Today Ban Maliwan contains the Asia/Pacific offices of the UN Food & Agriculture Organization. Since the entrance to Ban Maliwan faces the river, the architecture is best appreciated from the riverfront promenade.

Another international organisation, **Unicef**, occupies the former palace of HRH Prince Naresworarit, a son of King Rama IV and his Queen consort. Originally built during the Fourth regnum (1851-1868), the palace served as a command post for the Seri Thai (Free Thai) movement towards the end of WWII.

Just a bit farther south down Th Phra Athit, you'll pass under **Saphan Phra Pin Klao** and come to the well-staffed Bangkok Tourist Bureau. From here you can link to the Ko Ratanakosin walking tour described in this section, or you could walk back to Th Ratchadamnoen Klang or Th Khao San.

The Democracy Monument in among the city lights.

Phra Sumen Fort glows under Bangkok's night lights.

Fish to go – Trok Itsaranuphap is one of the busiest alleys in Bangkok's Chinatown.

Multi-instrumentalist Tewan Sapsanyakorn stands at the forefront of Thai jazz fusion.

Put on your dancing shoes and bust a move at one of Bangkok's bars.

# Places to Stay

Bangkok has perhaps the best variety and quality of places to stay of any Asian capital – which is one of the reasons why it's such a popular destination for roving world travellers. As accommodation is spread across the city it's easy to find a place close to where you want be – the tourist shopping ghettos of Thanon (Th) Sukhumvit, Th Silom and Th Surawong, the backpackers' ghetto of Banglamphu (north of Th Ratchadamnoen Klang), the centrally located Siam Square area, boisterous Chinatown, the elegant hotels along the river or the old travellers centre around Soi Ngam Duphli, off Th Phra Ram IV.

Chinatown (around Hualamphong station) and Banglamphu are the best all-round areas for seeing the real Bangkok, and are the cheapest districts for eating and sleeping. The Siam Square area is also well located, in that it's more or less in the centre of Bangkok and on both Skytrain lines. This, coupled with the good selection of city buses that pass through the Th Phra Ram I and Th Phayathai intersection, makes even more of the city accessible. In addition, this area has good bookshops, several banks, shopping centres, excellent mid-range restaurants, travel agencies and eight cinemas within a 10- to 15-minute walk.

## PLACES TO STAY – BUDGET
### Banglamphu (Map 3)

If you're really on a tight budget head for the Th Khao San (Khao San Rd) area, near the Democracy Monument, parallel to Th Ratchadamnoen Klang – ordinary bus Nos 3, 15, 30, 39, 44, 47, 53, 59 and 79 and air-con bus Nos 11 and 12 will get you there. The Airport Bus (route A-2) also stops nearby. The BTS Skytrain does not extend to Banglamphu, but the new subway under construction will – whenever it's completed. The best way to reach Banglamphu via the Skytrain is to take a Silom line train all the way to its south-western terminus at Saphan Sathon. Then take a Chao Phraya

River Express boat north along the river and get off at Tha Phra Athit. This is still very much the main travellers' centre and new guesthouses are continually springing up.

Rates in Banglamphu are the lowest in Bangkok and although some of the places are barely adequate (bedbugs are sometimes a problem), a few are excellent value if you can afford just a bit more. At the budget end, rooms are quite small, mattresses may be on the floor and the walls dividing the rooms are thin – in fact, most are indistinguishable from one another. Some places have small attached cafes with limited menus. Bathrooms are usually down the hall or out the back somewhere.

The least expensive rooms are 80/120B for singles/doubles, though these are hard to come by due to the hordes of people seeking them out. More common are the 120/160B rooms. Occasionally, triple rooms are available for as low as 180B and dorm beds for 70B. During most of the year, it pays to visit several guesthouses before making a decision, but in the high season, from December to February, when Th Khao San is bursting with life, you'd better take the first vacant bed you come across. The best time of day to find a vacancy is from around 9 to 10 am.

In the early 1980s, when I first stumbled onto Th Khao San, there were only two Chinese-Thai hotels on the road, the Nith Jaroen Suk (now called Nith Charoen Hotel) and the Sri Phranakhon (now the Khao San Palace Hotel). Now there are close to 100 guesthouses in the immediate vicinity (hundreds more off Th Khao San), far too many to list here. If you haven't already arrived with a recommendation in hand, you might best use the Banglamphu and Th Khao San area maps, Map 3 and Map 4 respectively, and simply pick a place at random for your first night. If you're not satisfied you can stow your gear and explore the area until something better turns up. Here's a tip: the guesthouses along Th Khao San tend to be cubicles in modern shophouses, while those in Banglamphu's quieter lanes and alleys are often housed in old homes, some of them with a lot of character.

In this chapter, budget accommodation has been taken to mean places costing 80B to 600B per night. At the cheaper places it's not worth calling ahead, since the staff usually won't hold a room for you unless you pay in advance. For places that *may* take phone reservations, the phone numbers have been included.

**Central Banglamphu (Map 4)** Many of the places on or just off Th Khao San are very similar to one another – small rooms with toilet and shower down the hall. This time around we still liked *Prakorp's House & Restaurant*, which offers singles/doubles for 90/180B in a teak house and perhaps the best guesthouse coffee on Khao San. Other OK digs were available at friendly *Bonny Guest House*, the strip's oldest, with singles/doubles for 140B or dorm beds for 60B. *Grand Guest House*, *Lek Guest House* and *Lucky Beer & Guest House*, all in the 100B to 250B range, continue to get good reviews. *Chada Guest House* has small but newly renovated rooms for 180/200B single/double. *Chart Guest House* adds air-con for 400B or fan for 100/130B. *Classic Place* boasts decent singles/doubles with fan for 200/250B, or air-con for 390/490B double/triple. *Sitdhi Guest House & Restaurant* is friendly and charges just 100/150B for singles/doubles with shared facilities. *CH I Guest House* was closed for renovation but the ongoing work indicates it will be a dandy hangout in the 150B to 300B range when open again.

Moving a little more upmarket, the friendly *Khao San Palace Hotel* (☎ 282 0578), set off down an alley at 139 Th Khao San, is well kept; rooms cost 280B to 390B with fan and private bath, 400B to 580B with air-con, TV and hot water. A deluxe room is 730B. Down a parallel alley, the *Nith Charoen Hotel* (☎ 281 9872) has rooms with bath and fan for 360B a single/double, 700B for air-con. The *Nana Plaza Inn* (☎ 281 6402), towards Th Khao San's eastern end, is a large, hotel-like enterprise built around a restaurant; air-con/hot-water rooms go for

500/700B single/double. The similar-looking *D&D Inn* costs 350/500B single/double. Each room has a TV and IDD phone. The four-storey *Siam Oriental* (☎ 620 0312, 190 Th Khao San) has decent singles with fan for 280B, up to 650B for air-con rooms that can accommodate up to four people. There's a large restaurant and a lift.

*Sawasdee Bangkok Inn* (☎ 280 1251, fax 281 7818, ⓔ sawasdee@sawasdeehotels .com, 126/2 Th Khao San) features three floors around a courtyard designed to look like early Ratanakosin but somehow coming off more like Creole New Orleans. A fan room with shared toilet is 200B. For 250B you can get an air-con room with shared facilities. Rooms with private bath cost 300B to 360B with fan, or 400B to 460B with air-con. All rooms have wooden floors, cable TV, hot-water showers and towels. There's an attached restaurant and Internet services.

Two narrow alleys between Th Khao San and Th Rambutri feature rows of cramped places with small, luggage-crammed lobbies and staircases leading to rooms layered on several floors. Nonetheless they manage to fill up since rates average only 80B to 160B. We've placed some of these guesthouses on the map for orientation (eg, Doll, Pro, Friendly), but can't recommend any in particular.

East down Th Khao San is a wider alley that's a bit more open, with the small *Pian Guest House & Traditional Massage Center & School* (rooms 120/180B) and the hotel-like *Marco Polo Hostel* (120B to 300B, most rooms with private bath). Farther south-east another alley has only one guesthouse, *New Royal* with basic rooms from 80/150B with shared bath, 200B to 250B with attached bath. A final, very narrow but quiet alley just before you come to Th Tanao has a couple of standard-issue places, the *Harn* and *VS*. The friendly and well-run VS offers singles/doubles for 120/150B and dorm rooms 60B, and a collective vegie dinner most nights.

Parallel to Th Khao San but much quieter is Trok Mayom, an alley reserved for mostly pedestrian traffic. *J & Joe* (☎ 281 2949, 281 1198) is a sprawling old teak complex with singles for 90B, doubles for 160B to 180B, triples for 230B, and sitting areas for hanging out; it's often full and a little noisy. There's also *New Joe* (☎ *281 2948, fax 281 5547*) on Trok Mayom, a rather modern-looking place set off the alley, with an outdoor cafe downstairs. Singles/doubles cost 200/280B with private bath, 380B air-con; and email and fax services are available. Up a tiny alley nearby, the relatively new *Barn Thai Guest House* (☎ *281 9041*) is very quiet and secure, and offers rooms in an old wooden house or newer wing for 300B to 350B with shared bath, 400B for a double with private bath. Although priced higher than normal for this neighbourhood, it's kept very clean and the front gate is locked nightly.

Up a narrow soi nearby, *Khao San Privacy Guest House* offers rooms with fan for 150/200B plus air-con at 380/440B. Farther east, towards Th Tanao, are *Ranee's Guest House* (120/220B for singles/doubles with shared bath, 350B air-con) and *7 Holder* (220B), which seems to cater to Japanese travellers and even has Japanese fonts on its Internet cafe computers.

Moving just slightly upscale, the friendly *Orchid House* (☎ *280 2691*), near the Viengtai Hotel on Th Ramburi (north of Th Khao San, and sometimes called Soi Rambutri), offers quiet, clean apartment-style rooms for 250B single with fan and hot water, 380/430B single/double with air-con, or 480B for larger air-con rooms.

Walking west along Th Ramburti you'll come to two side-by-side guesthouses in old restored wooden buildings with cheery paint jobs. *Au-Thong Restaurant & Guest House* (☎ *629 2172*, e *au_thong@hotmail.com, 78 Th Rambutri*) is more of a restaurant that just happens to have a few very simple rooms with shared toilet and shower for 200B. The garden restaurant at the front (there's also a small air-con dining room inside the old house) is one of the best Thai eateries in the neighbourhood if you know how to order Thai food. Next door, *Tuptim Bed & Breakfast* (☎ *629 1535, fax 629 1540*, e *mick@ksc.th.com, 82 Th Rambutri*) look similar but here the emphasis is on the rooms rather than the food. Tuptim has 19 air-con rooms with shared gender segregated toilets

and hot-water showers for 399/550B single/double, including breakfast. There are also two single rooms with fan available for 250B.

### West Banglamphu (Map 3)

Several long-running guesthouses are on sois between Th Chakraphong and Mae Nam Chao Phraya, putting them within walking distance of Tha Phra Athit where you can catch express boats. This area is also close to the Thonburi (Bangkok Noi) station across the river, the National Museum and the National Theatre.

West of Chakraphong on Soi Rambutri, *Sawasdee House* (☎ *281 8138, fax 629 0994*) follows the trend towards hotel-style accommodation in the Th Khao San area, with a large restaurant and bar downstairs and small to medium-sized rooms on several floors upstairs. Rooms with fan and shared facilities are 160B to 250B single, 320B to 360B double. Rooms with private bath and fan cost 400B, while air-con rooms go for 550B. Next along Th Rambutri is the *Chusri Guest House*, which offers adequate rooms for 100B to 120B per person.

Right around the bend along Soi Rambutri is the popular *Merry V Guest House* (☎ *282 9267*), with rooms from 120B to 350B. The cosy *Green Guest House* (☎ *926 2104*) is next door and is slightly less expensive at 100/140B single/double with shared facilities, 240B with private bath. At *My House* on the same soi, the Thai-style downstairs sitting area looks nice, and decent singles/doubles with shared bath are 120/200B, or 180/300B with private facilities. Air-con is available for 500B.

A rash of new and larger places have opened up towards the south-west end of Soi Rambutri and around the corner to the south on Soi Rong Mai. *Bella Bella House* (☎ *629 3090*), just past the soi that leads to New Siam Guest House, is a new five-storey building with a sheltered rooftop area and rooms for 150B single, 220B double. A few doors farther, *Sawasdee Krungthep Inn* (☎/fax *629 0072*) offers rooms in a new four-storey building for 350B a double with fan, 400/450B a single/double with air-con or 500/600B for a triple/quadruple. *Baan*

*Sabai* (☎ 629 1599, fax 629 1595) features a pleasant, large lobby on the ground floor, finished to resemble an old Bangkok-style building. The inn's 64 rooms cost 170B for a single with fan, 270B to 320B a double with fan and 450B to 480B a double with air-con.

Also in this vicinity, off the southern end of Th Rambutri, the family run *Chai's House* offers clean rooms for 100/200/300B single/double/triple, or 300B single/double with air-con, all with shared bath. It's a quiet, security-conscious place with a sitting area out the front. The food must be cheap and good, as it's a favourite gathering spot for local Thai college students on weekends.

Backtracking along Th Rambutri and turning left into Soi Chana Songkhram, you'll find the four-storey *New Siam Guest House* (☎ 282 4554, fax 281 7461), where quiet clean rooms cost 200/250B with shared bath, 300B with private bath, 495B with air-con; storage lockers are available downstairs. This place seems exceptionally well organised and offers good food in the downstairs cafe; it's almost always full.

Continue on towards the river and you'll reach Th Phra Athit. On the eastern side of the road the *Peachy Guest House* (☎ 281 6471) and *New Merry V* are more like small hotels than family-type guesthouses. Peachy has been completely renovated since we last stopped by. Rooms with shared bath are 150B single/double, while rooms with air-con and private hot-water bath are 350B. Dorm beds are available for 55B per person. The New Merry V, north of Peachy, has comfortable rooms with private hot-water showers for 250B, or with shared bath for 120B. Air-con rooms are 380B.

**East Banglamphu (Map 3)**  All guesthouses are located on Map 3, unless otherwise indicated. There are several guesthouses clustered in the alleys east of Th Tanao. In general, the rooms are bigger and quieter here than at the places around Th Khao San. *Central Guest House* (Map 4, ☎ 282 0667) is just off Th Tanao on Trok Bowonrangsi – look for the rather inconspicuous signs. Clean, simple rooms go for 80/130B single/double.

On a small road parallel to Ratchadamnoen Klang, is the *Sweety Guest House* (☎ 281 6756), with small windowless singles for 80B to 100B, larger doubles for 120B to 200B and air-con rooms for 350B. Sweety has a roof terrace for lounging and for hanging laundry. Opposite the Sweety and next to the post office is *CH II*, which is more like the Th Khao San standard issue with rooms for 100B to 150B single, 150B to 240B double.

*Prasuri Guest House* (☎/fax 280 1428), down Soi Phrasuli on the right, has quiet, clean singles/doubles/triples for 190/220/300B with fan, 330/360/390B with air-con – all rooms come with private bath.

**South Banglamphu (Map 3)**  On the other side of Ratchadamnoen Klang, south of the Th Khao San area, are a couple of independent hotels worth investigating. Walk south along Th Tanao from Ratchadamnoen Klang, then turn left at the first soi and you'll come to *Hotel Rajdamnoen* (☎ 224 1012). Formerly known as Hotel 90, it's now a bit more respectable; large, clean rooms with fan and private bath are 200/250B, 400B with air-con and TV.

Return west on this soi to Th Tanao, turn left and then take the right at Trok Sa-Ke towards the upper mid-range Royal Hotel, and after 50m or so you'll come to the *Palace Hotel* (☎ 224 1876), an all air-con version of the Rajdamnoen with singles/doubles at 330/400B.

**North Banglamphu (Map 3)**  The clean, friendly *PS Guest House* (☎ 282 3932), not far from the river, has light and airy rooms for 130/190/250B single/double/triple (all with shared facilities). A restaurant is downstairs, and upstairs at the back is a small seating area overlooking the canal.

Facing the north side of Khlong Banglamphu off Th Samsen (the northern extension of Th Chakraphong), the *New World House Apartments & Guest House* (☎ 281 5596) offers both short and long-term room rentals starting at 400B per night. Rooms come with private hot-water shower, air-con and a small balcony.

Also off Th Samsen, farther north of Khlong Banglamphu, is a small cluster of guesthouses in convenient proximity to Tha Samphraya river express landing. On Soi 1 Samsen, just off Th Samsen, the Th Khao San-style *Truly Yours Guest House* (☎ *282 0371*) offers fan rooms for 80B to 200B over a downstairs restaurant. Farther along Soi 1, *Villa Guest House* (☎ *281 7009*) is a quiet, leafy, private old teak house with 10 rooms from 200B to 450B; it's often full. Up on Soi 3 Samsen (also known as Soi Wat Samphraya) are the *River House* (☎ *280 0876*), *Home & Garden Guest House* (☎ *280 1475*) and *Clean & Calm Guest House*, each with small but clean rooms with shared bath for 70B to 150B. The latter place is quite popular with West Africans waiting for visas.

Farther north on Th Samsen, turn east on Soi 6 Samsen and you'll find *Nakorn Pink Hotel* (☎ *281 6574, fax 282 3727*), where a double-bed room costs 300B with fan or 400B with air-con. Rooms with two double beds cost 550B with fan and 700B with air-con. All have private bathroom, TV, phone and fridge. Nakorn Pink also provides a left-luggage service for 10B a day. *Rajata Hotel*, opposite, is a relatively new Thai-Chinese hotel with clean singles/doubles with air-con and TV for 360/480B. *Mitr Paisarn Hotel* (☎ *281 1235, fax 281 1994*) on the same soi looks like a classic Thai 'no-tell' motel, but seems clean and gets foreign trade for its 500/600B single/double rooms, with air-con, TV and private bath. Nearby *Vorapong Guest House* (*Worapong; ☎ 281 1992*) is similar though cheaper, with rooms for 300B to 470B; a 24-hour coffee shop is attached.

## Tha Thewet & National Library Area (Map 3)

All hotels are located on Map 3, unless otherwise indicated. The district north of Banglamphu near the National Library is another travellers enclave. Ordinary bus Nos 19 and 53 and air-con bus No 5 pass this intersection, or you can arrive via Chao Phraya River Express boats by getting off at Tha Thewet, at the end of Th Si Ayuthaya. If you're coming by taxi, tell the driver 'Wat Thewrat', which is near the pier.

Turn on Th Si Ayuthaya towards the river (west from Samsen), and on two parallel sois off the north side of Th Si Ayuthaya you'll find five inexpensive guesthouses run by various members of the same extended family. Standing out from the rest, the nicely decorated and well-run *Shanti Lodge* (*Map 2, ☎ 281 2497*), on the corner of one of the sois, costs a bit more – 200/230B for rooms with fan, 400/450B with air-con or 100B for a dorm bed. Shanti has the best cafe and sitting area of the lot – if it's full, give the others a try.

A sixth, independently run place on the same soi as Paradise is *Little Home Guest House* (*Map 2, ☎ 281 3412*), which is similar to the others in this area except that it has a busy travel agency at the front. Rooms are 150/300B single/double.

Nearby Tha Thewet, a Chao Phraya River Express pier, provides good access to the National Library area. From the pier walk east along Th Krung Kasem to Th Samsen, turn left, cross the canal and take another left onto Th Si Ayuthaya. Ordinary bus Nos 3, 16, 30, 31, 32, 33, 53, 64 and 90 and air-con bus Nos 5 and 6 pass Th Si Ayuthaya while going up and down Th Samsen. Air-con bus No 10 from the airport also passes close to the area along Th Ratwithi to the north, before crossing Saphan Krungthon.

East of Th Samsen you'll find the *Bangkok International Youth Hostel* (*Map 3, ☎ 282 0950, fax 628 7416, e bangkok@ tyha.org, 25/2 Th Phitsanulok*). A bed in the 16-bed fan dorm costs 70B a night, while in the air-con dorm it's 120B. Rooms with fan and private hot-water bath cost 250B double (no single fan rooms are available), while air-con rooms with private facilities cost 280/350B single/double. There's a cafeteria downstairs. In 1992 the hostel stopped accepting nonmembers as guests. Annual Hostelling International (formerly IYHF) membership costs 300B, or you can purchase a temporary membership for 50B. For each temporary membership fee paid, you receive a 'welcome stamp', six of which entitle you to a one-year membership.

If you want to be close to Ratchadamnoen Stadium, or simply away from the river guesthouse scene, have a look at *Venice House* (☎ 281 8262, fax 281 8762, 548-546/1 *Th Krung Kasem)*. This friendly, well-maintained guesthouse is next to Wat Somanat, just around the corner from Th Ratchadamnoen Nok (walk north on Ratchadamnoen Nok from the stadium, turn right on Krung Kasem and walk about 80m till you see a sign for Venice House). Aircon rooms cost 300/450B. It's about a 15-minute walk from the Tha Thewet landing.

## Chinatown & Hualamphong Area (Map 6)

All hotels are on Map 6, unless otherwise indicated. This area is central and colourful, although rather noisy. There are numerous cheap hotels but it's not a travellers centre like Soi Ngam Duphli or Banglamphu. Watch your pockets and bags around the Hualamphong area, both on the street and on the bus. The cream of the razor artists operate here as the train passengers make good pickings.

The *New Empire Hotel* (☎ 234 6990/6, fax 234 6997, 572 Th Yaowarat) is near the Th Charoen Krung intersection, a short walk from Wat Traimit. Air-con singles/doubles with hot water are 450B to 600B, with a few more-expensive rooms for up to 800B – a bit noisy, but a great location if you like Chinatown. The New Empire is a favourite among Chinese Thais from Thailand's southern regions.

Other Chinatown hotels of this calibre, most without English signs at the front, can be found along Th Yaowarat, Th Chakraphet and Th Ratchawong. The *Burapha Hotel* (*Map 3*, ☎ 221 3545/9, fax 226 1723), at the intersection of Th Mahachai and Th Charoen Krung, on the edge of Chinatown, is a notch better than the Empire and costs from 550B single/double.

Straddling the budget and mid-range price range is the *River View Guest House* (☎ 234 5429, 235 8501, fax 237 5428, e riverview@mailcity.com, 768 Soi Phanurangsi, Th Songwat) in the Talat Noi area south of Chinatown – wedged between Bangrak (Silom) and Chinatown. The building is behind the Jao Seu Kong Chinese shrine,

about 400m from the Royal Orchid Sheraton, in a neighbourhood filled with small machine shops. To get there, turn right from the corner of Th Si Phraya (facing the River City shopping complex), take the fourth left, then the first right. Large rooms are 490B with fan and private bath, 690B with air-con and hot water. As the name suggests, many rooms have a Mae Nam Chao Phraya view; the view from the 8th-floor restaurant is superb, even if you have to wake up the staff to get a meal. If you call from the River City complex, someone from the guesthouse will pick you up – it's near Tha Krom Chao Tha.

Nearby Tha Ratchawang on Th Songwat is the *Chao Phraya Riverside Guest House* (☎ 222 6344, 244 8450, fax 223 1696, 1128 Th Songwat), in the heart of a busy area filled with warehouses and trucks loading and unloading all day. It can be hard to find: from Th Ratchawong, turn left onto Th Songwat, then proceed for 75m and keep an eye out for a Chinese school on the left. Turn right into a soi opposite, and you'll find the guesthouse towards the end of the soi on the left. At the time of writing the place was closed for renovations, but when it reopens this will be a good riverside choice.

Closer to the River City shopping complex, and easier to find, *River City Guest House* (☎ 235 1429, fax 237 3127, 11/4-5 Soi 24 (Soi Rong Nam Khaeng), Th Charoen Krung) has decent rooms with two twin beds, clean bathroom with tub and hot water, TV, fridge, phone and air-con for 500B a night. There's a Chinese restaurant downstairs, and the management speaks better Mandarin than Thai.

Costing more but quieter and more secure is the *Krung Kasem Srikung Hotel* (☎ 225 0132, fax 225-4705, 1860 Th Krung Kasem), south-west of Hualamphong station. Clean, sizeable rooms cost 550B with fan, air-con and hot water. There's a small coffee shop downstairs.

## Siam Square (Map 5)

Several good places can be found in this central area, which has the additional advantage of being on the Khlong Saen Saep canal taxi route and both Skytrain lines. In addition, this area has good bookshops, several banks, shopping centres and eight cinemas within a 10- to 15-minute walk.

There are several upper-end budget places on or near Soi Kasem San 1, off Th Phra Ram I near Jim Thompson's House and the National Stadium. The eight-storey *Muangphol Mansion* (*Muangphon Mansion;* ☎ *215 0033, fax 216 8053)* on the corner of Soi Kasem San 1 and Th Phra Ram I has singles/doubles from 450B. It badly needs remodelling but remains relatively popular. Behind the Muangphol, off this soi, is the apartment-style *Pranee Building* (☎ *216 3181, fax 215 0364)*, which has one entrance next to the Muangphol and another on Phra Ram I. Rooms with private bath and fan are 300B; air-con rooms with hot water are 450B. The Pranee also offers long-term rental at a 10% discount.

*White Lodge* (☎ *216 8867, fax 216 8228, 36/8 Soi Kasem San 1)* is past the more expensive Reno Hotel and on the left. It offers clean if somewhat small rooms at 400B single/double. There's a pleasant terrace cafe out the front. The next one down on Soi Kasem San 1 is the three-storey *Wendy House* (☎ *216 2436, fax 216 8053)*, where small but clean rooms with air-con, hot-water shower and TV go for 350/450B. Rooms with fridges cost 550B. If you're carrying unusually heavy bags, note there's no lift. A small restaurant is on the ground floor.

Next up the soi is the ancient *Star Hotel* (☎ *215 0020, 36/1 Soi Kasem San 1)*, a classic mid-1960s Thai no-tell motel, with fairly clean, comfortable, air-con rooms with bath and TV for 500B double, (350B without TV)

Opposite the Star is *A-One Inn* (☎ *215 3029, fax 216 4771, 25/13-15 Soi Kasem San 1)*, a friendly place that gets a lot of return business. Fair-sized air-con doubles with bath, hot water and TV are 450B; spacious triples are 650B (rates may drop 100B in the low season). The similar *Bed & Breakfast Inn* (☎ *215 3004)* diagonally opposite has room rates that fluctuate from 380B to 650B depending on room size and demand; the air-con rooms are substantially smaller than those at the A-One Inn, but the rates include a European breakfast.

## Th Silom & Th Surawong Area (Map 6)

All hotels are located on Map 6, unless otherwise indicated. Though mainly a mid-range area, Th Silom and Th Surawong still have some budget guesthouses.

*Ryn's Café 'n Bed*, (*Map 7,* ☎ *632-1327, fax 632-1323, 44/16 Th Convent)* is a new boutique hostel/B&B in the heart of Th Convent's trendy café and bar scene. Under Swiss-Thai management, Ryn's offers dorm beds for 250B, doubles with shared bath for 350 to 400B, and doubles with private bath for 500 to 600B. A family room sleeping four is available for 800B. All rooms are air-conditioned. The attached indoor/outdoor café serves European and Thai cuisine from 6am till late. English, French and German are spoken.

On Soi 32 Th Charoen Krung just north of the main post office is *Woodlands Inn* (☎ *235 3894)*, where small air-con rooms with no lift access are 350B to 450B. Clean air-con rooms with hot water, phone, TV and fridge are 550/700B single/double. Downstairs is an air-con Indian restaurant called The Cholas.

On the south side of Th Silom is Soi Suksavitthaya (Seuksa Withaya or Soi 9), and the *Niagara Hotel* (*Map 7,* ☎ *233 5783/4, 26 Soi Suksavitthaya)*, where clean air-con rooms with hot water and telephone are a bargain at 550B to 600B; rooms with fan are available for 300B.

*Madras Lodge/Café* (*Map 7,* ☎ *235 6761)*, in Trok Vaithi off Th Silom, not far from the Sri Mariamman Temple, has somewhat unkempt rooms with fan starting at 220B. The proprietor is a friendly, retired gem dealer from Madras, and his kitchen serves delicious south Indian food.

## Soi Ngam Duphli (Map 7)

This area off Th Phra Ram IV is where most budget travellers used to come on their first trip to Bangkok back in the 1970s and early 1980s. With a couple of notable exceptions, most of the places here are not especially cheap and the area has become slightly seedy. Overall, the Banglamphu area has better-value accommodation, though some travellers still prefer Soi Ngam Duphli, which has less of a 'scene' and some good-value places. Several countries maintain embassies on nearby Th Sathon, so it's also a convenient location for those with visa/passport business at these embassies.

The entrance to the soi is on Th Phra Ram IV, near the Th Sathon Tai intersection, and within walking distance of the verdant Lumphini Park and the Th Silom business district. Ordinary bus Nos 13, 14, 74, 109, 115 and 116, and air-con bus No 7, all pass by the entrance to Soi Ngam Duphli along Th Phra Ram IV. The nearest Skytrain station is Sala Daeng, on Th Silom.

At the northern end of Soi Ngam Duphli near Th Phra Ram IV is *ETC Guest House* (☎ 286 9424, 287 1478), an efficiently run, multistorey building with a travel agency downstairs. The rooms are small and uninspiring but clean, and the rates are 140B single/double with fan and shared bath, or 180/280B with fan and private bath. All room rates include a breakfast of cereal, fruit, toast and coffee or tea.

*Madam Guest House* gets mixed reports for its 160B to 240B rooms with fan. Next door, the *Lee 3 Guest House* is pleasant enough, and has large rooms with fan and shared bath for 120/160B single/double, or 200B for private bath. The friendly *Sala Thai Daily Mansion* (☎ 287 1436) is at the end of the alley and has large, clean rooms for 200B to 350B, all with shared bath. A sitting area with TV on the 3rd floor makes for a pleasant gathering place, and there is a breezy rooftop terrace. The owner speaks English and her design background is evident in the tasteful furnishings. Many repeat or long-term guests fill the rooms here.

If you continue north along the main soi that passes the previously mentioned guesthouses you'll come to a left turn that deadends at Soi Saphan Khu (parallel to Soi Ngam Duphli). Turn right and you'll come to two rather more upscale guesthouses on your left, Charlie House (see Places to Stay – Mid-Range later in this chapter) and *PS Guest House (Map 3, ☎ 679 8822/4)*, formerly Four Brothers Guest House. PS costs 400B per day (6000B per month) for air-con rooms.

Back out on Soi Si Bamphen heading south is *Freddy 2*, a clean, well-run place with rooms for 100/180B.

South of the Tungmahamek Privacy on Soi Ngam Duphli is *Honey House (☎ 679 8112/3, fax 287 2035)*, an apartment building with OK air-con rooms for 370/400B single/double. Monthly rates are also available.

## Th Sukhumvit (Map 7)

All hotels are located on Map 7, unless otherwise indicated. Staying in this area puts you in the newest part of Bangkok and the farthest from old Bangkok near the river. Taxis take longer to get here because of the one-way street system. On the other hand the Skytrain runs all the way from the start of Th Sukhumvit at Th Ploenchit to well beyond the Eastern bus terminal. The majority of the hotels in this area are priced in the mid-range, but there are some budget options.

The oldest and most centrally located hotel in the Th Sukhumvit area is *The Atlanta (☎ 252 1650, 252 6069, fax 656 8123, 78 Soi 2 (Soi Phasak), Th Sukhumvit)*. Owned since its construction as The Atlanta Club in the 1950s by Dr Max Henn, a former secretary to the Maharajah of Bikaner and owner of Bangkok's first international pharmacy, the Atlanta is a simple but reliable standby with clean, comfortable rooms in several price categories. Rooms with private cold-water shower, fan and one single and/or double bed cost 330/450B single/double. Air-con rooms with hot-water shower go for 450/570/690B single/double/triple. A small air-con suite with two single beds and a small living room costs 500/620/740B, while a large air-con suite with a living room and two bedrooms sleeping up to four people is 1200B. All rooms have built-in personal safes. Children under 12 years can stay with their parents for 60B extra. Monthly stays paid in advance warrant a 10% discount.

The Atlanta's 1954-vintage swimming pool was the first hotel pool in Thailand; the original 1950s-era hotel lobby is occasionally used as a backdrop for Bangkok fashion shoots. The subdued, simply decorated coffee shop features a heavily annotated menu (itself a crash course in Thai cuisine), a selection of British, German and French newspapers, a sound system playing Thai, classical and jazz (including an hour of King Bhumibol's compositions beginning at noon), and evening video selections that include film classics with Thailand themes (eg, *Chang, Bridge on the River Kwai*). In the lobby area, letter-writing desks, each with its own light and fan, round out the offerings at this Bangkok institution. The Nana Skytrain station is about 15 minutes away on foot.

The L-shaped, aquamarine coloured *Golden Palace Hotel* (*Map 5, ☎ 252 5115, fax 254 1538, 15 Soi 1, Th Sukhumvit*) has a decent swimming pool, is well situated, and costs 490/520B for a single/double with air-con and bath. On the next soi east, the quiet *Best Inn* (*☎ 253 0573, 75/5-6 Soi 3, Th Sukhumvit*) provides smallish rooms with fan for 400B and air-con rooms for 500B. Also in the inner Th Sukhumvit area is *Thai House Inn* (*☎ 255 4698, fax 253 1780*) between sois 5 and 7. Rooms with air-con and hot water are 550B single or double; facilities include a safety-deposit service and a coffee shop.

Moving farther out on Th Sukhumvit, the *Miami Hotel* (*☎ 253 0369, fax 253 1266, e miamihtl@asiaaccess.net.th, 2 Soi 13, Th Sukhumvit*) dates back to the 1960s and 1970s Vietnam R&R period. The room and service quality seems to seesaw every three years or so but at the moment it's decent value at 400/500B single/double for clean air-con rooms with hot water and TV, plus a small swimming pool and coffee shop; discounts are given for long-term stays.

## PLACES TO STAY – MID-RANGE

Bangkok is saturated with small and medium-sized hotels in this category (from roughly 600B to 1800B per night). The clientele are a mixed bunch of Asian business travellers, Western journalists on slim expense accounts, economy-class tour groups, along with a smattering of independent tourists who seem to have chosen their hotels at random. Not quite 'international class', these places often offer guests a better sense of being in Thailand than the luxury hotels.

In the low season (March to November), you may be able to get a low-occupancy discount at these places. Many hotels in this category can also be booked through travel agencies or airport hotel desks for 20% to 40% less than the rates listed here.

### Banglamphu (Map 3)

All hotels are located on Map 3, unless otherwise indicated. Before Th Khao San was 'discovered', the most popular Banglamphu hotel was the *Viengtai Hotel* (*Map 4, ☎ 280 5434, fax 281 8153, 42 Th Rambutri*). Over the last decade or so the Viengtai has continually renovated its rooms and raised its prices until it now sits solidly in the mid-price range of Bangkok hotels. Standard singles/doubles/triples in the six-storey old wing are 1225/1575/1750B, while deluxe rooms in the remodelled nine-storey wing are 1575/1750/2275B; including breakfast. There is a swimming pool on the 3rd floor.

After the Oriental and the Atlanta hotels, the next oldest continually operating hotel in the city is the *Royal Hotel* (*☎ 222 9111/26, fax 224 2083*), which is still going strong on the corner of Th Ratchadamnoen Klang and Th Atsadang, about 500m from the Democracy Monument. The Royal's 24-hour coffee shop is a favourite local rendezvous and the daily buffet breakfast is quite good; this is one of the few upper mid-range places where there are as many Asian as non-Asian guests. Singles/doubles start at 960/1300B, including tax and service. Most taxi drivers know this hotel as the 'Ratanakosin' (as the Thai sign on top of the building reads), not as the Royal.

Another mid-range place in this area is the *Thai Hotel* (*☎ 282 2831/3, fax 280 1299, 78 Th Prachatipatai*), a good budget business hotel with singles/doubles for 900/1200B.

The next river express stop north, and the last in the Banglamphu district, is next to Th Wisut Kasat. The comfortable five-storey *Trang Hotel* (*☎ 282 2141, fax 280 3610, 99/1 Th Wisut Kasat*) has 181 rooms for 1200/1450B single/double with air-con, up to 4000B for a suite. It's east of Th Samsen, so it's a decent walk from the river.

## Chinatown (Map 6)

All hotels are located on Map 6, unless otherwise indicated. Mid-range hotels in Chinatown are tough to find. Best bets are the *Chinatown Hotel* (☎ 225 0230, fax 226 1295, e *malaysia@comnet3.ksc.net.th, 526 Th Yaowarat)*, which has rooms for 700B to 1800B, and the *Miramar Hotel (Map 3, ☎ 226 3579, fax 225 4994, 777 Th Ma-hachai)*, where standard singles/doubles cost 600B to 1800B. The *White Orchid Hotel* (☎ 226 0026, fax 255 6403, 409-421 Th Yaowarat)*, diagonally opposite the Chinatown Hotel, offers nicer accommodation beginning at 900B.

## Th Silom & Th Surawong Area (Map 7)

All hotels are located on Map 7, unless otherwise indicated. This area is packed with upper mid-range places; discounts are often given from April to October. Bangkok's YMCA and YWCA are both in this area. The *YMCA Collins International House* (☎ 287 1900, 287 2727, fax 287 1996, e *bkkmca@asiaaccess.net.th, 27 Th Sathon Tai)* has air-con rooms with TV, fridge, telephone, in-room safe and private bath for 1300B to 2300B; suites are 2700B. Credit cards are accepted. Guests may use the Y's massage room, gym, track and swimming pool, and there's a coffee shop on the premises. The recently remodelled *YWCA Hostel* (☎ 286 1936, 13 Th Sathon Tai)* offers rooms for 700/900B single/double, including breakfast.

On the south side of Th Silom *Sathorn Inn* (☎ 238 1655, fax 237 6668, 37 Soi Suk-savitthaya (also known as Soi 9 or Seuksa Withaya), Th Silom)* offers cosy rooms with air-con, TV and phone for 896B.

Classic mid-range hotels on Th Surawong include the *New Fuji* (☎ 234 5364, fax 233 4336)* at No 299-310, with rooms from 1124B to 1338B and a 24-hour bar and restaurant.

The recently renovated *New Trocadero Hotel (Map 6, ☎ 234 8920/8, fax 234 8929, e newtroc@ksc.th.com)* at No 343 has standard singles/doubles from 650B to 800B and deluxe rooms from 980B to

1190B. A family room is available for 1200B. All rates include breakfast. This hotel is a favourite of Arabs and Africans.

A newer entry at No 173/8-9, *La Rési-dence Hotel & Serviced Apartments* (☎ 266 5400, fax 237 9322, e *residence@loxinfo .co.th)* is a boutique-style place with a restaurant downstairs and room rates of 950/1400B single/double (1200/1800B dur-ing the high season). Monthly rates are 650B to 950B per day, depending on room size.

Close to the Th Silom shopping area, *Silom Village Inn* (☎ 635 6810, fax 635 6817, e *silom-village-inn@thai.com, Silom Village Trade Centre, 286 Th Silom)* charges from 1800B for its rooms, which all come with safe deposit box, air-con, IDD phone, TV and minibar. Discounts of up to 50% are often available.

*Tower Inn* (☎ 237 8300/4, fax 237 8286, e *towerinn@box1.a.net.net.th, 533 Th Silom)* is a multistorey hotel with a pool, gym and restaurant. Large and comfortable rooms start at 1500B.

The modern five-storey *Silom Golden Inn (Map 6, ☎ 238 2663, fax 238 2667, 41/4 Soi 19, Th Silom)* offers 60 modestly furnished air-con rooms with TV, IDD phone, hot-water shower and minibar for 850B single/double or 1300B for a king-size room.

*Bangkok Christian Guest House* (☎ 233 6303, fax 237 1742, e *bcgh@loxinfo.co.th, 123 Sala Daeng Soi 2, Th Convent)*, off Th Silom, has very nice air-con rooms for 704B to 2222B (plus 10% service), includ-ing breakfast. Lunch and dinner are also available at very low prices.

The friendly *Intown Residence (Map 6, ☎ 233 3596, fax 236 6886, 1086/6 Th Charoen Krung)*, on Th Charoen Krung be-tween Th Si Phraya and Soi 30, is a clean, modern, six-storey place with just 20 rooms, each with TV, air-con and phone, for 600B to 700B single, 700B to 800B double, in-cluding breakfast (subtract 50B per person from all rates if you don't want breakfast). Attached are a respectable coffee shop and a Thai-Chinese restaurant. Monthly rates are also available from 13,000B.

## Soi Ngam Duphli & Th Sathon (Map 7)

**Pinnacle Hotel** (☎ 287 0111, fax 287 3420, **e** pinhl@loxinfo.co.th, 17 Soi Ngam Duphli, Th Phra Ram IV) has rooms with published rates of 1800/2200B; discounts to 1100/1300B, including breakfast, are readily available. Amenities include a fitness centre with sauna, steam room and outdoor rooftop jacuzzi.

**Charlie House** (☎ 679 8330, fax 679 7308, 1034/36-37 Soi Saphan Khu), between Lumphini Tower and Soi Ngam Duphli, aims for a slightly more upscale, security-conscious market with carpeted rooms with air-con, phone and TV for 750/900B single/double (discounts up to 40% can be negotiated in the low-season months like June and September). There is a coffee shop, and smoking is prohibited throughout the hotel; a sign reads 'Decently dressed ladies, gentlemen and their children are welcome'.

## Siam Square, Th Ploenchit & Hualamphong Area (Map 5)

All hotels are located on Map 5, unless otherwise indicated. This area tends to offer either upper-end budget or top-end luxury hotels, with little in the middle. An old Siam Square standby, the **Reno Hotel** (☎ 215 0026, fax 215 3430) on Soi Kasem San 1 is a veteran from the Vietnam War days when a number of hotels opened in Bangkok named after US cities. Standard rooms are 600/720/840B single/double/triple, deluxe rooms are 900/1020B single/double and VIP rooms are 960/1080B. It also has a pool.

**Jim's Lodge** (Map 7, ☎ 255 3100, fax 253 8492), on Soi Ruam Rudi off Th Ploenchit, provides clean rooms with TV, fridge, air-con and carpeting in a six-storey building for 930B a night single/double.

The **Siam Orchid Inn** (☎ 255 3140, fax 255 3144, **e** siam_orchidinn@hotmail.com), on Ratchadamri, opposite the World Trade Center, offers well-appointed rooms with all the amenities for around 1100B, including breakfast.

Opposite the UK embassy on Th Withayu, a little north of Th Ploenchit, the **Holiday Mansion Hotel** (Map 7, ☎ 253 8016,

fax 253 0130, 53 Th Withayu) is a simple but well-run mid-range place where good-sized rooms come with air-con, IDD phone, stocked minifridge, TV and breakfast for around 1500B single/double. Other amenities include a pool, business centre and 24-hour coffee shop. It's only a three-minute walk from the Ploenchit Skytrain station.

## Pratunam (Map 5)

All hotels are located on Map 5, unless otherwise indicated. The quiet **Opera Hotel** (☎ 252 4031, fax 253 5360, 16 Soi Somprasong 1/Soi 11 Phetburi, Th Phetburi) is very near the heart of Pratunam and has air-con doubles with hot water from 590B to 740B. The Opera also has a swimming pool and coffee shop.

A long walk east along the soi opposite the Indra (off Th Ratchaprarop) leads eventually to **Borarn House** (☎ 253 2252, fax 253 3639, 487/48 Soi Wattanasin), a Thai-style apartment building with singles/doubles for 850/980B with air-con and TV. The old-fashioned **Siam Hotel** (Map 1, ☎ 252 5081, fax 254 6609, 1777 Th Phetburi Tat Mai) has OK singles/doubles costing 750/1200B.

## Th Sukhumvit (Map 7)

This area has hotels costing 800B to 1500B. Stick to the lower numbered sois to save cross-town travel time. Many of the Th Sukhumvit hotels in this price range were built as R&R hotels for soldiers on leave during the Vietnam War, 1962-74. Some hotels made the transition from the soldiers-on-leave clientele to a traditional tourist base with style and grace, while others continue to have a slightly rough image. The following don't cater to the girlie bar scene.

Up on Soi 3, the **Grand Inn** (☎ 254 9021, fax 254 9020) is a small apartment-style place with very decent rooms and security for 800B to 1100B. The well-run **Parkway Inn**, on Th Sukhumvit at Soi 4, near the Landmark Hotel, is also good value at 700B to 800B a night, if slightly noisier.

On Soi 5, but seemingly a world away from the girlie-bar crowd, the older **Fortuna Hotel** (☎ 251 5121, fax 253 6282) offers decent rooms with all the mod cons for 850B

**PLACES TO STAY**

to 1400B. The small, friendly **Premier Travellodge** (☎ *253 5078, 253-3201, fax 253 3195, 170-170/1 Soi 8 (Soi Prida), Th Sukhumvit*) has rooms with air-con, carpet, safe-deposit box, cable TV and video, refrigerator, phone and fax for a bargain 600B.

The **Federal Hotel** (☎/fax 253 5332, 27 Soi 11, Th Sukhumvit) has rooms for 650B to 1600B. The added-on rooms at ground level, which occasionally flood in the rainy season, aren't worth the price, so be sure to get one of the larger, older upstairs rooms. The small pool and American-style coffee shop are the main attractions. The Asoke Skytrain station is about a 10-minute walk away.

Dating back to the Vietnam War era, the **Manhattan Hotel** (☎ *255 0166, fax 255 3481, 13 Soi 15, Th Sukhumvit*) has 203 good-sized and fairly well-kept rooms starting at 1400B.

Anyone wanting to stay on busy Soi Asoke (Soi 21) can try the well-run **Carlton Inn** (☎ *258 0471, fax 258 3717, 22/2-4 Soi 21, Th Sukhumvit*), with decent rooms from 750B.

Favourites among middle-class business travellers are the two **City Lodges** on sois 9 (☎ *253 7705, fax 255 4667*) and 19 (☎ *254 4783, fax 255 7340*). Rooms at either are 2090B, and include air-con, telephone, minibar, TV and video.

A couple of hundred metres down Soi 20 (Soi Nam Phung), the **Premier Inn** (☎ *261 0401, fax 261 0414, 9/1 Soi 20, Th Sukhumvit*), opposite the Windsor Hotel, offers rooms and suites with hot water, satellite TV and video for 800B to 1200B, including breakfast. The nearest Skytrain station is Phrom Phong.

## Victory Monument Area (Map 5)

Just north of Siam Square, in the Victory Monument area, are several hotels, including the busy, semi-plush **Century Park Hotel** (☎ *246 7800, fax 246 7197, e century@ samart.co.th, 9 Th Ratchaprarop*). Rooms at this hotel are listed at 3600B but are readily discounted to half that amount. At the similar **Continental Hotel** (☎ *278 1385, fax 271 3547, 971/16 Th Phahonyothin*) singles/ doubles cost from 2400B, with discounts to

1200B available. The Vietnam War-era **Florida Hotel** (☎ *247 0990, fax 247 7419, 43 Phayathai Square, Th Phayathai*) is an average 1970s-style place, with air-con singles/ doubles for around 800B.

## Airport Area

Finding decent, moderately priced accommodation in the airport area is difficult. Most of the hotels charge nearly twice as much as comparable hotels in the city. Typical is **Don Muang Mansion** (☎ *566 3064, 118/7 Th Soranakom, Don Muang*), which looks classy on the outside but asks 1000B to 1200B for a small air-con room that in Bangkok would cost 500B to 750B. It's possible to negotiate a lower rate of 800B. This is a bargain for the airport area (only one place is less expensive; see We-Train International House later in this entry).

If you can spend more, better value is **Comfort Suites Airport** (☎ *552 8921/9, fax 552-8920, e pinap@loxinfo.co.th, 88/117 Vibhavadi (Wiphaawadi) Rangsit Hwy*), which is about five minutes south of the airport by car. Large rooms with all the amenities (satellite TV, air-con, hot-water bath and shower) cost 1400B to 1800B if you book through a Bangkok travel agent, or 2500B to 2600B for walk-ins. Best of all, the hotel provides a free shuttle to/from the airport every hour. Other facilities here include a coffee shop, pool, sauna and health club. One negative is that you can hear the planes landing and taking off until around 1 am.

For quite a bit less you could stay at the well-run **We-Train International House** (☎ *929 2222, 929 2301, fax 929 2300, e we-train@linethai.co.th, 501/1 Mu 3, Th Dechatungkha, Sikan, Don Muang*). Simple but clean rooms with two beds, fan, private hot-water bath, fridge and phone cost 180B single/double or 580B with air-con (extra beds cost 150B). You can also get a bed in a dorm with fan for 120B. To these rates add the usual 10% service charge but no tax since it's operated by the nonprofit Association for the Promotion of the Status of Women (but male guests are welcome). Facilities include a pool, Thai massage, laundry service, a coffee shop and beauty salon.

One major drawback to We-Train International House is its distance from the airport – you must get a taxi to cross the highway and railway, then go about 3km west along Th Dechatungkha to the Thung Sikan school *(rohng rian thûng sǐi-kan)*. If you don't have a great deal of luggage, walk across the airport pedestrian bridge to reach Don Muang Airport (or the Amari Airport Hotel), then get a taxi – it's much cheaper that way because you avoid the high taxi-desk fees. From the guesthouse there are usually no taxis in the area when you're ready to return to the airport or continue on to Bangkok, but transportation to/from the airport can be arranged on request for 200B one way, or 70B to/from the Amari Airport Hotel.

*Siam Rangsit Hotel (☎ 531 3394, 309/336 Viphavadi Rangsit Hwy)*, about 6km north of Bangkok International Airport, offers basic rooms with TV and shower for 200B single/double with fan or 300B with air-con.

### Thonburi
You could hardly be farther from the tourist track in Bangkok than at *The Artists Place (☎ 862 0056, 438 9653, 01-354 8354, fax 862 0074, 63 Soi Thiam Bunyang (off Soi Krung Thonburi 1), Th Krung Thonburi)*. Near a large traffic circle known as Wong Wian Yai, it can be a bit difficult to find, so call the guesthouse for directions. Or if you want to try it on your own, take air-con bus No 3 to Wong Wian Yai and then catch a túk-túk or meter taxi to the guesthouse. If you want to hike it, walk north-east from Wong Wian Yai along broad Th Lat Ya about 200m, and turn right on Soi Lat Ya 2. Continue south and after another 200m, turn left (east) on Soi Ratruam Charoen, and after another hundred metres or so, make a right (south) on Soi Thiam Bunyang and follow signs to the guesthouse, which is on the left side of the soi. This family-style place has a communal kitchen, rooftop sitting area and artist studio space, rates are 100/150/250B for dorm/single/double, 350B single/double air-con or 400B for a multi-bed family room. The guesthouse offers free laundry and luggage storage services.

### Saphan Khwai
*Liberty Hotel (Map 1, ☎ 618 6000, 271 2148, 215 Th Pratipat, Saphaan Khwai)*, in the central northern part of the city, has 209 singles or doubles for 700B to 1000B.

### Nonthaburi
North of central Bangkok in Nonthaburi – about 40 minutes away by Chao Phraya River Express – *Thai House (☎ 903 9611, fax 903 9354, e pip_thaihouse@hotmail.com, 32/4 Mu, 8 Tambon Bang Meuang, Amphoe Bang Yai)* is popular with repeat visitors for its traditional Thai decor and for the cooking courses taught on the premises. Rates are 1000B single, 1400B double. Thai House maintains a separate reservation office in Banglamphu at 22 Th Phra Athit. From Tha Chang, take a public boat (60B for tourists) to Bang Yai, Nonthaburi, via Khlong Bangkok Noi. Once you reach the public pier in Bang Yai, charter a boat for 80 to 100B to Thai House's own pier – all the boat pilots know it. For more information on boats to Bang Yai, see River & Canal Trips in the Things to See & Do chapter.

## PLACES TO STAY – TOP END
Bangkok has all sorts of international standard tourist hotels, from straightforward package places to some of Asia's most classic hotels – including two of the tallest hotels in the world. Several of Bangkok's luxury hotels have made worldwide top 10 or 20 lists in plush travel magazines.

Although there's no single area for top-end hotels, you'll find several around Siam Square, along Th Surawong and Th Silom, and the river, while many of the slightly less expensive 'international standard' places are scattered along Th Sukhumvit.

Since the 1997 devaluation of the baht, a few top-end places have begun quoting prices in US dollars, while others raised the baht prices to bring exchange levels back in line with 1996 prices. Since many hotels in this category rely on imported goods (and imported management staff), prices had to be adjusted to avoid massive losses.

Even so, you should still be able to negotiate discounts of up to 40% during the low season (anytime except December to March and July to August). Booking through a travel agency almost always means lower rates, or try asking for a hotel's 'corporate' discount. Several top-end hotels offer discounts of up to 60% when you make your reservation via the Internet. THAI airlines can also arrange substantial discounts if you hold a THAI air ticket.

A welcome trend in the past few years has been the appearance of several European-style 'boutique' hotels – small, business-oriented places of around 100 rooms or less with rates in the 2000B to 3000B range. Many Bangkok business travellers prefer this type of hotel because they get personal service for about 1000B less than the bigger hotels; also these smaller hotels don't accept tour groups, so regular guests don't have to wade through crowds in the lobby.

The hotels in this category will add a 10% service charge plus 7% tax to hotel bills.

## On the River (Map 6)

All hotels are located on Map 6, unless otherwise indicated. The 124-year-old **Oriental Hotel** (☎ 236 0400, 236 0420, fax 236 1937, e bscorbkk@loxinfo.co.th, 48 Th Oriental), right on Mae Nam Chao Phraya, is one of the most famous hotels in Asia, right up there with the Raffles in Singapore or the Peninsula in Hong Kong. What's more it's also rated as one of the best hotels in the world, as well as being just about the most expensive in Bangkok. The hotel management prides itself on providing highly personalised service through a staff of 1200 (for 35 suites and 361 rooms) – once you've stayed here the staff will remember your name, what you like to eat for breakfast, even what type of flowers you'd prefer in your room.

Nowadays the Oriental Hotel is looking more modern and less classic – the original Author's Wing is dwarfed by the Tower (built in 1958) and River (1976) wings. Authors who have stayed at the Oriental Hotel and had suites named after them include Joseph Conrad, W Somerset Maugham, Noël Coward, Graham Greene, John le Carré, James Michener, Gore Vidal and Bar-

bara Cartland. Room rates start at US$210 and suites are as much as 10 times this price. It's worth wandering in, if only to see the lobby (no shorts, sleeveless shirts or sandals allowed). A landscaped annexe directly across the river from the hotel harbours The Oriental Spa, Thai Health and Beauty Centre (including over 30 treatment programs and a meditation room), a sports centre with jogging track, air-conditioned tennis and squash courts (use of sportswear free of charge), and classrooms for the Thai Cooking School and Thai Culture Programme. Ten restaurants and bars offer Thai, Chinese, French and Italian cuisines; the legendary Bamboo Bar is one of the city's best jazz venues. The public areas off the lobby have a stiff, somewhat cold feel – the lounge in the Authors Wing is a better place to meet.

Another luxury gem along the river is the **Shangri-La Hotel** (☎ 236 7777, fax 236 8579, e slbk@shangri-la.com, 89 Soi Wat Suan Phlu, Th Charoen Krung). It has rooms and suites starting from US$190/210 single/double, with minibar, hair dryer, coffeemaker and security box. Facilities and services include helicopter transport from the airport (at extra cost), two outdoor swimming pools, two outdoor flood-lit tennis courts, two squash courts, fully equipped gym overlooking the river, sauna, steam bath, hydropool, two outdoor jacuzzis and nine restaurants (including one of the best Italian eateries in the city). The service is of a very high standard. The capacious lounge areas off the main lobby have a less formal and more relaxed feel than those at the Oriental, and are a favourite rendezvous spot even for non-hotel guests. The Shangri-La is close to the Saphan Taksin Skytrain station.

On the Thonburi bank of Mae Nam Chao Phraya, a bit south of central Bangkok, the tastefully appointed **Marriott Royal Garden Riverside Hotel** (Map 1, ☎ 476 0021, fax 476 1120, e marriottrgr@minornet.com, 257/1-3 Th Charoen Nakhon), near Saphan Krungthep, is highly valued for its serene atmosphere and expansive, airy public areas. The grounds encompass a large swimming pool, lush gardens, two lighted tennis courts and a world-class health club.

Trader Vic's and Benihana are among the Marriott Royal Garden Riverside Hotel's six restaurants; the *Manohra*, a luxury rice-barge dinner cruiser, is also moored here. A free water taxi service shuttles guests back and forth to Tha Oriental and Tha River City every hour from 7 am to 11 pm. The rack rates for spacious rooms are 4800B, or 5400B with a river view.

Also on the river, the **Royal Orchid Sheraton** *(ROS; ☎ 266 0123, fax 236 6656, e rosht@mozart.inet.co.th, 2 Soi Captain Bush, Th Si Phraya)* has rooms from 10,560B a night. It's known for crisp, efficient service, and the business centre is open 24 hours.

The **Menam Riverside** *(Map 1, ☎ 688 1000, fax 291 9400, e menamhtl@mozart .inet.co.th, 2074 Th Charoen Krung, Yannawa)*, towering over the river, has rooms from 1500B. The **Royal River** *(Map 1, ☎ 433 0300, fax 433 5880, 670/805 Th Charan Sanitwong, Thonburi)* has rooms from 2300B; it receives lots of tour groups.

The 370-room **Peninsula Hotel** *(☎ 861 2888, fax 861 1112, e pbk@peninsula.com, 333 Th Charoen Nakhon)* is the latest tower hotel to rim Mae Nam Chao Phraya. Facilities include handicapped-access rooms; oversized 'executive work desks' with dual-line phones with dataport, private fax number and voice mail; in-room laser/video/CD players; fitness centre; tennis courts; gym; swimming pool; helicopter service (for a hefty charge), Rolls-Royce limos; private boat pier; and river shuttle. Luxuriously appointed rooms are remarkably well priced at US$119 to US$129, and suites for US$154, but these rates will most likely increase as the hotel becomes more well known.

## Siam Square, Th Ploenchit & Pratunam (Map 5)

All hotels are located on Map 5, unless otherwise indicated. People accustomed to heady hotels claim the plush **Regent Bangkok** *(Map 7, ☎ 251 6127, fax 251 5390, e regent@bkkl.asiaaccess.net.th, 155 Th Ratchadamri)* tops the Oriental Hotel in quality for money. This is particularly true for business travellers because of the

Regent's efficient business centre and central location (and local calls are free at the Regent, probably the only luxury hotel in the city to offer this courtesy). The hotel also offers (for around 2000B an hour) an 'office on wheels', a high-tech, multi-passenger van equipped with computers, cell phones, fax machines, TVs and videos, and swivelling leather seats so that small conferences can be held while crossing town. The Regent's rooms start at 9600B. The Ratchadamri Skytrain station is within walking distance.

Another top executive choice is the **Hilton International Bangkok** *(☎ 253 0123, fax 253 6509, e bkkhitw@lox2.loxinfo .co.th, 2 Th Withayu)*, where you won't find tour groups milling around in the lobby; its rooms start at 8640B. The expansive grounds are a major plus; only Bangkok's older hotel properties are so fortunate. It's a 15-minute walk to the Ploenchit Skytrain station.

Another of this generation, the **Siam Inter-Continental** *(☎ 253 0355, fax 254 4388, e bangkok@interconti.com, 967 Th Phra Ram I)*, ensconced in 10.4 hectares (26 acres) of tropical gardens (filled with peacocks, geese, swans and parrots) near Siam Square, takes in a mix of well-heeled, pleasure and business travellers. Standard rooms start at 6000B. Rumour says the Inter-Continental is selling the valuable land it sits on and it may be replaced by a shopping centre.

The **Grand Hyatt Erawan** *(Map 7, ☎ 254 1234, fax 254 6308, e erawan@ksc.g.th .com)*, at the intersection of Th Ratchadamri and Th Ploenchit, was built on the site of the original Erawan Hotel with obvious ambitions to become one of the city's top-ranked hotels. The neo-Thai architecture has been well executed; inside is the largest collection of contemporary Thai art in the world. Adding to the elite atmosphere, the rooms in the rear of the hotel overlook the prestigious Bangkok Royal Sports Club racetrack. For most top-end visitors it vies with the Regent Bangkok or the Novotel Bangkok on Siam Square for having the best location vis-à-vis transport and proximity to shopping. Huge rooms start at

11,520B, though a rate of 7000/8200B single/double can usually be obtained through a travel agent. It's within easy walking distance of the Chit Lom Skytrain station.

The 34-storey *Amari Watergate* (☎ 653 9000, fax 653 9045, [e] watergate@amari.com) is right in the centre of Bangkok's busiest district, Pratunam, on Th Phetburi. The neoclassical interior design blends Thai and European motifs, guest rooms are large, and facilities include a 900-sq-metre Clark Hatch fitness centre, free-form pool, two squash courts, Thai massage, a 24-hour business centre, an American-style pub, and highly rated Cantonese and Italian restaurants. The Amari Watergate is on Th Phetburi near the Th Ratchaprarop intersection. Tour groups check in via a separate floor and lobby. Spacious rooms cost US$184/200 single/double; the top three floors contain more luxuriously appointed executive rooms for another US$40 or so.

Other Amari hotels in central Bangkok include the *Amari Atrium (Map 1,* ☎ 718 2000, fax 718 2002, [e] atrium@amari.com) on Th Phetburi Tat Mai, east of Soi Asoke, with rooms from US$134/142 single/double, and the *Amari Boulevard (Map 7,* ☎ 255 2930, fax 255 2950, [e] boulevard@amari.com, 2 Soi 5, Th Sukhumvit), with rooms from US$150 double. Amari also has an airport hotel – see the Airport Area entry later in this section for details.

Another extremely well-located hotel for business or leisure is the *Novotel Bangkok on Siam Square (Map 7,* ☎ 255 6888, fax 255 1824, [e] novotel@ksc.th.com) on Soi 6 in Siam Square. Just steps away from one of Bangkok's most vibrant shopping and entertainment districts, as well as the Siam Skytrain station, the Novotel boasts a full business centre, pool, bakery and various restaurants. The rooms are huge and start at 4961B.

Or try *Le Meridien President Hotel & Tower (Map 7,* ☎ 656 0444, fax 656 0555, [e] meridien@loxinfo.co.th, 135/26 Th Gaysorn), in the heart of the Th Ploenchit shopping area and near the Chit Lom Skytrain station, offers 758 well-appointed rooms and suites from 4200B. Amenities

include two pools, a health club, business centre and 10 restaurants and bars.

Dropping down a notch or two in price is the *Chateau de Bangkok (Map 7,* ☎ 651 4400, fax 651 4500, [e] chateau@infoneurs.co.th, 29 Soi Ruam Rudi, Th Ploenchit). Owned by French hotel group Accor, it offers serviced studios – one- and two-bedroom apartments, each with walk-in closet, IDD phone and fax – for 1300B to 3265B.

The *Asia Hotel (*☎ 215 0808, fax 215 4360, [e] techaru@mozart.inet.co.th, 296 Th Phayathai) is a huge place with large rooms starting at 3509B; it's in a good location, but is often full of tour groups and conventioneers. The *Indra Regent (*☎ 208 0033, fax 208 0388, [e] indra@cybeer-image.com, 120/126 Th Ratchaprarop), with rooms from 2000B, is similar.

The tallest hotel in the world, the 93-storey, 673-room *Baiyoke Sky Hotel (*☎ 656 3000, fax 656 3555, [e] baiyokegroup@baiyokehotels.co.th), is right behind the Indra Hotel off Th Ratchaprarop in Pratunam. Spacious rooms and junior suites with all the amenities – though not quite as luxurious as one might expect – cost 2200B and 3000B respectively, not a bad deal considering the altitude.

## Central Bangkok
Although there are no top-end hotels in the Banglamphu area, a little way east are a couple of highly recommended places. *Royal Princess Hotel (Map 3,* ☎ 281 3088, fax 280 1314, [e] larnluang@dusit.com, 269 Th Lan Luang) has rooms from 3300B, but discounts down to about half that are often available through travel agents. It's close to the main city THAI office and a short taxi ride from Banglamphu and the river.

Even nicer is the independently owned and operated *Siam City Hotel (Map 5,* ☎ 247 0123, fax 247 0165, [e] siamcity@siamhotels.com, 477 Th Si Ayuthaya). Large, well-maintained rooms with all the amenities are listed at 4272B but, as with the Royal Princess, good discounts are often available through Thai travel agents. The restaurants at the Siam City are highly regarded by Thai businesspeople.

## Th Silom, Th Surawong & Th Sathon (Map 7)

All hotels are located on Map 7, unless otherwise indicated. Another entry in the luxury/executive market is the **Sukhothai Hotel** (☎ 287 0222, res 285 0303, fax 287 4980, ℮ reservations@sukhothai.com or info@sukhothai.com, 13/3 Th Sathon Tai). The Sukhothai features an Asian minimalist decor, including an inner courtyard with lily ponds; the same architect and interior designer created Phuket's landmark Amanpuri. Superior rooms cost US$220, deluxe rooms US$264; there are also more-expensive suites.

**Westin Banyan Tree** (☎ 679 1200, fax 679 1199, ℮ westinbangkok@westin-bangkok .com) towers over Th Sathon Tai with 216 business suites. This ultra-modern hotel is ensconced on the lower two and top 28 floors of the 60-storey Thai Wah Tower II. The Westin Banyan Tree's huge rooms feature separate work and sleep areas, two-line speaker phones with data ports along with all the other amenities expected of lodgings that start at US$158 a night. The spa and fitness centre – the biggest such hotel facility in Bangkok – spans four floors.

Two top hotels in the district along Th Silom and Th Surawong are the very Thai **Montien** (☎ 233 7060, fax 236 5218, ℮ montien@ksc15.th.com, 54 Th Surawong), which has rooms from 4000B (entrance off Th Silom), and the great **Dusit Thani** (☎ 236 0450, fax 236 6400, ℮ dusit-bkk@dusit.com, 946 Th Phra Ram IV), with rooms from US$180/190 single/double.

Two upmarket Singaporean-style places offer more than 400 rooms and suites each: **Monarch-Lee Gardens Bangkok** (☎ 238 1991, fax 238 1999, ℮ monarch@ksc9.th .com, 188 Th Silom), which has rooms from 4000B to 16,000B; and **Mandarin Hotel** (☎ 238 0230, fax 234 3363, 662 Th Phra Ram IV), with rooms from 2700B to 3300B. All four of the preceding hotels are within walking distance of the Sala Daeng Skytrain station.

There are many hotels with similar functional amenities but, because of their location or smaller staff-to-guest ratios, are cheaper.

In the Th Silom and Th Surawong areas these include: the **Narai** (☎ 237 0100, fax 236 7161, ℮ narai@narai.com, 222 Th Silom), with rooms from 3267B; and the **Holiday Inn Crowne Plaza** (Map 6, ☎ 238 4300, fax 238 5289, ℮ admin@hicp-bkk.com, 981 Th Silom), which has rooms from US$149.

With only 57 rooms, the management at the **Swiss Lodge** (☎ 233 5345, fax 236 9425, 3 Th Convent) is able to pay close attention to service details such as cold refresher towels whenever you enter the lobby from outside. Data-ports and soundproof windows further enhance the attraction for people doing business. Facilities include a restaurant, pool and business centre. Discounted rates start at 2550B for a standard room.

Other top-end hotels in this area include the **Trinity Silom Hotel** (☎ 231 5050, ext 5, fax 231 5417, 150 Soi 5, Th Silom), a boutique-style place with rooms costing 2300B to 2500B (although substantially discounted rates are available via the Internet).

## Th Sukhumvit (Map 7)

The overpriced, musty and ramshackle **Ambassador Hotel** (☎ 254 0444, fax 254 4123, ℮ amtel@infonews.co.th, Soi 11, Th Sukhumvit) mostly plays host to Hong Kong and Taiwanese tourists on low budget package tours. We only list this hotel because many package tours get booked here, so if you have a choice you may want to stay elsewhere.

The tastefully decorated **Hotel Rembrandt** (☎ 261 7100, fax 261 7017, ℮ rembrandt@ siam.net, 19 Soi 18, Th Sukhumvit) has 407 large rooms. Starting prices are 2050B, though rack rates were listed at 3950B. Facilities include a swimming pool and the best Mexican restaurant in Bangkok, Señor Pico's of Los Angeles. Another advantage is the proximity to Queen Sirikit National Convention Centre, off Soi 16. The hotel is between the Asoke and Phrom Phong Skytrain stations.

The **Landmark Hotel** (☎ 254 0404, fax 253 4259, 138 Th Sukhumvit) has 415 well-appointed rooms with discounted rates starting at 2950B. The Landmark's business centre is one of the hotel's strong suits;

the heavy traffic along this stretch of Th Sukhumvit is not.

***Delta Grand Pacific Hotel*** *(☎ 651 1000, fax 255 2441, hotel@grandpacifichotel .com, Soi 17-19, Th Sukhumvit)* offers rooms from US$85. Its Soi 19 location is easy to reach from either Th Sukhumvit or Th Phetburi, and a nearby pedestrian bridge across Th Sukhumvit is an added bonus. The hotel bears the distinction of containing the highest karaoke lounge in the city, and is attached to Robinson department store, and close to the Asoke Skytrain station.

***Windsor Hotel*** *(☎ 258 0160, fax 258 1491,* e *varaporn@mozart.inet.co.th, 8-10 Soi 20 (Soi Nam Phung), Th Sukhumvit)* is a fairly deluxe place with standard rooms for 2000/2400B single/double, and superior rooms at 2400/2600B; rates include a cooked-to-order breakfast. Each of the rooms and suites have air-con, phone, TV, video and refrigerator. On the premises is a 24-hour coffee shop. Guests of the Windsor have use of all amenities at the ***Windsor Suites Hotel*** *(☎ 262 1234, fax 258 1522, varaporn@ mozart.inet.co.th),* which features spacious suites (each with two TVs). Amenities include a bakery, cafe, restaurant, fitness club, shopping arcade, swimming pool and jacuzzi. Official rates start at 6000/7000B but are heavily discounted via the Internet. A complimentary buffet breakfast is included. The nearest Skytrain station is Phrom Phong.

Accor's well-designed and relatively new ***Novotel Lotus Bangkok*** *(☎ 261 0111, fax 262 1700,* e *novotel@asiaaccess.net .th, 1 Soi 33, Th Sukhumvit)* contains plush rooms starting at 4100B a night; discounts are often available. Phrom Phong Skytrain station is nearby.

## Ratchada (Map 1)

This entertainment and business district in the Huay Khwang neighbourhood of northeast Bangkok features several flash hotels along Th Ratchadaphisek.

Managed by Singapore's Raffles International, the well-appointed ***Merchant Court Hotel*** *(☎ 694 222, fax 694 2223,* e *info@ merchantcourt.th.com, 202 Th Ratch- adaphisek)* occupies one of the two tower

blocks of Le Concorde Building. The second tower contains offices, including the TAT headquarters. Rates for superior room are 5000/5500B single/double, deluxe 6000/6500B and up to 20,500B double for a studio suite, excluding tax and service. Rooms on floors set aside for executives offer two phone lines, ergonomically designed writing desk and chair, and optional personal computer and fax/printer. Amenities include five restaurants and bars, a fitness centre, swimming pool and two squash courts. Nonsmoking floors are available. When the subway is finished, there will be a subway station right in front of this hotel.

One of the least expensive places, next to the Le Concorde building and close to several upscale 'entertainment centres', is the ***Siam Beverly Hotel*** *(☎ 215 4397, fax 215 4049, 188 Th Ratchadaphisek),* where rates are 1800B for a superior single to 2200B for deluxe double, including breakfast. It's not spectacular but the service is friendly and the rooms have all the amenities. The 3rd-floor coffee shop is well priced.

Roughly equivalent in price, the ***Chao- phya Park Hotel*** *(☎ 290 0125, fax 290 0167,* e *chaopark@asiaaccess.inet.th, 247 Th Ratchadaphisek)* is similar but a little farther out on the strip. At the lowest end of the scale along the neon-washed Ratchada strip is the ***Crystal Hotel*** *(☎ 274 6441, 274 6020, fax 274 6449, 65 Soi Nathong, Th Ratchadaphisek),* with rooms from 799B.

At the lower end of this spectrum, and a favourite with visiting Asian businessmen, is ***The Emerald*** *(☎ 276 4567, fax 276 4555,* e *em@emeraldhotel.com, 99/1 Th Ratch- adaphisek),* with rooms from 2800B.

## Airport Area (Map 1)

The ***Amari Airport Hotel*** *(☎ 566 1020, fax 566 1941,* e *airport@amari.com),* connected to the airport by an air-conditioned walkway, is obviously the closest hotel to Bangkok International Airport. The Amari offers nonsmoking rooms, a 'ladies' floor, rooms for disabled persons, and an executive floor with huge suites and 24-hour butler service. The rates start at US$182 for a standard double; discounts are rarely available, since rooms are very much in demand. However, passengers arriving/departing Bangkok by THAI receive a 50% discount when they show their current boarding pass or ticket. Amari also offers 'ministay' rates for stays of up to three hours for US$20, including tax and service provided the check-in time is between 8 am and 6 pm.

Another luxury-class hotel towards the airport is the *Central Grand Plaza Bangkok* (☎ *541 1234, fax 541 1087,* [e] *cpbsales@ samart.co.th, 1695 Th Phahonyothin),* overlooking the Railway Golf Course and Chatuchak Park. Rooms start at 6800B.

The *Asia Airport Hotel* (☎ *992 6999, fax 532 3193)* is north of the airport at Km 28. The rates for the comfortable rooms start at 2000B, but discounts to 1200B or 1500B are often available because the hotel often seems to be half empty – we're not sure why as it seems fine to us.

## LONG-TERM RENTALS

Several apartment complexes in Bangkok offer weekly and monthly rates. Many of these are 'serviced apartments' that include furniture, daily cleaning services, all bed and bath linens, minimal kitchen utensils and an operator-serviced phone line, all included in the basic rent.

Check the 'Property Guide' in the *Bangkok Post* on Thursday for rental advertisements and listings. Monthly rates average around 5000B for a one-room or studio apartment to 20,000B for a two- or three-bedroom apartment at the low to medium range, up to 60,000B or more for a luxury place.

Many short-term rental apartments are located on high-numbered sois off Th Sukhumvit and in the Khlong Toey area towards Mae Nam Chao Phraya. *Inter Court Apartment* (☎ *258 7967, 251 Soi 71, Th Sukhumvit)* has furnished studios with aircon, satellite TV, fridge and daily cleaning starting at a low 3000B per month. *Taiping Tower Condo* (☎ *253 7576, Soi 63, Th Sukhumvit)* offers furnished three-bedroom units with living room, kitchen, air-con, satellite TV and maid service for 20,000B per month. *Boss Tower* (☎ *661 3150, fax 661 3299, 3241 Th Phra Ram IV, Khlong Toey)* rents 31-sq-metre studio apartments for just 8500B per month, larger studios for 13,000B or one-bedrooms from 20,000B. It has a swimming pool, business centre, minimart, restaurant, sauna and fitness centre.

The Ratchada area of the Huay Khwang district in north-eastern Bangkok is another popular area for short-term rental apartments, and is conveniently connected to central Bangkok by an expressway. *Galleria Serviced Mansion* (☎ *276 4378, 24 Soi Pracharat Bamphen, Th Ratchadaphisek)* is a modern high-rise with apartments from 4000B to 12,000B a month, or 600B per day.

**PLACES TO STAY**

# Places to Eat

## DISTRICTS

No matter where you go in Bangkok you're almost never more than 50m from a restaurant or sidewalk food vendor. The variety of places to eat is simply astounding and defeats all but the most tireless food samplers in the quest to say they've tried everything. As with seeking a place to stay, you can find somewhere to eat in every price range in most districts – with a few obvious exceptions. Chinatown is naturally a good area for Chinese food, while Bangrak and Phahurat (both districts with high concentrations of Indian residents) are good for Indian and Muslim cuisine. Some parts of the city tend to have higher priced restaurants than others (eg, Siam Square, Thanon (Th) Silom, Th Surawong and Th Sukhumvit), while other areas are full of cheap eats (eg, Banglamphu and Ko Ratanakosin around Tha Maharat).

Because transport can be such a hassle in Bangkok, most visitors choose the most convenient place to eat rather than seeking out a specific restaurant – the majority of this chapter has therefore been organised by area, rather than cuisine. See also the special section 'Tastes of Bangkok' in this chapter for more on Thai cuisine and some nifty recipes to impress your friends back home!

## Th Khao San Area (Map 4)

This area near the river and old part of the city is one of the best for cheap eating. Many of the guesthouses on Th Khao San (Khao San Rd) have open-air cafes, which are packed with travellers from November to March and July to August. The typical cafe menu has a few Thai and Chinese standards plus travellers' favourites like fruit salads, muesli and yoghurt. None of them are particular standouts, though the side-by-side *Orm* and *Wally House* produce fair Thai, Western and vegetarian meals at cheap prices, while *Prakorp's House & Restaurant* makes good coffee. *Hello Restaurant* (not to be confused with the guesthouse of the same name across the street) and *Center Khao Sarn* on Th Khao

San are both quite popular, but the food's nothing special. *Arawy Det*, an old Hokkien-style noodle shop on the corner of Th Khao San and Th Tanao, has somehow managed to stay authentic amid the cosmic swirl. The English sign reads 'Khao San Seafood Restaurant', and for foreigners the restaurant has a special higher-priced seafood menu. If you want noodles or what the Thais are eating, just point. Opposite the eastern end of Th Khao San, on Th Tanao, *No 147 Thai Food* is also reasonably authentic.

Up at the intersection of Th Khao San and Th Chakraphong, the air-conditioned *Gulliver's Traveler's Tavern* (☎ 629 1988) serves cocktails, shots and beers, and has an international menu bearing comfort food such as Belgian fries, fried calamari, cottage pie and fish and chips. Prices range from 80B to 100B a dish, and the music is loud.

There are two Indian restaurants on the street housed over shops towards the northwestern end of Th Khao San, *Himalayan Kitchen* and *Namastee Indian Cuisine*.

For authentic (and cheap) Thai food check out the several *open-air restaurants* – actually simple vendor carts with clusters of tables and chairs – at the western end of Th Rambutri opposite Tuptum Bed & Breakfast.

A short string of street vendors offering reliable *noodle and curry dishes* can also be found along Th Chakraphong, about 50m south of Th Khao San.

*Chabad House* (☎ 282 6388), a Jewish place of worship on Th Rambutri, serves Israeli-style kosher food downstairs. It's open noon to 9 pm Sunday to Thursday, until 4.30 pm on Friday. Cheaper falafel and hummus can be found at *Chochana* (*Shoshana;* ☎ 282 9948), down a tràwk (alley) off Th Chakraphong, around the corner from Th Khao San. Right next door is *Sarah*, also serving Israeli dishes.

## Banglamphu & Thewet (Map 3)

A small shop called *Roti-Mataba* (☎ 282 2119), opposite the Phra Sumen Fort on the corner of Th Phra Athit and Th Phra Sumen near the river, offers delicious *roti* (fried Indian flatbread), *kaeng mátsàman* (Thai Muslim curry), chicken korma and chicken or vegetable *mátàbà* (a sort of stuffed Indian pancake), and has a bilingual menu; look for a white sign with red letters. An upstairs air-con dining area has recently been added. It's open 7 am to 8 pm, closed Monday. Two doors up from Roti-Mataba, *Kuay Tiaw Mae* serves good *kŭaytĭaw tôm yam* (rice noodles in a spicy lemongrass broth; it's made with pork but you can ask for it with tofu instead), real coffee and unique mushroom ice cream.

Along Th Phra Athit north of the New Merry V guesthouse are several small but up-and-coming Thai places with chic but casual decor and good food at prices local university students can afford. The *Raan Kin Deum* (☎ 629 0614), no roman-script sign, a few doors down from New Merry V, is a nice two-storey cafe with wooden tables and chairs, traditional Thai food and live folk music nightly; the laid-back atmosphere reaches its peak in the evenings when Thais and farang crowd the place. The bright and cheery *Saffron Bakery*, opposite the Food and Agriculture Organization (FAO) on Th Phra Athit, has good pastries but only a few tables.

Several other places along this strip of Th Phra Athit – *Hemlock*, *Suntana*, *Indy*, *To Sit*, *Apostrophe's*, *Dog Days*, *108 Yang* and *Joy Luck Club* – contribute to a neighbourhood cafe scene that has been hyperbolically compared with High Street Kensington or Greenwich Village by the Thai press. Tiny Joy Luck Club has the most interesting interior design – a collection of ₁hotos of old American bluesmen, contemporary Thai art and tables containing boxed art under glass. Despite their English names, all of these cafes see more Thai customers than farang, but staff usually speak a little English. The English language menus at some Th Phra Athit cafes conform to the Thais' worst expectations of what farang like to eat – if you can't read Thai, you won't be getting the best dishes on hand. If possible, go with someone who speaks Thai. Most are open in the evenings only.

One restaurant on the Phra Athit strip without 'tuppie' (Thai yuppie) pretensions is *Khrua Nopparat* (no roman-script sign) near 108 Yang. It's a plainly decorated place with air-con and a good menu of Thai dishes at very reasonable prices, making it popular with neighbourhood residents. It's open 10.30 am to 9.30 pm daily. *Ton Pho* (☎ 280 0452) (no roman sign), next to the Buddhist Association on Th Phra Athit, is another great spot for traditional, authentic Thai.

Many of the Th Khao San guesthouse cafes offer vegetarian dishes. For an all-vegie menu at low prices, seek out the string of *vegetarian restaurants* near Srinthip Guest House. To find these out-of-the-way places, turn left on Th Tanao at the eastern end of Th Khao San, cross the street and turn right down the first narrow alley, then left at Soi Wat Bowon. A very good Thai vegetarian place is *Arawy* (the roman-script sign reads 'Alloy'), south of Th Khao San, across Th Ratchadamnoen Klang at 152 Th Din So (opposite the Municipal Hall near a 7-Eleven store). This was one of Bangkok's first Thai vegetarian restaurants, inspired by ex-Bangkok Governor Chamlong Srimuang. It's open 7 am to 7 pm daily.

At the Democracy Monument circle on Th Ratchadamnoen Klang, there are a few air-con Thai restaurants, including the *Vijit* (VR; ☎ 282 0958) and the *Methavalai Sorn Daeng* (☎ 224 3088), which have reasonable prices considering the food and facilities. At lunch time on weekdays they're crowded with local government office workers. Both stay open until 11 pm or so.

Opposite River City shopping complex on the Thonburi side of the river, there's a very good floating seafood restaurant called *Yok Yor Khlongsan (Map 6, ☎ 437 1121)*. Especially good is the *hàw mòk* (fish curry). It also offers inexpensive evening dinner cruises (8 to 10 pm) – you order from the regular menu and pay a nominal 70B charge for the boat service. *Wang Ngar (Map 3, ☎ 226 5940)*, in west Banglamphu, next to the Saphan Phra Pin Klao, is another decent waterfront place.

For North-Eastern Thai food, try the *Isan restaurants* (North-Eastern Thai cuisine) next to Ratchadamnoen Boxing Stadium.

## Chinatown, Hualamphong & Phahurat (Map 6)

All restaurants are located on Map 6, unless otherwise indicated. Some of Bangkok's best Chinese and Indian food is found in these adjacent districts, but because few tourists stay in this part of town (for good reason – it's simply too congested) they rarely make any eating forays into the area. A few old Chinese restaurants have moved from Chinatown to locations with less traffic, the most famous being Hoi Tien Lao, now the excellent *Hoi Tien Lao Rim Nam*, adjacent to River House Condominium on the Thonburi bank of Mae Nam Chao Phraya, more or less opposite the Portuguese embassy and River City shopping complex. However, many places are still hanging on to their venerable Chinatown addresses, where the atmosphere is still part of the eating experience.

Most specialise in southern Chinese cuisine, particularly that of coastal Guangdong and Fujian provinces. This means seafood, rice noodles and dumplings are often the best choices. The large, banquet-style Chinese places are mostly found along Th Yaowarat and Th Charoen Krung, and include *Laem Thong* (38 Soi Bamrungrat), just off Th Charoen Krung, and *Shangarila Restaurant* (formerly Yau Wah Yuen), near the Th Yaowarat and Th Ratchawong intersection. Each has an extensive menu, including dim sum before lunch time. *Lie Kee* (☎ 224 3587, 360-362 Th Charoen Krung) is an excellent and inexpensive Chinese food centre on the 3rd floor of a building on the corner of Th Charoen Krung and Th Bamrungrat, a block west of Th Ratchawong. It's air-conditioned, yet it's difficult to spend more than 50B for lunch.

The best noodle and dumpling shops are hidden away on smaller sois and alleys. At 54 Th Bamrungrat is the funky *Chiang Kii*, where the 100B *khâo tôm plaa* (rice soup with fish) belies the casual surroundings – no place does it better. *Kong Lee* (☎ 224 5600, 137/141 Th Ratchawong) has a loyal clientele for its dry-fried wheat noodles *(bàmìi hâeng)* – again it's reportedly the best in Bangkok.

Another great noodle place, *Pet Tun Jao Tha* ( 945 Soi Wanit 2) is on the south-eastern edge of Chinatown near the River City shopping complex (this area is usually referred to as Talat Noi). The restaurant's name means 'Harbour Department Stewed Duck' – the speciality is rice noodles (kǔaytǐaw) served with duck or goose, either roasted or stewed. Other Thai and Chinese dishes are available as well – just name it and the cooks can probably make it.

All-night *food hawkers* set up along Th Yaowarat and along Th Ratchawong near where the two streets intersect. This is the least expensive place to dine out in Chinatown – and on weekends parts of these two streets are turned into a pedestrian-only mall.

Diagonally opposite About Studio/About Café on Th Maitrijit, unassuming *Pheng Phochana* serves perhaps the best *kǔaytǐaw khua kài* (rice noodles stir-fried with egg and chicken) in the city. It's open sunrise to midnight Monday to Saturday.

*Suki Jeh Yuu Jing* (the English sign reads 'Vegetarian'), a Chinese vegetarian restaurant just 70m down Th Phra Ram IV from Hualamphong station, serves excellent, if rather pricey, vegetarian food in a clean, air-con atmosphere; the fruit shakes are particularly refreshing. This is a great place to fortify yourself with food and drink while waiting for a train at Hualamphong station. Service can be slow, so leave plenty of time to make your train departure. It's open 6 am to 10 pm.

Over in Phahurat, the Indian fabric district, most places serve north Indian cuisine, heavily influenced by Moghul or Persian flavours and spices. One of the best north Indian restaurant in town is the *Royal India* (392/1 Th Chakraphet). It can be very crowded at lunch time, almost exclusively with Indian residents, so it might be better to go there after the standard lunch hour or at night. It has very good curries (both vegetarian and non-vegetarian), dal (curried lentils), Indian breads, raita, lassi etc, all at reasonable prices. Royal India also has a branch on Th Khao San in Banglamphu but it's not as good.

The ATM department store on Th Chakraphet near the pedestrian bridge has a food centre on the top floor that features several Indian vendors – the food is cheap and tasty and there's quite a good selection.

Running alongside the ATM Building on Soi ATM are several small **teahouses** with very inexpensive Indian and Nepali food, including lots of fresh chapatis and strong milk tea. In the afternoons, a Sikh man sets up a push-cart on the corner of Soi ATM and Th Chakraphet and sells **vegetarian samosas**, often cited as the best in Bangkok.

Wedged between the western edge of Chinatown and the northern edge of Phahu-rat, the three-storey **Old Siam Plaza** shopping centre (Map 6) houses a number of Thai, Chinese and Japanese restaurants. A food centre on the 3rd floor serves inexpensive Thai and Chinese meals from 10 am to 5 pm, and has reasonably priced, Thai-style coffee shops. Attached to the adjacent Chalermkrung Royal Theatre is a branch of the highly efficient, moderately priced **S&P Restaurant & Bakery** (Map 3), where the extensive menu encompasses everything from authentic Thai to well-prepared Japanese, European and vegetarian dishes, along with a selection of pastries and desserts.

**Vegetarian** During the annual Vegetarian Festival (centred around Wat Mangkon Kamalawat on Th Charoen Krung in September-October), Bangkok's Chinatown becomes a virtual orgy of vegetarian Thai and Chinese food. Restaurants and noodle shops in the area offer hundreds of different dishes. One of the best spreads is at **Hua Seng Restaurant** (☎ 222 9464), a few doors west of Wat Mangkon on Th Charoen Krung.

## Siam Square, Ploenchit & Th Withayu (Map 7)

All restaurants are located on Map 7, unless otherwise indicated. This shopping area is interspersed with several low and medium-priced restaurants as well as American fast-food franchises.

**S&P Restaurant & Bakery** on Soi 11 has high-quality fare and Häagen-Dazs ice cream at low to moderate prices. Dishes cost 45B to 75B, breakfast 35B to 65B.

Also on Soi 11, the Bangkok branch of London's **Hard Rock Café** (☎ 254 0830) serves good American and Thai food; prices are about the same as at other Hard Rocks

around the world. Look for the túk-túk captioned 'God is my co-pilot' coming out of the building's facade. The Hard Rock stays open till 2 am, later than many Siam Square eateries.

**Nooddi** (Map 7), about 25m from the Skytrain station on Siam Square Soi 4, is a modern noodle bar serving all kinds of fresh Thai and Italian pastas. Just to the right of the Siam Square's Scala cinema (Map 5), plunge into the alley that curves behind the Th Phayathai shops to find a row of cheap, good **food stalls**. A shorter alley with food stalls also leads off the north end of Siam Square's Soi 2.

On both sides of Th Phra Ram I in Siam Square and the Siam Center (Map 5) you'll find a variety of American fast-food franchises. Prices are close to what you would pay in the USA, UK or Australia. Siam Center contains a bevy of good **Thai coffee shops** on its upper floors.

On the 2nd floor of the relatively new Siam Discovery Center (Map 5, attached to the Siam Center by an enclosed walkway), the sleekly designed **Hartmannsdorfer Brau Haus** (☎ 658 0229) offers three types of home-brewed German beer and a long menu of German specialities, including home-made sausages. An international buffet of German, Italian and Thai dishes is served from 11 am to 3 pm Monday to Friday for 240B plus tax and service. **Les Artistes Restaurant & Pastry** (☎ 658 0214), on the same floor, features various baked goods and a large menu of Italian, Thai and French food served in a fun, modern decor. One major plus – it's open 7 am to midnight daily.

If you're staying on or nearby Soi Kasem San 1 (Map 5), you don't have to suck motorcycle fumes crossing Th Phra Ram I and Th Phayathai to find something to eat. Besides the typical hotel coffee shops found on the soi, there are also two very good, inexpensive **khâo kaeng vendors** with tables along the east side of the soi. No need to be fluent in Thai, they're used to the 'point-and-serve' system. Two outdoor cafes on either side of the White Lodge serve more expensive Thai and European food, burgers, pastries, coffees and breakfast.

Despite its farang name, *Sara-Jane's* (☎ *650 9992, Sindhorn Bldg, 130-132 Th Withayu)* serves very good Isan and Italian cuisine in a casual, air-con dining room. The restaurant is inside the Sindhorn Building towards the back. There's a second location on Th Narathiwat Ratchanakharin, near Th Sathon Tai.

*Fabb Fashion Café (☎ 658 2003, Mercury Tower, 540 Th Ploenchit)*, near the Chit Lom Skytrain station, serves good Thai-Italian fusion cuisine for lunch and dinner at moderate to high prices. In the same building, *Auberge DAB (☎ 658 6222)* goes all French with panfried French duck liver with raspberry dressing, poached French oysters wrapped in spinach leaf with champagne sauce, roast pigeon and fresh oysters from Brittany among the offerings. Dinner prices are quite high; the 295B three-course set lunch is better value.

### Mahboonkrong Shopping Centre (Map 5)

Another building studded with restaurants, Mahboonkrong (MBK) shopping centre is directly across from Siam Square at the intersection of Th Phayathai and Th Phra Ram I. A section on the ground floor called Major Plaza contains two cinemas and a good food centre. An older food centre is on the 7th floor; both places have vendors serving tasty dishes from all over Thailand, including vegetarian, at prices averaging 20B to 35B per plate. Hours are 10 am to 10 pm, but the more popular vendors run out of food as early as 8.30 or 9 pm – come earlier for the best selection. A beer garden on the terrace surrounding two sides of the 7th-floor food centre, with good views of the Bangkok nightscape, is open in the evening.

Scattered around other floors, especially the 3rd and 4th, are a number of popular medium-price places, including *13 Coins* (steak, pizza and pasta), *Kobune Japanese Restaurant* and other fast-food outlets.

### World Trade Center (Map 7)

This shopping complex on the corner of Th Ploenchit and Th Ratchadamri contains a few upmarket restaurants and the city's trendiest food centre. Located on the ground floor of this huge glossy building are *Kroissant House*, serving coffees, pastries and gelato, *La Fontana (☎ 255 9534)*, a bistro-style Italian eatery, and the always-satisfying *Vijit* (traditional Thai), a branch of the Democracy Circle restaurant of the same name. The 6th floor features *Lai-Lai* and *Chao Sua*, two sumptuous Chinese banquet-style places, plus the elegant, traditional Thai *Thanying* (a branch of the original Thanying on Th Silom) and the more casual *Narai Pizzeria*. There are also two *food centres* on the 7th floor serving standard Thai and Chinese dishes, which are only a little more expensive than the usual Bangkok food centre.

**Soi Lang Suan (Map 7)** East from Siam Square and off Th Ploenchit, Soi Lang Suan offers a number of medium-priced eating possibilities. The Italian-owned *Pan Pan Capri (☎ 252 7104, 45 Soi Lang Suan)* is very popular with Western residents for wood-fired pizza (takeaway orders accepted), pastas, salads, gelato (the best in Thailand) and pastries. A low-calorie vegetarian menu is available on request.

The *Whole Earth Restaurant (☎ 252 5574, 93/3 Soi Lang Suan)* is a good Thai vegetarian restaurant (non-veg dishes are also served) with service to match, but is a bit pricey if you're on a tight budget. The upstairs room features low tables with floor cushions. A *second branch (☎ 258 4900, 71 Soi 26, Th Sukhumvit)* has opened, and serves both Thai and Indian vegetarian dishes.

*Nguan Lee Lang Suan (☎ 251 8366)*, on the corner of Soi Lang Suan and Soi Sarasin, is a semi-outdoor place specialising in Chinese-style seafood and *kài lâo daeng* (chicken steamed in Chinese herbs).

### Th Silom, Th Surawong & Th Sathon Area (Map 7)

All restaurants are located on Map 7, unless otherwise indicated. This area represents the heart of the financial district, so it features a lot of pricey restaurants, along with cheaper ones that attract both office workers and the more flush. Many restaurants are found along the main avenues but there's an even greater number tucked away in sois and alleys. The river end of Th Silom and Th Surawong towards Th Charoen Krung (the Bangrak district) is a good hunting ground for Indian food.

**Thai & Other Asian** The *Soi Pradit (Soi 20) Night Market* (Map 6), which assembles each evening off Th Silom in front of the municipal market pavilion, is good for cheap eats. During the day there are also a few *food vendors* in this soi, but much better daytime fare can be found amid the mass of foodstalls purveying pots of curry and miles of noodles inside *Talat ITF* at the end of Soi 10.

The area to the east of Th Silom off Th Convent and Soi Sala Daeng is a Thai gourmets' enclave. Most of the restaurants tucked away here are very good, but a meal for two will cost 650B to 850B. One such upmarket spot is *Bussaracum* (☎ 266 6312, Sethiwan Bldg, 139 Th Pan) off Th Silom, pronounced 'boot-sa-ra-kam'. Bussaracum specialises in 'royal Thai' cuisine – recipes that were created for the royal court in days past, and kept secret from 'commoners' until late this century. Every dish is supposedly prepared only when ordered, from fresh ingredients and freshly ground spices. Live classical Thai music is played at a subdued volume. This is a fancy place, recommended for a splurge; call ahead to be sure of a table.

Very popular among Th Silom area businesspeople as well as Thai media/movie celebrities, *Anna's Café*, *(Map 7, ☎ 632-0620, 118 Soi Sala Daeng)* provides a creative menu of Thai and European dishes as well as fast, friendly service.

A great place for traditional Thai and Isan cuisine, at moderate prices, is *Ban Chiang (Map 6, ☎ 266 6994, 14 Soi Si Wiang, Th Pramuan)*, a restored wooden house in a leafy setting off Th Silom west of Wat Khaek. Owned by a Thai movie star, *Thanying (Map 6, ☎ 236 4361, 235 0371, 10 Soi Pramuan, Th Silom)* features elegant decor and very good, moderately expensive royal Thai cuisine. It's open 11 am to 11 pm daily; there's also a second branch *(☎ 255 9838)* at the World Trade Center on Th Ploenchit; open 11.30 am to 10.30 pm daily.

*Mango Tree* (☎ 236 2820), down Soi Than Tawan off Th Surawong, offers traditional Thai cuisine, music and historical decor. Recommended dishes include *plaa sǎmlii dàet diaw* (half-dried, half-fried cottonfish with spicy mango salad) and *kài bai toei* (chicken baked in pandanus leaves). Prices are moderate and it's open daily for lunch and dinner.

A good one-stop eating place is the Silom Village Trade Centre (Map 6), an outdoor shopping complex on Soi 24. Though it's basically a tourist spot with higher than average prices, the restaurants are of fine quality and plenty of Thais dine here as well. The centrepiece is *Silom Village*, with shaded outdoor tables where the emphasis is on fresh Thai seafood, sold by weight. The menu also has extensive Chinese and Japanese sections. For a quick and casual meal, *Silom Coffee Bar* makes a good choice.

*Chaii Karr* (Map 6, ☎ 233 2549), on Th Silom across from the Holiday Inn and a few shops west of Central department store, is simply decorated with Thai antiques. The medium-price menu is mostly Thai, with a few farang dishes, plus 19 varieties of brewed coffee; the Thai mango salad and spicy seafood soup are very good. Thai folk music plays in the background. Chaii Karr is open 10.30 am to 9.30 pm daily.

Towards the eastern end of Th Surawong, about a 10-minute walk west of Montien Hotel, is the famous *Somboon Seafood* (☎ 233 3104), a good, reasonably priced seafood restaurant known for having the best crab curry in town. Soy-steamed seabass *(plaa kràphong nêung sii-íu)* is also a speciality; open from 4 pm to midnight.

*Mizu's Kitchen* on Soi Patpong 1 has a loyal Japanese and Thai following for its inexpensive but good Japanese food, including Japanese-style steak. Another very good Japanese place, especially for sushi and sashimi, is *Goro (399/1 Soi 7, Th Silom)*; prices are reasonable.

**Indian, Muslim & Burmese** Towards the western end of Th Silom and Th Surawong in an area known as Bangrak, Indian eateries begin making an appearance. Unlike at

Indian restaurants elsewhere in Bangkok, the menus in Bangrak don't necessarily exhibit the usual, boring predilection towards north Indian Moghul-style cuisine. For authentic south Indian food (dosa, idli, vada etc), try the **Madras Café** (☎ 235 6761, 31/10-11 Trok Vaithi (Trok 13), Th Silom) in the Madras Lodge near the Narai Hotel. It's open 9 am to 10 pm daily. Across from the Narai Hotel, near the Sri Mariamman Temple, *street vendors* sometimes sell Indian snacks.

**Madura Restaurant** (Map 6, ☎ 635 6609, 68 Soi 22, Th Silom), down a small soi opposite the Sri Mariamman Temple, is a modest South Asian establishment with delicious vegetarian thalis. Although it's not a Sri Lankan restaurant per se, authentic string hoppers and a few other Sinhalese specialities are also on the menu.

**India Hut** (Map 6, ☎ 635 7876), a friendly place on Th Surawong diagonally opposite the Manohra Hotel (Map 6), specialises in Nawabi (Lucknow) cuisine. It's quite good, is moderate to medium-high in price (from 50B to 100B per dish) and has modern Indian decor. The vegetarian samosas and fresh prawns cooked with ginger are particularly good. The restaurant is three flights of steps off the street.

**Himali Cha-Cha** (Map 6, ☎ 235 1569, 1229/11 Th Charoen Krung) features north Indian cuisine at slightly higher prices. The founder, Cha-Cha, worked as a chef for India's last Viceroy; his son has taken over the kitchen here. It's open for lunch and dinner.

**The Cholas**, a small air-con place downstairs in the Woodlands Inn (Map 6) on Soi 32, Th Charoen Krung, just north of the main post office, serves decent, no-fuss north Indian food from 50B to 80B a dish. The open-air **Sallim Restaurant**, next door to the Woodlands Inn (Map 6), is a cheaper place with north Indian, Malay and Thai-Muslim dishes – it's usually packed.

Around the corner on Soi Phuttha Osot is the very popular but basic-looking *Naaz* (Naat in Thai), with the richest *khâo mòk kài* (Thai Muslim-style chicken biryani) in the city. The milk tea is also very good, and daily specials include chicken masala and mutton korma. For dessert, the house speciality is *firni,* a Middle Eastern pudding spiced with coconut, almonds, cardamom and saffron. It's open 7.30 am to 10.30 pm daily.

*Yogi* (Map 6), another shophouse stall also tucked away on Soi Phuttha Osot, serves delicious and inexpensive Indian vegetarian (and vegan, if you specify no ghee or butter) food. The nearby *New Restaurant* (NR Restaurant; Map 6) is similar but serves non-veg as well as veg. Finding this soi is a little tricky since an expressway bisected the original approach from Th Charoen Krung. The best way to reach these two is by walking north from Th Surawong along a soi opposite Th Mahesak and the New Fuji Hotel; turn left at Soi Phuttha Osot and you'll reach Yogi and NR a short walk down on the left.

Down near the intersection of Th Charoen Krung and Th Silom is the *Muslim Restaurant* (Map 6, 1356 Th Charoen Krung), one of the oldest in the area. The faded yellow walls and stainless steel tables aren't inspiring, but it's clean enough and you can fill yourself on curries and roti for 40B or less. On Soi 20 off Th Silom there's a mosque, Masjid Mirasuddeen (Map 6), so Muslim *food vendors* are common.

*Sun Far Myanmar Food Centre* (☎ 266 8787, 107/1 Th Pan), between Th Silom and Th Sathon Tai (near the Myanmar embassy), is an inexpensive place to sample authentic Burmese curries and *thok* (spicy Burmese-style salads). It's open 8 am to 10 pm daily.

**Vegetarian** *Rabianthong Restaurant* (Map 7, ☎ 237 0100), in the Narai Hotel on Th Silom, offers a very good vegetarian section in its luncheon buffet on *wan phrá* (full moon days) only for 250B.

*Tiensin* (Map 6, ☎ 233 8716, 1345 Th Charoen Krung), opposite the entrance of the soi that leads to the Shangri-La Hotel, serves very good Chinese vegetarian food, including many mock meat dishes. It's open from 7 am to 9 pm daily.

[continued on page 181]

Tastes of Bangkok

# FOOD

Thailand's intricate cuisine has become famous the globe over, from London and Montreal, to Melbourne. Thai dishes can be pungent and spicy with a lot of garlic and chillies used, especially *phrík khîi nǔu* (literally, mouse-shit peppers), small torpedo-shaped devils best pushed aside if you are timid about red-hot curries. Almost all Thai food is cooked with fresh ingredients, including vegetables, poultry, pork and some beef. Plenty of lime juice, lemon grass and fresh coriander leaf are added to give the food its characteristic tang, and fish sauce *(náam plaa)*, generally made from anchovies, or shrimp paste *(kà-pi)* to make it salty.

Other common seasonings include laos or galanga root *(khàa)*, black pepper, three kinds of basil, ground peanuts (more often a condiment), tamarind juice *(náam má-khǎam)*, ginger *(khǐng)* and coconut milk *(kà-thí)*. The Thais also eat a lot of what could be called Chinese food, which is generally, but not always, less spicy.

Rice *(khâo)* is eaten with most meals. 'To eat' in Thai is literally 'eat rice' or *kin khâo*. Thais can be very picky about their rice, insisting on the right temperature and cooking times. Ordinary white rice is called *khâo jâo* and there are many varieties and grades. The finest quality Thai rice is known as *khâo hǎwm málí* (jasmine-scented rice) for its sweet, inviting smell when cooked. In the North and North-East of Thailand, 'sticky' or glutinous rice *(khâo nǐaw)* is common and is traditionally eaten with the hands.

Most restaurants in Bangkok's tourist districts have bilingual or English menus; for those places outside the usual tourist venues, it's worthwhile memorising a small standard 'repertoire' of dishes. Many restaurants have their own local specialities in addition to the standards and you might try asking for 'whatever is good' *('mii à-rai náe nam mǎi')*, allowing the proprietors to choose for you. Of course, you might get stuck with a large bill this way, but with a little practice in Thai social relations you may get some very pleasant results.

The most economical places to eat – and the most dependable – are noodle shops *(ráan kǔaytǐaw)*, curry-rice shops *(ráan khâo kaeng)* and night markets *(ta-làat tôh rûng)*.

## Vegetarian

If you wish to avoid eating meat and seafood while in Thailand, you can do so with some effort. Vegetarian restaurants are increasing in number throughout the country, thanks largely to Bangkok's ex-Governor Chamlong Srimuang, whose strict vegetarianism has inspired a nonprofit chain of vegetarian restaurants *(ráan aahǎan mangsàwírát)* in Bangkok and several provincial capitals.

Many of these are sponsored by the Asoke Foundation, an ascetic (some would say heretic) Theravada Buddhist sect that finds justification

**Title page:** An evening market counter topped with varieties of Thai dishes. (Photograph by Jerry Alexander)

### Don't Be Like Lime Without Juice!

Food plays an important role in Thai idioms and proverbs whose intended meaning have nothing to do with eating.

**kin hâew** 'eat water chestnuts'; to fail at something
**kwàa thùa jà sùk ngaa kâw mâi** 'Before the peanuts are done, the sesame will burn'; an admonition to do things in the proper order. This saying offers added poetry in the way all words in the first clause – 'before the peanuts are done' – are spoken in parallel low tones, while two of three words in the second clause – 'the sesame will burn' – are falling tones.
**mâi kin sên** 'not eating noodles'; when two people refuse to speak to one another due to a falling out
**mánao mâi mii náam** 'like lime without juice'; dull
**phàk chii rawy nâa** 'coriander leaf sprinkled on top'; performing a deed for appearances only
**sên yài** 'big noodle'; important person
**wăan yen** 'sweet cool' (a type of iced Thai dessert); an easy-going person
**From Lonely Planet's *World Food Thailand***

for vegetarianism in the Buddhist *suttas* (discourses of the Buddha). Look for the green sign with large Thai numerals out the front of shops – each restaurant is numbered according to the order in which it was established. The food is usually served buffet style and is very inexpensive – typically 5B to 10B per dish. Most are open only from 7 or 8 am until noon. At an Asoke Foundation lecture I once attended in Chiang Mai, a spokesperson for the foundation said its objective is to *lose* money at these restaurants.

Other easy, though less widespread, venues for vegetarian meals include Indian restaurants, which usually feature a vegetarian section on the menu. Chinese restaurants are also a good bet since many Chinese Buddhists eat vegetarian food during Buddhist festivals.

More often than not, however, visiting vegetarians are left to their own devices at the average Thai restaurant. In Thai the magic words are *phŏm kin jeh* (for males), and *dìchăn kin jeh* (for females). Loosely translated this phrase means 'I eat only vegetarian food'. Like other Thai phrases, it's important to get the tones right – the key word, *jeh*, should rhyme with the English 'jay' without the 'y'. It might also be necessary to follow with the explanation *phŏm/dìchăn kin tàe phàk* ('I eat only vegetables'). Don't worry – this won't be interpreted to mean no rice, herbs or fruit.

In Thai culture, 'brown' or unpolished rice *(khâo klâwng)* is said to be reserved for prisoners! A few health-food shops also carry it.

Those interested in tapping into the Thai vegetarian movement can phone the Vegetarian Society of Bangkok (☎ 254 5444, 254 3502). The society usually meets monthly to share a vegetarian feast, swap recipes and discuss vegetarianism (in English).

# What to Order

Thai food is served with a variety of condiments and sauces, including ground red pepper *(phrík pòn)*, ground peanuts *(thùa pòn)*, vinegar with sliced chillies *(náam sôm phrík)*, fish sauce with chillies *(náam plaa phrík)*, a spicy red sauce called *náam phrík sǐi raachaa* (from Si Racha, of course) and any number of other dipping sauces *(náam jîm)* for particular dishes. Soy sauce *(náam sii-íu)* can be requested, though this is normally used as a condiment for Chinese food only.

Except for the 'rice plates' and noodle dishes, Thai meals are usually ordered family style, which is to say that two or more people order together, sharing different dishes. Traditionally, the party orders one of each kind of dish, eg, one chicken, one fish, one soup etc. One dish is generally large enough for two people. One or two extras may be ordered for a large party. If you come to eat at a Thai restaurant alone and order one of these 'entrees', you had better be hungry or know enough Thai to order a small portion. This latter alternative is not really too acceptable socially as Thais generally consider eating alone in a restaurant unusual – but then as a *farang* you're an exception anyway.

## How To Order Noodles

At most noodle stalls menus are non-existent, and vendors speak little if any English. This means attaining 'made to order' noodle creations can involve some experimentation. Because you must indicate the type of noodle desired, additional ingredients and style of preparation, the noodle experience can be a challenging and fun way to order a meal.

Sometimes the name of the dish will indicate its contents; other times it will refer to a famous style from a particular location in Thailand. Some typical Thai noodle dishes are *kǔaytǐaw phàt thai* (usually called *phàt thai* for short; thin rice noodles with dried or fresh shrimp, bean sprouts, fried tofu, peanuts, egg and seasonings), *kǔaytǐaw râat nâa* (or just *râat nâa*; braised noodles combined with pork or chicken, Chinese broccoli or Chinese kale and oyster sauce) and *kǔaytǐaw phàt khîi mao* (wide rice noodles, fresh basil leaves, chicken or pork, seasonings and a healthy dose of fresh sliced chillies).

Language failing, you can always point to the desired choices, or point to the tables of other diners. After a few noodle experiences, the observant traveller will begin to pick up a noodle vocabulary and should get better at ordering the types and styles of dishes desired.

Noodle vendors can be found on street corners, in alleys, along rivers, at markets and in canoes along canals. A good rule of thumb for choosing a noodle outlet is to find one that's crowded. Thai diners usually have good taste and their presence at a particular stall is often an indication that it is worth a try. But whatever you do, try noodles – a national dish that has been called 'the fuel that drives the engines of a kingdom'.

**By Steve Van Yodern, adapted from Lonely Planet's**
***World Food Thailand***

A cheaper alternative is to order dishes *râat khâo* (over rice). Curry *(kaeng)* over rice is called *khâo kaeng;* in a standard curry shop, khâo kaeng is only around 15B a plate. Another category of Thai food is called *kàp klâem* – dishes meant to be eaten while drinking alcoholic beverages. On some menus these are translated as 'snacks' or 'appetisers'. Typical kàp klâem include *thùa thâwt* (fried peanuts), *kài sǎam yàang* (literally 'three kinds of chicken', a plate of chopped ginger, peanuts, mouse-shit peppers and bits of lime – to be mixed and eaten by hand) and various kinds of *yam* – Thai-style salads made with lots of chillies and lime juice.

## Table Etiquette

Using the correct utensils and eating gestures will garner much respect from Thais, who generally view Western table manners as rather coarse.

Thais eat most dishes with a fork *(sâwm)* and tablespoon *(cháwn)*, except for Chinese noodles, which are eaten with chopsticks *(tà-kìap);* noodle soups are eaten with a spoon and chopsticks.

The fork is held in the left hand and used to push food onto the spoon, which you eat from. To the Thais, pushing a fork into one's mouth is uncouth. An exception to the fork-and-spoon routine is sticky rice, which is rolled into balls and eaten with the right hand, along with the food accompanying it.

When serving yourself from a common platter, put no more than one or two spoonfuls onto your plate at a time. It's customary at the start of a shared meal to eat a spoonful of plain rice first – a gesture that recognises rice as the most important part of the meal. If you're being hosted by Thais, they'll undoubtedly encourage you to eat less rice and more curries etc as a gesture of their generosity (since rice costs comparatively little). The humble guest, takes rice with every spoonful.

Don't pick a serving plate up to serve yourself. Proper Thai food etiquette involves reaching over to the serving plate with your spoon, and if you can't reach the platter at all, it's best to hand your plate to someone near the serving platter. Most Thais will do this automatically if they notice you're out of platter range. Whatever you do, don't tilt a serving plate over your own plate – this is considered very rude.

Always leave some food on the serving platters as well as on your plate – not to do so would be a grave insult to your hosts. This is why Thais tend to over-order at social occasions – the more food left on the table, the more generous the host appears.

## Recipes

### Yam Mét Má-Mûang Hìmáphaan (Spicy Cashew Nut Salad)

*Yam mét má-mûang hìmáphaan* makes a tasty *kàp klâem* (drinking food) dish. The most simple recipes consist of fried cashew nuts on a plate with little piles of chopped spring onions or shallots, sliced fresh chillies, wedges of lime, salt and sometimes dried shrimp on the side. The customers then squeeze the lime over the nuts and mix everything together.

Here's a more sophisticated cashew yam we dreamt up after several visits to a little Mekong view restaurant in Khong Jiam.

½ kilo cashews, fresh or dry roasted
8 fresh red and green chillies (any kind will do, depending on how hot you'd like this dish to be), sliced into small rounds
6 fresh cherry tomatoes
4 shallots, sliced into small wedges
¼ cup dried shrimp
1 teaspoon green peppercorns, fresh or bottled (but drained)
3 tablespoons lime juice
salt, to taste

Roast the cherry tomatoes in a hot oven or over an open flame until the skins blister and crack. Peel the tomatoes and set aside.

Fry the cashews in a small amount of cooking oil until fragrant and golden. Take care not to overcook or burn them.

Toss all the ingredients together. Serve with cold Singha Beer or iced Mekong whisky with lime and soda.

### Tôm Yam Kûng (Chilli & Lemongrass Soup with Shrimp)

Thailand's best-known dish is quick and easy to prepare. Reduce the number of fresh chillies in this simple, classic recipe if you're chilli-shy.

6 large whole shrimp
1½ tablespoons fresh chopped galangal
1 lemongrass stalk, thinly sliced
2 kaffir lime leaves, thinly sliced
15 phrík khîi nñu (mouse-shit chilli)
10 fresh straw mushrooms
3 tablespoons lime juice
2 tablespoons fish sauce

Remove the heads from the shrimp and make a stock by simmering them in 3¼ cups of boiling water for about 10 minutes. Strain the stock into a saucepan.

Add the shrimp, galangal and lemongrass to the stock and simmer for five minutes.

Stir in the remaining ingredients, remove from the heat and serve with plenty of white rice.

### Kaeng Phèt (Hot Curry)

Also known as *kaeng daeng* (red curry) and *kaeng phèt daeng* (red hot curry), this is the most traditional of Thai curries and is often used as a base to create other curries. This curry paste should be quite spicy, but the number of chillies can be reduced by half without affecting the overall flavour too much.

Two of the most well loved versions of kaeng phèt are *kaeng phèt pèt yâang* (roast duck curry), a recipe confined to the royal court until the

**Top:** Digging into an Isan meal in Bangkok.

**Middle:** The colours of Thai food – (clockwise from top left) basket of mackerel, parcels of pandanus leaves, red chillies and sweet coconut sweets.

**Bottom:** Roadside eatery in Bangkok's Chinatown.

JERRY ALEXANDER

KRAIG LIEB

JOHN HAY

JULIET COOMBE

JERRY ALEXANDER

PAUL BEINSSEN

FRANK CARTER

JULIET COOMBE

JERRY ALEXANDER

JOHN HAY

JERRY ALEXANDER

JOE CUMMINGS

**Top:** Spoilt for choice – a street restaurant near Banglamphu

**Middle:** (Clockwise from top left) Tom Yam Kung, barbecued fish, ingredients for phàt thai, and a basket of peanuts and mame nuts.

**Bottom:** Anyone for seconds? Vendors fry up a giant serve of kuaytiaw phàt thai.

mid 20th century, and *kaeng phèt kài nàw mái* (chicken and bamboo shoot curry), a working-class mainstay of many rice and curry shops.

### Khrêuang Kaeng Phèt (Hot Curry Paste)

15 dried *phrík chíi fáa* (sky pointing chillies)
15 green peppercorns
4 tablespoons chopped garlic
3 tablespoons chopped shallots
2 tablespoons sliced fresh lemongrass
2 teaspoons chopped coriander root
1½ tablespoons chopped fresh galangal
1½ teaspoons roasted coriander seed
½ teaspoon roasted cumin seed
1 teaspoon shrimp paste
1 teaspoon salt

Slice open the dried chillies, shake out and discard the seeds and soak the chillies in warm water until they are soft and flexible. Grind and mash all the ingredients together in a mortar until a thick, brick-red paste is formed.

### Kaeng Phèt Pèt Yâang (Roast Duck Curry)

1½ tablespoons vegetable oil
3 tablespoons hot curry paste
2½ cups coconut milk
1 roast duck, boned and sliced into 2-3cm pieces*
8-10 cherry tomatoes
1 cup whole Thai eggplants
¾ cup pineapple chunks
½ cup clear chicken stock
1 teaspoon palm sugar
2 tablespoons fish sauce
½ teaspoon salt
3 kaffir lime leaves, sliced lengthways into 3cm strips

*The duck skin may be removed, but much of the 'roast' flavour will be lost.

In a thick-bottomed saucepan, stirfry the curry paste in the vegetable oil on medium-high heat until fragrant. Add half the coconut milk, mix thoroughly, then add the duck and simmer for five minutes to allow the curry paste and coconut milk to permeate the meat.

Add the other half of the coconut milk and all the remaining ingredients except the kaffir lime leaves, and simmer another five minutes. Remove from the heat, garnish with sliced kaffir lime leaves and serve.

**All recipes from Lonely Planet's *World Food Thailand*,
by Joe Cummings**

# DRINKS
## Non-alcoholic Drinks

**Fruit Juices & Shakes** The incredible variety of fruits in Thailand means there's an abundance of nutritious juices and shakes.

Thais prefer to drink most fruit juices with a little salt mixed in. Unless a vendor is used to serving faràng, your fruit juice or shake will come slightly salted. If you prefer unsalted fruit juices, specify *mâi sài kleua* (without salt).

Sugar cane juice *(náam âwy)* is a Thai favourite and a very refreshing accompaniment to curry and rice plates. Many small restaurants or food stalls that don't offer any other juices will have a supply of freshly squeezed náam âwy on hand.

**Water** Purified water is simply called *náam dèum* (drinking water), whether boiled or filtered. *All* water offered to customers in restaurants or to guests in an office or home will be purified, so don't fret about taking a sip (see Health in the Facts for the Visitor chapter).

## Alcoholic Drinks

Drinking in Thailand can be expensive in relation to the cost of other activities. The Thai government has placed increasingly heavy taxes on liquor and beer, so that now about nearly half the price you pay for a large beer is tax. Whether this is an effort to raise more tax revenue (the result has been a sharp decrease in the consumption of alcohol and corresponding drop in revenue) or to discourage consumption, drinking can wreak havoc with your budget. One large 630mL bottle of Singha beer costs more than the minimum daily wage of a Bangkok worker.

According to the Food and Agriculture Organisation (FAO), Thailand ranks fifth worldwide in alcohol consumption, behind South Korea, the Bahamas, Taiwan and Bermuda, and well ahead of Portugal, Ireland and France.

**Beer** Several brands of beer are brewed in Thailand by Thai-owned breweries. Advertised with such slogans as *pràthêht rao, bia rao* (Our Land, Our Beer), the Singha label is considered the quintessential 'Thai' beer. Pronounced Sǐng (Lion) by the Thais, it claims an enviable 66% of the domestic market. It's a strong, hoppy-tasting brew thought by many to be the best beer in Asia. The rated alcohol content is a heady 6%. Singha is sometimes available on tap in pubs and restaurants.

Kloster, similarly inspired by German brewing recipes, is a notch smoother and lighter than Singha with an alcohol content of 4.7% and generally costs about 5B to 10B more per bottle. Kloster claims only about 5% of Thailand's beer consumption. Like Singha, it's available in cans as well as bottles.

Boon Rawd Breweries, makers of Singha, also produce a lighter beer called Singha Gold that only comes in small bottles; most people seem

## Crunch in a Can

Imagine the scenario: unexpected guests arrive on your doorstep demanding liquid refreshment and pre-dinner snacks. Need to impress? Dips and crackers are so passe, and potato crisps are old hat. Why not surprise your guests with the latest innovation to come out of Bangkok? – insects in a can! If you like your crickets crunchy and with a long shelf-life (and who doesn't?), this is the development you've been waiting for. The tinned bugs, invented by a Thai researcher, won awards at a recent technical exhibition held in Bangkok.

Protein-rich fried grasshoppers, locusts and other insects have long been sold in Bangkok's street stalls, and are a commonly eaten food in the country's North-East. The processed variety look set to take the market by storm. Be sure to keep your eyes peeled in Bangkok's supermarkets and stock up – one never knows when one will have to entertain those hard-to-please friends.

**Adapted from Lonely Planet Scoop travel news at
www.lonelyplanet.com/scoop**

to prefer either Kloster or regular Singha to Singha Gold, which is a little on the bland side. Better is Singha's new canned 'draught beer' – if you like cans.

Carlsberg, jointly owned by Danish and Thai interests, waded into the market in the early 1990s and proved to be a strong contender. As elsewhere in South-East Asia, Carlsberg used an aggressive promotion campaign, and when test marketing found that Thais perceived it to be too weak, the company adjusted its recipe to come closer to Singha's 6% alcohol content. In its first two years in business, Carlsberg managed to grab around 25% of the Thai market. Like Kloster, it has a smoother flavour than Singha, and is preferred by some drinkers during spells of hot weather.

As the beer wars heated up, Singha retaliated with advertisements suggesting that drinking a Danish beer was unpatriotic. Carlsberg responded by introducing Beer Chang (Elephant Beer), which matches the hoppy taste of Singha but ratchets the alcohol content up to 7%. Beer Chang has managed to gain an impressive market share mainly because it retails at a significantly lower price than Singha and thus easily offers more bang per baht. Predictably, the next offensive in the war was launched with the marketing of Boon Rawd's new cheaper brand, Leo. Sporting a black and red leopard label, Leo costs only slightly more than Chang but is similarly high in alcohol. To differentiate itself from the flavour of the competition, Boon Rawd gave Leo a maltier taste.

Dutch giant Heineken, which opened a plant in Nonthaburi in 1995, comes third after Singha and Carlsberg to most national palates, and holds a similar ranking in sales. Other Thailand-produced, European-branded beers you'll find in larger cities include a dark beer called Black Tiger, malty-sweet Mittweida and Amstel lager.

You'll also find various imported beers in Bangkok – everything from Mexico's Corona to Ireland's Guinness – in the city's more upscale bars and restaurants.

The Thai word for beer is *bia*. Draught beer is *bia sòt* (literally, fresh beer).

**Spirits** Rice whisky is a big favourite in Thailand and somewhat more affordable than beer for the average Thai. It has a sharp, sweet taste not unlike rum, with an alcoholic content of 35%. The most famous brand is Mekong (pronounced 'Mâe-khŏng'). In rural areas you'll find several other labels, including Kwangthong, Hong Thong, Hong Ngoen, Hong Yok and Hong Tho. Mekong costs around 120B for a large bottle *(klom)* or 60B for the flask-sized bottle *(baen)*. The Hong brands are less expensive.

More expensive Thai whiskies appealing to the can't-afford-Johnnie-Walker-yet set include Blue Eagle whisky and Spey Royal whisky, each with 40% alcohol. These come dressed up in shiny boxes, much like the far more expensive imported whiskies they're imitating.

One company in Thailand produces a true rum, that is, a distilled liquor made from sugar cane, called Sang Som. Alcohol content is 40% and the stock is supposedly aged. Sang Som costs several baht more than the rice whiskies, but for those who find Mekong and the like unpalatable, it is an alternative worth trying.

**Herbal Liquor** Currently, herbal liquors are fashionable throughout the country and can be found at roadside vendors, small pubs and in a few guesthouses. These liquors are made by soaking various herbs, roots, seeds, fruit and bark in *lâo khǎo* (a clear, colourless, distilled rice liquor) to produce a range of concoctions called *yaa dawng*. Many of the yaa dawng preparations are purported to have specific health-enhancing qualities. Some of them taste fabulous, while others are rank.

**Wine** Thais are increasingly interested in wine, but still manage only a minuscule one glass per capita average consumption per year. Wines imported from France, Italy, the USA, Australia, Chile and other countries are available in restaurants and wine shops, but a 340% government tax makes them just about out of reach for most of us – or at the very least a poor bargain. If the government drops the tax, wine could become very fashionable in Thailand.

Various businesses have attempted to produce wine in Thailand, most often with disastrous results. However, an exception is the Chateau de Loei winery, near Phu Reua in Loei Province. Its first grape variety, a Chenin Blanc, is quite drinkable, and its latest Cabernet Sauvignon release confirms Chaiyuth's reputation as a serious vintner. Both are available at many of the finer restaurants in Bangkok.

*[continued from page 170]*

**Other Cuisines** If you crave German or Japanese food, there are plenty of places on and around Th Patpong. *Bobby's Arms* (☎ 233 6828), an Aussie-British pub on the 1st floor of a multistorey car park off Soi Patpong 2, has good fish and chips. *Le Bouchon* (☎ 234 9109), on Soi Patpong 2, is a popular and reasonably authentic French bistro open only from 6 pm to midnight.

*O'Reilly's Irish Pub* (☎ 235 1572, 62/1-2 Th Silom), at the entrance to Thaniya Plaza, opens at 8 am and doesn't close until 1 or 2 am; it features a good menu of reasonably priced pub grub. *Shenanigans* (☎ 266 7160, 1-4 Sivadon Bldg, Th Convent), (formerly Delaney's Irish Pub) in the Th Silom district, serves a set lunch menu Monday to Friday, plus Western food for lunch and dinner daily.

*Folies Café-Patisserie (Map 7, ☎ 678 4100, 29 Th Sathon Tai)*, at the Alliance Française, serves inexpensive to moderately priced French dishes. It's open 8 am to 6 pm Monday to Saturday. *Coffee World (☎ 634 3140)*, on the north side of Th Silom near the mouth of Soi 10, serves a variety of coffees, teas, Italian sodas, sandwiches and pastries in a large, clean, California-style cafe setting. Foreign magazines and newspapers are available for reading. In the *CP Tower* on Th Silom are a cluster of air-con American and Japanese-style fast-food places; several are open late.

The tiny *Harmonique (Map 6, ☎ 630 6270, Soi 24, Th Charoen Krung 34)*, around the corner from the main post office, is a refreshing oasis in this extremely busy, smog-filled section of Th Charoen Krung. This unobtrusive little shop serves a variety of teas, fruit shakes and coffee on Hokkien-style marble-topped tables – a pleasant spot to read poste-restante mail while quenching your thirst. Well-prepared if pricey (60B to 150B per dish) Thai food is available. The shop discreetly sells silk, silverware and antiques. It's open 11 am to 10 pm daily, closed Sunday.

## Soi Ngam Duphli (Map 7)

Across from the Tungmahamek Privacy Hotel and beside the Malaysia Hotel, an out-door Thai place called *Just One (☎ 679 7932, 58 Soi 1, Th Sathon Tai)* is a popular lunch spot. On the 11th floor of *Lumphini Tower* on busy Th Phra Ram IV is a cafeteria-style food centre open from 7 am to 2 pm. Opposite Lumphini Tower on the same road is a warren of *food vendors* with cheap eats.

Another restaurant in the Soi Ngam Duphli area worth mentioning is *Ratsstube (☎ 287 2822)* in the Goethe Institut, also on Soi Atakanprasit. Home-made German sausages and set meals from 120B attract a large and steady clientele. The softly lit Euro-Asian decor borders on rococo. It's open 11 am to 2.30 pm and 5.30 to 10 pm Monday to Friday, 11 am to 10 pm on weekends.

## Th Sukhumvit (Map 7)

This avenue, stretching east all the way to the city limits, has hundreds of Thai, Chinese and Western restaurants to choose from, especially in areas around major hotels. Most are of average quality and slightly above-average prices, while some are outstanding in both quality and price.

**Thai & Other Asian** This central section of Th Sukhumvit is loaded with medium-priced Thai restaurants that feature modern decor but real Thai food. *Baan Suan (☎ 261 6650)*, next to Bei Otto restaurant on Soi 20, is a pleasant garden restaurant with excellent Isan food, including Khon Kaen-style *kài yâang*, chicken grilled over coconut husk coals.

Although it's a little grungy, the *Yong Lee Restaurant* on Soi 15, near Asia Books, has excellent Thai and Chinese food at reasonable prices and is a longtime favourite among Thai and farang residents alike. It has another branch between sois 35 and 37.

For nouvelle Thai cuisine, you can try the *Lemongrass (Map 2, ☎ 258 8637, 5/1 Soi 24, Th Sukhumvit)*, which has an atmospheric setting in an old Thai house decorated with antiques. The food is exceptional; try the *yam pèt* (duck salad). It's open 11 am to 2 pm and 6 to 11 pm daily.

Yet another hidden gem down Th Sukhumvit is *Laicram (☎ 204 1069)* on Soi 23. The food is authentic gourmet Thai, but not outrageously priced. One of the house specialities is *hàw mòk hǎwy,* an exquisite thick fish curry steamed with mussels inside the shell. *Sôm-tam* (spicy green papaya salad) is also excellent here, usually served with *khâo man* (rice cooked with coconut milk) and *bai toei* (pandanus leaf). Opening hours are 10 am to 9 pm Monday to Saturday, until 3 pm on Sunday.

The upscale *Le Dalat* (☎ 258 4192, 260 1849, 47/1 Soi 23, Th Sukhumvit) has the most celebrated Vietnamese cuisine in the city. A house speciality is *nǎem meuang,* grilled meatballs that you place on steamed rice-flour wrappers, then add chunks of garlic, chilli, ginger, starfruit and mango along with a tamarind sauce, and finally wrap the whole thing into a lettuce bundle before popping it in your mouth. It's open 11 am to 2.30 pm and 6 to 10 pm daily. There's another branches at 14 Soi 23, Th Sukhumvit (same hours). Also good for a stylish Vietnamese meal is *Pho (Map 5, ☎ 658 1199),* on the 4th floor of Siam Center. There is a second branch *(☎ 251 8945)* in the Alma Link Building, 25 Soi Chitlom, Th Ploenchit; both branches are open daily for lunch and dinner.

About a 50m walk down Soi 12, *Cabbages & Condoms (☎ 252 7349),* next to the PDA headquarters, offers fair Thai food for lunch and dinner in indoor and outdoor dining areas. Instead of after-meal mints, diners get packaged condoms; all proceeds go towards sex education/AIDS prevention programs in Thailand. Another 50m down the same soi, *Crepes & Co (☎ 653 3990)* serves high-quality crepes of all kinds, European-style breakfasts, and a very nice selection of Mediterranean, Moroccan and Spanish lunch and dinner specialities. It's air-conditioned and prices are moderate.

*The Emporium* shopping centre (Map 7), Soi 24, Th Sukhumvit, has several restaurants on its 4th, 5th and 6th floors, including a wood-panelled food centre with upmarket Thai vendors. If you go for the blonde wood and metal LA-cafe-bar-look, try the enormously trendy *Greyhound Café* on the 4th floor. The hybrid menu emphasises good, updated Thai supplemented by Italian and Mediterranean cuisine.

*Kuppa* (☎ 663 0450, Soi 16, Th Sukhumvit) is another very fashionable spot among Thais and expats, particularly for late breakfasts.

**Indian & Muslim** A restaurant with a good variety of moderately priced vegetarian and non-vegie Indian food (mostly north Indian) is *Mrs Balbir's (☎ 651 0498, 155/18 Soi 11/1),* behind the Siam Commercial Bank and next to the Swiss Park Hotel. A 150B buffet lunch is served daily. Owner Vinder Balbir has been teaching Indian and Thai cooking for many years, and has her own Indian grocery service as well. It's closed on Monday.

A few medium to expensive restaurants serving Pakistani and Middle Eastern food can be found in the 'Little Arabia' area of Soi 3 (Soi Nana Neua). The best value in the whole area is *Al Hussain*, a covered outdoor cafe on the corner of a lane (Soi 3/5) off the east side of Soi Nana Neua. It has a range of vegetarian, chicken, mutton and fish curries, along with dal, aloo gobi (spicy potatoes and cauliflower), nan and rice. Dishes cost 20B to 40B each. *Shiraz*, on the same soi, is a slightly pricier indoor place that provides hookahs (oriental pipes) for Middle Eastern gentlemen, who while away the afternoon smoking in front of the restaurant. Similar places in the vicinity include *Mehmaan*, *Akbar's (☎ 253 3479), Al Hamra* and *Shaharazad (☎ 251 3666).*

The splurge-worthy *Rang Mahal (☎ 261 7100),* a rooftop restaurant in the Rembrandt Hotel on Soi 18, offers very good north and south Indian 'royal cuisine' with overly attentive service and cityscape views. Most of the entrees are in the 150B to 230B range. In addition to its regular menu, it offers three set menus ranging from 700B to 950B per person. On Sunday the restaurant puts on a sumptuous Indian buffet from 11.30 am to 3 pm. An open-air observation platform on the same floor is reason enough for a visit.

**Western** The British-style downstairs bar at *Jool's Bar & Restaurant (☎ 252 6413)* on Soi 4 (Soi Nana Tai), past Nana Entertainment Plaza on the left walking from Th

Sukhumvit, is a favourite expat hang-out, while the dining room upstairs serves decent English food. On the west side of Soi 23, just around the corner from Soi Cowboy, the **Ship Inn** (no phone) is a small but authentic-looking British pub with food and libation.

Several rather expensive West European restaurants (Swiss, French, German etc) are also found on touristy Th Sukhumvit. **Bei Otto** (☎ 260 0892, 1 Soi 20 (Soi Nam Phung), Th Sukhumvit) is one of the most popular German restaurants in town and has a comfortable bar. Attached are a bakery, deli and butcher shop. **Haus München** (☎ 252 5775, 4 Soi 15, Th Sukhumvit) serves large portions of good German and Austrian food; prices are reasonable and there are recent German-language newspapers on hand. It's open daily for breakfast, lunch and dinner. Thailand's first microbrewery, **Bräuhaus-Bangkok** (☎ 661 1111, Ground floor, President Park, 99/27 Soi 24, Th Sukhumvit) serves German cuisine and fresh brewed beer in a huge air-con dining room or at outdoor tables. The average bill is around 400B.

Nostalgic visitors from the USA, especially those from the south, will appreciate the well-run **Bourbon St Bar & Restaurant** (☎ 259 0328), on Soi 22 (behind the Washington Theatre). The menu here emphasises Cajun and Creole cooking, but there are also some Mexican dishes on the menu; on some nights there is also free live music. A large dinner special for two costs 400B. It's also open for breakfast.

**Larry's Dive Center, Bar & Grill** (☎ 663 4563), a bright yellow two-storey building on Soi 22, serves American and Tex-Mex fare amid a kitsch sand-floor-and-potted-palms decor. The fake newspaper menu ('largest circulation of any newspaper on Soi 22') lists stuffed potato skins, salads, quesadillas, nachos, chilli, spicy chicken wings and Larry's food guarantee: 'Served in 30 minutes, or it's cold.' There's an attached dive shop, should you get the urge to go snorkelling in a nearby canal.

One of the top French restaurants in the city, and probably the best not associated with a luxury hotel, is **Le Banyan** (☎ 253 5556, 59 Soi 8 (Soi Prida), Th Sukhumvit) in a charming early Ratanakosin-style house. The kitchen is French-managed and the menu covers the territory from *ragout d'escargot* to *canard maigret avec foie gras*, complemented by a superb wine list. This is definitely a splurge experience, although the prices are moderate when compared with other elegant French restaurants in the city.

**Pomodoro** (☎ 254 5282), a place with floor-to-ceiling windows on the ground floor of the Nai Lert Building on Th Sukhumvit (between sois 3 and 5), specialises in Sardinian cuisine. The menu includes over 25 pasta dishes, and special set lunch menus are available for 180B to 250B. The wine list encompasses vintages from nine regions in Italy, along with others from France, Australia and the USA; the house red is particularly good considering the price.

**De Meglio** (☎ 651 3838), opposite Grand President Tower, Soi 11, is an elegant but comfortable Italian restaurant with a creative, seasonal menu, including a nice selection of vegetarian entrees. It's managed by the same company that operates Bräuhaus-Bangkok, so locally brewed German-style beer is available along with imported wines. A cigar lounge is attached.

If you're looking for Mexican food, the city's best can be found at **Señor Pico's of Los Angeles** (☎ 261 7100, 2nd floor, Rembrandt Hotel, Soi 18, Th Sukhumvit). This brightly decorated, festive restaurant offers reasonably authentic Tex-Mex cuisine, including fajitas, carnitas, nachos and combination platters. A live band provides Latin sounds; on Thursday evenings the staff teach free Latin dance lessons. Expect to spend around 500B for two.

## Victory Monument

The **Pickle Factory** (Map 5, ☎ 246 3036, 55 Soi 2, Thanon Ratwithi) occupies a 1970s-vintage Thai house that has been converted into a cosy restaurant, replete with indoor sofa-seating areas, outdoor tables, fully stocked bar and a swimming pool out the front – in short, the perfect place to kick back for an evening with friends. The menu includes Western dishes such as baked potatoes, smoked chicken wings, stuffed mussels, and roasted garlic and fetta cheese pizza, as well as Thai mango salads, *tôm yam kûng* and other Thai items. Prices run 60B to 120B per dish.

## DINNER CRUISES

There are a number of companies that run these. Prices range from 70B to 1200B per person depending on how far they go and whether dinner is included in the fare. See the River & Canal Trips section in the Things to See & Do chapter.

## HOTEL RESTAURANTS

For a splurge, many of Bangkok's grand luxury hotels provide memorable, if expensive, eating experiences. With Western cuisine particularly, the quality usually far exceeds anything found elsewhere in Bangkok. Some of the city's best Chinese restaurants are also located in hotels. If you're on a budget, check to see if a lunch-time buffet is available on weekdays; usually these are the best deals, ranging from 150B to 500B per person. Also check the *Bangkok Post* and *The Nation* for weekly specials presented by visiting chefs from far-flung corners of the globe – Morocco, Mexico City, Montreal – no matter how obscure, they've probably done the Bangkok hotel circuit.

The Oriental Hotel (Map 6) has six restaurants, all managed by world-class chefs, and several offer buffet lunches. *China House* (☎ 236 0400), set in a charming, restored private residence opposite the hotel's main wing, has one of the best Chinese kitchens in Bangkok, with an emphasis on Cantonese cooking. The lunch time dim sum is superb and is a bargain by luxury hotel standards. Reservations are recommended. The Oriental's river-view *Lord Jim's* (☎ 236 0400) is designed to imitate the interior of a 19th-century Asian steamer; the menu focuses on seafood (lunch-buffet available). During the cool season (December to February), the Oriental operates a Mediterranean garden-style restaurant known as *Ciao* (☎ 236 0400).

*Bai Yun* (☎ 679 1200), on the 60th floor of the Westin Banyan Tree (Map 7), specialises in nouvelle Cantonese – an East-West fusion.

*Chinatown* (☎ 236 0450) in the Dusit Thani Hotel (Map 7) focuses on Chiu Chau (Chao Zhou) cuisine as well as Cantonese. Dim sum lunch is available; it's a bit more expensive than the Oriental's, but the service (like the Oriental's) is impeccable. Dusit also has the highly reputed *Mayflower*, with pricey Cantonese cuisine, and the Vietnamese *Thien Duong* (☎ 236 0450).

For hotel dim sum almost as good as that at the Dusit Thani or Oriental – but at less than a third of the price – try the *Jade Garden* (☎ 233 7060) at the Montien Hotel (Map 7). Though not quite as fancy in presentation, the food is nonetheless impressive.

For French food, the leading hotel contenders are *Ma Maison* (☎ 253 0123) at the Hilton International (Map 5), *Le Normandie* (☎ 236 0400, ext 3380) at the Oriental Hotel (Map 6) and *Regent Grill* (☎ 251 6127) at the Regent Bangkok (Map 7). All are expensive but the meals and service are virtually guaranteed to be of top quality.

One of the best Italian dining experiences in the city can be found at the very posh and formal *Grappino Italian Restaurant* (☎ 653 9000) in the Amari Watergate hotel (Map 5), on Th Phetburi in the busy Pratunam district. All pasta and breads are prepared fresh on the premises daily, and the small but high-tech wine cellar is one of Bangkok's best – the grappa selection is, of course, unmatched. Grappino is open daily for lunch and dinner; reservations are recommended.

Of a similar quality – or perhaps better – and probably the busiest Italian restaurant in the city, the Regent Bangkok's (Map 7) *Biscotti* (☎ 255 5443) serves inventive dishes for relatively reasonable prices considering the location and the high quality of the cooking. As at Grappino, reservations are recommended.

The more relaxed *Angelini's* (☎ 236 7777, ext 1766), in the Shangri-La Hotel (Map 6), offers fine Italian cuisine in one of the most chic restaurants in Bangkok. Expect to pay 800B to 1000B for dinner for two. An array of upscale grappas is available at the sleek bar, where a good, live pop band is usually playing. It's open from 11 am till late.

The minimalist *Colonnade Restaurant* (☎ 287 0222) at the Sukhothai Hotel (Map 7) lays out a huge 900B brunch, including made-to-order lobster bisque, 11 am to 3 pm on Sunday. A jazz trio supplies background music; reservations are recommended.

Finally, if eating at one of these restaurants would mean spending your life savings, try this pauper's version of dining amid the bright hotel lights of Bangkok. Go to the end of the soi in front of the Shangri-La Hotel and take a ferry (2B) across the river to the wooden pier immediately opposite on the Thonburi shore. Wind through the narrow lanes opposite till you come to a main road (Th Charoen Nakhon), then turn left. About 200m down on your left, turn back towards the river until you come to the large, open-air *Thon Krueng* (Ton Khreuang; Map 6, ☎ 437 9671, 723 Th Charoen Nakhon). Here, you can enjoy a moderately priced Thai seafood meal outdoors with impressive night-time views of the Shangri-La and Oriental hotels opposite. To best take advantage of Thon Krueng's menu, it's best to share dishes in small groups, as this is definitely not a fried rice or fried noodles kind of place (though you'll find these dishes on the menu). Also the middle-class Thai clientele that dine here regularly do tend to dress up a bit, so don't wear your Th Khao San clothes. The ferry runs until around 2 am.

## OTHER VEGETARIAN RESTAURANTS

One of the oldest Thai vegetarian restaurants, operated by the Buddhist ascetic Asoke Foundation, is the branch at Chatuchak Weekend Market (Map 1) off Th Kamphaeng Phet (near the main local bus stop, a pedestrian bridge and a Chinese shrine – look for a sign reading 'Vegetarian' in green letters). It's open only on weekends 8 am to noon. Prices are almost ridiculously low – around 7B to 15B per dish. The *cafeteria* at the Bangkok Adventist Hospital (Map 3) at 430 Th Phitsanulok also serves inexpensive vegie fare. All the Indian restaurants in town also have vegetarian selections on their menus.

## HIGH TEA

Although Thailand was never a British colony (or anyone's colony for that matter), influences from nearby Kuala Lumpur and Singapore have made afternoon tea (or high tea) a custom at the more ritzy hotels. Prices average 300B to 500B per person. One of the best spreads is afternoon tea in the *Regent Bangkok* (Map 7) lobby from 2.30 to 5.30 pm on weekdays, where you'll find a selection of herbal, fruit, Japanese, Chinese and Indian teas, plus a variety of hot scones, Devonshire cream, jam, cakes, cookies and sandwiches. A live string quartet provides atmosphere.

At the *Authors Lounge* of the Oriental Hotel (Map 6) high tea consists of a range of sweet and savoury delights and one of the best tea assortments in Bangkok, all taken in the quasi-colonial atmosphere enjoyed by Maugham, Coward and Greene. Tea is served daily from 2 to 6 pm.

Amid the Asian minimalism of the *Sukhothai Hotel* (Map 7) lobby salon, the usual sandwiches, pastries and tea selections are served daily from 2.30 to 6 pm.

Afternoon tea is available in the relaxed lobby-lounge of the *Shangri-La Hotel* (Map 6) between 3 to 6 pm. Choose from a variety of teas, sandwiches and cakes. On Sunday, the Shangri-La does a more lavish 40-item 'high tea buffet' for a higher price.

PLACES TO EAT

# Entertainment

In their round-the-clock search for *khwaam sanùk* (fun), Bangkok residents have made their metropolis one that never sleeps. To get an idea of what's available, check the daily entertainment listings in the *Bangkok Post* and *The Nation* or the monthly *Bangkok Metro*. The latter maintains a good Web site (www.bkkmetro.com) listing current happenings in the city. Possibilities include classical music performances, rock concerts, videoteque dancing, touring Asian music or theatre ensembles, art shows and dinner theatre – virtually every type of event held in both the East and West.

## NIGHTLIFE

Bangkok's evening entertainment scene goes way beyond its overpublicised naughty nightlife image.

Today's Bangkok offers a heady assortment of entertainment venues, nightclubs, bars, cafes and discos appealing to every sort of proclivity. Many specialise in live music – rock, country & western, Thai pop music and jazz – while you'll hear the latest hits in the smaller neighbourhood bars, as well as in the mega-discos. Hotels catering to tourists and businesspeople often contain discos as well.

All bars and clubs are supposed to close at 1 or 2 am (the 2 am closing time applies to places with dance floors and/or live music), but in reality only some establishments obey the letter of the law.

## Live Music

Bangkok's live music scene has expanded rapidly over the past decade or so, with a multiplicity of great, new bands and clubs.

A casual spot to hear music is the open-air bar operated by *Ruang Pung Art Community* (☎ 513 7225), next to Chatuchak Weekend Market (Map 1). Thai rock, folk, blues and jam sessions attract an artsy Thai crowd; it's open 11 am to 10 pm on weekends.

Not to be overlooked is the strip of music bars along Th Sarasin (Map 7); *Brown Sugar* (mostly jazz) and *Old West* (folk and

Thai pop). *Blue's Bar* (☎ 252 7335), *Johnny Walker* and *Shakin'* usually feature recorded music, with occasional live bands on weekends.

*Concept CM2* (☎ 255 6888), a multi-themed complex in the basement of the Novotel in Siam Square (Map 7), hosts a rotation of live Western bands and Thai recording artists – generally focusing on what passes as alternative acts these days – interspersed with DJ dance music.

The talented house band at *Radio City* (Map 7, ☎ 266 4567), next to the Madrid Restaurant on Soi Patpong 1, performs oldies from the 1960s, '70s and '80s. The Thai Elvis Presley and Tom Jones impersonators who perform here nightly really get the crowd going.

*Dance Fever* (☎ 247 4295), a large club at 71 Th Ratchadaphisek in the burgeoning 'Ratchada' entertainment district, features a state-of-the-art sound and lighting system, giant video screens, a bar and restaurant. International touring bands like Bush, Blur and others have played there.

*Metal Zone* (Map 7, ☎ 255 1913), around the corner from Th Sarasin on Soi Lang Suan, just north of Lumphini Park, offers Thai heavy metal – with plenty of hair throwing and lip-jutting – nightly. Along with the dragons-and-dungeons decor is a regular lineup of bands ranging from thrash and gothic to speed metal. The volume level is perfect – loud enough for chest compression, but not so loud as to extract blood from the ears. *Rock Pub* (Map 5, ☎ 208 9664) on Th Phayathai opposite the Asia Hotel is similar.

Bangkok's better-than-average *Hard Rock Café* (Map 7, ☎ 254 0830), Siam Square, Soi 11, features live rock music most evenings from around 10 pm to 12.30 am, including occasional big names.

The spacious *Witch's Tavern* (☎ 391 9791, 306/1 Soi 55, Th Sukhumvit) features live pop music nightly.

*Imageries By The Glass* (Map 7, 2 Soi 24, Th Sukhumvit), owned by Thai composer-musician Jirapan Ansvananada, boasts a huge sound board and closed circuit TV for its stage shows, which welcome local as well as foreign bands of all genres.

An eclectic line-up of bands, including touring ones, also play nightly at *The Brewhouse* (see Brewery Pubs later in this section).

Many top-end hotels have bars with imported pop bands, of varying talent, who play mostly covers. *Angelini's* in the Shangri-La Hotel (Map 6) usually has one of the better cover bands, as does *Spasso* in the Grand Hyatt Erawan (Map 7).

## Jazz

The famous *Bamboo Bar* in the Oriental Hotel (Map 6) has live jazz nightly in an elegant atmosphere. The *Colonnade* at the Sukhothai Hotel (Map 7) offers jazz from Tuesday to Saturday.

*Fabb Fashion Café (Map 7, ☎ 658 2003, 540 Th Ploenchit)*, near the Chit Lom Skytrain station, features jazz piano and saxophone 8 pm to midnight Monday to Saturday.

## Latin

Clubs featuring all or mostly Latin dance music have exploded in Bangkok over the last couple of years. A Filipino band mixes up the salsa at *Baila Baila (☎ 714 1898)*, off Soi 63 (sub-Soi 4), Th Sukhumvit, where there are Latin dance lessons nightly.

At the flashier *El Niño (☎ 656 0160)*, in the President Tower Arcade (Map 7) on Th Ploenchit, a Colombian band plays nightly Monday to Saturday, dance lessons are available. The most serious venue for learning to salsa or cumbia is *The Salsa Club (☎ 216 3700)* in the Patumwan Princess Hotel, attached to Mahboonkrong shopping centre (Map 5), Th Phra Ram I. *La Havana (☎ 204 1166)*, in a small plaza area off Soi 22, Th Sukhumvit, features a small Cuban combo nightly they play late, so this is the place to go if the others start to fade early.

## Pubs & Bars

Trendy among Bangkok Thais these days are bars that strive for a sophisticated but casual atmosphere with good service, good drinks

and a good choice of music. The Thais often call them pubs but they bear little resemblance to the traditional English pub. Some are 'theme' bars, conceived around a particular aesthetic. All the city's major hotels feature Western-style bars as well.

In Banglamphu, *Gulliver's Traveler's Tavern* (Map 4), on the corner of Th Khao San (Khao San Road) and Th Chakraphong, is an air-conditioned place with the atmosphere of an American college hang-out. *Salvador Dali* (Map 3), a block north on Th Rambutri (towards the west end) and tucked away amid a row of noodle stands, is a comfortable, two-storey air-con bar with a quieter and more intimate feel.

The on and off (often closed during slow months) *Hole in the Wall* bar (Map 4, no phone), on a short, dead-end soi towards the western end of Th Khao San, is a cheap place to drink and chat with Th Khao San denizens.

More happening is the low-key *Susie Pub* (Map 4), in an alley off the north side of Th Khao San, and its sister pub down another alley off the south side of Th Khao San, *Austin Pub* (Map 4). Both pack in a heavily Thai clientele. If you want more of the Thai bar scene, head for Th Tanao south of Th Ratchadamnoen, where you'll find *Window Seat*, *Yellowish*, *Spicy*, *Go 6*, *Song Muai*, *Fifa Pub* and *Zoda*, all of which draw a young crowd.

*Shenanigans (Map 7, ☎ 266 7160, 1-4 Sivadon Building, Th Convent)*, (formerly Delaney's Irish Pub) also in the Th Silom district, is one of only two places in Bangkok that serves Guinness on tap; the interior wood panels, glass mirrors and bench seating were all custom-made and imported from Ireland. Bands of varying quality play from Tuesday to Saturday, and the place is often packed from 6 pm till closing. *O'Reilly's Irish Pub (Map 7, ☎ 632 7515, 62/1-2 Th Silom)*, at the entrance to Thaniya Plaza (corner of Th Silom and Soi Thaniya), draws a slow pint of Guinness or Kilkenny in a comparatively more low-key setting that resembles an old camera shop. Early drinkers will find O'Reilly's open at 11 am. Both pubs feature daily happy hours when their otherwise pricey beers are temporarily discounted.

ENTERTAINMENT

## One Night in Bangkok

### A Top 10 Sampler

It was not long ago that Bangkok's nightlife was synonymous with five-star hotel nightclubs and go-go bars. Finally, the city has grown up and is now home to some of Asia's slickest bars and clubs. The move of Q Bar from Ho Chi Minh City in 1999 to Bangkok heralded an entrepreneurial deluge and more and more places are spinning funky tunes in aesthetically pleasing surrounds. Thai students love to party and venturing to some of their favourite hangouts promises yet another take on this city that never seems to sleep.

### About Cafe

Map 6, ☎ 623 1742-3, 402-418 Th Maitreechit (between Wongwian 22 and Hualamphong Station)
Air-con bus No 7
Easy to find once you know where it is, About Cafe puts a new spin on venturing out in Chinatown and is a popular venue for Bangkok's art scene (it also houses the About Studio gallery upstairs). It's relaxed and low-key – like a home away from home with large comfy lounges, candle lighting and groovy house beats. At only 50B for a glass of vino, this is a prime place to guzzle the night away with a friend or three.

### Bangkok Bar

Map 3, ☎ 629 4443, 149 Soi Rambutri, Banglamphu
This small and friendly bar is a stone's throw away from Th Khao San, and attracts a cool Thai crowd and a sprinkling of travellers. Part of its appeal is the excellent music, varying from hip hop to techno depending on the night. Ideal for a few games of pool or a night out with some mates, Bangkok Bar is an intimate and sophisticated alternative to the surrounding backpacker bars. The higher than usual drink prices have rendered a tourist invasion unlikely.

### Lucifer

Map 7, ☎ 234 6902, 76/1-3 Soi 1, Patpong (Saladaeng Station)
Nestled in the heart of Patpong, Lucifer may sound devilish but it's heaven on earth for those needing a fix of hardcore techno. Typical of many Bangkok clubs with a multi-level design, Lucifer pulls a big crowd of ravers dedicated to the dance floor. The club built its reputation on being the place to go until the early hours of the morning. With stricter closing times being enforced recently, you may have to head there a bit earlier now.

### Narcissus

Map 7, ☎ 261 3991, 112 Soi 23, Th Sukhumvit (Asoke Station)
In keeping with its name, Narcissus is one of the city's most ostentatious clubs and has stood the test of time, remaining a favourite among Bangkok's elite. Here, mediocrity is a dirty word; with its overly grand Art Deco fit-out, awesome sound system and international playbill (Oakenfold has brought the house down here twice), this place means business.

### Q Bar

Map 7, ☎ 252 3274, 34 Soi 11, Th Sukhumvit (Nana Station)
Since its hyped opening in 1999, Q Bar has fast become Bangkok's bar of choice for anyone who's someone. Themed around a New York-style lounge club, Q Bar is slick and sophisticated with an air of pretence. The interior is quasi-industrial punctuated by sexy neon lighting and music that varies from soft house to trip hop. It boasts perhaps the largest range of drinks in Thailand – choose from 27 types of vodka and 41 brands of whisky/bourbon. If you've still got a cent left to your name, finish off the night with a potent mojito and Cuban cigar. Yes, this is the life.

## One Night in Bangkok

### Retro
Map 1, ☎ 714 1015, 70/9 Soi 4 Ekamai, Th Sukhumvit (Ekamai Station)
This smart and funky new bar is reminiscent of an *Austin Powers* set, where patrons ooze around the central bar surrounded by a tasteful combination of stainless steel, wood panelling and plastic. Retro is undeniably the theme here – where else in Bangkok can you order a Black Side Car or Beach Boys cocktail? But despite the temptation to overdo it on colour and lights, Retro keeps its cool with a minimalist yet warm approach. Similarly the music is not caught up in the past – DJs combine house and garage with a dash of 1970s funk. Drawing a mixed crowd of Thais and farang, Retro has all the ingredients of a Bangkok institution.

### Saxaphone Pub and Restaurant
Map 5, ☎ 246 5472, 3/8 Th Phayathai, Victory Monument (Victory Monument Station)
In a city that loves it pop, good jazz and blues aren't as easily come by, but over the years, Saxophone has hosted some of the best live jazz acts in Thailand. Rustic and barn-like, the acoustics at Saxophone are excellent and equally enjoyed from the cavernous alcoves downstairs or on floor cushions upstairs. The music changes each night – early on in the week you're likely to catch jazz bands, while Friday, Saturday and Sunday features a combination of folk, blues, ska and reggae bands.

### Silom Soi 2 & Soi 4 Area
Map 7, Soi 2 & Soi 4, Th Silom (Saladaeng Station)
With sexuality a prominent theme in this neck of the woods, Soi 4 is where homo meets hetero, attracting a mixed crowd to the clubs and bars spilling out into the soi. Each venue competes heavily for business, pushing its sound system to the limit and beckoning passers-by. You can hardly go wrong along here – small places like *Tapas* offer a more intimate vibe while long-timer *Balcony Bar* keeps people coming back for the cheap drinks, great service and prime vantage point for perving. Down on narrow Soi 2, the action hots up a bit more with a largely gay male clientele. Soi 2 has numerous venues worth a visit – *DJ Station* gets packed out with groovers out for a boogie while, opposite, the *Expresso Bar* brings an edge of sophistication to the soi with its designer decor, funky armchairs and mellow sounds.

### Skunk
Map 1, ☎ 390 0495, 1/1 Soi 2 Ekamai, Th Sukhumvit (Ekamai Station)
Discretely located off Soi Ekamai, Skunk is a recent addition to Bangkok's range of chilled-out bars playing quality dance music – here it's largely trance with some drum 'n bass. The decor is funky with a futuristic edge, featuring elongated vinyl couches and glass tabletops with creative installations underneath. Downstairs dig into excellent macrobiotic food – upstairs the post-indulgence room is perfect for sipping cocktails into the night engulfed by brilliant beats.

### Th Phra Athit Area
Map 3
Unbeknown to many travellers, the street running adjacent to Mae Nam Chao Phraya (two blocks west of Th Khao San) is home to a plethora of charming wooden shophouses converted into bars and cafes. Popular among Thai university students, Phra Ahtit has metamorphosised into a Bohemian retreat, with many places featuring live music – typically a one-man acoustic set. For a good Thai meal in congenial surrounds, *Hemlock* and *Commé* are sure winners – for a more raucous evening there are a string of good bars bunched together like *ToSit* and *Suntana*.

**Carly Hammond**

The latest Irish-style pub to open in Bangkok is the rustic *Dubliner*, in Washington Square (Map 7) on Th Sukhumvit between sois 22 and 24. An excellent blues band plays on Saturday night.

Three low-key, British-style taverns include *Jool's* (☎ 252 6413), on Soi 4 near Nana Plaza, the *Ship Inn* (Map 7, no phone), just around the corner from Soi Cowboy on the west side of Soi 23, and *Bull's Head & Angus Steakhouse* (☎ 259 4444, Soi 33/1, Th Sukhumvit), which tends to get very smoky inside if there's much of a crowd at all.

For slick aerial city views, the place to go is the 93-storey *Baiyoke Sky Hotel* on Th Ratchaprarop in Pratunam. On the 77th floor there's an *observation deck* that's open 24 hours, or you can scope the cityscape while dining in one of the restaurants on the 78th and 79th floors. The *Compass Rose*, a bar on the 59th floor of the Westin Banyan Tree (Map 7) on Th Sathon Tai, is also sky high; it's open 11.30 am to 1 am.

### Brewery Pubs
*The Brewhouse (Map 1, ☎ 661 3535, 61/2 Soi 26, Th Sukhumvit)*, associated with the Taurus dance club opposite, features four brews (including low-alcohol 'Dynamite Lite' and high-alcohol 'Naked Killer Ale'), in a split-level interior beneath a metallic dome.

In the Siam Discovery Center (attached to the Siam Center by an enclosed walkway), *Hartmannsdorfer Brau Haus (Map 5, ☎ 658 0229)* does fresh beer, sausages, cheeses and other stout German fare in a polished but pleasant atmosphere.

*Londoner Brew Pub (Map 7, ☎ 261 0238, basement, UBC II Bldg, Soi 33, Th Sukhumvit)* has recently begun serving its own beers and ales but the ambience is limp.

If you find yourself stuck at Bangkok International Airport, you could do a lot worse than the *Taurus Brewhouse (☎ 535 6861)*, towards the south end of Terminal 2 on the 4th floor, not far from the indoor carpark. The menu of sandwiches, burgers, salads, pastas, soups, pizza and Thai specials is quite good. It's open 6 pm to midnight daily.

**Cigar Bars** One half of the lobby in the *Regent Bangkok* (Map 7) is devoted to the smoker, with Dominican and Cuban brands (including Montecristo and Cohiba) available from the hotel's humidor. The Regent also claims the largest selection of single-malt whiskies in Asia – 64 of them, dating back to a 1940 Glenlivet.

*La Casa del Habano*, in The Oriental Hotel (Map 6), has 25 brands of Cuban cigars ranging from US$3 to US$120 per cigar, with a tiny lounge equipped with a select list of fine cognacs, port and single-malt whiskies. Other hotel cigar lounges include *Cigar Café* (Hilton International, Map 5), *Siam Havana* (Dusit Thani, Map 7) and *Club 54* (Montien Hotel, Map 7).

### Discos & Dance Clubs
Bangkok is famous for its huge high-tech discos that feature mega-watt sound systems, giant video screens and the latest in light-show technology. The clientele for these dance palaces is mostly young, moneyed Thais experimenting with lifestyles of conspicuous affluence, plus the occasional Bangkok celebrity and a sprinkling of bloodshot-eyed expats. Cover charges are typically 400B to 500B per person and include three drinks on weeknights, two drinks on weekends. The most 'in' disco of this nature continues to be *Phuture* (Map 1) on Th Ratchadapisek, attached to the north side of the Chaophya Park Hotel.

Another biggie is *Energy Zone* (☎ 433 7147, 14/4 Th Arun Amarin) in Thonburi.

The extremely popular *Taurus* (☎ 261 3991, Soi 26, Th Sukhumvit) offers a 'classic' pub and gourmet restaurant in addition to the lively disco, spread out over several levels.

A string of small dance clubs on *Silom Soi 2* and *Silom Soi 4* (Soi Jaruwan), both parallel to Patpong sois 1 and 2 (Map 7), off Th Silom, attracts a more mixed crowd in terms of age, gender, nationality and sexual orientation than either the hotel discos or the mega-discos. Expect to hear techno, trance, hip-hop and other current electonica. Main venues (some of which are small and narrow) include *Disco Disco (DD)*, *JJ Park* and *DJ Station* on Soi 2; *Icon*, *Deeper*, *Om*

*Trance*, *Hyper*, *Kool Spot*, *Speed* and *Sphinx* on Soi 4. If you tire of hip-hop and techno, slip into *Que Pasa* for recorded Latin dance sounds. The larger places collect cover charges of around 100B to 300B depending on the night of the week; the smaller ones are free. The clientele at these clubs was once predominantly gay but became more mixed as word got around about the great dance scene. Things don't get started here till relatively late – around midnight; in fact, on most nights the Soi 2 and Soi 4 dance clubs serve more as 'after hours' hang-outs since they usually stay open past the official 2 am closing time.

All the major hotels have international-style discos that cater to well-heeled tourists and business travellers. Only a few – those at the *Dusit Thani*, *Grand Hyatt*, *Regent Bangkok* (all Map 7) and the *Shangri-La* (Map 6) – can really be recommended as attractions in themselves. Cover charges are pretty uniform: around 300B on weekday nights and around 400B on weekends, including two drinks. Most places don't begin filling up until after 11 pm.

## Gay/Lesbian Venues

See the information on the Soi 2 and Soi 4, Th Silom dance club scene under Discos & Dance Clubs for places that attract a mixed gay/straight/bi clientele. In general the Soi 2 clubs are more gay than the Soi 4 bars, though Soi 4's *Telephone* and *The Balcony* are more exclusively gay than other bars on this street. *DJ Station* still boasts Soi 2's hottest gay dance scene, plus *kà-thoey* (transvestite) cabaret at midnight. *Khrua Silom*, in Silom Alley off Soi 2, attracts a young Thai gay and lesbian crowd; it's a 'kitchen disco' – you stand and dance next to your table. There's a cluster of seedier gay bars off Soi Anuman Ratchathon, off Soi Tantawan (Soi 6), which is off Th Surawong opposite the Tawana Ramada Hotel – more or less the gay equivalent of Patpong.

*Utopia* (☎ 259 9619, 116/1 Soi 23, Th Sukhumvit) is a combination bar, gallery, cafe and information clearing house for the local gay and lesbian community – the only place like it in South-East Asia. Friday night is des-ignated women's night, and there are regular film nights as well as Thai lessons. Special events, such as Valentine's Day candlelit dinners, are held from time to time. Utopia is open noon to 2 am daily. Nearby on Soi 23 are a sprinkling of other gay-oriented bars.

*Kitchenette* (☎ 381 0861, 1st floor, Dutchess Plaza, 289 Soi 55 (Soi Thong Lor), Th Sukhumvit) is a lesbian/mixed cafe with live music on weekends. Trendy, lesbian-owned *Vega* (☎ 258 8273, 662-6471) on Soi 39, Th Sukhumvit, is a casual pub/restaurant that also features live music and dancing, while upstairs there's karaoke.

Other lesbian venues include: *By Heart Pub* (☎ 570 1841, 117/697 Soi Sena Nikhom 1, Th Phahonyothin, Bang Kapi); *Be My Guest* (mixed crowd), around the corner from Utopia on Soi 31; and *Thumb Up* (mixed), Soi 31, Th Sukhumvit.

*Babylon Bangkok* (Map 7, ☎ 213 2108, 50 Soi Atakanprasit, Th Sathon Tai) is a four-storey gay sauna that has been called one of the top 10 gay men's saunas in the world. Facilities include a bar, roof garden, gym, massage room, steam and dry saunas, and jacuzzi baths. It's open 5 to 11 pm daily.

See Gay & Lesbian Travellers in the Facts for the Visitor chapter for more detail on Gay and Lesbian resources in Bangkok.

## Go-Go Bars

By and large these throwbacks to the Indochina War era are seedy, expensive and cater to men only, whether straight or gay. They're concentrated along Th Sukhumvit (Map 7, between sois 21 and 23), off Th Sukhumvit on Soi Nana Tai in the world-famous Patpong area, between Th Silom and Th Surawong.

Patpong's neon-lit buildings cover roughly four acres standing on what was once a banana plantation owned by the Bank of Indochina, which sold the land to the Hainanese-Thai Patpongphanit family for 60,000B (US$2400 at pre-1997 exchange rates) just before WWII. The Patpongphanit family collects a total of 10 million baht (over US$300,000) rent per month from Patpong tenants; a typical bar measures four by 12m deep.

ENTERTAINMENT

According to a *Bangkok Metro* interview with the late Patpongphanit patriarch himself, it wasn't American GIs who originally supported the Patpong bar business but rather airline staff from some 15 airline offices that established themselves in the area after WWII. Bangkok's first massage parlour, Bangkok Onsen, was established here in 1956 to serve Japanese expats and senior Thai police officers. By the 1960s, Soi Patpong had a flourishing local nightclub scene that was further boosted by the arrival of US and Australian soldiers in the early 1970s.

Patpong has calmed down a lot over the years and become a general tourist attraction. These days it has more of an open-air market feel as several of the newer bars are literally on the street, and vendors set up shop in the evening hawking everything from roast squid to fake designer watches. On Patpong's two parallel sois there are around 35 or 40 go-go bars, plus a sprinkling of restaurants, cocktail bars, discos and live music venues.

The downstairs clubs, with names like *King's Castle* and *Pussy Galore*, feature go-go dancing while upstairs more explicit performances are held behind closed doors. Women and couples are welcome. Avoid bars touting 'free' sex shows as there are usually hidden charges and doors are suddenly blocked by muscled bouncers when you try to ditch the outrageous bill. An exception is *Supergirls*, famous for its sex-on-a-flying-motorcycle show, as covered by *Rolling Stone*. The 1 am closing law is strictly enforced on Soi Patpong 1 and 2.

The gay men's equivalent can be found on nearby Soi Thaniya, Soi Pratuchai and Soi Anuman Ratchathon, where go-go bars feature in-your-face names like *Golden Cock*, as well as the more cryptic *Super Lex Matsuda*. Along with male go-go dancers and 'bar boys', several bars feature live sex shows, which are generally better choreographed than the hetero equivalents on Patpong. See Gay & Lesbian Venues in this chapter for other types of venues.

A more direct legacy of the R&R days is *Soi Cowboy* (Map 7), a single lane strip of 25 to 30 bars off Th Sukhumvit between sois 21 and 23. By and large it's seedier than Patpong, and you will see fewer women and couples in the crowd.

*Nana Entertainment Plaza*, off Soi 4 (Soi Nana Tai) Th Sukhumvit, is a three-storey complex with around 20 bars that have surged in popularity among resident and visiting oglers over the past five or more years. Nana Plaza (it's common shortened name) comes complete with its own guesthouses in the same complex, used almost exclusively by Nana Plaza's female bar workers for illicit assignations. The 'female' staff at Casanova consists entirely of Thai transvestites and transsexuals – this is a favourite stop for foreigners visiting Bangkok for sex reassignment surgery (see the boxed text 'Cut & Paste' in the Facts about Bangkok chapter).

Asian tourists – primarily Japanese, Taiwanese and Hong Kong males – flock to the *Ratchada entertainment strip*, part of the Huay Khwang district (Map 1), along wide Th Ratchadaphisek between Th Phra Ram IX and Th Lat Phrao. Lit up like Las Vegas, this stretch of neon boasts huge male-oriented massage-snooker-and-karaoke and go-go complexes with names like *Caesar's Sauna* and *Emmanuelle* – far grander in scale and more expensive than anything in Patpong.

## THEATRE & DANCE

Thailand's most traditional *lákhon* and *khŏn* performances are held at the *National Theatre (Map 3, ☎ 224 1342)* on Th Ratchini, north of the National Museum. The theatre's regular public roster schedules six or seven performances per month, usually on weekends. Admission fees are very reasonable at around 20B to 200B depending on the seating. Attendance at a khŏn performance (masked dance-drama based on stories from the *Ramakian*) is highly recommended.

Occasionally, classical dance performances are also held at the *Thailand Cultural Centre (Map 1, ☎ 245 7742)* on Th Ratchadaphisek and at the *College of Dramatic Arts (☎ 224 1391)* on Th Chao Fa near the National Theatre (Map 3). For background information see the Arts section in the Facts about Bangkok chapter.

[continued on page 198]

Traditional Thai Martial Arts

# Muay Thai (Thai Boxing)

Almost anything goes in this martial sport, both in the ring and in the stands. If you don't mind the violence (in the ring), a Thai boxing match is worth attending for the pure spectacle – the wild musical accompaniment, the ceremonial opening of each match and the frenzied betting around the stadium.

Thai boxing is also telecast on Channel 7 every Sunday afternoon; if you're wondering where everyone is, they're probably inside watching the national sport.

**History** Most of what is known about the early history of Thai boxing comes from Burmese accounts of warfare between Myanmar and Thailand during the 15th and 16th centuries. The earliest reference (1411 AD) mentions a ferocious style of unarmed combat that decided the fate of Thai kings. A later description tells how Nai Khanom Tom, Thailand's first famous boxer and a prisoner of war in Myanmar, gained his freedom by roundly defeating a dozen Burmese warriors before the Burmese court.

King Naresuan the Great (1555-1605) was supposed to have been a top-notch boxer, and he made *muay thai* a required part of military training for all Thai soldiers. Later another Thai king, Phra Chao Seua (the Tiger King), further promoted Thai boxing as a national sport by encouraging prize fights and the development of training camps in the early 18th century. There are accounts of massive wagers and bouts to the death during this time. Phra Chao Seua, himself, is said to have been an incognito participant in many of the matches during the early part of his reign. Combatants' fists were wrapped in thick horsehide for maximum impact with minimum knuckle damage. They also used cotton soaked in glue and ground glass and later hemp. Tree bark and sea shells were used to protect the groin from lethal kicks.

No one trained in any other martial art has been able to defeat a ranking Thai *nák muay* (fighter trained in muay thai) and many martial art aficionados consider the Thai style the ultimate in hand-to-hand fighting. On one famous occasion, in the 1970s, Hong Kong's top five kung fu masters were dispatched in less than 6½ minutes cumulative total, all knock-outs. Hong Kong, China, Singapore, Taiwan, Korea, Japan, the USA, the Netherlands, Germany and France have all sent their best, and none of the challengers has yet beaten a top-ranked Ratchadamnoen or Lumphini boxing stadium Thai boxer (except in non-stadium-sponsored bouts – see International Muay Thai later in this section). An American Dale Kvalheim trained in muay thai and won a North-Eastern championship around 25 years ago, becoming the first non-Thai to seize a regional title – but Isaan stadiums are a far cry from Bangkok's two muay thai crucibles, Ratchadamnoen and Lumphini.

Muay thai techniques are extensively incorporated into contemporary Thai military training, as well as by elite military units – such as US Navy SEAL teams – the world over.

**Title page:** Professional thai boxer. (Photograph by Paul Beinssen)

**Modern Thai Boxing** The high incidence of death and physical injury led the Thai government to institute a ban on muay thai in the 1920s, but in the 1930s the sport was revived under modern regulations based on the international Queensberry rules. Bouts were limited to five three-minute rounds separated by two-minute breaks. Contestants had to wear international-style gloves and trunks (always either red or blue) and their feet were taped – to this day no shoes are worn.

There are 16 weight divisions in Thai boxing, from mini-flyweight to heavyweight, with the best fighters said to be in the welterweight division (67kg maximum). As in international-style boxing, matches take place on a 7.3 sq metre canvas-covered floor with rope retainers supported by four padded posts, rather than the traditional dirt circle.

Today, in spite of these concessions to safety, all surfaces of the body are still considered fair targets and any part of the body except the head may be used to strike an opponent. Common blows include high kicks to the neck, elbow thrusts to the face and head, knee hooks to the ribs and low crescent kicks to the calf. A contestant may even grasp an opponent's head between his hands and pull it down to meet an upward knee thrust. Punching is considered the weakest of all blows and kicking merely a way to 'soften up' one's opponent; knee and elbow strikes are decisive in most matches.

The training of a Thai boxer, and particularly the relationship between boxer and trainer, is highly ritualised. When a boxer is considered ready for the ring, he is given a new name by his trainer, usually with the name of the training camp as his surname. For the public, the relationship is perhaps best expressed in the *ram muay* (boxing dance) that takes place before every match.

The ram muay ceremony usually lasts about five minutes and expresses obeisance to the fighter's guru *(khruu)*, the trainer, as well as to the guardian spirit of Thai boxing. This is done through a series of gestures and body movements performed in rhythm to the ringside musical accompaniment of Thai oboe *(pìi)* and percussion. Each boxer works out his own dance, in conjunction with his trainer and in accordance with the style of his particular training camp.

The woven headbands and armbands worn by fighters in the ring are sacred ornaments that bestow blessings and divine protection; the headband is removed after the ram muay ceremony, but the armband, which actually contains a small Buddha image, is worn throughout the match. After the bout begins, the fighters continue to bob and weave in rhythm until the action begins to heat up. The musicians play throughout the match and the volume and tempo of the music rise and fall along with the events in the ring.

Coloured belts denoting training ranks, such as those issued by karate schools, do not exist in muay thai. As one well-known muay thai trainer has said, 'The only belts Thai boxers are concerned with are the Lumphini Boxing Stadium and the Ratchadamnoen Boxing Stadium championship belts'. Lumphini and Ratchadamnoen, both in Bangkok, are Thailand's two main muay thai venues.

**Muay thai sparring partners.**

As Thai boxing has become more popular among Westerners (as both spectators and participants), there are increasing numbers of bouts staged for tourists in places like Pattaya, Phuket and Ko Samui. In these, the action may be genuine but amateurish, and the judging way below par. Nonetheless, dozens of authentic matches are held daily at the major Bangkok stadiums and in the provinces (there are about 60,000 full-time boxers in Thailand), and these are easily sought out.

Several Thai *nák muay* have won world championships in international-style boxing. Khaosai Galaxy, the greatest Asian boxer of all time, chalked up 19 WBA bantamweight championships in a row before retiring undefeated in December 1991. At any given time Thailand typically claims five international boxing champions – usually in the flyweight and bantamweight categories.

Meanwhile, in some areas of the country a pre-1920s version of muay thai still exists. In North-Eastern Thailand *muay boraan* is a very ritualised form that resembles *tai qi chuan* or classical dance in its adherence to set moves and routines. In pockets of southern Thailand, fighters practicing *muay katchii* still bind their hands in hemp, and a more localised southern style in Chaiya known as *muay chaiya* uses the elbows and forearms to good advantage. Each year around Songkhran (the lunar new year) in April, near the town of Mae Sot on the Thai-Myanmar border, a top Thai fighter challenges a Burmese fighter of similar class from the other side of the Moei River to a no-holds barred, hemp-fisted battle that ends only after one of the opponents wipes blood from his body.

**International Muay Thai** The World Muay Thai Council (WMTC), a relatively new organisation sanctioned by Thailand's Sports Authority and headquartered at the Thai Army Officers Club in Bangkok, has begun organising international muay thai bouts in Bangkok stadiums and elsewhere. The WMTC tracks training facilities as well as ranked fighters, and is the first entity to match champions from all muay thai camps. So far the largest number of WMTC-affiliated muay thai training facilities is found in the USA, followed by Australia, the Netherlands, Canada, Japan, France and the UK.

Although WMTC championship bouts have only been held since 1994, WMTC titles have the potential to carry more prestige than titles from Bangkok's two main stadiums because all athletes, whether Lumphini champions or Ratchadamnoen champions (or from elsewhere), can compete for WMTC belts. Prior to the establishment of the WMTC it wasn't ordinarily possible for a Ratchadamnoen champ to engage with a Lumphini counterpart.

Dutch fighter Ivan Hippolyte took the middleweight WMTC championship in November 1995 at Lumphini Boxing Stadium, reportedly the first foreigner ever to win a Lumphini fight. Holland is now widely considered to produce the world's best kickboxers after Thailand. However, recently many muay thai aficionados considered Cameroon's Danny Bille to be the best. International participation signals a new era for Thai boxing; some observers think it will upgrade the martial art by reconcentrating the focus on fight technique rather than ringside betting.

**Krabi-Krabong** Another traditional Thai martial art still practised in Thailand is *kràbìi-kràbawng* (literally, sword-staff). As the name implies, this sport focuses on hand-held weapons techniques, specifically the *kràbìi* (sword), *phlawng* (quarter-staff), *ngáo* (halberd), *dàap sǎwng meu* (a pair of swords held in each hand) and *mái sun-sàwk* (a pair of clubs). Although for most Thais krabi-krabong is a ritual artefact to be displayed at festivals or tourist venues, the art is still solemnly taught according to a 400-year-old tradition handed down from Ayuthaya's Wat Phutthaisawan. The King of Thailand's elite bodyguards are trained in krabi-krabong; many Thai cultural observers perceive it as a 'purer' tradition than muay thai.

Like muay thai of 70 years ago, modern krabi-krabong matches are held within a marked circle, beginning with a *wâi khruu* ceremony and accompanied throughout by a musical ensemble. Thai boxing techniques and judo-like throws are used along with weapons techniques. Although sharpened weapons are used, the contestants refrain from striking their opponents – the winner is decided on the basis of stamina and technical skill displayed. Although an injured fighter may surrender, injuries do not automatically stop a match.

For information on muay thai and krabi-krabong training courses in Thailand, see Courses in Things to See & Do chapter.

[continued from page 192]

## Chalermkrung Royal Theatre (Sala Chaloem Krung, Map 3)

The 1993 renovation of this Thai Deco building at the edge of the city's Chinatown-Pahurat district provided a striking new venue for khŏn performance in Thailand. When originally opened in 1933, the royally funded Chalermkrung was the largest and most modern theatre in Asia, with state-of-the-art motion picture projection technology and the first chilled-water air-con system in the region. Prince Samaichaloem, a former student of the École des Beaux-Arts in Paris, designed the hexagonal building.

The reborn theatre's 80,000-watt audio system, combined with computer-generated laser graphics, enables the 170-member dance troupe to present a technologically enhanced version of traditional khŏn. Although the special effects are reasonably impressive, the excellent costumes, set design, dancing and music are reason enough to attend.

When held, the khŏn performances last about two hours with intermission. Other Thai performing arts as well as film festivals may also be scheduled at the theatre. Check Bangkok newspapers for current performance schedules. For ticket reservations, call ☎ 222 0434 or visit the box office in person. The theatre requests that patrons dress respectfully, which means no shorts, tank tops or sandals. Bring a wrap or long-sleeved shirt in case the air-con is running full blast.

The Chalermkrung Royal Theatre is on the corner of Th Charoen Krung and Th Triphet, adjacent to the Old Siam Plaza complex. Air-con bus Nos 8, 48 and 73 pass the theatre (going west on Th Charoen Krung). You can also comfortably walk to the theatre from the western terminus of the Saen Saep canal ferry. Taxi drivers may know the theatre by its original name, Sala Chaloem Krung, which is spelt out in Thai in the lighted sign surmounting the front of the building.

## Kà-thoey Cabaret

Kà-thoey (transvestite) cabarets are big in Bangkok. *Calypso Cabaret* (☎ 261 6355, 216 8937, 296 Th Phayathai), in the Asia Hotel (Map 5), has the largest regularly performing transvestite troupe in Thailand, with nightly shows at 8.15 and 9.45 pm. Tickets cost 700B and include one drink. Although the audience is almost 100% tourists, the show is very good and includes plenty of Thai and Asian themes as well as the usual Broadway camp. *Mambo Cabaret*, in Washington Square (Map 7) on Th Sukhumvit between sois 22 and 24, is similar. Several of the gay bars on sois 2 and 4 off Th Silom also feature short drag shows during intermissions between dance sets.

## Dinner Theatres

Most tourists attend performances put on solely for their benefit at Thai classical dance/dinner theatres in the city. Admission prices at these evening venues average 200B to 500B per person and include a 'typical' Thai dinner (often toned down for farang palates), a couple of selected dance performances and a martial arts display.

The historic Oriental Hotel (Map 6) has its own dinner theatre, *Sala Rim Nam* (☎ 437 2918, 437 3080), on the Thonburi side of Mae Nam Chao Phraya, opposite the hotel. Admission is well above average but so is the food, the performance and the Thai pavilion decor (teak, marble and bronze); the river ferry between the hotel and restaurant is free. Dinner begins at 7 pm, the dance performance at 8.30 pm.

If you want to focus on the dining as much as the dance, and it's a weekend, your best choice is the upscale *Supatra River House* (Map 3, ☎ 411 0305, 266 Soi Wat Rakhang), next to Patravadi Theatre in Thonburi. It's opposite Tha Mahathat, from where the restaurant operates its own free ferry nightly. You won't find more authentic Thai food coupled with Thai dance in Bangkok, but note that dance performances – which meander through the restaurant's gardens rather than on a fixed stage – only take place from 8 to 9 pm on Friday and Saturday.

Other dinner theatres in Bangkok include:

*Baan Thai Restaurant* (☎ 258 5403) 7 Soi 32, Th Sukhumvit

*Maneeya Lotus Room* (Map 7, ☎ 251 0382)
518/5 Th Ploenchit
*Piman Thai Theatre Restaurant* (☎ 258 7866)
46 Soi 49, Th Sukhumvit
*Suwannahong Restaurant* (☎ 245 4448) Th Si
Ayuthaya

## Shrine Dancing

Free performances of traditional *lákhon kâe bon* can be seen daily at the Lak Meuang (Map 3) and Erawan (Map 7) shrines if you happen to arrive when a performance troupe has been commissioned by a worshipper. Although many of the dance movements are the same as those seen in classical lákhon, these relatively crude performances are specially choreographed for ritual purposes and don't represent true classical dance forms. But the dancing is colourful – the dancers wear full costume and are accompanied by live music – so it's worth stopping by to watch a performance if you're in the vicinity.

## CINEMAS

Dozens of cinemas around town show Thai, Chinese, Indian and Western films. The majority are comedies and shoot-'em-ups, with the occasional drama slipping through. These cinemas are air-conditioned and quite comfortable, with reasonable rates (70B to 120B). All movies in Thai cinemas are preceded by the Thai royal anthem. Everyone in the cinema is expected to stand quietly and respectfully for the duration of the anthem.

Movie ads appear daily in both *The Nation* and the *Bangkok Post*; listings in *The Nation* include addresses and session times. Movie Seer (www.movieseer.com) posts even more detailed listings for virtually every cinema screening English-language films in Bangkok. *Bangkok Metro* magazine carries details of film festivals or other special events when they are scheduled.

Foreign films are usually censored for nudity – and occasionally – violence.

Film buffs may prefer the regular (usually sub-titled) screenings at *Bangkok's Alliance Française* (Map 7) and *Goethe Institut* (Map 7). Admission is sometimes free, sometimes 30B to 40B. For contact details see Cultural Centres in the Facts for the Visitor chapter.

The main theatres showing commercial English-language films are:

*Grand EGV* (Map 5, ☎ 658 0458) Siam Discovery Centre
*Hollywood Theatre* (☎ 208 9194) Hollywood Street Centre, Th Phetburi
*Indra* (☎ 251 6230) Th Ratchaprarop
*Lido Multiplex* (Map 5, ☎ 252 6729) Siam Square, Th Phra Ram I
*MacKenna* (Map 5, ☎ 251 5256) 17/2 Th Phayathai
*Major Cineplex* (☎ 714 2828) Soi 63, Th Sukhumvit
*Micromack* (Map 5, ☎ 252 6215) Ground floor, MacKenna Theatre, Th Phayathai
*Pantip* (Map 5, ☎ 251 2390) Pantip Plaza, Th Phetburi Tat Mai
*Scala* (Map 5, ☎ 251 2161) Siam Square, Soi 1, Th Phra Ram I
*SF Cinema City* (Map 5, ☎ 611 6444) Mahboonkrong shopping centre, Th Phra Ram I
*Siam* (Map 7, ☎ 252 9975) Siam Square, Th Phra Ram I
*United Artists* (Map 7, ☎ 664 8771) 6th floor, The Emporium, Th Sukhumvit
*United Artists* (☎ 673 6060/88) 7th and 8th floor, Central Plaza, Th Ratchada-Th Phra Ram III
*Warner* (☎ 234 3700/9) 119 Th Mahesak
*World Trade 1, 2, 3* (Map 5, ☎ 256 9500) 6th floor, World Trade Center, corner of Th Ploenchit and Th Ratchadamri
*World Trade 4, 5* (Map 5, ☎ 255 9500) Basement floor, World Trade Center, corner of Th Ploenchit and Th Ratchadamri

Of these cinemas, the most state-of-the-art sound and projection facilities are at Grand EGV and United Artists (the Central Plaza and Emporium locations).

## VIDEO

Video rentals are very popular in Bangkok as they're cheaper than seeing a film at a cinema and often videos are available of films that the Thai censors won't pass for distribution. Average rental is 20B to 50B. Th Sukhumvit has the highest concentration of video shops; the better ones are found in the residential area between sois 39 and 55. *Blockbuster*, the world's largest video chain, has a branch on Soi 33/1, Th Sukhumvit, and plans to open many more branches throughout the capital.

*Vidéofrance (21/17 Soi 4, Th Sukhumvit)*, near the Hotel Rajah (Map 7) on Soi Nana Tai, has a good selection of French-language videos. Members of the *Alliance Française* (Map 7) may borrow videos from its French video library.

TVs and VCRs (both PAL and NTSC format) can be rented at *Silver Bell (☎ 236 2845, 113/1-2 Surawong Centre, Th Surawong).*

## SPECTATOR SPORTS
## Muay Thai (Thai Boxing)

*Muay thai* can be seen at two boxing stadiums, *Sanam Muay Lumphini* (Map 7), on Th Phra Ram IV near Th Sathon Tai, and *Sanam Muay Ratchadamnoen* (Ratchadamnoen Boxing Stadium, Map 3), on Th Ratchadamnoen Nok, next to the Tourist Authority of Thailand (TAT) information office. Admission fees vary according to seating: the cheapest seats in Bangkok are now around 220B for the outer circle or 920B to 1000B for ringside seats (Sunday shows at Ratchadamnoen are 50/500B). This is for eight fights of five rounds each. The outer circle seats are quite OK. On Monday, Wednesday, Thursday and Sunday the boxing is at Ratchadamnoen, while on Tuesday, Friday and Saturday it's at Lumphini. The Ratchadamnoen matches begin at 6 pm, except for the Sunday shows, which start at 4 and 8 pm. The Lumphini matches begin at 6.30 pm on Tuesday and Friday, and at 5 and 8.30 pm on Saturday. Aficionados say the best-matched bouts are reserved for Tuesday nights at Lumphini, and Thursday nights at Ratchadamnoen. The restaurants on the north side of Ratchadamnoen stadium are well known for their delicious *kài yâang* (grilled chicken) and other North-Eastern dishes.

For more details, see the special section 'Traditional Thai Martial Arts' in this chapter.

**Beware** At some programs a ticket mafia tries to steer every tourist into buying a 500B ringside seat, often claiming all other seats are sold out. Ignore the touts and head to a window ticket vendor, where you'll find seats as cheaply as 90B (prices are marked on windows).

A similar racket operates on Th Khao San, where touts sell 500B seats (including transport to/from Th Khao San) for inferior matches at Samrong or 'Lumprinee' stadium on Monday evening. Follow the aforementioned Ratchadamnoen and Lumphini schedules for the best fights; provide your own transport and go to the ticket windows yourself to avoid rip offs.

### Tàkrâw

Sometimes called Siamese football in old English texts, *tàkrâw* refers to a game in which a woven rattan ball about 12cm in diameter is kicked around. The rattan (or sometimes plastic) ball itself is called a *lûuk tàkrâw*. Tàkrâw is also popular in several neighbouring countries; it was originally introduced to the SEA Games by Thailand, and international championships tend to alternate between the Thais and Malays.

The traditional way to play tàkrâw in Thailand is for players to stand in a circle (the size of the circle depends on the number of players) and simply try to keep the ball airborne by kicking it soccer-style. Points are scored for style, difficulty and variety of kicking manoeuvres. A popular variation on tàkrâw – and the one used in intramural or international competitions – is played with a volleyball net, using all the same rules as in volleyball except that only the feet and head are permitted to touch the ball. It's amazing to see the players perform aerial pirouettes, spiking the ball over the net with their feet. Another variation has players kicking the ball into a hoop 4.5m above the ground – basketball without hands and without a backboard! Tàkrâw is most easily seen on the athletic fields at school grounds and university campuses around the city.

# Shopping

Regular visitors to Asia know that, in many ways, Bangkok beats Hong Kong and Singapore for deals on handicrafts, textiles, gems, jewellery, art and antiques – nowhere else will you find the same selection, quality and prices. The trouble is finding the good spots, as the city's intense urban tangle sometimes makes orientation difficult: *Nancy Chandler's Map of Bangkok* makes a good shopping companion, with annotations on all sorts of small, out-of-the-way shopping venues and markets. For information on packaging and shipping goods, see Post & Communications in the Facts for the Visitor chapter.

## WHAT TO BUY
### Antiques & Decorative Items
Real Thai antiques are rare and costly. Most Bangkok antique shops keep a few antiques around for collectors, along with lots of pseudo-antiques or traditionally crafted items that look like antiques. The majority of shop operators are quite candid about what's really old and what isn't. As Thai design becomes more popular abroad, many shops are now specialising in Thai home decorative items.

Your best one-stop shopping venue for old-world Asiana is the multi-storey River City Complex (Map 6), on the river and near the Royal Orchid Sheraton Hotel. Several high quality art and antique shops are found on the 3rd and 4th floors. Acala, shop 312, is a gallery of unusual Tibetan and Chinese artefacts. Old Maps & Prints (☎ 237 0077, ext 432), shop 432, proffers one of the best selections of one-of-a-kind, rare maps and illustrations, with a focus on Asia. The Oriental Plaza (Map 6) shopping complex also has several good, if pricey, antique shops.

Gaysorn Plaza (Map 7), along from Le Meridien President Hotel & Tower on Thanon (Th) Ploenchit, contains several shops specialising in furniture and home decor accessories, both antique and contemporary Thai. The Thai Craft Museum shop (☎ 656 1149) on the 2nd floor offers craft demonstrations, plus displays of Thai ceramics, textiles, jewellery and more. Triphum (☎ 656 1149), on the 2nd floor, features tasteful South-East Asian art and accessories.

Barang-Barang Antik (Map 7, ☎ 255 2461), 1047 Th Ploenchit, carries a well curated selection of Indonesian antiques and reproductions, mostly furniture.

Reliable antique shops (using the word 'antique' loosely) include:

**Artisan's** (☎ 237 4456) Silom Village Trade Centre (Map 6)
**Asian Heritage** (☎ 258 4157) 57 Soi 23, Th Sukhumvit
**Elephant House** (☎ 630 1586) Soi Phattana, Th Silom; (☎ 679 3122) 67/12 Soi Phra Phinit

For modern arts see Art Galleries in the Things to See & Do Chapter, or try this Web Site, which lists many of Bangkok's galleries: www.rama9art.org.

## Gems & Jewellery
Thailand is one of the world's largest exporters of gems and ornaments, rivalled only by India and Sri Lanka. The biggest importers of Thai jewellery are the USA, Japan and Switzerland. One of the results of the remarkable growth of the gem industry – in Thailand the gem trade has increased nearly 10% every year for the last decade – is that the prices are rising rapidly.

If you know what you are doing you can make some really good buys in both unset gems and finished jewellery. Gold ornaments are sold at a good rate as labour costs are low. The best bargains in gems are jade, rubies and sapphires. Buy from reputable dealers only, unless you're a gemologist. Be wary of special 'deals' that are 'one day only' or that set you up as a 'courier' in which you're promised big money. Many travellers end up losing big (see the boxed text 'Too Good to Be True' in this chapter).

At the time of writing, a Jewel Fest Club was introduced through the cooperation of the Tourist Authority of Thailand (TAT) and the Thai Gem and Jewellery Traders

## Too Good to Be True

Thais are generally so friendly and laid-back that some visitors are lulled into a false sense of security that makes them vulnerable to scams and con schemes of all kinds. Scammers tend to haunt first-time tourist spots, such as the Grand Palace area, Wat Pho or Siam Square (especially near Jim Thompson's House).

Most scams begin the same way: a friendly Thai male (or on rare occasion, a female) approaches a lone visitor – usually newly arrived – and strikes up a seemingly innocuous conversation. Sometimes the con man says he's a university student or teacher, at other times he may claim to work for the World Bank or a similarly distinguished organisation. If you're on the way to Wat Pho or Jim Thompson's House, for example, he may tell you it's closed for a holiday or repairs. Eventually the conversation works its way around to the subject of the scam – the better con men can actually make it seem as though you initiated the topic. That's one of the most bewildering aspects of the con – afterwards victims remember that the whole thing seemed to be their idea, not the con artist's.

The scam itself almost always involves gems, tailor shops or card playing. With gems, the victims are invited to a gem and jewellery shop – your new-found friend is picking up some merchandise for himself and you're just along for the ride. Somewhere along the way he usually claims to have a connection – often a relative – in your home country (what a coincidence!) with whom he has a regular gem export-import business. One way or another, victims are convinced (usually they convince themselves) that they can turn a profit by arranging a gem purchase and reselling the merchandise at home. After all, the jewellery shop just happens to be offering a generous discount today – it's a government or religious holiday, or perhaps it's the shop's 10th anniversary, or maybe they just take a liking to you! The latest ploy is to say it's a special 'Amazing Thailand' promotion. As one freshly scammed reader recently wrote in: 'Everybody we spoke to mentioned 'Amazing Thailand' before they ripped us off!'

There are a seemingly infinite number of variations on the gem scam, almost all of which end up with the victim purchasing small, low-quality sapphires and posting them to their home countries. (If they let you walk out with them, you might return for a refund after realising you'd been taken.) Once you return home, of course, the cheap sapphires turn out to be worth much less than what you paid for them (perhaps one-tenth to one-half). At one stage a jeweller in Perth, Australia, said he was seeing about 12 people a week who had been conned in Thailand. TAT says it receives over 1000 letters a year about such scams.

Many have invested and lost virtually all their savings; some admit they have been scammed even after reading warnings in this guidebook or ones posted by the TAT around Bangkok. As one letter-writer concluded his story: 'So now I'm US$500 poorer and in possession of potentially worthless sapphires – a very expensive lesson into human nature.'

Even if you were able to return your purchase to the gem shop in question (I knew one fellow who actually intercepted his parcel at the airport before it left Thailand), chances are slim to none they'd give a full refund. The con artist who brings the mark into the shop gets a commission of 10% to 50% per sale – the shop takes the rest.

The Thai police are usually of no help, believing that merchants are entitled to whatever price they can get. The main victimisers are a handful of shops who get protection from certain high-ranking

Association (TGJTA). When you purchase an item of jewellery from a shop that is clearly identified as a member of the Jewel Fest Club, a certificate detailing your purchase will be issued. It also guarantees a refund less 10% if you return the merchandise to the point of sale within 30 days. A refund less 20% is guaranteed if the items are returned after 30 days but within 45 days of purchase. A list of members offering government guarantees is available from the TAT.

## Too Good to Be True

government officials. These officials put pressure on police not to prosecute, or to take as little action as possible. Even the TAT tourist police have never been able to prosecute a Thai jeweller, even in cases of blatant, recurring gem fraud. In recent years a Thai police commissioner was convicted of fraud in an investigation into a jewellery theft by Thais in Saudi Arabia – the commissioner had replaced the Saudi gems with fakes! (See the Gems & Jewellery entry in this chapter for information on recent initiatives to protect consumers.)

With tailor shops the objective is to get you to order poorly made clothes at exorbitant prices. The tailor shops that do this sort of thing are adept at delaying delivery until just before you leave Thailand, so that you don't have time to object to poor workmanship. The way to avoid this scam is to choose tailor shops yourself, and not to part with any more money than a small deposit – no more than enough to cover the fabrics used – till you're satisfied with the workmanship.

The card-playing scam starts out much the same – a friendly stranger approaches the lone traveller on the street, strikes up a conversation and then invites him or her to the house or apartment of his sister (or brother-in-law etc) for a drink or meal. After a bit of socialising, a friend or relative of the con arrives on the scene; it just so happens a little high-stakes card game is planned for later that day. Like the gem scam, the card-game scam has many variations, but eventually the 'victim' is shown some cheating tactics to use with help from the 'dealer', some practice sessions take place and finally the game gets under way with several high rollers at the table. The mark is allowed to win a few hands first, then somehow loses a few, gets bankrolled by one of the friendly Thais and then loses the Thai's money. Suddenly your new-found buddies aren't so friendly any more – they want the money you lost. Sometimes the con pretends to be dismayed by it all. Sooner or later you end up cashing in most or all of your travellers cheques or making a costly visit to an ATM. Again the police won't take any action – in this case because gambling is illegal in Thailand – you've broken the law by playing cards for money.

The common denominator in all scams of this nature is the victims' own greed – the desire for an easy score. Other minor scams involve tuk-tuk drivers, hotel employees and bar girls who take new arrivals on city tours; these almost always end in high-pressure sales pushes at silk, jewellery or handicraft shops. In this case greed isn't the ruling motivation – it's simply a matter of weak sales resistance.

Follow the TAT's No 1 suggestion to tourists: disregard all offers of free shopping or sightseeing help from strangers – they will invariably take a commission from your purchases. I would add to this: beware of deals that seem too good to be true – they're usually neither good nor true. You might also try lying whenever a stranger asks how long you've been in Thailand – if it's only been three days, say three weeks! The con artists rarely prey on anyone except new arrivals.

You should contact the Tourist Police if you have any problems with consumer fraud. Telephone hotline number ☎ 1155 connects with the Tourist Police from any phone in Thailand.

---

Recommending specific shops is tricky, since to the average eye one coloured stone looks as good as the next, so the risk of a rip-off is greater than for most other popular shopping items. One shop that's been a longtime favourite with Bangkok expats for service and value in set jewellery is Johnny's Gems (☎ 224 4065), 199 Th Fuang Nakhon (off Th Charoen Krung). A dependable place specialising in unset stones is Lambert Holding (☎ 236 4343) at 807 Th Silom.

## Bronzeware

Thailand has the oldest bronze-working tradition in the world and there are several factories in Bangkok producing bronze sculpture and cutlery. Two factories that sell direct to the public (and where you may also be able to observe the bronze-working process) are Siam Bronze Factory ($\pi$ 234 9436), 1250 Th Charoen Krung, and Somkij Bronze ($\pi$ 251 0891), 1194 Th Phetburi Tat Mai (New Phetburi). Make sure any items you buy are silicon-coated, otherwise they'll tarnish.

To see the casting process for Buddha images, go to the Buddha Casting Foundry next to Wat Wiset Khan on Th Phrannok, Thonburi. To get there, take a river ferry from Tha Phra Chan or Tha Maharat on the Bangkok side to reach the foot of Th Phrannok (see the Chao Phraya River Express map).

Many vendors at Wat Mahathat's (Map 3) Sunday market sell old and new bronzeware – haggling is imperative.

## Handicrafts

Bangkok has excellent buys in Thai handicrafts, though for Northern hill-tribe materials you might be able to do better in Chiang Mai. Perhaps the most interesting places to shop for handicrafts are the smaller, independent handicraft shops, each of which has its own style and character.

Lao Song Handicrafts ($\pi$ 261 6627), 2/56 Soi 41, Th Sukhumvit, is a nonprofit place that sells village handicrafts to promote cottage industries. It buys directly from the villagers, cutting out middlemen thus the artisans receive higher wholesale prices.

Quality is high at Rasi Sayam ($\pi$ 258 4195), 32 Soi 23, Th Sukhumvit. Many of the items it carries, including wall-hangings and pottery, are made specifically for this shop; prices are moderate. A good one for lacquerware and fabrics is Vilai's ($\pi$ 391 6106), 731/1 Soi 55 (Thong Lor), Th Sukhumvit.

Nandakwang ($\pi$ 258 1962), 108/3 Soi 23 (Soi Prasanmit), Th Sukhumvit, sells high-quality woven cotton clothing and household wares (tablecloths, napkins etc) are its speciality.

*Khŏn* masks of intricately formed wire and papier mache can be purchased at Padung Cheep (no roman-script sign) on Th Chakraphong just south of the Th Khao San (Khao San Rd) intersection.

The International School Bangkok (Map 1, IBS; $\pi$ 583 5401), 39/7 Soi Nichadathani Samakhi, Th Chaeng Wattana, puts on a large charity sale of Thai handicrafts every sixth Saturday or so (except during its summer holiday from June to August). Quality varies from the rare to mundane. Call for the latest charity sale schedule.

For quality Thai celadon (a type of green or blue-glazed porcelain), check out Thai Celadon ($\pi$ 229 4383), 8/6-8 Th Ratchadaphisek Tat Mai. Inexpensive places to pick up new Thai pottery of all shapes and sizes at wholesale prices include two places on Soi On Nut, off Soi 77, Th Sukhumvit: United Siam Overseas ($\pi$ 721 6320) and Siamese Merchandise ($\pi$ 333 0680). Overseas shipping can be arranged.

Narayana Phand (Map 5, $\pi$ 252 4670) on Th Ratchadamri is a bit on the touristy side but has a large selection and good marked prices – no haggling is necessary. Central Department Store (Map 7) on Th Ploenchit has a Thai handicrafts section with marked prices.

## Nielloware & Damascene

Nielloware came from Europe via Nakhon Si Thammarat and has been cultivated in Thailand for over 700 years. Engraved silver is inlaid with niello – an alloy of lead, silver, copper and sulphur – to form striking black-and-silver jewellery designs, often based on Thai classical dance motifs.

For damascene ware *(khraam),* gold and silver wire is hammered into a cross-hatched steel surface to create exquisitely patterned bowls and boxes. Both kinds of metalwork are among Bangkok's best bargains. Look for them in Narayana Phand, Central Department Store (Map 7), and other upscale department stores and craft shops.

## Furniture

Rattan and hardwood furniture are often good buys and can be made to order. Teak furniture has become relatively scarce and expensive; rosewood is a more reasonable buy. Prinya Decoration (☎ 318 1824) at Th Phetburi Mai and Soi 63, Th Phetburi, stocks both rosewood and teak furniture.

Several rattan shops can be found along Th Sukhumvit between sois 35 and 43, including Corner 43, Hawaii, Pattaya, Pacific Design, Thai Home and Thai Pattana. Siam Rattan Furniture Shop (☎ 513 7995), 1576 Th Phahonyothin, opposite Soi 35, and Siam Rattan Works (☎ 316 7262), 222 Bang Na, Trat Hwy, specialise in made-to-order rattan furniture.

Anyone interested in the history of rattan furniture crafting in Thailand should also pay a visit to Nai Muan, over 100 years old, it is the oldest rattan shop in Thailand. It's near Wat Suthat (Map 3).

## Tailor-Made Clothes

Bangkok abounds in places where you can have shirts, trousers, suits and just about any other article of clothing designed, cut and sewn by hand. Workmanship ranges from shoddy to excellent, so it pays to ask around before committing yourself. Shirts and trousers can be turned around in 48 hours or less with only one fitting. But no matter what a tailor may tell you, it takes more than one or two fittings to create a good suit, and most reputable tailors will ask for two to five sittings. A custom-made suit will cost from US$175 (for synthetics or natural/synthetic blends) to US$400 (for 100% wool or cashmere). Bring your own fabric and it will cost even less.

Bangkok tailors can be particularly good at copying your favourite piece of clothing. Designer-made shirts costing upwards of US$100 at home can be knocked off for not much more than a tenth of the designer price. The one area where you need to be most careful is in fabric selection. If possible, bring your own personally selected fabric from home or abroad, especially if you want 100% cotton. Most of the so-called 'cotton' offered by Bangkok tailors is actually a blend of cotton and a synthetic; more than a few tailors will actually try to pass off full polyester or dacron as cotton. Good quality silk, on the other hand, is plentiful. Tailor-made silk shirts should cost no

more than US$20, depending on the type of silk (Chinese silk is cheaper than Thai).

A majority of the tailors working in Bangkok are of Indian or Chinese descent. Generally speaking, the best shops are those found along the outer reaches of Th Sukhumvit (out beyond Soi 20 or so) and on or off Th Charoen Krung. Th Silom also has some good tailors. The worst tailor shops tend to be those in tourist-oriented shopping areas in inner Th Sukhumvit, Th Khao San, the River City Complex and other shopping malls. 'Great deals' like four shirts, two suits, a kimono and a safari suit (!) all in one package almost always turn out to be of inferior materials and workmanship.

Recommended tailor shops include:

**Julie** 1279 Th Charoen, near Silom Center (Map 7)
**Marco Tailor** (☎ 252 0689) Soi 7, Siam Square (Map 7)
**Macway's Exporters** (☎ 235 2407) 715-717 Th Silom, opposite the Narai Hotel (Map 7)
**Siam Emporium** (☎ 251 9617) 2nd floor, Siam Center (Map 5)
**Alla Moda** (☎ 658 1093), 2nd floor, Siam Center (Map 5), opposite Siam Emporium

## Camera Supplies, Film & Processing

For a wide range of camera models and brands, you could try one of Sunny Camera's three branches: 1267/1 Th Charoen Krung (☎ 235 2123, 233 8378); 144/23 Th Silom (☎ 236 8627); and the 3rd floor of the Mahboonkrong shopping centre (Map 5, ☎ 217 9293).

Niks (☎ 235 2929), at 166 Th Silom on the north-west corner of Soi 12, sells all types of professional equipment, and services Nikon, Mamiya and Rollei.

Central Department Store (Map 7) on Th Ploenchit has a good camera department with surprisingly reasonable prices.

Film prices in Bangkok are generally lower than anywhere else in Asia, including Hong Kong. Both slide and print films are widely available. The highest concentration of photo shops can be found along Th Silom and Th Surawong. In Mahboonkrong shopping centre, FotoFile on the ground floor has the best selection of slide films, including refrigerated professional films.

Quick, professional quality processing of most film types is available at: Image Quality Lab (IQ Lab; ☎ 238 4001), 60 Th Silom opposite Silom Complex, or (☎ 714 0644), 9/33 Thana Arcade, Soi 63, Th Sukhumvit; and Eastbourne Professional Color Laboratories (☎ 235 5234), 134/4 Th Silom.

## Books & Magazines

Bangkok has many good bookshops, with probably the best selection in South-East Asia. You can find books in European languages at the following shops; most publications are in English, some in French or German, with limited – if any – material in Italian.

For new books and magazines, some good bookshop chains are Asia Books, Bookazine and Duang Kamol (DK) Book House. Asia Books lives up to its name by having Bangkok's best and largest selections of English-language titles on Asia. Its oldest branch (☎ 252 7277) is at 221 Th Sukhumvit at Soi 15 (Map 7). Other large branch shops are:

**Emporium complex** (Map 7)
**Landmark Plaza** (Map 7)
**Peninsula Plaza** 2nd floor (Map 7)
**Siam Discovery Center** (Map 5)
**Thaniya Plaza** 3rd floor (Map 7)
**Times Square** (Map 7)
**World Trade Centre** 3rd floor (Map 5 & 7)

Bookazine is a newer bookshop chain with a decent selection of English books and an excellent selection of magazines. Branches in Bangkok are:

**Siam Square** No 286, opposite Siam Center (Map 5)
**Silom Complex** 2nd floor (Map 7)
**Sogo department store** 3rd floor (Map 7)
**Th Sukhumvit** North side, half-way between sois 3 and 5

Teck Heng Bookstore (☎ 234 1836), 1326 Th Charoen Krung, between the Shangri-La and Oriental hotels (Map 6), is the best independent bookshop in this neighbourhood, carrying quite an up-to-date variety of books on South-East Asia. The owner is very helpful.

English-language books can be found in the Siam Square complex at the Book Chest (Soi 2) and Odeon Store (Soi 1). Kinokuniya in The Emporium shopping centre (Map 7), Soi 24, Th Sukhumvit, is quite good, and stocks reading material in Japanese and English.

Suksit Siam (Map 3, ☎ 225 9531), opposite Wat Ratchabophit at 113-5 Th Fuang Nakhon, specialises in books on Thai politics, especially those representing the views of leading Thai social critic, Sulak Sivaraksa, and the progressive Santi Pracha Dhamma Institute (which has offices next door). The shop also has mainstream titles on Thailand and Asia, both in English and Thai.

**Used & Rare Books** Along Th Khao San (Map 4) you'll find several book stores; Shaman Books (☎ 629 0418), 71 Th Khao San, carries a good mixture of new and used guidebooks, maps, novels and books on spirituality in several languages, although prices are a bit higher than the norm for Bangkok. Much smaller, but with an attached outdoor cafe, is Banana Leaf Books & Café. Aporia Books, also offers an extensive selection of new and used books. There's also at least three streetside vendors specialising in used paperback novels and guidebooks.

Merman Books (☎ 231 3155), 191 Th Silom, Silom Complex (Map 7), is a bookshop for the true lover of Asiana. Operated by a former *Bangkok Post* editor, it collects all manner of out-of-print and rare books on Asia, along with plenty of new titles.

Global Books on Soi 32, Th Sukhumvit, carries lots of used travel guides and offers a discount if you buy more than one book. Elite Used Books, 593/5 Th Sukhumvit at Soi 33/1 (near Villa supermarket) and at 1/12 Soi 3, Th Sukhumvit, stocks a decent selection of used foreign-language titles, including English, Chinese, French, German and Swedish. The Chatuchak Weekend Market in Chatuchak Park is also a source of used, often out-of-print books in several languages.

## Fake or Pirated Goods

In all the various tourist centres, eg, Patpong, Th Sukhumvit and Th Silom, there is black market street trade in fake designer goods; particularly Benetton pants and sweaters, Lacoste (crocodile logo) and Ralph Lauren polo shirts, Levi's jeans, and Rolex, Dunhill and Cartier watches. No one pretends they're the real thing, not even the vendors. Western manufacturers are applying heavy pressure on Asian governments to get this stuff off the street, so it may not be around for much longer.

In some cases, foreign name brands are legally produced under licence in Thailand and represent good value. A pair of legally produced Levi's 501s, for example, typically costs US$10 from a Thai street vendor – compared to US$35 to US$45 in Levi's home town of San Francisco! Careful examination of the product usually reveals tell-tale characteristics that confirm or deny the item's legality.

### Music

Cassette tapes of Thai music are readily available throughout the country in department stores, cassette shops and from street vendors. The average price for a Thai music cassette is 90B. Western bootlegged tapes are cheaper (35B to 55B each), but the days of pirate tapes in Thailand are numbered now that the US music industry is enforcing international copyright laws. Licensed Western music tapes cost 110B to 119B, still a good deal by the pricing standards of most Western nations.

Music CDs are much more expensive, averaging 400B to 500B per disc for licensed versions, 100B to 180B for pirated ones. Aside from being illegal, bootleg CDs vary highly in quality – some are fine, while some skip or won't play at all. For about 200B, you can also buy CDs on which 12 to 15 CDs have been compressed into MP3 format.

Tower Records, on level 4 in the Siam Center (Map 5), carries the best selection of CDs in Bangkok. A Thai chain called Mang Pong found throughout the city is good for Thai CDs.

Blank audio tapes (60, 90 and 120 minutes) CDs and mini-CDs are also widely available in Bangkok.

## WHERE TO SHOP
### Chatuchak Weekend Market

Known in Thai as Talat Jatujak, this is the Disneyland of Thai markets; on weekends 8672 vendor stalls cater to an estimated 200,000 visitors a day. Everything is sold here, from live chickens and snakes to opium pipes and herbal remedies. Thai clothing such as the *phâakhamáa* ('sarong' for males) and the *phâasîn* ('sarong' for females), *kaang keng jiin* (Chinese pants) and *sêua mâw hâwm* (blue cotton farmer's shirt) are good buys. You'll also find musical instruments, hill-tribe crafts, religious amulets, antiques, flowers, clothes imported from India and Nepal, camping gear and military surplus.

The best bargains of all are household goods like pots and pans, dishes, drinking glasses etc. If you're moving to Thailand for an extended period, this is the place to pick up stuff for your kitchen. Don't forget to try out your bargaining skills.

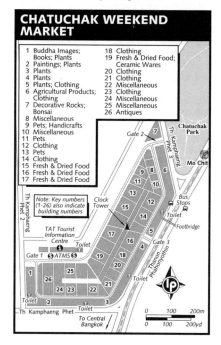

**CHATUCHAK WEEKEND MARKET**

1  Buddha Images; Books; Plants
2  Paintings; Plants
3  Plants
4  Plants
5  Plants; Clothing
6  Agricultural Products; Clothing
7  Decorative Rocks; Bonsai
8  Miscellaneous
9  Pets; Handicrafts
10  Miscellaneous
11  Pets
12  Clothing
13  Pets
14  Clothing
15  Fresh & Dried Food
16  Fresh & Dried Food
17  Fresh & Dried Food
18  Clothing
19  Fresh & Dried Food; Ceramic Wares
20  Clothing
21  Clothing
22  Miscellaneous
23  Clothing
24  Miscellaneous
25  Miscellaneous
26  Antiques

Note: Key numbers (1-26) also indicate building numbers

There is plenty of interesting and tasty food for sale if you're feeling hungry, and live music in the early evening. And if you need some cash, a couple of banks have ATMs and foreign-exchange booths at the Chatuchak Park offices, near the northern end of the market's sois 1, 2 and 3. Plan to spend a full day, as there's plenty to see and do.

The main part of the Weekend Market is open from around 8 am to 6 pm on weekends, though some places may stay open as late as 8 pm. There are a few vendors out on weekday mornings and a daily vegetables/plants/flowers market opposite the market's south side. One section of the latter, known as the Aw Taw Kaw Market, sells organically grown (no chemical sprays or fertilisers) fruits and vegetables.

The Weekend Market lies at the southern end of Chatuchak Park, off Th Phahonyothin and south of the Northern bus terminal. Air-con bus No 2, 3, 9, 10 or 13, and a dozen other ordinary city buses (including No 3 from Th Phra Athit in Banglamphu), all pass the market – just get off before the Northern bus terminal. Air-con bus No 12 and ordinary bus No 77 conveniently terminate right next to the market. The Skytrain runs direct to Mo Chit Skytrain station, which stands almost in front of the market.

### Nailert (Nai Loet) Market (Map 5)

This market complex, opposite the Amari Watergate Hotel, is a good alternative to Chatuchak Weekend Market for residents or visitors located near the city centre. The array of goods for sale is similar and the foodstalls, especially those serving Thai seafood, are particularly good.

### Flower Markets & Nurseries

Tropical flowers and plants are available at Thewet Market (Map 3) to the north-west of Banglamphu. The city's largest wholesale flower source is Pak Khlong Market (Map 6) near Tha Ratchchini. Pak Khlong is also a big market for vegetables. The largest plant market, known as Talat Phahonyothin (Phahonyothin Market), is opposite the south side of Chatuchak Weekend Market (Map 1).

The best area for nursery plants, including Thailand's world-famous orchid varieties, is Thonburi's Phasi Charoen district, which is accessible via the Phetkasem Hwy north of Khlong Phasi Charoen itself. The latter is linked to Mae Nam Chao Phraya via Khlong Bangkok Yai. Two places with good selections are Eima Orchid Co (☎ 454 0366, fax 454 1156), 999/9 Mu 2, Bang Khae, Phasi Charoen, and Botanical Gardens Bangkok (☎ 467 4955), 6871 Kuhasawan, Phasi Charoen. Ordinary bus Nos 7 and 80, plus air-con bus No 9, stop in the Phasi Charoen district.

Bo-Be Market (Map 3), off Th Rong Meuang, east of Banglamphu, doesn't get started until after midnight and then continues until dawn, selling mostly fresh produce and flowers that have been trucked in from outside Bangkok.

You can also buy fresh strands of night-blooming jasmine flower buds – called *phuang malai* (jasmine chains) for 5B to 10B each all over Bangkok. They make great natural air fresheners for malodorous hotel rooms.

### Other Thai Markets

Under the expressway at the intersection of Th Phra Rama IV and Th At Narong in the Khlong Toey district is the Khlong Toey Market, (Map 1) possibly the cheapest all-purpose market in Bangkok (best on Wednesday).

The similar Penang Market (Map 1), so called because a lot of the goods 'drop off' cargo boats from Penang, is located adjacent to the Chatuchak Weekend Market.

Pratunam Market (Map 5), at the intersection of Th Phetburi and Th Ratchaprarop, runs daily and is very crowded, but has great deals in new, cheap clothing. You won't see it from the street – you'll need to look for one of the unmarked entrances that lead back behind the main storefronts. While browsing Pratunam you can easily visit Nailert Market also (see the Nailert Market entry earlier).

The huge Banglamphu Market (Map 3) spreads over several blocks, a short walk from the Th Khao San guesthouse area. This is probably the most comprehensive

Fresh orchids are available at stalls and markets throughout Bangkok.

The hustle and bustle of a street market

A walk on the wild side – Thanon Khao San

Oodles of noodles

KAREN TRIST

JERRY ALEXANDER

JERRY ALEXANDER

PAUL BEINSSEN

JOHN HAY

Looking for fruit and vegetables, a bunch of flowers, service with a smile, a little music or a place to unwind? Everything and anything can be found at one of Bangkok's many markets.

shopping district in the city as it encompasses everything from street vendors to upmarket department stores. Nearby you'll find the Thewet flower market (see the previous Flower Markets & Nurseries entry).

Soi Lalaisap (Map 7), the 'money-dissolving soi', actually Soi 5, Th Silom, has a number of vendors selling all sorts of cheap clothing, watches and housewares during the day.

The Phahurat and Chinatown districts (Map 3) have interconnected markets selling tonnes of well-priced fabrics, clothes and household wares, as well as a few places selling gems and jewellery (see the 'Walking Tours' special section in the Things to See & Do chapter).

The Wong Wian Yai Market (Map 6) in Thonburi, next to the large roundabout directly south-west of Phra Phut Yot Fa (Memorial) Bridge, is another all-purpose market – but this one rarely gets tourists.

### Tourist Markets

Th Khao San (Map 4), the main guesthouse strip in Banglamphu, has itself become a shopping bazaar offering cheap audio tapes, used books, jewellery, beads, clothing, Thai axe pillows (a traditional Thai wedge-shaped pillow), T-shirts, tattoos, body piercing and just about any other product or service you can think of.

At night, Patpong sois 1 and 2 (Map 7) fill up with vendors selling cheap tourist junk, inexpensive clothing, fake watches – you name it. Along both sides of Th Sukhumvit (Map 7) between sois 1 and 5 there are also lots of street vendors selling similar items.

### Shopping Centres & Department Stores

The growth of large and small shopping centres has accelerated over the past few years into a virtual boom. Central department store (Map 7) is generally regarded as the all-round best of the bunch, for quality and selection, with 12 branches in Bangkok. The flagship store on Th Ploenchit near the Chit Lom Skytrain station (Map 7) is probably the best of the bunch; in addition to designer clothes, Western cosmetics, cassette tapes,

fabrics, furniture, handicrafts and an attached supermarket, the store offers free alteration on all clothing purchases and free delivery to Bangkok hotels. There's also a fix-it area for watch, shoe and clothing repairs. Central's main competitor, Robinsons (Map 7), also has branches throughout the city.

Oriental Plaza (Soi Oriental, Th Charoen Krung) and River City Complex (Map 6), near Tha Si Praya, are centres for high-end consumer goods. River City has good quality art and antique shops on the 3rd and 4th floors.

Along Th Ploenchit and Th Sukhumvit (Map 7) you'll find many newer shopping centres including Sogo, Landmark Plaza and Times Square, but these Tokyo clones tend to be expensive and not that exciting. Peninsula Plaza on Th Ratchadamri (Map 7) has a more exclusive selection of shops – many of which have branches at River City and Oriental Plaza – and a good-sized branch of Asia Books. Promenade Decor, in front of the Hilton International Bangkok (Map 5) on Th Withayu, is a posh mall offering jewellery, cafes, antiques, furniture, art galleries and quality modern Thai art.

The much smaller Silom Village Trade Centre (Map 6) on Th Silom has a few cheaper antique and handicraft shops. Anchored by Central department store, the six-storey Silom Complex nearby remains one of the city's busiest shopping centres. Also on Th Silom is the posh Thaniya Plaza, a newer arcade housing clothing boutiques, bookshops, jewellery shops and more.

The eight floors of the World Trade Centre (WTC, Map 5 & 7) is a shoppers' paradise, featuring the Zen department store, which has clothing shops reminiscent of Hong Kong's high-end boutiques. On the 8th floor is Bangkok's premier antidote to the tropics, the **World Ice Skating Center**. If you're looking for clothing or toys for kids, ABC Babyland on WTC's 2nd floor has just about everything.

Siam Square (Map 5), on Th Phra Ram I near Th Phayathai, is a network of some 12 sois lined with shops selling mid-price designer clothes, books, sporting goods and antiques. On the opposite side of Th Phra Ram I is Thailand's first shopping centre, built in 1976, the four-storey Siam Center (Map 5). It features designer and brand-label clothing shops – Benetton, Quicksilver, Chaps, Esprit, Lacoste, Timberland and Guy Laroche to name a few – as well as coffee shops, travel agencies, banks and airline offices.

Next to the Siam Center, and connected by an enclosed pedestrian bridge, Siam Discovery Center contains yet more designer stores such as Calvin Klein, Nine West, Yves Saint Laurent, Armani, plus Asia Books, Habitat and several large restaurants.

One of the most varied and affordable shopping centres is the Mahboonkrong (MBK) shopping centre (Map 5) near Siam Square. It's all air-con, but there are many small, inexpensive stalls and shops in addition to the middle-class Tokyu department store. Bargains can be found here if you look. The Travel Mart on MBK's 3rd floor stocks a reasonable supply of travel gear and camping equipment – not the highest quality but useful in a pinch.

North of Siam Square on Th Phetburi, Pantip Plaza (Map 5) specialises in computer equipment and software.

Old Siam Plaza (Map 6), north of Tha Saphan Phut, is the first new development of any significance in the Chinatown-Phahurat area in over a decade. Along with the renovation and reopening of the adjacent Chalermkrung Royal Theatre, this old Bangkok-style shopping centre represents a minor renaissance for an otherwise shabby and congested district. Most of the shops purvey Thai-style goods or services; one whole side is devoted to gun dealers, another to gem and jewellery shops, the rest to Thai handicrafts, furniture, restaurants and coffee shops.

## GUARANTEES

Guarantees are an important consideration if you're buying expensive items like gems or electronic goods. Make sure the guarantee is international – usually this is no problem but check it out before you start haggling. A national guarantee is next to useless – are you going to return with a gem to Bangkok if you discover it's fake? Finally, make sure that the guarantee is filled out correctly with the shop's name and, if appropriate, the serial number of the item. For electronic goods, check the item's compatibility back home. You don't want a brand or model that has never found its way to your home country.

# Excursions

When you've had enough of Bangkok's intensity, there are several spots outside the city you can escape to for day trips or overnight visits. Within a 150km radius, you have a choice of 16th- to 18th-century temple ruins in Ayuthaya, the two tallest Buddhist monuments in the world at Phutthamonthon and Nakhon Pathom, and the world famous 'Bridge on the River Kwai' in Kanchanaburi.

But even just outside Bangkok a host of artificial tourist attractions provides either the 'see the whole country in an hour' theme or the standard Western-style amusement park. If these attractions appeal to you, it's often worth arranging tickets through travel agencies if the booking includes round-trip transport from your lodgings. See the following West, North, North-East and South of Bangkok entries for details on these attractions.

## WEST OF BANGKOK

Thirty-two kilometres west of Bangkok, on the way to Nakhon Pathom, the **Rose Garden Country Resort** (☎ 253 0295, 295 3261) is a canned Thai 'cultural village' (with demos of handicrafts, dancing, traditional ceremonies and martial arts). There's also a resort hotel, swimming pools, tennis courts, a three-hectare lake, elephant rides and a golf course. Admission to the 24-hectare garden – which boasts 20,000 rose bushes – is 10B; it's another 220B for the 2.45 pm performance in the cultural village. The resort and rose garden are open from 8 am to 6 pm daily, the cultural village from 10.30am to 5 pm. Shuttle buses run between the resort and major Bangkok hotels.

Just 1km north of the Rose Garden, at the nine-hectare **Samphran Elephant Ground & Zoo** (☎ 284 1873), you can see elephant 'roundups' and crocodile shows; a number of other animals can also be observed in zoo-like conditions; it's the sort of place kids generally like. It's open daily from 8 am to 5.30 pm, with crocodile wrestling

shows at 12.45 and 2.20 pm, elephant shows at 1.45 and 3.30 pm weekdays, a magic show at 1.15 and 3 pm, plus additional shows on weekends and holidays. Admission is 220B for adults, 120B children.

## NORTH OF BANGKOK

Ko Kret, an island in the middle of the Mae Nam Chao Phraya (Chao Phraya River) at Bangkok's northern edge, is home to one of Thailand's **oldest Mon settlements**. The Mon, who between the 6th and 10th centuries AD were the dominant culture in central Thailand, are skilled potters and Ko Kret remains one of the oldest and largest sources of earthenware in the region. An exhibit of local pottery can be seen at the island's Ancient Mon Pottery Centre; there are also plenty of opportunities to watch the local crafting pottery. A Mon Buddhist temple called **Wat Porami Yikawat**, also known simply as 'Wat Mon', contains a Mon-style marble Buddha.

To reach Ko Kret, take a Chao Phraya River Express boat to Tha Nonthaburi, then switch to a Chao Phraya Express boat with a green flag (these run from 6.30 to 7.30 am to 4.30 to 6.30 pm daily) and ride to Tha Wat Poramai at Wat Poramai Yikawat on the island. Chao Phraya River Express also offers a cruise to Ko Kret (departs 9 am, returns 3 pm) for 220B (150B for children). The cruise departs from Tha Maharat.

If you have time to kill in Pak Kret, you can get a good, low-cost **massage** at the School for the Blind, which has a training program in massage therapy.

Every Sunday, Chao Phraya River Express runs an excursion boat to Ko Kret from Tha Maharat at 9 am. The tour takes in Wat Poramai, the Ancient Mon Pottery House, Baan Khanom Thai (to watch Thai sweets being made) and Wat Chaloem Phrakiat. The tour leaves from Wat Chaloem Phrakiat at 2 pm, arriving back at Tha Maharat at 3 pm. Tour prices are 300B per adult, 150B per child.

On the east bank of the Mae Nam Chao Phraya in Pathum Thani Province is Wat

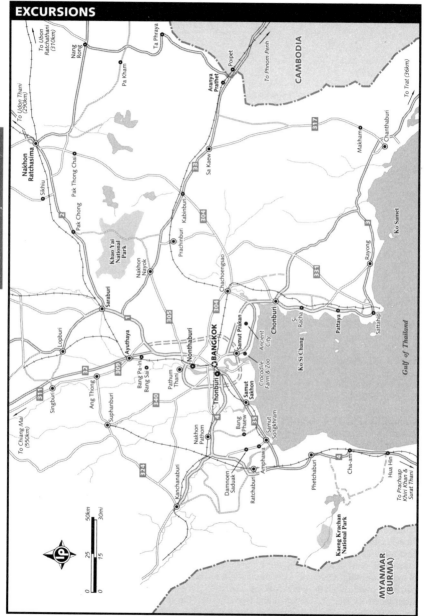

EXCURSIONS

Phailom. This old, wooden Mon wat is noted for the tens of thousands of open-billed storks that nest in bamboo groves opposite the temple area from December to June. The temple is 51km from the centre of Bangkok in Pathum Thani's Sam Kok district. Take a Pathum Thani-bound bus (12B) from Bangkok's Northern bus terminal and cross the river by ferry to the wat grounds.

Bus No 33 from Sanam Luang goes all the way to Phailom and back. Chao Phraya Express tours from Tha Maharat to Bang Pa-In each Sunday also make a stop at Wat Phailom (see River & Canal Trips in the Things to See & Do chapter).

## NORTH-EAST OF BANGKOK

In Minburi, 10km north-east of Bangkok, the 69-hectare **Safari World** (Map 1, ☎ 518 1000) wildlife park is said to be the largest 'open zoo' in the world. It's divided into two portions, the drive-through Safari Park and the walk-through Marine Park. The 5km drive-through Safari Park (aboard air-con coaches or your own vehicle) intersects eight distinct habitats featuring giraffes, lions, zebras, elephants, orangutans, and other African and Asian animals (75 mammal and 300 bird species in all). A panda house displays rare white pandas. The Marine Park focuses on trained animal performances by dolphins and the like. Safari World is open daily from 9 am to 5 pm; the 'foreigner admission price' is 400B for adults, 300B for children. It's at 99 Ramindra 1, 45km east of central Bangkok; for public transport catch a No 26 bus from the Victory Monument to Minburi, then a *songthaew* (small pick-up truck) to the park.

## SOUTH OF BANGKOK
## Ancient City (Meuang Boran)

เมืองโบราณ

Billed as the largest open-air museum in the world, the Ancient City (☎ 323 9253) covers more than 80 hectares and presents 109 scaled-down facsimiles of many of the kingdom's most famous monuments. The grounds follow Thailand's general geographical outline, with the monuments placed accordingly. The main entrance

places visitors at the country's southern tip, from where you work your way to the 'northernmost' monuments. A sculpture garden focusing on episodes from the *Ramakian* can also be seen on the premises.

For anyone with an interest in Thai architecture or those who won't be able to tour the real thing, it's worth a day's visit (it takes an entire day to cover the area). It's also a good place for long, undistracted walks, as it's usually quiet and never crowded. A new zone, occupying almost half as much space as the older zone, contains nine new sites, including replicas of Bangkok's Sao Ching-Cha (Giant Swing), Golden Mount and a canal with a stationary display of the Royal Barge procession, plus lots of open space for picnics. You can buy noodles and other snacks for boat vendors paddling along the canal.

The Ancient City Co (☎ 226 1936, fax 226 1227) also publishes a lavish bilingual periodical devoted to Thai art and architecture called *Muang Boran*. The journal is edited by some of Thailand's leading art historians. The owner of both the journal and park is Bangkok's largest Mercedes Benz dealer, who has an avid interest in Thai art.

Ancient City is 33km from Bangkok along the Old Sukhumvit Hwy. Opening hours are from 8 am to 5 pm; admission is 50/25B. Public bus No 25 (3.50B) or air-con bus No 7, 8 or 11 (12B to 16B) to the Samut Prakan terminal can take up to two hours depending on traffic. From the terminal take minibus No 36 (5B), which passes the entrance to Ancient City. Transport can also be arranged through the Bangkok office (☎ 224 1057) at 78 Democracy Monument circle, Thanon (Th) Ratchadamnoen Klang.

## Samut Prakan Crocodile Farm & Zoo

ฟาร์มจระเข้สมุทรปราการ

Nearby the Ancient City is the Samut Prakan Crocodile Farm & Zoo (☎ 387 0020). Over 30,000 crocs reside here (including the largest-known Siamese croc, a male named Yai who's 6m long and weighs 1114kg), along with elephants, monkeys and snakes. The farm is open from 7 am to 6 pm daily, with trained animal shows (including croc wrestling) every hour between 9 and 11 am and 1 and 4 pm. Elephant shows take place at 9.30 and 11.30 am, while the reptiles usually get their dinner between 4 and 5 pm. Admission is 300B for adults, 200B for children (50/30B for Thais). Convention on International Trade in Endangered Species (CITES) certified items – handbags, belts, shoes – made from crocodile hide are available from the farm's gift shop. You can reach the crocodile farm via air-con bus No 7, 8 or 11, changing to songthaew No S1 or S80.

## AYUTHAYA
พระนครศรีอยุธยา

About 85km north of Bangkok, lies the Unesco World Heritage Site of Thailand's old capital, Ayuthaya (current population 62,100). The capital was transferred from U Thong to Ayutha in 1350 and lasted until 1767. Accounts say it was a splendid period during this time – prior to that it was a Khmer outpost. The city was named for Ayodhya (Sanskrit for 'unassailable' or 'undefeatable'), the home of Rama in the Indian epic *Ramayana*. Its full Thai name is Phra Nakhon Si Ayuthaya (Sacred City of Ayodhya).

The Sukhothai period is often referred to as Thailand's 'golden age', but in many ways the Ayuthaya era was the kingdom's true historical apex; in terms of global influence, geographic rule (sovereignty extended well into present-day Laos, Cambodia and Myanmar) and dynastic endurance (over 400 years). Thirty-three kings of various Siamese dynasties reigned in Ayuthaya until it was conquered by the Burmese. During its heyday, Thai culture and international commerce flourished in the kingdom and Ayuthaya was courted by Dutch, Portuguese, French, English, Chinese and Japanese merchants. By the end of the 17th century, Ayuthaya's population had reached one million – foreign visitors reportedly claimed it to be the most illustrious city they had ever seen.

### Orientation & Information
The present-day city is located at the confluence of three rivers, the Chao Phraya, the Pa Sak and the smaller Lopburi. A wide canal joins them and makes a complete circle around the town.

Ayuthaya's historic temples are scattered throughout this once magnificent city and along the encircling rivers. Several of the more central ruins – Wat Phra Si Sanphet, Wat Mongkhon Bophit, Wat Phra Ram, Wat Thammikarat, Wat Ratburana and Wat Mahathat – can easily be visited on foot if you avoid the hottest part of the day – 11 am to 4 pm. Or you could enlarge your itinerary by touring on a rented bicycle. For visitors who want to 'do it all', you can bicycle around the central temples and charter a longtail boat for the outlying ruins along the river from the boat landing across from Chan Kasem Palace for a tour around the river/canal; several of the old wat ruins (Wat Phanan Choeng, Wat Phutthaisawan, Wat Kasatthirat and Wat Chai Wattanaram) may be glimpsed from the canal, along with picturesque views of river life. Apart from the historic ruins and museums, there's not a lot to do in Ayuthaya. See Getting Around in this section for details on different modes and rates of transport. At many of the ruins a 20B to 30B admission fee is collected 8 am to 6.30 pm.

**Tourist Office** The Tourist Authority of Thailand (TAT; ☎ 035-246076, 01-239 8616) has an office (open from 8 am to 4.30 pm daily) next to the Tourist Police office (☎ 035-241446, 1155) on Th Si Sanphet.

**Post & Communications** Post office hours are 8.30 am to 4.30 pm on weekdays, and 9 am to noon Saturday. The international card phone and overseas phone service upstairs operates between 8 am and 8 pm daily.

### National Museums
There are two museums, the main one is **Chao Sam Phraya National Museum**, near the intersection of Th Rotchana (Ayuthaya's main street) and Th Si Sanphet, near the centre of town. It features your basic roundup of Thai Buddhist sculpture with an emphasis, naturally, on Ayuthaya pieces. A selection of books on Thai art and archaeology can be bought at the ticket kiosk. The museum is

open 9 am to 4 pm Wednesday to Sunday; entry is 30B.

**Chantharakasem National Museum** (Chan Kasem Palace or Phra Ratchawang Chan Kasem) is a museum piece itself, built by the 17th king of Ayuthaya, Maha Thammarat, for his son Prince Naresuan. Among the exhibits is a collection of gold treasures from Wat Phra Mahathat and Wat Ratburana. Chan Kasem Palace is in the northeast corner of town, near the river. Opening hours are 9 am to noon and 1 to 4 pm Wednesday to Sunday; entry is also 30B.

## Wat Phra Si Sanphet

วัดพระศรีสรรเพชญ์

This was the largest temple in Ayuthaya in its time, and was used as the royal temple/palace by several Ayuthaya kings. Built in the 14th century, the compound once contained a 16m standing Buddha covered with 250kg of gold, which was melted down by the Burmese conquerors. It is mainly known for the *chedis* (stupas) erected in the quintessential Ayuthaya style, which has come to be identified with Thai art more than any other single style. Admission is 30B.

## Wat Phra Mongkhon Bophit

วัดมงคลบพิตร

This monastery near Wat Si Sanphet contains one of Thailand's largest Buddha images, a blackened 15th-century bronze casting. The present *wíhăan* (Buddhist image house) was built in 1956.

## Wat Phra Mahathat

วัดพระมหาธาตุ

This wát, on the corner of Th Chee Kun and Th Naresuan, dates back to the 14th century, to the reign of King Ramesuan. Despite extensive damage – not much was left standing by the Burmese hordes – the *prang* (Khmer-style stupa) is still impressive. The wat grounds contain one of the most photographed sites in Ayuthaya – a Buddha head around which tree roots have grown. Admission is 30B.

## Wat Ratburana

วัดราชบูรณะ

The Ratburana ruins are the counterpart to Wat Phra Mahathat across the road. The chedis, however, contain murals and are not quite as dilapidated. Admission is 30B.

## Wat Thammikarat

วัดธรรมิกราช

To the east of the old palace grounds, inside the river loop, Wat Thammikarat features overgrown chedi ruins and lion sculptures.

## Wat Phanan Choeng

วัดพนัญเชิง

South-east of town on the Mae Nam Chao Phraya, this wat was built before Ayuthaya became a Siamese capital. It's not known who built the temple, but it appears to have been constructed in the early 14th century, so it's possibly Khmer. The main wihăan contains a highly revered 19m sitting Buddha image from which the wat derives its name.

The easiest way to get to Wat Phanan Choeng is by ferry from the pier near Phom Phet fortress, inside the south-east corner of the city centre. For a few extra baht you can take a bicycle with you on the boat.

## Wat Na Phra Mehn

วัดหน้าพระเมรุ

Across from the old royal palace *(wang lŭang)* grounds is a bridge that can be crossed to arrive at Wat Na Phra Mehn. This temple is notable because it escaped destruction in the 1767 Burmese capture, though it has required restoration over the years. The main *bòt* (central chapel) was built in 1546 and features fortress-like walls and pillars. During the 18th-century Burmese invasion, Burma's King Along Phaya chose this site to fire a cannon at the palace; the cannon exploded and the king was fatally injured, thus ending the sacking of Ayuthaya.

The bòt interior contains an impressive carved wooden ceiling and a splendid Ayuthaya-era crowned sitting Buddha, 6m

EXCURSIONS

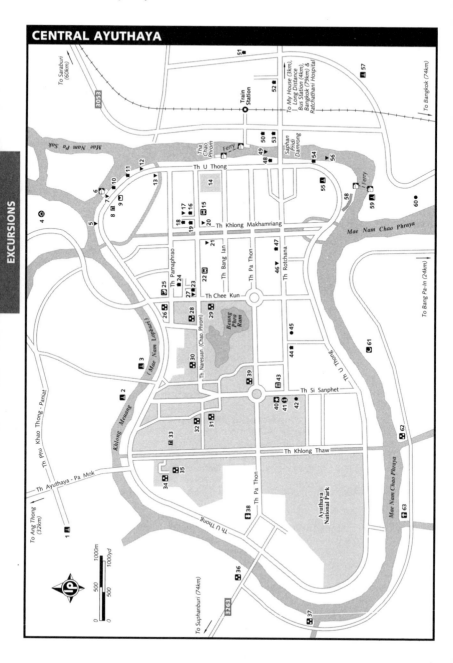

CENTRAL AYUTHAYA

## CENTRAL AYUTHAYA

**PLACES TO STAY**
10 U-Thong Hotel
11 Cathay Hotel
16 Ayothaya Hotel
18 Ayuthaya Guest House; Toto Guest House; BJ1 Guest House; PU Guest House
19 TMT Guest House; Good Luck Restaurant
23 New BJ Guest House
24 PS Guest House
44 Suan Luang (Royal Garden) Hotel
47 Wieng Fa Hotel
48 Reuan Doem
50 Tevaraj Tanrin Hotel
51 Ayuthaya Grand Hotel
52 U-Thong Inn
53 Krungsri River Hotel
54 Phaesri Thong Guest House

**PLACES TO EAT**
5 Hua Raw Night Market
7 Night Market
12 Chainam
13 Rodeo

14 Chao Phrom Market
17 Moon Cafe; Sun Cafe
20 Duangporn
21 Vegetarian Restaurant
27 Malakor
46 Moradok-Thai
49 Ruenpae; Rueuan Doem
56 Phae Krung Kao

**OTHER**
1 Phu Khao Thong Temple (Golden Mount Chedi)
2 Wat Phra Mehn
3 Wat Kuti Thong
4 Elephant Kraal
6 Tha Chan Kaem
8 Chan Kasem Palace
9 Main Post Office
15 Bus Station
22 Air-Con Minivans to Bangkok
25 Chinese Shrine
26 Wat Suwannawat
28 Wat Ratburana
29 Wat Phra Mahathat
30 Wat Thammikarat

31 Wat Mongkhon Bophit
32 Wat Phra Si Sanphet
33 Royal Palace
34 Wat Chetharam
35 Wat Lokaya Sutha
36 Wat Kasatthirat
37 Wat Chai Wattanaram
38 Queen Suriyothai Memorial Pagoda
39 Wat Phra Ram
40 Tourist Police
41 TAT Office
42 City Hall
43 Chao Sam Phraya National Museum
45 Ayuthaya Historical Study Centre
55 Wat Suwan Dararam
57 Wat Yai Chai Mongkhon
58 Phom Phet Fortress
59 Wat Phanan Choeng
60 Ayuthaya Historical Study Centre (Annexe)
61 Mosque
62 Wat Phutthaisawan
63 St Joseph's Cathedral

**EXCURSIONS**

in height. Inside a smaller wíhǎan behind the bòt is a green-stone, European-pose (sitting in a chair) Buddha from Ceylon, said to be 1300 years old. The walls of the wíhǎan show traces of 18th- or 19th-century murals. Admission to Wat Na Phra Mehn is 20B.

### Wat Yai Chai Mongkhon
วัดใหญ่ชัยมงคล

Wat Yai, as the locals call it, is south-east of the town proper, but can be reached by minibus for 3B to 4B. It's a quiet old place built in 1357 by King U Thong and was once famous as a meditation centre. The compound contains a very large chedi from which the wat takes its popular name (yài means big), and there is a community of mâe chii (Buddhist nuns) residing here. Admission is 20B.

### Elephant Kraal
เพนียดคล้องช้าง

This is a restored version of the kraal (wooden stockade) once used for the annual roundup of wild elephants. A huge

fence of teak logs planted in the ground at 45 degree angles enclosed the elephants. The king had a special raised pavilion from which to observe the thrilling event.

### Boat Trips

Longtail boats can be rented from Tha Chan Kasem to do a semicircular tour of the island and see some of the less accessible ruins. A longtail boat that will take up to eight people can be hired for 400B for a two- to three-hour trip with stops at Wat Phutthaisawan, Wat Phanan Choeng and Wat Chai Wattanaram. Or, if you happen to be in town during the full moon, check out the ruins by moonlight on boat tours arranged by PS Guest House. (See Places to Stay in this section for details.)

### Festivals

Ayuthaya holds one of the country's largest **Loi Krathong** festivals on the full moon of the 12th lunar month, usually November. The festival, held on full moon night, is peculiarly Thai and probably originated in the northern city of Sukhothai. Celebrations are held at several spots in Ayuthaya; the largest spectacle takes place at **Beung Phra Ram**, the large lake in the centre of the city between Wat Phra Ram and Wat Mahathat. Thousands of people, many from Bangkok, flock to the event to crowd around five outdoor stages offering *lí-keh* (often bawdy folk plays with dancing and music), Thai pop, cinema and *lákhon chaatrii* (dance-drama) all at the same time – the din can be deafening! Fireworks are a big part of the show and there are lots of food vendors on site.

More low-key and traditional is the celebration at the **Chan Kasem pier**, where families launch their *krathong* (small lotus-shaped floats made from banana leaves and topped with incense, flowers, coins and candles) onto the junction of the Lopburi and Pa Sak rivers. Krathong can be purchased at the pier (or you can make your own from materials for sale); for a few baht you can board one of the many waiting canoes at the pier and be paddled out to launch your krathong in the middle of the river. Thai tradition says that any couple who launch a krathong together are destined to be lovers – if not in this lifetime then the next.

Another large Loi Krathong festival takes place at the Royal Folk Arts & Crafts Centre in Bang Sai, about 24km west of Ayuthaya. Here the emphasis is on traditional costumes and hand-made krathong. If you can put together a small group, any of the hotels or guesthouses in Ayuthaya can arrange a trip to the Loi Krathong in Bang Sai for around 250B or less per person.

During the 10 days leading to the **Songkran Festival**, the lunar New Year celebration held in mid-April, there is a sound-and-light show with fireworks over the ruins.

## Places to Stay – Budget

There are several budget accommodation options in Ayuthaya, many of which rent bicycles for around 50B per day. As elsewhere in Thailand, *tuk-tuk* (motorised pedicab) and *samlor* (three-wheeled pedicab) drivers will tell you anything to steer you towards guesthouses that pay commissions (about 35B a head).

*PU Guest House* (☎ 035-251213, 20/1 Soi Thaw Kaw Saw), off Th Naresuan, is a relatively new place with two floors of clean rooms for 140B. Shared bathrooms are outside in a separate building. The friendly owner speaks English and Japanese. Cheap food and drink is available, and there are bicycles/motorbikes for rent for 50/250B per day.

Just down the road, the *TMT Guest House* (☎ 035-251474) has small but clean rooms for 100/140B single/double. The place also has a small restaurant and is popular with Japanese travellers.

Almost directly across the river from the train station in an 80-year-old teak house is the *Reuan Doem* (☎ 035-241978, 48/2 Th U Thong), formerly known as Ayuthaya Youth Hostel. Rustic and atmospheric rooms with ceiling fans and shared bath cost 250B. A very good floating restaurant extends from the river side of the house; it is open from 10 am to 11 pm. If you can put up with some ambient noise from the restaurant, it's not a bad choice.

*Phaesri Thong Guest House* (☎ 035-246010, 8/1 Th U Thong), near Wat Suwan Dararam on the river, is a spotless place with a common balcony sitting area on every level. The top floor has a huge room with dorm beds for 200B per night, while the 1st and 2nd floors offer spacious private rooms with air-con, TV and private bath for 500B to 600B. The breezy indoor/outdoor restaurant that overlooks the river offers Thai and *farang* (Western) food. The owner speaks English, and the guesthouse has a boat that can be chartered for tours around Ayuthaya for 150B per person.

Near the PU Guesthouse, *Ayuthaya Guest House* (☎ 035-232658) charges 120/160B single/double for plain rooms, with shared bath in a house. Next door is *Toto Guest House* (☎ 035-251468), which offers similar fan rooms for 100B to 140B, or 500B for air-con and TV. Next door, a branch of the same family runs the *BJ1 Guest House* (☎ 035-251526), with fan rooms for 100/140B in a private house. All three offer minimal food service.

Another BJ relative operates the *New BJ Guest House* (☎ 035-244046, 19/29 Th Naresuan). Rooms cost 120/150B with fan or dorm beds are 60B, and there's a simple dining area at the front. It's right on Th Naresuan – traffic noise may be distracting.

The hospitable **PS Guest House** is a two-storey house off Th Chee Kun. Fan and air-con rooms (with shared bath) are 150B and 250B. Home-cooked meals, including vegetarian food, are served on request. The owner is an ex-student whose former students put on a classical Thai dance show on Friday evening. On full-moon nights, boat trips to view the ruins by moonlight are offered for 100B per person.

There are two standard Thai-Chinese-style hotels at the junction of the Mae Nam Lopburi and Mae Nam Pa Sak that have been accommodating Ayuthaya visitors for over two decades now, and it shows. Both places are pretty run-down. The **U-Thong Hotel** (☎ 035-251136), on Th U Thong near Hua Raw Night Market and Chan Kasem Palace, is the better choice. It has adequate rooms with fan for 300/370B single/double, or with air-con, TV and hot-water shower for 380/450B.

## Places to Stay – Mid-Range & Top End

The **Wieng Fa Hotel** (☎ 035-241353, 1/8 Th Rotchana) is a friendly, cosy two-storey place with clean, relatively quiet rooms around a garden courtyard for 450B to 500B. All rooms come with TV, fridge and air-con; English is spoken.

**Suan Luang Hotel** (Royal Garden; tel/fax 035-245537) is a five-storey hotel training facility beside the Ayuthaya Historical Study Centre. Decent air-con rooms with fridge and TV cost a moderate 500B; a couple of six-bed air-con rooms are available for 600B. All rooms have cold-water showers and TV.

**My House** (☎ 035-335493, fax 335494), on Th Rotchana out towards Ratchathani Hospital, has decent rooms with fan for 420B; the isolated location is a definite drawback.

The **Ayothaya Hotel** (☎ 035-232855, fax 251018, 12 Soi 2, Th Thetsaban), just off Th Naresuan, is more upmarket. It charges 900B for singles/doubles with air-con, bath-

tub, fridge and cable TV. There's a swimming pool.

Moving towards the top end, the **U-Thong Inn** (☎ 035-242236, fax 242235) offers comfortable air-con rooms in the old wing for 1200B, while rooms in the newer wing with separate sitting areas go for 1400B. The new wing is better value. Facilities include a pool, sauna and massage room. Discounts of up to 45% are given in the low season. It's out on Th Rotchana past the turn-off for the train station.

Farther out, the six-storey **Ayuthaya Grand Hotel** (☎ 035-335483, fax 335492, 55/5 Th Rotchana) features rooms with all the mod cons for 1200B to 1500B (900B to 1200B low season). There's a coffee shop, cocktail lounge, nightclub and a large swimming pool.

Ayuthaya's flashiest digs are the 202-room, nine-storey **Krungsri River Hotel** (☎ 035-244333, fax 243777, 27/2 Th Rotchana), where rooms cost 1650B to 2000B, suites from 5000B to 10,000B. Facilities include a pub/coffee house, Chinese restaurant, beer garden, fitness centre, pool, bowling alley and snooker club.

Next door to the Krungsri, the 102-room **Tevaraj Tanrin Hotel** (☎ 035-234873, fax 244139) has similar rooms with river views starting at 1200B single/double (with breakfast), a floating restaurant and beer garden.

## Places to Eat

The most dependable and least expensive places to eat are the **Hua Raw Night Market**, on the river near Chan Kasem Palace, and the **Chao Phrom Market**, opposite the ferry piers along the east side of the island. The **Chainam** near Chan Kasem Palace and U-Thong Hotel has tables on the river, a bilingual menu and friendly service; it's also open for breakfast.

The **Malakor**, on Th Chee Kun opposite Wat Ratburana, is located in a two-storey wooden house with a charming view of the temple, and offers good, cheap Thai dishes in the 35B to 50B range, plus an excellent selection of coffees.

Next to the TMT guest House is **Good Luck**, an open-air restaurant under some shady mango trees. Prices are 40B to 60B per dish for Thai and farang food, and the portions are generous.

The *Moon Cafe* and *Sun Cafe*, tiny spots on the same soi, serve Thai and faràng snacks for 60B to 80B per dish. *Duangporn* on Th Naresuan near the main bus terminal is an indoor air-con place with Thai and Chinese food in the 70B to 180B range. A *vegetarian restaurant* can be found around the corner from the Duangporn on the opposite side of the canal.

A few restaurants can be found on Th Rotchana, including *Moradok-Thai*, a Thai food establishment that is very popular with Thai tourists. Dishes cost 60B to 120B, and there is also a selection of wines. It's a good place to soak up the air-con after touring the ruins.

There are four floating restaurants on the Mae Nam Pa Sak, three on either side of Saphan Pridi Damrong on the west bank, and one on the east bank north of the bridge. Of these, the *Phae Krung Kao* – on the south side of the bridge on the west bank – has the better reputation; it's open 10 am to 2 am. North of the bridge on the west bank, *Ruenpae* is similar. The floating *Reuan Doem*, on the river behind the guesthouse of the same name, is also quite good and has the most intimate atmosphere of the riverside places.

In the evenings a *night market* comes to life near the pier *(thâa)* opposite Chan Kasem Palace. Quite a few of the vendors sell Thai-Muslim dishes – look for the green crescent and star on the signs.

For entertainment with your food, try the air-con *Rodeo* on Th U Thong. Despite the name and old-west decor, the food is mostly Thai cocktail snacks (an English menu is available); it's only open at night, when a small band plays Thai and international folk music.

## Getting There & Away

**Bus** Ordinary buses run between the Northern bus terminal in Bangkok and Ayuthaya's main terminal on Th Naresuan every 20 minutes between 5 am and 7 pm. The fare is 34B and the trip takes around two hours. Air-con buses operate along the same route every 20 minutes from 5.40 am to 7.20 pm and cost 47B; the trip takes 1½ hours when traffic north of Bangkok is light, two hours otherwise. Across the street from the BJ1 Guest House is a minivan service to Bangkok that runs every 20 minutes from 4 am to 5 pm for 40B.

If you're arriving by bus from some place other than Bangkok or cities nearby, you may be dropped off at the long-distance bus terminal, 5km east of Saphan Pridi Damrong at the Hwy 32 junction.

*Songthaews* (pickup trucks used as buses or taxis) to/from Bang Pa-In leave from the same area on Th Naresuan and cost 10B; it's about 45 minutes away.

**Train** Trains to Ayuthaya leave Bangkok's Hualamphong station every hour or so between 4.20 am and 10.10 pm. The 3rd-class fare is 15B for the 1½-hour trip; it's hardly worth taking a more expensive class, rapid or express, for this short trip and most 2nd- and 1st-class tickets will already be taken up by long distance travellers. Train schedules are available from the information booth at Hualamphong station.

From Ayuthaya's train station, the quickest way to reach the old city is to walk straight west to the river, where you can take a short ferry ride across to Tha Chao Phrom for 1B. Alternatively, a tuk-tuk to any point in old Ayuthaya should be around 30B.

Upon arrival at Bangkok International Airport, savvy visitors to Thailand sometimes choose to board a north-bound train direct to Ayuthaya rather than head south into the Bangkok maelstrom. The last train to Ayuthaya leaves Bangkok's Hualamphong station at 10.10 pm. There are frequent 3rd-class trains throughout the day between Don Muang station (opposite Bangkok International Airport) and Ayuthaya.

**Boat** There are no scheduled or chartered boat services running between Bangkok and Ayuthaya.

Several companies in Bangkok operate luxury cruises to Bang Pa-In, with side trips by bus to Ayuthaya, for around 1500B to 1800B per person, including a lavish luncheon. Longer two-day trips in converted rice barges start at 4800B. See the River & Canal Trips section in the Things to See & Do chapter.

### Getting Around

Songthaews and shared tuk-tuks ply the main city roads for 5B to 10B per person depending on the distance. A tuk-tuk from the train station to any point in old Ayuthaya should be around 30B; on the island itself figure to pay no more than 20B per trip.

For touring the ruins, your most economical and ecological option is to rent a bicycle from one of the guesthouses (about 50B a day), or walk. You can hire a samlor, tuk-tuk or songthaew by the hour or by the day to explore the ruins, but prices are quite high by Thai standards (200B per hour for anything with a motor, 500B all day when things are slow). Many drivers ask upwards of 700B for a day's worth of sightseeing – it's much cheaper to take separate rides from site to site.

### BANG PA-IN

บางปะอิน

Twenty kilometres south of Ayuthaya is Bang Pa-In, which has a curious collection of palace buildings in a wide variety of architectural styles. It's a nice boat trip from Bangkok if you're taking one of the cruise tours, although in itself it's not particularly noteworthy. The palace is open from 8.30 am to 3.30 pm daily; admission is 50B.

### Palace Buildings

The postcard stereotype here is a pretty little Thai pavilion in the centre of a small lake by the palace entrance. Inside the palace grounds, the Chinese-style **Wehat Chamrun Palace** is the only building open to visitors. The **Withun Thatsana** building looks like a lighthouse with balconies. It was built to give a fine view over gardens and lakes. There are various other buildings, towers and memorials in the grounds, plus an interesting topiary garden where the bushes have been trimmed into the shape of a small herd of elephants.

## Wat Niwet Thamaprawat

วัดนิเวศธรรมประวัติ

Across the river and south from the palace grounds, this unusual wat looks much more like a Gothic Christian church than anything from Thailand. It was built by Rama V (Chulalongkorn). You get to the wat by crossing the river in a small trolley-like cable car. The crossing is free.

### Getting There & Away

Bang Pa-In can be reached by minibus (it's really a large songthaew truck) around the corner from Ayuthaya's Chao Phrom Market on Th Naresuan, for 10B; the trip takes about 45 minutes. From Bangkok there are buses every half-hour or so from the Northern bus terminal and the fare is 23B ordinary, 34B air-con. You can also reach Bang Pa-In by train from Bangkok for 12B in 3rd class.

The Chao Phraya River Express Boat Co (☎ 222 5330, 225 3002/3) does a tour every Sunday, from Tha Maharat in Bangkok, that goes to Wat Phailom in Pathum Thani (November to June) or Wat Chaloem Phrakiat (July to October), as well as Bang Pa-In and Bang Sai's Royal Folk Arts & Crafts Centre. The trip leaves Bangkok at 8 am and returns at 5.30 pm. The price is 300B, excluding lunch, which you arrange in Bang Pa-In. For more expensive, all-inclusive river cruises to Bang Pa-In, which include tours of old Ayuthaya, see the River & Canal Trips section of the Things to See & Do chapter.

## NAKHON PATHOM

อ.เมืองนครปฐม

Only 56km west of Bangkok, Nakhon Pathom (population 46,400) is often referred to by Thais as the oldest city in Thailand – the name is derived from the Pali 'Nagara Pathama', meaning 'First City'. At one time it functioned as the centre of the Dvaravati kingdom, a loose collection of Mon city states that flourished between the 6th and 11th centuries AD in the Mae Nam Chao Phraya valley. Some historians speculate that the area may have been inhabited before India's Ashokan period (3rd century

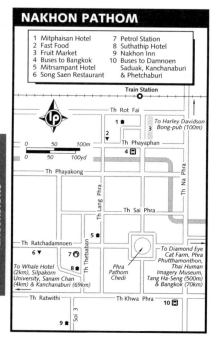

**NAKHON PATHOM**

1 Mitphaisan Hotel
2 Fast Food
3 Fruit Market
4 Buses to Bangkok
5 Mitrsampant Hotel
6 Song Saen Restaurant
7 Petrol Station
8 Suthathip Hotel
9 Nakhon Inn
10 Buses to Damnoen
   Saduak, Kanchanaburi
   & Phetchaburi

Train Station

Th Rot Fai

To Harley Davidson
Bong-pub (100m)

Th Phayaphan

Th Phayakong

Th Lang Phra

Th Na Phra

Th Sai Phra

Th Ratchadamnoen

Th Thetsaban

Phra
Pathom
Chedi

To Diamond Eye
Cat Farm, Phra
Phutthamonthon,
Thai Human
Imagery Museum,
Tang Ha-Seng (500m)
& Bangkok (70km)

To Whale Hotel
(2km), Silpakorn
University, Sanam Chan
(4km) & Kanchanaburi (69km)

Th Ratwithi

Th Khwa Phra

Soi 3

BC), as it is theorised that Buddhist missionaries from India visited Nakhon Pathom at that time. Although one could point out that other areas of Thailand were inhabited earlier, Nakhon Pathom may very well be the longest continually inhabited place within Thailand's current borders.

Today's Nakhon Pathom is a typical provincial Thai city whose only visible link to its glorious past is the Phra Pathom Chedi.

## Phra Pathom Chedi
พระปฐมเจดีย์

The central attraction in Nakhon Pathom is the famous Phra Pathom Chedi, the tallest Buddhist monument in the world, rising to 127m. The original monument, buried within the massive orange-glazed dome, was erected in the early 6th century by the Theravada Buddhists of Dvaravati (possibly at the same time as Myanmar's famous Shwe Dagon stupa), but in the early 11th

century the Khmer king, Suryavarman I of Angkor, conquered the city and built a Brahman prang over the sanctuary. The Burmese of Bagan, under King Anuruddha, sacked the city in 1057 and the prang lay in ruins until King Mongkut had it restored in 1860.

The king built a larger chedi over the remains according to Buddhist tradition, adding four wíhǎan, a bòt, a replica of the original chedi, *sala* (open-sided pavilions), and assorted prang and embellishments. There's a Chinese temple attached to the outer walls of the chedi, next to which outdoor *lí-keh* (Thai folk opera) is sometimes performed.

On the eastern side of the monument, in the bòt, is a Dvaravati-style Buddha seated in a European pose similar to the one in Wat Na Phra Mehn in Ayuthaya. It may, in fact, have come from Phra Mehn.

The wat surrounding the chedi enjoys the kingdom's highest temple rank, Ratchavoramahavihan, one of only six temples so honoured in Thailand. Rama VI's ashes are interred in the base of the Sukhothai-era Phra Ruang Rochanarit, a large standing Buddha image in the wát's northern wíhǎan.

Opposite the bòt is a museum, open 9 am to 4 pm Wednesday to Sunday, which contains some interesting Dvaravati sculpture; admission is 20B.

## Other Attractions

Besides the chedi, the other focuses of the town are **Silpakorn University**, west of the chedi off Phetkasem Hwy, and **Sanam Chan**, adjacent to the university. Sanam Chan, formerly the grounds of Rama VI's palace, is a pleasant park with a canal passing through it. The somewhat run-down palace still stands in the park, but entry is not permitted.

South-east of the city towards Bangkok, between the districts of Nakhon Chaisi and Sam Phran, stands **Phra Phutthamonthon** (from the Pali 'Buddhamandala'). This 40.7m Sukhothai-style Buddha is reportedly the world's tallest. It's surrounded by an expansive landscaped park containing replicas of important Buddhist pilgrimage spots in India and Nepal. All Bangkok to Nakhon Pathom buses pass the access road to the park (signposted in English and Thai); from there you can walk or flag one of the frequent songthaews into the park itself.

The **Diamond Eye Cat Farm** (☎ 034-441 1619), just before Phra Phutthamonthon on Th Pinklao-Nakhon Chaisi (the highway to Bangkok), affords a glimpse of the very rare *maew khǎo manii* (white jewel cat). This unusual breed consists of less than 200 individual cats, all descended from a single family kept and bred by Thailand's Chakri dynasty. By royal decree of Rama V, these cats must not be crossed with any other feline breed, nor may they be bought or sold (one that was sold illegally in 1993 fetched 150 million baht). The khǎo manii has all-white fur and features either one green eye and one light blue eye or one yellow and one blue. In addition to the royal cats, visitors can view exhibits of rare religious amulets and various royal heirlooms. Also on the grounds are 14 old Thai teak homes. Admission is 300/ 200B for foreign tourists/children, 50/20B for Thais and residents of Thailand/children.

The **Thai Human Imagery Museum** (☎ 034-332607), a bit out of town at Km 31, Th Pinklao-Nakhon Chaisi, contains exhibits of life-like resin sculptures. A group of Thai artists reportedly spent 10 years studying their subjects and creating the figures, which fall into four sections: famous Buddhist monks of Thailand, former kings of the Chakri dynasty, Thai lifestyles and chess playing. It's open 9 am to 5.30 pm weekdays, 8.30 am to 6 pm weekends; admission for foreigners is 200B.

### Places to Stay

Budget accommodation in Nakhon Pathom can be a bit on the dreary side. Some visitors prefer passing through to spending the night, while others may find the town of interest for its typical provincialism. The *Mitphaisan Hotel* (Mitr Paisal; ☎ 034-242422) is on the right as you walk directly down the street opposite the train station. Rooms are 250B for fan and bath, 350B with air-con. Near the west side of Phra Pathom Chedi, on Th Lang Phra, the *Mitrsampant* (Mitsamphan; ☎ 034-241422) offers smaller but clean rooms with fan and bath for 200B. Both of the 'Mit' hotels are owned by the same family.

A few blocks south-west of Phra Pathom Chedi is the *Suthathip Hotel* (☎ 034-242242, 24/22 Th Thetsaban), with a boisterous Chinese restaurant downstairs. Rooms seem like an afterthought here and cost 150/200B for one/two beds with fan and bath, or 300B for air-con.

Mid-range/top-end accommodation includes the *Nakhon Inn* (☎ 034-251152, fax 254998, 55 Soi 3, Th Ratwithi), which is a pleasant air-con hotel where rooms with TV are 525B, or 675B for larger rooms with fridge.

The newer *Whale Hotel* (☎ 034-251020, fax 253864, 151/79 Th Ratwithi), south-west of the monument, offers good air-con rooms in four separate buildings from 480B to 600B. Facilities and services include a coffee shop, restaurant, karaoke, snooker club, golf driving range, sauna and massage.

### Places to Eat

Nakhon Pathom has an excellent *fruit market* along the road between the train station and the Phra Pathom Chedi; the *khâo lǎam* (sticky rice and coconut steamed in a bamboo joint) is reputed to be the best in Thailand. There are many good, inexpensive food vendors and restaurants in this area.

An old standby on Th Thesa, east of the chedi, is the inexpensive Chinese *Tang Ha-Seng* (no roman-script sign); there are two branches, one at No 71/2-3 and another at No 59/1-2.

*Song Saeng*, on Th Ratchadamnoen a few blocks directly west of Phra Pathom Chedi, offers a pleasant Thai sala setting with good, medium-priced Thai food.

In the evenings you can get decent Thai food at *Harley Davidson Bong-Pub*, just north of the train station. Though really more of a bar than a restaurant, the menu has a good selection of *kàp klâem* (finger food) and live music on Friday and Saturday.

There's *fast-food outlets* on the corner of Th Lang Phra and Th Phayaphan.

### Getting There & Away

**Bus** Buses for Nakhon Pathom leave the Southern bus terminal in Bangkok every 10 minutes from 5.45 am to 9.10 pm; the fare is 20B for the one-hour trip. Air-con buses are 34B and leave about every 20 minutes between 6 am and 10.30 pm. There are two bus routes; be sure to take the *săi mài* (new route) buses, as the 'old route' buses take a half-hour longer. In the opposite direction, ordinary (No 83) and air-con (No 997) buses depart for Bangkok from Th Phayaphan on the canal side of the road close to the Mitphaisan Hotel.

The location of bus stops in Nakhon Pathom seems to change between every edition of this guide. At this visit, buses to Kanchanaburi left throughout the day from Th Khwa Phra, south-east of Phra Pathom Chedi – get bus No 81. Buses to Damnoen Saduak floating market (No 78) and to Phetchaburi (No 73) leave from the same stop. Buses leave about every 30 minutes.

**Train** Ordinary trains (3rd class only) leave Thonburi (Bangkok Noi) station daily at 7.45 am and 1.30 and 2 pm, arriving in Nakhon Pathom in about an hour and 10 minutes. The fare is 14B.

There are also rapid and express trains to Nakhon Pathom from Hualamphong station roughly hourly between 12.20 and 10.50 pm. The 2nd-class fare is 31B and 1st class is 60B (add 40B and 60B respectively for rapid and express service). While rapid trains from Hualamphong take 1½ hours, the express is only 10 minutes faster. There are no longer any ordinary trains to Nakhon Pathom from Hualamphong station.

## AROUND NAKHON PATHOM
## Damnoen Saduak Floating Markets

ตลาดน้ำดำเนินสะดวก

The lively floating markets *(talàat náam)* on Khlong Damnoen Saduak in Ratchaburi Province, 104km south-west of Bangkok, between Nakhon Pathom and Samut Songkhram, have become well known.

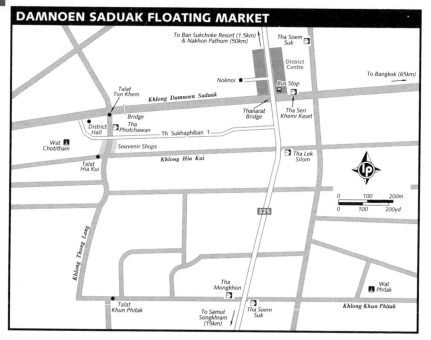

**Talat Ton Khem** is the main, 100-year-old market on Khlong Damnoen Saduak Canal, while **Talat Hia Kui**, just south on the parallel Khlong Hia Kui, gets the most tourists – one area has been set aside for tourists, with a large open shop with souvenirs for bus tours as well as souvenir-laden boats. There is a third, less crowded market on a smaller canal, a bit south of Khlong Damnoen Saduak, called **Talat Khun Phitak**. To get there, take a water taxi going south from the pier on the east side of Khlong Thong Lang Canal, which intersects Damnoen Saduak near the larger floating market, and ask for Talat Khun Phitak. You can rent a boat to tour the canals and all three markets for 150B for half an hour or 300B per hour. Try to arrive by 8 am at the latest – by 9 am the package tours are in full evidence.

Less touristed floating markets can be reached by boating south from Damnoen Saduak to Amphawa district in Samut Songkhram Province (see the Samut Songkhram section later in this chapter for details).

**Places to Stay** One sure way to beat the tour buses from Bangkok is to spend the night in Damnoen Saduak itself and get up before the hordes of tourists arrive. There's enough to see to justify spending a night and a day, perhaps longer.

Try the clean and quiet *Noknoi (Little Bird;* ☎ 032-254382), where rooms cost 170/300B fan/air-con. It's about a 15-minute walk from Talat Ton Khem.

*Ban Sukchoke Resort* (☎ 032-254301) offers comfortable bungalows set over the canal for 450/700B single/double. There is also a small house that sleeps 10 for 1,600B. Ban Sukchoke is 1.5km north-west of Damnoen's market area.

**Getting There & Away** Bus No 78 goes direct from Bangkok's Southern bus terminal to Damnoen Saduak every 20 minutes, beginning at 6.20 am, but you'll have to get one of the first few buses to arrive in Damnoen Saduak by 8 or 9 am, when the market's at its best. Air-con buses start at 6 am. The trip lasts just short of two hours under normal road conditions. The fare is 55B for air-con or 35B for an ordinary bus.

From the bus terminal, head to Tha Seri Khani Kaset, take a 20B water taxi to the floating market or simply walk 10 minutes west and south from the terminal along the canal until you come to the Hia Kui market area, where most of the rental boats are found.

Some people spend the night in Nakhon Pathom and catch an early morning bus to Samut Songkhram, asking to be let out at Damnoen Saduak.

It is also possible to get to Damnoen Saduak by bus (8B) from Samut Songkhram, a trip of around 25 minutes; Samut Songkhram is much closer to Damnoen Saduak (20 minutes by bus), and some people find it a better place to stay. A songthaew to/from Ratchaburi costs 25B.

One interesting way to return to Bangkok from Damnoen Saduak is by boat via Samut Sakhon. From Khlong Damnoen Saduak, take a 30km trip by longtail boat to Bang Yang lock (around 400B for up to four people), where you can catch a bus or songthaew to Samut Sakhon (you may have to change in Kratum Baen along the way). From there, you can take bus or train to Bangkok. (See the Samut Sakhon section for details.)

## SAMUT SAKHON
### อ.เมืองสมุทรสาคร

Twenty-eight kilometres south-west of Bangkok, Samut Sakhon (Ocean City; population 57,500) is popularly known as Mahachai because it straddles the confluence of the Mae Nam Tha Chin and Khlong Mahachai. Just a few kilometres from the Gulf of Thailand, this busy port features a lively market area and a pleasant breezy park around the crumbling walls of **Wichian Chodok Fort**. A few rusty cannons pointing towards the river testify to the fort's original purpose of guarding the mouth of the Mae Nam Chao Phraya from foreign invaders. Before the arrival of European traders in the 17th century, the town was known as Tha Jiin (Chinese Pier) because of the large number of Chinese junks that called here.

Samut Sakon set a macabre world record in December 1997 when the skeletal remains of 21,347 unclaimed road accident victims (many from Bangkok) were cremated in a specially built electric crematorium at the edge of town. The cremation of the corpses, which had been collected over an 11-year period by the Paw Tek Teung Foundation (a Chinese benevolent society dedicated to this purpose), took seven days of constant burning to complete.

A few kilometres west of Samut Sakhon, along Hwy 35, is the Ayuthaya-period **Wat Yai Chom Prasat**, which is known for the finely carved wooden doors on its bòt. You can easily identify the wat from the road by the tall Buddha figure standing at the front. To get here from Samut Sakhon, take a westbound bus (3B) heading towards Samut Songkhram. The wat is only a 10-minute ride from the edge of town.

In Ban Phaew district, around 30km northwest of Samut Sakhon via Hwy 35 (west) and Route 3079 (north), **Khlong Pho Hak Floating Market** (talàat náam khlawng phoh hàk) convenes daily except on wan phrá (full and new moon days) from 4 am to 7.30 or 8 am. To get there, take a songthaew or bus to Ban Phaew (around 10B), then catch a longtail boat along Khlong Pho Hak to the market 8km away – if you share with a group of Thais going to the market the fare should be no more than 10B each. It may also be possible to reach this market by chartered longtail boat from Samut Sakhon through a network of canals. The market is also known as talàat náam làk hâa (Km 5 floating market).

The Jao Mae Kuan Im Shrine at **Wat Chawng Lom** is a 9m-high fountain in the shape of the Mahayana Buddhist Goddess of Mercy, and popular with regional tour groups. The colourful image, which pours a constant stream of water from a vase in the goddess's right hand, rests on an artificial hill into which a passageway is carved leading to another Kuan Im shrine.

To get there from the ferry terminal at the harbour end of Th Sethakit (Tha Mahachai), take a ferry (1B) to Tha Chalong, and from there take a motorcycle taxi (10B) for the 2km ride to Wat Chawng Lom.

## Places to Stay & Eat

Inland from the park, Samut Sakhon is basically a gritty urban satellite of Bangkok. The selection of places to stay is pretty downbeat and we don't recommend an overnight here. Nonetheless if you're stuck, you can try the **Wiang Thai Hotel** (☎ 034-411151, 821/5 Th Sukhonthawit), where grubby rooms with fans cost 240B.

Towards the harbour, Th Norasing (off Th Sethakit) fills with *food stalls* at night, making it a great spot for inexpensive seafood dinners. **Tarua Restaurant** (Tha Reua Restaurant), on three floors of the ferry terminal building at the harbour end of Th Sethakit, has good seafood dishes from 60B to 200B and an English-language menu. A five-minute walk from Wat Chong Lom, down the road running along the side of the temple opposite the Kuan Im statue, is **Khrua Chom Ao** (☎ 034-422997), an open-air seafood restaurant with a view of the gulf. Prices are similar to those at Tarua, though locals reckon Khrua Chom Ao is better.

**New Rot Thip** (formerly New Sathip) and **Wang Nam Khem** at 927/42 and 927/179 Th Sethakit serve standard Thai and Chinese dishes at reasonable prices.

## Getting There & Away

**Bus** Ordinary buses to Samut Sakhon (25B) depart from Bangkok's Southern bus terminal all day long. The trip takes about an hour. Buses between Samut Sakhon and Samut Songkhram cost 14B and take about half an hour.

**Train** Samut Sakhon is nearly midway along the 3rd-class, short-line 'Mahachai' train route that runs between Thonburi's Wong Wian Yai station and Samut Songkhram. You won't find the Mahachai short line listed on any published State Railway of Thailand (SRT) schedule, whether English or Thai, as it's strictly a local proposition.

The fare to/from either Thonburi or Samut Songkhram is 10B; there are four departures a day: 7.30 and 10.10 am and 1.30 and 4.40 pm heading south, and at similar times heading north from Samut Sakhon.

You can continue to Samut Songkhram by train from Samut Sakon by crossing the river at Ban Laem.

## Getting Around

Samlors and motorbike taxis around town cost 20B to 30B depending on the distance.

## SAMUT SONGKHRAM

## อ.เมืองสมุทรสงคราม

Wedged between Ratchaburi, Samut Sakhon and Phetburi, 416-sq-km Samut Songkhram (population 35,000) is Thailand's smallest province. Commonly known as 'Mae Klong', the capital lies along a sharp bend in the Mae Nam Mae Klong, 74km south-west of Bangkok and just a few kilometres from the Gulf of Thailand. Due to flat topography and abundant water sources, the area surrounding the capital is well suited for the steady irrigation needed to grow guava, lychee and grapes. Along the highway from Thonburi, visitors will pass a string of artificial sea lakes used in the production of salt. A profusion of coconut palms makes the area look unusually lush, considering its proximity to Bangkok.

Samut Songkhram would make a good jumping-off point for early morning forays to Damnoen Saduak floating markets, 20 minutes away by bus. It has some decent – and less touristed – floating markets of its own as well.

## Information

The Thai Farmers Bank at 125/5 Th Prasitphatthana offers foreign exchange services 10 am to 4 pm weekdays.

## Things to See

The capital itself is a fairly modern city with a large market area between the train line and bus terminal. The sizeable **Wat Phet Samut Worawihan**, in the centre of town near the train station and river, contains a renowned Buddha image called Luang Phaw Wat Ban Laem – named after the *phrá sàksìt* (holy monk) who dedicated it, thus transferring mystical powers to the image.

At the mouth of the Mae Nam Mae Klong, not far from town, is the province's most famous tourist attraction, a bank of fossilised shells known as **Don Hoi Lot**. These shells come from *hǎwy làwt*, clams with a tube-like shell. The shell bank is best seen late in the dry season when the river surface has receded to its lowest height (typically April and May). Many seafood restaurants have been built at the edge of Don Hoi Lot, encroaching on a crab-eating macaque habitat. About 200 remaining monkeys are threatened by the development. To get to Don Hoi Lot you can hop a songthaew in front of Somdet Phra Phuttalertla Hospital at the intersection of Th Prasitwatthana and Th Thamnimit; the trip takes about 15 minutes. Or you can charter a boat from the Mae Klong Market pier *(thâa talàat mâe klawng)*, a scenic journey of around 45 minutes.

**Wat Satthatham**, 500m down the road to Don Hoi Lot, is notable for its bòt constructed of golden teak and decorated with 60 million baht worth of mother-of-pearl inlay. The inlay completely covers the temple's interior and depicts scenes from the jataka above the windows and the *Ramakian* below.

**King Buddhalertla (Phuttha Loet La) Naphalai Memorial Park**, a 10-minute walk from Amphawa Floating Market, is a museum housed in a collection of traditional central Thai houses set on four landscaped acres. Dedicated to King Rama II, a native of Amphawa district, the museum contains a library of rare Thai books, antiques from early 19th-century Siam and an exhibition of dolls depicting four of Rama II's theatrical works *(Inao, Manii Phichai, Ramakian, Sang Thong)*. Behind the houses is a lush botanical garden and beyond that is a dramatic arts training hall. To get there from Amphawa Floating Market, walk over the bridge and follow the road through the gardens of Wat Amphawan Chetiyaram. The park is open 9 am to 6 pm daily, and the museum is only open 9 am to 4 pm Wednesday to Sunday; admission is 10B.

**Ban Benjarong** This is a small factory (☎ 034-751322) in a modern house that produces top quality *benjarong,* the traditional five-coloured Thai ceramics. Here you can watch craftsmen painting the intricate arabesques and ornate floral patterns for which benjarong is known. This isn't the glossy stuff you see at Chatuchak Weekend Market in Bangkok, but the real thing. Prices start at about 1000B and a showroom displays various styles. Ban Benjarong is only about 1km from the park, but it's better to take a 10B motorcycle taxi from there as it's easy to get lost; it's open daily.

Another local attraction is the **Orchid Farm**, 4km north of town on the road to Damnoen Saduak. In spite of its basic commercial function – and side function as a tourist trap – the farm is really quite impressive for its colour. A bus to the farm costs 5B and takes about 10 minutes.

Some of the most picturesque countryside I've seen this close to Bangkok lies along Rte 325 between Damnoen Saduak and Samut Songkhram. Coconut plantations interspersed with small wooden houses line the road and add to the tropical-pastoral atmosphere.

**Floating Markets** Samut Songkhram Province is crisscrossed with canals intersecting the lazy bends of the Mae Nam Mae Klong, creating the perfect environment for traditional Thai floating markets. Three of the better ones are held in Amphawa district, about 7km north-west of the Samut Songkhram city via the Mae Nam Mae Klong. The **Amphawa Floating Market** (talàat náam ampháwaa) convenes daily in front of Wat Amphawa from 6 to 8 am but is best on weekends. The other two meet only six days a month following the traditional lunar calendar: **Bang Noi Floating Market** takes place in nearby Bang Noi from 6 to 11 am on the third, eighth and 13th days of both the waxing and waning moons, while the **Tha Kha Floating Market** meets on the second, seventh and 12th days of the waxing and waning moons. The latter convenes along an open, breezy khlong lined with greenery and older wooden houses – well worth seeking out.

Any common Thai calendar, available for a few baht in a housewares market, will show you which days of the solar month coincide with this lunar schedule. These floating markets can be visited by chartered longtail boat from the Mae Klong Market pier – figure on paying 150B to 200B per hour depending on negotiation, or 300B for all morning, a price usually agreed upon without negotiation.

## Places to Stay & Eat

There are four hotels in the centre of the city, none of them very quiet. The cheapest is the **Thai Sawat** (☎ 034-711205, 524 Th Phet Samut), where basic rooms with fan and shared bath cost 100B. Also inexpensive is the nearby **Mae Klong Hotel** (☎ 034-711150, 546/10-13 Th Phet Samut), opposite Wat Phet Samut Worawihan on Th Si Champa. The owners speak some English and can provide information about the area. The rooms are fairly clean and cost 180B with a fan or 300B with air-con, or 400B with air-con and TV.

Somewhat better, the **Alongkorn 1 Hotel** (☎ 034-711017, 541/15 Th Kasem Sukhum) and **Alongkorn 2 Hotel** (☎ 034-711709, 540 Th Pomkaew) are only separated by the cinema on busy Th Kasem Sukhum. They have very similar rooms and standards, and cost 150B with fan and 200B with air-con.

In front of Mae Klong Market are several **food stalls** open all day and evening. There is also a lively **night market** in the square near the bus and taxi stands along Th Prasitphatthana. **Suan Ahan Tuk**, at Don Hoi Lot, offers an extensive Thai and Chinese menu.

In the Chinese shophouse, the friendly **Meng Khao Mu Daeng** (☎ 034-713422, 467 Th Phet Samut) offers excellent khâo mǔu daeng as well as khâo nâa pèt (clippings from a Matichon restaurant review on the wall attest to the duck's greatness). All dishes cost 20B. There is no roman-script sign.

**Isan Tai** (☎ 034-716503), an open-air restaurant on Th Ekachai opposite the telephone office, offers a wide range of Isan food. The grilled catfish is recommended; prices are 30B to 60B per dish. There is no roman-script sign.

**The Dollars Pub** (☎ 034-711344), near Wat Phet Samut, is an old-west-style restaurant/pub that offers Thai food from 80B per dish. It also has a band on weekends and is open 7 pm to midnight.

On weekends, the more adventurous might try *Jungle Home Pub*, a Thai-folk-style cafe set in a rambling garden at the end of Soi Thanai Khong, off Th Ekachai. It's hard to find on your own, but a túk-túk from the market should only cost 15B. It's run by a bohemian Thai couple and is a good spot to enjoy a beer or herbal liquor at the end of the day. It's only open from 4 pm Friday, Saturday and Sunday evening.

### Getting There & Away

**Bus** Buses and taxis park at the intersection of Th Ratchayat Raksa and Th Prasit-phatthana. Buses from Bangkok's Southern bus terminal to Damnoen Saduak also stop here, but some buses from Bangkok may drop you off on the main highway, from where you can either walk or take a samlor or a songthaew (5B). Air-con buses to Bangkok leave from the Damnoen Tour office next to Bangkok Bank. The fare is 35B in an ordinary bus or 55B for a bus with air-con; either takes about 1½ hours. There are also many daily buses to Samut Sakhon for 14B, taking about an hour.

**Train** Samut Songkhram is the southernmost terminus of a 70km railway that originates at Thonburi (Wong Wian Yai) station, a journey of about an hour. The all 3rd-class train to/from Bangkok costs 20B (10B to/from Samut Sakhon) and there are four departures per day (see the Samut Sakhon Getting There & Away section for current times). From Samut Songkhram trains depart at 6.20, 9 and 11.30 am and 3.30 pm. The train station is a five-minute walk from the bus terminal, where Th Kasem Sukhum terminates at Th Prasitphatthana near the river.

## KANCHANABURI

อ.เมืองกาญจนบุรี

Kanchanaburi (population 38,100) lies 130km west of Bangkok in the slightly elevated valley of the Mae Nam Mae Klong amid hills and sugar cane plantations. It was originally established by Rama I as a first line of defence against the Burmese who, it was commonly believed, might use the old invasion route through the Three Pagodas Pass on the Thai-Burmese border. It's still a popular smuggling route into Burma today.

During WWII, the Japanese used Allied prisoners of war to build the infamous Death Railway along this same invasion route, though in reverse, along the Mae Nam Khwae Noi (Little Tributary River) to the pass. Thousands and thousands of prisoners died as a result of brutal treatment by their captors, a story chronicled by Pierre Boulle's book *The Bridge on the River Kwai* and popularised by a movie based on the same. The bridge is still there (still in use, in fact) and so are the graves of the Allied soldiers. The river is actually spelled and pronounced Khwae, like 'quack' without the '-ck'.

The town itself has a certain atmosphere, and whatever you may think of its war history, it's a fine place to hang out for a while. The weather is slightly cooler than in Bangkok and the evenings are especially pleasant. Although Meuang Kan (as the locals call it; also Kan'buri) gets enough tourists to warrant its own tourist office, not many Western visitors make it here – most are Thai, Japanese, or Hong Kong and Singapore Chinese, who blaze through on air-con buses, hitting the River Khwae Bridge, the cemetery on Th Saengchuto, the River Kwai Hotel, and then hurry off to the nearby sapphire mines or one of the big waterfalls before heading north to Chiang Mai or back to Bangkok.

The Mae Nam Mae Klong itself is a focus for much weekend and holiday activity among the Thais. In recent years the city has given the waterfront area a face-lift, planting casuarina trees and moving most of the floating restaurants offshore. A new bridge spanning the river, another bridge on the way and a new highway bypass north-east of town signify that development has arrived in what was previously a provincial backwater.

### Death Railway Bridge

สะพานข้ามแม่น้ำแคว

The so-called 'Bridge on the River Kwai' looks quite ordinary, but its dramatic story may be of interest. The bridge spans the Mae

EXCURSIONS

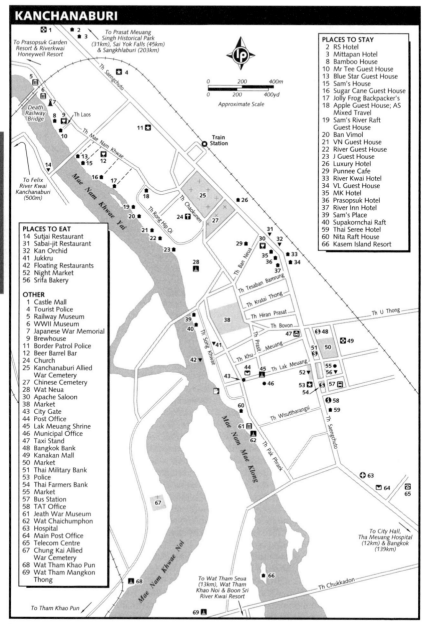

# KANCHANABURI

To Prasopsuk Garden
Resort & Riverkwai
Honeywell Resort

To Prasat Meuang
Singh Historical Park
(31km), Sai Yok Falls (45km)
& Sangkhlaburi (203km)

Death
Railway
Bridge

Th Laos

Th Mae Nam Khwae

To Felix
River Kwai
Kanchanaburi
(500m)

Mae Nam Khwae Yai

Th Saengchuto

Train
Station

Th Chaokunen

Th Rong Hip Oi

Th Ban Neua

Th Tesaban Bamrung

Th Kratai Thong

Th Hiran Prasat

Th U Thong

Th Bovon

Th Prasit Meuang

Th Khu

Th Lak Meuang

Th Song Khwae

Mae Nam Mae Klong

Th Pak Phraek

Th Saengchuto

Th Wisuttharangsi

Mae Nam Khwae Noi

Th Chukkadon

To City Hall,
Tha Meuang Hospital
(12km) & Bangkok
(139km)

To Wat Tham Seua
(13km), Wat Tham
Khao Noi & Boon Sri
River Kwai Resort

To Tham Khao Pun

## PLACES TO STAY
2 RS Hotel
3 Mittapan Hotel
8 Bamboo House
10 Mr Tee Guest House
13 Blue Star Guest House
15 Sam's House
16 Sugar Cane Guest House
17 Jolly Frog Backpacker's
18 Apple Guest House; AS
   Mixed Travel
19 Sam's River Raft
   Guest House
20 Ban Vimol
21 VN Guest House
22 River Guest House
23 J Guest House
26 Luxury Hotel
29 Punnee Cafe
33 River Kwai Hotel
34 VL Guest House
35 MK Hotel
36 Prasopsuk Hotel
37 River Inn Hotel
39 Sam's Place
40 Supakornchai Raft
59 Thai Seree Hotel
60 Nita Raft House
66 Kasem Island Resort

## PLACES TO EAT
14 Sutjai Restaurant
31 Sabai-jit Restaurant
32 Kan Orchid
41 Jukkru
42 Floating Restaurants
52 Night Market
56 Srifa Bakery

## OTHER
1 Castle Mall
4 Tourist Police
5 Railway Museum
6 WWII Museum
7 Japanese War Memorial
9 Brewhouse
11 Border Patrol Police
12 Beer Barrel Bar
24 Church
25 Kanchanaburi Allied
   War Cemetery
27 Chinese Cemetery
28 Wat Neua
30 Apache Saloon
38 Market
43 City Gate
44 Post Office
45 Lak Meuang Shrine
46 Municipal Office
47 Taxi Stand
48 Bangkok Bank
49 Kanakan Mall
50 Market
51 Thai Military Bank
53 Police
54 Thai Farmers Bank
55 Market
57 Bus Station
58 TAT Office
61 Jeath War Museum
62 Wat Chaichumphon
63 Hospital
64 Main Post Office
65 Telecom Centre
67 Chung Kai Allied
   War Cemetery
68 Wat Tham Khao Pun
69 Wat Tham Mangkon
   Thong

Approximate Scale

0    200    400m
0    200    400yd

Nam Khwae Yai, a tributary of the Mae Nam Mae Klong, 3km from Kanchanaburi's *làk meuang* (town pillar/phallus). Khwae Yai literally translates as 'large tributary'.

The materials for the bridge were brought from Java by the Imperial Japanese Army during their occupation of Thailand. In 1945 the bridge was bombed several times and was only rebuilt after the war – the curved portions of the bridge are original. The first version of the bridge, completed in February 1943, was all wood. In April of the same year a second bridge of steel was constructed.

It's estimated 16,000 prisoners of war (POWs) died building the Death Railway to Myanmar, of which the bridge was only a small part. The objective of the railway was to secure an alternative supply route for the Japanese conquest of Burma and other Asian countries to the west. Construction of the railway began on 16 September 1942 at existing terminals in Thanbyuzayat, Myanmar and Nong Pladuk, Thailand. Japanese engineers at the time estimated that it would take five years to link Thailand and Myanmar by rail, but the Japanese army forced the POWs to complete the 415km, 1m-gauge railway (of which roughly two-thirds ran through Thailand) in 16 months. Much of the railway was built in difficult terrain that required high bridges and deep mountain cuttings. The rails were finally joined 37km south of Three Pagodas Pass; a Japanese brothel train inaugurated the line. The River Khwae Bridge was in use for 20 months before the Allies bombed it in 1945. Only one POW is known to have escaped, a Briton who took refuge among pro-British Karen guerrillas.

Although the number of POWs who died during the Japanese occupation is horrifying, the figures for the labourers, many from Thailand, Myanmar, Malaysia and Indonesia, are even worse. It is thought that 90,000 to 100,000 coolies died in the area.

Today little remains of the original railway. West of Nam Tok, Karen and Mon minorities carried off most of the track to use in the construction of local buildings and bridges.

Train enthusiasts may enjoy the **railway museum** in front of the bridge, with engines used during WWII on display. Every year during the first week of December there is a nightly sound-and-light show at the bridge, commemorating the Allied attack on the Death Railway in 1945. It's a big scene, with the sounds of bombers and explosions, fantastic bursts of light and more. The town gets a lot of Thai tourists during this week, so book early if you want to witness this spectacle.

There are a couple of large outdoor restaurants near the bridge on the river, but these are for tour groups that arrive en masse throughout the day. If you're hungry, you can save money by eating with the tour bus and songthaew drivers in the little noodle places at the northern end of Th Pak Phraek.

**Getting There & Away** The best way to get to the bridge from town is to catch a songthaew along Th Pak Phraek (parallel to Th Saengchuto towards the river) heading north. Regular songthaews are 5B and stop at the bridge, which is about 3km from the *làk meuang* (town pillar/phallus). You can also take a train from Kanchanaburi train station to the bridge for 2B.

## Allied War Cemeteries

สุสานทหารสงครามโลกครั้งที่ ๒

There are two cemeteries containing the remains of Allied POWs who died in captivity during WWII; one is north of town off Th Saengchuto, just before the train station, and the other is across the Mae Nam Mae Klong west of town, a few kilometres down the Mae Nam Khwae Noi.

The **Kanchanaburi Allied War Cemetery** is better cared for, with green lawns and healthy flowers. It's usually a cool spot on a hot Kanchanaburi day. It's only a 15-minute walk from the River Kwai Hotel or you can catch a songthaew or orange minibus (No 2) anywhere along Th Saengchuto going north – the fare is 5B. Jump off at the English sign in front of the cemetery on the left, or ask to be let off at the *sùsǎan* (cemetery). Just before the cemetery on the same side of the road is a colourful **Chinese cemetery** with burial mounds and inscribed tombstones.

To get to the **Chung Kai Allied War Cemetery**, take a 5B ferry boat from the pier at the west end of Th Lak Meuang across the Mae Klong, then follow the curving road through picturesque corn and sugar cane fields until you reach the cemetery on your left. This is a fairly long walk, but the scenery along the way is very pleasant. You can also easily take a bicycle over the new bridge here. Like the more visited cemetery north of town, the Chung Kai burial plaques carry names, military insignia, and short epitaphs for Dutch, British, French and Australian soldiers. This cemetery sees fewer tourists than the other one.

About 1km south-west of the Chung Kai cemetery is a dirt path that leads to **Wat Tham Khao Pun**, one of Kanchanaburi's many cave temples. The path is approximately 1km long and passes through thick forest with a few wooden houses along the way. This wat became notorious in late 1995 when a drug-addicted monk living at the wat murdered a British tourist and disposed of her corpse in a nearby sinkhole. Kanchanaburi residents – like the rest of Thailand – were mortified by the crime and many now refer to the cave as 'Johanne's Cave' in memory of the victim. The monk was de-frocked and sentenced to death (commuted to life imprisonment without parole by the king in 1996).

### JEATH War Museum
พิพิธภัณฑ์สงคราม

This odd museum next to Wat Chaichumphon (Wat Tai) is worth visiting just to sit on the cool banks of the Mae Klong. Phra Maha Tomson Tongproh, a Thai monk who devotes much energy to promoting the museum, speaks some English and can answer questions about the exhibits, and supply information about sight-seeing around Kanchanaburi. The museum itself is a replica example of the bamboo huts used to house Allied POWs during the occupation. The long huts contain various photographs taken during the war, drawings and paintings by POWs, maps, weapons and other war memorabilia. The acronym JEATH represents the fated meeting of Japan, England,

Australia/America, Thailand and Holland at Kanchanaburi during WWII.

The war museum is at the end of Th Wisuttharangsi (Visutrangsi), near the TAT office. The common Thai name for this museum is *phíphítháphan sŏngkhram wát tâi* (Wat Tai War Museum). It's open 8.30 am to 6 pm daily; admission is 30B.

### Lak Meuang Shrine
ศาลหลักเมือง

Like many other older Thai cities, Kanchanaburi has a làk meuang (town pillar/phallus) enclosed in a shrine at what was originally the town centre. Kanchanaburi's Lak Meuang Shrine is appropriately located on Th Lak Meuang, which intersects Th Saengchuto two blocks north of the TAT office.

The bulbous-tipped pillar is covered with gold leaf and is much worshipped. Unlike Bangkok's Lak Meuang you can get as close to this pillar as you like – there's no curtain.

Within sight of the pillar, towards the river, stands Kanchanaburi's original **city gate**.

### WWII Museum
พิพิธภัณฑ์สงครามโลกครั้งที่ ๒

Also called Art Gallery & War Museum, this new, somewhat garish structure just south of the famous bridge on the river looks like a Chinese temple on the outside. The larger, more lavishly built of the two buildings has nothing to do with WWII and little to do with art unless you include the garish murals throughout. The bottom floor contains Burmese-style alabaster Buddhas and a *phrá khrêuang* (sacred amulets) display. Upper floors exhibit Thai weaponry from the Ayuthaya period and a fair collection of historic and modern ceramics. Brightly painted portraits of all the kings in Thai history fill the 4th floor. Finally, on the 5th and uppermost floor – above the royal portraits (flirting with lese-majesty) – is the history of the Chinese family who built the museum, complete with a huge portrait of the family's original patriarch in China.

A smaller building opposite contains WWII relics, including photos and sketches made during the POW period, and a display of Japanese and Allied weapons. Along the front of this building stand life-size sculptures of historical figures associated with the war, including Churchill, MacArthur, Hitler, Einstein, de Gaulle and Hirohito. The English captions are sometimes unintentionally amusing or disturbing – a reference to the atomic bomb dropped on Hiroshima, for example, reads 'Almost the entire city was destroyed in a jiffy'. Inside, a glass case contains 106 skeletons unearthed in a mass grave of Asian labourers. The gossip around town says these remains were stolen from a municipal excavation. The museum is open 9 am to 6 pm daily; entry is 30B.

## Wat Tham Mangkon Thong
วัดถ้ำมังกรทอง

The Cave Temple of the Golden Dragon is well known because of the 'floating nun' – a *mâe chii* (Thai Buddhist nun) who meditates while floating on her back in a pool of water. If you are lucky you might see her, but she seems to be doing this less frequently nowadays (try a Sunday). A nun now in her early 80s began the floating tradition and has passed it on to a younger disciple. Thais come from all over Thailand to see the younger nun float and to receive her blessings. A sizeable contingent of young Thai nuns stay here under the old nun's tutelage.

A long and steep series of steps with dragon-sculpted handrails lead up the craggy mountainside behind the main bòt to a complex of limestone caves. Follow the string of light bulbs through the front cave and you'll come out above the wat with a view of the valley and mountains below. One section of the cave requires crawling or duck-walking, so wear appropriate clothing. Bats squeak away above your head and the smell of guano permeates the air.

Another cave wat is off this same road about 1km to 2km from Wat Tham Mangkon Thong towards the pier. It can be seen on a limestone outcrop back from the road some 500m or so. The name is **Wat Tham Khao**

**Laem**. The cave is less impressive than that at Wat Tham Mangkon Thong, but there are some interesting old temple buildings on the grounds.

**Getting There & Away** Heading southeast down Th Saengchuto from the TAT office, turn right on Th Chukkadon (marked in English – about halfway between the TAT and main post office), or take a songthaew (5B) from the town centre to the end of Th Chukkadon. A bridge has replaced the river ferry that used to cross here; wait for any songthaew crossing the bridge and you can be dropped off in front of the temple for 5B.

The road to the wat passes sugar cane fields, karst formations, wooden houses, cattle and rock quarries. Alternatively you could ride a bicycle from town – the road can be dusty in the dry season but at least it's flat.

## Wat Tham Seua & Wat Tham Khao Noi
วัดถ้ำเสือและวัดถ้ำเขาน้อย

These large hill-top monasteries about 15km south-east of Kanchanaburi are important local pilgrimage spots, especially for Chinese Buddhists. Wat Tham Khao Noi (Little Hill Cave Monastery) is a Chinese temple monastery similar in size and style to Penang's Kek Lok Si. Adjacent is the half-Thai, half-Chinese-style Wat Tham Seua (Tiger Cave Monastery). Both are built on a ridge over a series of small caves. Wat Tham Khao Noi isn't much of a climb, since it's built onto the side of the slope. Seeing Wat Tham Seua, however, means climbing either a steep set of *naga* (mythical giant sea serpent) stairs or a meandering set of steps past the cave entrance.

A climb to the top is rewarded with views of the Mae Nam Khwae on one side and rice fields on the other. Wat Tham Seua features a huge sitting Buddha facing the river, with a mechanical conveyor belt that carries money offerings to a huge alms bowl in the image's lap. The easier set of steps to the right of the temple's naga stairs leads to a cave and passes an aviary with peacocks and other exotic birds. The cave itself has the usual assortment of Buddha images.

**Getting There & Away** By public transport, you can take a bus (5B) to Tha Meuang (12km south-east of Kanchanaburi), then a motorcycle taxi (30B) from near Tha Meuang Hospital directly to the temples.

If you're travelling by motorcycle or bicycle, take the right fork of the highway when you reach Tha Meuang, turn right past the hospital onto a road along the canal and then across the dam (Meuang Dam). From here to Wat Tham Seua and Khao Noi is another 4km. Once you cross the dam, turn right down the other side of the river and follow this unpaved road 1.4km, then turn left towards the pagodas, which can easily be seen in the distance at this point. The network of roads leading to the base of the hill offers several route possibilities – just keep an eye on the pagodas and you'll be able to make the appropriate turns.

By bicycle, you can avoid taking the highway by using back roads along the river. Follow Th Pak Phraek and Th Mae Nam Khwae in Kanchanaburi south-east and cross the bridge towards Wat Tham Mangkon Thong, then turn left on the other side and follow the gravel road parallel to the river. Eventually (after about 14km) you'll see the Kheuan Meuang (Meuang Dam) up ahead – at this point you should start looking for the hill-top pagodas on your right. This makes a good day trip by bicycle – the road is flat all the way and avoids the high-speed traffic on the highway. You can break your journey at Ban Tham, a village along the way with its own minor cave wát.

### Boat Trips
**Rafts** Several small-time enterprises offer raft trips up and down the Mae Nam Mae Klong and its tributaries. The typical raft is a large affair with a two-storey shelter that will carry 15 to 20 people. The average rental cost per raft is 1500B for half a day or 3500B for an overnight trip, divided among as many people as you can fit on the boat. Such a trip would include stops at Hat Tha Aw, Wat Tham Mangkon Thong, Khao Pun Cave and

the Chung Kai Allied War Cemetery, plus all meals and one night's accommodation on the raft. Alcoholic beverages are usually extra. Bargaining can be fruitful as there are said to be over 500 rafts available in the city.

Inquire at any guesthouse, the TAT office or at the main pier at the end of Th Lak Meuang about raft trips. Perhaps the best are those arranged by groups of travellers who get together and plan their own raft excursions with one of the raft operators.

**Longtail Boats** One way to see the same river sights at a lower cost is to hire a longtail boat instead of a raft. Longtails cost around 400B per hour and can take up to six passengers. For 800B, a group could take a two-hour longtail trip to the JEATH Museum, Wat Tham Khao Pun, Chung Kai Allied War Cemetery and the Death Railway Bridge. Longtails can be hired from the boat pier off Th Song Khwae or at the JEATH Museum.

### Places to Stay – Budget
Kanchanaburi has numerous places to stay in every price range but especially in the guesthouse category. Those along the river can be a little noisy on weekends and holidays due to the floating disco traffic (although they now stop by 11 pm), so choose your accommodation carefully. Inevitably, there are even karaoke rafts now!

The popularity of floating accommodation has seen a profusion of 'raft rooms' being added to the choice of accommodation at riverfront guesthouses. These are essentially rooms constructed on a platform that rests on steel pontoons. Some guesthouses that offer raft rooms are trying to cut their expenses by pumping river water into their guests' bathrooms – not a healthy situation if you consider that waste water and sewage are dumped directly into the river. A few guesthouses have gone to great trouble to hide their illicit plumbing from guests. At other establishments the set up is in plain view. If you are in doubt, before agreeing to take a room simply fill the bathroom sink with water. It will be readily apparent if the water came from the river or not.

Samlor drivers get a 50B to 100B commission for each foreign traveller they bring to guesthouses from the bus or train station (on top of what they charge you for the ride), so don't believe everything they say with regard to 'full', 'dirty' or 'closed' – see for yourself. Most guesthouses will provide free transport from the bus or train station if you call.

**On the River** Down on the river, at the junction of the Mae Nam Khwae and Mae Nam Khwae Noi, is *Nita Raft House* (☎ 034-514521, 27/1 Th Pak Phraek), where older singles/doubles with mosquito net are 60B, doubles with fan 100B, or with private shower 150B. It's basic but quite well run, though you should heed the warning about floating discos on weekends and holidays. The manager speaks English and can provide information on the local sights and activities.

Near the floating restaurants is *Sam's Place* (☎ 034-513971, fax 512023, 7/3 Th Song Khwae), a rambling affair of linked raft houses. A room with fan and private bath is 150B for a single or double. For 300B you can get a room with air-con. The raft has a small coffee shop. A drawback to Sam's is that it's within range of the floating discos.

Next to Sam's Place is *Supakornchai Raft* (☎ 034-512055, 7/4 Th Song Khwae), which is similar but not quite as nice. Raft rooms with fan and bath are 150B to 200B for a large bed, or 300B to 400B for two large beds.

Two places a little closer to the city centre are the *River Guest House* (☎ 034-512491, 42 Soi Rong Hip Oi 2, Th Mae Nam Khwae)* and the *J Guest House* (☎ 034-620307). Both are located in a hyacinth-choked lagoon and have raft rooms with shared bath for 40B to 80B single and 120B to 150B double.

Just upriver is the *VN Guest House* (☎ 034-514082, 44 Soi Rong Hip Oi 2, Th Mae Nam Khwae), where small, basic raft rooms are 50B to 70B, with bath 150B and with air-con 300B. All are in the same vicinity on the river, not far from the train station. They tend to get booked out in the high season.

*Ban Vimol* (☎ 034-514831, 48/5 Soi Rong Hip Oi 2, Th Mae Nam Khwae) is along the river just upriver from the VN guesthouses. Tastefully decorated bamboo accommodation with fan and private bath costs 300B on the river, 250B back from the river. A bit farther north on the river, *Sam's River Raft Guest House* has raft rooms with private bath, fan or air-con for 250B and 350B. There is also a restaurant and sunbathing platform.

Continuing along a bend in the river road, *Apple Guest House* (☎ 034-512017), not actually on the river but under a huge mango tree near the intersection of Th Mae Nam Khwae and Th Rong Hip Oi, offers one-bed bungalows for 150B and two-bed bungalows for 200B, all with clean toilet and shower, fan and screened doors to allow for better ventilation. The guesthouse restaurant gets rave reviews and one-day Thai cooking courses are offered. The guesthouse is locally owned and very friendly.

North along Th Mae Nam Khwae is the *Jolly Frog Backpacker's* (☎ 034-514579, 28 Soi China), a comparatively huge, 50-room 'bamboo motel' with good security and a popular but nothing-special restaurant. Singles/doubles with shared bath are 60/110B (120B for a double room on the river); doubles with private bath are 150B. For samlor transport to any guesthouse in this vicinity, you shouldn't pay more than 20B from the train station, or 30B from the bus terminal.

About 100m upriver is the newly built *Sugar Cane Guest House* (☎ 034-624520, 22 Soi Pakistan, Th Mae Nam Khwae), which has comfortable rooms on a raft with a wide veranda as well as bungalows and a riverside restaurant. Raft rooms are all doubles with private bath and cost 200B and 400B, depending on the size of the room. Bungalow doubles with private bath are 150B or 250B for a larger room. The management is friendly and helpful.

A bit farther north-west, near the bridge that crosses over to Sutjai Restaurant, *Sam's House* (☎ 034-515956, fax 512023) features a variety of accommodation – from raft rooms to rooms in an L-shaped stone building to bungalows. Prices are 150B for fan and private bath to 300B for air-con. As

EXCURSIONS

at the original Sam's Place, there is a terrace restaurant.

Nearby is the newly opened **Blue Star Guest House** (☎ 034-512161), which has A-frame bungalows, all with private bath, for 150/300B for fan cooled singles/doubles and 380B for air-con singles. Discounts are offered for long-term stays. There is also an open-air restaurant on the premises with acoustic Thai music in the evenings.

Continuing upriver, at the end of Th Laos, is quiet **Mr Tee Guest House** (☎ 034-625103), another two-storey thatched bamboo place. Rooms upstairs are 150B without bath, while downstairs rooms are 200B with private bath; all with fans. The guesthouse dining area sits on a floating raft moored to the shore, and there are pleasant sitting areas on the grounds.

If you want to stay out near the Mae Nam Khwae bridge (and away from the floating discos), the locally owned and well-kept **Bamboo House** (☎ 034-624470, 3-5 Soi Vietnam, Th Mae Nam Khwae), on the river about 1km before the Japanese war memorial, costs 200B per room with shared bath, 300B with fan and private bath, 500B with air-con, or 800B with TV and fridge. The owners are very friendly and the setting is peaceful.

**In Town** The three-storey **VL Guest House** (☎ 034-513546), across the street from the River Kwai Hotel, has clean, spacious rooms with fan, TV and hot-water shower for 250B single/double, 350B single/double with air-con. The VL has a small dining area downstairs and there is a generous 2 pm checkout.

Next door is the similar **Prasopsuk Hotel** (☎ 034-511777). Rooms with fan and TV cost 200/300B, air-con singles with phone are 400B and air-con doubles (no phone) are 550B. The restaurant serves inexpensive Thai dishes.

South of the River Kwai Hotel on Saengchuto, on the site of what once held an earlier version of the same hotel, the **River Inn Hotel** (☎ 034-621056) has decent air-con rooms with TV and hot-water shower from 360B.

The **Sri Muang Kan** (☎ 034-511609, 313/1-3 Th Saengchuto), at the northern end of Saengchuto, with clean singles/doubles with fan and bath for 200B, or 370B with air-con, and the **Thai Seree Hotel** (☎ 034-511128) at the southern end of the same road, near the Th Visutrangsi intersection and the TAT office, with somewhat dilapidated but adequate rooms with fan for 150B or 250/350B for air-con singles/doubles.

The bungalow-style **Luxury Hotel** (☎ 034-511168, 284/1-5 Th Saengchuto) is a couple of blocks north of the River Kwai Hotel, and not as centrally located. All rooms have air-con and cost 350B to 800B.

## Places to Stay – Top End

Kanchanaburi's original 1st-class hotel, the **River Kwai Hotel** (☎ 034-513348, fax 511269, 284/3-16 Th Saengchuto), offers semi-deluxe rooms with air-con, hot-water shower, fridge, telephone and TV from 960B. Facilities include a coffee shop, karaoke bar, disco and swimming pool. Next door is the huge River Paradise massage parlour, bearing a sign on the door that reads 'No women allowed' (working masseuses are exempted, of course).

South of the River Kwai Hotel, the relatively new multistorey, 52-room **MK Hotel** (☎ 034-621143/4) on Th Saengchuto has two-bed air-con rooms for 250B; for 50B more you can add either TV or hot-water shower. Rooms with all the amenities are available for 400B (500B with breakfast).

Farther north along Th Saengchuto, past the train station, is the four-storey **Mittapan Hotel** (☎ 034-515904, fax 514499). Standard rooms with all the amenities cost 650B to 5000B. A large massage parlour and snooker club are next door.

Next comes the nicer **RS Hotel** (☎ 034-625128, fax 514499, 264 Th Saengchuto). Rooms cost 700B to 6000B and there's a swimming pool.

The luxurious **Felix River Kwai Kanchanaburi** (☎ 034-515061, fax 515095; in Bangkok ☎ 255 3410, fax 255 5767) sits on the west bank of the river, about 2km north of the new one-lane bridge. The nicely landscaped grounds include two swimming pools. Spacious rooms and suites with IDD phones, cable TV, fridge and personal safe cost 3000B to 20,000B. Nonguests may use the pool for 50B.

**River Resorts** The *Kasem Island Resort* (☎ *034-513359; in Bangkok* ☎ *255 3604*) sits on an island in the middle of the Mae Nam Mae Klong just about 200m from Tha Chukkadon. The tastefully designed thatched cottages and house rafts are cool, clean, quiet and go for 750B to 1300B. There are facilities for swimming, fishing and rafting, as well as an outdoor bar and restaurant. The resort has an office near Tha Chukkadon where you can arrange for a free shuttle boat out to the island; shuttle service stops at 10 pm.

North of the Death Railway Bridge are several river resorts of varying quality, most featuring standard wooden bungalows for about 800B. Just above the bridge, 2km before the turn-off for Rte 323, is the 50-room *Prasopsuk Garden Resort* (☎ *034-513215*) with air-con townhouse doubles for 600B, air-con bungalows with two bedrooms for 1200B and large bungalows sleeping 10 people for 4000B per night. The *Riverkwai Honeywell Resort* (☎ *034-515413; in Bangkok* ☎ *221 5472*) offers 20 bungalows with private bath on the river bank for 600B to 800B.

On the river, opposite Wat Tham Mangkon Thong to the south, the similar *Boon Sri River Kwai Resort* (☎ *034-515143; in Bangkok* ☎ *415 5875, 420 8518*) charges 350B to 800B a night.

## Places to Eat

The greatest proliferation of inexpensive restaurants in Kanchanaburi is along the northern end of Th Saengchuto near the River Kwai Hotel. From here south, to where Th U Thong crosses Saengchuto, are many good Chinese, Thai and Isan-style restaurants. As elsewhere in Thailand, the best are generally the most crowded.

The air-conditioned *Kan Orchid*, next to the River Kwai Hotel on Th Saengchuto, has a good selection of Thai food and also offers reasonably priced sandwiches, baked goods and ice cream. It's a good place to escape the midday heat.

The restaurant at *Apple Guest House*, about 100m south of Jolly Frog, goes way above and beyond normal guesthouse fare. Both the *kaeng mátsàman* (Muslim-style curry) and *phàt thai* are highly recommended. Apple also does what is perhaps the best banana pancake in Thailand.

Good, cheap eating places can be found in the *markets* along Th Prasit. In the evenings, a sizeable *night market* convenes along Th Saengchuto near the Th Lak Meuang intersection.

The *Sabai-jit Restaurant*, north of the River Kwai Hotel on Th Saengchuto, has an English menu. Beer and Mekong whisky are sold here at quite competitive prices and the food is consistently good. Other Thai and Chinese dishes are served apart from those listed on the English menu. If you see someone eating something not listed, point.

*Punnee Cafe & Bar* (☎ *034-513503*) on Th Ban Neua serves Thai and European food according to expat tastes and advertises the coldest beer in town. Lots of information on Kanchanaburi is available here; there are also used paperback books for sale or trade. If you're in the mood for Western food and air-con ambience, there are fast-food outlets at both Kanakan Mall near the bus terminal and Castle Mall on Th Saengchuto on the northern outskirts of town.

Down on the river are several large floating restaurants where the quality of the food varies but it's hard not to enjoy the atmosphere. Most cater to Thais out for a night of drinking and snacking, so if you go, don't expect Western food or large portions – if you know what to order, you could have a very nice meal here. Recommended is the *Mae Nam*. Across from the floating restaurants, along the road, are several restaurants that are just as good but less expensive; the best on this row is *Jukkru* (no roman-script sign – look for blue tables and chairs). Although it's a little out of the way, one of the better riverside restaurants in town is *Sutjai*, a garden-style place on the west bank of the river next to the one-lane bridge.

There are also *food vendors* on both sides of Th Song Khwae along the river near the new park where you can buy inexpensive

EXCURSIONS

takeaway and picnic on mats along the riverbank. This is a festive and prosperous town and people seem to eat out a lot.

The *Srifa Bakery* on the north side of the bus terminal has everything from Singapore-style curry puffs to French-style pastries.

## Entertainment

If the floating discos and karaoke bars on the river or the disco at the River Kwai Hotel don't appeal to you, try the *Apache Saloon* opposite the Sabai-jit Restaurant on Th Saengchuto. This large, old-West-style bar/restaurant offers live folk-rock music nightly. *The Raft*, in front of the River Kwai Hotel, also features live Thai bands.

The *Beer Barrel Bar*, 100m north of Sugar Cane Guest House on Th Mae Nam Khwae, is a nicely done outdoor beer garden with good prices. Between Mr Tee's and Bamboo House on the corner of Th India and Th Mae Nam Khwae is another beer garden called *Brew House*.

## Getting There & Away

**Bus** Ordinary buses leave Bangkok daily from the Southern bus terminal in Thonburi every 20 minutes (first bus 5 am, last at 10 pm) for Kanchanaburi. The trip takes about three hours and costs 41B. Return buses to Bangkok leave Kanchanaburi between the same hours. Air-con (2nd class) buses cost 55B; leaving at similar intervals

First-class air-con buses leave Bangkok's Southern bus terminal every 15 minutes from 5.30 am to 10.30 pm for 68B. These same buses depart from Kanchanaburi for Bangkok from opposite the police station on Th Saengchuto – not from the bus terminal. Air-con buses only take about two hours to reach Bangkok. The first bus out is at 4 am; the last one to Bangkok leaves at 7 pm.

Buses leave frequently throughout the day from nearby Nakhon Pathom, cost 25B and take about 1½ hours. For travellers heading south, Nakhon Pathom makes a good connecting point – this way you avoid having to go back to Bangkok. Other frequent direct bus services are available to/from Ratchaburi (No 461, 31B, 2½ hours) and Suphanburi (No 411, 34B, 2½ to three hours).

**Train** Ordinary trains leave Thonburi (Bangkok Noi) station at 7.45 am and 1.45 pm, arriving at 10.55 am and 4.35 pm. Only 3rd-class seats are available and the fare is 25B. Trains return to Bangkok (Thonburi) from Kanchanaburi at 7.27 am and 2.50 pm, arriving at 10.35 am and 6.10 pm. Ordinary train tickets to Kanchanaburi can be booked on the day of departure only. There are no trains between Bangkok's Hualamphong station and Kanchanaburi.

You can also take the train from the Kanchanaburi station out to the Death Railway Bridge, a three-minute ride for 2B. There are three trains per day at 6.11 am (No 485), 11.01 am (No 257) and 4.37 pm (No 259).

The same trains continue to the end of the railway at Nam Tok, which is near Nam Tok Sai Yok (Sai Yok Falls). You can catch the train in Kanchanaburi as mentioned earlier, or at the bridge at 6.18 and 11.08 am and 4.44 pm; the fare is the same (17B). Nam Tok is 8km from Nam Tok Khao Pang and 18km from Hellfire Pass and the Mae Nam Khwae village. The trip to Nam Tok takes about two hours. Coming back from Nam Tok, there are trains at 5.25 am and 1 and 3.15 pm. The early morning trains between Kanchanaburi and Nam Tok (6.11 am) do not run on weekends and holidays.

**Tourist Train** The State Railway of Thailand (SRT) has a special tourist train from Bangkok's Hualamphong station on weekends and holidays that departs around 6.30 am and returns at 7.55 pm. The one-way/return fare is 250B for adults, 120B for children. It includes an hour-long stop in Nakhon Pathom to see the Phra Pathom Chedi, an hour at the Death Railway Bridge, a minibus to Prasat Meuang Singh Historical Park for a short tour, a walk along an elevated 'Death Railway' bridge (no longer in use), a three-hour stop at the river for lunch and a bat cave visit, before returning to Bangkok with a one-hour stopover at one of the war cemeteries. Also on weekends and holidays there's a direct steam train between Kanchanaburi to Wang Pho (10.25 am departure, 2 pm return, with a 90-minute stopover at the waterfall), no stops, for 100B one way or 150B return. These tickets should be booked in advance, although it's worth trying on the day even if you're told it's full. The SRT changes the tour itinerary and price from time to time. Call ☎ 034-561052 for further information or check out the SRT Web site at www.srt.motc.go.th.

**Share Taxi & Minivan** You can also take a share taxi from Th Saengchuto to Bangkok for 60B per person. Taxis leave throughout the day whenever five passengers accumulate at the taxi stand. These taxis will make drops at Th Khao San or in the Phahurat district. Kanchanaburi guesthouses also arrange daily minivans to Bangkok for 100B per person. Passengers are dropped at Th Khao San.

## Getting Around

The easiest way to get around town is on foot or by bicycle. If you're not up to it, samlor rides should cost around 20B per kilometre; however, drivers may try and charge up to 10 times that amount! A samlor or motorcycle taxi from the bus or train stations to the river area and most guesthouses should cost 20B to 30B. Songthaews run up and down Th Saengchuto and Th Pak Phraek for 5B per passenger.

Bicycles and motorcycles can be rented at some guesthouses, at the Suzuki dealer near the bus terminal, at the Punnee Cafe and at the motorcycle repair shop near Sam's Place. Expect to pay 150B to 250B per day for a motorbike (more for a dirt bike), 50B a day for bicycles. Punnee Cafe also rents mountain bikes for 80B per 24 hours.

The river ferry across the Mae Klong costs 5B per person. Sometimes there's an extra few baht charge for bikes (motor or push) taken on the ferry, though usually it's included in the 5B fare.

## KO SAMET

เกาะเสม็ด

This T-shaped island earned a permanent place in Thai literature when classical Thai poet Sunthorn Phu set part of his epic *Phra Aphaimani* on its shores. The story follows the travails of a prince exiled to an undersea kingdom ruled by a lovesick female giant. A mermaid aids the prince in his escape to Ko Samet where he defeats the giant by playing a magic flute. Formerly Ko Kaew Phitsadan (Vast Jewel Isle) – a reference to the abundant white sand – this island became known as Ko Samet (Cajeput Isle) after the cajeput *(samèt)* tree that grows in abundance here and is very highly valued as firewood throughout South-East Asia. Locally, the samet tree has also been used in boat building.

In the early 1980s, the tiny 13.1-sq-km island began receiving its first visitors interested in more than cajeput trees and sand – young Thais in search of a retreat from city life. At that time there were only about 40 houses on the island, built by fisherfolk and Ban Phe locals. Rayong and Bangkok speculators saw the sudden interest in Ko Samet as a chance to cash in on an up-and-coming Phuket and began buying up land along the beaches. No one bothered about the fact that Ko Samet, along with Laem Ya and other nearby islands, had been a national marine park since 1981.

When farangs started coming to Ko Samet in greater and greater numbers, spurred on by rumours that Ko Samet was similar to Ko Samui '10 years ago' (one always seems to miss it by a decade, eh?), the National Parks Division stepped in and built a visitors office on the island, ordered that all bungalows be moved back behind the tree line and started charging a 5B admission into the park.

This entry fee has since risen to 200B for foreigners (100B for children 14 and under) and 20B for Thais. There are separate park units at each beach in charge of fees collection. There are now plenty of vehicles on the island, more frequent boat services from Ban Phe and a much improved water situation. Ko Samet is a very dry island (which makes it an excellent place to visit during the rainy season). Before they started trucking water to the bungalows you had to bathe at often muddy wells. Now most of the bungalow places have proper Thai-style bathrooms and Ko Samet is a much more comfortable place to visit, though it sometimes becomes overcrowded.

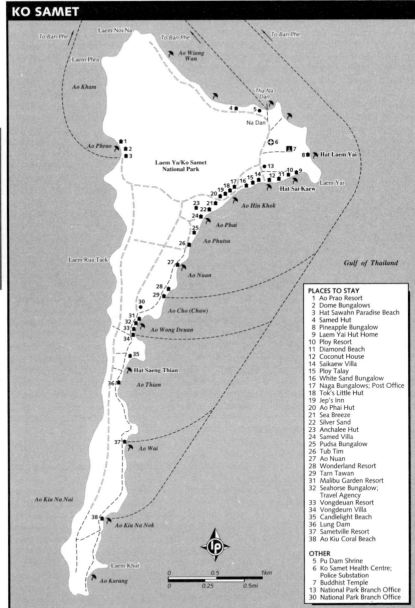

# KO SAMET

EXCURSIONS

**PLACES TO STAY**
1 Ao Prao Resort
2 Dome Bungalows
3 Hat Sawahn Paradise Beach
4 Samed Hut
8 Pineapple Bungalow
9 Laem Yai Hut Home
10 Ploy Resort
11 Diamond Beach
12 Coconut House
14 Saikaew Villa
15 Ploy Talay
16 White Sand Bungalow
17 Naga Bungalows; Post Office
18 Tok's Little Hut
19 Jep's Inn
20 Ao Phai Hut
21 Sea Breeze
22 Silver Sand
23 Anchalee Hut
24 Samed Villa
25 Pudsa Bungalow
26 Tub Tim
27 Ao Nuan
28 Wonderland Resort
29 Tarn Tawan
31 Malibu Garden Resort
32 Seahorse Bungalow;
   Travel Agency
33 Vongdeuan Resort
34 Vongdeurn Villa
35 Candlelight Beach
36 Lung Dam
37 Sametville Resort
38 Ao Kiu Coral Beach

**OTHER**
5 Pu Dam Shrine
6 Ko Samet Health Centre;
   Police Substation
7 Buddhist Temple
13 National Park Branch Office
30 National Park Branch Office

Entrance to ruins of Wat Ratburana, Ayuthaya

GLENN BEANLAND

Withun Thatsana, Bang Pa-In

TOM COCKREM

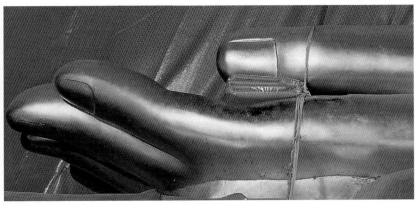

A monk's saffron robe placed in buddha's hand, Wat Phra Mongkhon Bophit, Ayuthaya.

FRANK CARTER

The Death Railway Bridge over River Kwai, Kanchanaburi

PATRICK HORTON

View from the end of a pier at Ao Cho, Ko Samet

FRANK CARTER

Because of a ban on new accommodation (except where it replaces old sites), bungalows are spread thinly over most of the island, with the north-east coast being the most crowded. The beaches really are lovely, with the whitest, squeakiest sand in Thailand. There is even a little **surf** occasionally (best months are December to January).

In spite of the fact that the island is supposedly under the protection of the National Parks Division, on recent trips to Ko Samet I have been appalled at conditions in the Na Dan and Hat Sai Kaew areas. Piles of rubbish and construction materials spoil the island's charm at the northern end. Once you get away from this end of the island, however, things start looking a bit better.

Ko Samet can be very crowded during Thai public holidays (see Public Holidays & Special Events in the Facts for the Visitor chapter). During these times there are people sleeping on the floors of beach restaurants, on the beach – everywhere. September gets the lowest number of visitors (average 2500), March the most (around 40,000, approximately 36,000 of them Thai). Thais in any month are more prevalent than foreigners but many are day visitors; most stay at Hat Sai Kaew or Ao Wong Deuan in more upmarket accommodation.

It should also be pointed out that Ko Samet has what is probably Thailand's largest and most loathsome collection of stray dogs, many of them with advanced cases of mange. They can be especially disturbing during meal times when, hopeful for a handout, the crusty curs park themselves nearby and stare longingly at your food. And if that weren't enough, once night falls the dogs sometimes raise such an astounding din that some visitors find that only by drinking large quantities of alcohol are they able to fall asleep.

A couple of times the Forestry Department has temporarily closed the park to all visitors in an effort to halt encroachment on national park lands; so far they've always reopened the island within a month or less in response to protests by resort operators. Developers objected that if Ko Samet is to be closed, then so must Ko Phi Phi. Court hearings continue with no verdict in sight; until a decision is reached, a permanent moratorium on new developments remains in place in order to preserve the island's forested interior.

## Information

The park has a main office near Hat Sai Kaew, and a smaller one at Ao Wong Deuan. An excellent guide to the history, flora and fauna of Ko Samet is Alan A Alan's 94-page *Samet,* published by Asia Books. Instead of writing a straightforward guidebook, Alan has woven the information into an amusing fictional travelogue involving a pair of Swedish twins on their first trip to the island.

**Post & Communications** A small post office next to Naga Bungalows has poste restante. It's open 8.30 am to noon and 1 to 4.30 pm weekdays, and 8.30 am to noon Saturday. There is Internet access at a shop next to the post office.

**Travel Agencies** There are several small travel agencies near Na Dan and on Hat Sai Kaew and Ao Wong Deuan that can arrange long-distance phone calls, bus and train reservations, and air ticketing.

**Medical Services** The Ko Samet Health Centre, a small public clinic, is located midway between the village harbour and Hat Sai Kaew. English-speaking doctors are on hand to help with problems like heat rash, or bites from poisonous sea creatures or snakes.

*Malaria* Ko Samet, like much of coastal Thailand along the eastern shore of the Gulf, carries a higher risk of malaria than most other parts of the country. You may want to consider taking preventive medication before vacationing here, particularly during the rainy season months (June to October). If not, take a little extra care.

## Activities

Most of the bungalows on the island can arrange boat trips to nearby reefs and uninhabited islands. Ao Phutsa, Naga Beach (Ao Hin Khok), Hat Sai Kaew and Ao Wong Deuan have **windsurfing-equipment** rental places that do boat trips as well. Typical day trips to Ko Thalu, Ko Kuti etc cost about 400B per person, including food and beverages (minimum of 10 people). Sailboards, **boogie boards** and inner tubes can be rented from a number of guesthouses.

## Places to Stay

The two most developed beaches are Hat Sai Kaew and Ao Wong Deuan. All of the other spots are still rather peaceful. Every bungalow operation on the island has at least one restaurant and most now have running water and electricity. Most places have electric power from 5 or 6 pm until 6 am; only the more upmarket places have 24-hour power.

Thanks to healthy competition, even the most expensive places offer accommodation discounts during the high season. Very basic small huts cost 100B to 120B, similar huts with fan and bath start from 150B to 200B. Bungalows with furniture and air-con start at 600B. Most places offer discounts for stays of four or more days, while on weekends and public holidays most will raise their rates to meet the demand – sometimes dramatically.

Some resorts, mostly around the Hat Sai Kaew area, have also been known to boot out foreigners without warning to make room for free-spending Thai tour groups. You won't need to worry about this at reputable spots, like Naga Bungalows and Samed Villa. But even so, if possible avoid Ko Samet during peak times, especially public holidays.

Since this is a national park, *camping* is allowed on any of the beaches. In fact, this is a great island for camping as it hardly ever rains, there's plenty of room (most of the island is uninhabited) and, so far, tourism is pretty much restricted to the north-eastern and north-western beaches.

## Places to Stay – East Coast

**Hat Sai Kaew** Samet's prettiest beach, 'Diamond Sand', is 1km or so long and 25 to 30m wide. The bungalows here happen to be the most commercial on the island, with videos in the restaurants at night and lots of electric lights. They're all very similar and offer a range of accommodation from 120B (in the low season) for simple huts without

fan or bath, 200B to 600B with fan, mosquito net and private bath, or as high as 2500B with air-con. All face the beach and most have outdoor restaurants serving a variety of seafood. Like elsewhere in Thailand, the daily rate for accommodation can soar suddenly with demand, though the more scrupulous places don't hike rates by much.

*Coconut House* (☎ 038-651661) has 30 bungalows. Prices are 350B with fan to 800B with air-con, TV and fridge. *Diamond Beach* (☎ 038-652514) offers fan bungalows for 350B or with air-con for 500B to 900B. Another option is *Ploy Talay* (☎ 01-218 7636), with rooms for 400B to 800B, all with private bath. There is also a disco but it doesn't seem to get much use. Prices at the *White Sand Bungalow* (☎ 038-653154) cost 300B for a fan room or 400B to 1500B for air-con. Also along this stretch are the *Ploy Resort,* with concrete bungalows, all with private bath, for 300B with fan and 600B to 800B for air-con. (Breakfast is included with air-con rooms.) A better choice is *Laem Yai Hut Home* (☎ 038-651956), which has spacious wooden bungalows with verandas. Rooms with fan and bath are 700B.

*Saikaew Villa* (☎/fax 038-651852) is a huge top-end complex off the prettiest part of the beach with fan rooms from 700B to 1300B, 1650B and up for air-con and TV. Breakfast is included. It boasts 24-hour power – try to get a room away from the noisy generators. Discounts for long-term stays are available.

**Ao Hin Khok** The beach here is about half the size of Hat Sai Kaew but just as pretty – the rocks that give the beach its name add a certain character. It's separated from Hat Sai Kaew by a rocky point surmounted by a mermaid statue, a representation of the mermaid that carried the mythical Phra Aphaimani to Ko Samet in the Thai epic of the same name. Ao Hin Khok and Ao Phai, the next inlet south, offer the advantage of having among the least expensive huts on the island along with reasonably priced restaurants serving good food.

Two of Samet's original bungalow operations still reign here – *Naga* (☎ 01-218

*5372)* and *Tok's Little Hut*. Naga offers simple bungalows set on a hill overlooking the sea for 100B and decent ones with a good mattress from 120B. Its restaurant sells great bread (it is distributed to several other bungalows on the island), cookies, cakes, pizzas and other pastries. There is also Internet access, a bar and a tatty pool table. Bungalows at Tok's Little Hut are a little more solid and have fan and bath, and go for 200B to 300B, depending on proximity to the generator.

Farther down the road is *Jep's Inn*, with nicely designed, clean bungalows with bath and fan for 350B and 500B. Its restaurant (no videos) is also quite good, and there's a nice shaded dining area right at the edge of the beach. Jep's is probably the most pleasant accommodation in the area.

Farther down the beach you may see what looks like a Thai 'gathering of the tribes' – a colourful outpost presided over by Chawalee, a free-spirited Thai woman who has lived on this beach since long before the bungalows came.

**Ao Phai** Around the next headland is another shallow bay with a nice wide beach, though it can get fairly crowded. At the northern end is the friendly *Ao Phai Hut (☎ 01-213 6392),* which has screened bungalows with bath and fan for 300B, 400B and 1000B, depending on size. Air-con bungalows are 700B, 800B and 2000B; weekends and holidays add 200B. Electricity is available from 5 pm to 6 am. The staff organise tours around the island, and it has an international telephone and basic postal services.

Next door, *Sea Breeze (☎/fax 01-239 4780)* has rather closely spaced bungalows, all with bath, for 400B with fan and 650B air-con. Adjacent is a small shop and a bookshop and library (no exchanges), and international phone and fax services. Next is *Silver Sand (☎ 01-218 5195),* which has fan bungalows for 250B to 300B and air-con for 400B to 800B, all with attached bath and 24-hour electricity.

Swiss-run *Samed Villa (☎ 01-494 8090)* has very clean, screened, well-maintained tree-shaded bungalows with large verandas from 600B for smaller units with private bath to 1000B for family accommodation – 24-hour electricity is offered. The food is quite good, and some of the bungalows have great sea views. This is also one of the few places in the area that doesn't screen videos at night.

About 30m behind Samed Villa in a small compound is *Anchalee Hut*, with clean wooden bungalows with fan and bath for 150B to 300B.

Near Sea Breeze the main road south to Ao Wong Deuan turns inland and heads down the middle of the island. A little farther along the road from here is where the cross-island road to Ao Phrao on the west coast starts.

**Ao Phutsa** On Ao Phutsa, also known as Ao Thap Thim, you'll find *Pudsa Bungalow (☎ 01-663 1371),* where huts with fan and bath cost 350B and 400B. Some of the huts are close to the water, making them good value for money. At the southern end of the beach *Tub Tim (☎ 01-218 6425)* has fan bungalows on a hillside for 200B to 700B, while air-con bungalows cost 1200B. All bungalows have attached bath.

After Ao Phutsa, the remaining beaches south are separated from one another by fairly steep headlands. To get from one to the next, you have a choice of negotiating rocky paths over the hilly points or walking west to the main road that goes along the centre of the island, then cutting back on side roads to each beach.

**Ao Nuan** If you blink, you'll miss this beach, which is one of the more secluded places to stay without having to go to the far south of the island. The bungalows at *Ao Nuan* have shared bath and intermittent electricity and vary in size. Some are little more than bamboo huts. Prices are 150B to 400B. The food is quite good here and the eating area is set in an imaginatively arranged garden. It's a five-minute walk over the headland from Ao Phutsa.

**Ao Cho (Chaw)** A five-minute walk across the next headland from Ao Nuan, this bay has its own pier and can be reached directly from Ban Phe on the boat, *White Shark,* or aboard the supply boat. Though just north of crowded Ao Wong Deuan, it's fairly quiet here, though the beach is not among Ko Samet's best.

At the northern end of the beach, **Wonderland Resort** (☎ *01-438 8409*) has basic, rather scruffy bungalows with shower and toilet for 150B to 500B, more on weekends and holidays. Huts with fan and bath at **Tarn Tawan** are quite OK and cost 400B to 600B. The restaurant at Tarn Tawan specialises in Isan food.

**Ao Wong Deuan** This once gorgeous bay is now filled with speedboats and jet skis, and there's a lot of accommodation packed into a small area, making things a bit cramped. The crescent-shaped beach is still nice, but it is noisy and often crowded. The best of the lot is **Vongdeuan Resort** (☎ *038-651777, fax 651819)*, with bungalows for 800B, complete with running water, flush toilet and fan. Air-con costs 1100B to 1200B.

**Vongduern Villa** (☎ *038-652300)* is similar in amenities but all bungalows have air-con, with prices from 650B to 2500B.

The **Malibu Garden Resort** (☎ *038-651057)* has well-built brick or wood bungalows with fan for 800B to 1100B, air-con for 1500B to 2200B; the more expensive rooms have TV. Breakfast is included. If you tire of the scene at the beach, this place even has a swimming pool.

**Seahorse Bungalow** (☎ *01-451 5184)* has practically taken over the beach-front with two restaurants, a travel agency, and bungalows with fan and bath for 600B. Air-con bungalows go for 800B to 1000B.

Three boats go back and forth between Ao Wong Deuan and Ban Phe – the *Malibu, Seahorse* and *Vongduern*.

**Ao Thian** From this point south things start to get much quieter. Better known by its English name, 'Candlelight Beach', the bay is quite scenic, and rocky outcrops break up the beach, though there's plenty of sand to stretch out upon. Unfortunately, the bungalow operations here are no great shakes.

On the bay's northern end is **Candlelight Beach** (☎ *01-218 6934)* with fan and bath bungalows for 400B to 700B, depending on proximity to the beach. Electricity is on from 6 pm to 6 am. At the southern end of the bay, **Lung Dam** (☎ *01-458 8430)* charges 200B for quite roughly built huts with shared bath and 400B for huts with attached bath. There is also an interesting treehouse you can rent for 150B per night. Keep in mind you're captive of only two guesthouse kitchen choices here; you may want to bring some of your own food from the village on the northern tip of the island.

**Other Bays** You really have to be determined to get away from it all to go farther south on the east coast of Ko Samet, but it can be well worth the effort. Lovely **Ao Wai** is about 1km from Ao Thian and can be reached by the boat *Phra Aphai* from Ban Phe, which sails once a day and charges 50B per person. There's only one bungalow operation here, the very private **Sametville Resort** (☎ *038-651681;* in Bangkok ☎ *246 3196)*, which offers a fine combination of upscale accommodation and isolation. Two-bed bungalows with attached bath cost 800B to 900B with fan, or 1300B with air-con. Most bookings are done by phone, but you can try your luck by contacting someone on the *Phra Aphai* at the Ban Phe piers.

A 20-minute walk over the rocky shore from Ao Wai, **Ao Kiu Na Nok** had only one place to stay at the time of writing – the friendly and clean **Ao Kiu Coral Beach** (☎ *01-218 6231)*. Bamboo huts are 200B, unattractive but better equipped cement huts cost 300B to 600B. **Tents** may be rented for 100B a night. The beach here is gorgeous, one of the nicest on the island. Another plus is that it's a five minute walk to the western side of the island and a view of the sunset.

## Places to Stay – West Coast

**Hat Ao Phrao** This is the only beach on the west side of the island, and it has nice sunset views. In Thai the name means 'Coconut Bay Beach' but bungalow operators tend to use the clichéd 'Paradise Beach' moniker. So far there are no jet-skis on this side of the island, so it tends to be quieter than the island's east coast. Local bungalow operators also do a good job of keeping the beach clean.

At the northern end of the beach is *Ao Prao Resort* (☎ *438 9771)*, where attractive air-con bungalows with large verandas are surrounded by lush landscaping. Amenities include cable TV and hot-water attached bath, and perhaps the best restaurant on the island. Rates are 1900B to 3150B. Add 500B on weekends and holidays. **Ao Prao Divers** at the resort offers diving, windsurfing, kayaking and boat trips.

In the middle of the beach is *Dome Bungalows* (☎ *038-651377, fax 652600)*, which has nice fan and bath bungalows on the hillside for 800B to 900B, or 1000B to 1100B for air-con. Breakfast is included. There's a pleasant restaurant serving Thai and international dishes.

At the southern end near the cross-island trail is the friendly *Hat Sawahn Paradise Beach* (☎ *01-912 4587)*, where rustic wooden bungalows with fan and bath cost 400B. Electricity is on from 6 pm to 8 am. An attached restaurant serves Thai and international food.

There is a daily boat between Ban Phe and Ao Phrao for 80B per person.

### Places to Stay – Na Dan Area
To the north-west of Ko Samet's main pier is a long beach, Ao Wiang Wan, where several rather characterless bungalows are set up in straight lines facing the mainland. Here you get neither sunrise nor sunset. The best place is *Samed Hut* (☎ *01-818 3051; in Bangkok* ☎ *678 4645)*, which is shady and New Mexican in style with fan singles/doubles for 800B to 900B and air-con for 1000B to 1100B. All rooms have attached bath.

Between Na Dan and Hat Sai Kaew, along the north-east corner of the island, are a couple of small beach bays with bungalow operations. Hardly anyone seems to stay here. *Pineapple Bungalow* at Laem Yai beach (also known as Ao Yon) charges 300B per bungalow. When we visited this looked like it was soon to be abandoned.

### Places to Eat
All bungalows except Anchalee Hut, Laem Yai Hut Home and Pineapple have restaurants offering mixed menus of Thai and traveller food; prices are typically 30B to 50B per dish. Fresh seafood is almost always available and costs around 60B to 150B per dish. The pleasant *Bamboo Restaurant* at Ao Cho, behind Tarn Tawan, offers inexpensive but tasty food and good service. It's open for breakfast, lunch and dinner. *Naga* on Ao Hin Khok has a very good bakery with all kinds of breads and cakes. Ao Wong Deuan has a cluster of restaurants serving Western and Thai food: *Oasis*, *Nice & Easy* and *Tom's Restaurant*. At the southern tip of the beach, the *Vongduern Villa* restaurant is a bit more expensive, but both the food and the location are quite nice.

On Hat Sai Kaew, the *White Sands Restaurant* has good seafood in the 100B range. For cheaper fare on this beach, try the popular *Toy Restaurant*, next to Saikaew Villa. *Samet Beach Restaurant* next to Diamond Hut has also been recommended for good food with reasonable prices and friendly staff. Probably the best eatery on the island is the fancy open-air terrace restaurant at Ao Prao Resort.

### Getting There & Away
**Bus** Many Th Khao San agencies in Bangkok organise transport to Ko Samet, including boat, for 170B (300B return). This is more expensive than doing it on your own, but it's convenient for travellers who don't plan to go anywhere else on the east coast.

If you want the flexibility and economy of arranging your own travel, take a bus to Ban Phe in Rayong Province, then catch a boat to Ko Samet. There are regular buses to Rayong throughout the day from the Eastern bus terminal, but if your destination is Ban Phe (for Ko Samet) it's better to take one of the direct Ban Phe buses, which only cost 7B more; a songthaew to Ban Phe from Rayong costs 15B. The Bangkok to Rayong air-con bus is 101B, Bangkok to Ban Phe is 108B. Cheaper is the ordinary bus to Rayong (87B) and then a local bus to Ban Phe. Buses from Bangkok stop in Ban Phe in front of the restaurant opposite Tha Saphan Nuan Tip. Air-con buses between Rayong and Bangkok's Eastern bus terminal take around 3½ hours, ordinary buses about an hour longer.

Ordinary buses to Chanthaburi from Rayong cost 52B and take about 2½ hours. To get one of these, you need to catch a motorcycle taxi (10B) to the bus stop on Th Sukhumvit (Hwy 3).

Minibuses to Bangkok's Th Khao San and Pattaya can be arranged through several of the guesthouses on Samet or through travel agencies in Ban Phe. Minibuses to Bangkok leave at 10 am and 2 pm and cost 200B. Minibuses to Pattaya leave at 10 am and 1.30 and 5 pm and cost 150B. All leave from the vicinity of Saphan Sri Ban Phe pier.

**Boat** There are various ways to get to/from the island by boat.

*To Ko Samet* There are three piers: Saphan Nuan Tip for the regularly scheduled passenger boat; Saphan Mai for supply boats; and Saphan Sri Ban Phe for tour groups. Saphan Nuan Tip is usually the only one you'll need, but if you arrive between passenger-boat departure times you can try for a ride aboard one of the cargo boats from Saphan Mai (you must still pay the regular passenger fare). Saphan Nuan Tip is also where buses from Bangkok arrive and depart. It's best to avoid the Saphan Sri Ban Phe pier: without a doubt there are more sharks at the ticket booths here than in the surrounding waters.

Passenger boats to Ko Samet leave at regular intervals throughout the day starting at around 8 am and ending around 5 pm. Frequency depends on having sufficient passengers and/or cargo to make the trip profitable; departures are more frequent in the high season (December to March). At least three or four boats a day go to Na Dan and Ao Wong Deuan year-round.

It can be difficult to find the boat you need, as agents and boat owners are intensely aware of their competitors. In most cases they'll be reluctant to tell you about another boat. Some travellers have reported being hassled by 'agents' who present photo albums of bungalows on Samet, claiming that they must book a bungalow for several days in order to get onto the island. This is false; ignore these touts and head straight for the boats. Report any problems to the TAT office in Rayong.

Probably the best place to head is the Saphan Nuan Tip ticket office, behind all the food and souvenir stalls. They sell tickets for a number of different boat operators, and also provide information on private resort boats.

For Hat Sai Kaew, Ao Hin Khok, Ao Phai and Ao Phutsa, catch a boat to Na Dan. These generally leave as soon as there are at least 20 passengers: the round-trip fare is 80B. Ignore touts or ticket agents who claim the fare is 100B or more. Simply climb into one of these boats and wait to pay the ticket collector directly. From Na Dan you can either walk to these beaches (10 to 15 minutes) or take one of the trucks that go round the island. See the Getting Around section for standard fares.

The Saphan Nuan Tip ticket office also has boats to Ao Wong Deuan (50B one way), Ao Phrao (80B) and Ao Wai (80B). All boats need at least seven people before they'll depart.

The Saphan Sri Ban Phe ticket office also sells tickets for Na Dan (40B), as well as Ao Wong Deuan (50B), Ao Wai (80B), Ao Kiu Na Nok (100B), Ao Phrao (80B), Ao Nuan and Ao Thian (50B). Again, go directly to the ticket office and ignore what touts tell you.

If you arrive in Ban Phe at night and need a boat to Samet, you can usually charter a one-way trip at the Ban Phe pier but prices are steep: plan on about 1500B to Na Dan.

*From Ko Samet* Samet Tour seems to run a monopoly on return trips from Na Dan and boats leave only when full – a minimum of 18 people for some boats, 25 for others – unless someone contributes more to the passage. The usual fare is 40B.

These days it's so easy to get boats back from the main beaches to Ban Phe that few tourists go to Na Dan to get a boat. There are four daily boats each from Ao Wong Deuan and Ao Cho, plus at least one daily boat from Ao Wai, Ao Kiu and Ao Phrao.

While waiting for a boat back to the mainland from Na Dan, you may notice a shrine not far from the pier. This *săan jâo phâw* (guardian deity shrine) is a spirit shrine to Puu Dam (Grandfather Black), a sage who once lived on the island. Worshippers offer statues of *reusĭi* (hermit sages), flowers, incense and fruit.

## Getting Around

If you take the boat from Ban Phe to the village harbour, Na Dan, you can easily walk the distance to Hat Sai Kaew, Ao Phai or Ao Phutsa. Don't believe the taxi operators who say that these beaches are a long distance away. If you're going farther down the island, or have a lot of luggage, you can take the taxi (which is either a truck or a three-wheeled affair with a trailer) as far as Ao Wong Deuan.

Set fares for transport around the island from Na Dan are posted on a tree in the middle of a square in front of the Na Dan harbour: 15B per person to Hat Sai Kaew (or 100B charter); 25B to Ao Phai or Ao Phutsa (150B to charter); 35B to Ao Wong Deuan or Ao Phrao (200B to charter); 45B to Ao Thian or Ao Wai (300B and 400B charter); and 60B to Ao Kiu Na Nok (500B charter). Exactly how many people it takes to constitute 'public service' rather than a 'charter' is not a hard and fast number. Figure on 30B per person for six to eight people to anywhere between Na Dan and Ao Cho. If there aren't enough people to fill the vehicle, they either won't go, or passengers will have to pay up to 200B to charter the vehicle.

There are trails from Ao Wong Deuan all the way to the southern tip of the island, and a few cross-island trails as well. Taxis will make trips to Ao Phrao when the road isn't too muddy.

Motorbikes can be rented from a number of bungalow operations on Hat Sai Kaew, Ao Phai and Ao Phrao. Figure on about 500B per day or an hourly rate of 150B.

# Language

Learning some Thai is indispensable for travelling in the kingdom; naturally, the more language you pick up, the closer you get to Thailand's culture and people. Foreigners who speak Thai are so rare in Thailand that it doesn't take much to impress most Thais with a few words in their own language.

Your first attempts to speak the language will probably meet with mixed success, but keep trying. When learning new words or phrases, listen closely to the way the Thais themselves use the various tones – you'll catch on quickly. Don't let laughter at your linguistic forays discourage you; this apparent amusement is an expression of appreciation. Thais are among the most supportive people in the world when it comes to foreigners learning their language.

Travellers, both young and old, are particularly urged to make the effort to meet Thai college and university students. Thai students are, by and large, eager to meet visitors from other countries. They will often know some English, so communication is not as difficult as it may be with shop owners, civil servants etc, plus they are generally willing to teach you useful Thai words and phrases.

For a handy pocket-size guide to Thai, get a copy of Lonely Planet's excellent *Thai phrasebook*; it contains a section on basic grammar and a broad selection of useful words and phrases for travel in Thailand.

Many people have reported modest success with *Robertson's Practical English-Thai Dictionary* (Charles E Tuttle Co, Tokyo), which has a phonetic guide to pronunciation with tones and is compact in size. If you have difficulty finding it, write to the publisher at 2-6 Suido 1-chome, Bunkyo-ku, Tokyo, Japan.

More serious learners of the language should get Mary Haas' *Thai-English Student's Dictionary* (Stanford University Press, Stanford, California) and George McFarland's *Thai-English Dictionary* (also Stanford University Press) – the cream of the crop. Both of these require that you know the Thai script. The US State Department's *Thai Reference Grammar* by RB Noss (Foreign Service Institute, Washington, DC, 1964) is good for an in-depth look at Thai syntax.

Other learning texts worth seeking out include:

*AUA Language Center Thai Course: Reading & Writing* (two volumes) – AUA Language Center (Bangkok), 1979

*AUA Language Center Thai Course* (three volumes) – AUA Language Center (Bangkok), 1969

*Foundations of Thai* (two volumes) – by EM Anthony, University of Michigan Press, 1973

*A Programmed Course in Reading Thai Syllables* – by EM Anthony, University of Hawaii, 1979

*Teaching Grammar of Thai* – by William Kuo, University of California at Berkeley, 1982

*Thai Basic Reader* – by Gething & Bilmes, University of Hawaii, 1977

*Thai Cultural Reader* (two volumes) – by RB Jones, Cornell University, 1969

*Thai Reader* – by Mary Haas, American Council of Learned Societies, Program in Oriental Languages, 1954

*The Thai System of Writing* – by Mary Haas, American Council of Learned Societies, Program in Oriental Languages, 1954

*A Workbook for Writing Thai* – by William Kuo, University of California at Berkeley, 1979

An interactive CD-ROM called *Learning Thai Script* (Allen & Unwin, 1997) is also an excellent resource for teaching yourself to read and write the Thai script.

For information on language courses, see Language under Courses in the Facts for the Visitor chapter.

## Dialects

Thailand's official language is Thai as spoken and written in central Thailand. This dialect has successfully become the lingua franca of all Thai and non-Thai ethnic groups in the kingdom. Of course, native Thai is spoken with differing tonal accents and with slightly differing vocabularies as you move from one part of the country to the next, especially in a north to south direction. But it is the central Thai dialect that is most widely understood.

All Thai dialects are members of the Thai half of the Thai-Kadai family of languages and are closely related to languages spoken in Laos (Lao, northern Thai, Thai Lü), northern Myanmar (Shan, northern Thai), north-western Vietnam (Nung, Tho), Assam (Ahom) and pockets of south China (Zhuang, Thai Lü). Modern Thai linguists recognise four basic dialects within Thailand: central Thai (spoken as a first dialect through central Thailand and throughout the country as a second dialect); northern-Thai (spoken from Tak Province north to the Myanmar border); north-eastern Thai (north-eastern provinces towards the Lao and Cambodian borders); and southern Thai (from Chumphon Province south to the Malaysian border). Each of these can be further divided into subdialects; north-eastern Thai, for example, has nine regional variations easily distinguished by those who know Thai well. There are also a number of Thai minority dialects such as those spoken by the Phu Thai, Thai Dam, Thai Daeng, Phu Noi, Phuan and other tribal Thai groups, most of whom reside in the north and north-east.

## Vocabulary Differences

Like most languages, Thai distinguishes between 'vulgar' and 'polite' vocabulary, so that *thaan*, for example, is a more polite everyday word for 'eat' than *kin*, and *sĭi-sà* for 'head' is more polite than *hŭa*. When given a choice, foreigners are better off learning and using the polite terms since these are less likely to lead to unconscious offence.

A special set of words, collectively called *kham raachaasàp* (royal vocabulary), is set aside for use with Thai royalty within the semantic fields of kinship, body parts, physical and mental actions, clothing and housing. For example, in everyday language Thais use the word *kin* or *thaan* for 'eat', while with reference to the royal family they say *sà wŏey*. For the most part these terms are used only when speaking to or referring to the king, queen and their children, hence as a foreigner you will have little need to learn them.

## Script

The Thai script, a fairly recent development in comparison with the spoken language, consists of 44 consonants (but only 21 separate sounds) and 48 vowel and diphthong possibilities (32 separate signs). Experts disagree as to the exact origins of the script, but it was apparently developed around 800 years ago using Mon and possibly Khmer models, both of which were in turn inspired by south Indian scripts. Like these languages, written Thai proceeds from left to right, though vowel signs may be written before, after, above, below, *or* 'around' (before, after *and* above) consonants, depending on the sign.

Though learning the alphabet is not difficult, the writing system itself is fairly complex, so unless you are planning a lengthy stay in Thailand it should perhaps be foregone in favour of actually learning to speak the language. The names of major places included in this book are given in both Thai and Roman script, so that you can at least 'read' the names of destinations at a pinch, or point to them if necessary.

## Tones & Pronunciation

In Thai the meaning of a single syllable may be altered by means of different tones – in standard Central Thai there are five: low tone, level or mid tone, falling tone, high tone and rising tone. For example, depending on the tone, the syllable *mai* can mean 'new', 'burn', 'wood', 'not?' or 'not'; ponder the phrase *mái mài mâi mâi măi* (New wood doesn't burn, does it?) and you begin to appreciate the importance of tones in spoken Thai. This makes it a rather tricky language to learn at first, especially for those of us unaccustomed to the concept of tones. Even when we 'know' what the correct tone in Thai should be, our tendency to denote emotion, verbal stress, the interrogative etc, through tone modulation often interferes with producing the correct tone. Therefore the first rule in learning to speak Thai is to divorce emotions from your speech, at least until you have learned the Thai way to express them without changing essential tone value.

The following is visual representation in chart form to show relative tone values:

**Thai Tones**

| Low | Mid | Falling | High | Rising |
|-----|-----|---------|------|--------|

The following is a brief attempt to explain the tones. The only way to really understand the differences is by listening to a native or fluent non-native speaker. The range of all five tones is relative to each speaker's vocal range so there is no fixed 'pitch' intrinsic to the language.

1 The low tone is 'flat' like the mid tone, but pronounced at the relative *bottom* of one's vocal range. It is low, level and with no inflection, eg, *bàat* (baht – the Thai currency).

2 The level or mid tone is pronounced 'flat', at the relative middle of the speaker's vocal range, eg, *dii* (good); no tone mark used.

3 The falling tone is pronounced as if you were emphasising a word, or calling someone's name from afar, eg, *mâi* (no/not).

4 The high tone is usually the most difficult for westerners. It is pronounced near the relative top of the vocal range, as level as possible, eg, *máa* (horse).

5 The rising tone sounds like the inflection used by English speakers to imply a question – 'Yes?', eg, *sǎam* (three).

Words in Thai that appear to have more than one syllable are usually compounds made up of two or more word units, each with its own tone. They may be words taken directly from Sanskrit, Pali or English, in which case each syllable must still have its own tone.

The following is a guide to the phonetic system that has been used for the words and phrases included in this chapter (and throughout the rest of the book when transcribing directly from Thai). It's based on the Royal Thai General System (RTGS), except that it distinguishes: between short and long vowels (eg, 'i' and 'ii'; 'a' and 'aa'; 'e' and 'eh'; 'o' and 'oh'); between 'o' and 'aw' (both would be 'o' in the RTGS); between 'u' and 'eu' (both would be 'u' in the RTGS); and between 'ch' and 'j' (both would be 'ch' in the RTGS).

## Consonants

The majority of consonants correspond closely to their English counterparts. Here are a few exceptions:

| | |
|---|---|
| k | as the 'k' in 'skin'; similar to 'g' in 'good', but unaspirated (no accompanying puff of air) and unvoiced |
| p | as the 'p' in 'stopper', unvoiced and unaspirated (not like the 'p' in 'put'); actually sounds closer to an English 'b', its voiced equivalent |
| t | as the 't' in 'forty', unaspirated; similar to 'd' but unvoiced |
| kh | as the 'k' in 'kite' |
| ph | as the 'p' in 'put' (never as the 'ph' in 'phone') |
| th | as the 't' in 'tea' |
| ng | as the 'nging' in 'singing'; can occur as an initial consonant in (practise by saying 'singing' without the 'si') |
| r | similar to the 'r' in 'run' but flapped (tongue touches palate); in everyday speech often pronounced like 'l' |

## Vowels

| | |
|---|---|
| **i** | as the 'i' in 'it' |
| **ii** | as the 'ee' in 'feet' |
| **ai** | as the 'i' in 'pipe' |
| **aa** | as the 'a' in 'father' |
| **a** | half as long as **aa**, as the 'a' in 'about' |
| **ae** | as the 'a' in 'bat' or 'tab' |
| **e** | as the 'e' in 'hen' |
| **eh** | as the 'a' in 'hate' |
| **oe** | as the 'er' in 'fern' (without the 'r' sound) |
| **u** | as the 'u' in 'flute' |
| **uu** | as the 'oo' in 'food', longer than **u** |
| **eu** | as the 'u' in 'fur' |
| **ao** | as the 'ow' in 'now' |
| **aw** | as the 'aw' in 'jaw' or 'prawn' |
| **o** | as the 'o' in 'bone' |
| **oh** | as the 'o' in 'toe' |
| **eua** | a combination of **eu** and **a** |
| **ia** | as 'ee-ya', or as the 'ie' in French *rien* |
| **ua** | as the 'ou' in 'tour' |
| **uay** | sounds like 'oo-way' |
| **iu** | as the 'ew' in 'yew' |
| **iaw** | as the 'io' in 'Rio' or Italian *mio* |
| **aew** | like a Cockney pronunciation of the 'ow' in 'now' |
| **ehw** | as 'air-ooh' |
| **awy** | as the 'oi' in 'coin' |

Here are a few extra hints to help you with the alphabetic tangle:

- **ph** is never pronounced as the 'ph' in phone but like the 'p' in 'pound' (the 'h' is added to distinguish this consonant sound from the Thai 'p' which is closer to the English 'b'). This can be seen written as **p**, **ph**, and even **bh**.
- to some people, the Thai **k** sounds closer to the English 'g' than the English 'k'. The standard RTGS chooses to use 'k' to represent this sound to emphasise that it is not a 'voiced' sound, but more a glottal stop.
- there is no 'v' sound in Thai; *Sukhumvit* is pronounced Sukhumwit and *Viang* is really Wiang
- **l** and **r** are always pronounced as an 'n' when word-final, eg, *Satul* is pronounced as Satun, *Wihar* as Wihan. The exception

to this is when 'er' or 'ur' are used to indicate the sound 'oe', as in 'ampher' *(amphoe)*. In the same way 'or' is sometimes used for the sound 'aw', as in 'Porn' *(phawn)*.

- **l** and **r** are often interchanged in speech and this shows up in some transliterations. For example, *naalíkaa* (clock) may appear as 'narika' and *râat nâa* (a type of noodle dish) might be rendered 'laat naa' or 'lat na'.
- **u** is often used to represent the short 'a' sound, as in *tam* or *nam*, which may appear as 'tum' and 'num'. It is also used to represent the 'eu' sound, as when *beung* (swamp) is spelt 'bung'.
- phonetically, all Thai words end in a vowel (**a**, **e**, **i**, **o**, **u**), semi-vowel (**w**, **y**), nasal (**m**, **n**, **ng**) or one of three stops (**p**, **t**, **k**). That's it. Words transcribed with 'ch', 'j', 's' or 'd' endings – like Panich, Raj, Chuanpis and Had – should be pronounced as if they end in 't', as in Panit, Rat, Chuanpit and Hat. Likewise 'g' becomes 'k' (Ralug is actually Raluk) and 'b' becomes 'p' (Thab becomes Thap).
- the 'r' in *sri* is always silent, so the word should be pronounced 'sii' (extended 'i' sound, too). Hence 'Sri Racha' really comes out 'Si Racha'.

## Transliteration

Writing Thai in Roman script is a perennial problem – no wholly satisfactory system has yet been devised to assure both consistency and readability. The Thai government uses the Royal Thai General System of transcription for official government documents in English and for most highway signs. However, local variations crop up on hotel signs, city street signs, menus and so on in such a way that visitors often become confused. Add to this the fact that even the government system has its flaws. For example, 'o' is used for two very different sounds ('o' and the 'aw' in the Vowels section above), as is 'u' (for 'u' and 'eu' above). Likewise for 'ch', which is used to represent two different consonant sounds ('ch' and 'j'). The government transcription system also does not distinguish between short and long vowel sounds, which affect the tonal value of every word.

To top it off, many Thai words (especially names of people and place) have Sanskrit and Pali spellings but their actual pronunciation bears little relation to that spelling if Romanised strictly according to the original Sanskrit/Pali. Thus Nakhon Si Thammarat, if transliterated literally, becomes 'Nagara Sri Dhammaraja'. If you tried to pronounce it using this Pali transcription, very few Thais would be able to understand you.

Generally, names in this book follow the most common practice or, in the case of hotels for example, simply copy their Roman script name, no matter what devious process was used in its transliteration! When this transliteration is markedly different from actual pronunciation, the pronunciation is included (according to the system outlined in this section) in parentheses after the transliteration. Where no Roman model was available, names have been transliterated phonetically, directly from Thai. Of course, this will only be helpful to readers who bother to acquaint themselves with the language – and it's surprising how many people manage to stay for great lengths of time in Thailand without learning a word of Thai.

Problems often arise when a name is transliterated differently, even at the same location. 'Thawi', for example, can be seen as Tavi, Thawee, Thavi, Tavee or various other versions. Outside the International Phonetic Alphabet, there is no 'proper' way to transliterate Thai – only wrong ways. The Thais themselves are incredibly inconsistent in this matter, often using English letters that have no equivalent sound in Thai: Faisal for Phaisan, Bhumibol for Phumiphon, Vanich for Wanit, Vibhavadi for Wiphawadi. Sometimes they even mix literal Sanskrit transcription with Thai pronunciation, as in King Bhumibol (which is pronounced Phumiphon and if transliterated according to the Sanskrit would be Bhumibala).

Here are a few words that are often spelt in a way that encourages native English speakers to mispronounce them:

| Common Spelling | Pronunciation | Meaning |
|---|---|---|
| *bung* | beung | pond or swamp |
| *ko* or *koh* | kàw | island |
| *muang* | meuang | city |
| *nakhon* or *nakorn* | nákhawn | large city |
| *raja* | usually râatchá if at the beginning of a word, râat at the end of a word | royal |

## Greetings & Civilities

When being polite, the speaker ends his or her sentence with *khráp* (for men) or *khâ* (for women). It is the gender of the speaker that is being expressed here; it is also the common way to answer 'yes' to a question or show agreement.

Greetings/Hello.
    *sàwàt-dii*          สวัสดี
    *(khráp/khâ)*   (ครับ/ค่ะ)
How are you?
    *sàbai dii rěu?*   สบายดีหรือ?
I'm fine.
    *sàbai dii*       สบายดี
Thank you.
    *khàwp khun*     ขอบคุณ
Excuse me.
    *khǎw thôht*     ขอโทษ

I/me
    *phǒm*         ผม
    (for men)
    *dì-chǎn*      ดิฉัน
    (for women)
you
    *khun*         คุณ
    (for peers)
    *thâan*       ท่าน
    (for elders and people in authority)

What's your name?
*khun chêu àrai?*    คุณชื่ออะไร?

My name is ...
*phǒm chêu ...*    ผมชื่อ...
(men)
*dì-chǎn chêu ...*    ดิฉันชื่อ...
(women)

Do you have ...?
*mii ... mǎi?/*    มี...ไหม/
*... mii mǎi?*    ...มีไหม?

No.
*mâi châi*    ไม่ใช่

No?
*mǎi?/châi mǎi?*    ไหม?/ใช่ไหม?

(I) like ...
*châwp ...*    ชอบ...

(I) don't like ...
*mâi châwp ...*    ไม่ชอบ...

(I) would like ...
(+ verb)
*yàak jà ...*    อยากจะ...

(I) would like ...
(+ noun)
*yàak dâi ...*    อยากได้...

When?
*mêua-rai?*    เมื่อไร?

It doesn't matter.
*mâi pen rai*    ไม่เป็นไร

What is this?
*nîi àrai?*    นี่อะไร?

go
*pai*    ไป

come
*maa*    มา

## Language Difficulties

I understand.
*khâo jai*    เข้าใจ

I don't understand.
*mâi khâo jai*    ไม่เข้าใจ

Do you understand?
*khâo jai mǎi?*    เข้าใจไหม?

A little.
*nít nàwy*    นิดหน่อย

What do you call
this in Thai?
*nîi phaasǎa thai*    นี่ภาษาไทย
*rîak wâa àrai?*    เรียกว่าอะไร?

## Getting Around

I'd like to go ...
*yàak jà pai ...*    อยากจะไป...

Where is (the) ...?
*... yùu thîi nǎi?*    ...อยู่ที่ไหน?

airport
*sànǎam bin*    สนามบิน

bus station
*sàthǎanii khǒn sòng*    สถานีขนส่ง

bus stop
*thîi jàwt rót*    ที่จอดรถ
*pràjam thaang*    ประจำทาง

train station
*sàthǎanii rót fai*    สถานีรถไฟ

taxi stand
*thîi jàwt rót*    ที่จอดรถแท็กซี่
*tháek-sîi*

I'd like a ticket.
*yàak dâi tǔa*    อยากได้ตั๋ว

What time will the ...
leave?
*... jà àwk kìi*    ...จะออกกี่
*mohng ?*    โมง?

What time will the ...
arrive?
*... jà maa thěung*    ...จะมาถึงกี่
*kìi mohng ?*    โมง?

bus
*rót meh/rót bát*    รถเมล์/รถบัส

car
  *rót yon*            รถยนต์
motorcycle
  *rót maw-toe-sai*    รถมอเตอร์ไซค์
train
  *rót fai*            รถไฟ
straight ahead
  *trong pai*          ตรงไป
left
  *sái*                ซ้าย
right
  *khwăa*              ขวา
far/not far/near
  *klai/mâi klai/*     ไกล/ไม่ไกล/
    *klâi*             ใกล้

## Accommodation
hotel
  *rohng raem*         โรงแรม
guesthouse
  *bâan phák*          บ้านพัก
    *(kèt háo)*        (เกสต์เฮาส์)
Do you have a
room available?
  *mii hâwng wâang*    มีห้องว่าง
    *măi?*             ไหม?
How much is it
per night?
  *kheun-lá thâo rai?* คืนละเท่าไร?
bathroom
  *hâwng náam*         ห้องน้ำ
toilet
  *hâwng sûam*         ห้องส้วม
room
  *hâwng*              ห้อง
hot
  *ráwn*               ร้อน
cold
  *yen*                เย็น
bath/shower
  *àap náam*           อาบน้ำ

blanket
  *phâa hòm*           ผ้าห่ม
towel
  *phâa chét tua*      ผ้าเช็ดตัว

## Around Town
Can (I/we) change money here?
  *lâek ngoen thîi níi dâi măi?*
  แลกเงินที่นี่ได้ไหม?
What time does it open?
  *ráan pòet mêua rai?*
  ร้านเปิดเมื่อไร?
What time does it close?
  *ráan pìt mêua rai?*
  ร้านปิดเมื่อไร?

bank
  *thánaakhaan*        ธนาคาร
beach
  *hàat*               หาด
market
  *tàlàat*             ตลาด
museum
  *phíphítháphan*      พิพิธภัณฑ์
post office
  *praisànii*          ไปรษณีย์
restaurant
  *ráan aahăan*        ร้านอาหาร
tourist office
  *sămnák ngaan*       สำนักงาน
    *thâwng thîaw*     ท่องเที่ยว

## Shopping
How much?
  *thâo rai?*          เท่าไร?
too expensive
  *phaeng pai*         แพงไป
How much is this?
  *nîi thâo rai?/*     นี่เท่าไร?/
    *kìi bàat?*        กี่บาท?
cheap, inexpensive
  *thùuk*              ถูก

## Health

chemist/pharmacy
*ráan khǎi yaa* ร้านขายยา

dentist
*mǎw fan* หมอฟัน

doctor
*mǎw* หมอ

hospital
*rohng pháyaabaan* โรงพยาบาล

aspirin (pain killer)
*yaa kâe pùat* ยาแก้ปวด

bandage
*phâa phan* ผ้าพัน

bleeding
*lêuat àwk* เลือดออก

condom
*thǔung yaang ànaamai* ถุงยางอนามัย

mosquito repellent
*yaa kan yung* ยากันยุง

sanitary napkins
*phâa ànaamai* ผ้าอนามัย

Please call a doctor.
*kàrúnaa rîak mǎw nòi*
กรุณาเรียกหมอหน่อย

I'm allergic to penicillin.
*pháe yaa phenísinlin*
แพ้ยาเพนิซิลลิน

I'm pregnant.
*tâng khan láew/mee tháwng*
ตั้งครรภ์แล้ว/มีท้อง

It hurts here.
*jèp trong née*
เจ็บตรงนี้

I feel nauseous.
*róosèuk khlêun sâi*
รู้สึกคลื่นไส้

I keep vomiting.
*aajian bòi bòi*
อาเจียนบ่อยๆ

## Emergencies

I need a doctor.
*tâwng-kaan mǎw* ต้องการหมอ

Help!
*chûay dûay!* ช่วยด้วย

Stop!
*yùt!* หยุด

Go away!
*pai sí!* ไปซิ

I'm lost.
*chǎn lǒng thaang* ฉันหลงทาง

I feel faint.
*róosèuk jà pen lom*
รู้สึกจะเป็นลม

I have diarrhoea.
*tháwng rûang*
ท้องร่วง

I have a fever.
*pen khâi*
เป็นไข้

I have a headache.
*pùat hǔa*
ปวดหัว

I have indigestion.
*tháwng fóe*
ท้องเฟ้อ

I have period pain.
*pùat pràjam deuan*
ปวดประจำเดือน

I have a stomachache.
*pùat tháwng*
ปวดท้อง

I have a toothache.
*pùat fan*
ปวดฟัน

## Time, Days & Numbers

What's the time?
  *kìi mohng láew?*   กี่โมงแล้ว?

today
  *wan níi*   วันนี้

tomorrow
  *phrûng níi*   พรุ่งนี้

yesterday
  *mêua waan*   เมื่อวาน

Sunday
  *wan aathít*   วันอาทิตย์

Monday
  *wan jan*   วันจันทร์

Tuesday
  *wan angkhaan*   วันอังคาร

Wednesday
  *wan phút*   วันพุธ

Thursday
  *wan phréuhàt*   วันพฤหัสฯ

Friday
  *wan sùk*   วันศุกร์

Saturday
  *wan săo*   วันเสาร์

| 0 | *sŭun* | ศูนย์ |
| 1 | *nèung* | หนึ่ง |
| 2 | *săwng* | สอง |
| 3 | *săam* | สาม |
| 4 | *sìi* | สี่ |
| 5 | *hâa* | ห้า |
| 6 | *hòk* | หก |
| 7 | *jèt* | เจ็ด |
| 8 | *pàet* | แปด |
| 9 | *kâo* | เก้า |

| 10 | *sìp* | สิบ |
| 11 | *sìp-èt* | สิบเอ็ด |
| 12 | *sìp-săwng* | สิบสอง |
| 13 | *sìp-săam* | สิบสาม |
| 20 | *yîi-sìp* | ยี่สิบ |
| 21 | *yîi-sìp-èt* | ยี่สิบเอ็ด |
| 22 | *yîi-sìp-săwng* | ยี่สิบสอง |
| 30 | *săam-sìp* | สามสิบ |
| 40 | *sìi-sìp* | สี่สิบ |
| 50 | *hâa-sìp* | ห้าสิบ |
| 100 | *ráwy* | ร้อย |
| 200 | *săwng ráwy* | สองร้อย |
| 300 | *săam ráwy* | สามร้อย |
| 1000 | *phan* | พัน |
| 10,000 | *mèun* | หมื่น |
| 100,000 | *săen* | แสน |
| one million | *láan* | ล้าน |
| one billion | *phan láan* | พันล้าน |

## FOOD
## Ordering

(For 'I' men use *phŏm*; women use *di-chăn*)

I eat only vegetarian food.
  *phŏm/di-chăn kin jeh*
  ผม/ดิฉันกินเจ

I can't eat pork.
  *phŏm/di-chăn kin mŭu mâi dâi*
  ผม/ดิฉันกินหมูไม่ได้

I can't eat beef.
  *phŏm/di-chăn kin néua mâi dâi*
  ผม/ดิฉันกินเนื้อไม่ได้

(I) don't like it hot & spicy.
  *mâi châwp phèt*
  ไม่ชอบเผ็ด

(I) like it hot & spicy.
*châwp phèt*
ชอบเผ็ด

(I) can eat Thai food.
*kin aahăan thai pen*
กินอาหารไทยเป็น

What do you have that's special?
*mii a-rai phí-sèt?*
มีอะไรพิเศษ?

I didn't order this.
*nîi phŏm/di-chăn mâi dâi sàng*
นี่ผม/ดิฉันไม่ได้สั่ง

Do you have ...?
*mii ... măi?*
มี ...ไหม?

## Food Glossary

The following list gives standard dishes in Thai script with a transliterated pronunciation guide, using the system outlined at the beginning of this chapter.

**Soups**    *(súp)*    ชุป

mild soup with vegetables & pork
*kaeng jèut*
แกงจืด

mild soup with vegetables, pork & bean curd
*kaeng jèut tâo-hûu*
แกงจืดเต้าหู้

soup with chicken, galanga root & coconut
*tôm khàa kài*
ต้มข่าไก่

prawn & lemon grass soup with mushrooms
*tôm yam kûng*
ต้มยำกุ้ง

fish-ball soup
*kaeng jèut lûuk chín*
แกงจืดลูกชิ้น

rice soup with fish/chicken/shrimp
*khâo tôm plaa/kài/kûng*
ข้าวต้มปลา/ไก่/กุ้ง

**Egg**    *(khài)*    ไข่

hard-boiled egg
*khài tôm*
ไข่ต้ม

fried egg
*khài dao*
ไข่ดาว

plain omelette
*khài jiaw*
ไข่เจียว

omelette with vegetables & pork
*khài yát sâi*
ไข่ยัดไส้

scrambled egg
*khài kuan*
ไข่กวน

**Noodles**    *(kŭaytĭaw/*    ก๋วยเตี๋ยว/
            *bà-mìi)*    บะหมี่

rice noodle soup with vegetables & meat
*kŭaytĭaw náam*
ก๋วยเตี๋ยวน้ำ

rice noodles with vegetables & meat
*kŭaytĭaw hâeng*
ก๋วยเตี๋ยวแห้ง

rice noodles with gravy
*râat nâa*
ราดหน้า

thin rice noodles fried with tofu, vegetables egg & peanuts
*phàt thai*
ผัดไทย

fried noodles with soy sauce
*phàt sii-íu*
ผัดซีอิ๊ว

wheat noodles in broth with vegetables & meat
*bà-mìi náam*
บะหมี่น้ำ

wheat noodles with vegetables & meat
*bà-mìi hâeng*
บะหมี่แห้ง

**Rice** *(khâo)* ข้าว

fried rice with pork/chicken/shrimp
*khâo phàt mǔu/kài/kûng*
ข้าวผัดหมู/ไก่/กุ้ง

boned, sliced Hainan-style chicken with
marinated rice
*khâo man kài*
ข้าวมันไก่

chicken with sauce over rice
*khâo nâa kài*
ข้าวหน้าไก่

roast duck over rice
*khâo nâa pèt*
ข้าวหน้าเป็ด

'red' pork with rice
*khâo mǔu daeng*
ข้าวหมูแดง

curry over rice
*khâo kaeng*
ข้าวแกง

**Curries** *(kaeng)* แกง

hot Thai curry with chicken/beef/pork
*kaeng phèt kài/néua/mǔu*
แกงเผ็ดไก่/เนื้อ/หมู

rich & spicy, Muslim-style curry with
chicken/beef & potatoes
*kaeng mátsàman kài/néua*
แกงมัสมั่นไก่/เนื้อ

mild, Indian-style curry with chicken
*kaeng karìi kài*
แกงกะหรี่ไก่

hot & sour, fish & vegetable ragout
*kaeng sôm*
แกงส้ม

'green' curry with fish/chicken/beef
*kaeng khǐaw-wǎan plaa/kài/néua*
แกงเขียวหวานปลา/ไก่/เนื้อ

savoury curry with chicken/beef
*kaeng phánaeng kài/néua*
แกงพะแนงไก่/เนื้อ

chicken curry with bamboo shoots
*kaeng nàw mái kài*
แกงหน่อไม้ไก่

catfish curry
*kaeng plaa dùk*
แกงปลาดุก

**Seafood** *(aahǎan tháleh)* อาหารทะเล

steamed crab
*puu nêung*
ปูนึ่ง

steamed crab claws
*kâam puu nêung*
ก้ามปูนึ่ง

shark-fin soup
*hǔu chàlǎam*
หูฉลาม

crisp-fried fish
*plaa thâwt*
ปลาทอด

fried prawns
*kûng thâwt*
กุ้งทอด

batter-fried prawns
*kûng chúp pâeng thâwt*
กุ้งชุบแป้งทอด

grilled prawns
*kûng phǎo*
กุ้งเผา

steamed fish
*plaa nêung*
ปลานึ่ง

grilled fish
*plaa phǎo*

ปลาเผา

whole fish cooked in ginger,
onions & soy sauce
*plaa jǐan*

ปลาเจี๋ยน

sweet & sour fish
*plaa prîaw wǎn*

ปลาเปรี้ยวหวาน

cellophane noodles baked with crab
*puu òp wún-sên*

ปูอบวุ้นเส้น

spicy fried squid
*plaa mèuk phàt phèt*

ปลาหมึกผัดเผ็ด

roast squid
*plaa mèuk yâang*

ปลาหมึกย่าง

oysters fried in egg batter
*hǎwy thâwt*

หอยทอด

squid
*plaa mèuk*

ปลาหมึก

shrimp
*kûng*

กุ้ง

fish
*plaa*

ปลา

saltwater eel
*plaa lòt*

ปลาหลด

spiny lobster
*kûng mangkawn*

กุ้งมังกร

green mussel
*hǎwy málaeng phûu*

หอยแมลงภู่

scallop
*hǎwy phát*

หอยพัด

oyster
*hǎwy naang rom*

หอยนางรม

**Miscellaneous**

stir-fried mixed vegetables
*phàt phàk ruam*

ผัดผักรวม

spring rolls
*pàw-pía*

เปาะเปี๊ยะ

beef in oyster sauce
*néua phàt náam-man hǎwy*

เนื้อผัดน้ำมันหอย

duck soup
*pèt tǔn*

เป็ดตุ๋น

roast duck
*pèt yâang*

เป็ดย่าง

fried chicken
*kài thâwt*

ไก่ทอด

chicken fried in holy basil
*kài phàt bai kà-phrao*

ไก่ผัดใบกะเพรา

grilled chicken
*kài yâang*

ไก่ย่าง

chicken fried with chillies
*kài phàt phrík*

ไก่ผัดพริก

chicken fried with cashews
*kài phàt mét má-mûang*
ไก่ผัดเม็ดมะม่วง

morning-glory vine fried in garlic, chilli &
bean sauce
*phàk bûng fai daeng*
ผักบุ้งไฟแดง

skewers of barbecued meat (satay)
*sà-té*
สะเต๊ะ

spicy green papaya salad
(North-Eastern speciality)
*sôm-tam*
ส้มตำ

noodles with fish curry
*khànom jiin náam yaa*
ขนมจีนน้ำยา

prawns fried with chillies
*kûng phàt phrík phǎo*
กุ้งผัดพริกเผา

chicken fried with ginger
*kài phàt khǐng*
ไก่ผัดขิง

fried wonton
*kíaw kràwp*
เกี๊ยวกรอบ

cellophane noodle salad
*yam wún sên*
ยำวุ้นเส้น

spicy chicken or beef salad
*lâap kài/néua*
ลาบไก่/เนื้อ

hot & sour, grilled beef salad
*yam néua*
ยำเนื้อ

fried chicken with bean sprouts
*kài phat thùa ngâwk*
ไก่ผัดถั่วงอก

fried fish cakes with cucumber sauce
*thâwt man plaa*
ทอดมันปลา

**Vegetables** *(phàk)* ผัก

bitter melon
*márá-jiin*
มะระจีน

brinjal (round eggplant)
*mákhěua pràw*
มะเขือเปราะ

cabbage
*phàk kà-làm* (or *kà-làm plii*)
ผักกะหล่ำ(กะหล่ำปลี)

cauliflower
*dàwk kà-làm*
ดอกกะหล่ำ

Chinese radish
*phàk kàat hǔa*
ผักกาดหัว

corn
*khâo phôht*
ข้าวโพด

cucumber
*taeng kwaa*
แตงกวา

eggplant
*mákhěua mûang*
มะเขือม่วง

garlic
*kràthiam*
กระเทียม

lettuce
*phàk kàat*
ผักกาด

long bean
*thùa fàk yao*
ถั่วฝักยาว

okra ('ladyfingers')
*krà-jíap*
กระเจี๊ยบ

onion (bulb)
*hŭa hăwm*
หัวหอม

onion (green, 'scallions')
*tôn hăwm*
ต้นหอม

peanuts (ground nuts)
*tùa lísŏng*
ถั่วลิสง

potato
*man faràng*
มันฝรั่ง

pumpkin
*fák thawng*
ฟักทอง

taro
*phèuak*
เผือก

tomato
*mákhĕua thêt*
มะเขือเทศ

**Fruit** *(phŏn-lá-mái)* ผลไม้
banana – over 20 varieties (year-round)
*klûay*
กล้วย

coconut (year-round)
*máphráo*
มะพร้าว

custard-apple
*náwy nàa*
น้อยหน่า

durian
*thúrian*
ทุเรียน

guava (year-round)
*fa-ràng*
ฝรั่ง

jackfruit
*kha-nŭn*
ขนุน

lime (year-round)
*má-nao*
มะนาว

longan – 'dragon's eyes'; similar to rambutan (July to October)
*lam yai*
ลำใย

mandarin orange (year-round)
*sôm*
ส้ม

mango – several varieties & seasons
*má-mûang*
มะม่วง

mangosteen
*mang-khút*
มังคุด

papaya (year-round)
*málákaw*
มะละกอ

pineapple (year-round)
*sàp-pàrót*
สับปะรด

pomelo
*sôm oh*
ส้มโอ

rambeh – small, reddish-brown and apricot-like (April to May)
*máfai*
มะไฟ

rambutan
*ngáw*
เงาะ

rose-apple – apple-like texture; very fragrant
(April to July)
*chom-phûu*

ชมพู่

tamarind – sweet and tart varieties
*mákhǎam*

มะขาม

sapodilla – small and oval; sweet but
pungent (July to September)
*lámút*

ละมุด

watermelon (year-round)
*taeng moh*

แตงโม

**Sweets** *(khǎwng wǎan)* ของหวาน
Thai custard
*sǎngkha-yǎa*

สังขยา

coconut custard
*sǎngkha-yǎa ma-phráo*

สังขยามะพร้าว

sweet shredded egg yolk
*fǎwy thawng*

ฝอยทอง

egg custard
*mâw kaeng*

หม้อแกง

banana in coconut milk
*klûay bùat chii*

กล้วยบวชชี

fried, Indian-style banana
*klûay khàek*

กล้วยแขก

sweet palm kernels
*lûuk taan chêuam*

ลูกตาลเชื่อม

Thai jelly with coconut cream
*ta-kôh*

ตะโก้

red sticky rice with coconut cream
*khâo nǐaw daeng*

ข้าวเหนียวแดง

sticky rice in coconut cream with ripe mango
*khâo nǐaw má-mûang*

ข้าวเหนียวมะม่วง

## DRINKS
**Beverages** *(khrêuang dèum)* เครื่องดื่ม
plain water
*náam plào*

น้ำเปล่า

hot water
*náam ráwn*

น้ำร้อน

boiled water
*náam tôm*

น้ำต้ม

bottled drinking water
*náam dèum khùat*

น้ำดื่มขวด

cold water
*náam yen*

น้ำเย็น

ice
*náam khǎeng*

น้ำแข็ง

soda water
*náam soh-daa*

น้ำโซดา

orange soda
*náam sôm*

น้ำส้ม

iced lime juice with sugar
(usually with salt too)
*náam mánao*

น้ำมะนาว

no salt (command)
*mâi sài kleua*

ไม่ใส่เกลือ

plain milk
*nom jèut*
นมจืด

Chinese tea
*chaa jiin*
ชาจีน

weak Chinese tea
*náam chaa*
น้ำชา

iced Thai tea with milk & sugar
*chaa yen*
ชาเย็น

iced Thai tea with sugar only
*chaa dam yen*
ชาดำเย็น

no sugar (command)
*mâi sài náam-taan*
ไม่ใส่น้ำตาล

hot Thai tea with sugar
*chaa dam ráwn*
ชาดำร้อน

hot Thai tea with milk & sugar
*chaa ráwn*
ชาร้อน

hot coffee with milk & sugar
*kaafae ráwn*
กาแฟร้อน

traditional filtered coffee
with milk & sugar
*kaafae thǔng* (*ko-píi* in the South)
กาแฟถุง (โกปี๊)

iced coffee with sugar, no milk
*oh-líang*
โอเลี้ยง

Ovaltine
*oh-wantin*
โอวันติน

bottle
*khùat*
ขวด

glass
*kâew*
แก้ว

# Glossary

**abidhamma** – teachings of higher philosophy and Buddhist psychology
**ao** – bay or gulf
**axe pillow** – traditional Thai wedge-shaped pillow

**baht** – *bàat*; Thai currency/unit of measure equalling 15g
**bhikkhu** – *phíksù*; Buddhist monk
**bòt** – central sanctuary in a Thai temple used for official business of the Order *(sangha)* of monks, such as ordinations; from Pali term *uposatha*

**chaa** – tea
**chao leh** – sea gypsies; also *chao náam*
**chedi** – (from the Pali *cetiya*) stupa; monument erected to house a Buddha relic

**damascene ware** – metal ornamented by etching or inlaying, usually with gold or silver

**farang** – Western, Westerner

**hat** – *hàat*; beach

**Isan** – *isǎan*; general term for North-Eastern Thailand, from the Sanskrit name for the medieval kingdom Isana, which encompassed parts of Cambodia and North-Eastern Thailand

**jataka** – stories of the Buddha's past lives

**kàthoey** – transvestites and transsexuals
**kèp plai-thaang** – reverse charges telephone call
**khlong** – *khlawng;* canal
**kràthǎwm** – a leaf of the Mitragyna speciosa tree, used by workers and students as a stimulant; illegal and said to be addictive
**Krung Thep** – 'City of Angels', Bangkok

**lákhon** – classical Thai dance-drama
**làk meuang** – city pillar/phallus
**lék** – little, small (in size)

**mâe chii** – Buddhist nun
**mâe náam** – river; literally, water mother
**mát-mìi** – a technique for tie-dying cotton or silk threads before weaving, similar to Indonesian ikat
**metta** – *mêt-taa;* Buddhist practice of loving kindness
**muay thai** – Thai boxing

**naga** – *nâak;* a mythical serpent-like being with magical powers
**niello ware** – an object decorated with niello, a black compound used to incise designs on metal surfaces

**phâakhamáa** – sarong (for men)
**phâasîn** – sarong (for women)
**phrá phim or phrá khrêuang** – Buddha images or amulets, sometimes worn on a chain around the neck
**prang** – Khmer-style tower on temples
**prasada** – blessed food offered to Hindu or Sikh temple attendees

**Ratanakosin** – Bangkok period of Thai history; style of architecture late 19th to early 20th century, which combines traditional Thai and European forms; also known as 'old Bangkok'
**reua hǎang yao** – longtail boat
**rót dùan** – express trains
**rót rehw** – rapid trains
**rót thamadaa** – ordinary government-run buses

**sǎalaa** – open-sided, covered meeting hall or resting place; from Portuguese term *sala,* literally 'room'; also *sala*
**samatha** – meditation techniques aimed at calming the mind and developing concentration
**samlor** – *sǎam-láw;* three-wheeled pedicab
**satipatthana** – 'the bases of mindfulness'; a style of meditation
**soi** – *sawy;* lane, small street
**songthaew** – *sǎwngthǎew;* small pick-up truck, literally meaning 'two rows' – a

reference to the wooden benches; common form of public transport outside Bangkok

**tàlàat** – market
**tàlàat náam** – floating markets
**Tha** – *thâa*; pier
**tháeksii miitôe** – metered taxi
**thanŏn** – street
**thorásàp ráwàang pràthêt** – international long-distance call
**Tripitaka** – Theravada Buddhist scriptures
**trok** – *tràwk*; alleyway
**túk-túk** – motorised pedicab
**tuppie** – moneyed and materialistic Thai youth; coined from English 'Thai yuppie'

**vipassana** – *wípàtsàna;* meditation that develops insight into reality

**wâi** – palms-together Thai greeting
**wát** – temple, monastery
**wíhăan** – counterpart to *bòt* in Thai temple that contains Buddha images

**yaan líphao** – a type of intricately woven basket made from a hardy grass that grows in Southern Thailand

## ACRONYMS

**BKK** – International Airport Code for Bangkok International Airport, but commonly used as an abbreviated for Bangkok
**BMA** – Bangkok Metropolitan Administration; the city's local government
**BMTA** – Bangkok Metropolitan Transit Authority; operates the city's public bus system
**BTS** – Bangkok Transit System; private company operating the Skytrain
**CAT** – Communications Authority of Thailand
**CITES** – Convention on International Trade in Endangered Species
**FAO** – Food & Agriculture Organisation
**IMF** – International Monetary Fund
**MRTA** – Metropolitan Rapid Transit Authority; state enterprise in charge of subway construction
**SRT** – State Railway of Thailand
**TAT** – Tourist Authority of Thailand
**THAI** – Thai Airways International
**TOT** – Telephone Organisation of Thailand
**UNEP** – United Nations Environment Programme
**WHO** – World Health Organization

# Thanks

Many thanks to the travellers who used the last edition and wrote to us with helpful hints, useful advice and interesting anecdotes. Your names follow:

Donna Acord, Martin Alan Searle, Sarah Anderson, Steve Archer, Dennis G Arnold, Luli Arroyo, Sven Assarsson, John & Esther Atwell, Jorg Ausfelt, Chris Bagley, Chris Bain, Tereza Bakesova, Wayen Barley, Stuart Barlow, Roger Bayliss, Roger Beattie, Glenn Behrman, Mila Benedicto, C Bergener, Joy & Michael Berkowitz, Kees Beukelman, Lennard Bijl, Terry Blackburn, Shannon Blackmore, John Bloomfield, Andris Blums, Manuel Bonmati, Markus Borner, Frank Brockmann, Roland Broda, Allison Burke, Dave Burke, Brian Burns, Kathy Butts, Xavier Cazauran, Aimee Chan, Polly Chapman, Dr JD Chaudhuri, Sally Claiborne, Amy Clements, David Cocksedge, Mike Craig, Fraser Crayford, Carl Crosado, Zsolt Csok, Karen Cushman, Monique de Jong, Marie-Aline de Lavau, Martin Dujmovic, Iain Dunlop, Chris Dunning, Rob Earney, Peter Edan, Bert Eijnthoven, Hugh Elsol, Michelle Enticknap, C Erwin, Robert Evangelisti, Honor Fallon, Janet Fenton, Hans & Anne Fix, Kieron Flynn, Alan Foster, Megan Foster, Andrew Gannon, Stuart Gebbie, Paul H Geissler, Kate Gibbs, Alice Gifford, Albert D Goldson, Josil C Gonzales, Diane B Goodpasture, Kirsty Gray, Ralph Grosse, Gil Hahn, Lucette Hansen, Kevin Bryah Harrison, Richard Harvey, Mike Harzha, Jeff Haugh, Andreas Hefti, Hans Heintze, Jason & Michelle Heppenstall, Carsten Herzog, TE Hesse, Wanda Hoerning, Mark Holloway, Damien Horigan, Shane Howard, L Hurley, Gwen James, Robert Jan Van Mulst, Teresa Johnson, MA Johnston, Jennifer Jolley, Khatijah Abdul Kadir, Katrin Kegel, Julia Keller, Julie Kinsey, Jenny Kirby, Jochen Klaschka, Malte Klesen, Angela Knox, Amy Kolczak, Steven Kram, Nicholas B Kronwall, Bill Larson, Tony Le, Mark Leach, Colin Lee, Heikki Lehikoinen, Wolfgang Lofi, Mark Lydon, Anthony Lynch, Mhairi-Clare Lyons, Padraig MacDonnchadha, Kelly McCarthy, Michael McWhirter, Susie Mesure, Lynn Mikami, Paul Moffett, Dean Moore, Simon Moore, Andrew Morgan, Marjorie Morkham, Anna Muir, Randi Munkeby, Edmond J Murphy, James Murray, Chris Nevmever, Gail O'Keeffe, Henning Otto Karlsen, Renate Pelzl, Seth Petchers, Katherine Potter, Stuart Ray, Mark Reed, Leontien Reedijk, AF & Mr Robilliard, Maarten Rooij, Vilai Roongroj, Nathalie Ruhmann, Elizabeth Savir, Astrid Schinharl, HJ Schmid, Martin Schmidt, Stephan Schneider, Ken Schubauer, Peter Scott, Hamish Scott-Brown, Margaret Shallcross, Mark Siemelink, Bruce Silvers, A Smithee, Sammy Southall, Eduardo Spaccasassi, Kellie Spicknell, Rachael Stead, Elliot Steel, Peter Steiner, Dave Stone, Tom Stringell, Tobias Strollo, Josep M Suelves, Theerada Suphaphong, Bill Taylor, Lilian Teunissen, Sue & Ian Timbrell, Kevin Troy, Marty Tunney, Elisabeth Ugel, Juha Valimaki, Melissa Vallillo, Jeroen van Bijsterveld, Age van Lemel, Rachel Vine, NH & Rene Voyer, Robert Vriesman, Lorenzo Ward, Sachiko Washimi, Rosie Watson, Brad Wetmore, Steve Whitehead, Shannon Williams, Terry Williams, Penny Wincer, Pak Yue Wing, Joanna Wiseman, Leung-hee Woo, Paul Wood, Tonia Wood, Nick Woodman, Delores Woosnam, Andrew Wright, Jim Wright, Bronwyn Wyatt, Paul Yurewicz.

# LONELY PLANET

You already know that Lonely Planet produces more than this one guidebook, but you might not be aware of the other products we have on this region. Here is a selection of titles that you may want to check out as well:

**South-East Asia on a shoestring**
ISBN 1 86450 158 8
US$21.99 • UK£12.99

**Hill Tribes phrasebook**
ISBN 0 86442 635 6
US$5.95 • UK£3.99

**South-East Asia phrasebook**
ISBN 0 86442 435 3
US$6.95 • UK£3.99

**Thailand**
ISBN 1 86450 251 7
US$24.99 • UK£14.99

**Thailands Islands & Beaches**
ISBN 0 86442 728 X
US$15.95 • UK£9.99

**Thai phrasebook**
ISBN 0 86442 658 5
US$6.95 • UK£4.50

**Diving & Snorkeling Thailand**
ISBN 1 86450 201 0
US$16.99 • UK£10.99

**Citysync**
ISBN 1 86450 228 2
US$49.99 • UK£29.99

**Healthy Travel Asia & India**
ISBN 1 86450 051 4
US$5.95 • UK£3.99

**Thailand, Vietnam, Laos & Cambodia Road Atlas**
ISBN 1 86450 102 2
US$14.99 • UK£8.99

**Bangkok City Map**
ISBN 1 86450 004 2
US$5.95 • UK£3.99

**World Food Thailand**
ISBN 1 86450 093 X
US$11.99 • UK£6.99

Available wherever books are sold

# LONELY PLANET

## Guides by Region

**L**onely Planet is known worldwide for publishing practical, reliable and no-nonsense travel information in our guides and on our Web site. The Lonely Planet list covers just about every accessible part of the world. Currently there are 16 series: Travel guides, Shoestring guides, Condensed guides, Phrasebooks, Read This First, Healthy Travel, Walking guides, Cycling guides, Watching Wildlife guides, Pisces Diving & Snorkeling guides, City Maps, Road Atlases, Out to Eat, World Food, Journeys travel literature and Pictorials.

**AFRICA** Africa on a shoestring • Cairo • Cairo City Map • Cape Town • Cape Town City Map • East Africa • Egypt • Egyptian Arabic phrasebook • Ethiopia, Eritrea & Djibouti • Ethiopian Amharic phrasebook • The Gambia & Senegal • Healthy Travel Africa • Kenya • Malawi • Morocco • Moroccan Arabic phrasebook • Mozambique • Read This First: Africa • South Africa, Lesotho & Swaziland • Southern Africa • Southern Africa Road Atlas • Swahili phrasebook • Tanzania, Zanzibar & Pemba • Trekking in East Africa • Tunisia • Watching Wildlife East Africa • Watching Wildlife Southern Africa • West Africa • World Food Morocco • Zimbabwe, Botswana & Namibia
**Travel Literature:** Mali Blues: Traveling to an African Beat • The Rainbird: A Central African Journey • Songs to an African Sunset: A Zimbabwean Story

**AUSTRALIA & THE PACIFIC** Auckland • Australia • Australian phrasebook • Australia Road Atlas • Cycling Australia • Cycling New Zealand • Fiji • Fijian phrasebook • Healthy Travel Australia, NZ & the Pacific • Islands of Australia's Great Barrier Reef • Melbourne • Melbourne City Map • Micronesia • New Caledonia • New South Wales • New Zealand • Northern Territory • Outback Australia • Out to Eat – Melbourne • Out to Eat – Sydney • Papua New Guinea • Pidgin phrasebook • Queensland • Rarotonga & the Cook Islands • Samoa • Solomon Islands • South Australia • South Pacific • South Pacific phrasebook • Sydney • Sydney City Map • Sydney Condensed • Tahiti & French Polynesia • Tasmania • Tonga • Tramping in New Zealand • Vanuatu • Victoria • Walking in Australia • Watching Wildlife Australia • Western Australia
**Travel Literature:** Islands in the Clouds: Travels in the Highlands of New Guinea • Kiwi Tracks: A New Zealand Journey • Sean & David's Long Drive

**CENTRAL AMERICA & THE CARIBBEAN** Bahamas, Turks & Caicos • Baja California • Belize, Guatemala & Yucatán • Bermuda • Central America on a shoestring • Costa Rica • Costa Rica Spanish phrasebook • Cuba • Dominican Republic & Haiti • Eastern Caribbean • Guatemala • Havana • Healthy Travel Central & South America • Jamaica • Mexico • Mexico City • Panama • Puerto Rico • Read This First: Central & South America • World Food Mexico • Yucatán
**Travel Literature:** Green Dreams: Travels in Central America

**EUROPE** Amsterdam • Amsterdam City Map • Amsterdam Condensed • Andalucía • Austria • Baltic States phrasebook • Barcelona • Barcelona City Map • Belgium & Luxembourg • Berlin • Berlin City Map • Britain • British phrasebook • Brussels, Bruges & Antwerp • Brussels City Map • Budapest • Budapest City Map • Canary Islands • Central Europe • Central Europe phrasebook • Copenhagen • Corfu & the Ionians • Corsica • Crete • Crete Condensed • Croatia • Cycling Britain • Cycling France • Cyprus • Czech & Slovak Republics • Denmark • Dublin • Dublin City Map • Eastern Europe • Eastern Europe phrasebook • Edinburgh • England • Estonia, Latvia & Lithuania • Europe on a shoestring • Europe phrasebook • Finland • Florence • France • Frankfurt Condensed • French phrasebook • Georgia, Armenia & Azerbaijan • Germany • German phrasebook • Greece • Greek Islands • Greek phrasebook • Hungary • Iceland, Greenland & the Faroe Islands • Ireland • Italian phrasebook • Italy • Krakow • Lisbon • The Loire • London • London City Map • London Condensed • Madrid • Malta • Mediterranean Europe • Mediterranean Europe phrasebook • Moscow • Munich • Netherlands • Normandy • Norway • Out to Eat – London • Out to Eat – Paris • Paris • Paris City Map • Paris Condensed • Poland • Polish phrasebook • Portugal • Portuguese phrasebook • Prague • Prague City Map • Provence & the Côte d'Azur • Read This First: Europe • Rhodes & the Dodecanese • Romania & Moldova • Rome • Rome City Map • Russia, Ukraine & Belarus • Russian phrasebook • Scandinavian & Baltic Europe • Scandinavian phrasebook • Scotland • Sicily • Slovenia • South-West France • Spain • Spanish phrasebook • St Petersburg • St Petersburg City Map • Sweden • Switzerland • Tuscany • Ukrainian phrasebook • Venice • Vienna • Walking in Britain • Walking in France • Walking in Ireland • Walking in Italy • Walking in Spain • Walking in Switzerland • Western Europe • World Food France • World Food Ireland • World Food Italy • World Food Spain
**Travel Literature:** After Yugoslavia • Love and War in the Apennines • The Olive Grove: Travels in Greece • On the Shores of the Mediterranean • Round Ireland in Low Gear • A Small Place in Italy

## Mail Order

**L**onely Planet products are distributed worldwide. They are also available by mail order from Lonely Planet, so if you have difficulty finding a title please write to us. North and South American residents should write to 150 Linden St, Oakland, CA 94607, USA; European and African residents should write to 10a Spring Place, London NW5 3BH, UK; and residents of other countries to Locked Bag 1, Footscray, Victoria 3011, Australia.

**INDIAN SUBCONTINENT & THE INDIAN OCEAN** Bangladesh • Bengali phrasebook • Bhutan • Delhi • Goa • Healthy Travel Asia & India • Hindi & Urdu phrasebook • India • Indian Himalaya • Karakoram Highway • Kerala • Madagascar • Maldives • Mauritius, Réunion & Seychelles • Mumbai (Bombay) • Nepal • Nepali phrasebook • Pakistan • Rajasthan • Read This First: Asia & India • South India • Sri Lanka • Sri Lanka phrasebook • Tibet • Tibetan phrasebook • Trekking in the Indian Himalaya • Trekking in the Karakoram & Hindukush • Trekking in the Nepal Himalaya
**Travel Literature:** The Age of Kali: Indian Travels and Encounters • Hello Goodnight: A Life of Goa • In Rajasthan • Maverick in Madagascar • A Season in Heaven: True Tales from the Road to Kathmandu • Shopping for Buddhas • A Short Walk in the Hindu Kush • Slowly Down the Ganges

**MIDDLE EAST & CENTRAL ASIA** Bahrain, Kuwait & Qatar • Central Asia • Central Asia phrasebook • Dubai • Farsi (Persian) phrasebook • Hebrew phrasebook • Iran • Israel & the Palestinian Territories • Istanbul • Istanbul City Map • Istanbul to Cairo • Istanbul to Kathmandu • Jerusalem • Jerusalem City Map • Jordan • Lebanon • Middle East • Oman & the United Arab Emirates • Syria • Turkey • Turkish phrasebook • World Food Turkey • Yemen
**Travel Literature:** Black on Black: Iran Revisited • The Gates of Damascus • Kingdom of the Film Stars: Journey into Jordan

**NORTH AMERICA** Alaska • Boston • Boston City Map • Boston Condensed • British Columbia • California & Nevada • California Condensed • Canada • Chicago • Chicago City Map • Florida • Great Lakes • Hawaii • Hiking in Alaska • Hiking in the USA • Las Vegas • Los Angeles • Los Angeles City Map • Louisiana & the Deep South • Miami • Miami City Map • Montreal • New England • New Orleans • New York City • New York City City Map • New York City Condensed • New York, New Jersey & Pennsylvania • Oahu • Out to Eat – San Francisco • Pacific Northwest • Rocky Mountains • San Francisco • San Francisco City Map • Seattle • Southwest • Texas • Toronto • USA • USA phrasebook • Vancouver • Virginia & the Capital Region • Washington, DC • Washington, DC City Map • World Food New Orleans
**Travel Literature:** Caught Inside: A Surfer's Year on the California Coast • Drive Thru America

**NORTH-EAST ASIA** Beijing • Beijing City Map • Cantonese phrasebook • China • Hiking in Japan • Hong Kong • Hong Kong City Map • Hong Kong Condensed • Hong Kong, Macau & Guangzhou • Japan • Japanese phrasebook • Korea • Korean phrasebook • Kyoto • Mandarin phrasebook • Mongolia • Mongolian phrasebook • Seoul • Shanghai • South-West China • Taiwan • Tokyo • World Food Hong Kong
**Travel Literature:** In Xanadu: A Quest • Lost Japan

**SOUTH AMERICA** Argentina, Uruguay & Paraguay • Bolivia • Brazil • Brazilian phrasebook • Buenos Aires • Chile & Easter Island • Colombia • Ecuador & the Galapagos Islands • Healthy Travel Central & South America • Latin American Spanish phrasebook • Peru • Quechua phrasebook • Read This First: Central & South America • Rio de Janeiro • Rio de Janeiro City Map • Santiago de Chile • South America on a shoestring • Trekking in the Patagonian Andes • Venezuela
**Travel Literature:** Full Circle: A South American Journey

**SOUTH-EAST ASIA** Bali & Lombok • Bangkok • Bangkok City Map • Burmese phrasebook • Cambodia • Hanoi • Healthy Travel Asia & India • Hill Tribes phrasebook • Ho Chi Minh City • Indonesia • Indonesian phrasebook • Indonesia's Eastern Islands • Java • Lao phrasebook • Laos • Malay phrasebook • Malaysia, Singapore & Brunei • Myanmar (Burma) • Philippines • Pilipino (Tagalog) phrasebook • Read This First: Asia & India • Singapore • Singapore City Map • South-East Asia on a shoestring • South-East Asia phrasebook • Thailand • Thailand's Islands & Beaches • Thailand, Vietnam, Laos & Cambodia Road Atlas • Thai phrasebook • Vietnam • Vietnamese phrasebook • World Food Thailand • World Food Vietnam

**ALSO AVAILABLE:** Antarctica • The Arctic • The Blue Man: Tales of Travel, Love and Coffee • Brief Encounters: Stories of Love, Sex & Travel • Chasing Rickshaws • The Last Grain Race • Lonely Planet ... On the Edge: Adventurous Escapades from Around the World • Lonely Planet Unpacked • Not the Only Planet: Science Fiction Travel Stories • Sacred India • Travel Photography: A Guide to Taking Better Pictures • Travel with Children

# Index

## Text

### A

Abhisek Dusit Throne Hall 113
accomodation 145-63
  airport area 156-7, 162-3
  budget 145-53
  long-term rentals 163
  mid-range 153-7
  Thai vocabulary 254
AIDS 71-2
air travel 87-92
  departure tax 87
  glossary 90
  to/from Asia 91
  to/from Australasia 88
  to/from Europe/UK 88-9
  to/from USA/Canada 89-91
airlines
  domestic 87-8
  international 92
airports
  accomodation 156-7, 162-3
  domestic 88
  international 101-2
Alcoholics Anonymous 68
Alliance Française 78
allied war cemeteries 231-2
ambulance 68
American University Alumni 78
animals 16, 31-2, 125, 211, 213-14, 223
antiques 201, 206, see also shopping
  exportation of 45-6
Architecture 17-19
  of Chinatown 123-4
  traditional examples of 111, 112, 113, 115, 117, 136-44, 214, 221
area codes 53
art galleries 110-12, 114-15
arts 17-25, see also entertainment, culture
  artistic elephants 16
  ceramics 211, 227
  cinema 24-5
  literature 58-9
  music 20-3

painting 19-20
  theatre & dance 23-4
Author's Lounge & Oriental Hotel 158, 185
Ayuthaya 214-21, **216-17**
  festivals 217-18
  getting there & away 220-1
  places to eat 219-21
  places to stay 218-19

### B

backpackers
  accommodation 145-53
  cafes 164
  markets 209
Banglamphu, Old 142-4
Bang Pa-In 221
beaches 239-47
beauty treatments 64-5
boat travel
  around Bangkok 109
  to/from China 100
  to/from Laos 100
  to/from Malaysia 100
  to/from Myanmar 100
  trips 217, 234, 245
  royal barges 113
books 57-60
  Buddhism 37, 134
  cooking 59
  health guides 66-7
  learning Thai 248
  literature 58-9
  bookshops 206
border crossings, see bus travel, train travel
British Council 78
Buddhism 34-7
  floating nuns 233
  meditation courses 134
  place of worship 115
  soccer worship 122
  monasteries 233
  tattoo festival 83
bus travel
  around Bangkok 104-5
  quirks of 105
  safety 93-4, 105

terminals 94
  to/from Cambodia 95
  to/from China 95-6
  to/from Laos 95
  to/from Malaysia 94-5
  to/from Myanmar 95
  within Thailand 92-4
business 84-6
  business hours 81-2
  fax services 55
  postal & courier services 51-2
  public holidays 82-4
  rental accomodation 163
  telephone services 54-5
  visas 40-2

### C

camping 210, 242, 244
car travel 107
  platform shoes 107
  vehicle importation 46
ceramics 211, 227-8
Chao Phraya River Express 127, 211-13, **128**
Chatuchak Weekend Market 207-8, **207**
children
  ABC Babyland store 209
  cinemas 199
  Crocodile Farm & Zoo 213-14
  Diamond Eye Cat Farm 223
  doll factory 114
  ice skating 209
  kite flying 125
  planetarium 114
  railway museum 114
  Safari World 213
  science museum 114
  snake farm 125-6
  sport & swimming facilities 131
  tourist train 238-9
  travel with 77
  wax works 223
  zoos 125, 213
Chinatown 123-4, 139-42, 166-7

**Bold** indicates maps.

churches 123
cinemas 199, see also film
climate 13-14
consulates 43-5
courier services 51-2
courses 132-4
  cooking 133
  martial arts 133-4
  meditation 134
  Thai language 132
cuisine, see food
cultural centres 78-9
culture 25-34, 211, see also
    arts, religion, entertainment
  cuisine 172-80
  books about 58
  courses 132-4
  festivals 82-4
  pop-culture 21-3, 61
  tattoos 83
customs 45-6

**D**

Damnoen Saduak Floating
    Markets 130, 224-5, **224**
dance 23-4, see also theatre &
    dance, entertainment
Death Railway Bridge 229-31
dental clinics 68
department stores, see
    shopping
departure tax 87
disabled travellers 76-7
diving 245
Doll Factory & Museum 114
drinks 178-80
  alcoholics anonymous 68
  Thai vocabulary 262-3
driving licence 42
drugs 79, 80-1
dry-cleaning 63-4
Dusit Zoo 125

**E**

Eastern & Oriental Express 99
ecology 14
economy 12-13, 15-16
education 17
electricity 63
elephant farm & zoo 211
elephants 16, 211, 217
email 55-6
embassies 43-5

Emerald Buddha, the 116
entertainment 186-200
  bars 187-91
  cabaret (Kà-thoey) 198
  dinner theatre 198-9
  discos & dance clubs 188-91
  gay & lesbian 191
  Go-Go bars 191-2
  jazz music 187
  Latin music 187
  live music 186-7
  pubs 187-90
  spectator sports 194-7
environmental issues 14,
    239-41, see also responsible
    tourism
ethnicity 17
etiquette 27-31, 175
exchange rates 46
excursions 211-47, see also
    tours
  Ancient Village 213
  Ayuthaya 214
  Bang Pa-In 221
  culltural village 211
  Kanchanaburi 229-39
  Ko Samet 239-47
  Nakhon Pathom 221-4
  Samut Sakhon 225-7
  Samut Songkhram 227-9
  waterfalls 238

**F**

fax services 55
festivals 82-4, 217-18
film 24-5
  cinemas 199
fitness centres 131
floating markets 130-1, 224-5,
    228
food
  Thai cuisine 172-80
  American 167, 183
  health issues 67
  backpacker hangouts 164
  Burmese 169-70
  cafes 165, 167, 168, 169,
    181
  Chinese 166-67, 184
  cook books 59-60
  cooking classes 133
  dinner cruises 184
  dinner theatres 198-9
  drinks 178-80
  French 167, 168, 181, 183,
    184
  German 167, 183

high tea 185
  Indian 166-7, 170, 182
  Israeli 164
  Italian 167, 168, 182, 183,
    184
  Japanese 167, 169, 181
  Mediterranean 183
  Mexican 183
  Middle Eastern 164, 170, 182
  Muslim 170, 182
  nouvelle Thai 181
  places to eat 164-85
  pub food 181, 183
  recipes 175-8
  royal Thai 169
  table ettiquette 175
  Thai vocabulary 256-62
  teahouses 167, 185
  vegetarian 165, 166-7, 168,
    170, 185
  Vietnamese 182, 184
Friendship Bridge 95, 99

**G**

gardens 112, 211, 221, 228,
    see also parks
gay & lesbian travellers 75-6
  entertainment 189, 191
  queer cabaret 198
geography 13
Goethe-Institut 79
glossary 264-5
Golden Mount & Wat Saket
    119
government 10-13, 14-15
Grand Palace & Wat Phra
    Kaew 115-17
guesthouses, see
    accommodation

**H**

hairdressers 64-5
health 65-74
  medical services 68
  Thai vocabulary 255
history 10-13, 214, 229-31
  books about 57-8
HIV 71-2
hospitals 68
hotels, see accommodation
Hualamphong train station
    96-9, 124

**I**

immigration 40-2
immunisations 65-74

insurance 42
internet
    access to 55-6
    useful sites 56-7
intineraries 38, 110

## J

Jim Thompson's House 111-12

## K

Kanchanaburi 229-39, **230**
    boat trips 234
    Death Railway Bridge
        229-31
    entertainment 238
    getting around 239
    getting there & away 238-9
    places to eat 237-8
    places to stay 234-6
    swimming pools 236-7
    things to see 229-33
Ko Samet 239-47, **240**
    getting around 247
    getting there & away 245-7
    medical services 241
    places to eat 245
    places to stay 242
    watersports 241, 245
Krabi-Krabong 134

## L

Lak Meuang (City Pillar) 120
laundry 63-4
legal matters 34
    drugs 80-1
    visas 40-2
lesbian travellers 75-6, see also
    gay & lesbian travellers
libraries 77-8
literature 58-9

## M

magazines 60
malaria 66
malls, see shopping
maps 38-9
markets 207-8
    floating 130-1, 224-5, 228
martial arts 133-4, 200, 194-7
massage 117, 131-2, 211
measures 63
media
    censorship of 60, 69
    magazines 60
    newspapers 60

radio 60
    TV 60-2
medical services 68
    Ko Samet 241
meditation 134
military 11
Mon, the 211-13, 221
monarchy 10-13, 28-9
    festivals 82-4
    ploughing ceremony 84
money 46-51
    ATMs 47-8
    bargaining 49-50
    costs 49
    credit cards 47-8
    exchange rates 46
    exchanging 47-8
    security 79
    tipping 49-50
Monk's Bowl Village 126
monks 36
    monasteries 233-4
motorcycle travel 107
Muay Thai 133-4, 200, 194-7
museums 110-15, 214-15
    Abhisek Dusit Throne Hall
        113
    Ancient City 213
    Ayuthaya 214-15
    Jim Thompson's House
        111-12
    National Museum 110-11,
        **111**
    Science 114
    Royal Barges 113
    Royal Elephant 113
    Royal Thai Airforce 114
    Samut Songkhram 227-8
    Siam Society & Ban
        Kamthieng 114
    Vimanmek Teak Mansion
        112-13
    Wang Suan Phakkat
        (Lettuce Farm Palace)
        112
    war museums, Kanchanburi
        232
    wax works 223
music 16, 20-3, see also arts,
    entertainment, shopping

## N

Nakhon Pathom 221-4, **222**
    attractions 222-3
    floating markets 224-5
    getting there & away 223-4
    Phra Pathom Chedi 222

    places to eat 223
    places to stay 223
National Parks
    Ko Samet 239-47
newspapers 60
night-life, see entertainment
nuns 36, 233

## O

Orchid Farm 228
Oriental Hotel & Author's
    Lounge 158, 185

## P

painting 16, 19-20
parks, see also gardens
    Lumphini 124
    Rama IX Royal 125
    Sanam Luang 125
passports 40
Phahurat 124, 139-42
photography 62-3
    supplies 205-6
Phra Pathom Chedi 222
Phra Sumen Fort 126-7
places to stay, see
    accommodation
places to eat, see food
police 80, 81
politics 10-13, 14-15
    books 57-8
pollution 14
popstars 21-3
population 17
postal services 51-2
POWs historic sites 229-33
prisons 81
prostitution 32-4
public holidays 82-4

## Q

Queen Saovabha Memorial
    Institute (snake farm) 125-6

## R

rabies 73, 126
radio 60
railways, see also train travel
    railway museum 114
    Death Railway Bridge 229,
        231
religion 29-30, 34-7, see also
    Buddhism
    modern worship 122
    tattoos 83

responsible tourism 14, *see also* etiquette, environmental issues
  charity restaurant 182
  volunteer work 33, 86
restaurants, *see* food
river & canal trips 126-7, 211-13
road travel 92-6
Royal Barges National Museum 113
Royal Elephant Museum 113

**S**
Safari World 213
safe travel 79-80
  emergency vocabulary 255
  money 48-9
Samut Prakan Crocodile Farm & Zoo 213-14
Samut Sakhon 225-7
  getting there & away 226-7
  places to stay & eat 226
Samut Songkram 227-9
  getting there & away 229
  places to stay & eat 228-9
  things to see 227-8
senior travellers 77
sex industry 32-4
shopping 201-10
  antiques 201, 206, 209-10
  books & magazines 206
  buyers tips 59-60
  camping 210
  ceramics 227
  children 209-10
  clothes 205, 209-10
  flowers & nurseries 208
  furniture 204-5
  gems 201-3
  guarantees 210
  hair & beauty 64-5
  handicrafts 204
  music 207
  photographic supplies 205-6
  pirated goods 206-7
  scams 202-3, 210
  shopping centres 209-10
  tailors 205
  Thai crafts 204, 209

touts 79-80
  vocabulary 254
shrines 115-23
  Lak Meuang (City Pillar) 120
Siam Society & Ban Kamthieng 114
sight-seeing 110-34, 136-44
Skytrain 105-6
snake farm 125-6
society 17, 25-34, 58
  books 58
spectator sports 200
sporting facilities 131
sports 200
Sri Mariamman 120-1
student riots 11, 12
student travel 43
subway 106
swimming pools 131

**T**
tailors, *see* shopping
tampons 75
taxis 107-8
telephone services 54-5
temples & shrines 115-23, *see also* wats
  Sri Mariamman 120-1
tennis courts 131
Thai boxing 133-4, 200, 194-7
Thai language 248-63
  accommodation 254
  dialects 249
  emergencies 255-63
  food 256-62
  glossary 264-5
  greetings 252-3
  health 255
  idioms 173
  pronunciation 249-50
  script 249
  shopping 254
theatre & dance 23-4
  venues 192, 198-9
time 63
toilets 64
tourist offices 39-40
  tourist police 81
tours 211, 234, 238
  walking tours 136-44
  dinner cruises 129-30
  river & canals 126-31
train travel 96-100
  bookings & charges 96-7

to/from China 100
  to/from Laos 99
  to/from Malaysia 99
  within Thailand 96-9
  tourist train 238-9
transport 80-6
  boat 109
  bus touts 80
  car & motorcycle rental 107
  motorcycle taxi 108
  river & canals 126-31
  Skytrain 105-6
  subway 106
  to/from airport 101-2
  tuk-tuk 108-9
  vocabulary 253-4
túk-túk 108-9
TV 60-62

**U**
universities 78

**V**
vegetarian food 172-3
video 62-3
  rentals 199-200
Vietnam/American War 11
Vimanmek Teak Mansion 112-13
visas 40-2
volunteer work 86

**W**
walking 109
walking tours 136-44
  Chinatown-Phahurat 139-42, **140**
  Old Banglamphu 142-4, **143**
  temples & river 136-9, **137**
Wang Suan Phakkat (Lettuce Farm Palace) 112
Wat Phra Kaew & Grand Palace 115-17
watersports 241, 245
waterfalls 238
wats 115-23
  Arun 118-19
  Ayuthaya's historic 214-17
  Benchamabophit 119
  Bowonniwet 120
  definition of 115
  Emerald Buddha, the 116
  Mahathat 118
  Pho 117-18

**Bold** indicates maps.

*wats continued*
  Phra Kaew & Grand Palace
    115-17
  Phra Pathom Chedi 222
  Ratchanatda 120
  Saket & Golden Mount 119
  Satthaatham 227
  Thammamongkhon 121
  Tham Mongkon Thong 233

  Tham Seua & Wat Tham
    Khao Noi 233-4
  Traimit 118
wax works 223
weights 63
women
  attitudes towards 74-5
  safe travel 74-5, 79
  what to bring 75

work 85-6
WWII 11-12
  sites 229, 231-3

**Y**
youth hostels 42-3

**Z**
zoos 125, 213

## Boxed Text

All Trunked Up But Nowhere
  to Go 16
Area Codes 53
Bangkok's Big Smoke 69
Crunch in a Can 179
Cut & Paste 26
Don't Be Like Lime Without
  Juice! 173
Emerald Buddha, The
  (Phra Kaew) 116

Finding Addresses 39
Get Soapy 61
Green Travel 14
How To Order Noodles 174
How You Can Help 33
Kickstart to Enlightenment 122
Lûuk Thûng – Truckin' Music 22
More Than Skin Deep 83
Mutt Mayhem 31
Novelty Bussing 105

One Night in Bangkok 188-9
Original Siamese Twins, The 11
Platform Shoes Banned 107
Rama V Cult 29
Royal Ploughing Ceremony,
  The 84
Thai Art Styles 18
Too Good to Be True 202-3
Túk-Túk Wars 108
What's a Wat 115

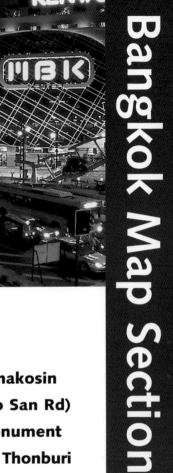

Bangkok Map Section

MAP 1    Greater Bangkok

MAP 2    Central Bangkok

MAP 3    Banglamphu & Ko Ratanakosin

MAP 4    Thanon Khao San (Khao San Rd)

MAP 5    Pratunam & Victory Monument

MAP 6    Chinatown - Bang Rak - Thonburi

MAP 7    Lumphini Park - Th Ploenchit -
         Samyan

# MAP 1 – GREATER BANGKOK

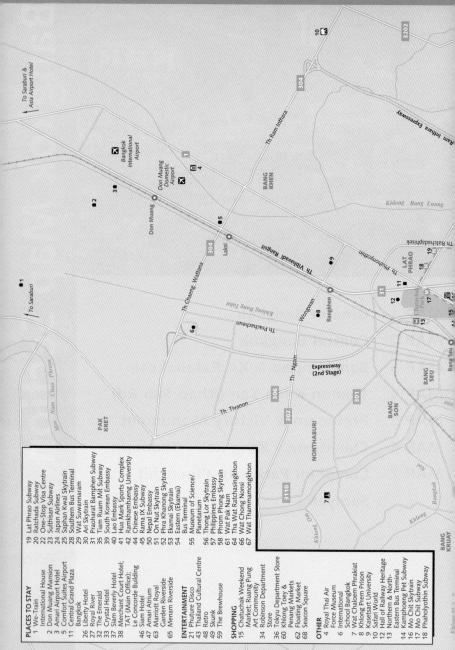

**PLACES TO STAY**
1 We-Train
2 International House
3 Don Muang Mansion
5 Amari Airport Hotel
6 Comfort Suites Airport
11 Central Grand Plaza
   Bangkok
26 Liberty Hotel
27 Royal River
32 The Emerald
33 Crystal Hotel
37 Siam Beverly Hotel
38 Merchant Court Hotel;
   TAT (Main Office);
   Le Concorde Building
46 Siam Hotel
47 Amari Atrium
63 Marriott Royal
   Garden Riverside
65 Menam Riverside

**ENTERTAINMENT**
21 Phuture Disco
43 Thailand Cultural Centre
48 Retro
49 Skunk
59 The Brewhouse

**SHOPPING**
15 Chatuchak Weekend
   Market; Ruang Pung
   Art Community
34 Robinson Department
   Store
36 Tokyu Department Store
60 Khlong Toey &
   Penang Markets
64 Floating Market
68 Seacon Square

**OTHER**
4 Royal Thai Air
   Force Museum
6 International
   School Bangkok
7 Wat Chaloem Phrakiat
8 Khlong Prem Prison
9 Kasetsart University
10 Safari World
12 Hall of Railway Heritage
13 Northern & North-
   Eastern Bus Terminal
14 Kamphoeng Pet Subway
16 Mo Chit Skytrain
17 Mo Chit Subway
18 Phaholyothin Subway

19 Lat Phrao Subway
20 Ratchada Subway
22 One-Stop Visa Centre
23 Sulthisan Subway
24 Japan Airlines
25 Saphan Kwai Skytrain
28 Southern Bus Terminal
29 Wat Suwannaram
30 Ari Skytrain
31 Praohrat Bamphen Subway
35 Tiam Ruam Mit Subway
39 South Korean Embassy
40 Lao Embassy
41 Hua Mark Sports Complex
42 Ramkhamhaeng University
44 Chinese Embassy
45 Rama IX Subway
50 Nepal Embassy
51 On Nut Skytrain
52 Phra Khanong Skytrain
53 Ekamai Skytrain
54 Eastern (Ekamai)
   Bus Terminal
55 Museum of Science/
   Planetarium
56 Thong Lor Skytrain
57 Philippines Embassy
58 Phirom Phong Skytrain
61 Wat Pak Nam
64 Tha Wat Ratchasingkhon
66 Wat Chong Nonsi
67 Wat Thammamongkhon

RICHARD NEBESKY

Dusit Hall at the Grand Palace

JULIET COOMBE

Wat Arun (Temple of Dawn)

Wat Phra Kaew (Temple of the Emerald Buddha)

Reclining buddha at Wat Pho

# MAP 2 – CENTRAL BANGKOK

# MAP 3 – BANGLAMPHU & KO RATANAKOSIN

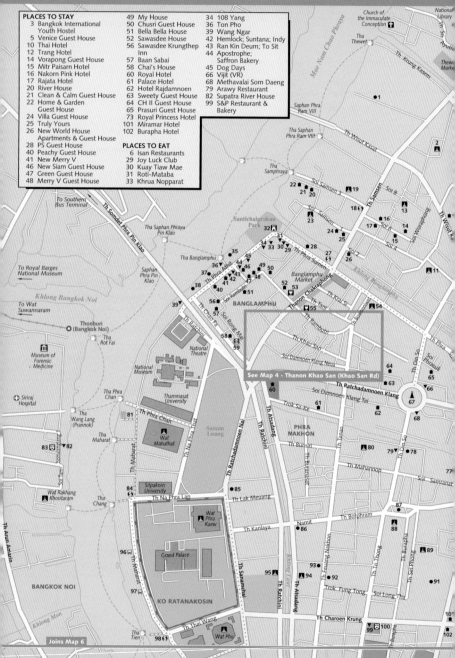

**PLACES TO STAY**
- 3 Bangkok International Youth Hostel
- 5 Venice Guest House
- 10 Thai Hotel
- 12 Trang Hotel
- 14 Vorapong Guest House
- 15 Mitr Paisarn Hotel
- 16 Nakorn Pink Hotel
- 17 Rajata Hotel
- 20 River House
- 21 Clean & Calm Guest House
- 22 Home & Garden Guest House
- 24 Villa Guest House
- 25 Truly Yours
- 26 New World House Apartments & Guest House
- 28 PS Guest House
- 40 Peachy Guest House
- 41 New Merry V
- 46 New Siam Guest House
- 47 Green Guest House
- 48 Merry V Guest House
- 49 My House
- 50 Chusri Guest House
- 51 Bella Bella House
- 52 Sawasdee House
- 56 Sawasdee Krungthep Inn
- 57 Baan Sabai
- 58 Chai's House
- 60 Royal Hotel
- 61 Palace Hotel
- 62 Hotel Rajdamnoen
- 63 Sweety Guest House
- 64 CH II Guest House
- 65 Prasuri Guest House
- 73 Royal Princess Hotel
- 101 Miramar Hotel
- 102 Burapha Hotel

**PLACES TO EAT**
- 6 Isan Restaurants
- 29 Joy Luck Club
- 30 Kuay Tiaw Mae
- 31 Roti-Mataba
- 33 Khrua Nopparat
- 34 108 Yang
- 36 Ton Pho
- 39 Wang Ngar
- 42 Hemlock; Suntana; Indy
- 43 Ran Kin Deum; To Sit
- 44 Apostrophe; Saffron Bakery
- 45 Dog Days
- 66 Vijit (VR)
- 68 Methavalai Sorn Daeng
- 79 Arawy Restaurant
- 82 Supatra River House
- 99 S&P Restaurant & Bakery

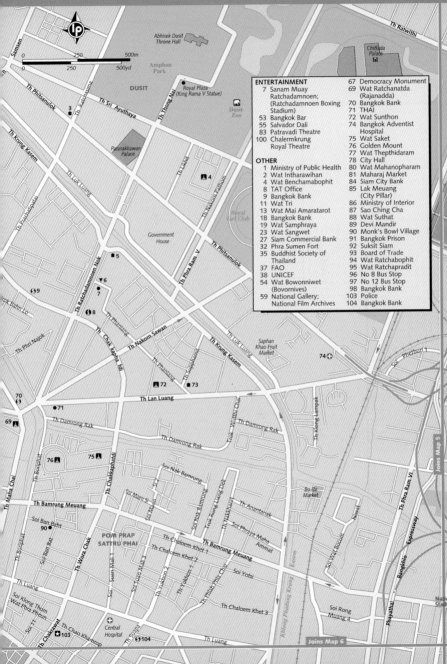

**ENTERTAINMENT**
7 Sanam Muay
  Ratchadamnoen;
  (Ratchadamnoen Boxing
  Stadium)
53 Bangkok Bar
55 Salvador Dali
83 Patravadi Theatre
100 Chalermkrung
  Royal Theatre

**OTHER**
1 Ministry of Public Health
2 Wat Intharawihan
4 Wat Benchamabophit
8 TAT Office
9 Bangkok Bank
11 Wat Tri
13 Wat Mai Amaratarot
18 Bangkok Bank
19 Wat Samphraya
23 Wat Sangwet
27 Siam Commercial Bank
32 Phra Sumen Fort
35 Buddhist Society of
  Thailand
37 FAO
38 UNICEF
54 Wat Bowonniwet
  (Bovornives)
59 National Gallery;
  National Film Archives

67 Democracy Monument
69 Wat Ratchanatda
  (Rajanadda)
70 Bangkok Bank
71 THAI
72 Wat Sunthon
74 Bangkok Adventist
  Hospital
75 Wat Saket
76 Golden Mount
77 Wat Thepthidaram
78 City Hall
80 Wat Mahanopharam
81 Maharaj Market
84 Siam City Bank
85 Lak Meuang
  (City Pillar)
86 Ministry of Interior
87 Sao Ching Cha
88 Wat Suthat
89 Devi Mandir
90 Monk's Bowl Village
91 Bangkok Prison
92 Suksit Siam
93 Board of Trade
94 Wat Ratchabophit
95 Wat Ratchapradit
96 No 8 Bus Stop
97 No 12 Bus Stop
98 Bangkok Bank
103 Police
104 Bangkok Bank

# MAP 4 – THANON KHAO SAN (KHAO SAN RD)

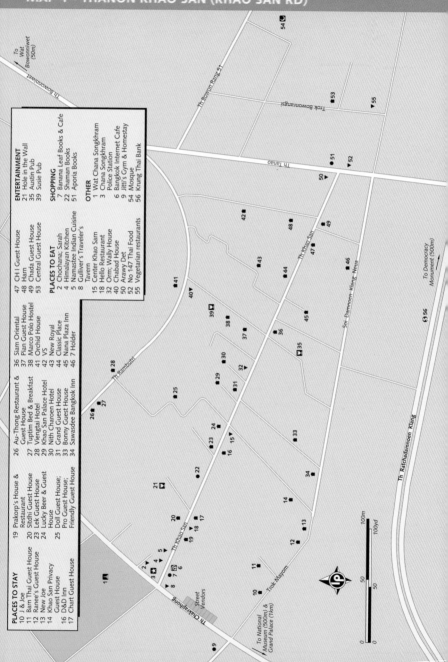

## PLACES TO STAY
10 J & Joe
11 Barn Thai Guest House
12 Ranee's Guest House
13 New Joe
14 Khao San Privacy Guest House
16 D&D Inn
17 Chart Guest House

19 Prakorp's House & Restaurant
20 Sitdhi Guest House
23 Lek Guest House
24 Lucky Beer & Guest House
25 Doll Guest House; Pro Guest House; Friendly Guest House

26 Au-Thong Restaurant & Guest House
27 Tuptim Bed & Breakfast
28 Viengtai Hotel
29 Khao San Palace Hotel
30 Nith Charoen Hotel
31 Grand Guest House
33 Bonny Guest House
34 Sawasdee Bangkok Inn

36 Siam Oriental
37 Pian Guest House
38 Marco Polo Hostel
41 Orchid House
42 VS
43 New Royal
44 Classic Place
45 Nana Plaza Inn
46 7 Holder

47 CH I Guest House
48 Harn
49 Chada Guest House
53 Central Guest House

## PLACES TO EAT
2 Chochana; Sarah
4 Himalayan Kitchen
5 Namastee Indian Cuisine
8 Gulliver's Traveler's Tavern
15 Center Khao Sam
18 Hello Restaurant
32 Orm; Wally House
40 Chabad House
50 Arawy Det
52 No 147 Thai Food
55 Vegetarian restaurants

## ENTERTAINMENT
21 Hole in the Wall
35 Austin Pub
39 Susie Pub

## SHOPPING
7 Banana Leaf Books & Cafe
22 Shaman Books
51 Aporia Books

## OTHER
1 Wat Chana Songkhram
3 Chana Songkhram Police Station
6 Bangkok Internet Cafe
9 Jitti's Gym & Homestay
54 Mosque
56 Krung Thai Bank

Snacks on standby at Thanon Khao San

Hair-raising experience along Thanon Khao San

Travel hub by day, reggae dub by night – Thanon Khao San is a tourist's delight.

# MAP 5 – PRATUNAM & VICTORY MONUMENT

PHAYATHAI

Th Sawankalok

Th Phra Ram V

Khlong Samsen

Sanam Pao

Skytrain

Th Phetchaburi

2

Th Ratwithi

Soi 2

1

Soi Sermak

Th Yothi

Phayathai – Bangkhlo Expressway

Ministry of
Science Technology
& Environment

Mahidol
University

Ministry of
Industry

Department
of Foreign
Affairs

Victory
Monument

Victory
Monument

3

Asoke – Rachadapisek

Th Ratwithi

Th Phayathai

Soi Loed Panya

4

RATCHATHEWI

Th Rangnam

Soi Subolprasoen

Th Si Ayuthaya

Soi Phet Panya

Joins Map 3

9

Th Si Ayuthaya

10

6

11

Phayathai

Soi Ko Lit

8  7

Soi 3

Soi Mansin 4

Soi Mansin 3

Soi 10

Th Phetburi 7

Soi Phetburi 12

Th Phetburi

Skytrain

Th Phayathai

Soi 9

Th Phetburi 13

Th Phetburi 15

Th Phetburi 19

12

13

Th Ratchaprarop

Pratunam
Market

Soi Rong Rian
Sudarak

Th Phaya Nak

Th Ban Phai Thong

Soi Phetburi 12

Th Phetburi 8

Ratchathewi

19
20

21

18

Th Phetburi

17

15

16

Chalaem
Market

Charoen
Nakhon
Market

Nai Lert
Market

Expressway

Khlong Saen Saep

(2nd Stage)

22

23

25
26
27
24
28
29

Soi Kasem San 3

Soi Kasem San 2

Soi Kasem San 1

To Banglamphu

National
Stadium

Th Phra Ram I

Siam Square
Mahboonkrung
Intersection

32
33
35
36

34

30
31

Siam
Square

37

Th Ratchadamri

39

40

World
Trade
Centre

Soi Ratchadamri

38

Th Gaysorn

Soi 32

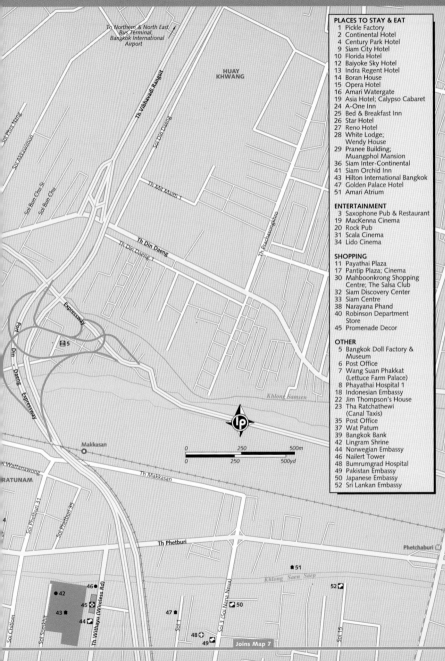

**PLACES TO STAY & EAT**
1 Pickle Factory
2 Continental Hotel
4 Century Park Hotel
9 Siam City Hotel
10 Florida Hotel
12 Baiyoke Sky Hotel
13 Indra Regent Hotel
14 Boran House
15 Opera Hotel
16 Amari Watergate
19 Asia Hotel; Calypso Cabaret
24 A-One Inn
25 Bed & Breakfast Inn
26 Star Hotel
27 Reno Hotel
28 White Lodge;
   Wendy House
29 Pranee Building;
   Muangphol Mansion
36 Siam Inter-Continental
41 Siam Orchid Inn
43 Hilton International Bangkok
47 Golden Palace Hotel
51 Amari Atrium

**ENTERTAINMENT**
3 Saxophone Pub & Restaurant
19 MacKenna Cinema
20 Rock Pub
31 Scala Cinema
34 Lido Cinema

**SHOPPING**
11 Payathai Plaza
17 Pantip Plaza; Cinema
30 Mahboonkrong Shopping
   Centre; The Salsa Club
32 Siam Discovery Center
33 Siam Centre
38 Narayana Phand
40 Robinson Department
   Store
45 Promenade Decor

**OTHER**
5 Bangkok Doll Factory &
   Museum
6 Post Office
7 Wang Suan Phakkat
   (Lettuce Farm Palace)
8 Phayathai Hospital 1
18 Indonesian Embassy
22 Jim Thompson's House
23 Tha Ratchathewi
   (Canal Taxis)
35 Post Office
37 Wat Patum
39 Bangkok Bank
42 Lingram Shrine
44 Norwegian Embassy
46 Nailert Tower
48 Bumrumgrad Hospital
49 Pakistan Embassy
50 Japanese Embassy
52 Sri Lankan Embassy

# MAP 6 – CHINATOWN - BANG RAK - THONBURI

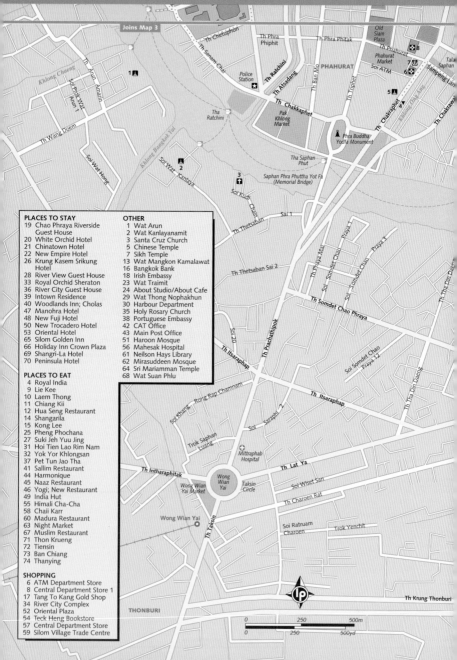

Joins Map 3

Th Chetuphon
Th Phra Phiphit
Th Phra Phitak
Th Phra Phiphit
Old Siam Plaza
Th Sanam Chai
Th Ratchini
Th Atsadang
Th Ban Mo
PHAHURAT
Th Phahurat
Phahurat Market
Soi ATM
Police Station
Th Chakkaphet
Th Triphet
Th Chakrawat
Tala Saphan
Sampeng Lane
Khlong Chaeng
Soi Phak Wan
Soi Phak Wan
Th Arun Amarin
Th Wang Doem
Soi Wat Home
Tha Ratchini
Pak Khlong Market
Th Chakkaphet
Khlong Ong Ang
Khlong Bangkok Yai
Soi Wat Kanlaya
Phra Buddha Yodfa Monument
Tha Saphan Phut
Soi Kudi Chiin
Saphan Phra Phuttha Yot Fa
(Memorial Bridge)
Sai 1
Th Thetsaban
Th Thetsaban Sai 2
Th Phaya Mai
Soi Somdet Chao Praya 1
Soi Somdet Chao Praya 3
Th Tha Din Daeng
Th Somdet Chao Phraya
Soi Somdet Chao Praya 12
Th Prachathipok
Th Itsaraphap
Th Itsaraphap
Th Tha Din Daeng
Soi Khang Rong Rap Chamnan
Soi Saraphi 2
Trok Saphan Luang
Mittraphap Hospital
Th Intharaphitak
Wong Wian Yai Market
Wong Wian Yai
Taksin Circle
Th Lat Ya
Soi Wiset San
Th Charoen Rat
Wong Wian Yai
Th Taksin
Soi Ratruam Charoen
Trok Yenchit
THONBURI
Th Krung Thonburi

**PLACES TO STAY**
19 Chao Phraya Riverside Guest House
20 White Orchid Hotel
21 Chinatown Hotel
22 New Empire Hotel
26 Krung Kasem Srikung Hotel
28 River View Guest House
33 Royal Orchid Sheraton
36 River City Guest House
39 Intown Residence
40 Woodlands Inn; Cholas
47 Manohra Hotel
48 New Fuji Hotel
50 New Trocadero Hotel
53 Oriental Hotel
61 Silom Golden Inn
66 Holiday Inn Crown Plaza
69 Shangri-La Hotel
70 Peninsula Hotel

**PLACES TO EAT**
4 Royal India
9 Lie Kee
10 Laem Thong
11 Chiang Kii
12 Hua Seng Restaurant
14 Shangarila
15 Kong Lee
25 Pheng Phochana
27 Suki Jeh Yuu Jing
31 Hoi Tien Lao Rim Nam
32 Yok Yor Khlongsan
37 Pet Tun Jao Tha
41 Sallim Restaurant
44 Harmonique
45 Naaz Restaurant
46 Yogi; New Restaurant
49 India Hut
55 Himali Cha-Cha
58 Chaii Karr
60 Madura Restaurant
63 Night Market
67 Muslim Restaurant
71 Thon Krueng
72 Tiensin
73 Ban Chiang
74 Thanying

**OTHER**
1 Wat Arun
2 Wat Kanlayanamit
3 Santa Cruz Church
5 Chinese Temple
7 Sikh Temple
13 Wat Mangkon Kamalawat
16 Bangkok Bank
18 Irish Embassy
23 Wat Traimit
24 About Studio/About Cafe
29 Wat Thong Nophakhun
30 Harbour Department
35 Holy Rosary Church
38 Portuguese Embassy
42 CAT Office
43 Main Post Office
51 Haroon Mosque
56 Mahesak Hospital
61 Neilson Hays Library
62 Mirasuddeen Mosque
64 Sri Mariamman Temple
68 Wat Suan Phlu

**SHOPPING**
6 ATM Department Store
8 Central Department Store 1
17 Tang To Kang Gold Shop
34 River City Complex
52 Oriental Plaza
54 Teck Heng Bookstore
57 Central Department Store
59 Silom Village Trade Centre

0    250    500m
0    250    500yd

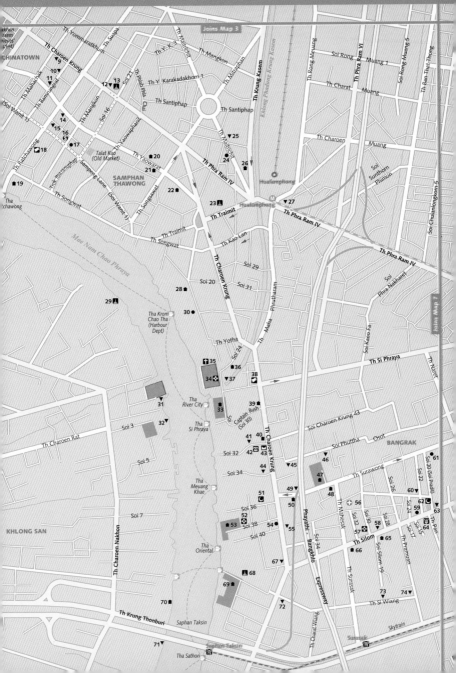

# MAP 7 – LUMPHINI PARK - TH PLOENCHIT - SAMYAN

Joins Map 5

17
18
19
20
21

Th Ploenchit
Skytrain
Ploenchit
22

23

26
31
30
29
28
27

85

Soi Ruam Rudi

Soi Sanam Khli

Soi Polo

lumphini

Sanam Muay Lumphini
(Boxing Stadium)

151
152
153
154
157 156 155
158
160 159
161

162

163
164
165
166

Th Phra Ram IV

Port-Din Daeng Expressway

Th Withayu (Wireless Rd)

Soi Tonson

Soi Ruam Rudi

Soi Polo 5

Soi 16

Soi Sarphin Duphi

Soi Athakhaprasit

Soi Ngam Duphi

Soi Si Bamphen

Soi Ngam Duphi

Soi Suwan Sawat

32

33
34
35
36
37
38
39
40
41
42
43
44
45
46
47
Nana
48
49 51
50
52
53
54
55
56
57
58
59
60
61
62
63
64
65
66

Th Sukhumvit

Soi 3 (Soi Nana Neua)
Soi 4 (Nana Tai)
Soi 2
Soi 5
Soi 7
Soi 9
Soi 11
Soi 13
Soi 15
Soi 19
Soi 16
Soi 18

Soi Asoke (Soi 21)
Soi 23

Th Sukhumvit

Joins Inset

**Joins Main Map**

84
M
Sukhumvit
Asoke
83
Soi Cowboy
82
81
80
79
78
77
76
75
74
73
72
71 70
69
68
67

Soi 23
Soi 35
Soi 33
Soi 31
Soi 29
Soi 27 (Paphatson)
Soi 25
Soi 18
Soi 20 (Ruam Phung)
Soi 22

Soi 33 (Daeng Udom)
Soi 31 (Sawadi)
Soi 29

Th Sukhumvit

To Eastern
Bus
Terminal

To Wat
Thammamongkhon

Phrom Phong
M

Benjasiri
Park

Same scale as main map

KHLONG
TOEY

Queen Sirikit
National
Convention
Centre

Sirikit Centre
167

Th Ratchadaphisek

Th Ratchadaphisek

Soi 16

Bon Kai
Market

Bon Kai
M

Klong
Toey
Market

# MAP 7 – LUMPHINI PARK - TH PLOENCHIT - SAMYAN

## PLACES TO STAY
5 Novotel Bangkok on Siam Square
6 Regent Bangkok
8 Grand Hyatt Erawan
12 Le Meridien President Hotel & Tower
21 Holiday Mansion Hotel
30 Chateau de Bangkok
31 Jim's Lodge
32 The Atlanta
35 Best Inn
36 Grand Inn
38 Fortuna Hotel
39 Amari Boulevard
41 Parkway Inn
44 Landmark Hotel & Gallery; Asia Books
46 Thai House Inn
47 City Lodge
48 Federal Hotel
52 Ambassador Hotel
54 Miami Hotel
55 Manhattan Hotel
59 Delta Grand Pacific Hotel
60 City Lodge
63 Premier Travellodge
67 Novotel Lotus Bangkok
76 Hotel Rembrandt
77 Windsor Hotel
78 Windsor Suites Hotels
79 Premier Inn
93 Mandarin Hotel
94 Montien Hotel
109 Dusit Thani Hotel; Cyber Pub
112 Bangkok Christian Guest House
114 Swiss Lodge
121 La Résidence Hotel
122 Narai Hotel; Rabianthong Restaurant
123 Monarch-Lee Gardens Bangkok
124 Tower Inn
128 Trinity Silom Hotel
131 Sathorn Inn
132 Niagara Hotel
140 Ryn's Café 'n Bed
146 YMCA Collins International House
147 Westin Banyan Tree
148 Sukhothai Hotel
149 YWCA Hostel
153 ETC Guest House
154 PS Guest House
156 Charlie House
157 Pinnacle Hotel
158 Malaysia Hotel
162 Honey House
163 Madam Guest House
164 Lee 3 Guest House
165 Sala Thai Daily Mansion
166 Freddy 2 Guest House

## PLACES TO EAT
1 Hard Rock Café
2 S&P Restaurant & Bakery
3 Nooddi
14 Fabb Fashion Café; Auberge DAB
17 Pho
24 Pan Pan Capri
25 Whole Earth Restaurant
34 Mehmaan; Akbar's; Al Hamra; Shaharazad
37 Al Hussain; Shiraz
40 Pomodoro
49 De Meglio
53 Mrs Balbir's
56 Yong Lee Restaurant
57 Haus München
64 Le Banyan
65 Cabbages & Condoms
66 Crepes & Co
73 Bourbon St Bar & Restaurant
74 Larry's Dive Center, Bar & Grill
75 Kuppa
80 Bei Otto; Baan Suan
82 Le Dalat
86 Nguan Lee Lang Suan
95 Somboon Seafood
100 Mizu's Kitchen
103 Bobby's Arms
104 Le Bouchon
111 Anna's Café
118 Mango Tree
119 Talat ITF
120 Coffee World
127 Goro
129 Bussaracum
133 Madras Café/Madras Lodge
134 Sun Far Myanmar Food Centre
138 Sara-Jane's
159 Just One
160 Babylon Bangkok

## ENTERTAINMENT
4 Siam Cinema
43 Jool's Bar & Restaurant
50 Q Bar
70 Imageries By the Glass
72 Washington Square (Mambo Cabaret; Dubliner)
81 Narcissus
83 Ship Inn
87 Metal Zone
88 Brown Sugar; Old West
89 Blue's Bar; Johnny Walker; Shakin'
101 Lucifer
102 Radio City
106 O'Reilly's Irish Pub
115 Shenanigans
152 Goethe Institut; Ratsstube

## SHOPPING
7 Peninsula Plaza
11 Gaysorn Plaza
13 Sogo Department Store
18 Central Department Store
22 Barang-Barang Antik
33 Ploenchit Centre; Cyber Cafe
42 Nana Entertainment Plaza
58 Asia Books
61 Times Square
62 Sukhumvit Plaza
69 The Emporium
105 Thaniya Plaza
107 Silom Complex
108 Silom Center; Robinson Department Store
125 Silom Plaza

## OTHER
9 Police Station
10 Erawan Shrine (Saan Phra Phrom)
15 Maneeya Centre; FCCT
16 Telephone Organisation of Thailand (TOT)
19 UK & North Ireland Embassy
20 Swiss Embassy
23 Vietnamese Embassy
26 Netherlands Embassy
27 US Embassy
28 Spanish Embassy
29 New Zealand Embassy
45 Swedish Embassy
51 Grand President Tower
68 UBC II Building; Londoner Brew Pub
71 World Fellowship of Buddhists
84 Siam Society & Ban Kamthieng
85 Sindhorn Building
90 American University Alumni (AUA)
91 Malaysian Embassy
92 Cambodian Embassy
96 Eve House
97 Charn Issara Tower
98 Wallstreet Tower
99 Marble House; Arima Onsen
110 Canadian Embassy
113 Bangkok Nursing Home
116 CP Tower
117 Bangkok Christian Hospital
126 Thai Airways International (THAI)
130 Belgian Embassy
135 Myanmar Embassy
136 St Louis Hospital
137 Empire Building
139 Singaporean Embassy
141 Christ Church
142 USIS
143 Immigration Bureau
144 Australian Embassy
145 French Consulate; Alliance Française
150 German Embassy
151 Danish Embassy
155 Lumphini Tower
161 Austrian Embassy
167 Bangkok Airways Head Office

Bangkok's modern city skyline in the eve of the night.

Travellers enjoy the bright and busy cafe scene along Soi Patpong 4, near Thanon Silom.

## MAP LEGEND

### CITY ROUTES

| | |
|---|---|
| Freeway ......... Freeway | ......... Unsealed Road |
| Highway ......... Primary Road | ......... One Way Street |
| Road ......... Secondary Road | ......... Pedestrian Street |
| Street ......... Street | ......... Stepped Street |
| Lane ......... Lane | ......... Tunnel |
| ......... On/Off Ramp | ......... Footbridge |

### REGIONAL ROUTES

......... Freeway
......... Primary Road
......... Secondary Road
......... Minor Road

### BOUNDARIES

......... International
......... Provincial
......... Disputed
......... Wall

### HYDROGRAPHY

| | |
|---|---|
| ......... River, Creek | ......... Lake |
| ......... Canal | ......... Spring; Waterfalls |

### TRANSPORT ROUTES & STATIONS

| | |
|---|---|
| ......... Train | ......... Walking Trail |
| ......... Skytrain | ......... Walking Tour |
| ......... Subway | ......... Path |
| ......... Ferry | ......... Pier or Jetty |

### AREA FEATURES

| | | |
|---|---|---|
| ......... Building | ......... Market | ......... Beach | ......... Campus |
| ......... Park, Gardens | ......... Sports Ground | ......... Cemetery | ......... Plaza |

### POPULATION SYMBOLS

| | | |
|---|---|---|
| ◎ CAPITAL ......... National Capital | ● CITY ......... City | ● Village ......... Village |
| ◉ CAPITAL ......... Provincial Capital | ● Town ......... Town | ......... Urban Area |

### MAP SYMBOLS

| | | |
|---|---|---|
| ■ ......... Place to Stay | ▼ ......... Place to Eat | ● ......... Point of Interest |

| | | |
|---|---|---|
| ......... Airport | ......... Hospital | ......... Police Station | ......... Telephone |
| ......... Bank | ......... Internet Cafe | ......... Post Office | ......... Temple (Buddhist) |
| ......... Bus Terminal, Stop | ......... Kraal | ......... Pub or Bar | ......... Temple (Hindu) |
| ......... Camping Area | ......... Monument | ......... Ruins | ......... Temple (Sikh) |
| ......... Church | ......... Mosque | ......... Shopping Centre | ......... Temple (Taoist) |
| ......... Cinema | ......... Museum | ......... Stately Home | ......... Theatre |
| ......... Dive Site | ......... National Park | ......... Swimming Pool | ......... Tourist Information |
| ......... Embassy | ......... Pagoda | ......... Taxi or Tuk-Tuk | ......... Zoo |

*Note: not all symbols displayed above appear in this book*

---

## LONELY PLANET OFFICES

### Australia
Locked Bag 1, Footscray, Victoria 3011
☎ 03 8379 8000  fax 03 8379 8111
email: talk2us@lonelyplanet.com.au

### UK
10a Spring Place, London NW5 3BH
☎ 020 7428 4800  fax 020 7428 4828
email: go@lonelyplanet.co.uk

### USA
150 Linden St, Oakland, CA 94607
☎ 510 893 8555  TOLL FREE: 800 275 8555
fax 510 893 8572
email: info@lonelyplanet.com

### France
1 rue du Dahomey, 75011 Paris
☎ 01 55 25 33 00  fax 01 55 25 33 01
email: bip@lonelyplanet.fr
www.lonelyplanet.fr

**World Wide Web: www.lonelyplanet.com *or* AOL keyword: lp**
**Lonely Planet Images: lpi@lonelyplanet.com.au**